The Bird
Almanac

The Bird Almanac

A Guide to Essential Facts and Figures of the World's Birds

COMPLETELY REVISED AND UPDATED

David M. Bird, Ph.D.

FIREFLY BOOKS

A FIREFLY BOOK

Published by Firefly Books (U.S.) Inc. 2004

First Printing

Publisher Cataloging-in-Publication Data (U.S.)

Bird, David Michael.
    The bird almanac : a guide to essential facts and figures of the world's birds : completely revised and updated / David M. Bird.
    [480] p. : ill. , maps ;   cm.
    Includes bibliographical references and index.
    Summary: Comprehensive guide to all aspects of avian biology, including anatomy, reproduction and mortality of bird species worldwide.
    ISBN 1-55297-925-3 (pbk.)
    1. Birds. 2. Birds -- Anatomy. 3. Birds — Behavior. I. Title.
    598 22   QL697.B57   2004

Published in the United States in 2004 by
Firefly Books (U.S.) Inc.
P.O. Box 1338, Ellicott Station
Buffalo, New York, USA
14205

Published in Canada in 2004 by Key Porter Books Limited.

Design: Peter Maher
Electronic formatting: Jean Lightfoot Peters

Printed and bound in Canada

Contents

Preface

Why an almanac on birds? The idea actually took root because of the phone calls. As a regular columnist on birds for *The Gazette* of Montreal for two decades and on bird behavior for *Bird Watchers' Digest* for over a decade, I get numerous phone calls on a weekly basis concerning birds. While many are desperately seeking solutions to problems with unwanted pigeons or are looking for a cheaper place to buy cracked corn to feed pigeons, still others simply want to know more about birds in their backyard. For instance, what's the incubation period for those robin eggs sitting in the nest over their front porch light? What kind of flowers attract hummingbirds? What kind of foods can one offer to the birds? Perhaps a caller's child is looking for information for a school project on birds. What is the rate of a bird's heartbeat? How fast does a bird fly? How long do they live? Or maybe someone's trying to settle a bet or answer a trivia question. What's the world's largest bird or the smallest egg? How much weight can a bird carry? Maybe the caller is merely searching for places to go bird-watching or for some tips on buying binoculars.

Oh yes, there are indeed many fine books and scientific journals out there on the market that provide answers to these questions and more. But I longed to have just one resource book by my telephone or in my briefcase that could answer most of the kinds of questions I am often asked. In searching about for a model for this book, I came across the "almanac," i.e. a soft-cover book that is reasonably compact, user-friendly, relatively up-to-date, but most important of all, fairly inexpensive. They are often used to provide a quick, ready answer to questions that pop up from time to time. The famous *Farmers' Almanac*, and in more recent years, *The Universal Almanac* published by Andrews and McMeel (Kansas and New York) come to mind as examples. There now exist almanacs for a variety of subjects ranging from fishing to the Civil War. However, much to my surprise, no such almanac existed for birds and bird-lovers!

There is no shortage of bird-lovers out there either, whether professional or amateur. Several professional organizations in both North America and the U.K. have grown from as little as a dozen founding members to several thousand in a century's time. For example, the American Ornithologists' Union founded in 1884 now has over 4,000 members from countries throughout the world, while the British Ornithologists' Union established in 1858 has over 2,000 members worldwide.

Birds, with their wide distribution around the world, their amazing mobility and powers of flight, and a fascinating array of species and colors, have clearly caught the attention of the public-at-large as well. One in every five North Americans now casually watches birds and bird-watching is second only to gardening as the number one recreation worldwide. Recent demographic analyses show that bird-watching will be the fastest growing activity in the world from 1996 to 2011. Yet, in a sad twist of irony, no less than 12 percent of the world's 9,750 bird species are at risk of global extinction!

According to a U.S. Fish and Wildlife Service survey of 62.9 million people in 2001, bird-watchers attracted the biggest following of all wildlife-watching activities. In that year, 40 million people observed birds around the home and 18 million took trips to see birds. Over 2.3 million wild-bird enthusiasts kept birding life lists, i.e. a tally of bird species seen by a birder in his or her lifetime, in 2001. And what were the favored species for those taking trips to see birds? More than 14.4 million people observed waterfowl such as ducks and geese, 12.9 million liked songbirds best, 12.5 million preferred raptors such as hawks, falcons, and eagles, 10.3 million favored herons, pelicans, and other waterbirds, and finally, 7.9 million were attracted to pheasants and turkeys. Of the 46 million birders, 74 percent could identify up to 20 different kinds of birds, 13 percent could identify 21 to 40 types of birds, and almost 4 million could identify 41 or more species.

Bird-watching can have quite an impact on a country's economy. In 2003, the U.S. Fish and Wildlife Service released an economic report on birding in the U.S., which revealed that 46 million bird-watchers (defined specifically as people who travelled more than a mile mainly to see birds or who closely observed birds at home) across America spent $32 billion in 2001. Spending on items like travel,

in a small way a love for birds in those living in other less developed countries, who could ask for more?

In compiling the information for the book, I hasten to acknowledge that there could be errors or perhaps information that could be added. My research assistants and I relied heavily on the internet for searching for organizations, products, and so on. I am aware too that there are other important ornithological awards out there that should be included and I have likely omitted a number of famous, deceased ornithologists from the who's who list. Records for the most species seen and addresses also change frequently with time. If I have inadvertently left out (and I am sure that I have) the name of a prominent organization, company, or product, please do not hesitate to inform me.

In any case, I humbly ask you, the reader, to help me ensure that the contents of this book are factual, up-to-date, and useful to as wide a bird-loving audience as possible. Lastly and most importantly, it was never my intention for *The Bird Almanac* to be quoted as a scientific reference text and I beseech anyone even considering doing this to refer instead to the original sources of information, i.e. the many excellent ornithological textbooks and scientific journals available on the market and in libraries.

Whether *The Bird Almanac* successfully fills a niche, time will tell. But, as Pete Dunne, one of North America's top birders, wisely said to me when I informed him of this book's imminent publication, "There can never be too many books on birds in the world."

Acknowledgments

No book of this sort was ever published without a great deal of help. In no particular order of importance, I gratefully acknowledge the kind assistance of Eleanor MacLean and Ann Habbick of the Blacker-Wood Library at McGill University, Bruce Grainger of the library on McGill's Macdonald campus, ornithological historians Marianne Ainley and C. Stuart Houston, Keith Bildstein of the Hawk Mountain Sanctuary Association, Pete Dunne and Sheila Lego of the Cape May Bird Observatory, Frank Gill of the National Audubon Society, David Nettleship of the Canadian Wildlife Service, Larry Bryan of Savannah River Ecology Laboratory, Charles Duncan of the Institute of Field Ornithology, Mary Victoria McDonald of the University of Central Arkansas, Gary Duke of the University of Minnesota, Richard Clark of York University, Gregory Butcher, Blake Maybank, Fred Lohrer and Glen Woolfenden of the Archbold Biological Station, Kathy Merk of the Cooper Ornithological Society, Allen Fish of the Golden Gate Raptor Observatory, Derek Turner of the UK400 Club, Alistair Gammell and Chris Martin of the Royal Society for the Protection of Birds (BirdLife Partner in the U.K.), David Stroud of the U.K government, author John K. Terres, Bill Thompson III, editor of *Bird Watchers' Digest*, Sheila Hardie, Josep del Hoyo and Andy Elliott, editors of *Handbook of the Birds of the World*, Judith Vickery, Rodger Titman of McGill University, and Elise Titman of Wildlifers nature store. For this new edition, I am additionally indebted to Allison Wells of the Cornell Laboratory of Ornithology, Phil Currie, Curator of Dinosaurs at the Royal Tyrrell Museum of Paleontology, Michael Pinhorn of the Royal Society for the Protection of Birds, Judy Kellogg Markowsky, Bill S. Evans, Pete Thayer, David Diehl, Fred Paquet and Linda Paetow of the Ecomuseum, Buzz Hull of the Golden Gate Raptor Observatory, Ed Henckel, Jim Fitzpatrick, Laurie Goodrich of the Hawk Mountain Sanctuary Association, Paul Green, Michael Ord, Richard Payne, Ann Stone, Bettie Harriman, Paul Baicich, and Mark Dennis. I am especially indebted to C. Stuart Houston for generously giving his valuable time to take on the painstaking task of correcting and updating the section dedicated to brief obituaries of those having made major contributions to the biology and conservation of birds.

I have saved some very special people to the end. I was fortunate enough to have several highly resourceful and hard-working research assistants. For the original version, Melanie Simard was assigned the difficult task of seeking out biographical information on famous, deceased ornithologists from all over the world and distilling their myriad accomplishments into a handful of short phrases. *The Bird Almanac* could not have been achieved without the services of Oliver Love whose brain melded with mine to give me exactly what I asked of him and more. I cannot speak highly enough of this energetic young man whose unwavering enthusiasm for the project and amazing ability to surf the Web helped me bring the book to life. Oliver in turn would like to thank The Science College of Concordia University and the Semeniuks of Kirkland, Quebec for their support. For this current edition, I was fortunate enough to find yet another energetic squad of research assistants, including Veera Harnal, Jean and Richard Gregson, and the dynamic duo of Marie-Anne Hudson and Isabel Julian affectionately known as my "golf girls."

Every book has its publication editor. I was incredibly lucky to be blessed with Michael Mouland, Senior International Editor for Key Porter, who was understanding and laid back enough to leave me to the job, yet continually and even humorously cheered on my efforts to make the book a reality. It was indeed a real pleasure working with him and I look forward to future collaborations. I am also grateful to the rest of the hardworking souls at both Key Porter Books and Firefly Books, who brought considerable professionalism to the book. I am especially thankful to Anna Porter, owner of Key Porter, and Lionel Koffler, owner of Firefly Books, for believing in me and this project.

Finally, there are no words to express my gratitude to my life partner and loving wife, Toni. She shared each and every one of my high and low points while working on the almanac, not to mention typing the lion's share of its text. When it comes to her, there is no luckier man on earth!

David M. Bird, September 22, 2003

*To the memory of my father, David Archibald Bird (1924–1975),
who knew long before I did that I would become a writer about wildlife.
Seldom a day passes that I do not think of him.*

How to Use the World Checklist

Shading denotes common names of birds shown on previous (light shading, left side), current (dark shade, centre) and following pages (light shade, right side)

Common and Latin names for birds; indexed alphabetically on page 436

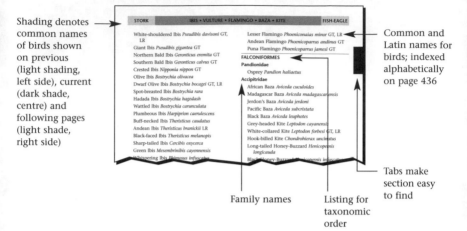

Family names

Listing for taxonomic order

Tabs make section easy to find

Fossil History of Birds

Geological Era	Geological Period	Epoch	MYA	Appearance of Modern Orders and Families	Extinct Birds Known fron Fossil Record (Millions of years ago)
		Recent	0.011	Modern birds; Passeriformes are dominant order.	Moas, such as *Dinornis maximus,* extinct.
	Quaternary	Pleistocene	2	All modern orders and families represented; 50% of modern species appear during this time.	
		Pliocene	7	Species numbers reach maximum; larks, buntings, thrushes, fringillid sparrows, swallows, nuthatches appear.	*Opisthocomus hoazin* (5 mya)
			13	Moas and tinamous appear.	*Argentavis magnificens* (Teratorn) (10 mya)
		Miocene	25	Most modern families and genera are present. Falcons, nighthawks, mousebirds, shrikes, North American wood warblers.	*Osteodontornis* (giant seabird)
			37	Families present: petrels, shearwaters, boobies, gannets, pigeons, goatsuckers, turkey, kingfishers, swifts, parrots, Old World warblers, sparrows, dabbling ducks, New World vultures.	
		Eocene	53	More than 20 modern orders now present. Penguins, ostriches, rheas, albatrosses, herons, storks, avocets, ducks, hawks, eagles, kites.	*Phororhacos* (giant flightless predatory bird) (40 mya) *Aepyornis* *Diatryma gigantea* (45–55 mya) *Presbyornis* (50 mya)
Cenozoic	Tertiary	Paleocene	65	Grouse, crane, pheasants, bustards, gulls & terns, auks, cuckoos, true owls, woodpeckers, rollers, hornbills, kingfishers, trogons, starlings, titmice.	

MYA=Millions of years ago

Geological Era	Geological Period	Epoch	MYA	Appearance of Modern Orders and Families	Extinct Birds Known fron Fossil Record (Millions of years ago)
		Cretaceous	145	The earliest fossils resemble loons, cormorants, pelicans, grebes, ibises, sandpipers, flamingos, and rails.	Emergence and extinction of toothed birds: *Baptornis advenus*, *Neogaeornis*, *Hesperonis regalis* and *Ichthyornis dispar* *Avimimus portentosus* (80 mya) *Gobipteryx minuta* (80 mya) *Ileropteryx* (125 mya)
		Jurassic	205		*Archaeopteryx lithographica* (140 mya)
Mesozoic		Triassic	240	Emergence of dinosaurs	
		Permian	270		
Paleozoic		Cambrian	600	Appearance of most kinds of invertebrates.	

SOURCES: C. Leahy, *The Birdwatcher's Companion: An Encyclopedic Handbook of North American Birdlife* (New York: Bonanza Books, 1983)

N.S. Proctor and P.J. Lynch, *Manual of Ornithology. Avian Structure and Function* (New Haven, CT: Yale University Press, 1993)

J.C. Welty, and L. Baptista, *The Life of Birds*, 4th ed. (Orlando, FL: Harcourt Brace Jovanovich College Publishers, 1990)

Dr. Phil Currie, Royal Tyrrell Museum of Paleontology, Personal communication

Anatomy

Terms for Anatomical Characteristics of Birds

Bill Characteristics

Style	Characteristic
acute:	bill tapering to a sharp point, e.g. warbler
bent:	bill deflected at an angle, e.g. flamingo
chisel-like:	bill tip beveled, e.g. woodpecker
compressed:	bill mostly higher than wide, e.g. puffin
conical:	bill cone-shaped, e.g. redpoll
crossed:	mandible tips crossing over one another, e.g. crossbill
decurved:	bill curving downward, e.g. curlew
depressed:	bill wider than high, e.g. duck
gibbous:	bill with a pronounced hump, e.g. scoter
hooked:	upper mandible longer than lower, with its tip bent over the tip of the lower, e.g. falcon
lamellate:	mandibles with transverse, tooth-like ridges on the tomia, e.g. geese
long:	bill longer than head, e.g. heron
notched:	bill with a slight nick in the tomia of one or both mandibles, e.g. thrush
recurved:	bill curving upward, e.g. godwit
serrate:	bill with saw like tomia, e.g. merganser
short:	bill shorter than head, e.g. redpoll
spatulate:	bill widened toward the tip, e.g. spoonbill
stout:	bill high and wide, e.g. grouse
straight:	line along which mandibles close following axis of head, e.g. heron
swollen:	mandible sides convex, e.g. finch
terete:	bill circular in cross section, e.g. hummingbird
toothed:	upper mandible tomium with one tooth, e.g. falcon, or several teeth, e.g. trogon

Tail Characteristics

Style	Characteristic
double-rounded:	central and outermost pairs of tail feathers are shorter than the intermediate ones producing a double-convex profile
emarginate:	retrices increasing in length from the middle to the outermost pair, e.g. finch
forked:	retrices increasing in length successively and in gradation from middle pair to outside pair, e.g. tern

Style	Characteristic
graduated:	retrices shortening successively from outside to inside, e.g. cuckoo
lanceolate:	lance-shaped tail feather, i.e. two sides evenly graduating to a point
pointed:	middle retrices longer than than the others, e.g. pheasant
rounded:	retrices shortening successively from inside to outside, e.g. crow
square:	retrices all the same length, e.g. sharp-shinned hawk

Wing Characteristics

Style	Characteristic
broad:	both primaries and secondaries long throughout the wing, e.g. red-tailed hawk
concave:	extreme curvature of spread wing convex above and concave below, e.g. grouse
flat:	slight curvature of spread wing, e.g. swift
long:	distance from the bend to the tip longer than the trunk, e.g. falcon
narrow:	primaries and secondaries short throughout the wing, e.g. gull
pointed:	outermost primaries longest, e.g. gull
rounded:	middle primaries longest and remainder graduated, e.g. sparrowhawk
short:	distance from the bend to the tip is the same or shorter than the trunk, e.g. grebe
spurred:	bend of the wing has a horny structure like a spur, e.g. jacana

Leg and Feet Characteristics

Style	Characteristic
acute:	nails extremely curved and sharp-pointed, e.g. woodpecker
anisodactyl:	digits 2, 3 and 4 pointing forward, 1 backward, e.g. most songbirds
booted:	tarsus covered with several long continuous platelike scales instead of small overlapping ones, e.g. thrush
elevated:	hind toe or hallux inserted high on the metatarsus such that its tip does not reach ground, e.g. rail
flattened:	nails extremely flattened and broadened, e.g. grebe
heterodactyl:	digits 3 and 4 forward, 1 and 2 backward, e.g. trogon
incumbent:	hind toe or hallux inserted on the metatarsus at the same level as the other three toes, e.g. meadowlark
lengthened:	nails straight, elongated, and sharp-pointed, e.g. horned lark
lobate:	anisodactyl with digits 2, 3 and 4 edged with lobes of skin that expand or contract during swimming, e.g. grebe
obtuse:	nails less curved and blunt, e.g. grouse
palmate:	anisodactyl with digits 2, 3 and 4 fully webbed, e.g. most waterfowl
pamprodactyl:	zygodactyl with digits 1 and 4 pivoting freely forward and backward, e.g. swift
pectinate:	nails with serrated edges, e.g. heron

Style	Characteristic
raptorial:	anisodactyl with strong digits armed with sharp claws or talons, e.g. hawks
reticulate:	tarsus and foot covered with a fine, net-like patchwork of small, irregularly shaped plates, e.g. falcons
scutellate:	tarsus and foot covered with a layer of overlapping or imbricated horny keratin scales, e.g. songbirds
scutellate-booted:	upper part of tarsus and foot scutellate and bottom of tarsus booted, e.g. catbird
scutellate-reticulate:	upper part of tarsus and foot scutellate and bottom part reticulate, e.g. pigeon
semipalmate:	anisodactyl with digits 2, 3 and 4 partially webbed, e.g. grouse
spurred:	back side of tarsus modified to form a spur, e.g. pheasant
syndactyl:	anisodactyl with digits 2 and 3 partly fused, e.g. kingfisher
totipalmate:	anisodactyl with all four digits webbed, e.g. gannet
zygodactyl:	digits 2 and 3 forward, 1 and 4 backward, e.g. owls

General Anatomical References for Birds

Style	Characteristic
abdominal:	region between thorax and pelvis
abductor:	muscles drawing away from the body's midline
adductor:	muscles drawing toward the body's midline
alar:	area of the wing
antebrachium:	forearm composed of radius and ulna
anterior:	toward the head
axillary:	armpit area
brachial:	upper arm composed of humerus
buccal:	cheek area
carpal:	wrist area
caudad:	toward the tail
celiac:	stomach area
cephalad:	toward the head
cervical:	neck area
costal:	rib area
cranial:	head area
cranially:	toward the head
crural:	leg area
digital:	finger remnants in wing
distal:	farther from the body's midline or point of attachment
dorsal:	top or back side
dorsum:	back surface

Style	Characteristic
extensor:	muscles that extend a part away from the body's midline
flexor:	muscles that pull a part toward the body's midline
inferior:	lower or ventral
interscapular:	upper back between the shoulders
lateral:	farther from the body's midline
medial:	closer to the body's midline
nasal:	area of nares or nostrils
nuchal:	area of the nape
occipital:	nape area where the spine meets the skull
orbital:	area of the eye sockets
pectoral:	chest and breast area between the sternum and shoulder
plantar:	sole of the feet
posterior:	toward the tail
pronator:	muscles that rotate wing bones forward and ventrally
proximal:	closer to the body's midline or point of attachment
rostral:	toward the head
sacral:	pelvic area
sternal:	breastbone area
superior:	upper or dorsal
supinator:	muscles that rotate the wing bones backward and dorsally
tarsal:	lower part of the leg
terminally:	toward the tail
ventral:	lower or abdominal side
vertebral:	spinal column

Skeleton

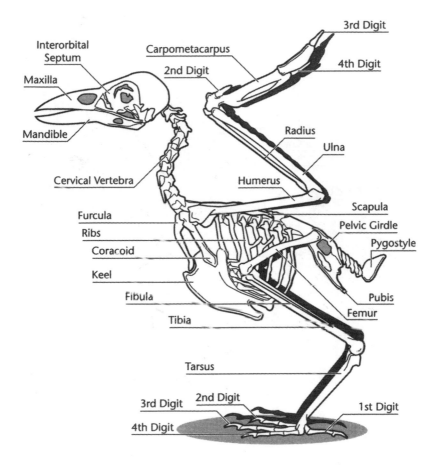

Interorbital Septum

Maxilla

Mandible

Carpometacarpus

2nd Digit

3rd Digit

4th Digit

Radius

Ulna

Cervical Vertebra

Humerus

Furcula

Ribs

Coracoid

Keel

Fibula

Tibia

Scapula

Pelvic Girdle

Pygostyle

Pubis

Femur

Tarsus

3rd Digit

2nd Digit

4th Digit

1st Digit

Topography

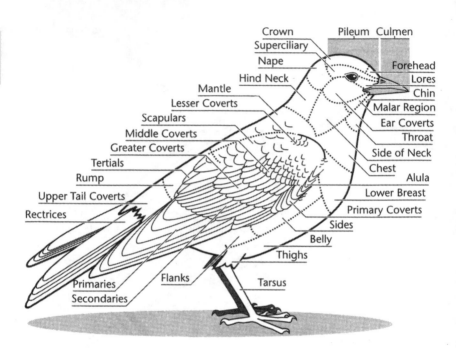

Measurements

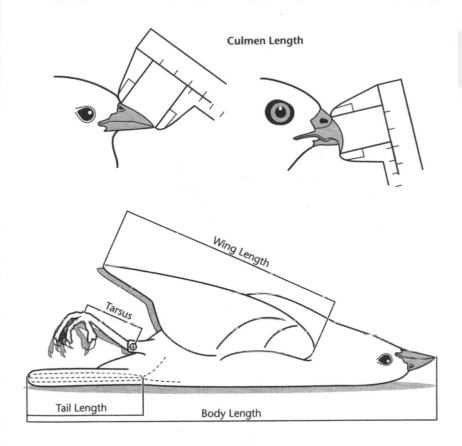

Culmen Length

Wing Length

Tarsus

Tail Length

Body Length

Physiology

Circulatory System

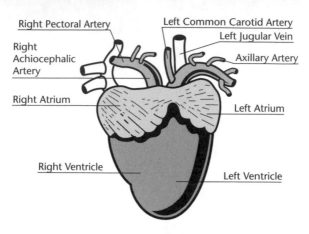

Heart

Heart Weight of Selected Birds Relative to Body Weight

	Body Weight (g)	Heart Weight (g)	% Body Weight
Ostrich	123,000	120	0.1
Emu	37,500	319	0.8
Goose	6,900	37	0.5
Chicken	3,120	14	0.4
Peking duck	2,900	23	0.8
Vulture	2,040	17	0.8
Duck	1,685	12	0.7
Pheasant	1,200	6	0.5
Common raven	1,200	12	1.0
Pigeon	297	4	1.3
Ptarmigan	258	3	1.2
Turtle dove	153	1.3	0.8
Budgerigar	35	.45	1.3
Bluebird	29	.5	1.7
Mango hummingbird	7.7	.2	2.6

SOURCES: 1. P.D. Sturkie, ed., *Avian Physiology*, 4th ed. (New York: Springer-Verlag, 1986); 2. J.C. Welty, and L. Baptista, *The Life of Birds*, 4th ed. (Orlando, FL: Harcourt Brace Jovanovich College Publishers, 1990)

Approximate Heartbeat Rates of Selected Adult Birds at Rest

	Body Weight (gm)	Heart Beat (per min)
Turkey	8,750	93
Brown pelican	7,500	150
Anser sp. (geese)	3,420	113
Mallard	2,670	118
Turkey vulture	2,000	132
Herring gull	930	218
Domestic pigeon	382	166
Crow	337	342
California quail	138	250
Mourning dove	130	135
Blue jay	77	307
Robin	69	328–384
Brown thrasher	59	303–465
Wood thrush	47	303
Cardinal	40	375
Catbird	28	307–427
House sparrow	28	350
Song sparrow	20	450
Black-capped chickadee	12	480
House wren	11	450
Ruby-throated hummingbird	4	615

SOURCES: W.A. Calder, *Condor* 70 (1968) :358–365; J.R. Simons in *Biology and Comparative Physiology of Birds*, ed. A.J. Marshall; (New York: Academic Press, 1969); A.R. Lewis, *Auk* 84 (1967) :131

Approximate Blood Volumes of Selected Birds

	Body Weight (g)	Total Blood Volume (ml/100g)	Plasma Volume (ml/100g)
Great horned owl	1,495	6.4	3.4
Pheasant	1,190	6.7	4.5
Red-tailed hawk	925	6.2	3.5
Coot	550	9.5	5.1
Pigeon	310	9.2	4.4
Quail	98	7.4	4.7

SOURCE: Adapted from: P.D. Sturkie, ed., *Avian Physiology*, 4th ed. (New York: Springer-Verlag, 1986)

Approximate Erythrocyte (Red Corpuscle) Numbers in Selected Birds in Millions per Cubic Millimeter

Blackbird	3.2
Dabbling duck	2.2
Dark-eyed junco	3.2
Diving duck	3.6
Great horned owl	3.1
Guinea fowl	4.5
Jackdaw	6.4
Ostrich	6.2
Peacock	6.7
Pigeon	2.6
Red-tailed hawk	1.8
Red-throated loon	2.8
Ring-necked pheasant	3.2
Rock partridge	2.0
Ruby topaz hummingbird	3.0

SOURCE: Adapted from: P.D. Sturkie, ed., *Avian Physiology*, 4th ed. (New York: Springer-Verlag, 1986); J. Dorst, *The Life of Birds*, Vol. 1 (New York: Columbia University Press, 1974)

Approximate Number of Leukocytes and Thrombocytes in Bird Blood

	Number (x 10³/mm³)		Differential count (%)				
	Leukocytes	Thrombocytes	Lymphocytes	Heterophils	Eosinophils	Basophils	Monocytes
Canada goose	–	–	46.0	39.0	7.0	2.0	6.0
Ring-necked pheasant	–	–	34.0	48.0	1.0	10.0	8.0
Pigeon	13.0	–	65.6	23.0	2.2	2.6	6.6
Ostrich	21.0	10.5	26.8	59.1	6.3	4.7	3.0
Quail	23.1	132	71.6	21.8	4.3	0.2	2.1
Red-winged blackbird	–	–	55.0	30.0	3.0	2.5	8.0

SOURCE: Adapted from: P.D. Sturkie, ed., *Avian Physiology*, 4th ed. (New York: Springer-Verlag, 1986)

**Approximate Total Plasma (or Serum) Proteins, "Albumins,"
"Globulins," and "A/G" Ratio in Selected Birds**

	Total protein (g/100 ml)	"Alb" (g/100 ml)	"Glob" (g/100 ml)	A/G
Guinea fowl	3.52	1.45	1.98	0.73
Pheasant	4.90	2.29	2.62	0.87
Rock partridge	4.66	1.66	2.98	0.56
Bankiva	4.43	1.95	2.47	0.79
Peacock	4.36	2.41	1.94	1.24
Guan	3.69	2.03	1.60	1.27
Rook	4.10	0.81	2.69	0.30
Crow	4.40	1.30	2.80	0.46
Jackdaw	4.60	1.20	2.80	0.43
Magpie	4.30	1.00	2.50	0.40
Jay	4.80	1.12	3.16	0.35

SOURCE: Adapted from: P.D. Sturkle, ed., *Avian Physiology*, 4th ed. (New York: Springer-Verlag, 1986)

Digestive System

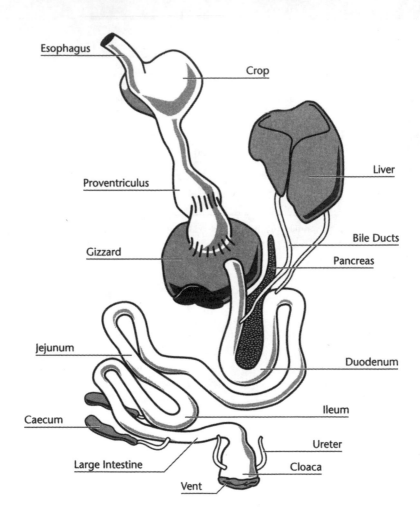

Composition of Avian Esophageal Fluids

	Protein (%)	Lipid (%)	Carbohydrates (%)
Pigeon	23	10	0.0
Flamingo	8	18	0.2
Penguin	59	29	5.5

SOURCE: F. Gill, *Ornithology*, 2nd ed. (New York: W.H. Freeman and Co., 1995)

Respiratory System

Approximate Breathing Rates of Resting Birds Relative to Body Weight

	Average Body Weight (g)	Breathing Rate (breaths per minute)
Ostrich	100,000	5
Swan	10,000	10
Pheasant	1,000	16
Kestrel	100	28
Wren	10	100
Hummingbird	3	250

SOURCE: Adapted from: J.C. Welty and L. Baptista, *The Life of Birds*, 4th ed (Orlando, FL: Harcourt Brace Jovanovich College Publishers, 1990)

Relative Respiratory Volumes in the Chicken

Air Spaces	Volume (ml)
Cervical (both)	20
Clavicular (single)	55
Cranial thoracic (both)	50
Caudal thoracic (both)	24
Abdominal (both)	110
Lungs (both)	35
Skeletal air space	4
Total respiratory volume	298

SOURCE: A.S. King. Structural and functional aspects of the avian lungs and air sacs. *International Review of General and Experimental Zoology*, Vol. 2. (1986): 171

Major Air Sacs

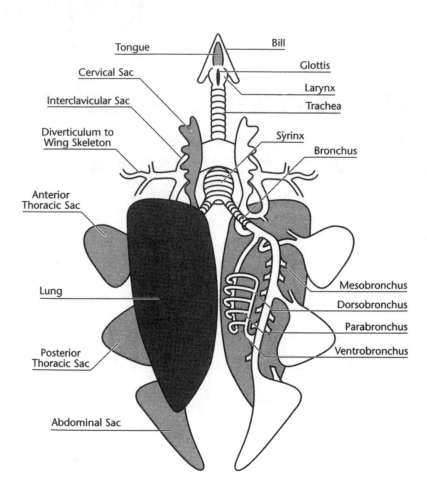

Approximate Diving Depths of Selected Diving Birds

	Mass (kg)	Maximum Dive Depth (m)
Emperor penguin	34	540
King penguin	13	300
Gentoo penguin	6	150
Adélie penguin	4	170
Common murre	1	180
Thick-billed murre	1	150
Razorbill	0.75	140
Sooty shearwater	0.80	65
Short-tailed shearwater	0.60	70
Peruvian diving petrel	0.25	80
Common diving petrel	0.20	60

SOURCE: Adapted from: E.A. Schreiber and J. Burger, *Biology of Marine Birds* (New York, NY: CRC Press, 2002)

Diving Durations for Selected Underwater Birds

	Estimated Time (sec.)
Common loon	480–600
Gentoo penguin	108–145
Adélie penguin	105–141
Chinstrap penguin	71–103
Oldsquaw	48–70
Surf scoter	33–65
Pelagic cormorant	24–60
Red-breasted merganser	42–47
Common goldeneye	25–41
Horned grebe	29–40
Ruddy duck	17–22
Pied-billed grebe	6–16
American coot	2–12

SOURCE: Drawn from various sources

Urogenital System

Male and Female

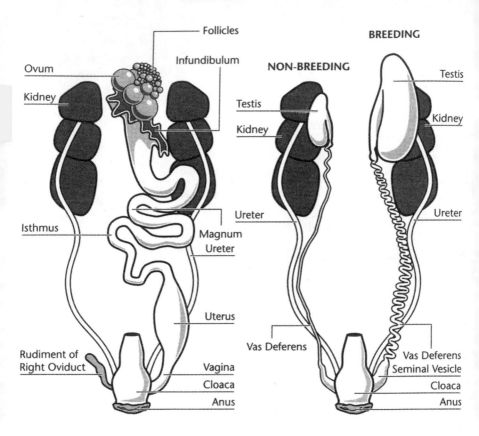

Approximate Total Body Water of Selected Birds Relative to Body Weight

	Body weight (g)	% Body Weight in Water
Emu	32,700	63
Duck	3,090	69
Pigeon	360	64
Japanese quail	105	67
Zebra finch	13	63

SOURCE: Adapted from: P.D. Sturkie, ed. *Avian Physiology*, 4th ed. (New York: Springer-Verlag, 1986)

Metabolism and Thermoregulation

Metabolic Rates of Selected Birds Relative to Body Weight

	Weight (g)	Kcal/kg/24h	Kcal/24h
Bennett's cassowary	17,600	29.3	516
Trumpeter swan	8,880	47.1	418
Brown pelican	3.510	75.2	264
Golden eagle	3,000	34	102
Great blue heron	1,870	68.4	128
Raven	850	108	92
Domestic pigeon	311	105.9	32.9
Kestrel	108	157	17.0
Quail	97	235	23
White-crowned sparrow	26.4	324	8.55
Yellowhammer	26.4	354	9.35
House sparrow	24.3	449	10.90
Great tit	18.5	451	8.36
House wren	10.8	589	6.36
Anna's hummingbird	4.07	1,410	5.83
Rufous hummingbird	3.53	1,601	5.67

SOURCE: J. Dorst, *The Life of Birds*, Vol.1 (New York: Columbia University Press, 1974)

Deep-Body Temperature of Selected Birds Relative to Body Weight*

	Body mass (g)	Deep-body temp. (°C)
Ostrich	100,000	38.3
Emu	38,300	38.1
Rhea	21,700	39.7
Mute swan	8,300	39.5
Domestic goose	5,000	41.0
Gentoo penguin	4,900	38.3
Peruvian penguin	3,900	39.0
Adélie penguin	3,500	38.5
Chinstrap penguin	3,100	39.4
Brown pelican	3,100	40.3
Little penguin	900	38.4
Brown-necked raven	610	39.9
Willow ptarmigan	573	39.9
Domestic pigeon	300	42.2
California quail	139	41.3
Mourning dove	120	42.7
American kestrel	119	39.3
Evening grosbeak	60	41.0
Speckled mousebird	53	39.0
Common redpoll	15	40.1
Zebra finch	12	40.3
Ruby-throated hummingbird	3	38.9

* at rest, under thermoneutral conditions

SOURCE: P.D. Sturkie, ed. *Avian Physiology*, 4th ed., (New York: Springer-Verlag, 1986); J. Dorst, ed., *The Life of Birds*, Vol. 1 (New York: Columbia University Press, 1974)

Senses

Brain

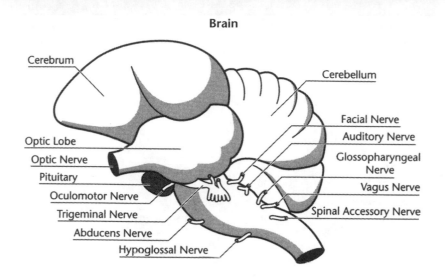

Eyeball

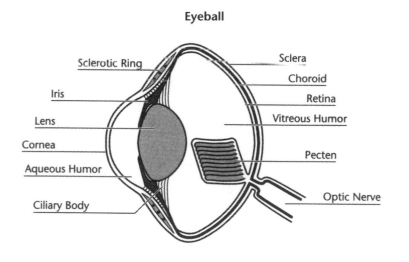

Approximate Hearing Range of Selected Birds

	Lower limit (Hz)	Highest sensitivity (Hz)	Upper limit (Hz)
Ring-billed gull	100	500–800	3,000
Canvasback	190		5,200
Great horned owl	60		7,000
Snow bunting	400		7,200
Prairie horned lark	350		7,600
Crow	300	1,000–2,000	8,000
Eagle owl	60	1,000	8,000
Mallard	300	2,000–3,000	8,000
American kestrel	300	2,000	10,000
Canary	250	2,800	10,000
Ring-necked pheasant	250		10,500
Pigeon	50	1,800–2,400	11,500
Budgerigar	40	2,000	14,000
Cape penguin	100	600–4,000	15,000
Starling	700		15,000
House sparrow			18,000
Long-eared owl	100	6,000	18,000
Greenfinch			20,000
Red crossbill			20,000
Black-billed magpie	100	800–1,600	21,000
Robin			21,000
Tawny owl	100	3,000–6,000	21,000
Bullfinch	200	3,200	20,000–25,000
Chaffinch	200	3,200	29,000

SOURCE: Adapted from P.D. Sturkie, ed., *Avian Physiology*, 4th ed. (New York: Springer-Verlag, 1986)

Sizes of Tympanic Membranes and Columellas in Selected Birds Relative to Body Size

	Body area (=weight 2/3) (cm²)	Tympanic membrane (cm²)	Columella base area (cm²)
Chiffchaff	4.0	0.078	0.0036
Willow warbler	4.5	0.004	0.0034
Common tit	5.0	0.089	0.0039
Blue tit	5.1	0.084	0.0032
Icterine warbler	5.7	0.086	0.0030
Black-cap warbler	6.6	0.126	0.0044
Barn swallow	7.4	0.171	0.0038
Chaffinch	7.9	0.114	0.0041
Great tit	7.9	0.104	0.0042
Common bullfinch	9.0	0.117	0.0048
House sparrow	9.6	0.091	0.0042
Blackbird	20.9	0.160	0.0073
Black-billed magpie	35.5	0.265	0.0116
Common gallinule	41.7	0.132	0.0078
Long-eared owl	44.9	0.480	0.0120
Pigeon	46.8	0.204	0.0116
Carrion crow	65.5	0.347	0.0151
Tawny owl	66.4	0.594	0.0198
Mallard	82.5	0.285	0.0109
Common coot	84.0	0.209	0.0106
Great crested grebe	86.0	0.140	0.0095
Common buzzard	86.1	0.330	0.0180
Ring-necked pheasant	113.0	0.368	0.0133
Common crane	245.0	0.418	0.0169

SOURCE: Adapted from P.D. Sturkie, ed., *Avian Physiology*, 4th ed. (New York: Springer-Verlag, 1986)

Frequency Ranges of Song Signals in Selected Birds

	Frequency range of signal (kHz)	Frequency range of maximal acoustic energy (kHz)
Bittern	1	0.5
Cuckoo	0.2–1.7	0.25–0.5
Wren	2.5–10.0	
Robin	1.5–11.0	4–7
Nightingale	1–9	
Bonelli's warbler	2.7–7.0	3.5–6.0
Willow warbler	2–7	
Wood warbler	2.8–9.0	4.5–8.0
White-crowned sparrow	2.2–6.8	
Chipping sparrow	2.4–7.0	
Song sparrow	2.5–6.7	

SOURCE: Adapted from J. Dorst, *The Life of Birds*, Vol. 1 (New York: Columbia University Press, 1974)

Approximate Numbers of Taste Buds in Selected Birds

Blue tit	24
Pigeon	37–75
Bullfinch	46
Barbary dove	54
Japanese quail	62
Starling	200
Chicken	250–350
Duck	375
Parrot	300–400

SOURCE: Adapted from P.D. Sturkie, ed., *Avian Physiology*, 4th ed. (New York: Springer-Verlag, 1986)

Flight

Wing

(Dorsal View)

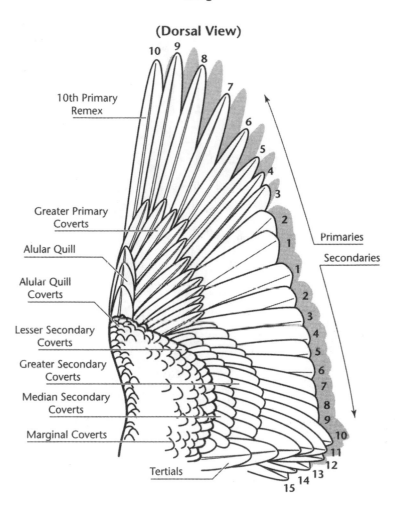

10th Primary Remex

Greater Primary Coverts

Alular Quill

Alular Quill Coverts

Lesser Secondary Coverts

Greater Secondary Coverts

Median Secondary Coverts

Marginal Coverts

Tertials

Primaries

Secondaries

Feather

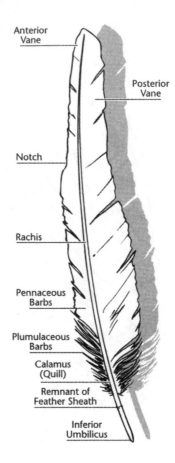

Anterior Vane

Posterior Vane

Notch

Rachis

Pennaceous Barbs

Plumulaceous Barbs

Calamus (Quill)

Remnant of Feather Sheath

Inferior Umbilicus

Feather Tracts

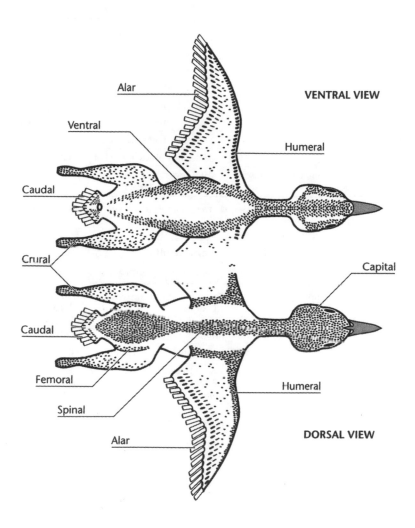

Alar

VENTRAL VIEW

Ventral

Humeral

Caudal

Crural

Capital

Caudal

Femoral

Spinal

Humeral

Alar

DORSAL VIEW

Major Adaptations of Birds for Flight

Weight Reductions	Power Increases
1. thin, hollow bones	1. warm-bloodedness
2. fusion of bones in the pectoral and pelvic girdles and spinal column	2. insulative coat of feathers
3. no teeth or heavy jaws	3. energy-rich diet
4. absence of tail vertebrae	4. rapid and efficient digestion
5. reduced number of digits	5. high glucose levels in the blood
6. light feathers	6. high metabolic rate
7. air sacs	7. four-chambered heart for double circulation
8. few skin glands	8. rapid, high-pressure circulation
9. laying of eggs	9. highly efficient respiratory system
10. reduced gonads in non-breeding season	10. synchronization of respiratory movements with wing beats

SOURCE: Adapted from J.C. Welty and L. Baptista, *The Life of Birds*, 4th ed. (Orlando, FL: Harcourt Brace Jovanovich College Publishers, 1990)

Plumages and Molts

Plumage		Molt		
Traditional (Dwight)	Humphrey & Parks	Traditional (Dwight)	Extent	Humphrey & Parks
Natal down	Natal down	Postnatal molt	complete	Prejuvenal molt
Juvenal plumage	Juvenal plumage	Postjuvenal molt	partial	1st prebasic molt
1st winter plumage	1st basic plumage	1st prenuptial molt	partial	1st prealternate molt
1st nuptial plumage	1st alternate plumage	1st postnuptial molt	complete	2nd prebasic molt
2nd winter plumage	2nd basic plumage	Prenuptial molt	partial	2nd prealternate molt
2nd nuptial plumage	2nd alternate plumage	2nd postnuptial molt	complete	2nd prebasic molt

SOURCES: J. Dwight, Jr., *Ann. N.Y. Acad. Sci.* 13(1900): 73–360; P.S. Humphrey and K.C. Parkes, *Auk* 76 (1959): 1–31

Flight Feather Counts of Selected Bird Groups

	Primary	Secondary	Tail
Quail, pheasants	10	10–18	12–18
Ducks, geese, swans	11	15–24	12–24
Woodpeckers	10	11	12
Trogons	10	11	12
Kingfishers	10–11	11–14	12
Cuckoos	10	11	8–10
Parrots, macaws	10	8–14	12
Swifts	10	8–11	10
Hummingbirds	10	6–7	10
Owls	10	11–19	12
Nighthawks	10	12–15	10
Pigeons, doves	10	11–15	12
Cranes	11	~16	12
Rails, gallinules	10–11	~15	8–14
Sandpipers	10	11	12
Plovers	10	11	12
Gulls, terns, alcids	11	11	12
Hawks, eagles, osprey	10	15–20	12–14
Falcons, caracaras	10	16	12–14
Grebes	12	~22	–
Cormorants	11	~20	12–14
Herons	11	23	8–12
Pelicans	11	20	22–24
New World vultures	10	18–25	12–14
Loons	11	22–23	16–20
Songbirds	9–10	9–11	12

SOURCE: Adapted from N.S. Proctor and P.J. Lynch, *Manual of Ornithology. Avian Structure and Function.* (New Haven, CT: Yale University Press, 1993)

Approximate Wingbeats per Second in Selected Birds

	Beats per second		Beats per second
Amethyst woodstar hummingbird	78	Capercaillie	4.6
Ruby-throated hummingbird	70	Peregrine falcon	4.3
Blue-tailed hummingbird	41.5	Wood pigeon	4.0
Black jacobin hummingbird	25	Turnstone	4.0
Swallow-tailed hummingbird	22	Cormorant	3.9
Pheasant	9.0	Magpie	3.0
Black guillemot	8.0	Black kite	2.8
Great crested grebe	6.3	Herring gull	2.8
Coot	5.8	Mute swan	2.7
Puffin	5.7	Heron	2.5
Blackbird	5.6	Mourning dove	2.5
Ringed plover	5.3	Belted kingfisher	2.4
Wigeon	5.1	Lapwing	2.3
Starling	5.1	Rook	2.3
Mallard	5.0		

SOURCE: J. Dorst, *The Life of Birds*, Vol. 1 (New York: Columbia University Press, 1974)

Wing Loading in Selected Birds

	Weight (g)	Wing Area (cm²)	Wing Area (cm²/g)
Ruby-throated hummingbird	3.0	12.4	4.2
House wren	11.0	48.4	4.4
Black-capped chickadee	12.5	76.0	6.1
Barn swallow	17.0	118.5	7.0
Chimney swift	17.3	104.0	6.0
Whitethroat	18.6	87.1	4.7
Chaffinch	21.1	102.0	4.8
Great tit	21.4	102.0	4.7
Song sparrow	22.0	86.5	3.9
Leach's petrel	26.5	251.0	9.5
Swift	36.2	165.0	4.5
Purple martin	43.0	185.5	4.3
Dunlin	44.0	126.0	2.8
Red-winged blackbird	70.0	245.0	3.5
Great spotted woodpecker	73.0	238.0	3.3
European starling	84.0	190.3	2.2

Wing Loading in Selected Birds (cont'd)

	Weight (g)	Wing Area (cm²)	Wing Area (cm²/g)
Blackbird	91.5	260.0	2.8
Snipe	95.5	244.0	2.5
Common tern	118.0	563.0	4.8
Mourning dove	130.0	357.0	2.7
Magpie	214.0	640.0	3.0
Kestrel	245.0	708.0	2.9
Pied-billed grebe	343.5	291.0	0.8
Partridge	387.0	433.0	1.1
Carrion crow	470.0	1,058.0	2.2
Common barn owl	505.0	1,683.0	3.3
American crow	552.0	1,344.0	2.4
Herring gull	850.0	2,006.0	2.4
Buzzard	1,072.0	2,691.0	2.5
Peregrine falcon	1,222.5	1,342.0	1.1
Mallard	1,408.0	1,029.0	0.7
Black vulture	1,702.0	3,012.0	1.8
Great blue heron	1,905.0	4,436.0	2.3
Common loon	2,425.0	1,358.0	0.6
Greylag goose	3,065.0	2,697.0	0.9
White stork	3,438.0	4,951.0	1.4
Crane	4,175.0	5,553.0	1.3
Golden eagle	4,664.0	6,520.0	1.4
Canada goose	5,662.0	2,820.0	0.5
Whooper swan	5,925.0	3,377.0	0.6
Griffon vulture	7,269.0	10,540.0	1.4
Great bustard	8,950.0	5,728.0	0.6
Mute swan	11,602	6,808.0	0.6

SOURCES: Adapted from J.C. Welty and L. Baptista, *The Life of Birds*, 4th ed. (Orlando, FL: Harcourt Brace Jovanovich College Publishers, 1990); J. Dorst, *The Life of Birds*, Vol. 1 (New York, Columbia University Press, 1974)

Suggested Weight-Carrying Capacities of Selected Bird Species

	Approx. Body Weight (g)*	Item Carried	Approx. Weight of Item (g)	Percent of Body Weight
House finch	21	cloth rag	5	23
American kestrel	165	rat	240	145
Chestnut-collared longspur	20	nestling	14	70
Calliope hummingbird	2.5	mate	2.9	116
Osprey	1,800	fish	1,800	100
Pallas's fish eagle	3,700	carp	5,900	160
Bald eagle	6,300	mule deer	6,800	108
Golden eagle	4,309	UID prey item	900	21
Harpy eagle	9,000	sloth	5,900	65
Steller's sea-eagle	8,600	seal	9,100	105

* In all cases, a maximum weight was assigned based on the literature

SOURCES: B.P. Martin, *World Birds* (Enfield, Middlesex: Guinness Books, 1987); J. Terres, ed., *The Audubon Society Encyclopedia of North American Birds* (New York: Alfred A. Knopf, 1987)

Flight Morphology of Selected Soaring Birds Species

	Mass (kg)	Span (kg) (kg)	Wing Area (m²)	Wing Load* (N/m²)	Aspect** Ratio
Sharp-shinned hawk	0.14	0.51	0.057	24.05	4.57
Broad-winged hawk	0.46	0.81	0.118	35.42	5.61
Red-tailed hawk	1.36	1.08	0.222	49.68	5.20
Osprey	1.68	1.49	0.297	54.75	7.20
Lanner falcon	0.57	1.01	0.132	42.39	7.72
Black vulture	1.80	1.38	0.331	53.45	5.70
White-backed vulture	5.39	2.18	0.690	76.50	6.90
Andean condor	10.05	2.88	1.050	93.50	7.90
Common crane	5.50	2.40	0.720	80.00	8.00
Rock dove	0.40	0.67	0.063	52.20	6.50
Fulmar	0.73	1.10	0.121	58.93	10.02

* Weight supported by unit wing area
** Wing span squared, divided by area

SOURCE: Adapted from P. Kerlinger, *Flight Strategies of Migrating Hawks* (Chicago: University of Chicago Press, 1989)

Flight Speeds of Banded Wild Birds During Migration Between Two Locations

	Distance Covered (km)	Elapsed Time of Flight (days)	Km per Day
Manx shearwater	9,500	17	559
Mallard	890	2	445
Blue-winged teal	4,800	35	140
Peregrine falcon	1,600	21	76
Lesser kestrel	8,785	61	144
Ruddy turnstone	4,655	4	1,164
Lesser yellowlegs	3,100	7	443
Red knot	5,640	8	705
Ruff	6,500	32	203
Arctic tern	14,000	114	123
Barn swallow	8,800	35	251
Great tit	1,200	21	57
Redwing	2,400	4	600
Yellow-rumped warbler	725	2	362
White-crowned sparrow	500	12 hrs	1,000

SOURCES: Adapted from J.C. Welty and L. Baptista, *The Life of Birds*, 4th ed. (Orlando, FL: Harcourt Brace Jovanovich College Publishers, 1990)

Flight Speeds of Experimentally Displaced Birds Returning to Their Nests

	Distance Displaced (km)	Elapsed Time of Flight (days)	Km per Day
Laysan albatross	5,150	10.0	515
Manx shearwater	5,300	12.5	424
White stork	2,260	11.9	190
Herring gull	1,400	4.1	341
Noddy tern	1,739	5.0	348
Homing pigeon	1,620	1.5	1,080
Alpine swift	1,620	3.0	540

SOURCE: J.C. Welty and L. Baptista, *The Life of Birds*, 4th ed. (Orlando, FL: Harcourt Brace Jovanovich College Publishers, 1990)

Flight Speeds for Selected Birds Relative to Mass, Aspect Ratio, and Wing Loading

	Mass (g)	Aspect Ratio*	Wing Loading**	Speed (m/s)	Speed (km/h)
Red-throated diver	960	12.1	106	17	61
Wandering albatross	8,700	15	140	15	54
Wilson's petrel	38	8	19.4	11	40
Grey heron	1,320	7.8	39.8	12	43
Bewick's swan	6,200	9.2	147	20	72
Barnacle goose	1,150	10.1	98	19	68
White-fronted goose	1,720	10.8	92	15	54
Mallard	1,010	9.1	113	18	65
Eider duck	2,180	8.4	194	21	76
Sparrowhawk	188	6.5	28.1	12	43
Osprey	1,100	8.9	38.5	13	47
Kestrel	200	7.9	30.7	9	32
Pheasant	1,200	5.5	123	15	54
Crane	4,800	7.3	85	19	68
Oystercatcher	420	9.7	64	14–16	50–58
Dunlin	45	8.6	29.8	13	47
Herring gull	1,000	10	49.9	10–11	36–40
Common tern	121	13.2	24.5	9–12	32–43
Wood pigeon	461	6.6	57.5	17	61
Swift	420	10.5	29.1	6.5	23
Swallow	22	8	16.1	9	32
Blue tit	10	6.8	16.8	8	29
Chaffinch	22	5.9	20.2	10–14	36–50
House sparrow	28	5.5	26.4	8–11	29–40
Starling	76	7.2	36.6	9–10	32–36
Crow	460	6.8	36.7	14	50

* Wing span squared, divided by area
** Weight supported by unit wing area

SOURCE: B. Campbell and E. Lack, *A Dictionary of Birds* (Vermillion, SD: Buteo Books, 1985)

Average Flight Speeds (m/sec) of Selected Bird Species During Daytime and Evening Measured by Doppler Radar

	Midday	Evening
Mourning dove	9.9	12.0
Chimney swift	10.3	12.3
Purple martin	8.5	11.1
Cliff swallow	9.9	8.7
Tree swallow	10.0	9.2
Northern mockingbird	10.0	9.3
American robin	7.2	10.4
Red-winged blackbird	10.0	11.3
Common grackle	10.2	11.7
Eastern meadowlark	8.4	12.0
European starling	10.0	12.7
House sparrow	10.2	12.3

SOURCE: T.R. Evans and L.C. Drickamer, *Wilson Bull*. 106 (1994): 156–162

Abilities of Birds to Return to the Site of Capture After Transport to a Distant, Unfamiliar Release Site

	Number of Birds	Distance (km)	Return (%)	Speed (km/day)
Leach's storm-petrel	61	250–870	67	56
Manx shearwater	42	491–768	90	370
Laysan albatross	11	3,083–7,630	82	370
Northern gannet	18	394	63	185
Herring gull	109	396–1,615	90	112
Common tern	44	422–748	43	231
Barn swallow	21	444–574	52	278
European starling	68	370–815	46	46

SOURCE: F.B. Gill, *Ornithology* (New York, NY: W.H. Freeman and Co, 1990)

Penguin Swimming Speeds at Sea

	Speed (m/sec)
Adélie penguin	2.2
Chinstrap penguin	2.2
Gentoo penguin	2.2
Macaroni penguin	2.1
Rockhopper penguin	2.1
Jackass penguin	1.6
King penguin	2.4

SOURCE: L.S. Davis and J.T. Darby, *Penguin Biology* (New York: Academic Press, 1990)

Minimum Daily Flight Distance of Selected Migrating Raptors

	Total Migration Distance (km)	Days	Minimum Daily Distance (km)
Sharp-shinned hawk	2,000	30	67
Broad-winged hawk	6,000	40	150
Swainson's hawk	8,000	50	160
Lesser spotted eagle	6,000	40	150
Bald eagle	2,500	35	74
Eleonora's falcon	7,000	50	140

SOURCE: Adapted from P. Kerlinger, *Flight Strategies of Migrating Hawks* (Chicago: University of Chicago Press, 1989)

Average Air Speeds and Ground Speeds of Some Migrating Hawks

	Air Speed (mps)		Ground Speed (mps)	
	Stopwatch	Radar	Stopwatch	Radar
Sharp-shinned hawk	14.2	22.5	10.8	22.7
Cooper's hawk	16.6	21.3	13.1	20.6
Goshawk	–	22.5		20.7
Broad-winged hawk	13.7	24.2	11.1	23.7
Red-tailed hawk	16.6	23.9	13.1	24.4
Red-shouldered hawk	12.2	21.8	15.5	21.6
Osprey	16.2	24.9	13.8	23.7
Northern harrier	12.9	18.7	10.8	19.4
American kestrel	14.4	–	10.8	–

SOURCE: Adapted from P. Kerlinger, *Flight Strategies of Migrating Hawks* (Chicago, IL: University of Chicago Press, 1989)

Mean Altitudes (m) Flown by Migrating Raptors in Autumn

| | Method of Detection | |
	Motor Glider	Radar
American kestrel	640	746
Broad-winged hawk	855	791
Cooper's hawk	–	792
Goshawk	–	803
Merlin	457	–
Northern harrier	–	774
Osprey	818	831
Red-shouldered hawk	–	749
Red-tailed hawk	457	839
Sharp-shinned hawk	610	755

SOURCE: P. Kerlinger, *Flight Strategies of Migrating Hawks* (Chicago: University of Chicago Press, 1989)

Circling Performance of Selected Bird Species

	Circling Radius (m)	Bank Angle	Circle Time (sec)	Air Speed (mps)
Black vulture	17.1	24.7	12.5	8.8
	24.4	20–30	14.1	10.9
Brown pelican	18.0	22.9	13.3	8.6
Magnificent frigatebird	12.0	23.7	10.6	7.?
	12.5	20–30	10.1	7.8
Turkey vulture	12.5	20–30	10.1	7.8
Lappet-faced vulture	15.0	35.0	9.4	10.0
Indian white-backed vulture	40–50	?	13–16	10.0
Kite (*Milvus* sp.)	12.0	?	7–9	5.0
Broad-winged hawk	15.4	24.5	13.9	7.0
Sharp-shinned hawk	5.7–11.5	?	9–12	6.0

SOURCE: Adapted from P. Kerlinger, *Flight Strategies of Migrating Hawks* (Chicago, IL: Univ. Of Chicago Press, 1989)

Reproduction

Territory

Relative Territory Sizes (hectares) in Selected Birds*

Black-headed gull	.00003	Prothonotary warbler	1.7
King penguin	.00005	Yellow-bellied sapsucker	2.1
Least flycatcher	.07	Downy woodpecker	2.6
European blackbird	.12	Hairy woodpecker	2.8
American robin	.12	Hazel grouse	4.0
Willow warbler	.15	Song thrush	4.0
Snow bunting	.24	Black-capped chickadee	5.3
Red-winged blackbird	.30	Western meadowlark	9.0
Mockingbird	.32	Great horned owl	50
Coot	.40	Mistle thrush	50
House wren	.40	Red-tailed hawk	130
American redstart	.40	Bald eagle	250
Chaffinch	.40	Crowned hornbill	520
Song sparrow	.40	Ivory-billed woodpecker	700
European robin	.60	Powerful owl	1,000
Chestnut-collared longspur	.60	Golden eagle	9,300
Red-eyed vireo	.84	Bearded vulture	20,000
Ovenbird	1.0		

* will vary according to many factors, e.g. year, locality, season, food availability, etc.

SOURCE: Various ornithology and bird books

Initiation of Singing Before Sunrise (min.)*

Blackbird	44
Song thrush	43
Robin	34
Turtle dove	27
Willow warbler	22
Wren	22
Great tit	17
Chaffinch	9
Whitethroat	7

* note that this can vary according to light intensity and weather conditions

SOURCE: Adapted from J. Dorst, *The Life of Birds*, Vol. 1 (New York: Columbia University Press, 1974)

Song-Type Repertoire Sizes in Selected Songbirds

	Repertoire size
Ovenbird	1
White-crowned sparrow	1
Chingolo sparrow	1
European redwing	1
Splendid sunbird	1
Chaffinch	1–6
Ring ouzel	2–4
Great tit	2–8
Dark-eyed junco	3–7
Western meadowlark	3–12
Cardinal	8–12
Starling	21–67
Red-eyed vireo	12–117
European blackbird	22–48
Marsh wren	33–162
Mockingbird	53–150
Nightingale	100–300
Song thrush	138–219
Five-striped sparrow	159–237
Brown thrasher	2,000+

SOURCE: C.K. Catchpole and P.J.B. Slater, *Bird Song: Biological Themes and Variations* (Cambridge University Press, U.K., 1995)

Classifications of Nest Types

platform: floor of loosely assembled plant materials with a shallow depression for eggs located on ground, in tree, on cliff, or on human-made structure, e.g. osprey

ground: scraped-out depression or platform of plant materials, e.g. loon

floating: platform of plant materials lying on surface of water, e.g. grebe

cavity: burrow in ground (e.g. burrowing owl), as well as hole in tree, cliff, bank or human-made structure, e.g. kestrel

cupped: nest with true structure consisting of materials arranged and compacted for the bottom and sides as well as softer materials for inside lining, e.g. many songbirds

statant: cupped nest supported mainly from below with rims standing firmly upright, e.g. hummingbird

domed: statant nest with sides extended to form an arched roof, e.g. magpie

pensile: cupped nest suspended from branches by stiffly woven rims and sides, e.g. vireos

pendulous: deeply cupped nest swinging freely from branches by rims and flexibly woven sides, e.g. orioles

adherent:	cupped nests built with adhesive substances to attach to cliffs and other vertical surfaces (e.g. swallows) or built on the ground (e.g. larks) or in preformed cavities (e.g. titmice) or in excavated cavities (e.g. bank swallow)
half-cupped adherent:	half of a cup using saliva to stick nest materials together, e.g. swift
pit or mound:	pile of rotting vegetable matter placed over eggs to warm and incubate them, e.g. megapodes

Gametes

Spermatozoa

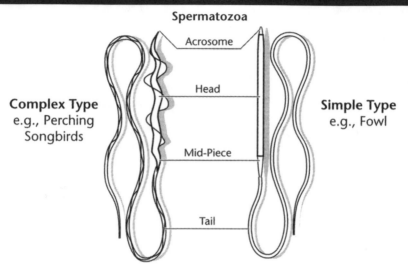

Complex Type
e.g., Perching Songbirds

Simple Type
e.g., Fowl

Acrosome

Head

Mid-Piece

Tail

Approximate Number of Sperm-Storage Tubules in Selected Birds

	Total No. of Sperm-Storage Tubules	Total No. of Branches
Pheasant	3,864	4,101
Japanese quail	3,467	3,467
Chicken	13,533	13,533
Turkey	20,000	20,000
Goose	7,030	7,683
Mallard	1,467	1,491
Pigeon	2,310	3,301
Ring dove	5,067	20,621
Budgerigar	512	522
Zebra finch	1,499	1,750
Bengalese finch	1,511	1,926

SOURCE: Adapted from T.R. Birkhead and A.P. Moller, *Sperm Competition in Birds* (London: Academic Press, 1992)

Sperm Storage Duration, Sperm Numbers, Clutch Size, and Spread of Laying in Selected Birds

	Sperm Storage Duration (days)	Sperm Number (x 10⁶) per Ejaculate	Clutch Size	Spread of Laying (days)
Goose	9.7	0.093	12	12
Domestic duck	10.3	–	17	17
Mallard	9.9	1,020	11	11
American kestrel	8.1	0.53	4.6	9
Pheasant	21.0	150	11.8	16.5
Japanese quail	6.3	157	8	10
Chicken	12.0	773	12	12
Turkey	42.0	1,577	17	25
Willow ptarmigan	7.8	–	7.5	8
Bobwhite quail	8.3	–	14	19
Guineafowl	7.0	67.3	14	14
Capercaillie	24.0	–	7	9
Pigeon	8.0	5.6	2	3
Ring dove	8.0	–	2	3
Budgerigar	11.0	10	6	12
Zebra finch	10.0	–	6	6
Bengalese finch	8.0		6	6

SOURCE: Adapted from T.R. Birkhead and A.P. Moller, *Sperm Competition in Birds* (London: Academic Press, 1992)

Egg

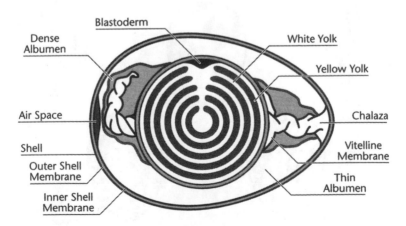

41

Nutritional Composition of a Chicken Egg

	Yolk	Albumen	Shell
Proteins (%)	16.6	10.6	3.3
Carbohydrates (%)	1.0	0.9	–
Fats (%)	32.6	Trace	0.03
Minerals (%)	1.1	0.6	95.10

SOURCE: A.L.Romanoff and A.J. Romanoff, *The Avian Egg* (New York: John Wiley & Sons, 1949)

Egg Patterns

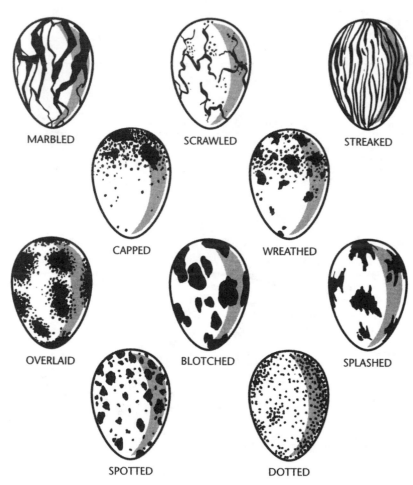

MARBLED

SCRAWLED

STREAKED

CAPPED

WREATHED

OVERLAID

BLOTCHED

SPLASHED

SPOTTED

DOTTED

Egg Shape

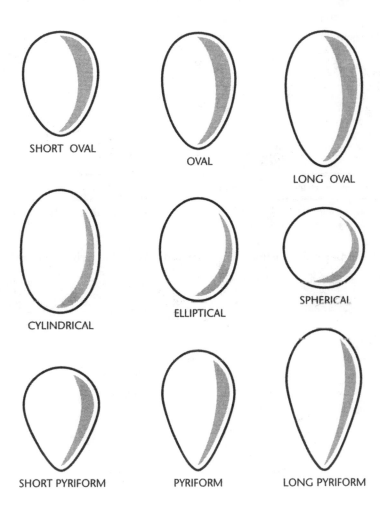

SHORT OVAL

OVAL

LONG OVAL

CYLINDRICAL

ELLIPTICAL

SPHERICAL

SHORT PYRIFORM

PYRIFORM

LONG PYRIFORM

Egg-Laying

Approximate Egg-laying Intervals in Selected Bird Species*

24 hours	songbirds, most ducks, geese, woodpeckers, small shorebirds and grebes, turkeys
38 to 48 hours	ostriches, rheas, large shorebirds and grebes, gulls, ducks, swans, herons, bitterns, storks, cranes, pigeons and doves, falcons, small hawks, owls, cuckoos, hummingbirds, swifts, kingfishers, ravens
62 hours	cuckoos, goatsuckers
3 days	emus, cassowaries, penguins
3 to 5 days	large raptors
5 days	condors, kiwis
5 to 7 days	boobies, hornbills
4 to 8 days	mound-builders

* There are exceptions in almost every bird group.

SOURCE: Adapted from J.C. Welty and L. Baptista, *The Life of Birds*, 4th ed. (Orlando, FL: Harcourt Brace Jovanovich College Publishers, 1990).

Egg Weight as a Proportion of Female Body Weight in Selected Bird Species

	Adult Female Body Weight (g)	Egg Weight (g)	Egg weight/ Body Weight (%)
Ostrich	90,000	1,600	1.8
Emperor penguin	30,000	450	1.5
Mute swan	9,000	340	3.8
Snowy owl	2,000	83	4.1
Little spotted kiwi	1,200	310	26.0
Peregrine falcon	1,100	52	4.7
Mallard	1,000	54	5.4
Herring gull	895	82	9.2
Puffin	500	65	13.0
American crow	450	34	7.6
Grey partridge	390	26	6.7
Northern bobwhite	180	18	10.0
American robin	100	8	8.0
Northern cardinal	45	8.6	19.1
Snow bunting	42	6.3	15.0
Fox sparrow	32	7.1	22.2
House sparrow	30	3	10.0

Egg Weight as a Proportion of Female Body Weight in Selected Bird Species (cont'd)

	Adult Female Body Weight (g)	Egg Weight (g)	Egg weight/ Body Weight (%)
American goldfinch	13	2.3	17.7
House wren	9	1.3	14.4
Vervain hummingbird	2	0.2	10.0

SOURCE: J. Faaborg, *Ornithology. An Ecological Approach* (Englewood Cliffs, NJ: Prentice-Hall, 1988); J.K. Terres, *The Audubon Society Encyclopedia of North American Birds* (New York: Alfred A. Knopf, 1987)

Incubation

Duration of Incubation of Selected Birds (days)

Ostrich	42	Barn owl	30–32
Emu	56–60	Eagle owl	33–36
Brown kiwi	75–80	Rock dove	17–19
Emperor penguin	62–66	Great spotted woodpecker	12–13
Great crested grebe	26–29	Silvery-cheeked hornbill	40
Cormorant	23–25	Hummingbirds	11–23
Gannet	43–45	Swift	17–22
Manx shearwater	51–53	Eastern phoebe	16
Yellow-nosed albatross	78	Skylark	11–12
Heron	25–26	Swallow	12–14
Mallard	22–28	Pied white wagtail	12–14
Greylag goose	27–29	Wren	13–20
Quail	17–20	Robin	12–14
Partridge	21–25	Ovenbird	12
Pheasant	23–25	Garden warbler	12–13
Redshank	23–25	Great tit	11–15
Herring gull	25–27	Starling	12–13
Black-headed gull	23–24	Rook	16–18
Lammergeier	52	Magpie	17–18
Common buzzard	28–31	House sparrow	12–13
Sparrowhawk	35–38		

SOURCE: J. Dorst, *The Life of Birds*, Vol. 1 (New York: Columbia University Press, 1974)

Estimated Clutch Sizes, Incubation Periods, and Ages at Fledging in Selected Groups of Birds

	Clutch Size	Incubation Period (in days)	Age at First Flight (in days)
Loons	2	28–30	70–80
Grebes	3–5	20–25	?
Albatrosses	1	64–65	140–165
Shearwaters, petrels, fulmars	1	51–53	70–97
Storm-petrels	1	41–42	63–70
Tropic-birds	1	41–42	70–80
Pelicans	2–3	28–36	60–65
Gannets	1	43–45	95–107
Cormorants	3–6	28–31	46–53
Anhingas	3–4	25–28	?
frigatebirds	1	44–55	170–190
Herons, bitterns	3–5	17–28	30–60
Storks	3–4	28–32	50–55
Ibises, spoonbills	2–4	21–24	50–56
Flamingos	1–2	28–32	75–78
Ducks, geese	3–14	22–31	34–77
Swans	5–6	33–37	100–108
New World vultures	2	38–41	70–80
Hawks, kites	2–5	28–38	23–45
Eagles	2	43–45	70–84
Osprey	2–3	32–35	51–59
Falcons	2–5	28–32	25–42
Grouse, ptarmigan, prairie chickens	9–12	22–24	7–10
Quail	10–15	22–23	10–18
Pheasants	7–10	23–25	7–8
Turkeys	11–13	27–29	11–17
Cranes	2	28–36	60–70
Limpkin	5–7	?	?
Rails, coots	5–12	18–24	?
Oystercatchers	3	24–27	34–37
Plovers, lapwings	3 or 4	21–27	27–40
Sandpipers, turnstones	4	17–28	14–21
Stilts, avocets	3–5	22–25	25–28?
Phalaropes	4	18–20	?
Skuas, jaegers	2 or 2–3	25–28	35–45
Gulls	1–5	20–29	35–50
Terns	1–3	20–25	28–35
Skimmers	4–5	30–32	38–42

Estimated Clutch Sizes, Incubation Periods, and Ages at Fledging in Selected Groups of Birds (cont'd)

	Clutch Size	Incubation Period (in days)	Age at First Flight (in days)
Auks	1 or 2	21–39	38–40
Pigeons, doves	1 or 2	13–19	14–28
Cuckoos	2–5	14–18	15–16?
Barn owl	5–7	32–34	42–50
Owls	2–8	21–34?	23–60
Nightjars	2	19–20	20–25
Swifts	4–5	19–21	29–31
Hummingbirds	2	16–17	19–22
Kingfishers	5–7	23–24	29–35?
Woodpeckers	3–10	11–14	24–28
Flycatchers	3–5	12–16	13–16
Larks	3–5	11–14	10–12
Swallows	4–6	12–16	18–26
Crows, jays, magpies	4–6	16–21	26–40
Nutcrackers	2–3	17–18	24–28
Tits	4–8	11–15	14–18
Nuthatches	5–8	12–16	18–21
Treecreepers	5–6	14–15	14–15
Dippers	4–5	15–17	24–25
Wrens	5–8	12–16	13–22
Mimic thrushes	3–5	12–15	11–18
Thrushes	3–6	11–16	11–18
Old World warblers, kinglets, gnatcatchers	4–9	13–15	10–14
Wagtails, pipits	4–5	13–14	12–13
Waxwings	3–6	12–16	14–18
Silky flycatchers	2–3	14–16	18–19
Shrikes	4–6	11–16	19–20
Starlings, mynas	4–6	11–13	19–22
Vireos	4	12–14	11–12
New World warblers	3–6	11–14	8–12
Weavers	4–6	11–14	12–15
New World blackbirds, meadowlarks	3–5	11–14	9–20
Tanagers	4–5	13–14	10–12
Siskins, crossbills	3–5	11–15	9–14
Sparrows	3–5	11–15	9–14

SOURCE: Adapted from O.S. Pettingill, Jr., *Ornithology in Laboratory and Field* (Minneapolis, MN: Burgess Publishing Co., 1970)

Average Periods On and Off the Nest for Ten Incubating Female Songbirds

	Avg. Off (min.)	Avg. On (min.)	% Time on Nest
Song sparrow	8.8	28.5	75
Marsh tit	7.1	37.9	84
European dipper	8.1	30.9	78
Chiffchaff	8.2	34.3	77
Becard	8.5	12.0	60
Sulphur-bellied flycatcher	8.5	17.0	67
Scarlet finch	9.2	48.5	84
American robin	11.0	44.0	80
European nuthatch	11.3	31.1	73
Hedge sparrow	14.6	29.7	66

SOURCE: M.M. Nice, *Studies in the Life History of the Song Sparrow*, Vol. II (New York: Dover Publications, 1943)

Hatching

Maturity of Young Birds at Hatching

Precocial

Eyes open, down-covered, leave nest first day or two	1. Completely independent of parents,	e.g. megapodes
	2. Follow parents but find own food,	e.g. ducks, shorebirds
	3. Follow parents and are shown food,	e.g. quails, chickens
	4. Follow parents and are fed by them,	e.g. grebes, rails

Semiprecocial

Eyes open, down-covered, stay at nest although able to walk, fed by parents		e.g. gulls, terns

Semialtricial

Down-covered, unable to leave nest, fed by parents	1. Eyes open	e.g. herons, hawks
	2. Eyes closed	e.g. owls

Altricial

Eyes closed, little or no down, unable to leave nest, fed by parents		e.g. passerines

SOURCE: J.C. Welty and L. Baptista, *The Life of Birds,* 4th ed. (Orlando, FL: Harcourt Brace Jovanovich Publishers, 1990)

Embryonic Development

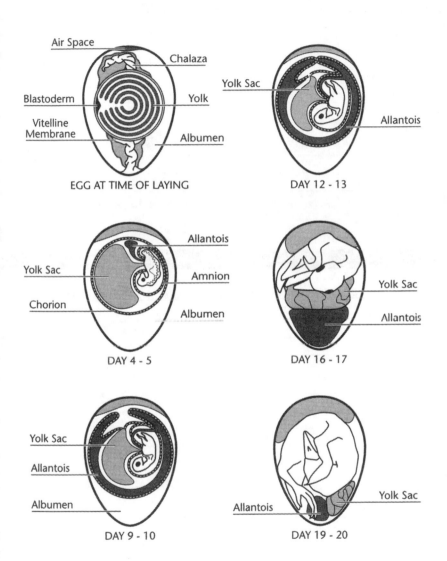

49

A Comparison of Organs of Precocial and Altricial Young at Hatching

Type & Species	Percentages of Total Body Weight		
	Eyes	Brain	Intestines
Precocial young			
Snowy plover	10.7	7.2	6.6
Japanese quail	5.5	6.2	9.7
Ring-necked pheasant	4.2	4.2	6.5
Water rail	4.5	6.2	10.5
Altricial young			
Pigeon	4.9	2.9	10.3
Alpine swift	6.1	3.1	14.6
Jackdaw	5.5	3.6	13.1
European starling	4.0	3.2	14.1

SOURCE: J.C. Welty and L. Baptista, *The Life of Birds*, 4th ed. (Orlando. FL: Harcourt Brace Jovanovich College Publishers, 1990)

Sex Ratios

Sample Sex Ratios in Selected Species of Adult Wild Birds

	Total Number of Birds	Percent Males	Percent Females
American crow	1,000	53	47
Blue-winged teal	5,090	59	41
Boat-tailed grackle	5,333	33	67
Bobwhite quail	45,452	53	47
Brown-headed cowbird	4,281	74	26
House sparrow	20,931	55	45
Mallard	21,723	52	48
Pintail	5,707	66	34
Purple finch	1,380	57	43
Red-winged blackbird	6,480	74	26

SOURCE: J.C. Welty and L. Baptista, *The Life of Birds*, 4th ed. (Orlando. FL: Harcourt Brace Jovanovich College Publishers, 1990)

Mortality

Longevity Records for Selected Wild Birds

	Maximum Age (yrs)*		Maximum Age (yrs)*
American goldfinch	11	Brown-throated sunbird	12
American robin	14	Buff-backed heron	23
American crow	15	Bullfinch	18
American coot	22	Bulwer's petrel	24
American white pelican	26	Buzzard	24
American kestrel	12	Canada goose	23
Arctic tern	34	Capercaillie	9
Arctic skua	18	Carrion crow	19
Atlantic puffin	52	Chaffinch	14
Bald eagle	28	Chimney swift	15
Barn owl	34	Chinstrap penguin	11
Bay-backed shrike	8	Cliff swallow	11
Black vulture	25	Collared dove	16
Black-and-white warbler	11	Common snipe	12
Black guillemot	20	Common raven	13
Black-capped chickadee	12	Common grackle	22
Black-footed albatross	28	Common murre	26
Black-headed gull	32	Common starling	22
Black-throated diver	27	Crested myna	11
Blackbird	20	Cuckoo	13
Blue jay	18	Dark-eyed junco	11
Blue tit	21	Dipper	8
Blue-faced booby	23	Dunlin	24
Blue-gray tanager	9	Dunnock	9
Blue-winged teal	17	Eurasian tree sparrow	13
Bobwhite quail	7	Eurasian collared-dove	14
Bohemian waxwing	12	Eurasian treecreeper	8
Bristle-thighed curlew	24	Eurasian kestrel	16
Brown booby	26	Eurasian jay	16
Brown pelican	43	Eurasian curlew	31
Brown-headed cowbird	16	Glaucous gull	21

Longevity Records for Selected Wild Birds (cont'd)

	Maximum Age (yrs)*		Maximum Age (yrs)*
Goldcrest	7	Monk parakeet	6
Golden oriole	15	Mourning dove	19
Golden eagle	32	Mute swan	27
Grasshopper sparrow	7	Nightingale	8
Gray catbird	11	Northern mockingbird	8
Gray partridge	5	Northern harrier	16
Great blue heron	23	Northern fulmar	50
Great cormorant	22	Northern cardinal	16
Great tit	15	Northern gannet	21
Great frigatebird	34	Olive-winged bulbul	12
Great gray owl	13	Osprey	25
Great horned owl	29	Oystercatcher	36
Great spotted woodpecker	10	Peregrine falcon	19
Greenfinch	12	Pied flycatcher	9
Hairy woodpecker	16	Pied wagtail	11
Herring gull	32	Pink-footed goose	22
Honey buzzard	29	Purple heron	25
Horned lark	8	Purple martin	14
House finch	12	Red-bellied woodpecker	12
House martin	14	Red-footed booby	22
House sparrow	13	Red-tailed hawk	21
House wren	7	Red-throated loon	24
Kea	14	Red-winged blackbird	14
Killdeer	11	Reed warbler	12
Kookaburra	12	Ring-billed gull	32
Lapwing	25	Ring-necked pheasant	18
Laysan albatross	53	Robin	13
Leach's petrel	36	Rock pigeon	20
Little blue penguin	19	Rook	20
Little grebe	13	Royal albatross	58
Long-eared owl	28	Ruby-throated hummingbird	9
Long-tailed tit	8	Ruddy duck	14
Magpie	21	Sanderling	13
Mallard	29	Scarlet tanager	10
Manx shearwater	26	Shag	21
Mistle thrush	11	Short-eared owl	13

Longevity Records for Selected Wild Birds (cont'd)

	Maximum Age (yrs)[*]		Maximum Age (yrs)[*]
Short-tailed shearwater	30	Turkey vulture	17
Siberian tit	7	Warbling vireo	13
Silvereye	11	Waved albatross	38
Skylark	10	White wagtail	10
Snowy owl	9	White stork	26
Song sparrow	10	White-breasted nuthatch	10
Sooty tern	34	White-browed babbler	12
Spoonbill	28	White-crowned sparrow	13
Spotted sandpiper	12	Willow tit	9
Spruce grouse	13	Willow ptarmigan	9
Tengmalm's owl	11	Yellow warbler	9
Tree swallow	11	Yellow-eyed penguin	18
Trumpeter swan	24	Yellow-rumped warbler	7

SOURCE: Taken from various textbooks and scientific journals, but mostly from The Birds of North America series published by the Academy of Natural Sciences, Washington, DC and the American Ornithologists' Union, and from the Royal Society for the Protection of Birds

[*] Ages of 6 months or greater were rounded off to the next year; also note that some birds were still alive when their ages were recorded

Maximum Known Ages of Selected Captive Bird Species

	Maximum age recorded (years)		Maximum age recorded (years)
American kestrel	14	House sparrow	23
Andean condor	77	Monk parakeet	15
Bald eagle	36	Mute swan	21
Bateleur eagle	55	Northern cardinal	22
Blue jay	26	Northern mockingbird	20
Canada goose	33	Red-crowned parrot	20
Common caracara	55	Red-tailed hawk	29
Common raven	80	Saw-whet owl	17
Common starling	17	Siberian white crane	62
Eagle owl	68	Snowy owl	28
Garden warbler	24	Sulphur-crested cockatoo	80
Golden eagle	46	Trumpeter swan	32
Herring gull	44	White pelican	52

SOURCE: J. Dorst, The Life of Birds. Vol. 1 (New York: Columbia University Press, 1974); The Birds of North America series published by the Academy of Natural Sciences, Washington, DC and the American Ornithologists' Union

Potential Average Longevity of Popular Birds

	years		years
Kestrels	2–10	Juncos	3–11
Blackbirds	4–16	Nuthatches	5–9
Grackles	4–16	Orioles	6–8
Bluebirds	3–6	Martins	4–8
Tree creepers	3–5	Small owls	6–13
Cardinals	4–13	Sparrows	2–3
Tits	3–12	Starling	5–20
Crows	6–14	Swallows	4–16
Doves and pigeons	6–17	Tanagers	3–9
Finches	4–12	Thrushes	3–12
Flycatchers	6–11	Towhees	4–14
Grosbeaks	4–13	Waxwings	3–7
Hummingbirds	5–12	Woodpeckers	4–20
Jays	5–15	Wrens	3–7

SOURCE: Approximations based on J.K. Terres, *The Audubon Society Encyclopedia of North American Birds* (New York: Alfred A. Knopf, 1987)

Estimated Annual Mortality Rate (%) of Selected Birds*

Yellow-eyed penguin	10	Buzzard	19
Manx shearwater	5	Mourning dove	69
Pintado petrel	5–6	Swift	18
Snow petrel	4–7	Swallow	63
Sooty shearwater	7	White-bearded manakin	11
Mallard	40–64	Redstart	56
Redshank	25	Robin	57–66
Ringed plover	25–30	Blackbird	42
Common tern	30	American robin	48
Heron	31	Starling	50–63
Mute swan	38	Great tit	46
Pheasant	72	Blue tit	41–73
Bobwhite quail	87	Song sparrow	44
Herring gull	30	Red-billed firefinch	70–75

* decreases with age and experience

SOURCE: J. Dorst. *The Life of Birds*, Vol. 1 (New York: Columbia University Press, 1974)

Relative Annual Human-Related Mortality of Birds in the U.S.

Cause	Estimated Annual Mortality (millions)
Recreational hunting	120
Nuisance bird control	2
Scientific research	0.02
Indirect pesticide poisoning	72
Collisions with:	
Motor vehicles	60–80
Power lines	0.1–174
Communication towers	4–50
Buildings	100–1,000
Wind generators	0.01–0.04
Electrocution	0.01–0.1
Cat predation	118

SOURCE: Adapted from R.C. Banks, *Human-related Mortality of Birds in the United States* Special Scientific Report—Wildlife No. 215,. U.S. Dept. Interior (Washington, D.C., 1979); F.B. Gill, *Ornithology* (Englewood Cliffs, NJ: Prentice-Hall, 1990); D.A. Klem, *Biology of Collisions Between Birds and Windows*, Ph.D. Thesis, Southern Illinois University, 1979; J.S. Coleman, S.A. Temple, and S.R. Craven, *Cats and Wildlife. A Conservation Dilemma* (Madison WI: Cooperative Extension Publ., 1997); D.M. Bird, unpublished data; W.P. Erickson, unpublished data; A. Manville, unpublished data

Threatened and Endangered Bird Species

Endangered Bird Species in Canada as of 2003

Extinct (3):

Great auk

Labrador duck

Passenger pigeon

Extirpated (2):

Greater prairie-chicken`

Greater sage grouse (subspecies *phaios*)

Endangered (21):

Acadian flycatcher

Barn owl

Burrowing owl (eastern population)

Eskimo curlew

Greater sage-grouse (subspecies *urophasianus*)

Henslow's sparrow

King rail

Kirtland's warbler

Eastern loggerhead shrike (subspecies *migrans*)

Mountain plover

Northern bobwhite

Northern spotted owl

Piping plover (subspecies *circumcinctus, melodus*)

Prothotonary warbler

Roseate tern

Sage thrasher

Western screech-owl (subspecies *macfarlanei*)

Western yellow-breasted chat

Whooping crane

White-headed woodpecker

Threatened (8):

Hooded warbler

Least bittern

Marbled murrelet

Northern goshawk (subspecies *laingi*)

Peregrine falcon (subspecies *anatum*)

Prairie loggerhead shrike (subspecies *excubitorides*)

Ross's gull

Sprague's pipit

Special Concern (22):

Eastern yellow-breasted chat

Long-billed curlew

Harequin duck (eastern population)

Peregrine falcon (subspecies *pealei* and *tundrius*)

Barrow's goldeneye (eastern population)

Ivory gull

Ferruginous hawk

Red-shouldered hawk

Great blue heron (subspecies *fannini*)

Ancient murrelet

Barn owl (western population)

Flammulated owl

Short-eared owl

Yellow rail

Western screech-owl (subspecies *kennicottii*)

Savannah sparrow (subspecies *princeps*)

Bicknell's thrush

Cerulean warbler

Louisiana waterthrush

Lewis's woodpecker

Red-headed woodpecker

Endangered Bird Species in the U.S. as of 2003

Endangered (78):

Hawaii akepa (honeycreeper)

Maui akepa (honeycreeper)

Kauai akialoa (honeycreeper)

Akiapola'au (honeycreeper)

Short-tailed albatross

Yellow-shouldered blackbird

Masked bobwhite (quail)

Guam broadbill

Cahow

Hawaiian coot

Mississippi sandhill crane

California condor

Whooping crane

Hawaii creeper

Molokai creeper

Oahu creeper

Hawaiian crow ('alala)

Mariana crow (aga)

White-necked crow

Eskimo curlew

Hawaiian duck (koloa)

Laysan duck

Oahu elepaio

Northern aplomado falcon

Laysan finch (honeycreeper)

Nihoa finch (honeycreeper)

Southwestern willow flycatcher

Hawaiian goose

Hawaiian hawk

Puerto Rican broad-winged hawk

Puerto Rican sharp-shinned hawk

Crested honeycreeper

Guam Micronesian kingfisher

Everglade snail kite

Mariana mallard

Micronesian megapode

Nihoa millerbird (Old World warbler)

Hawaiian common moorhen

Mariana common moorhen

Puerto Rican nightjar

Nukupu'u (honeycreeper)

Kauai 'O'o (honeycreeper)

'O'u (honeycreeper)

Palila (honeycreeper)

Puerto Rican parrot

Maui parrotbill (honeycreeper)

Brown pelican

Hawaiian dark-rumped petrel

Puerto Rican plain pigeon

Piping plover

Po'ouli (honeycreeper)

Attwater's greater prairie-chicken

Cactus ferruginous pygmy-owl

California clapper rail

Guam rail

Light-footed clapper rail

Yuma clapper rail

San Clemente loggerhead shrike

Cape Sable seaside sparrow

Florida grasshopper sparrow

Hawaiian stilt

Wood stork

Mariana gray swiftlet

California least tern

Least tern

Roseate tern

Large Kauai thrush (kamao)

Molokai thrush

Small Kauai thrush (puaiohi)

Black-capped vireo

Least Bell's vireo

Bachman's warbler

Golden-cheeked warbler

Kirtland's warbler

Reed nightingale warbler (Old World warbler)

Bridled white-eye

Ivory-billed woodpecker

Red-cockaded woodpecker

Threatened (16):

Inyo California towhee

Roseate tern

Newell's Townsend's shearwater

San Clemente sage sparrow

Western snowy plover

Piping plover

Northern spotted owl

Mexican spotted owl

Marbled murrelet

Tinian monarch (Old World flycatcher)

Audubon's crested caracara

Bald eagle

Spectacled eider

Steller's eider

Coastal California gnatcatcher

Florida scrub jay

Experimental Populations Essential/Non-essential (3):

California condor

Whooping crane

Guam rail

Birds of Conservation Concern in the U.K. (2002–2007)

Red List Species: High Conservation Concern (40)

Aquatic warbler

Bittern

Black grouse

Black-tailed godwit

Bullfinch

Capercaillie

Cirl bunting

Common scoter

Corn bunting

Corncrake

Grasshopper warbler

Grey partridge

Hen harrier

House sparrow

Lesser spotted woodpecker

Linnet

Marsh tit

Marsh warbler

Nightjar

Quail

Red-backed shrike

Red-necked phalarope

Reed bunting

Ring ouzel

Roseate tern

Savi's warbler

Scottish crossbill

Skylark

Song thrush

Spotted flycatcher

Starling

Stone-curlew

Tree sparrow

Turtle dove

Twite

White-tailed eagle

Willow tit

Woodlark

Wryneck

Yellowhammer

Amber List Species: Medium Conservation Concern (121)

Arctic tern

Avocet

Bar-tailed godwit

Barn owl

Barnacle goose

Bean goose

Bearded tit

Bewick's swan

Black redstart

Black guillemot

Black-headed gull

Black-necked grebe

Black-throated diver

Bluethroat

Brent goose

Chough

Common gull
Common rosefinch
Cormorant
Crane
Cuckoo
Curlew
Dartford warbler
Dotterel
Dunlin
Dunnock
Eider
Fieldfare
Firecrest
Fulmar
Gadwall
Gannet
Garganey
Goldcrest
Golden oriole
Golden eagle
Goldeneye
Great northern diver
Great skua
Green woodpecker
Green sandpiper
Grey wagtail
Grey plover
Greylag goose
Guillemot
Hawfinch
Herring gull
Honey buzzard
House martin
Kestrel
Kingfisher
Kittiwake
Knot
Lapwing
Leach's petrel
Lesser redpoll
Lesser black-backed gull
Little egret
Little tern
Long-tailed duck
Manx shearwater

Marsh harrier
Meadow pipit
Mediterranean gull
Merlin
Mistle thrush
Montagu's harrier
Mute swan
Nightingale
Osprey
Oystercatcher
Parrot crossbill
Peregrine falcon
Pink-footed goose
Pintail
Pochard
Puffin
Purple sandpiper
Razorbill
Red grouse
Red kite
Red-necked grebe
Red-throated diver
Redshank
Redstart
Redwing
Ringed plover
Ruff
Sand martin
Sandwich tern
Scaup
Serin
Shag
Shelduck
Short-eared owl
Shoveler
Slavonian grebe
Snipe
Snow bunting
Spoonbill
Spotted crake
Spotted redshank
Stock dove
Stonechat
Storm petrel
Swallow

Teal	Whooper swan
Temminck's stint	Wigeon
Tree pipit	Willow warbler
Turnstone	Wood sandpiper
Velvet scoter	Wood warbler
Water rail	Woodcock
Whimbrel	Yellow wagtail
White-fronted goose	

SOURCE: Royal Society for the Protection of Birds

Bird Species Presumed Extinct Since 1600

Aepyornis (*Aepyornis maximus*)

Slender moa (*Dinornis torosus*)

Great broad-billed moa (*Euryapteryx gravis*)

Lesser megalapteryx (*Megalapteryx didinus*)

Atitlan grebe (*Podilymbus gigas*)

Guadalupe storm petrel (*Oceanodroma macrodactyla*)

Spectacled cormorant (*Phalacrocorax perspicillatus*)

Rodrigues night heron (*Nycticorax megacephalus*)

Labrador duck (*Camptorhynchus labradorius*)

Auckland Islands merganser (*Mergus australis*)

Pink-headed duck (*Rhodonessa caryophyllacea*)

Korean crested shelduck (*Tadorna cristata*)

Guadalupe caracara (*Polyborus lutosus*)

New Zealand quail (*Coturnix novae-zelandiae*)

Himalayan mountain quail (*Ophrysia superciliosa*)

Chatham Islands rail (*Rallus modestus*)

Wake Island rail (*Rallus wakensis*)

Tahitian red-billed rail (*Rallus pacificus*)

Ascension Island rail (*Atlantisia elpenor*)

Kusaie Island crake (*Porzana monasa*)

Hawaiian rail (*Porzana sandwichensis*)

Samoan wood rail (*Gallinula pacifica*)

Lord Howe swamphen (*Porphyrio albus*)

Mauritius red hen (*Aphanapteryx bonasia*)

Leguat's gelinote (*Aphanapteryx leguati*)

Great auk (*Alca impennis*)

Eskimo curlew (*Numenius borealis*)

Javanese lapwing (*Vanellus macropterus*)

White-winged sandpiper (*Prosobonia leucoptera*)

Liverpool pigeon (*Caloenas maculata*)

Rodrigues pigeon (*?Columba rodericana*)*

Bonin wood pigeon (*Columba versicolor*)

Pigeon hollandaise (*Alectroenas nitidissima*)

Bird Species Presumed Extinct Since 1600 (con't)

Forster's dove of Tanna (*?Gallicolumba ferruginea*)*

Marquesas fruit pigeon (*Ptilinopus mercerii*)

Choiseul crested pigeon (*Microgoura meeki*)

Passenger pigeon (*Ectopistes migratorius*)

Dodo (*Raphus cucullatus*)

Rodrigues solitary (*Pezophaps solitaria*)

Paradise parrot (*Psephotus pulcherrimus*)

Society parakeet (*Cyanoramphus ulietanus*)

Black-fronted parakeet (*Cyanoramphus zealandicus*)

Newton's parakeet (*Psittacula exsul*)

Mascarene parrot (*Mascarinus mascarinus*)

Broad-billed parrot (*Lophopsittacus mauritianus*)

Rodrigues parrot (*Necropsittacus rodericanus*)

Cuban Red macaw (*Ara tricolor*)

Glaucus macaw (*Anodorhynchus glaucus*)

Carolina parakeet (*Conuropsis carolinensis*)

Delalande's coucal (*Coua delalandei*)

Rodrigues little owl (*Athene murivora*)

Laughing owl (*Sceloglaux albifacies*)

Jamaica least pauraqué (*Siphonorhis americanus*)

Ryukyu kingfisher (*Halcyon miyakoensis*)

Ivory-billed woodpecker (*Campephilus principalis*)

Imperial woodpecker (*Campephilus imperialis*)

Stephen Island wren (*Xenicus lyalli*)

New Zealand bush wren (*Xenicus longipes*)

Bay thrush (*?Turdus ulietensis*)*

Grand Cayman thrush (*Turdus ravidus*)

Kittlitz's thrush (*Zoothera terrestris*)

Piopio (*Turnagra capensis*)

Aldabran brush warbler (*Nesillas aldabranus*)

Lord Howe Island white-eye (*Zosterops strenua*)

Kioea (*Chaetoptila angustipluma*)

Hawaii 'o'o (*Moho nobilis*)

Oahu 'o'o (*Moho apicalis*)

Molokai 'o'o (*Moho bishopi*)

Kauai 'o'o (*Moho braccatus*)

Bachman's warbler (*Vermivora bachmanii*)

Ula-ai-Hawane (*Ciridops anna*)

Koa 'finch' (*Rhodacanthus palmeri*)

Kona Grosbeak 'finch' (*Chloridops kona*)

Greater amakihi (*Hemignathus sagittirostris*)

Akialoa (*Hemignathus obscurus*)

Mamo (*Drepanis pacifica*)

Black mamo (*Drepanis funerea*)

Bird Species Presumed Extinct Since 1600 (con't)

Bonin Islands grosbeak (*Chaunoproctus ferreirostris*)

Kusaie Island starling (*Aplonis corvina*)

Mysterious starling (*Aplonis mavornata*)

Norfolk and Lord Howe starling (*Aplonis fusca*)

Bourbon crested starling (*Fregilupus varius*)

Rodrigues starling (*Fregilupus rodericanus*)

Huia (*Heteralocha acutirostris*)

? denotes species unsure

SOURCE: E. Fuller, *Extinct Birds* (Ithaca, NY: Comstock Publishing Associates, 2001)

Mascot Birds

Official and Unofficial National Birds

Anguilla	Mourning dove
Argentina	Rufous hornero
Australia	Emu
Austria	Barn swallow
Bahamas	Greater flamingo
Belgium	Kestrel
Belize	Keel-billed toucan
Bermuda	White-tailed tropicbird
Bolivia	Andean condor
Bonaire	Greater flamingo
Brazil	Golden parakeet
British Virgin Islands	Mourning dove
Canada	Common loon
Cayman Islands	Cayman parrot
Chile	Andean condor
China:	
Shaanxi Province	Crested ibis
Ningxia Province	Blue-eared pheasant
Shanxi Province	Brown-eared pheasant
Colombia	Andean condor
Costa Rica	Clay-colored robin
Cuba	Cuban trogon
Denmark	Mute swan
Dominica	Imperial parrot
Dominican Republic	Palm chat
Ecuador	Andean condor
Estonia	Barn swallow
Faeroe Islands	Eurasian oystercatcher
Finland	Whooper swan
France	Gallic rooster (Red jungle fowl)
Germany	White stork
Grenada	Grenada dove
Guatemala	Quetzal
Guyana	Hoatzin or canje "pheasant"
Haiti	Hispaniolan trogon
Honduras	Yellow-naped Amazon parrot
Hungary	Great bustard
Iceland	Gyrfalcon
India	Peacock
Indonesia	Javan hawk eagle
Jamaica	Red-billed streamer tail

Official and Unofficial National Birds (cont'd)

Japan	Kiyi or green pheasant
Jordan	Sinai rosefinch
Korea	Black-billed magpie
Latvia	White wagtail
Liberia	Pepper bird
Lithuania	White stork
Luxembourg	Goldcrest
Malta	Blue rock thrush
Mexico	Crested caracara
Montserrat	Montserrat oriole
Myanmar	Burmese peacock
Namibia	Crimson-breasted shrike
Nepal	Impeyan pheasant
New Caledonia	Kagu
Nicaragua	Turquoise-browed motmot
Nigeria	Black-crowned crane
Norway	Dipper
Panama	Harpy eagle
Pakistan	Chukar partridge
Paraguay	Bare-throated bellbird
Peru	Andean cock-of-the-rock
Philippines	Philippine eagle
Puerto Rico	Puerto Rican woodpecker
St Kitts and Nevis	Brown pelican
St Lucia	St Lucian parrot
St Vincent and Grenadines	St Vincent parrot
Sao Tomé and Principe	African grey parrot
Singapore	Crimson sunbird
South Africa	Blue crane
Sri Lanka	Ceylon jungle fowl
Sweden	Eurasian blackbird
Thailand	Siamese fireback pheasant
Trinidad and Tobago	Scarlet ibis
Turkey	Redwing
Uganda	Crested crane
United Kingdom	(European) Robin
USA	Bald eagle
Venezuela	Troupial
Virgin Islands	Bananaquit
Zambia	Fish eagle
Zimbabwe	Fish eagle

Canadian Provincial Birds

Alberta	Great horned owl
British Columbia	Steller's jay
Manitoba	Great grey owl
New Brunswick	Black-capped chickadee
Newfoundland	Atlantic puffin
Northwest Territory	Gyrfalcon
Nova Scotia	Osprey
Nunavut Territory	Rock ptarmigan
Ontario	Common loon
Prince Edward Island	Blue jay
Quebec	Snowy owl
Saskatchewan	Sharp-tailed grouse
Yukon Territory	Raven

State Birds (U.S)

Alabama	Northern flicker
Alaska	Willow ptarmigan
Arizona	Cactus wren
Arkansas	Northern mockingbird
California	California quail
Colorado	Lark bunting
Connecticut	American robin
Delaware	Blue hen chicken
District of Columbia	Wood thrush
Florida	Northern mockingbird
Georgia	Brown thrasher
Hawaii	Hawaiian goose or nene
Idaho	Mountain bluebird
Illinois	Northern cardinal
Indiana	Northern cardinal
Iowa	American goldfinch
Kansas	Western meadowlark
Kentucky	Northern cardinal
Louisiana	Brown pelican
Maine	Black-capped chickadee
Maryland	Baltimore oriole
Massachusetts	Black-capped chickadee
Michigan	American robin
Minnesota	Common loon
Mississippi	Northern mockingbird
Missouri	Eastern bluebird
Montana	Western meadowlark

State Birds (U.S.) (cont'd)

Nebraska	Western meadowlark
Nevada	Mountain bluebird
New Hampshire	Purple finch
New Jersey	American goldfinch
New Mexico	Greater roadrunner
New York	Eastern bluebird
North Carolina	Northern cardinal
North Dakota	Western meadowlark
Ohio	Northern cardinal
Oklahoma	Scissor-tailed flycatcher
Oregon	Western meadowlark
Pennsylvania	Ruffed grouse
Rhode Island	Rhode Island red chicken
South Carolina	Carolina wren
South Dakota	Ring-necked pheasant
Tennessee	Northern mockingbird
Texas	Northern mockingbird
Utah	California gull
Vermont	Hermit thrush
Virginia	Northern cardinal
Washington	America goldfinch
West Virginia	Northern cardinal
Wisconsin	American robin
Wyoming	Western meadowlark

Symbolic Birds

Bluebird	happiness
Cuckoo	rain prophet
Dove	gentleness, peace
Eagle	bravery, courage, emblem of war
Game cock	aggressiveness
Goose	stupidity
Kingfisher (European)	calm seas, still air
Jay	false pride
Little bird	carrier of secret information
Ostrich	self-deception
Owl	wisdom, ill omen
Pelican	loneliness
Peacock	pride, vanity

SOURCE: A.D. Cruickshank and H. Cruickshank, *1001 Questions Answered About Birds* (New York, NY: Dover Publications, 1958)

Automobiles Named After Birds

Bird	Firebird	Silver hawk
Crow	Golden hawk	Sun Bird
Crow-Elkhart Black	Gull wing	Superbird
Duck	Hawkeye	Tercel
Eagle	Power hawk	Thunderbird
Eaglet	Road Runner	Wing
Falcon	Silverbird	

Assemblages of Birds

Affliction	starlings
Alacrity	pipits
Annoyance	house sparrows
Apology	sparrows
Aristocracy	waxwings
Bazaar	guillemots, murres
Beaker	pelicans
Bevy	quail, swans
Boil	hawks
Bouquet	pheasants
Brace	pheasants, mallards, birds (on ground)
Brood	hens, chicks
Bubbling	wrens
Bugle	cranes
Building	rooks
Cast	falcons, hawks
Chain	bobolinks
Charm	finches, hummingbirds, magpies
Chatter	chickadees
Chattering	chickadees, starlings
Cheer	vireos
Clamour	rooks
Clan	crows
Cleavage	shearwaters
Cluster	knots
Clutch	chicks
Colony	gulls, penguins
Commotion or covert	coots
Company	wigeon, parrots
Congregation	cardinals, plovers
Convocation	eagles
Coven	vultures
Cover	coots
Covey	grouse, quail, partridge
Creep	nuthatches
Crowd	ibises
Deceit or desert	lapwings
Descent	woodpeckers
Dissimulation	birds
Duet	turtle (doves)
Dule	doves

Elegance	terns
Exalting/exaltation	larks
Fall	woodcock
Farce	jays
Feint	killdeer
Flamboyance, flurry	flamingos
Flight	doves, swallows
Flute	thrushes
Flock	geese or ducks (in air)
Gaggle	geese
Galaxy	gulls
Gang	turkeys
Gatling	woodpeckers
Glide	harriers
Glister	goldfinches
Gulp	cormorants, magpies, swallows
Herd	curlews or geese
Horde	crows
Host	sparrows
Jubilee	eagles
Kettle	hawks
Knob	teal
Leash	merlins
Loomery	guillemots
Motley	magpies
Murder	crows, magpies
Murmuration	starlings
Muster	peacocks
Mustering	storks
Mutation	thrushes
Nest	pheasants
Nide	pheasants
Nye	pheasants
Ostentation	peacocks
Pack	grouse
Paddling	ducks
Parlance	chats
Parliament	owls
Party	jays
Peck	doves
Peep	chickens

Piracy	jaegers	Squall	snow buntings
Pitying	turtle doves	Stand	flamingos
Plump	waterfowl, woodcocks	Stealth	cowbirds
Pod	pelicans	Strand	silky flycatchers
Quandary	evening grosbeaks	Strut	buntings
Raft	ducks (on water)	Team	ducks
Rafter	turkeys	Teeter	stilts
Rainbow	grosbeaks	Tiding(s)	magpies
Rant, rabble	ravens	Tinkle	water thrushes
Reel	virginia rails	Tittering	magpies
Regency	kingbirds	Trip	dotterel
Richness	martins	Unkindness	ravens
Rotundity	robins	Volary	birds (in air)
Rookery	seabirds	Wake	buzzards
Salt	gannets	Walk or wisp	snipe
Scold	blackbirds, jays	Watch	kingfishers, nightingales
Scratch	thrashers	Wave	snow buntings
Screw	hawks	Wedge	swans
Sedge	bitterns, cranes, herons	Whiteness	swans
Siege	bitterns, cranes, herons	Wing	plovers
Skein	geese (in air)	Wish	willets
Solitude	soras	Wreck	seabirds
Sord or suite	mallards	Yellowing	warblers
Spring	teal	Zipper	flycatchers

Records in the Bird World

Anatomy

heaviest and tallest bird: ostrich at maximum 156 kg (345 lb) and 2.7 m (9 ft)

heaviest flying bird: great bustard at maximum 21 kg (46.3 lb)

tallest flying bird: sarus crane at 1.8 m (6 ft)

largest extinct bird: *Dromornis stirtoni* of Australia at 454 kg (1,000 lb) and 3 m (10 ft)

tallest extinct bird: giant moa of New Zealand at 3.7 m (12 ft)

greatest wingspan: wandering albatross at up to 3.63 m (11 ft 11 in)

greatest wingspan of landbirds: Andean condor and marabou stork tied at 3.2 m (10.5 ft)

tallest bird: greater flamingo at 145 cm (57 in)

smallest bird: bee hummingbird at 5.7 cm (2.24 in) and 1.6 g (0.056 oz)

smallest flightless bird: Inaccessible Island rail at 12.5 cm (5 in) and 34.7 g (1.2 oz)

longest legs: ostrich

longest legs relative to body length: black-winged stilt at 23 cm (9 in) or 60 % of its height

absolute shortest legs: virtually non-existent in swifts (*Apodidae*)

longest toes relative to body length: northern jacana at 10 cm (4 in)

longest bill relative to body length: sword-tailed hummingbird at 10.5 cm (4.13 in)

absolute longest bill: Australian pelican at 47 cm (18.5 in)

absolute shortest bill: glossy swiftlet at just a few mm

most oddly bent bill: wrybill with its beak bent to one side; crossbill with upper and lower mandibles crossing over one another

only bird capable of moving its beak in two different directions: crossbills for prying open pine cones

largest and fleshiest tongue: flamingo

longest tongue relative to body size: wryneck at 66% of its body length excluding the tail

smallest hearts relative to body size: Central and South American tinamous at 1.6–3.1 % of body weight

longest feathers: onagadori, a domestic strain of red jungle fowl, at 10.59 m (34.75 ft)

longest tail feathers: crested argus pheasant at 173 cm (5.7 ft)

longest tail coverts: Indian and green peafowl at 160 cm (5.24 ft)

widest tail feathers: crested argus pheasant at 13 cm (5.1 in)

longest tail feathers relative to body length: fork-tailed flycatcher at 27 cm (10.75 in), 77% of its body length

longest primary feathers relative to body length: pennant-winged nightjar at 60 cm (2 ft)

shortest tails: virtually non-existent in kiwis, emus, rheas, cassowaries

greatest number of feathers: whistling swan at 25,216

lowest number of feathers: ruby-throated hummingbird at 940

most secondary flight feathers: wandering and royal albatrosses with 40 secondaries and 11 primaries on each wing

most unique individual plumage variation within a species: no two male ruffs alike

best camouflaged bird: American woodcock, nightjars

largest eyeball: ostrich with a diameter of 5 cm (2 in)

Locomotion

fastest moving bird*: diving peregrine falcon reliably measured at 320 km/h (200 mph)

fastest flapping flight*: white-throated needle-tailed swift at 170 km/h (106 mph)

fastest level flight*: red-breasted merganser at 161 km/h (100 mph)

fastest moving racing pigeon*: 177 km/h (110 mph)

slowest flying bird: American woodcock at 8 km/h (5 mph)

fastest wingbeat: hummingbirds, e.g. amethyst woodstar and horned sungem at 90/sec slowest wingbeat: vultures at 1/sec

longest soaring bird: albatross and condor

smallest soaring bird: swift

highest recorded altitude: Ruppell's griffon vulture hitting a jetliner at 11,274 m (7 mi)

highest altitude regularly flown: bar-headed goose and demoiselle crane at 5,500 m (18,000 ft)

most aerial bird: sooty tern at 3 to 10 years without landing

most aerial landbird: common swift at 3 years without landing

longest one-way migration (assuming a coastal route): common tern at 26,000 km (16,210 mi) in January 1997

longest two-way annual migration: Arctic tern nesting in the Arctic and wintering in the Antarctic up to 17,700 km (11,000 mi.) each way

longest distance flown non-stop relative to a small body size: 800 km (500 mi) by ruby-throated hummingbird migrating across the Caribbean Gulf

most aquatic bird: penguins with 75% of their lives spent in the sea

bird with the least connection to land: ancient murrelet

fastest running bird: ostrich at 97.5 km/h (60 mph)

fastest running flying bird: greater roadrunner at 42 km/h (26 mph)

furthest distance walked by a migrating bird: emu in Australia at 515 km (320 mi)

fastest underwater swimming bird: gentoo penguin at 36 km/h (22.3 mph)

deepest dive for non-flying bird: emperor penguin at 540 m (1,772 ft)

deepest dive for a flying bird: thick-billed murre at 210 m (689 ft)

deepest dive for a flying bird under 210 g (7 oz): Peruvian diving petrel at 83 m (272 ft)

longest submergence: emperor penguin at 18 min

greatest weight-carrying capacity feat: Pallas's fish eagle (3,700 g or 8 lb) lifting a carp (5,900 g or 13 lb), i.e. 160% of its body weight

---

* flight speeds for birds must be quoted with caution; speed recorded depends on many factors, e.g. tail-winds, method of measurement used, etc.

Physiology

keenest sense of smell: kiwi, turkey vulture, petrel

keenest sense of hearing: barn owl (the best tested), screech owl, boreal owl, great grey owl

highest visual acuity: diurnal raptors with over 1 million cones per sq. mm in the retinal fovea

best light-gathering capacity at night: owls, e.g. tawny owl

greatest G-force (acceleration due to gravity): beak of red-headed woodpecker hitting bark at 20.9 km/h (13 mph)

highest daily frequency of pecking: 12,000 times by black woodpecker

most intelligent bird: African grey parrot, crow family, "bait-fishing" green and striated herons

most talkative bird: African grey parrot with a vocabulary of 800 words

greatest bird mimic: marsh warbler with up to 84 songs

most songs sung per unit time: 22,197 in 10 hours by a red-eyed vireo

bird with the farthest carrying sound: boom of the kakapo of New Zealand heard 6.4 km (4 mi) away

birds capable of echolocation: cave swiftlets and oilbirds

greatest hibernator: poorwill with body temperature lowered to 18–20 degrees C (64.4–68 degrees F)

fastest heartbeat: hummingbird at 16 beats per second

coldest temperature regularly endured by a bird: average temperatures of –45.6 degrees C (–50 degress F) for emperor penguins

coldest temperature endured by a bird: –62.5 degrees C (–80.5 degrees F) by snowy owls

coldest temperature of land where a bird has been recorded: –89.6 degrees C (–129 degrees F) in Vostok, Russia for south polar skua

warmest temperature regularly endured by a bird: larks and wheatears at 44–45 degrees C (111–113 degrees F)

highest wintering altitude: giant coot in South America in excess of 1,370 m (4,500 ft)

greatest weight gain relative to its body size: sedge warbler from 11 to 22 g (0.35–0.70 oz) just prior to migration

busiest eater: sand grouse at 5,000 to 80,000 seeds per day

Reproduction

largest recorded nesting bird colony: 136 million passenger pigeons nesting in an area in Wisconsin covering 1,942 sq km (750 sq mi)

most abundant wild bird: red-billed quelea at up to 100 billion

lowest altitude for nesting: little green bee-eater at 400 m (1,307 ft) below sea-level in the Dead Sea

highest altitude for nesting: Himalayan snow-cock at 5,000 m (15,000 ft)

most northerly nesting bird: ivory gull at edge of pack ice about 650 km (400 mi) south of the North Pole

longest fasting period: 134 days for incubating male emperor penguins

bird with the safest nesting ground: Providence petrel on Lord Howe Island off Australia (no predators)

bird with the most dangerous nesting ground: Japanese white-naped crane in the DMV between North and South Korea

largest ground nest: dusky scrubfowl nest at 11 m (36 ft) wide and 4.9 m (16 ft) high with over 2,700 kg (300 tons) of forest floor litter

largest tree nest: bald eagle in Florida at 6.1 m (20 ft) deep, 2.9 m (9.5 ft) wide and weighing 2,722 kg (almost 3 tons)

largest social nest: African social weavers with a 100-chamber nest structure 8.2 m (27 ft) in length and 1.8 m (6 ft) high

largest roofed nest: hammerhead stork at 2 m (6.5 ft) wide and 2 m (6.5 ft) deep

longest nest burrow: rhinoceros auklet at 8 m (26 ft)

highest tree nest: black-crowned heron at 53 m (160 ft)

smallest nest: Cuban bee and vervain hummingbirds at 1.98 cm (0.78 in) in breadth and 1.98–3.0 cm (0.78–1.2 in) deep

most skilled tailor during nest-building: golden-headed cisticola in Australia

most beautiful architectural nest creation: 9 months of building by the Volegkopf bowerbird of New Guinea

foulest smelling nest: Eurasian hoopoe

greatest number of sperm storage tubules in the oviduct: turkey at 20,000

greatest longevity of sperm inside a female: turkey at 42 days

longest penis relative to body size: Argentine stiff-tailed duck at 20 cm (8 in), half its body length

longest copulation time: buffalo weaver at about 30 minutes

largest egg laid by bird existing today: ostrich; 17.8 by 14 cm (7 by 4.5 in)

heaviest recorded egg laid by any bird ever: extinct elephant bird; 6.7 kg (18 lb)

largest egg laid by a passerine (perching song-bird): 57 g (2 oz) by Australian lyrebirds

largest egg laid relative to body weight: little spotted kiwi and storm petrel at 25%

smallest egg laid relative to body weight: ostrich egg at 1–1.5%

smallest egg: West Indian vervain hummingbird at 10 mm (0.39 in) in length and 0.375 g (0.0132 oz)

roundest egg: owl, tinamou

longest interval between eggs laid: maleofowl at 10–12 day intervals

largest clutch laid by a nidicolous species: 19 eggs laid by a European blue tit

largest clutch laid by a nidifugous species: 28 by a bobwhite quail

largest average clutch size: 15–19 by a grey partridge

smallest clutch size: 1 egg laid every 2 years by albatrosses

greatest number of eggs laid consecutively: 146 by a mallard

longest uninterrupted incubation period: emperor penguin at 64–67 days

longest interrupted incubation period: wandering albatross and brown kiwi at 85 days

longest incubation period by a passerine species: 50 days for Australian lyrebird

shortest incubation period: 11 days by small passerines

largest hatchling in a flying bird: mute swan

largest hatchling relative to body size: brown kiwi at 25% of its body weight

most precocial chick: hatched torrent ducklings fledging into fast-flowing rivers in the Andes

longest fledging period of flying birds: wandering albatross at 278 days

greatest number of broods raised in one year: 21 by zebra finch pair

fastest to breeding maturity: common quail at 5 weeks

slowest to breeding maturity: royal and wandering albatrosses at 6–10 years

slowest breeder: albatross with one chick every 2 to 3 years

longest-lived wild bird: royal albatross at over 58 years

longest-lived captive bird: sulphur-crested cockatoo and common raven at over 80 years

tamest wild bird: Providence petrel on Lord Howe Island

Human-Related

largest collection of bird skins: British Museum of Natural History with 1.25 million

most valuable bird: 8 billion domestic chickens produce 562,000 billion eggs annually

most valuable bird droppings: guanay cormorants producing guano for harvest in Peru

most valuable nest: grey-rumped swiftlet for bird's nest soup

largest domesticated bird: ostrich

earliest domesticated bird: jungle fowl at 3,200 BCE

heaviest domestic turkey: 37 kg (81 lb)

country with the most endangered birds: Indonesia with 136 (Brazil second with 103)

country with the highest percentage of its bird species endangered: New Zealand with 30%

country with the most introduced species: state of Hawaii with 68

most recent species of bird to be declared extinct: flightless Atitlan grebe of Guatemala in 1984

most recent North American bird to be declared extinct: dusky seaside sparrow, a race of seaside sparrow, in 1987

rarest bird in the world: ivory-billed woodpecker, Jerdon's courser among the rarest

highest price paid for a bird book: $3.96 million U.S. for a set of John James Audubon's *The Birds of America* in 1989

highest price paid for a mounted bird: £9,000 for an extinct great auk by the Natural History Museum of Iceland in 1971

highest price paid for a live bird: US$ 175,000 for a white saker falcon

highest price paid for a cage bird: £5,000 for a hyacinth macaw

highest price paid for an egg: 1,000 pounds for an egg of extinct *Aepyornis maximus*

first bird featured on a U.S. postage stamp: bald eagle

SOURCES: B. Martin, *World Birds* (Enfield, Middlesex: Guinness Superlatives Ltd, 1987); F.S. Todd, *10,001 Titillating Tidbits of Avian Trivia* (Vista, CA: Ibis Publishing Co., 1994); D. Attenborough, *Life of Birds* (Princeton, NJ: Princeton University Press, 1998) and many other ornithological textbooks and reference books.

Who's Who in Bird Biology and Conservation

Abert, James William (1820–1897): While collecting birds for Spencer F. Baird, he discovered a towhee that was later given the scientific name *Pipilo aberti*.

Adams, Edward (1824–1856): British surgeon, naturalist, and collector; involved in two polar expeditions to North America; the yellow-billed loon species name *adamsii* honors him.

Aiken, Charles Edward Howard (1850–1936): Ornithologist, taxidermist, and traveler; discovered two birds: the white-winged junco, *Junco aikeni*, and a subspecies of the screech owl, *Otus asio aikeni*.

Aldrich, John Warren (1906–1995): Curator of ornithology at the Cleveland Museum of Natural History; chief of the Section of Distribution and Migration of Birds of the U.S. Fish and Wildlife Service; editor of *Audubon Field Notes*; research associate of the Smithsonian Institution; helped form the Buffalo Ornithological Society; member of many organizations including serving as president of the American Ornithologists' Union.

Alexander, Horace Gundry (1889–1989): Known for his interest in birds, especially leaf-warblers; contributed to the *Handbook of British Birds* by writing about song periods and identification; authored *Some Notes on Asian Leaf Warblers* and *Seventy Years of Birdwatching*.

Alexander, Christopher (1887–1917): Known for his interest in natural history; originated a method to count breeding birds and map territories; acknowledged that different birds occupied different altitudes in mountain areas.

Alexander, Wilfrid Backhouse (1885–1965): Research officer; director of the library at the Edward Grey Institute; author of *Birds of the Ocean*.

Ali, Salim (1896–1987): Indian ornithologist who fought for environmental awareness; considered to be the father of Asian ecological understanding; honorary fellow of the American Ornithologists' Union; published *Handbook of the Birds of India and Pakistan*; recipient of several awards including the Gold Medal of the British Ornithologists' Union.

Allen, Arthur Augustus (1885–1964): Educator, research scientist, writer, lecturer, bird photographer and fellow of the American Ornithologists' Union; first in America to bear the title of Professor of Ornithology; taught at Cornell University where he remained for over 50 years; co-founder of the Cornell Laboratory of Ornithology; pioneered study of wild bird songs and calls; author of several books including *The Book of Bird Life* and *Stalking Birds with Color Camera*; a medal bearing his name is given to those widening popular interest in birds and for distinguished service to ornithology.

Allen, Charles Andrew (1841–1930): Bird collector; memorialized by Allen's hummingbird.

Allen, Robert Porter (1905–1963): Ornithologist; National Audubon Society conservationist; known for his interest in raptor migration; author of several studies on North American wading birds; wrote *On the Trail of Vanishing Species*.

Allen, Joel Asaph (1838–1921): The first curator of birds at Harvard's Museum of Comparative Zoology; a founder of the Nuttall Ornithological Club in Cambridge in 1873 and the American Ornithologists' Union (AOU) in 1883; the first president of the AOU, and the first editor of its journal, *The Auk*; studied geographic variation in birds and devised Allen's Rule.

Alvarez del Toro, Miguel (1917–1996): Taxidermist, Museum of Natural History, Tuxtla Gutiérrez; author of *Birds of Chiapas*; received the Paul Getty Prize for Conservation of Nature. (CSH)

Arbib, Robert S., Jr. (1915–1987): Ornithologist; editor of the *Linnaean Newsletter* and *American Birds*; president of the Federation of New York State Bird Clubs and the Linnaean Society of New York; elective member of the American Ornithologists' Union; helped initiate the Hawk Migration Association of North America; co-authored *The Hungry Bird Book* and *Enjoying Birds around New York City*; recipient of the Burroughs Medal.

Archbold, Richard (1907–1976): Naturalist; member of several expeditions; collected in New Guinea; established the Archbold Biological Station in Florida.

Arminjon, Vittorio (1830–1897): Captain and commander of the first Italian vessel to sail around the world; on this voyage the South Trinidad petrel was discovered and named *Pterodroma arminjoniana* in his honor.

Armstrong, Edward Allworthy (1900–1978): Irish naturalist; studied the wren; corresponding fellow of the American Ornithologists' Union; vice-president of the British Ornithologists' Union; published several books including *Birds of the Grey Wind* which received the Burroughs Medal, *Bird Display and Behaviour*, and *The Way Birds Live*.

Aschoff, Jürgen (1913–1998): Director of the Vogelwarte Radolfzell; physiologist; pioneer in biological rhythms; made German ornithology a respected science. (CSH)

Audubon, John James (1785–1851): Formally trained as an artist in France and then migrated to the United States in 1803; traveled widely throughout North America east of the Rockies, observing and shooting birds and painting life-sized watercolors of them; besides being responsible for the famous elephant folio prints, Audubon also published a five-volume *Ornithological Biography, or an Account of the Habits of the Birds of the United States*; widely regarded as a great pioneering student of bird biology and the artistic father of American ornithology.

Austin, Oliver L., Jr. (1903–1988): Professor of zoology; Curator Emeritus in Ornithology at the Florida Museum of Natural History; introduced the Japanese mist net to the U.S.; a founder and director of the Austin Ornithological Research Station at Wellfleet; fellow of the American Ornithologists' Union; editor of *The Auk*; published *The Birds of Korea* and *Birds of the World*.

Axtell, Harold H. (1904–1992): Naturalist, biologist; curator of biology in the Buffalo Museum of Science; devoted his time to field identification of birds; elective member of the American Ornithologists' Union; fellow of the Buffalo Ornithological Society.

Bachman, Rev. John (1790–1874): Naturalist and clergyman associated with Audubon; co-author of *The Viviparous Quadrupeds of North America*; memorialized by the black oystercatcher, *Haematopus bachmani*, Bachman's sparrow, and Bachman's warbler.

Bailey, Florence Merriam (1863–1948): Ornithologist, writer; promoter of nature education; first woman to be elected a fellow of the American Ornithologists' Union; associated with the United States Biological Survey; participated in the founding of the Audubon Society of the District of Columbia; member of several expeditions in the company of her husband; authored several books including *Birds through an Opera Glass*; published the *Handbook of Birds of the Western United States*, *Birds of New Mexico*; awarded the Brewster Medal by the American Ornithologists' Union.

Baillie, James L. (1904–1970): Wrote a weekly bird column in the *Toronto Telegram*; assistant curator in the Royal Ontario Museum; participated in the provincial Faunal Survey trips; elective member of the American Ornithologists' Union; president of the Toronto Field Naturalists' Club; a founder of the Toronto Ornithological Club; director of the Federation of Ontario Naturalists; secretary-treasurer of the Canadian Audubon Society; published over 300 papers and articles; life member and recipient of the Ontario Conservation Trophy from the Federation of Ontario Naturalists; recipient of the Centennial Medal.

Baird, Spencer Fullerton (1823–1887): Participated in the establishment of the Smithsonian Institution, which became a major scientific center; in part, helped expand the museum's bird collection; co-authored, along with Thomas Brewer and Robert Ridgway, *A History of North American Birds*; influential zoologist who founded the "Baird school" of ornithology; named Lucy's warbler, Grace's warbler, and Virginia's warbler after acquaintances; memorialized by Baird's sandpiper and Baird's sparrow.

Balph, David Finley (1931–1990): Teacher of animal behavior at Utah State University; studied social behavior and feeding strategies of birds; elective member of the American Ornithologists' Union.

Bannerman, David Armitage (1886–1979): British ornithologist; chairman of the British Ornithologists' Club; worked for the British Museum (Natural History); published many papers on birds of many countries, primarily Africa; wrote eight volumes of *The Birds of Tropical West Africa* and 12 volumes of *The Birds of the British Isles*, as well as many other books on birds; received many honors.

Baptista, Luis Felipe (1941–2000): Curator of the Moore Laboratory of Zoology, Occidental College, Los Angeles; his studies of White-crowned sparrows expanded our knowledge of bird song; fellow of the American Ornithologists' Union. (CSH)

Barclay-Smith, Phyllis (?–1980): British ornithologist; linguist; served as secretary to numerous ornithological bodies; later became the secretary-general and a main builder of the International Council for Bird Preservation; editor of *Aviculture Magazine*; wrote sereval books on birds; awarded many medals in several countries.

Barrow, Sir John (1764–1848): Chief founder of the Royal Geographical Society; remembered for his Arctic travels; commemorated in Barrow's goldeneye and a subspecies of the glaucous gull.

Barth, Edvard K. (1913–1996): Norwegian ornithologist; field zoologist; photographer and writer; curator of birds at the Zoological Museum in Oslo; produced over 200 publications; known for his interest in the systematics of the Laridae.

Bartram, William (1739–1823): Known as the grandfather of ornithology; described various aspects of bird biology in *Travels through North and South Carolina, Georgia, East and West Florida,* which contained information on such aspects as nesting and migration; an inspiration to Wilson; honored by Bartram's sandpiper.

Bartram, Sir John (1699–1777): Quaker botanist; explorer; sent specimens to his friend, Linnaeus; memorialized by *Bartramia longicauda*.

Baumgartner, Frederick M. (1910–1996): Teacher at Wisconsin State University at Stevens Point; areas of study included owls, bobwhite quail, and birds of prey; elective member of the American Ornithologists' Union; editor of *Audubon Field Notes*; president of the Oklahoma Ornithological Society; co-authored *Oklahoma Bird Life*.

Beebe, C. William (1877–1962): Professional ornithologist; one of the pioneers in the early conservation movement in the U.S.; known for his interest in the coloration of birds, e.g. the dichromatism in birds such as snow geese, murres, and peacocks; author of *The Bird, Its Form and Function*.

Bell, John Graham (1812–1889): Naturalist and pioneer taxidermist; friend of early American ornithologists; gave lessons to U.S. president Theodore Roosevelt; Bell's vireo and the sage sparrow, *Amphispiza belli*, honor his name.

Bendire, Charles (1836–1897): A German immigrant and surgical assistant who received medals for bravery in both the Civil and Indian Wars; his fascination with eggs led to his becoming the curator of oology at the United States Museum; authored *Life Histories of North American Birds, with Special Reference to their Breeding Habits and Eggs*; memorialized by Bendire's thrasher.

Benson, Constantine ("Con") Walter (1909–1982): Sportsman; ornithologist; head of the Cambridge Bird Club; studied birds of Malawi; made major contributions to African ornithology; published over 350 articles; sorted out the collection of the Museum of Zoology in Cambridge; described seven new species and several races; published approximately 400 titles including *A Check List of the Birds of Nyasaland* and *The Birds of the Comoro Islands*; awarded the Order of the British Empire; given the Union Medal by the British Ornithologists' Union and the Gill Memorial Medal by the South African Ornithological Society.

Bent, Arthur Cleveland (1866–1954): A businessman and amateur ornithologist; made many contributions to *The Auk* regarding distribution and nesting habits of a wide variety of bird species; recognized today as having spent a great deal of time editing and, to a large extent, writing the 26-volume series *Life Histories of North American Birds* that had been started by Bendire.

Berger, Andrew J. (1915–1995): Instructor of anatomy; conservationist; studied avian musculature; fellow of the American Ornithologists' Union and the American Association for the Advancement of Science; authored *Hawaiian Birdlife* and two ornithology textbooks; participated in the writing of *Fundamentals of Ornithology*.

Bewick, Thomas (1753–1828): English artist and wood engraver; wrote and illustrated *A History of British Birds*; memorialized by Bewick's wren.

Biswas, Biswamoy (1923–1994): Chief of the Bird and Mammal Section, then director, of the Zoological Survey of India; author of *Birds of Nepal* and co-author of *Birds of Bhutan*. (CSH)

Blackburne, Anna (1726–1793): English botanist; maintained a bird museum at her home that was later used in Pennant's *Arctic Zoology*; honored by the Blackburnian warbler, *Motacilla blackburniae*.

Blair, Hugh Moray Sutherland (1901?–1986): British ornithologist; oologist; known for his interest in waders and birds in Scandinavia; major contributor to the 12 volumes of *Birds of the British Isles*.

Blake, Charles Henry (1901–1981): Professor of biology at Massachusetts Institute of Technology; bird bander; known for his "extensive knowledge of a bookish kind" on almost any topic; applied his mathematical skills to his many articles about band wear, tarsus diameters, longevity, and returns and recoveries. (CSH)

Blakiston, Thomas Wright (1832–1891): Magnetic observer with the Palliser expedition that surveyed the Canadian prairies and Rocky Mountain passes; ornithologist; collected 100 bird species and observed 29 more near Carlton, Saskatchewan, providing unsurpassed knowledge of pre-settlement bird life. (CSH)

Bleitz, Donald Louis (1915–1986): Bird photographer; elective member of the American Ornithologists' Union; member of the Eastern and Western Bird Banding Association; founder of the Bleitz Wildife Foundation; over 600 photographs of North American Birds; life member of the Cooper Ornithological Society and the Wilson Ornithological Club.

Bonaparte, Charles Lucien (1803–1857): Napoleon's nephew; made systemic and zoogeographical contributions to supplemental volumes of Wilson's *American Ornithology*; known for his work in *Conspectus Generum Avium*, has been known as the father of systemic ornithology; commemorated by Bonaparte's gull.

Bond, James (1900–1989): Ornithologist, naturalist; specialist in the birds of the West Indies; published over 100 papers; authored the *Checklist of the Birds of the West Indies*; recipient of the Brewster Medal from the American Ornithologists' Union; Ian fleming's fictional superhero is named after him.

Bonelli, Franco Andrea (1784–1830): Italian entomologist, zoologist, and naturalist; professor; founded the Turin Museum in 1811 that contributed greatly to ornithology in Italy; memorialized by Bonelli's eagle and Bonelli's warbler, *Phylloscopus bonelli*.

Borror, Donald J. (1907–1988): Entomologist interested in bird songs; pioneer of bioacoustics; fellow of the American Ornithologists' Union; 15,000 recordings; over 50 publications on avian communication, most of which concentrate on North American bird species.

Botteri, Matteo (1808–1877): Dalmatian botanist; collector; Professor of Natural History in Veracruz, Mexico; collected Botteri's sparrow which was named after him.

Boulton, W. Rudyerd (?–1983): Ornithologist in Africa; elective member of the American Ornithologists' Union; founded the Atlantica Foundation; worked for the American Museum of Natural History, the Carnegie Museum, and the Field Museum of Natural History.

Bourlière, François (1913–1993): French ecologist and gerontologist; promoter of conservation; editor-in-chief of *Revue d'Écologie*; corresponding fellow of the American Ornithologists' Union; president of the International Union for Conservation of Nature and Natural Resources; president of the Société Nationale de la Protection de la Nature; recipient of several honors including the Dutch Royal Order of the Golden Ark.

Brandt, Johann Friedrich (1802–1879): German zoologist; director of the Zoological Museum in St. Petersburg; published over 300 papers; described several mammals and birds such as Brandt's cormorant.

Barclay-Smith, Phyllis (?–1980): British ornithologist; linguist; served as secretary to numerous ornithological bodies; later became secretary general and a main builder of the International Council for Bird Preservation; editor of *Avicultural Magazine*; wrote several books on birds; awarded many medals in several countries.

Brewer, Thomas (1814–1880): A physician who became a dedicated birder; helped, like Spencer Fullerton Baird, connect the early and modern era of ornithology; is known not only for his book on bird eggs, *North American Oology*, but also for his defense of the house sparrow when it was introduced in the United States; co-author of *A History of North American Birds*; memorialized by Brewer's blackbird and Brewer's sparrow.

Brewster, William (1851–1919): Conservationist, ornithologist; one of the founders and presidents of the American Ornithologist's Union and the Nuttall Ornithological Club of Cambridge; author of over 300 papers; author of *October Farm and Concord River*; honored by Brewster's warbler; a medal named in his honor and awarded annually by the American Ornithologists' Union.

Brodkorb, Pierce (1908–1992): Bird collector; professor at the University of Florida in Gainesville; studied paleontology and osteology; went on several expeditions; compiled the *Catalogue of Fossil Birds*; fellow of the American Ornithologists' Union; recipient of the Brewster Medal.

Broley, Charles Lavelle (1879–1959): Amateur ornithologist especially known for his bald eagle banding project in Florida; wrote *Eagle Man*.

Brooks, Maurice (1900–1993): Professor of Wildlife Management, University of Western Virginia; author of *The Appalachians*; honored by the state legislature as West Virginia Man of the Year; fellow of the American Ornithologists' Union. (CSH)

Broun, Maurice (1906–1979): Earliest protector and eventual Curator Emeritus of Hawk Mountain Sanctuary; involved in conservation of raptors; elective member of the American Ornithologists' Union; produced over 100 publications; author of *Hawks Aloft: The Story of Hawk Mountain*.

Brown, Leslie (1917–1980): Agriculturist, ecologist, and ornithologist; prolific writer with over a dozen books; specialist on birds of prey; coauthored *Eagles, Hawks and Falcons of the World*; awarded an Union Medal by the British Ornithologists' Union.

Browne, Sir Thomas (1605–1682): Britain naturalist; put forward the possibility that birds migrated to warmer climates; using dissections, contributed to our comprehension of the anatomy and physiology of birds and mammals.

Buller, Sir Walter Lawry (1838–1906): New Zealand lawyer with an interest in ornithology; collected and studied New Zealand birds; author of *History of Birds of New Zealand* and *Manual of Birds of New Zealand*; fellow of the Royal Society; commemorated by Buller's shearwater, *Puffinus bulleri*.

Bullock, William (1775–?): English traveler; proprietor of Bullock's Museum in London; collected several new species of birds in Mexico; memorialized by Bullock's oriole.

Bulwer, James (1794–1879): Diplomat and ambassador to Washington, D.C.; memorialized by genus *Bulweria* and especially Bulwer's petrel, *Bulweria bulwerii*.

Burkitt, James Parson (1870–1959): Revolutionized the study of bird movement by placing metal bands on the legs of robins; specialized in territorial behavior and songs.

Burroughs, John (1837–1921): Popularized the study of nature in America; known as the Hudson River naturalist, wrote 25 books including *Wake Robin*; possessed an innate ability to recognize bird songs; participated in a trip to Yellowstone Park with Theodore Roosevelt; awarded honorary degrees from Yale, Colgate, and the University of Georgia; John Burroughs Medal for the best natural history book commemorates him.

Buss, Irvin O. (1908–1993): Professor of wildlife biology, Washington State University at Pullman; author of *A Half Century of Change in Bird Populations of the Lower Chippewa River, Wisconsin* and *Elephant Life*. (CSH)

Buxton, John (1912–1989): University teacher; ornithologist; carried out bird observations as a POW in Nazi Germany and later published them; first person to bring a mist net into the U.K.

Campbell, Bruce (1912–1993): Naturalist; ornithologist; conducted long-term nestbox study of pied flycatchers; secretary of the British Trust for Ornithology; co-edited *A Dictionary of Birds*; awarded many medals for his work.

Carnes, Betty (1905–1987): Bird photographer; banded many birds; first woman to band a peregrine falcon; president of the New Jersey State Garden Club and the New Jersey Audubon Society; first woman to be elected a member of the American Ornithologists' Union; and later became a patron; a scholarship bears her name.

Carson, Rachel (1907–1964): While a marine biologist and having never studied birds, used her considerable writing skills to present the whole story of the misuse of pesticides, such as DDT in a readable fashion in a book entitled *Silent Spring* in 1962.

Cassin, John (1813–1869): Curator of ornithology at the Academy of Natural Sciences of Philadelphia; described and named 26 new bird species north of the Rio Grande River; only American in his time to be recognized as an ornithologist; published *Illustrations of the Birds of California, Texas, Oregon, British and Russian America*; Cassin's sparrow and Cassin's finch honor his name.

Catesby, Mark (1682–1749?): Regarded as the first real American naturalist; the founder of American ornithology; fellow of the Royal

Society; wrote and illustrated *Natural History of Carolina, Florida, and the Bahama Islands.*

Cetti, Francesco (1726–1780): Italian jesuit; zoologist; published *Natural History of Sardinia*; memorialized by Cettis warbler.

Chance, Edgar (1881–1955): Amateur naturalist who specialized in the behavior of cuckoos; known for his remarkable field observations; authored *The Cuckoo's Secret* and *The Truth about the Cuckoo.*

Chapman, Frank Michler (1864–1945): Popularizer; collected in Florida; research specialized on neo-tropical birds; assistant to the director of the American Museum in New York; curator of the Department of Birds; authored 17 books and 225 articles including *Handbook of Birds of Eastern North America*; honored by an award from American Museum of Natural History.

Cheng, Tso-Hsin (1906–1998): Curator of birds at Academia Sinica, then founder of the Peking Natural History Museum; author of *Zoogeographical Regions of China* and many volumes of *Fauna Sinica: Aves.* (CSH)

Chesterfield, Norman (1913–1996): Canadian birder; held the top Canadian bird species list since 1977 and was at one time the world's record holder for species seen.

Clark, William (1770–1838): Captain of the famous expedition across the continent; published *History of the Expedition under the Commands of Captain Lewis and Captain Clark;* memorialized by Clark's nutcracker, (formerly Clark's crow) which he discovered in Idaho.

Clarke, William Eagle (1858–1938): Keeper of Natural History in the Royal Scottish Museum; specialized in migration and faunistics; served on the Committee of the British Association for the Advancement of Science; editor of the *Annals of Scottish Natural History* and *Scottish Naturalist*; president of the British Ornithologists' Union; authored *Studies in Bird Migration*; received the Godman-Salvin medal awarded by the British Ornithologists' Union.

Coffey, Ben B., Jr. (1904–1993): Known for his interest in mid-South bird distribution patterns and the phenology of migration and nesting; recorded bird songs; fellow of the American Ornithologists' Union; member of the Wilson Ornithological Society and the Inland and Northeastern bird banding associations; president of the Tennessee Ornithological Society; editor of *The Migrant.*

Cooper, William (1798?–1864): One of the founders and secretary of the New York Lyceum of Natural History; first American to become a member of the London Zoological Society; named and described the evening grosbeak; collected Cooper's hawk which was later named after him; father of James G. Cooper.

Cooper, James Graham (1830–1902): Surgeon, naturalist, ornithologist, and bird collector; published *Ornithology in California*; honored by the Cooper Ornithological Society.

Cory, Charles Barney (1857–1921): One of the founders and presidents of the American Ornithologists' Union; bird curator at the Field Museum of Natural History; leading authority on West Indian birds; authored *A Naturalist in the Magdalen Islands*; Cory's shearwater bears his name.

Costa, Louis Marie Pantaleon (1806–1864): French collector of hummingbirds; honored by Costa's hummingbird, *Calypte costae.*

Cottam, Clarence (1899–1974): Professor; worked for the U.S. Fish and Wildlife Service; studied food habits of birds; fought against pesticide use; first director of the Rob and Bessie Welder Wildlife Foundation; president of The Wildlife Society, Texas Ornithological Society, National Parks Association, and the Council of Southwest Foundations; authored over 250 publications; recipient of many awards.

Coues, Elliot (1842–1899): Army officer who collected bird specimens for observations; one of the founders of the American Ornithologists' Union; authored *Birds of the Northwest, Birds of the Colorado Valley*; made a major contribution to ornithology by publishing the *Key to North American Birds*; honored by an annual award for the American Ornithologists' Union.

Coward, Thomas Alfred (1867–1933): Popularizer who broadcasted on natural history; co-authored *The Vertebrate Fauna of Cheshire and Liverpool Bay*; authored *Birds of the British Isles and their Eggs.*

Cramp, Stanley (1913–1987): British ornithologist; chief editor of the seven volumes of the handbook *The Birds of the Western Palearctic*; senior editor of journal *British Birds*; co-authored *The Seabirds of Britain and Ireland*; President and Union Medallist of the British Ornithologists' Union; received several other awards as well.

Crandall, Lee Saunders (1887–1969): General Curator Emeritus of the New York Zoological Society; known as "the zoo man"; member of several expeditions; fellow of the American Ornithologists' Union; served on several committees; published 250 articles and four books; recipient of the Everly Gold Medal of the American Association of Zoological Parks and Aquariums.

Craveri, Frederico (1815–1890): Italian professor of chemistry who collected birds for the Turin Academy of Science; collected Craveri's murrelet that bears his name.

Cruickshank, Allan Dudley (1907–1974): Teacher; photographer; editor of *Christmas Bird Counts*; National Audubon Society staff member from 1935, lecturing to nearly 3 million people; awarded the Arthur A. Allen Medal. (CSH)

Cruickshank, Helen Gere (1907–1995): Educator, traveler, photographer; authored several books including *Bird Islands Down East* and *Flight into Sunshine* which was awarded the John Burroughs Medal by the American Ornithologists' Union.

Curry-Lindahl, Kai (1917–1990): Swedish zoologist, conservationist, and naturalist; lecturer at the University of Stockholm; editor of *Acta Vertibratica*; honorary fellow of the American Ornithologists' Union; participated in committees and organizations related to ornithology and conservation including the International Council for Bird Preservation and the World Wildlife Fund; published over 600 papers and 100 books.

Darwin, Charles (1809–1882): Put forward the theory of evolution by natural selection; the most important scientist in the history of biology; a naturalist; traveled on the H.M.S. *Beagle* in an exploratory journey around the globe; particular interest in the Galapagos finches; wrote the famous book *On the Origin of Species by Means of Natural Selection or the Preservation of Favored Races in the Struggle for Life*, as well as other books on biology.

Dathe, Heinrich (1910–1991): East German ornithologist who influenced Saxony ornithology; founded and developed the Tierpark Berlin; founder and editor of *Beiträge zur Vogelkunde*; corresponding fellow of the American Ornithologists' Union.

Davis, David E. (1913–1994): Chair of zoology, University of Raleigh; studied populations; editor of *Wilson Bulletin*. (CSH)

Davis, John (1916–1986): Research zoologist and manager, Hastings Natural History Reservation, California; wrote about birds of the Hastings Reservation and Latin America, and the life cycle of the house sparrow; co-author of *The Bird Year*; fellow of the American Ornithologists' Union. (CSH)

Dawson, William Leon (1873–1928): Photographer of birds; author of *Birds of Ohio, Birds of Washington,* and *Birds of California.*

Dear, Colonel L.S. (1883–1959): Naturalist, conservationist; first president of the Thunder Bay Field Naturalists' Club; later named honorary president; published *The Breeding Birds of the Region of Thunder Bay.*

Degland, Côme Damien (1787–1856): Director of the Musée d'Histoire Naturelle in Lille, France; known for his work on European birds; author of *Ornithologie Européene*; the white-winged scoter, *Melanitta fusca deglandi*, bears his name.

Delacour, Jean (1890–1985): Ornithologist; familiar with birds of all faunistic regions; promoted international conservation; collector of rare living birds; owned a private zoo; founder and editor of *L'Oiseau*; several tropical expeditions; discovered several new species; founder and president of the International Council for Bird Preservation; several books including the *Pheasants of the World and Wild Pigeons and Doves.*

Dexter, Ralph Warren (1912–1991): Teacher at Kent State University; conducted a long-term study of chimney swifts; fellow of the American Association for the Advancement of Science; president of the Ohio Academy of Sciences; elective member of the American Ornithologists' Union.

Diaz, Augustin (1829–1893): Mexican soldier; engineer; geographer who helped establish the U.S.-Mexican border; mapped out Mexico for his government; honored by Mexican duck, *Anas diazi.*

Doubleday, Neltje Blanchan (1865–1918): Birdwatcher; published *Bird Neighbors, Birds that Hunt and are Hunted, How to Attract the Birds* and *Birds Worth Knowing.*

Douglas, David (1799–1834): Botanist; named Franklin's subspecies of spruce grouse, collected near Jasper House; gave first description of California condor. (CSH)

Dresser, Henry Eeles (1838–1915): Egg collector; secretary of the British Ornithologists' Union; author of *Eggs of the Birds of Europe* and *A History of the Birds of Europe*.

Drummond, Thomas (c1780–1835): Botanist; collector of birds and mammals; assistant naturalist to Richardson on the second Franklin expedition; collected type specimens of the white-tailed ptarmigan, black-backed woodpecker, and Forster's tern. (CSH)

Drury, William Holland (1921–1992): Professor at the College of the Atlantic; conservationist, artist; first director of the Hatheway School of Conservation Education; first to identify the transoceanic migration of the blackpoll warbler; studied herring gulls; fellow of the American Ornithologists' Union.

Duncan, Sir Arthur Bryce (1928–1984): Scottish ornithologist; helped form the Cambridge Bird Club; first chairman of the Scottish Ornithologists' Club; chairman of the Nature Conservancy in the U.K.

Dunnet, George Mackenzie (1928–1995): Scottish ornithologist; ecologist; created Culterty Field Station at Aberdeen University; known for his interest in seabirds; first chairman of the Seabird Group; leading authority of fleas as parasites of birds in Australia and Antarctic; president of the British Ecological Society; awarded the Godman-Salvin Medal by the British Ornithologists' Union.

Durrell, Gerald (1925–1995): writer and television raconteur; zoo collector; conservationist; founded the Jersey Wildlife Preservation Trust; wrote many popular books on wildlife; honored by the Durrell Institute of Conservation by the University of Kent.

Dwight, Jonathan, Jr., (1858–1929): Doctor; fellow, treasurer, and president of the American Ornithologists' Union; studied bird plumages; author of *Sequence of Plumage and Moults of the Passerine Birds of New York*.

Eckelberry, Don Richard (1921–2001): Superb bird artist and illustrator of field guides; a conservationist who helped save Corkscrew Swamp; fellow of the American Ornithologists' Union. (CSH)

Eckstorm, Fannie Hardy (1865–1946): Went on several expeditions with her father; founded a College Audubon Society at Smith College; authored *The Bird Book* and *Woodpeckers*.

Eisenmann, Eugene (1906–1981): Lawyer with an interest in birds; research associate of the American Museum of Natural History; president of the Linnean Society of New York; member of the International Commission on Zoological Nomenclature; vice president of the American Ornithologists' Union; editor of *The Auk*; vice-chairman of the Pan-American Section of the International Council for Bird Preservation; author of *The Species of Middle American Birds*.

Elliott, Daniel Giraud (1835–1915): One of the founders and presidents of the American Ornithologists' Union; representative of the American Museum; curator at the Field Museum in Chicago; worked on monographs concerning different groups of birds; wrote and illustrated the two-volume *Birds of North America*.

Elliott, Sir Hugh (1913–1989): collector; ornithologist; studied birdlife in Tanganyika and made important contributions to wildlife conservation there; co-author of *Herons of the World*; president of the British Ornithologists' Union.

Emlen, John Thompson, Jr. (1908–1997): Professor of zoology at the University of Wisconsin; a pioneer in ethology and ecology; a founder of the Animal Behavior Society; mentor to 39 doctoral students; fellow of the American Ornithologists' Union. (CSH)

Etchécopar, Robert Daniel (1905–1990): Honorary fellow of the American Ornithologists' Union; secretary-general of the Société Ornithologique de France; director of the banding center in the Paris Museum; founder and president of Euring.

Falla, Sir Robert (1901–1979): New Zealand ornithologist; known for his interest in petrels and moas; named several petrel species; president of the Royal Society of New Zealand and the Royal Australian Ornithologists' Union; awarded the Polar Medal for his Antarctic work.

Farner, Donald S. (1915–1988): Emeritus Professor of zoology at Washington State University; interest in photoregulation, reproductive biology, and endocrinology; president of the American Ornithologists' Union and the International Union of Biological Sciences; honorary member of the Cooper Ornithological Society; editor of *The Auk*; author of 260 publications; recipient of the Brewster Medal.

Farrand, John, Jr. (1937–1994): Zoologist at the Smithsonian Institution; curatorial assistant in ornithology at the American Museum of Natural History; editor-in-chief of *American Birds*; elective member of the American Ornithologists' Union; president of the Linnean Society of New York; author of several books including *The Audubon Society Master Guide to Birding* and *Masterpieces of Bird Art*; a Pliocene lily-trotter, *Jacana farrandi*, honors his name.

Fischer, Johann Gotthelf, von Waldheim (1771–1853): German professor of zoology in Moscow; doctor and geologist; remembered for his work in Russia on natural history; memorialized by the species name of the spectacled eider, *Somateria fischeri*.

Fisher, Albert Kenrick (1856–1948): One of the founders and presidents of the American Ornithologists' Union; helped found an economic ornithology branch in the federal Division of Entomology; ornithologist on a few expeditions, notably to the Southwest, Alaska, and the Pinchot South Seas; wrote *The Hawks and Owls of the United States and Their Relation to Agriculture*.

Fisher, James Maxwell McConnell (1912–1970): Helped popularize interest in natural history; assistant curator of the Zoological Society of London; known for his interest in seabirds; published several books and papers including *Wild America*, which he wrote with Peterson; awarded the Union Medal by the British Ornithologists' Union, the Tucker medal, Arthur Allen Medal from Cornell University, the Gold Medal by the Royal Society for the Protection of Birds, and the Bernard Tucker Medal.

Fisher, Harvey Irvin (1916–1994): Professor and chair of the zoology department at the University of Illinois; studied the laysan albatross; known for his interest in the functional anatomy of birds; studied footedness in birds; fellow of the American Ornithologists' Union; editor of *The Auk*; founding editor of *Pacific Science*.

Fleming, James Henry (1872–1940): Ontario bird collector; self-taught ornithologist; member of the Great Lakes Ornithological Club; member of the Brodie Club; president of the American Ornithologists' Union; published over 40 papers; authored *Birds of Toronto*; Honorary Curator of Ornithology at the National Museum of Canada and the Royal Ontario Museum.

Fleming, Sir Charles (1916–1987): Studied birds of New Zealand and the surrounding areas; participated in the formation of the Ornithological Society of New Zealand; member of the Royal Society of New Zealand.

Forbush, Edward Howe (1858–1929): Ornithologist, writer, lecturer, and conservationist of New England; fellow of the American Ornithologists' Union; past president of the Massachusetts Audubon Society; also presided over the New England Bird Banding Association and the Federation of Bird Clubs of New England; State Ornithologist of Massachusetts for eight years; author of the classic book *The Birds of Massachusetts and Other New England States*; also authored *Useful Birds and Their Protection* and *A History of Game Birds, Wild-Fowl and Shorebirds of Massachusetts and Adjacent States*.

Ford, Julian R. (1932–1987): Australian expert on geographic variation and hybrid zones in birds; corresponding fellow of the American Ornithologists' Union; recipient of many awards and grants.

Forster, Johann Reinhold (1729–1798): German naturalist; accompanied Cook on his second voyage around the world; authored the first book that attempted to cover North American fauna: *A Catalogue of Animals of North America*; collected and described many new bird species; honored by Forster's tern, *Sterna forsteri*.

Foster, William (1852–1924): Bird illustrator; member of the Watercolor Society; illustrated *Game Birds of India*.

Franklin, Sir John (1786–1847): English navigator and explorer who collected birds; died while seeking the Northwest Passage in the Canadian Arctic; his name is preserved in Franklin's gull.

Friedmann, Herbert (1900–1987): Studied parasitic birds, especially cowbirds; head curator of zoology at the Smithsonian Institution; president of the American Ornithologists' Union; elective member of the National Academy of Sciences; author of 17 books and 315 papers and articles, including *The Cowbirds: A Study in the Biology of Social Parasitism*; recipient of the Elliot Medal from the National Academy of Sciences; also awarded the Leidy Medal.

Frohawk, Frederick William (1861–1946): Bird illustrator; fellow of the Entomological Society; contributed to the *Encyclopedia Britannica*; produced over 1,000 drawings in books about birds.

Fuertes, Louis Agassiz (1874–1927): Great American bird painter considered to be the father of modern bird art; birder; lecturer at Cornell University; illustrated many books.

Fuggles-Couchman, Robin (?): Ornithologist and bird collector in Africa; life member of the British Ornithologists' Union; memorialized in two subspecies of birds, a bush warbler and a flycatcher.

Gabrielson, Ira Noel (1889–1977): First director of the newly named U.S. Fish and Wildlife Service; biologist and conservationist; author of *Wildlife Conservation* and co-author of *Birds of Oregon* and *Birds of Alaska*; fellow of the American Ornithologists' Union. (CSH)

Gambel, William (1819?–1849): Ornithologist and protégé of Thomas Nuttall; bird collector; his name is preserved in Gambel's quail and the mountain chickadee, *Parus gambeli*.

Godfrey, W. Earl (1910–2002): Curator of Ornithology at the National Museum of Canada; ultimate authority on the distribution and taxonomy of Canadian birds; author of two English and two French editions of *Birds of Canada*; fellow of the American Ornithologists' Union; first-ever recipient of the Doris Huestis Speirs Award, the top honor in Canadian ornithology. (CSH)

Godman, Frederick Du Cane (1834–1919): Associated with Osbert Salvin; went on an expedition to Jamaica and wrote *Biologia Centrali-Americana*; helped found the British Ornithologists' Union where he was secretary and later president; author of *A Monograph of the Petrels*; awarded the Gold Medal by the British Ornithologists' Union.

Gould, John (1804–1881): Curator and preserver of the Zoological Society of London Museum and later elected a Fellow; concentrated on the lithography and sketching of birds that followed the production of the *Birds of Europe*, *Birds of Australia*, *Birds of Asia*, and *Birds of Great Britain*; explored and collected in Australia; honored by the Gould League of Bird Lovers formed to help protect Australia birds.

Graham, Andrew (c1733–1815): Hudson's Bay Company fur trader; ethnologist; collected type specimens of great grey owl, boreal chickadee, blackpoll warbler, and white-crowned sparrow; his *Observations on Hudson's Bay* were not published until 1969. (CSH)

Greenewalt, Crawford H. (1902–1993): Helped develop high-speed photography capable of "freezing"; studied flight; elective member of the American Ornithologists' Union; life member of the Cooper Ornithological Society and the Wilson Ornithological Society; author of *Hummingbirds and Dimensional Relationships for Flying Animals*.

Greenway, James C., Jr. (1903–1989): Conservationist; worked for the Museum of Comparative Zoology and the American Museum of Natural History; member of several expeditions; fellow of the American Ornithologists' Union; participated in the American Committee for International Wildlife Protection and the International Council for Bird Preservation; published *Extinct and Vanishing Birds of the World*.

Grimes, Samuel A. (1906–1996): Ornithologist, bird photographer; his photographs appear in many books and journals; elective member of the American Ornithologists' Union; first honorary member of the Florida Ornithological Society; President Emeritus of the Tall Timbers Research Station.

Grinnell, Joseph (1877–1939): Ornithologist; director of Museum of Vertebrate Zoology at University of California in Berkeley; editor of *The Condor*; known for his interest in avifauna of California; elected the youngest fellow of the American Ornithologists' Union and later its president; produced over 500 publications; honored by Grinnell's waterthrush and *Lanius ludovicianus grinnelli*.

Griscom, Ludlow (1890–1959): Ornithologist at the American Museum of Natural History; patron saint of modern bird-watching; known for his interest in Mexican and Central American birdlife; extensive writings; many protégés; his chief contribution was to show that shooting was not necessary to identify birds.

Gronvold, Henrik (1858–1940): Bird illustrator known for his egg drawings; illustrated *Birds of Australia* and *The British Warblers*.

Gudmundsson, Finnur (1909–1979): Icelandic ornithologist; conservationist; limnologist; studied the status of many Icelandic bird species; worked at the Natural History Museum of Iceland; known for his interest in ptarmigan; translated the *Field Guide to the Birds of Britain and Europe* for use in Iceland.

Gullion, Gordon W. (1923–1991): Professor at the University of Minnesota; long-term study of ruffed grouse; wrote over 160 articles; recipient of many awards.

Gunn, William Walker Hamilton (1913–1984): Known for his bird-sound recordings, his research on bird migration, and the application of radar use to prevent avian-aircraft collisions; executive director of the Federation of Ontario Naturalists; president of the Wilson Ornithological Society; recipient of the Arthur A. Allen Award by Cornell University and the Douglas H. Pimlott Conservation Award by the Canadian Nature Federation.

Hagar, Joseph Archibald (1896–1989): Ecologist, biologist; studied raptors and birds of the northeast wetlands; first to associate eggshell thinning with the reduction in population numbers of the peregrine falcon; elective member of the American Ornithologists' Union.

Hamerstrom, Frances (1907–1998): A rebellious daughter of wealthy parents; first female graduate student in wildlife ecology; only female graduate student of Aldo Leopold; author of an outstanding children's book, *Walk When the Moon is Full*, and 12 others, notably *Harrier, Hawk of the Marshes*; hostess and mentor to numerous "gabboons" (raptor interns); fellow of the American Ornithologists' Union. (CSH)

Hamerstrom, Frederick Nathan (1909–1990): Project leader of the Prairie Grouse Management Research Unit in Wisconsin that concentrated on the prairie chicken and the sharp-tailed grouse; also interested in hawks and owls; fellow of the American Ornithologists' Union; president of the Wisconsin Society of Ornithology; vice-president of the Wisconsin Academy of Science, Letters and Arts; received many awards in addition to being twice recipient of the Wildlife Society's Award for his publications; honored along with his wife, Fran, by an award of the Raptor Research Foundation.

Hammond, William Alexander (1829–1900): Physician who collected birds; Hammond's flycatcher bears his name.

Harcourt, Edward William Vernon (1825–1891): English traveler and writer who described Harcourt's petrel; author of *Sketch of Madeira*.

Harlan, Richard (1796–1843): Physician and naturalist; authored *Fauna Americana*; honored by Harlan's hawk.

Harris, Edward (1799–1863): Member of the Yellowstone expedition with Audubon; commemorated by Harris's hawk and Harris's sparrow.

Hartert, Ernst Johannes Otto (1859–1933): Director of the Tring Museum; authored an important taxonomical work, *Die Vogel der Palaarktischen Fauna*; recognized that birds had geographical forms; established the trinomial system; participated in *The Catalogue of Birds of the British Museum*.

Harting, James Edmund (1841–1928): Helped establish the library at the British Museum of Natural History; editor of *The Field* and *The Zoologist*; founded the New Hawking Club; librarian and assistant secretary at the Linnean Society; authored several books including *Habits and Mangement of Hawks* and *Our Summer Migrants*.

Hartshorne, Charles (1897–2000): Philosophy professor at Chicago, Atlanta, and Austin; author of *Born to Sing: An Interpretation and World Survey of Bird Song*; believed that birds, in addition to sexual and territorial purposes, also sing for sheer pleasure. (CSH)

Haverschmidt, François (1906–1987): Ornithologist of the Netherlands; known for his interest in meadow birds; active in conservation; corresponding member of the American Ornithologists' Union; authored *Birds of Surinam*; wrote 350 papers and 6 books; received several honors.

Heermann, Adolphus Lewis (1827?–1865): Physician who collected birds and their eggs for Spencer F. Baird; attached to the Pacific Railroad-Surveys; honored by Heermann's gull.

Henshaw, Henry Wetherbee (1850–1930): Ornithologist and naturalist; a founder of the American Ornithologists' Union; chief of the U.S. Biological Survey; discovered that the male and female Williamson's sapsucker were of the same species; known for his rapid preparation of bird skins.

Henslow, John Stevens (1796–1861): Professor of botany who taught Charles Darwin in England; friend of Audubon; honored by Henslow's sparrow.

Herrick, Francis Hobart (1858–1940): Biologist and bird photographer; fellow of the American Ornithologists' Union; studied bald eagles, which led to articles in *The Auk* and a book, *The American Eagle*; authored the first Audubon biography, *Audubon: The Naturalist*; wrote *The Home Life of Wild Birds*.

Hickey, Joseph J. (1907–1993): Ornithologist, conservationist; professor at the University of Wisconsin; researched the effects of pesticides; helped the cause of the declining peregrine falcon population; founder and secretary of The Nature Conservancy; editor of several journals such as *Journal of Wildlife Management*; president of the American Ornithologists' Union; author of *A Guide to Bird Watching*; recipient of many awards including the Aldo Leopold Medal, the Arthur A. Allen Medal, and the Elliott Coues Award.

Hochbaum, Hans Albert (1911–1988): Director of the Delta Waterfowl Research Station; artist; fellow of the American Ornithologists' Union; authored *The Canvasback on a Prairie Marsh* for which he received a Literary Award and the Brewster Medal; also received a Literary Award for *Travels and Traditions of Waterfowl*; recipient of several other awards.

Höhn, E. Otto (1919–1997): Arctic ornithologist, avian endocrinologist, and professor at the University of Alberta; studied the relationship between the hormonal and behavioral status of birds. (CSH)

Holboell, Carl Peter (1795–1856): Governor of South Greenland with an interest in natural history; named and described several species of birds; memorialized in a subspecies of the red-necked grebe, formerly known as Holboell's grebe.

Holgersen, Holger (1914–1996): Norwegian ornithologist; director of the Stavanger Museum; participated in the ringing schemes of Norway and Europe; editor of *Sterna*; honorary member of the Norwegian Ornithological Society; corresponding fellow of the American Ornithologists' Union; published about 200 articles.

Hoogstraal, Harry (1917–1986): Entomologist and ornithologist; Egyptologist; compiled a major bibliography on ticks and tick-borne diseases in migratory birds; honored by the Hoogstraal Collection and Tick Study Centre in Washington, D.C.

Hope, Clifford (1910–1953): Bird collector; worked for the Royal Ontario Museum of Zoology where he became Chief Preparator in the Division of Ornithology; participated in several expeditions; studied the effects of DDT and budworm on birds.

Hornemann, Jens Wilken (1770–1841): Danish professor of botany; honored by the species name of the hoary redpoll, *Acanthis hornemanni*.

Howard, Eliot (1873–1940): Amateur naturalist who specialized on warblers; authored *The British Warblers* and *Introduction to the Study of Bird Behaviour*; vice-president of the British Ornithologists' Union.

Howard, Hildegarde (1901–1998): Chief curator of science at the University of California, Los Angeles; honored by the Hildegarde Howard Hall of Cenozoic Life; avian paleontologist who analysed 14,000 specimens from the Rancho La Brea tarpits; fellow of the American Ornithologists' Union. (CSH)

Hudson, William Henry (1841–1922): Ornithologist, writer; interest in wildlife of the Pampas; co-authored *Argentine Ornithology* and wrote *Birds of La Plata*; promoted bird protection and was a member of the first committee of the Royal Society for the Protection of Birds.

Hutchins, Thomas (c1742–1790): Hudson's Bay Company surgeon; meteorologist; first described the small (Hutchins's) subspecies of the Canada goose. (CSH)

Hutton, William (?): Collector of birds around Washington, D.C.; discovered Hutton's vireo which was later named in his honor.

Huxley, Sir Julian (1887–1975): Zoologist, professor; specialized on bird courtship; member of the British Ornithologists' Union; fellow of the Royal Society; secretary of the Zoological Society of London; secretary-general of UNESCO; authored books on different subjects; recipient of a Hollywood Oscar for a film on the gannet.

Imhof, Thomas A. (1920–1995): Chemist; author of two editions of *Alabama Birds*. (CSH)

Immelmann, Klaus (1935–1987): Professor of biology; director of the Institute of Ethology at the University of Bielefeld; studied the ontogeny behavior of birds and mammals; honorary fellow of the American Ornithologists' Union; president of the German Ornithological Society and the German Zoological Society; has written over 100 publications and many books.

Ingram, Captain Collingwood (1880–1981): British ornithologist; horticulturist; a member of the British Ornithologists' Union for 80 years; known for his interest in Japanese birds; wrote *The Birds of the Riviera*.

Isham, James (c1716–1761): Hudson's Bay Company fur trader; collected type specimens of 13 species of birds, which were painted by George Edwards and given Latin binomial names by Linnaeus. (CSH)

Ivor, Hance Roy (1880–1979): Self-trained ornithologist; among first to realize the importance of studying comparative behavior of semi-tame and wild birds; pioneered "anting" behavior.

Jacques, Florence Page (1890–1972): Author of natural history travelogs such as *Canoe Country, The Geese Can Fly, As Far as the Yukon, Birds Across the Sky; Snow Shoe Country*; was awarded the John Burroughs Medal from the American Ornithologists' Union.

Jenkinson, Marion Anne (1937–1994): Adjunct curator of ornithology in the Museum of Natural History, University of Kansas; developed a world-class avian skeletal collection.; organized improved library resources for 100 universities in Latin America; fellow of the American Ornithologists' Union; Marion Jenkinson AOU Service Award is presented annually in her honor. (CSH)

Johansen, Hans Christian (1897–1973): Zoologist, teacher; worked at the Zoological Museum of Copenhagen University; studied waders; corresponding fellow of the American Ornithologists' Union; recipient of a Danish Royal Medal.

Johnson, Alfred W. (1894–1979): Chilean ornithologist; known for his early interest in the Humboldt penguin; wrote *The Birds of Chile and Adjacent Regions of Argentina, Bolivia and Peru* and *Las Aves de Chile*; received several awards including the Brewster Award from the American Ornithologists' Union.

Jones, Lynds (1865–1951): Started his career as teacher of ecology; professor of zoology at Oberlin College who taught the first ever ornithology course in an American college or university; known for his interest in bird migration; a founder and president of the Wilson Ornithological Society; editor of the *Wilson Bulletin*; fellow of the American Ornithologists' Union.

Jourdain, Francis Charles Robert (1865–1940): Traveler, egg collector; part of an expedition to Spitsbergen; authority on Western Palearctic birds; editor of *British Birds*; vice-president of the British Ornithologists' Union.

Kale, Herbert W., II (1931–1995): Ornithologist; vice-president of ornithology at the Florida Audubon Society; organized and directed the Florida Breeding Bird Atlas project; fought for the protection of Florida birds; fellow of the American Ornithologists' Union; founder and president of the Florida Ornithological Society and the Colonial Waterbird Society; associate editor of *The Auk*; editor of *Colonial Waterbirds*.

Keeton, William (1933–1980): Entomologist; professor at Cornell University who influenced many students of biology; pioneer and world authority in avian navigation; known for his interest in using homing pigeons; Fellow of the American Ornithologists' Union; the recipient of many awards.

Kendeigh, Samuel Charles (1904–1986): Professor Emeritus of zoology at the University of Illinois; studied the ecology and physiology of birds; editor of *The Ecology of North America*; helped found the Illinois Nature Preserves Commission, the Nature Conservancy, and the Animal Behavior Society; president of the Wilson Ornithological Society and the Ecological Society of America; vice-president of the American Ornithologists' Union; president of the Champaign County Audubon Society; author of *Physiology of the Temperature of Birds*; has written over 90 publications; recipient of the Brewster Award from the American Ornithologists' Union and the Eminent Ecologist Award from the Ecological Society of America.

Keulemans, John Gerrard (1842–1912): Illustrator with special interest in natural history; produced many autolithographs; author of *Natural History of Cage Birds*.

Keve, Andrew (1909–1984): Hungarian ornithologist; researcher at the Hungarian Institute of Ornithology; worked on birds in the Carpathian Basin; fellow of the Natural History Museum of Vienna, Austria, and Hungary; corresponding member of the British Ornithologists' Union and the American Ornithologists' Union.

Kilham, Lawrence (1910–2000): Virologist at Dartmouth Medical School; leading authority on the behavioral ecology of woodpeckers; fellow of the American Ornithologists' Union. (CSH)

Kincaid, Edgar Bryan, Jr. (1921–1985): Rancher; spent 12 years editing Oberholser's *The Bird Life of Texas* and preparing it for publication. (CSH)

King, James R. (1927–1991): Professor of zoophysiology at Washington State University; studied avian biology and environmental physiology; president of the American Ornithologists' Union and the Council of the Cooper Ornithological Society; editor of *The Condor*; co-editor of *Avian Biology*; recipient of the Brewster Medal.

Kirtland, Jared Potter (1793–1877): Physician, teacher, horticulturist, and naturalist who was especially involved with fishes of Ohio; honored by Kirtland's warbler, which he collected.

Kittlitz, Friedrich Heinrich (1779–1874): German explorer-naturalist; member of an expedition to Kamchatka; memorialized by Kittlitz's murrelet.

Koplin, James R. (1934–1987): Zoologist, educator who influenced many students despite a short life; studied woodpecker predation; improved our knowledge of raptors; elective member of the American Ornithologists' Union; travel award named after him by the Raptor Research Foundation.

Kortright, Francis Herbert (1887–1972): President of the Canadian National Sportsmen's Show, the Conservation Council of Ontario, and the Toronto Anglers' and Hunters' Association; recipient of the Brewster Medal for his book on North American waterfowl; received several other awards; a waterfowl park, a nature centre, a lake in the Ontario region bear his name.

Lack, David Lambert (1910–1973): Helped develop radar during World War II; studied bird migration; a major part of his career was spent as director of the Edward Grey Institute of Field Ornithology at Oxford; his work consisted mostly of island bird faunas, especially that of Darwin's Galapagos finches; published *The Natural Regulation of Animal Numbers* and *Population Studies of Birds*, among others.

Laing, Hamilton Mack (1883–1982): Worked for the Museum of Canada and the Royal British Columbia Museum; elective member of the American Ornithologists' Union; author of 900 articles; a subspecies of the northern goshawk, *Accipiter gentilis laingi*, bears his name.

Lawrence, George Newbold (1806–1895): One of the founders of the American Ornithologists' Union; worked with birds of tropical America; author of *Catalogue of Birds Observed in New York*; participated as author in Volume IX of Spencer F. Baird's *Reports of Exploration and Surveys for a Railroad Route from the Mississippi River to the Pacific Ocean*; honored by Lawrence's goldfinch.

Lawrence, Louise de Kiriline (1894–1992): Studied ornithology; authored *A Comparative Life History of Four Species of Woodpeckers*; her book *The Lovely and the Wild* was awarded the John Burroughs Medal by the American Ornithologists' Union; regarded by Ernst Mayr as one of the best life-history researchers in North America.

Lawrence, Newbold Trotter (1855–1928): Amateur ornithologist; Lawrence's warbler was named after him but later discovered to be a hybrid.

Laybourne, Roxy C. (1911–2003): forensic ornithologist who worked for 50 years at the Smithsonian Museum of Natural History; her specialty was identifying feathers and other bird remains, especially for criminal cases and bird strikes on aircraft; given a lifetime achievement award by the Air Force Bird Strike Committee.

Løppenthin, Bernt H.O.F. (1904–1994): Curator of the Copenhagen University Library; foremost authority on Danish birds. (CSH)

Leach, William Elford (1790–1836): Zoologist at the British Museum in London; authority on crustaceans; Leach's storm-petrel honors his name.

Lear, Edward (1812–1888): Bird illustrator; specialized in members of the parrot family; associated with the Linnean Society; first to portray all the members of one family in *Illustrations of the Family Psittacidae or Parrots*.

LeConte, John Lawrence (1825–1883): Physician and entomologist; honored by LeConte's sparrow, *Ammospiza leconteii*, and by LeConte's thrasher.

Lekagul, Boonsong (1907–1992): Artist, biologist, conservationist of Thailand; started the Bangkok Bird Club; participated in the International Committee for Bird Protection and the World Wildlife Fund; corresponding fellow of the American Ornithologists' Union; author of *Bird Guide of Thailand*; recipient of the Getty Award.

Leopold, Aldo (1886–1948): Professor of University of Wisconsin who influenced many students in ornithology; pioneer in wildlife conservation; developed the theory of game management; wrote *A Sand County Almanac and Sketches Here and There*, as well as many other publications and books on wildlife management.

Leopold, A. Starker (1913–1983): Wildlife biologist, naturalist, conservationist; professor of zoology at the University of California; director of the Museum of Vertebrate Zoology; known for his interest in Mexico and game birds; elected to the Academy of Sciences; fellow of the American Ornithologists' Union; president of the Board of Governors in the Cooper Ornithological Society; president and honorary member of the Wildlife Society; author of *Wildlife of Mexico: The Game Birds and Mammals*; recipient of the Wildlife Publication Award for his book *The California Quail* as well as many other awards including the Aldo Leopold medal.

Lesson, René Primavère (1794–1849): French naturalist; collected and described several bird species; gave the species name, *clemenciae*, to the blue-throated hummingbird to honor his wife.

Lewis, Meriwether (1774–1809): Secretary of Thomas Jefferson; commanded an exploring expedition, the Lewis and Clark expedition, to the Pacific Ocean; discovered Lewis's woodpecker which was later named after him.

Lichtenstein, M. Heinrich (1780–1857): director of zoology at the Berlin Museum; commemorated by Lichtenstein's oriole.

Lincoln, Thomas (1812–1833): Accompanied Audubon on his Labrador expedition where he collected Lincoln's sparrow, which was later named after him.

Linnaeus, Carolus (1707–1778): A botanist and bird biologist; became known as the father of biological taxonomy; professor of medicine and botany at Uppsala University; developed the Linnaean system of binomial nomenclature which is still widely used today; described and gave scientific names to a large number of birds that live in North America; *Systema Naturae* is the starting point of zoological nomenclature.

Lloyd, Hoyes (1888–1978): Ornithologist, conservationist; helped create a number of sanctuaries; head of the Migratory Birds Unit, later named Superintendent of Wild Life Protection; president of the American Ornithologists' Union; president of the Ottawa Field-Naturalists' Club; served on many other committees, organizations, and congresses; honorary member of the Ottawa Field-Naturalists' Club and, along with his wife, the Wildlife Society; recipient of the Aldo Leopold Memorial Medal from the Wildlife Society and the Seth Gordon Award of the International Association of Game, Fish, and Conservation Commissioners.

Lodge, George Edward (1860–1953): Bird illustrator, taxidermist; had a special interest in birds of prey; falconer; his garden was a bird sanctuary.

Lorenz, Konrad (1903–1989): Influenced the study of animal behavior; imprinted graylag geese on himself; studied social corvids; honorary fellow of the American Ornithologists' Union; recipient of many honors including the Nobel Prize.

Lowery, George H., Jr. (1913–1978): Boyd Professor of Zoology at the Louisiana State University; director of the Louisiana State University Museum of Natural Science; president of the American Ornithologists' Union; studied the nocturnal migration of birds for which he received a Brewster Award; recipient of an Outstanding Conservationist of the Year Award from the Outdoor Writers Association and Conservation Educator of the Year by the Louisiana Wildlife Federation; memorialized by a species of owl, *Xenoglaux loweryi*.

Lueshen, Willetta (1914–1989): Teacher; housewife; bird bander, the mainstay of the Inland Bird Banding Association for 27 years; editor of the *Auk* index for five years. (CSH)

M'Dougall, Patrick (1770–1817?): Doctor; credited with shooting the type specimen of the roseate tern; memorialized by *Sterna dougallii*.

MacArthur, Robert (1930–1972): A major force in changing how ecologists think about the world; brought mathematical theory into ecology; his work focused on competition in birds; co-founded the concept of island biogeography.

MacFarlane, Roderick Ross (1833–1920): Hudson's Bay Company fur trade manager; oologist; studied or collected 33 nests or egg sets of Eskimo curlew, 170 of American golden-plover, 70 of red-necked phalarope; two subspecies of mammals and one of the Western screech-owl are named for him. (CSH)

MacGillivray, William (1796–1852): Scottish ornithologist, lecturer, and professor who participated in Audubon's ornithological biography; authored *History of British Birds*; honored by MacGillivray's warbler.

Macoun, James Melville (1862–1920): Canadian naturalist; president of the Ottawa Field-Naturalists' Club; editor of *The Ottawa Naturalist*; memorialized by *Papaver macounii*, a pepper.

Macoun, John (1831–1920): Botanist; first chief of Biological Division, Geological Survey of

Canada; laid the foundation for the National Museum of Canada; author of *Manitoba and the Great North-West*, *Catalogue of Canadian Plants*, and *Catalogue of Canadian Birds*. (CSH)

Manning, Thomas Henry (1911–1998): Arctic ornithologist and mammalogist; won the Patron's Medal of the Royal Geographic Society, Massey Medal of the Canadian Geographic Society, and Doris Huestis Speirs award, the top honor in Canadian ornithology. (CSH)

Marshall, Alan John "Jock" (1911–1967): Australian field zoologist; professor and dean; avian physiologist; interest in seasonal cycles of birds; pioneer of ecological endocrinology; wrote *Bower-birds: Their Display and Breeding Cycles, Biology and Comparative Physiology of Birds* as well as several other books; memorialized by a dedication in *Avian Biology* series and the Jock Marshall Zoology Reserve at Monah University.

Mason, Charles Russell (1921–1985): Horticulturist; executive director of the Massachusetts and then the Florida Audubon Societies; instrumental in establishing the Asa Wright Nature Center in Trinidad and the Cerro Punta Sanctuary in Panama. (CSH)

Mathews, Gregory Macalister (1876–1949): known for his interest in Australian birds; published *Birds of Australia*; co-authored *The Manual of Australian Birds*; compiled *Systema Avium Australasinarum*.

Mauri, Ernesto (1791–1836): Italian botanist; director of the Botanical Gardens of Rome; helped produce *Iconografia della Fauna Italica*; honored by the western sandpiper, *Caladris mauri*.

Mayaud, Noël (1899–1989): Studied France avifauna; a founder and editor/coeditor of *Alauda*; research associate at the Centre National de la Recherche Scientifique; honorary fellow of the American Ornithologists' Union; published *Inventaire des Oiseaux de France*.

Maynard, Charles Johnson (1845–1929): Naturalist and traveler who collected birds; a Florida subspecies of the mangrove cuckoo, Maynard's cuckoo, and a subspecies of the white-eyed vireo, *Vireo griseus maynardi*, are named after him.

McAtee, Waldo Lee (1883–1962): The leading economic ornithologist in the nation in his time; became an expert on the food habits of birds and other vertebrates; his work includes over 1,200 books, articles, reviews, and letters.

McCabe, Robert A. (1914–1995): Wildlife scientist; chairman of the Department of Wildlife Management at the University of Wisconsin; first to use egg-white electrophoresis, the precursor to DNA/RNA analyses, to study phylogenetic relationships among birds; one of the first to use radio isotopes to study movement and distribution and also one of the first to use infrared light for night observation; built North America's first duck decoy trap; fellow of the American Ornithologists' Union; president of The Wildlife Society and the Wisconsin Society for Ornithology; recipient of several awards including the Aldo Leopold Medal.

McCown, John (1815?–1879): Collected birds while on military service; honored by McCown's longspur, which he collected.

McGregor, Richard Crittenden (1871–1936): Australian fellow of the American Ornithologists' Union; published *Index to the Genera of Birds of the World*; a subspecies of the house finch, McGregor's house finch, was named after him.

McIlwraith, Thomas (1824–1903): Collector of birds; sent specimens to the Smithsonian Institution; superintendent of the Committee of Migration of birds for Ontario; a founder of the American Ornithologists' Union, published *Birds of Ontario*.

McKay, Charles Leslie (?–1883): Collector of birds for the U.S. National Museum; memorialized by McKay's bunting.

McKinney, Frank (1928–2001): Curator of Ethology and professor of Ecology, Evolution, and Behavior at the University of Minnesota, 1963–2000; world's foremost authority on the social behavior of dabbling ducks; fellow of the American Ornithologists' Union. (CSH)

Mead, Chris (1940–2003): Ornithologist; eminent bird ringer (bander) who caught and ringed over 250,000 birds in 20 different countries; head of the UK's National Ringing Scheme and secretary-general of EURING; helped devise the first computerized system for ringing information; awarded the Union Medal by the British Ornithologists' Union.

Mendall, Howard Lewis (1909–1994): Leader of the Maine Cooperative Wildlife Research Unit; wrote books and monographs on the ring-necked duck, double-crested cormorant, and American woodcock; fellow of the American Ornithologists' Union. (CSH)

Mengel, Robert M. (1921–1990): Professor at the University of Kansas; had diverse interests; bird painter; fellow of the American Ornithologists' Union; editor of *The Auk*; editor of the AOU monographs.

Merriam, Clinton Hart (1855–1942): Zoologist and naturalist; first director of U.S. Biological Survey; president of the American Ornithologists' Union; brother of Florence Merriam Bailey.

Mewaldt, Leonard Richard (1917–1990): Professor of zoology at San Jose State University; studied nutcrackers and *Zonotrichia* sparrows; involved with bird research stations and observatories; fellow of the American Ornithologists' Union; president and honorary member of the Cooper Ornithological Society; president of the Western Bird Banding Association.

Meyer de Schauensee, Rudolphe (1901–1984): Ornithologist; worked at the Academy of Natural Sciences; produced over 120 publications; author of *The Species of Birds of South America, The Birds of China* and other books; recipient of the Brewster Medal from the American Ornithologists' Union.

Middendorff, Alexander von (1815–1894): German scientist who explored Russia; first to suggest that birds could detect the magnetic poles; described and named Middendorff's grasshopper warbler.

Miller, Olive Thorne (1831–1918): Bird-watcher and bird writer; author of 11 books on birds including *A Bird Lover in the West* and *With the Birds in Maine*.

Miller, Alden H. (1906–1965): A leader in the field of bird ecology, behavior, and physiology from the 1930s through the 1950s; professor at the University of California at Berkeley and, for some time, director of its Museum of Vertebrate Zoology; published several hundred papers.

Miner, John Thomas (1865–1944): Naturalist dedicated to conservation education; one of the pioneer banders; founder of the Jack Minor Bird Sanctuary on Lake Erie; National Wildlife Week, in the month of April, honors him.

Mitchell, Margaret Howell (1901–1988): Canada's first woman ornithologist of international repute; volunteered in the bird department of the Royal Ontario Museum, where she worked on the passenger pigeon inquiry; published *The Passenger Pigeon in Ontario*; elective member of the American Ornithologists' Union.

Monroe, Burt L., Jr. (1930–1994): Expert on the systematics and distribution of the world's birds; learned the Latin names of North American birds; a president of the American Ornithologists' Union; co-authored *Distribution and Taxonomy of the Birds of the World*; compiled the Ten-Year Index to the *Auk*; known as the "keeper" of Kentucky ornithology; served on many boards and committees.

Moltoni, Edgardo (1896–1980): Italian ornithologist; worked mostly at the Civic Museum of Natural History in Milan; studied avifauna of Italy; principal editor of *Rivista Italiana di ornitologia*; over 450 publications.

Montagu, George (1751–1815): Author of *Ornithological Dictionary,* which was the best handbook at the time; described the roseate tern.

Moreau, Reginald Ernest (1897–1970): Specialized in African ornithology and in the ecology of tropical forests and savannahs; editor of *The Ibis*; president of the British Ornithologists' Union; authored *The Palaearctic-African Bird Migration Systems*; recipient of the Godman-Salvin medal.

Mousely, William Henry (1865–1949): Civil engineer; best all-round naturalist-ornithologist in Canada in first half of 20th century; known for his interest in nesting behavior of shorebirds and warblers; proponent of the "territory theory."

Moynihan, Martin Humphrey (1928–1996): Director of the Smithsonian Tropical Research Institute, which became exceptionally productive under his guidance; studied aggressive postures of gulls, social mimicry, mixed-species flocks, displays, and the relative evolutionary success of temperature versus tropical animals; fellow of the American Ornithologists' Union. (CSH)

Muir, John (1838–1914): Mountain naturalist; conservationist of wildlife; helped found the Sierra Club of which he was president for 22 years; wrote *A Thousand Mile Walk to the Gulf*; the father of American conservation; initiated the national park and national forests movements.

Murphy, Joseph Robison (1925–1992): Ecologist; professor at Brigham Young University; known for his interest in raptors; president of the Raptor Research Foundation; editor of the *Journal of Raptor Research*; elective member of the American Ornithologists' Union.

Murphy, Robert Cushman (1887–1973): Naturalist; prominent American ornithologist; undertook a voyage on the Antarctic waters where he became the expert on marine birds; a junior colleague of Chapman's; wrote the classic *Oceanic Birds of South America*.

Murton, Ron (1932–1978): British ornithologist; wrote *The Woodpigeon* and *Man and Birds*; studied circadian rhythms in birds and wrote *Avian Breeding Cycles*.

Naik, Ramesh Maganbhai (1931–1991): Head of the Department of Biosciences at India's Saurashtra University; studied the structure and physiology of avian flight muscles; interested also in the house swift; helped develop the study of ornithology in India; corresponding fellow of the American Ornithologists' Union; a founder and editor of *Pava*.

Naumann, Johann Andreas (1744–1826): German naturalist; wrote authoritative treatises on birds; memorialized by Naumann's thrush and *Falco naumanni*.

Neboux, Adolphe Simon (?): The blue-footed booby, *Sula nebouxii*, was named in his honor after he collected it from an expedition around the world.

Nethersole-Thompson, Desmond (1908–1989): British egg collector; ornithologist; author of *The Greenshank*, four monographs on snow buntings, dotterels, pine crossbills, and greenshanks, *Waders, Their Breeding Haunts and Watchers*, and *Highland Birds*.

Newman, Robert James (1907–1988): Curator of birds, Louisiana State University; with George Lowery he involved 2,500 participants from 300 localities in studying nocturnal migration as birds crossed the moon. (CSH)

Newton, Alfred (1829–1907): Doyen of British ornithologists; zoology professor at Cambridge; help found the British Ornithologists' Union and *The Ibis*; supported the Protection of Birds Act; author of *The Dictionary of Birds*; received the Gold Medal from the Royal Society.

Nice, Margaret Morse (1883–1974): To date the most important female scholar in the history of ornithology; intensively studied birds from her house and authored over 60 articles on various aspects of avian ecology and behavior, especially the role of territoriality and the development of precocial birds; her autobiography was entitled *Research is a Passion with Me*; her most enduring work was an eight-year study of color-banded song sparrows in Ohio; could search the ornithological literature in seven languages.

Nordmann, Alexander V. (1803–1866): Russian zoologist; memorialized by *Glareola nordmanni*.

Nuttall, Thomas (1786–1859): Self-taught naturalist; authored the first field guide to the birds of North America entitled *A Manual of the Ornithology of the United States and Canada*; honored by Nuttall's woodpecker and the Nuttall Ornithological Club.

Nutting, Charles Cleveland (1858–1927): Professor of zoology at the University of Iowa; collector for museums; honored by Nutting's flycatcher, which he collected.

Oberholser, Harry Church (1870–1963): Biologist of the U.S. Fish and Wildlife Service; expert in bird identification; published over 900 papers on ornithology and bird life of Louisiana; author of *The Bird Life of Texas*; memorialized by the dusky flycatcher, *Empidonax oberholseri* and a subspecies of the curve-billed thrasher.

Olendorff, Richard R. (1943–1994): Raptor biologist and conservationist; Endangered Species Coordinator of the Bureau of Land Management; participated in the recovery programs of the California condor, bald eagle, and peregrine falcon; established the Raptor Research and Technical Assistance Center in Idaho; elective member of the American Ornithologists' Union; help found the American Falconers' Association; president of the Raptor Research Foundation, which honored him with the President's Award.

Olrog, Claes Christian (1912–1985): Neotropical ornithologist; studied birds in Argentina, Bolivia, and Brazil; member of several expeditions; produced over 100 publications; author of *Las Aves Argentinas*, a field guide.

Ord, George (1781–1866): Early American naturalist; editor and biographer for Alexander Wilson.

Orr, Robert Thomas (1908–1994): Curator, California Academy of Sciences; author of five editions of *Vertebrate Zoology*; fellow of the American Ornithologists' Union. (CSH)

Ouellet, Henri Roger (1938–1999): Curator of birds, Natural Museum of Natural Sciences, Ottawa; zoogeographer; secretary-general of the 19th International Congress of Ornithology in Ottawa in 1986, which launched the Society of Canadian Ornithologists; co-chair of the International Commission on French names of birds; his studies elevated Bicknell's thrush to full species rank; fellow of the American Ornithologists' Union. (CSH)

Owre, Oscar T. (1917–1990): Teacher of ornithology; founder of the University of Miami bird reference collection; president of the Tropical Audubon Society, which has a fund named after him; helped found Biscayne National Park; elective member of the American Ornithologists' Union.

Pallas, Peter Simon (1741–1811): German professor, zoologist, and explorer; participated in many expeditions, especially in Russia; responsible for describing many new bird species; *Zoographia Rosso-Asiatica* published posthumously; memorialized by Pallas's reed bunting and Pallas's sea-eagle.

Palmgren, Pontus (1907–1993): Finnish biologist; studied the autoecology of bird species and other subjects including the anatomy of bird legs and Zugunruhe with respect to meteorological factors; honorary fellow of the American Ornithologists' Union; secretary of the Finnish Society of Sciences; editor of *Ornis Fennica*.

Parker, Theodore A. III (1953–1993): Major contributor to neotropical ornithology; interest in vocalization; elective member of the American Ornithologists' Union.

Parmelee, David Freeland (1924–1998): Director of the Lake Itasca Forestry and Biological Station, then Curator of Birds, Bell Museum, University of Minnesota; Arctic and Antarctic ornithologist and collector; fellow of the Explorers' Club. (CSH)

Peakall, David B. (1931–2001): Chief, Toxic Chemicals Division, Canadian Wildlife Service; made important contributions to the toxicology of fish-eating raptors and gulls, demonstrating the inverse relationship between DDE content and eggshell thickness in peregrines; founding co-editor of the journal *Ecotoxicology*. (CSH)

Pennant, Thomas (1726–1798): Gave the bean goose its name because he liked beans.

Peterson, Roger Tory (1908–1996): Educator, artist, writer, photographer, filmmaker, conservationist; inventor of the modern field guides; produced the first pocket-sized bird guide, *A Field Guide to the Birds*, which enables users to pinpoint species characteristics; popularized bird-watching like no one before him; director and senior lecturer of education for the National Audubon Society; recipient of many awards; memorialized by the species name of the cinnamon screech-owl, *Otus petersoni*.

Pettingill, Olin Sewall, Jr. (1907–2001): Cinematographer; ornithologist; author of *Ornithology in Laboratory and Field*, the most widely used ornithological text in American colleges for 50 years; winner of the Arthur A. Allen Medal, Ludlow Griscom Award, and Eugene Eisenmann Medal; fellow of the American Ornithologists' Union. (CSH)

Pettingill, Eleanor Rice (1908–1977): Freelance ornithologist and photographer; went on a photographic expedition to film penguins in the Falkland Islands; author of *Penguin Summer*.

Phelps, William H., Jr. (1902–1988): Venezuelan ornithologist who explored his country; helped develop neotropical ornithology; built the Colección Ornitológica Phelps, the largest bird collection in Latin America; honorary fellow of the American Ornithologists' Union; a founder and president of Sociedad Venezolana de Ciencias Naturales; wrote over 65 papers and books; recipient of the Explorers' Club Medal and the David Livingstone Centennial Medal.

Phillips, Allan R. (1914–1996): American ornithologist; wrote over 170 publications, among them four books, including *The Known Birds of North and Middle America*; mentor of many students of ornithology; specialist in alpha taxonomy of birds; named or renamed 160 avian taxa.

Pierce, Fred J. (1902–1992): Natural history bookseller who had the largest catalog business in North America, with 14,000 circulation; editor of *Iowa Bird Life* for 30 years (CSH)

Powys, Thomas Lyttleton (Lord Lilford) (1833–1896): Known for his interest in birds, especially birds of prey; traveled around the Mediterranean; author of *The Coloured Figures of the Birds of the British Islands*.

Preble, Edward Alexander (1871–1957): Senior biologist, U.S. Biological Survey; ornithologist, mammalogist; described 19 new taxa of mammals; author of biological investigations of the Hudson Bay region and the Athabasca-Mackenzie regions; an island in great Slave Lake and a bay in Great Bear Lake bear his name. (CSH)

Preston, Frank W. (1896–1989): Glass technologist and engineer; applied his mathematical skills to the shapes and measurements of birds' eggs, heights of nests, and bird migration; fellow of the American Ornithologists' Union. (CSH)

Prestt, Ian (1929–1995): Zoologist; studied toxic chemicals in British birds, mainly raptors; director and later the president of the Royal Society for the Protection of Birds; became first Member of Honour for BirdLife International.

Prigogine, Alexandre (1913–1991): Explorer; collector of more than 20,000 bird specimens from the Congo; first to apply concept of para- and allospecies to bird taxonomy in central Africa; described five bird species and many races; memorialized by four bird species in the genera *Pholidus, Caprimulgus, Chlorocichlia,* and *Nectarinia.*

Quay, Wilbur Brooks (1927–1994): Mammalogist, teacher; studied the pineal gland and avian reproduction; pioneered the technique of cloacal lavages; helped found and edit the *Journal of Pineal Research*; life member of the American Ornithologists' Union, the Cooper Ornithological Society, and the Wilson Ornithological Society; president of the Western Bird Banding Association; produced over 400 publications.

Rabor, Dioscoro S. (1911–1996): Father of Philippine conservation; 69 new bird taxa have been named from his collections; alerted the world to the endangered status of the Philippine monkey-eating eagle. (CSH)

Rahn, Hermann (1912–1990): Physiology professor; studied the respiratory physiology of avian eggs; elective member of the American Ornithologists' Union; produced over 225 publications; elected to the National Academy of Sciences; recipient of many awards including the Elliott Coues Award.

Rand, Austin L. (1905–1982): Ornithologist; acting chief of the Biological Division of the National Museum of Canada; chief curator of zoology at the Field Museum of Natural History; president of the American Ornithologists' Union; elective member of the International Ornithological Committee; published 103 papers

on a variety of subjects; author of four books including *Ornithology: an Introduction.*

Raitt, Ralph J. (1929–2000): Curator of birds at New Mexico State University; editor of *Condor* and of *Studies in Avian Biology*; authority on birds of Mexico and Central America; fellow of the American Ornithologists' Union. (CSH)

Raveling, Dennis G. (1939–1991): Faculty member of the University of California; studied the nestling ecology of Canada geese; researched the Arctic nesting geese in the Pacific Flyway; fellow of the American Ornithologists' Union and the American Association for the Advancement of Science; president of the California Wetlands Foundation; recipient of several awards for his contributions to wetland and waterfowl conservation.

Richdale, Lancelot Eric (1900–1983): New Zealand ornithologist; known for his interest in seabirds; corresponding fellow of the American Ornithologists' Union; wrote two books on penguins; received several awards; memorialized by The Richdale Observatory at Taiaroa Head; studied yellow-eyed penguins for 18 years and sooty shearwaters for 17 years; awarded the Order of the British Empire. (CSH)

Richardson, Sir John, MD (1787–1865): Foremost surgeon-naturalist in the history of the British Empire; explorer; botanist; author of two volumes of *Fauna Boreali-Americana*; named many plants, mammals, birds, and 43 still-extant genera of fish. (CSII)

Richmond, Charles W. (1868–1932): Scholar; bibliographer; helped Ridgway with *The Birds of North and Middle America*; created the card catalogue of the bird collection at the National Museum; memorialized by *Richmondena cardinalis.*

Ridgway, Robert (1850–1929): Curator at the Smithsonian Institution and then at the U.S. National Museum; one of the founders and presidents of the American Ornithologists' Union; co-authored *A History of North American Birds*; a leading American ornithologist of his generation; helped produce the first *Checklist of North American Birds*; produced hundreds of publications and the eight-volume book *Birds of North and Middle America*; memorialized by the species name of the buff-collared nightjar, *Caprimulgus ridwayi*, and a few subspecies of North American birds.

Ripley, S. Dillon (1913–2001): One of the greatest secretaries of the Smithsonian Institution; independently wealthy, he came to work in a Rolls-Royce; together with his co-author, Salim Ali, the leading authority on the birds of India and Pakistan; fellow of the American Ornithologists' Union. (CSH)

Robertson, William B., Jr. (1924–2000): Biologist at Everglades National Park; an authority on the birds of Florida; fellow of the American Ornithologists' Union. (CSH)

Ross, Sir James Clark (1800–1862): British explorer; navigated in the Arctic on five expeditions, one of which was an attempt to find and rescue Sir John Franklin; honored by Ross's gull.

Ross, Bernard Rogan (1827–1874): Chief Factor of the Hudson's Bay Company and correspondent with the Smithsonian Institution; contributed a fair number of bird specimens; Ross's goose is named after him.

Rothschild, Lord Walter (1868–1937): Bird collector who maintained a museum at Tring; authored several books including *Novitates Zoological*, *Extinct Birds*, and *A Monograph of the Genus Casuarius*.

Rowan, William (1891–1957): Important Canadian ornithologist; worked on bird migration; studied gonads of juncos; initiated the study of breeding seasons, daylength, and avian reproductive physiology as well as the physiological basis of migration.

Ruppell, E.S. (1794–1884): African zoologist; described a number of new species; memorialized by Ruppell's vulture, Ruppell's warbler, Ruppell's long-tailed starling, and Ruppell's black chat.

Ruschi, Augusto (1915–1986): Brazilian who studied Atlantic coastal rain-forest fauna and flora; promoted the conservation of the rain forest; founder and director of the Museu de Biologia Professor Mello Leitão. in Santa Teresa; corresponding fellow of the American Ornithologists' Union; author of *Aves do Brasil*; published over 400 papers.

Sabine, Joseph (1770–1837): Older brother of Sir Edward; member of an Arctic expedition; honored by a subspecies of the ruffed grouse, *Bonasa umbellus sabini*.

Sabine, Sir Edward (1788–1883): British astronomer and physicist; studied specimens brought back by Franklin expedition to the Arctic; honored by Sabine's gull.

Salmon, H. Morrey (1892?–1985): Ornithologist; conservationist; father of British photography and used it to count seabirds in colonies and pioneered the use of flash on nocturnal species; wrote *Birds in Britain Today*; awarded the Gold Medal from the British Ornithologists' Union.

Salomonsen, Finn (1909–1983): Contributed to Greenland ornithology; chief curator of the Zoological Museum in Copenhagen; corresponding fellow of the American Ornithologists' Union; president and editor of the journal of the Danish Ornithological Society; author of over 200 publications.

Salvin, Osbert (1835–1898): associated with Frederick Godman; known for his interest in neotropical birds; editor of *The Ibis* where he co-authored the first paper in the first issue; one of the founding members of the British Ornithologists' Union and its treasurer; contributed to *The Catalogue of Birds in the British Museum*; awarded the Gold Medal by the British Ornithologists' Union.

Sauer, Edgar Gustav Franz (1925–1979): Zoologist; professor at the University of Florida; studied stellar orientation in birds; known for his interest in plovers, bobolinks, and ostriches; fellow of the American Ornithologists' Union; director of the Zoologishes Forschungsinstitute und Museum Alexander Koenig in Bonn.

Saunders, William Edwin (1861–1943): Pharmacist; ornithologist, conservationist, naturalist; president of the Wilson Ornithological Club; helped found and presided over the Ornithological Section of the Entomological Society of Ontario and the Federation of Ontario Naturalists.

Say, Thomas (1787–1834): Entomologist who went on an expedition to the Rocky Mountains to report on birds observed; memorialized by Say's phoebe, *Sayornis saya*, as well as the genus name of the phoebes, *Sayornis*.

Saunders, Howard (1835–1907): Amateur ornithologist; specialized in gulls and terns as well as the birds of Spain; vice-president of the Zoological Society and the Linnean Society; secretary of the British Ornithologists' Union; contributed to *The Catalogue of Birds in the British*

Museum; published *An Illustrated Manual of British Birds*.

Saunders, Aretas Andrews (1884–1970): Naturalist; teacher; observed birds in Montana, New York, and the Adirondacks; studied bird songs; fellow of the American Ornithologists' Union; authored *Birds of Montana, Guide to Bird Song*, and *The Lives of Wild Birds*; a memorial fund honors his name.

Schlegel, Gustav (1840–1903): Eminent sinologist and naturalist; memorialized by *Anthus gustavi*.

Schorger, Arlie William (1884–1972): Known for his interest in birds and natural history; bird and mammal collector; fellow of the American Ornithologists' Union; author of *Handbook of the Birds of Eastern North America* and *The Wild Turkey: Its History and Domestication*; received the Brewster Award for *The Passenger Pigeon: Its History and Domestication*.

Schreiber, Ralph W. (1942–1988): Scientist; curator; conservationist; world authority on seabirds with over 100 publications; head of the Section of Birds and Mammals at the Natural History Museum of Los Angeles County; active in the International Council for Bird Preservation; awarded the Elliot Coues Award by the American Ornithologists' Union.

Schüz, Ernst (1901–1990): German ornithologist; headed the Vogelwarte Rossitten, a world-famous bird ringing and research station; a leading authority of bird migration research; wrote the *Grundriss der Vogelzugskunde*; co-founded Der Vogelzug; honorary fellow of the American Ornithologists' Union; published the *Atlas of Bird Migration* as well as over 100 papers.

Sclater, Philip Lutley (1829–1913): British ornithologist and zoogeographer; known for his interest in neotropical birds; editor of *The Ibis*; fellow of the Royal Society; secretary of the Zoological Society of London; one of the founders of the British Ornithologists' Union; author of *The Geographic Distribution of the Members of the Class Aves*; 1,300 articles and books; honored by the Mexican chickadee, *Parus sclateri*.

Scott, Winfield (1786–1866): Great American general and war hero; memorialized by Scott's oriole.

Scott, Sir Peter Markham (1909–1989): Author; illustrator; conservationist; Life Fellow of the Zoological Society of London; known for his interest in wildfowl; helped to found the World Wildlife Fund; authored and illustrated *A Coloured Key to the Wildfowl of the World*; illustrated *The Waterfowl of the World*; author of *Wild Geese and Eskimos* and co-author of A *Thousand Geese*.

Seebohm, Henry (1832–1895): Amateur ornithologist; authored *The Geographical Distribution of the Family Charadriidae, or the Plovers, Sandpipers, Snipes and their Allies*; also authored *A Monograph of the Turdidae, or Family of Thrushes*.

Selby, Prideaux John (1788–1867): Published *Illustrations of British Ornithology*; editor of the *Magazine of Zoology and Botany*.

Selous, Edmund (1858–1934): Considered to be the founder of modern studies of behavior; author of *Realities of Bird Life*; also authored *The Birdwatcher in the Shetlands, Thought Transference in Birds, Bird Life Glimpses*, and *Evolution of Habit in Birds*.

Serle, William (1912–1992): Minister; ornithologist; collector of bird skins and eggs; known for his interest in Scottish and African birds; wrote *The Collins Field Guide to the Birds of West Africa*.

Serventy, Dominic Louis (1904–1988): Australian ornithologist; studied the short-tailed shearwater; honorary fellow of the American Ornithologists' Union; authored hundreds of publications.

Seton, Ernest Thompson (1860–1946): Scientist; artist; editor of the *Proceedings of the Ornithological Subsection of the Biological Section of the Canadian Institute*; author of numerous books including a monograph on the birds of Manitoba; parks in the Toronto and Manitoba regions honor his name; recipient of several awards.

Sharpe, Richard Bowdler (1847–1909): Headed the bird section of the British Museum of Natural History; member of the Yarkand Mission; founder of the British Ornithologists Club; published numerous articles, papers, and books; contributed largely to *The Catalogue of Birds in the British Museum*.

Sherman, Althea (1853–1943): Amateur ornithologist; author of many articles and essays in ornithological journals; remembered for having built a swift observation tower at her home.

Shortt, Terrence (1910–1986): Artist; ornithologist; naturalist; worked at the Royal Ontario Museum for 45 years; participated in 36 field expeditions; elective member of the American Ornithologists' Union; author of *Not as the Crow Flies* and over 30 papers on birds; produced many paintings and illustrations.

Sibley, Charles Gard (1917–1998): Professor of Biology and curator of birds, Yale University; pioneer in field studies of hybridizing bird species, using serum electrophoresis of egg-white proteins, and later DNA-DNA hybridization; co-author of *Distribution and Taxonomy of the Birds of the World* and of *Phylogeny and Classification of Birds of the World*; president and Fellow of the American Ornithologists' Union. (CSH)

Sick, Helmut (1910–1991): German ornithologist who specialized in Brazilian birdlife; authored over 200 publications, including *Ornitologia Brasileira, uma Introdução*; pioneered the establishment of modern ornithology in Brazil.

Singer, Arthur Bernard (1917–1990): Wildlife artist; his paintings can be seen in *Birds of the World* by Oliver Austin and *Birds of North America* by Robbins, Bruun, and Zim as well as several other books; designed a series of stamps; elective member of the American Ornithologists' Union; recipient of the Augustus St. Gaudens Medal by the Cooper Union and the Hal Borland Medal by the National Audubon Society.

Smith, Gideon B. (1793–1867): Baltimore physician; friend and correspondent of Audubon; Smith's longspur bears his name.

Smith, Joseph (1836–1929): Bird illustrator; illustrations in *Exotic Ornithology*; contributed to *The Catalogue of Birds in the British Museum*.

Smithe, Frank B. (1892–1989): Manufacturer; author of *Birds of Tikal* and *Naturalist's Color Guide* (which followed the Munsell Color System). (CSH)

Snetsinger, Phoebe (1931–1999): Began birding at 34; diagnosed with cancer in 1981; first person to see over 8,000 birds; holds the world record for bird species seen—nearly 85 percent of the world's 10,000 species; her life story is told in *Birding on Borrowed Time* published in 2003.

Snyder, Lester L. (1894–1968): Conservationist; curator of birds and later associate director of zoology in the Royal Ontario Museum; headed field expeditions in the province; fellow of the American Ornithologists' Union; founded the Brodie Club; helped organize the Toronto Field-Naturalists and the Federation of Ontario Naturalists which he directed.

Southern, Harry Melville "Mick" (1909?–1986): British naturalist; bird photographer; mammalogist; known for work on predator-prey relationships involving owls; editor of *Bird Study* and the *Journal of Animal Ecology*; awarded the Union Medal by the British Ornithologists' Union, as well as other awards.

Speirs, Doris Louise Huestis (1894–1989): Founder of the Margaret Nice Ornithological Club; edited Margaret Nice's autobiography; helped found the Pickering Naturalists' Club; known for her interest in the evening grosbeak; an award of the Society of Canadian Ornithologists bears her name.

Spencer, Robert (1923–1994): British ornithologist; head of the National Bird Ringing Scheme for 29 years; served on the staff of the British Trust for Ornithology; contributed immensely to bird ringing; pioneered the movement for bird observatories; helped found EURING; principal editor of *The New Atlas of Breeding Birds in Britain and Ireland:1988–1991*; awarded several medals.

Spofford, Walter (1908–1995): Teacher; falconer; passion for birds of prey, especially peregrine falcons and golden eagles.

Sprague, Isaac (1811–1895): Botanical artist whose interest in birds led him to accompany Audubon on the Missouri R. expedition; honored by Sprague's pipit, *Anthus spragueii*.

Sprunt, Alexander, Jr. (1898–1973): Contributed to the ornithology of South Carolina; participated in the second supplement to Arthur T. Waynes's *Birds of South Carolina*; fellow of the American Ornithologists' Union; nature columnist for a local newspaper; a bird sanctuary is named after him.

Stanwood, Cordelia (1865–1958): Photographer; specialized on the nesting behavior of woodland species; her home is now a nature center; her photographs are preserved by the Wildlife Foundation which bears her name.

Steller, Georg Wilhelm (1709–1746): German zoologist and traveler; ship surgeon and mineralogist of the Arctic expedition on the *St. Peter*; first European to set foot in Alaska; collected Steller's crow which bears his name and the species name *stelleri*; honored also by Steller's sea eagle and by Steller's eider; the only naturalist to see the spectacled cormorant alive.

Stewart, Robert Earl, Sr. (1913–1993): Wildlife research biologist; studied waterfowl in the Chesapeake Bay; initiated the Audubon Winter Bird Population Study; fellow of the American Ornithologists' Union; author of *Waterfowl Populations in the Upper Chesapeake Region.*

Stewart, Paul A. (1909–1994): Studied the ecology and management of the wood duck; known for his interest in blackbird roosts and black vultures; elective member of the American Ornithologists' Union; published 130 papers.

Stirrett, George Milton (1899–1982): Wildlife biologist with the Canadian Wildlife Service; worked with waterfowl; participated in the formation of the Federation of Ontario Naturalists; Chief Parks Naturalist of National Parks of Canada; recipient of a Heritage Canada Foundation Award and a Paul Harris Fellow Award.

Stoddard, Herbert Lee (1889–1968): Ornithologist, naturalist; fellow of the American Ornithologists' Union; author of *The Bobwhite Quail*; awarded the Brewster Medal.

Stone, Witmer (1866–1939): Ornithologist, naturalist; worked at the Academy of Natural Sciences for 50 years; special interest in migration, molts, and plumages; helped found the Delaware Valley Ornithological Club; president of the American Ornithologists' Union, the Pennsylvania Audubon Society, and the National Association of Audubon Societies; editor of *The Auk*

Stratton-Porter, Gene , (1863–1924): Bird photographer and writer; authored *The Song of the Cardinal.*

Stresemann, Erwin (1889–1972): German ornithologist; teacher; explorer; collector; curator of birds at Berlin Zoological Museum; many important contributions to avian taxonomy; interest in molts and plumages; wrote *Aves*, a monumental 900-page handbook on ornithology; editor of *Journal für Ornithologie.*

Stroud, Robert (?–1963): Life prisoner for 54 years; self-trained pathologist specializing in bird diseases; wrote *Stroud's Digest on the Diseases of Birds*; known widely as the "Birdman of Alcatraz."

Sutter, Ernst (1914–1999): Curator of the bird collection, Natural History Museum, Basle, Switzerland; discovered new bird taxa in Indonesia; began one of first radar studies of nocturnal bird migration. (CSH)

Sutton, George Miksch (1898–1982): One of the most beloved ornithologists of this century; artist; wrote dozens of books, including *Eskimo Year*, hundreds of papers, and produced hundreds of paintings and drawings of birds; spent part of his life as curator of birds at Cornell University, later at the Museum of Zoology at the University of Michigan at Ann Arbor.

Swainson, William (1789–1855): English naturalist, ornithologist, traveler, writer, and illustrator; fellow of the Linnaean Society; fellow of the Royal Society; named and described more than 20 species of North American birds; produced many publications including *Fauna Boreali-Americana* and *Zoological Illustrations*; memorialized by Swainson's hawk, Swainson's warbler, and Swainson's thrush.

Swanson, Gustav A. (1910–1995): Professor; head of the Department of Conservation at Cornell University; head of the Department of Fisheries and Wildlife Biology at Colorado State University; fellow of the American Ornithologists' Union; founding member of the Minnesota Bird Club and the Minnesota Ornithologists' Union; founder and president of the Wildlife Society; editor of *Journal of Wildlife Management.*

Tanner, James T. (1914–1991): Studied the ivory-billed woodpecker; elective member of the American Ornithologists' Union; founder of the ecology program at the University of Tennessee; president and curator of the Tennessee Ornithological Society; editor of *The Migrant*; recipient of the Distinguished Service Award.

Taverner, Percy Algernon (1875–1947): Originator of the first co-operative banding scheme in North America; conservationist who helped create the Point Pelee National Park and Bonaventure Island Bird Sanctuary; worked for the National Museum of Canada; president of the Ottawa Field-Naturalists' Club; several books including *Birds of Canada.*

Temminck, Coenraad Jacob (1778–1858): Dutch zoologist; memorialized by Temminck's stint, *Calidris temminckii.*

Thaxter, Celia Leighton (1835–1894): Participated in nature education for children by writing poems that were mostly about birds; wrote an influential anti-plume-hunting essay.

Thayer, John Eliot (1862–1933): Ornithologist; established the Thayer Museum in Lancaster, Massachusetts, which contained a large private collection of birds and an ornithological library; honored by Thayer's gull, *Larus thayeri*.

Thomas, Betsy Trent (1923–1998): Wife of an American highway engineer working in South America; main force in founding Sociedad Conservacionista Audubon de Venezuela; student of Venezuelan birds. (CSH)

Thomson, Arthur Landsborough (1890–1977): Specialized in bird migration; helped organize bird ringing in Britain; edited *The New Dictionary of Birds*; president of the British Ornithologists' Union; promoted the protection of birds; authored several books including *Problems of Bird Migration*; recipient of the Buchanan Medal, Godman-Salvin medal, and Bernard Tucker medal.

Thorburn, Archibald (1860–1935): Bird illustrator; illustrated plates for *The Coloured Figures of the Birds of the British Museum*; published *British Birds* and illustrated many other books.

Thorpe, William Homan (1902–1986): Entomologist; ornithologist; widely acclaimed expert on bird song; known for his interest in duetting in birds; also interested in learning and imprinting in birds; wrote *Learning and Instinct in Animals* as well as two major books on bird song; president of the British Ornithologists' Union and later received the Godman-Salvin Medal from them.

Tinbergen, Nikolaas (1907–1988): Biologist; helped found ethology; professor of animal behavior at Oxford University; concentrated his work on a variety of animals into his most remarkable work on herring gulls; a Nobel Prize winner; authored several books including *Study of Instinct* and *Social Behaviour of Animals*.

Todd, Walter Edmond Clyde (1874–1969): Curator Emeritus of the Carnegie Museum in Pittsburgh; studied the birds of southern Saskatchewan and Labrador; the only person to be twice recipient of the Brewster Medal; three bird taxa honor his name.

Townsend, John Kirk (1809–1851): Ornithologist known for his *Narrative of a Journey Across the Rocky Mountains*; bird collector and member of the Academy of Natural Sciences in Philadelphia; became a curator in 1837; was later hired by the National Institute of Washington, D.C.; commemorated by Townsend's solitaire which he collected; also honored by Townsend's warbler and in subspecies of the dark-eyed junco, rock ptarmigan, fox sparrow, and snow bunting.

Townsend, Charles Haskins (1859–1944): Worked for the U.S Fish Commission where he was chief of the Division of Fisheries; director of the New York Aquarium; described several species of birds including Townsend's shearwater which honors his name.

Traill, Thomas Stewart, M.D. (1781–1862): Scottish naturalist; a founder of the Royal Institution of Liverpool; professor of medical jurisprudence who edited *Encyclopaedia Britannica's* 8th edition; memorialized by Traill's flycatcher.

Trautman, Milton Bernhard (1899–1991): Biologist; author of *Birds of Buckeye Lake* and three Ohio state bird lists; fellow of the American Ornithologists' Union. (CSH)

Tristram, Canon Henry Baker (1822–1906): Bird collector; specialized in birds of North Africa and the Middle East; author of *Fauna and Flora of Palestine*; memorialized by Tristram's grackle and Tristram's warbler.

Trudeau, James de Bertz (1817–1887): Physician; collected Trudeau's tern which bears his name.

Tuck, Leslie Mills (1911–1979): Canadian naturalist, nature photographer; Newfoundland Dominion Wildlife Officer; studied the reproductive biology of murres; interest in the Wilson's snipe; founded the Newfoundland Natural History Society; helped in the protection of Funk Island by having it declared a sanctuary; fellow of the American Ornithologists' Union; twice recipient of the Wildlife Society's Outstanding Publication of the Year Award with his books *The Murres, Their Distribution, Populations and Biology* and *The Snipes*.

Tucker, Bernard William (1901–1950): Central figure of British ornithology; professional zoologist; reader of ornithology at Oxford University; editor of *British Birds*; vice-president British Ornithologists' Union; president of the Oxford Ornithological Society; participated in the foundation of the British Trust for Ornithology and the Edward Grey Institute of Field Ornithology; corresponding fellow of the American Ornithologists' Union.

Udvardy, Miklos D.F. (1919–1998): Professor of zoology at the University of British Columbia, then Professor of biological sciences at California

State University, Sacramento; helped develop the British Columbia Nest Records Scheme; world leader in zoogeography; wrote one of the first National Audubon Society bird field guides; fellow of the American Ornithologists' Union. (CSH)

Vallisnieri, Antonio (1661–1730): Italian naturalist and professor of medicine; the species name of the canvasback duck, *valisineria* (which is misspelled), honors him since he named the genus of the plant that the duck is fond of eating.

Van Tyne, Josselyn (1902–1957): Important ornithologist in North America; president of the American Ornithologists' Union and the Wilson Ornithological Society; editor of the *Wilson Bulletin*; studied birds in Michigan and tropical America; senior author of an ornithological textbook.

Vaurie, Charles (1906–1975): Taxonomist; curator at the American Museum of Natural History; author of more than 150 papers as well as *Birds of the Palearctic Fauna* and *Tibet and its Birds*.

Vaux, William Sansom (1811–1882): Vice-president of the Philadelphia Academy of Natural Sciences; honored by Vaux's swift.

Verreaux, Jules Pierre (1807–1873): French explorer and collector; directed, along with his brother, the most important shop in the world dealing in natural history; collected exotic specimens; honored by the species name of the white-fronted dove, *verreauxi*.

Viellot, Louis Jean Pierre (1748–1831): Master taxonomist in France; named 26 genera and 32 species of North American birds; wrote books on birds of North America, tropical birds, and ornithology in France.

Von Haartman, Lars (1919–1998): Leading star of Finnish ornithology; artist; poet; editor of *Ornis Fennica*; president of the 18th International Ornithological Congress; made a lifelong study of the pied flycatcher. (CSH)

Wagler, Johann Georg (1800–1832): German systematist; professor of zoology at the newly founded University of Munich; director of its museum; published *Systema Avium*; memorialized by Wagler's oriole, *Icterus wagleri*, which is now called the black-vented oriole.

Walkinshaw, Lawrence Harvey (1904–1993): Dentist; author; bird bander; student of cranes and Kirtland's warblers (he documented 330 nests of the latter); fellow of the American Ornithologists' Union. (CSH)

Ward, Peter (1934–1979): British ornithologist; renowned expert on the ecology of red-billed queleas, especially their control as a crop pest in Africa.

Welty, Joel Carl (1901–1986): Ornithologist, teacher; elective member of the American Ornithologists' Union; remembered for his textbook *The Life of Birds*, which has undergone several editions and received the Borzoi Book Award.

Wetmore, Alexander (1886–1978): The sixth secretary of the Smithsonian Institution and the second ornithologist to hold that position; president and honorary president of the American Ornithologists' Union; described 189 new species and subspecies; his publications include work on bird migration, taxonomy, biogeography, and paleontology; by involving many scientific organizations, he promoted the study of bird biology; replaced Ridgway as the leading ornithologist in North America; a glacier in Antarctica is named after him.

White, Charles Matthew Newton (1914–1978): Ornithologist; anthropologist; naturalist; studied African birds, especially in northern Rhodesia; known for his interest in systematics.

White, Gilbert (1720–1793): Naturalist and author of *The Natural History of Selborne*; interested in the migration of birds.

Whitney, Josiah Dwight (1819–1896): State geologist; director of the Geological Survey of California; Sturgis Hooper professor of geology at Harvard University; honored by the species name of the elf owl, *whitneyi*.

Wied, Alexander Phillip Maximilian (1782–1867): German traveler and naturalist; discovered and described a subspecies of the turkey vulture, and the pinon jay (also known to some as Maximilian's jay); memorialized by Wied's crested flycatcher.

Wilkinson, William Henry Nairn (1932–1996): Gamehunter; British ornithologist; interest in the white-fronted goose; helped found the Ornithological Society of Turkey which later evolved into the Ornithological Society of the Middle East.

Williamson, Robert Stockton (1824–1882): Headed one of the Pacific Railroad exploratory expeditions to the far west; during this expedition, Williamson's sapsucker was collected.

Wilson, Alexander (1766–1813): Considered to be the scientific father of American ornithology; traveled through the eastern states collecting bird specimens for later observations; drew and painted birds; the author of the nine-volume classic book *American Ornithology or The Natural History of the Birds of the United States*; memorialized by Wilson's storm-petrel, Wilson's phalarope, Wilson's snipe, Wilson's plover, Wilson's warbler, and in the genus name of several North American wood warblers.

Wilson, Edward (1872–1912): Studied the fluctuation in population numbers of a bird species; specialized in the red grouse; co-authored *The Grouse in Health and Disease*.

Witherby, Harry Forbes (1873–1944): British amateur zoologist; joined the family publishing firm H.F.& G. Witherby which published many important British ornithology books; founder of the national ringing scheme; founded and edited *British Birds Magazine*; edited and contributed to the writing of *The Practical Handbook of British Birds*; president of the British Ornithologists' Union; honorary treasurer and secretary of the British Ornithologists' Club; awarded the Godman-Salvin medal.

Wolf, Josef (1820–1899): Bird illustrator; first to make a lifetime career as an illustrator of wildlife; focused on birds in motion; worked for the Zoological Society in London; illustrated *Genera of Birds* and other books.

Wolters, Hans Edmund (1915–1991): Head of the Department of Ornithology at the Alexander Koenig Zoological Research Institute and Museum; editor of *Bonner zoologische Beiträge* and *Bonner zoologische Monographien*; concentrated his studies on the systematics of families in the passeriformes; one of the first to use cladistic principles to reconstruct the avian phylogeny; honorary member of the German Ornithological Society; honorary fellow of the American Ornithologists' Union.

Wood, Merrill (1908–1992): Instructor of zoology and ornithology at Penn State; organizer and vice president of the Eastern Bird Banding Association; treasurer of the Wilson Ornithological Society; patron of the American Ornithologists' Union; published *Birds of Pennsylvania* and *A Bander's Guide to Determining the Age and Sex of Birds*; recipient of the Distinguished Service Award from the College Alumni Society of Penn State.

Worthen, Charles Kimball (1850–1909): Naturalist located in New Mexico who collected and sold natural history specimens; honored by Worthen's sparrow, *Spizella wortheni*.

Wright, Charles (1811–1885): Botanist and field collector of plants and birds; made important contributions to the botany of Texas; collected the gray flycatcher, *Empidonas wrightii*, which was named after him.

Wright, Philip L. (1914–1997): Chair of zoology, University of Montana; museum there named for him; taught many ornithology and mammalogy students. (CSH)

Wright, Mabel Osgood (1859–1934): Conservationist; associate editor of *Bird Lore*; founded and headed the Connecticut Audubon Society; director of the National Audubon Society; author of several books such as *Birdcraft*; developed the Birdcraft Museum and Sanctuary.

Wyatt, Claude Wilmott (1842–1900): Traveler; collector; illustrator; ornithologist on the Sinai expedition; published and illustrated *British Birds*.

Wynne-Edwards, Vero Copner (1906–1997): British marine zoologist; botanist; Arctic ornithologist; Regius Chair of Zoology, University of Aberdeen; developed an early interest in seabirds, especially trans-Atlantic movements; pioneer of marine ornithology; wrote *Animal Dispersion in Relation to Social Behaviour*; championed controversial "group selection" mechanism; co-editor of *Journal of Applied Ecology*; many honorary memberships in ornithological societies; president of British Ornithologists' Union; awarded many prizes and medals.

Xantus, John (1825–1894): Hungarian bird collector who described several new species of birds such as Hammond's flycatcher, the spotted owl, and a subspecies of the solitary vireo; honored by Xantus's hummingbird and Xantus's murrelet, both of which he collected.

Yamashina, Yoshimaro (1900–1989): Japanese ornithologist; studied cytology, systematics, and distribution of birds; founder and Marquis of the Yamashina Institute for Ornithology; described a new species of flightless rail; honorary fellow of the American Ornithologists' Union; author of *Birds of Japan*; recipient of the Jean Delacour Prize and the Golden Ark Award.

Yarrell, William (1784–1856): Founder of the Entomological Society; Fellow of the Linnean Society; vice-president of the Zoological Society; author of *A History of British Birds*.

Zénaide, Princess Zénaide Charlotte Julie Bonaparte (1801–1854): Eldest daughter of the King of Spain, cousin and wife of Charles Lucien Bonaparte; honored by *Zenaida* the generic name of several dove species, and the Zenaida dove.

Updated as of October 1, 2003; obituaries followed by CSH were graciously supplied by C. Stuart Houston

Presidents of Major Ornithological Societies in North America and the U.K.

Canada

Society of Canadian Ornithologists

(founded in 1982; ca. 275 members)

1982–1985	M.R. Lein	1994–1995	H.R. Ouellet
1986–1987	S.G. Sealy	1996–1997	D.N. Nettleship
1988–1989	E.H. Dunn	1998–1999	A.W. Diamond
1990–1991	J.C. Barlow	2000–2002	K.Martin
1992–1993	J.B. Falls	2002–	J.-P. Savard

United States

American Ornithologists' Union

(founded 1883; ca. 4,400 members)

1883–1889	J.A. Allen	1948–1950	R.C. Murphy
1890–1891	D.G. Elliot	1951–1953	J. Van Tyne
1892–1894	E. Coues	1953–1956	A.H. Miller
1895–1987	W. Brewster	1957–1959	E. Mayr
1898–1899	R. Ridgway	1959–1962	G.H. Lowery Jr.
1900–1903	C.H. Merriam	1962–1964	A.L. Rand
1903–1904	C.B. Corey	1964–1966	D. Amadon
1905–1908	C.F. Batchelder	1966–1968	H.F. Mayfield
1908–1910	E.W. Nelson	1968–1970	J. Aldrich
1911–1913	F.M. Chapman	1970–1972	R.W. Storer
1914–1916	A.K. Fischer	1972–1973	J.J. Hickey
1917–1919	J.H. Sage	1973–1975	D.S. Farner
1920–1922	W. Stone	1975–1976	J.T. Emlen
1923–1925	J. Dwight	1976–1978	W.E. Lanyon
1926–1929	A. Wetmore	1978–1980	H.B. Tordoff
1929–1931	J. Grinnell	1982–1984	T.R. Howell
1932–1933	J.H. Fleming	1984–1986	F.C. James
1935–1937	A.C. Bent	1986–1988	C.G. Sibley
1937–1939	H. Friedmann	1988–1990	G.E. Woolfenden
1939–1942	J.P. Chapin	1990–1992	B. Munroe Jr.
1942–1945	J.L. Peters	1992–1994	B. Kessel
1945–1948	H. Lloyd	1994–1996	R.C. Banks

1996–1998	N.K. Johnson	2000–2002	J.W. Fitzpatrick
1998–2000	F.B. Gill	2002–2004	F. Cooke

Cooper Ornithological Society

(founded 1893, incorporated 1944; ca. 2,900 members)

1942–1948	H. Robertson	1981–1983	N.K. Johnson
1948–1951	A. Miller	1983–1985	R.W. Schreiber
1952–1959	J.R. Pemberton	1985–1987	C.J. Ralph
1960–1963	W.J. Sheffler	1987–1989	R.P. Balda
1963–1964	E.N. Harrison	1989–1991	J. Verner
1964–1966	T.R. Howell	1991–1993	M.L. Morton
1967–1969	R.T. Orr	1993–1995	L.F. Kiff
1970–1971	L.R. Mewaldt	1995–1997	S.A. Mahoney
1972–1973	W.H. Behle	1997–1999	J.M. Scott
1974–1975	H.F. Mayfield	1999–2001	G.E. Walsberg
1976–1977	S. Russell	2001–2003	T.D. Rich
1978–1980	D.M. Power	2003–	B.S. Bowen

Wilson Ornithological Society

(founded in 1888; ca. 2,600 members)

1888–1889	J.B. Richards	1950–1952	M. Brooks
1890–1893	L. Jones	1952–1954	W.J. Breckenridge
1894	W.N. Clute	1954–1956	B.L. Monroe, Sr.
1894–1901	R.M. Strong	1956–1958	J.T. Emlen, Jr.
1902–1908	L. Jones	1958–1960	L.H. Walkinshaw
1909–1911	F.L. Burns	1960–1962	H.F. Mayfield
1912–1913	W.E. Saunders	1962–1964	P.B. Street
1914–1916	T.C. Stephens	1964–1966	R.T. Peterson
1917	W.F. Henninger	1966–1968	A.M. Bagg
1918–1919	M.H. Swenk	1968–1969	H.L. Batts, Jr.
1920–1921	R.M. Strong	1969–1971	W.W.H. Gunn
1922–1923	T.L. Hankinson	1971–1973	P.B. Hofslund
1924–1926	A.F. Ganier	1973–1975	K.C. Parkes
1927–1929	L. Jones	1975–1977	A.J. Berger
1930–1931	J.W. Stack	1977–1979	D.A. James
1932–1934	J.M. Shaver	1979–1981	G.A. Hall
1935–1937	J. Van Tyne	1981–1983	A.B. Gaunt
1938–1939	M.M. Nice	1983–1985	J.A. Jackson
1940–1941	L.E. Hicks	1985–1987	C.E. Braun
1942–1943	G.M. Sutton	1987–1989	M.H. Clench
1943–1945	S.C. Kendeigh	1989–1991	J.C. Barlow
1946–1947	G.M. Sutton	1991–1993	R.C. Banks
1948–1950	O.S. Pettingill	1993–1995	R.N. Conner

1995–1997	K.L. Bildstein	2001–2003	W.E. Davis
1997–1999	E.H. Burtt, Jr.	2003–	C.R. Blem
1999–2001	J.C. Kricher		

Association of Field Ornithologists

(founded in 1922; ca. 2,400 members)

1982–1984	G.A. Clark, Jr.	1992–1994	G. Butcher
1984–1986	J. Kricher	1994–1996	E. Landre
1986–1988	W.E. Davis	1996–1999	C.D. Duncan
1988–1990	P. Cannell	2000–2002	J. Jackson
1990–1992	E.H. Burtt, Jr.	2002–	S.A. Sutcliffe

Raptor Research Foundation, Inc.

(founded in 1966; ca. 1,200 members)

1966–1974	B.E Harrell	1990–1993	R. Clark
1975–1977	J.R. Murphy	1994–1995	M. Collopy
1977–1981	R.R. Olendorff	1996–1997	D.M. Bird
1981–1987	J.L. Lincer	1998–2002	M. Kochert
1988–1989	G.E. Duke	2002–	B. Millsap

The Waterbird Society

(founded in 1976; ca. 850 members)

1978–1979	J.C. Ogden	1992–1993	K.L. Bildstein
1980–1981	P.A. Buckley	1994–1995	D.N. Nettleship
1982–1983	J. Burger	1996–1997	J.A. Kushlan
1984–1985	R.M. Erwin	1998–1999	I.C.T. Nisbet
1986–1987	W.E. Southern	2000–2001	R. Butler
1988–1989	D.A. McCrimmon, Jr.	2002–2003	P.C. Frederick
1990–1991	H.W. Kale II		

United Kingdom

British Ornithologists' Union

(founded in 1858; ca. 2,000 members)

1859–1867	Col. H.M. Drummond-Hay	1955–1960	W.H. Thorpe
1867–1896	Lord Lilford	1960–1965	R.E. Moreau
1896–1913	F. Du Cane Godman	1965–1970	V.C. Wynne-Edwards
1913–1918	Col. R.G. Wardlaw-Ramsay	1970–1975	G. Mountfort
1918–1921	W.E. Clarke	1975–1979	Sir H. Elliott
1921–1922	H.J. Elwes	1979–1983	S. Cramp
1923–1928	Lord Rothschild	1983–1987	J.F. Monk
1928–1933	W.L. Sclater	1987–1990	D.W. Snow
1933–1938	H.F. Witherby	1990–1994	J. Kear
1938–1943	P.R. Lowe	1995–1999	J.P. Croxall
1943–1948	Sir N.B. Kinnear	1999–2003	I. Newton
1948–1955	Sir A.L. Thomson	2003–	C. Perrins

Scottish Ornithologists' Club

(founded in 1936; ca. 2,200 members)

1936–1948	E.V. Baxter	1975–1978	A.T. Macmillan
	L.J. Rintoul	1978–1981	V.M. Thom
1948–1951	A.B. Duncan	1981–1984	I.T. Draper
1951–1954	J. Berry	1984–1987	J.M.S. Arnott
1954–1957	V.C. Wynne-Edwards	1987–1988	J. Greenwood
1957–1960	C.G. Connell	1988–1990	S. Da Prato
1960–1963	M.F.M. Meiklejohn	1990–1993	F.D. Hamilton
1963–1966	I.D. Pennie	1993–1996	R.D. Murray
1966–1969	W.J. Eggeling	1996–1999	I.M. Darling
1969–1972	A.D. Watson	1999–2001	B. Downing
1972–1975	G. Waterston	2001–	I.J. Andrews

British Trust for Ornithology

(founded in 1933; ca. 25,000 members)

1958–1960	R.C. Holmes	1981–1984	S.M. Taylor
1961–1964	C.A. Norris	1985–1989	J.A. Hancock
1965–1968	R.C. Holmes	1990–1993	R.P. Howard
1969–1972	I.J. Ferguson-Lees	1994–1996	W. Wilkinson
1973–1976	R.A.O. Hickling	1997–2001	F. Holliday
1977–1980	J.M. McMeekling	2002–	M. Blakenham

Presidents of Major Bird-Watching Societies

United States

American Birding Association

(founded 1969; ca. 20,500 members)

1970–1976	G.S. Keith	1993–1997	D.T. Williams, Jr.
1976–1979	A. Small	1997–1999	A.R. Keith
1979–1983	J.W. Taylor	1999–2003	R. Payne
1983–1989	L.G. Balch	2003–	P. Green*
1989–1993	A.R. Keith		

* in 2003 Executive Director also serves as President

United Kingdom

Royal Society for the Protection of Birds

(founded 1889; ca. members 1,010,000)

1949–1954	Duchess of Portland	1980–1985	E.M. Nicholson
1955–1961	Lord Forester	1985–1990	M. Magnusson
1961–1966	Lord Hurcomb	1990–1991	Sir D. Barber
1966–1970	Sir T. Beamish	1991–1994	I. Prestt
1970–1975	R. Dougall	1994–2001	J. Pettifer
1975–1980	Lord Donaldson	2001–	J. Dimbleby

Distinguished Ornithology Award Recipients

Society of Canadian Ornithologists

Doris Huestis Speirs Award

(for outstanding contributions to Canadian ornithology)

1986	W.E. Godfrey	1995	R.W. Nero
1987	F.G. Cooch	1996	J. Murray
1988	H.A. Hochbaum	1997	H.J. Boyd
1989	C.S. Houston	1998	I. McTaggart-Cowan
1990	J.B. Falls	1999	H.R. Ouellet
1991	L. de K. Lawrence	2000	J.N.M. Smith
1992	T.H. Manning	2001	D. Hussell
1993	F. Cooke		E. Dunn
1994	A.J. Erskine	2002	N. David
		2003	R.J. Robertson

American Ornithologists' Union

William Brewster Memorial Award

(for the most meritorious body of written work on birds of the Western Hemisphere published during the ten calendar years preceding a given A.O.U. meeting)

1921	R. Ridgway	1948	D. Lack
1923	A.C. Bent	1950	A.F. Skutch
1925	M.A. Carriker Jr.	1951	S.C. Kendeigh
	J.C. Phillips	1952	J.T. Zimmer
	W.E.C. Todd	1953	T.E. Howard
1929	C.E. Hellmayr	1954	J. Bond
1931	A.M. Bailey	1955	W.H. Phelps, Sr.
1933	F.M. Chapman	1956	G.H. Lowery
1935	H.E. Stoddard	1957	A.A. Allen
1937	R.C. Murphy	1958	A.W. Schorger
1938	T.S. Roberts	1959	A. Wetmore
1939	W. Stone	1960	D.S. Farner
1940	J.L. Peters	1961	H. Mayfield
1941	D.R. Dickey	1962	A. Wolfson
	A.J. Van Rossem	1963	R.S. Palmer
1942	M.M. Nice	1964	H. Friedmann
1943	A.H. Miller	1965	E. Mayr
1944	R.T. Peterson	1966	G.A. Bartholomew
1945	H.A. Hochbaum	1967	W.E.C. Todd
1947	F.H. Kortright	1968	W.E. Lanyon

1971	C. Sibley	1986	V. Nolan
1972	B. Snow	1987	J. Brown
	D.W. Snow	1988	R.B. Payne
1973	A.W. Johnson	1989	N. Snyder
	R.A. Phillipi	1990	F. Cooke
1974	J.R. King	1991	L. Oring
1975	J. Haffer	1992	N.K. Johnson
1976	G.H. Orians	1993	R.T. Holmes
1977	R. Meyer de Schauensee	1994	F. McKinney
1978	P. Brodkorb	1995	E.S. Morton
1979	W. Dawson	1996	K. Able
1980	F. Pitelka	1997	J.C. Avise
1981	W.A. Keeton	1998	F. Gill
1982	R. Ricklefs	1999	W.D. Koenig
1983	P.R. Grant	2000	C. Carey
1984	S.T. Emlen	2001	S.I Rothstein
1985	J. Fitzpatrick	2002	J.N.M. Smith
	G. Woolfenden	2003	D. Mock

Elliott Coues Award

(for contributions that have had an important impact on the study
of birds in the Western Hemisphere)

1972	N. Tinbergen	1986	F. Nottebohm
	A. Wetmore	1987	J. Wingfield
1973	J.T. Emlen	1988	R. Schreiber
1974	R.H. MacArthur	1989	P. Berthold
1975	W.J. Bock	1991	J. Wiens
	R.F. Johnston	1992	F.C. James
	R.K. Selander	1993	J. Cracraft
1976	P. Marler	1994	W. Wiltschko
1977	J. Delacour	1995	I. Newton
	E. Mayr	1996	E.D. Ketterson
1978	J.J. Hickey	1997	C.H. Robbins
1980	E. Collias	1998	J. Diamond
	N. Collias	1999	J.R. Krebs
1981	A. Ar	2000	T.E. Martin
	C. Paganelli	2001	R.A. Paynter
	H. Rahn		M.A. Traylor Jr.
1983	M. Konishi	2002	J.R. Walters
1984	T.J. Cade	2003	D. Kroodsma
1985	T.R. Howell		

Association of Field Ornithologists

Alexander F. Skutch Medal

(for excellence in neotropical ornithology)

1997	F.G. Stiles	1999	H.A. Raffaele

Wilson Ornithological Society

Margaret Morse Nice Medal

(for lifetime of contributions to ornithology)

1997	E.C. Collias	2000	S.M. Smith
	N.E. Collias	2001	G.E. Woolfenden
1998	E.D. Ketterson	2002	R.T. Holmes
	V. Nolan Jr.	2003	R.E. Ricklefs
1999	F.C. James		

Raptor Research Foundation

President's Award

(for lifetime contributions to raptors and/or to the Raptor Research Foundation)

1980	F. Hamerstrom	1997	E. Henckel
1991	R.R. Olendorff		J. Henckel

Cornell Laboratory of Ornithology

Arthur A. Allen Award

(for the widening of popular interest in birds and for distinguished service to ornithology)

1967	R.T. Peterson	1978	K.H. Maslowski
1968	J. Fisher	1979	C.S. Robbins
1969	G.M. Sutton	1982	W.W.H. Gunn
1970	A. Wetmore	1983	A.F. Skutch
1971	P. Scott	1984	S.D. Ripley
1972	A.D. Cruickshank	1985	R.S. Arbib, Jr.
1973	O.L. Austin, Jr.		S.R. Drennan
	E. Austin	1989	T.J. Cade
1974	O.S. Pettingill, Jr.	1990	H.F. Mayfield
1975	W.J. Breckenridge	1992	C. Greenewalt
1976	J.J. Hickey	1995	K. Anderson
1977	J.T. Delacour		

American Birding Association

ABA Roger Tory Peterson Award

(for promoting the cause of birding)

2001	P. Dunne	2002	D. Sibley

British Ornithologists' Union

Founders' Gold Medal

(presented to the four original members surving at the Jubilee Celebration, December 9, 1908)

F.D. Godman	W.H. Hudleston	P.S. Godman	P.L. Sclater

Union Medal

(may be awarded by the Council to any member in recognition of eminent services to ornithology and to the Union)

1912	W. Goodfellow	1973	B.P. Hall
	C.H.B. Grant	1975	K.H. Voous
	G.C. Shortridge	1976	K. Williamson
	A.F.R. Wollaston	1979	K.E.L. Simmons
1948	W.P. Lowe	1980	G.V.T. Matthews
1953	A.W. Boyd	1984	S. Cramp
1959	W.B. Alexander		P.A.D. Hollom
	E.A. Armstrong		G. Mountfort
	D.A. Bannerman	1987	I. Newton
	E.V. Baxter	1988	J.F. Monk
	P.M. Scott	1989	R. Spencer
1960	C.W. Benson	1991	F.B.M. Campbell
1967	S. Ali	1992	M.P. Harris
1968	J.M.M. Fisher	1993	R.M. Lockley
	C.R.S. Pitman	1995	R. Tory Peterson
1969	C.W. Mackworth-Praed	1996	C.J. Mead
1970	L.H. Brown		R.A.F. Gillmor
1971	S. Marchant	1997	J.S. Ash
	H.N. Southern	1998	J. Kear
	B. Stonehouse		
1972	D. Goodwin		
	N.W. Moore		

Godman-Salvin Medal

(may be awarded by the Council to any person as a signal honour for
distinguished ornithological work)

1922	W.E. Clarke	1969	N. Tinbergen
1929	E. Hartert	1973	J.S. Huxley
1930	W.L. Sclater	1977	V.C. Wynne-Edwards
1936	H. Lynes	1982	D.W. Snow
1938	H.F. Witherby	1988	C.M. Perrins
1946	P.R. Lowe	1990	G.H. Dunnet
1951	R. Melnertzhagen	1991	D.A. Ratcliffe
1959	D.L. Lack	1992	J.C. Coulson
	A. Landsborough Thomson	1995	E. Mayr
1962	E.M. Nicholson	1996	P.R. Evans
1966	R.B. Moreau	1999	G.R. Potts
1968	W.H. Thorpe		

Bird-Watching Record Holders

500+ Birdwatchers in the U.K. and Ireland*

514	R. Johns	502	M. Billington
513	S. Webb	501	P. Flint
510	S. Gantlett	499	D. Filby
508	C. Heard	499	L. Evans
502	R. Millington	498	J. Hewitt

* this represents the latest information gleaned from various sources for 2003 and is not to be considered an official list

Top Ten ABA World Listing Leaders as of January 2002*

8,195	T. Gullick (Spain)	7,222	J. Gee (U.S.)
7,716	G. Winter (U.S.)	7,121	J. Clements (U.S.)
7,666	P. Kaestner (Brazil)	7,102	B. Rapp (U.S.)
7,493	J.D. Danzenbaker (U.S.)	7,095	H. Buck (Cyprus)
7,370	M. Edwards (Canada)	7,073	P. Rostron (U.S.)

* still living (P. Snetsinger had 8,618 at the time of her passing in 1999)

SOURCE: The *2002 ABA Big Day Report*, Vol. 35(3), American Birding Association

Top Ten ABA Area Listers (906 species) as of January 2002*

862	M. Smith (U.S.)	838	P. Sykes (U.S.)
852	B. Basham (U.S.)	836	W. Rydell (U.S.)
848	T. Koundakjian (U.S.)	831	L. Peavler (U.S.)
844	C. Koundakjian (U.S.)	825	D. Nairns (U.S.)
842	S. Komito (U.S.)	819	F. Carley (U.S.)

* still living

SOURCE: The *2002 ABA Big Day Report*, Vol. 35(3), American Birding Association

Top Ten ABA Canada Listers (620 species) as of January 2002*

512	R. Foxall (Canada)	479	E. Tull (Canada)
511	J. MacKenzie (Canada)	478	T. Hofmann (Canada)
511	H. MacKenzie (Canada)	476	M. Force (Canada)
482	D. Stirling (Canada)	476	D. Mark (U.S.)
481	M. Toochin (Canada)	467	C. Escott (Canada)

* still alive (N. Chesterfield had 523 at the time of his passing in 1996)

SOURCE: The *2002 ABA Big Day Report*, Vol. 35(3), American Birding Association

Top Ten ABA U.S. Listers (984 species) as of January 2002*

907	M. Smith (U.S.)	862	L. Peavler (U.S.)
902	B. Basham (U.S.)	860	B. Johnson (U.S.)
894	P. Sykes (U.S.)	850	E. Greaves (U.S.)
869	G. Wachtler (U.S.)	850	M. Gambill (U.S.)
868	R. Wachtler (U.S.)	850	C. Gambill (U.S.)
865	B. Barrett (U.S.)		

* still living

SOURCE: The *2002 ABA Big Day Report*, Vol. 35(3), American Birding Association

7000+ World Listers

8,618	P. Snetsinger (U.S.)	7,121	J. Clemens (U.S.)
8,195	T. Gullick (Spain)	7,102	B. Rapp (U.S.)
7,666	P. Kaestner (Brazil)	7,095	H. Buck (Cyprus)
7,596	J. Hornbuckle (U.K.)	7,073	P. Rostron (U.S.)
7,493	J. Danzenbaker (U.S.)	7,067	G. Graves (U.S.)
7,370	M. Edwards (Canada)	7,017	D. Fisher (U.K.)
7,421	K. Turner (U.K.)	7,001	M. Van Beirs (Belgium)
7,222	J. Gee (U.S.)		

SOURCE: A composite list based on the *2002 ABA Big Day Report*, Vol. 35(3), American Birding Association and the U.K. 400 Club Listing, http://www.uk400clubonline.co.uk/list_world.htm (updated to March 2003)

New Jersey Audubon Society's World Series of Birding

Urner-Stone Cup Award Recipients

Year	Total Species	Team	Team Members
1984	201	Zeiss Optics	R.T. Peterson, P. Dunne, L. Dunne, D. Sibley, P. Bacinski, W. Boyle
1985	182	D.V.O.C.	A. Brady, C. Danzenbaker, A. Hill, M. Danzenbaker, K. Brethwaite
1986 D.	199 (tie)	Bausch & Lomb Leica	G. Hanisek, J. Dowdell, J. Zamos, J. DeMarrais R. Kane, A. Keith, P. Buckley, W. Wander, D. Harrison
1987	205	Bausch & Lomb	G. Hanisek, J. Dowdell, J. Zamos, J. DeMarrais
1988	200	Zeiss Optics	P. Dunne, P. Bacinski, M. Gustafson, B. Peterjohn
1989	201	Bausch & Lomb	G. Hanisek, J. Dowdell, J. Zamos, J. DeMarrais
1990	210	Zeiss Optics	P. Dunne, L. Dunne, P. Bacinski, R. Radis, D. Freiday
1991	199	Bausch & Lomb	G. Hanisek, J. Dowdell, J. Zamos, J. DeMarrais
1992	205	Minolta Corp	D. Miranda, R. Crossley, S. Angus, J. Panzinger, J. Farber
1993	215	Kowa Optimed	T. Hince, P. Pratt, B. DiLabio
1994	218	Birders World Magazine	D. Wormer, C. Aquila, D. Dendler
1995	221	Birders World Magazine	D. Wormer, C. Aquila, D. Dendler
1996	229	Birders World Magazine	D. Wormer, C. Aquila, D. Dendler
1997	217	Kowa Optimed	T. Hince, G. Gervais, P. Pratt, B. DiLabio
1998	200	Phillipsburg Riverview Org.	D. Dunlop, M. King, M. Yoo, J. Walker, R. Johnson
1999	223	Nikon/D.V.O.C.	P. Guris, M. Fritz, A. Binns, B. Stocku
2000	219 (tie)	Nikon/D.V.O.C.	P. Guris, M. Fritz, A. Binns, B. Stocku, M. Edwards
		Carl Zeiss/C.M.B.O.	P. Dunne, R. Crossley, D. Freiday, W. Russell
2001	214 (tie)	Nikon/D.V.O.C.	P. Guris, M. Fritz, A. Binns, B. Stocku
		Swarovski Optik/C.L.O.	K. Rosenberg, S. Kelling, J. Wells, J. Fitzpatrick, K. McGowan
2002	224	Swarovski Optic/C.L.O.	K. Rosenberg, S. Kelling, J. Wells, J. Fitzpatrick, K. McGowan
2003	231	Nikon/D.V.O.C	P. Guris, M. Fritz, A. Binns, B. Stocku

SOURCE: Cape May Bird Observatory, Northwood Center, 701 East Lake Drive, P.O. Box 3, Cape May Point, NJ 08212

Great Texas Birding Classic Winners

Year	Total Species	Team	Members
1997	298	Compaq Computer Corp./ Houston Audubon Society	D. Peake, R. Weeks, G. Beaton, R. Breedlove
1998	298	WildBird Magazine	A. Farnsworth, N. Brinkley, M. Iliff
1999	312	WildBird Magazine	A. Farnsworth, D. Cooper, M. Iliff
2000	302	Kowa Optimed	T. Hince, P. Pratt, B. DiLabio, E. Meleg
2001	307	WildBird Magazine	N. Black, C. Cox, M. Retter, M. Andersen
2002	325	WildBird Magazine	N. Black, G. Gips, M. Hafner, C. Nunes
2003	329	WildBird Magazine/ Swift Instruments	N. Black, M. Haffner, P. Hosner, M. Retter

For more details, visit www.tpwd.state.tx.us/gtbc

Taverner Cup Winners (Canada)

Year	Total Species	Team	Team Members
1997	180	Bushnell Nighthawks	B. DiLabio, C. Traynor, J.Harris, D.Pierson
1998	171	Lee Valley Sawbills	M. Runtz, D.McRae, P. Burke, C. Jones, M.Borer
1999	183	Bushnell Nighthawks	B. DiLabio, C. Traynor, R. Harris A. Charron
2000	183	Lee Valley Sawbills	M. Runtz, P. Burke, C. Jones, M. Borer, D. Sutherland
2001	180	Bushnell Nighthawks	B. DiLabio, C. Traynor R. Harris, A. Charron
2002	193	Bushnell Nighthawks	B. DiLabio, C. Traynor, R. Harris
2003	161	Bushnell Nighthawks	B. DiLabio, C. Traynor, R. Harris

For more details, visit www.web-nat.com/taverner/

Ward World Bird-Carving Champions

Year	Category	Artist	Work
1971	Decorative Lifesize	Jules Iski	Oldsquaws
	Decorative Decoy Pair	J.B. Garton	Blue-winged Teal
1972	Decorative Lifesize	John Scheeler	American Kestrels
	Decorative Decoy Pair	John Scheeler	Red-breasted Mergansers
1973	Decorative Lifesize	John Scheeler	Peregrine Falcon w/ Green-winged teal
	Decorative Decoy Pair	Jim Foote	Gadwalls
1974	Decorative Lifesize	Wm. Koelpin	White-fronted Goose w/ Teal
	Decorative Decoy Pair	Paul Burdette	Redhead
1975	Decorative Lifesize	John Scheeler	Prairie Falcon w/ Dove
	Decorative Decoy Pair	Jim Foote	Wigeon
1976	Decorative Lifesize	John Scheeler	Long-eared Owl and Mouse
	Decorative Decoy Pair	Pat Godin	Goldeneyes
1977	Decorative Lifesize	Wm. Schultz	Bittern w/ Marsh Wren
	Decorative Decoy Pair	Tan Brunet	Pintails
1978	Decorative Lifesize	A.J. Rudisill	Clapper Rails w/ Snail
	Decorative Decoy Pair	Tan Brunet	Mallards
1979	Decorative Lifesize	Lynn Forehand	Red Jungle Fowl
	Decorative Decoy Pair	Randy Tull	Buffleheads
	Decorative Miniature	E. Muehlmatt	Woodcocks
1980	Decorative Lifesize	John Scheeler	Ruffed Grouse
	Decorative Decoy Pair	Pat Godin	Black Ducks
	Decorative Miniature	Gary Yoder	Pheasants
1981	Decorative Lifesize	John Scheeler	Goshawk and Crow
	Decorative Decoy Pair	Tan Brunet	Canvasbacks
	Decorative Miniature	E. Muehlmatt	Least Bittern
1982	Decorative Lifesize	Pat Godin	Along the Grand—Black Ducks and Muskrat
	Decorative Decoy Pair	Tan Brunet	Green-winged Teal
	Decorative Miniature	Gary Yoder	Mallards in Flight
1983	Decorative Lifesize	A.J. Rudisill	Black-crowned Night Heron
	Decorative Decoy Pair	Tan Brunet	Redheads
	Decorative Miniature	Bob Ptashnik	Avocets
1984	Decorative Lifesize	E. Muelmatt	Bobwhite Quail
	Decorative Decoy Pair	Pat Godin	Wigeon
	Decorative Miniature	Robert Guge	Mourning Dove

Year	Category	Artist	Work
1985	Decorative Lifesize	Larry Barth	Snowy Owl and Bonaparte's Gull
	Decorative Decoy Pair	Jett Brunet	Ruddy Ducks
	Decorative Miniature	Gary Yoder	Cooper's Hawk and Flicker
1986	Decorative Lifesize	Larry Barth	Terns in Flight
	Decorative Decoy Pair	Marcus Schultz	Cinnamon Teal
	Decorative Miniature	Robert Guge	Puffins
1987	Decorative Lifesize	Gordon Hare	Bluejays
	Decorative Decoy Pair	Jett Brunet	Scaups
	Decorative Miniature	Bob Guge	Eastern Bluebirds
	Natural Finish	Martin Gates	Snowy egret—"Snowy Essence"
1988	Decorative Lifesize	Gordon Hare	Kestrel
	Decorative Decoy Pair	Kent Duff	Wood Ducks
	Decorative Miniature	Peter Kaune	Robins
	Natural Finish	John Sharp	Three Goldeneyes
1989	Decorative Lifesize	Gary Yoder	Robins
	Decorative Decoy Pair	Chris Bonner	American Mergansers
	Decorative Miniature	Philip Galatas	Peregrine falcon—"Watch On"
	Interpretive	Leo and Lee Osborne	Goose sleeping—"Gentle Rest"
1990	Decorative Lifesize	Todd Wohlt	Black duck and pied-billed grebe—"Dive"
	Decorative Decoy Pair	D. Schroeder	Shovelers
	Decorative Miniature	Philip Galatas	Red-tailed hawk
	Interpretive	Vankeuren Marshall	"Courting Kestrels"
1991	Decorative Lifesize	Larry Barth	Loggerhead shrike and hawthorn—"Vantage Point"
	Decorative Decoy Pair	D. Scroeder	Oldsquaws
	Decorative Miniature	Bob Guge	Cardinal
	Interpretive	John Sharp	Cormorants
1992	Decorative Lifesize	Greg Woodard	Preening kestrel on cactus—"Cactus Flower"
	Decorative Decoy Pair	Victor Paroyan	Blue-winged Teal
	Decorative Miniature	Pete Zaluzec	Yellow Rails
	Interpretive	John Sharp	Canada Geese
1993	Decorative Lifesize	Larry Barth	Least bittern and marsh wren—"In the Cattails"
	Decorative Decoy Pair	Jude Brunet	Ringnecks
	Decorative Miniature	Pete Zaluzec	Plate-Billed Mountain Toucan
	Interpretive	John Sharp	Road Kill Pheasant
	Shootin' Rig	Tom Christie	Mallard Pair and Wigeon

Year	Category	Artist	Work
1994	Decorative Lifesize	Glenn Ladenberger	Male Northern Goshawk
	Decorative Decoy Pair	Jon Jones	Emperor Goose
	Decorative Miniature	Pete Zaluzec	Bateleur
	Interpretive	John Sharp	City Pigeons
	Shootin' Rig	Keith Mueller	Black Duck Pair and Mallard
1995	Decorative Lifesize	Pat Godin	American woodcock—"Descent Through the Alders"
	Decorative Decoy Pair	Jude Brunet	Gadwalls
	Decorative Miniature	Gary Yoder	Steller's Sea Eagle
	Interpretive	Jeff Muhs	Anhinga—"Sun Worshipper"
	Shootin' Rig	Mike Harde	Common Eiders
1996	Decorative Lifesize	Todd Wohlt	Kestrel
	Decorative Decoy Pair	Keith Mueller	Common Eiders
	Decorative Miniature	Michael Arthurs	Roseate spoonbills—"Evening Flight"
	Interpretive	Jeff Muhs	Barn owl and crows "Moonlight Run"
	Shootin' Rig	Alan Bell	Redheads (Two hens and a drake)
1997	Decorative Lifesize	Larry Barth	Great Reed Warbler
	Decorative Decoy Pair	Victor Paroyan	Pintails
	Decorative Miniature	Todd Wohlt	Indigo Bunting
	Interpretive	John Sharp	Bird-Watching
	Shootin' Rig	Weldon Bordelon, Jr.	Gadwalls (Two hens and a drake)
1998	Decorative Lifesize	Glenn Ladenberger	Harris's hawk—"Desert Reign"
	Decorative Decoy Pair	Victor Paroyan	Hooded Merganser Pair
	Decorative Miniature	Jeff Rechin	King penguins—"Three Kings"
	Interpretive	John T. Sharp	Dove pair—"Muddy Road"
	Shootin' Rig	Del Herbert	Two White-fronted Geese and One Ross's Goose
1999	Decorative Lifesize	Larry Barth	Green Heron
	Decorative Decoy Pair	Russell Martin, Jr.	Mute Swan (single)
	Decorative Miniature	Pat Godin	Ruffed grouse— "Otter Creek Courtship"
	Interpretive	John T. Sharp	Flying buffleheads —"Open Water"
	Shootin' Rig	Tom Christie	Redheads (Two drakes and a hen)

Year	Category	Artist	Work
2000	Decorative Lifesize	Larry Barth	Ruddy turnstone & purple sandpipers—"Tidal Companions"
	Decorative Decoy Pair	Russell Martin, Jr.	Surf Scoter Pair
	Decorative Miniature	Jeff Rechin	Eastern Turkeys
	Interpretive	Greg Woodard	Prairie falcon and cliff swallows —"Hunting the Adobe"
	Shootin' Rig	Thomas Matus	Red-breasted Mergansers (Two drakes and a hen)
2001	Decorative Lifesize	Larry Barth	Broad-winged Hawk and Green Snake
	Decorative Decoy Pair	Richard Reeves	Mallard Pair
	Decorative Miniature	Pat Godin	"Spruce Grouse on the North River"
	Interpretive	Daniel Burgette	White-throated swifts— "Chasing the Next Generation"
	Shootin' Rig	Pat Godin	Black Duck Pair and Hybrid Black Duck Mallard
2002	Decorative Lifesize	Larry Barth	"Winter Sanderlings"
	Decorative Decoy Pair	Jamie Welsh	Black-bellied Whistling Ducks
	Decorative Miniature	Pat Godin	Greater prairie chicken— "Prairie Dance"
	Interpretive	Phil Galatas	Macaw—"Queen of Hearts"
	Shootin' Rig	Tom Christie	

SOURCE: Ward Museum, 909 S. Schuumaker Dr., Salisbury, MD 21804 Tel: (410) 742-4988

United States Federal Duck Stamp Artists

Year	Artist	Work
1934–35	J.N. "Ding" Darling	Mallard pair landing
1935–36	Frank W. Benson	Three canvasbacks in flight
1936–37	Richard E. Bishop	Three Canada geese in flight
1937–38	Joseph D. Knap	Three Canada geese in flight
1938–39	Roland H. Clark	Pintail pair landing
1939–40	Lynn Bogue Hunt	Resting green-winged teal pair
1940–41	Francis Lee Jacques	Two black ducks in flight
1941–42	Edwin R. Kalmbach	Ruddy ducks with young
1942–43	Alden L. Ripley	Flock of American wigeon
1943–44	Walter H. Bohl	Wood duck pair in flight
1944–45	Walter A. Weber	Three white-fronted geese landing
1945–46	Owen J. Gromme	Three shovelers in flight
1946–47	Robert W. Hines	Male redhead landing
1947–48	Jack Murray	Two flying snow geese
1948–49	Maynard Reece	Three buffleheads in flight
1949–50	Roger E. Preuss	Pair of goldeneyes descending
1950–51	Walter A. Weber	Two trumpeter swans flying
1951–52	Maynard Reece	Two gadwall leaping into flight
1952–53	John H. Dick	Pair of harlequin ducks in flight
1953–54	Clayton B. Seager	Flock of blue-winged teal
1954–55	Harvey D. Sandstrom	Two ring-necked ducks landing
1955–56	Stanley Stearns	Three "blue" phase snow geese climbing into the air
1956–57	Edward J. Bierly	Two American mergansers in flight along river
1957–58	Jackson Miles Abbott	Two drake eiders flying above breaking surf
1958–59	Leslie C. Kouba	Three Canada Geese in a cornfield
1959–60	Maynard Reece	Labrador retriever shown holding a dead mallard
1960–61	John A. Ruthven	Male and female redhead with chicks
1961–62	Edward A. Morris	Hen mallard with chicks
1962–63	Edward A. Morris	Two pintail drakes landing on a marsh
1963–64	Edward J. Bierly	Two brant descending on coastal waters
1964–65	Stanley Stearns	Two Hawaiian geese grazing on grass
1965–66	Ron Jenkins	Three drake canvasbacks skimming rough water

Year	Artist	Work
1966–67	Stanley Stearns	Two tundra swans flying
1967–68	Leslie C. Kouba	Pair of oldsquaws sitting on ice floe
1968–69	Claremont Gale Prichard	Pair of hooded mergansers sitting on a fallen log
1969–70	Maynard Reece	Pair of white-winged scoters running
1970–71	Edward J. Bierly	Two Ross's geese
1971–72	Maynard Reece	Three cinnamon teal dropping in for a landing
1972–73	Arthur M. Cook	Two adult emperor geese landing
1973–74	Lee LeBlanc	Pair of Steller's eiders standing along rocky shore
1974–75	David Maass	Two wood ducks rising in front of dead tree
1975–76	James P. Fisher	Weathered canvasback decoy
1976–77	Alderson Magee	Pair of Canada geese guarding their four goslings
1977–78	Martin R. Murk	Two Ross's geese in flight
1978–79	Albert Earl Gilbert	Drake hooded merganser gliding
1979–80	Ken Michaelson	Pair of green-winged teal
1980–81	Richard W. Plasschaert	Pair of mallards flying over cattail marsh
1981–82	John S. Wilson	Pair of ruddy ducks sitting on quiet water
1982–83	David Maass	Three canvasbacks landing on a windy lake
1983–84	Phil V. Scholer	Pair of pintails
1984–85	William C. Morris	Pair of American wigeon swimming
1985–86	Gerald Mobley	Single drake cinnamon teal
1986–87	Burton E. Moore Jr.	Single fulvous whistling duck swimming
1987–88	Arthur G. Anderson	Two drake redheads and a single hen
1988–89	Daniel Smith	Single adult snow goose flying
1989–90	Neal R. Anderson	Two lesser scaup swimming among reeds
1990–91	James Hautman	Black-bellied whistling ducks
1991–92	Nancy Howe	King eiders
1992–93	Joseph Hautman	Spectacled eider
1993–94	Bruce Miller	Canvasbacks
1994–95	Neal R. Anderson	Red-breasted mergansers
1995–96	James Hautman	Mallards
1996–97	Wilhelm Goebel	Surf scoters
1997–98	Robert Hautman	Canada goose
1998–99	Robert Steiner	Barrow's goldeneye
1999–00	James Hautman	Greater scaup
2000–01	Adam Grimm	Mottled duck
2001–02	Robert Hautman	Northern pintail

Year	Artist	Work
2002–03	Joseph Hautman	Black scoter
	Ron Louque	Snow goose

SOURCE: S. Weidensaul, *Duck Stamps—Art in the Service of Conservation* (New York: Gallery Books, 1989; U.S. Fish and Wildlife Service http://www.fws.gov/~r9dso/dkhome.html

Bird-Watching

American Birding Association

Code of Birding Ethics

1. **Promote the welfare of birds and their environment.**

   1a) Support the protection of important bird habitat.

   1b) To avoid stressing birds or exposing them to danger, exercise restraint and caution during observation, photography, sound recording, or filming.

   Limit the use of recordings and other methods of attracting birds, and never use such methods in heavily birded areas, or for attracting any species that is Threatened, Endangered, or of Special Concern, or is rare in your local area.

   Keep well back from nests and nesting colonies, roosts, display areas, and important feeding sites. In such sensitive areas, if there is a need for extended observation, photography, filming, or recording, try to use a blind or hide, and take advantage of natural cover.

   Use artificial lighting sparingly for filming or photography, especially close-ups.

   1c) Before advertising the presence of a rare bird, evaluate the potential for disturbance to the bird, its surroundings, and other people in the area, and proceed only if access can be controlled, disturbance minimized, and permission has been obtained from private landowners. The sites of rare nesting birds should be divulged only to the proper conservation authorities.

   1d.) Stay on roads, trails, and paths where they exist; otherwise keep habitat disturbance to a minimum.

2. **Respect the law and the rights of others.**

   2a) Do not enter private property without the owner's explicit permission.

   2b) Follow all laws, rules, and regulations governing use of roads and public areas, both at home and abroad.

   2c) Practice common courtesy in contacts with other people. Your exemplary behavior will generate goodwill with birders and non-birders alike.

3. **Ensure that feeders, nest structures, and other artificial bird environments are safe.**

   3a) Keep dispensers, water, and food clean and free of decay or disease. It is important to feed birds continually during harsh weather.

   3b) Maintain and clean nest structures regularly.

   3c) If you are attracting birds to an area, ensure the birds are not exposed to predation from cats and other domestic animals, or dangers posed by artificial hazards.

4. **Group birding, whether organized or impromptu, requires special care.**

   Each individual in the group, in addition to the obligations spelled out in Items #1 and #2, has responsibilities as a Group Member.

   4a) Respect the interests, rights, and skills of fellow birders, as well as people participating in other legitimate outdoor activities. Freely share your knowledge and experience, except where code c) applies. Be especially helpful to beginning birders.

   4b) If you witness unethical birding behavior, assess the situation, and intervene if you think it prudent. When interceding, inform the person(s) of the inappropriate action, and attempt, within reason, to have it stopped. If the behavior continues, document it, and notify appropriate individuals or organizations.

Code of Birding Ethics (Cont'd)

Group Leader Responsibilities (amateur and professional trips and tours)

4c) Be an exemplary ethical role model for the group. Teach through word and example.

4d) Keep groups to a size that limits impact on the environment, and does not interfere with others using the same area.

4e) Ensure everyone in the group knows of and practices this code.

4f) Learn and inform the group of any special circumstances applicable to the areas being visited (e.g., no tape recordings allowed).

4g) Acknowledge that professional tour companies bear a special responsibility to place the welfare of birds and the benefits of public knowledge ahead of the company's commercial interests. Ideally, leaders should keep track of tour sightings, document unusual occurrences, and submit records to appropriate organizations.

American Birding Association
P.O. Box 6599
Colorado Springs, CO 80934-6599
(800) 850-2473 or (719) 578-1614
fax: (800) 247-3329 or (719) 578-1480
e-mail: member@aba.org

Royal Society for the Protection of Birds

Code of Conduct for Bird-Watchers

Today's bird-watchers are a powerful force for nature conservation. The number of those of us interested in birds rises continually and it is vital that we take seriously our responsibility to avoid any hardship to birds.

We must also present a responsible image to non-bird-watchers who may be affected by our activities and particularly those on whose sympathy and support the future of birds may rest.

There are 10 points to bear in mind:

1. The welfare of the birds must come first.

2. Habitats must be protected.

3. Keep disturbance to birds and their habitat to a minimum.

4. When you find a rare bird, think carefully about whom you should tell.

5. Do not harass rare migrants.

6. Abide by the bird protection laws at all times.

7. Respect the rights of landowners.

8. Respect the rights of other people in the countryside.

9. Make your records available to the local bird recorder.

10. Behave abroad as you would when bird-watching at home.

This code has been drafted after consultation between the British Ornithologists' Union, British Trust for Ornithology, The Royal Society for the Protection of Birds, the Scottish Ornithologists' Club, the Wildfowl and Wetlands Trust, and the editors of *British Birds*.

Checklist of Birding Gear

Alarm clock/watch

Binoculars

Bird checklist for the region/state/province/country

Bird guide(s)

Bottled water

Copy of your itinerary (leave one with family or friend for emergencies)

Customs certificates for binoculars, cameras, lenses to indicate ownership

Extra plastic bags of all sizes for protection of equipment from sand, saltwater, etc.

Camera (35 mm/digital)

Film/memory cards/charged batteries

First aid kit: Band-Aids, antacid pills, pain relief pills, laxative, Lomotil, water-purifying tablets, cortisone cream, gravol, eye and ear drops, vitamins, snakebite kit, lip balm, malaria pills

Flashlight with extra batteries

Hat

Insect repellent

Items of personal hygiene

Maps

Notebooks

Passport and spare copy

Pencils and pens

Poncho

Scarf/bandana

Spare pair of mini-binoculars

Spare eyeglasses and prescription for them

Sunglasses

Sunscreen

Survival whistle

Survival kit: nylon cord, super glue, rubber bands, needle and thread, safety pins

Swiss army knife

Telescope and tripod

Toilet paper roll

Vaccination booklet

Twenty Tips for Choosing Binoculars

1. Always buy the best you can afford.
2. Buy them to best suit the kind of birding you will mostly use them for, e.g. rugged, backyard, marine, etc.
3. Ensure that they feel good in your hands, whether mini- or regular-sized.
4. Roof prism binoculars are more expensive, but easier to hold and more rugged than porro prism versions.
5. Binoculars weighing over a pound and a half (700 g) can get heavy in time.
6. For rugged use, armoured binoculars are better.
7. High-quality optics are denser and heavier than low-quality ones, but preferred for a sharper image.
8. Fast-focusing binoculars are invaluable for fast-moving birds.
9. Focus wheels are superior to levers because the latter require two hands and are less durable.
10. Non-focusing binoculars will not permit close-focusing; close-focusing binoculars are very useful in woodland birding and for looking at beetles and butterflies.
11. Magnification between 7 to 10 times is preferable, as higher magnifications can increase hand-shake and provide a smaller field of view, a darker image, and a shallower depth of field.
12. Zoom binoculars generally offer inferior optics and a lower field of view.
13. "Fully multi-coated" optics cut glare and reduce light loss.
14. A wide field of view is preferable for fast-flying birds, scanning a vista quickly, and locating small birds in thick cover.
15. A generous depth of field minimizes the need to continually focus on birds moving closer or farther away.
16. Eyeglass-wearers need binoculars with a minimum of 15 mm of eye relief.
17. Well-sealed binoculars with internal focusing will minimize entry of dust, pollen, and moisture; fully waterproof binoculars are usually heavier and more expensive.
18. Custom-fitted rain guards are useful to protect the lens and adjustable, wide leather straps are recommended to relieve neck strain.
19. A lifetime warranty will ensure that your binoculars last you—a lifetime.
20. When shopping for binoculars, insist on taking them outside for a quick try-out.

Optical Terminology

alignment	the precise coordination of mechanical and optical elements with one another
armoured	covered with shock-absorbing rubber or polyurethane to protect internal elements
automatic-focus	having a mechanism that sets the focus on the object in view
brightness	amount of light admitted by the binoculars that is a function of the power and diameter of the objective lens
center-focusing	both barrels of the binocular are adjusted simultaneously by wheel or lever
close-focus	binoculars that allow focusing on objects that appear within 3 meters (10 ft)
coated optics	coating of all optical surfaces with a transparent chemical, e.g. magnesium fluoride), to reduce glare
de-alignment	a shift in the position of the lenses due to blows or jarring
depth of view	span of distance in front of and beyond an object in which the object remains in focus
dioptic correction	the adjustment of the optical instrument to the varying visual acuity of one's eyes
exit pupil	circle of light seen in the eyepiece from a distance of about 25 cm (10 in)
eye relief	distance between the ocular lens and the human eye measured in mm, e.g. important to eyeglass-wearers
eyecups	rubber rings covering each ocular lens which can be rolled down to accommodate eyeglass-wearers
field of view	the breadth of the view at a standard distance, e.g. a breadth of 100 m (328 ft) at a distance of 1000 m (1,000 yd)
focusing wheel	round knob used to adjust the focus on an object
individual ocular adjustment	each eyepiece can be adjusted separately
interior focusing	exterior objective and ocular elements do not move and thus, no air, dust, or moisture is drawn into the system while focusing
objective lens	larger lens (larger end) whose diameter is measured in millimeters by the second part of the numerical formula engraved on the binoculars, e.g. 7 × 35 mm, 8 × 40 mm
ocular lens	smaller lens (smaller end) to which one places one's eyes
optical quality	high quality lenses generally made from barium crown glass and low quality lenses from less expensive boro-silicate glass
permanent-focus	non-focusing binoculars used for spotting objects over 15 m (50 ft) away
porro prism	wide-bodied binoculars where the objective lens and the ocular lens are offset, e.g. not aligned along a vertical axis
power	amount of magnification expressed in first part of the numerical formula engraved on binoculars, e.g. 7 (times) × 35, 8 (times) × 40
quick-focusing	has flat lever operated by a finger on each hand holding the binoculars to fast-focus on an object

Optical Terminology (cont'd)

roof prism	longer, sleeker binoculars in which the objective and ocular lenses are aligned along the same tube
water-resistant binoculars	well-sealed optics that keep out water from splashes or light rainfall, but not immersion, heavy rainfall, or exceptionally high humidity
waterproof binoculars	optics that are able to stay completely dry inside when completely immersed in water
zoom binoculars	optics that offer the capability of quickly increasing the power from one level to a much higher one, e.g. 7 to 15 times

Attracting Birds to the Backyard

Top Ten Most Frequently Reported Species in the 2003 Great Backyard Bird Count in North America

Northern cardinal	American goldfinch	House sparrow
Mourning dove	Downy woodpecker	American crow
Dark-eyed junco	House finch	
Blue jay	Tufted titmouse	

SOURCE: www.birdsource.org/gbhc, Cornell Laboratory of Ornithology and National Audubon Society

Most Common and Most Numerous Bird Species in the 2003 Big Garden Birdwatch in the U.K.

Species	Number of birds recorded	Birds per Gardens (average number)
Starling	744,518	4.9
House sparrow	738,442	4.8
Blue tit	474,303	3.1
Blackbird*	414,957	2.7
Chaffinch	333,419	2.2
Greenfinch	284,938	1.9
Collared dove	257,140	1.7
Great tit	223,303	1.5
Robin	208,035	1.4
Woodpigeon	201,783	1.3
Dunnock	164,636	1.1
Magpie	145,541	1.0
Coal tit	104,627	0.7
Wren	72,515	0.5
Song thrush	72,515	0.4

* found in 93% of all gardens

SOURCE: Royal Society for the Protection of Birds

Six General Tips for Enjoying Backyard Birds

1. How can I attract more birds to my property?

   Offer year-round an array of feeders for several kinds of food, e.g. sunflower seed, peanuts, Nyjer seed, suet; set up a bird bath or build a pond; install nest boxes catering to several species; plant flowers, shrubs, and trees that provide food and shelter at varying times of year.

2. How can I prevent cats from killing my backyard birds?

   Hang feeders out of reach and away from cover where cats can hide; harass offending cats with water spray; ask cat owners to restrain their pets; live-trap repeat offenders and take them to a humane shelter.

3. How can I prevent birds from hitting my windows?

   Break up the reflection from the window by affixing stickers of hawk or falcon silhouettes on the outside, misting with weak detergent solution, covering the window with plastic cling wrap, hanging ornaments such as wind chimes, planters, or wind socks in front of the window; installing awnings, eave extensions, window screens, or tight bird netting; hanging domestic bird feathers on strings also works well.

4. How do I stop woodpeckers from drilling into my wooden house?

   Offer a nestbox as an alternative roosting site; place sheet metal or aluminum foil or a rubber snake over the affected area; hang moving aluminum pie plates; repeatedly harass offending bird; call fish and game officials to remove the bird.

5. What do I do if I find a baby bird, injured bird, or dead bird in my yard?

   Often "baby" birds have just left the nest and are best left alone; prefledged birds should be put back into the nest; hand-feeding baby birds leads to improper imprinting and poor survival; injured birds should be taken to local wildlife rehabilitation organization, humane society, or town animal control officer; dead birds can be left alone for scavengers or placed in the trash (wear gloves); if there is a virus alert in the newspaper, government biologists may be interested in the carcass

6. Why are there no birds at my feeders?

   More often than not, prevailing weather conditions will dictate the numbers and kinds of customers at your feeders. Inclement weather, e.g. extreme cold or rain, drives birds into deeper cover. Certain times of year are better for some species. The sudden presence of a predator like a hawk or cat can drive birds away temporarily. Birds visit feeders in more than one yard and thus competition from a neighbor's feeders with fresher seed, greater variety of offerings, better hygiene, or a safer environment can attract your birds elsewhere.

Housing

Ten Tips for Installing Nest Boxes

1. Do some homework and ensure that the habitat in which you wish to install the nest box is appropriate for the kind of bird you wish to attract.

2. Functional homes will attract birds to use them; cute bird houses will usually not, especially if they are conspicuous to predators.

3. Well-insulated houses are preferred by birds because they keep the cold out and the heat in; walls should be at least 3/4 inch (2 cm) thick.

4. Nest boxes should be made of wood that naturally sheds water, such as cedar; using waterproof stain or paint is okay as long as it is on the outside; earthy colors, e.g. greens, grays, or browns, work best.

5. The bottom of the cavity should be at least 8 inches (20 m) below the entrance hole to prevent predators from reaching in; cutting grooves or providing ladder-like steps will assist the young in leaving the box.

6. Since nest boxes stand out more than natural cavities, it is important to install baffles to thwart predators. By installing the box on a galvanized pole which does not rust, you can employ the same kind of conical or tubular baffles used to keep squirrels and raccoons out of feeders. These will also prevent bull and rat snakes from gaining access. The worst place to install a nest box is on a tree or on a fence post. The ideal height at which to install a typical nest box is 5 feet (1.5 m) or at eye-level.

7. An all-purpose bird house has sides 4 inches (10 m) wide, an interior depth of at least 8 inches (20 m) measured from the bottom of the hole downward, and a hole diameter of 1 1/4 inches (20 m).

8. Nest boxes can be put up at any time of year, so that the local birds get accustomed to it. Some may be used for winter roosting

9. Minimize your visits to examine the nest box; parents will desert their eggs during incubation if bothered frequently, but not their young; young over 10 days, i.e. with well-developed wing feathers, may jump prematurely out of the nest.

10. Whether to clean out the nest box each year is controversial; generally it is safe to remove the old nest if it is exceptionally messy

Specifications for Nest Boxes for North American Cavity-Nesting Birds

Species	Interior Floor Size of Box (in.)	Interior Height of Box (in.)	Entrance Hole Diameter (in.)	Mount Box this High (ft.)
American kestrel	9×9	16–18	3	12–30
Ash-throated flycatcher	6×6	12	$1 \, ^3/_4$–2	6–20
Barn owl	12×36	16	6×7	15–30
Barred owl	14×14	28	8	15–30
Boreal owl	8×8	18	3	8–30
Bufflehead	7×7	17	3	5–15
Carolina wren	4×4	9–12	1–$1 \, ^1/_2$	5–10
Chickadees	4×4	9–12	$1 \, ^1/_8 \times 1 \, ^1/_2$	5–15
Common merganser	12×12	24	5×6	8–20
Downy woodpecker	4×4	12	$1 \, ^1/_2$	5–20
Eastern bluebird	4×4	12	$1 \, ^1/_2$	5–6
Goldeneye	12×12	24	$3 \, ^1/_4 \times 4 \, ^1/_4$	15–20
Golden-fronted woodpecker	6×6	14	2	8–20
Great crested flycatcher	6×6	12	$1 \, ^3/_4$–2	6–20
Hairy woodpecker	6×6	14	$1 \, ^1/_2$	8–20
Hooded merganser	12×12	24	3×4	5–30
House finch	5×5	10	$1 \, ^1/_2$	5–10
House wren	4×4	6–8	1–$1 \, ^1/_4$	6–10
Mountain bluebird	5×5	12	$1 \, ^9/_{16}$	5–6
Northern flicker	7×7	16–24	$2 \, ^1/_2$	10–20
Pileated woodpecker	12×12	24	4	15–25
Prothonotary & Lucy's warbler	4×4	12	$1 \, ^1/_4$	5–12
Purple martin	6×6	6	$2 \, ^1/_8$	15–25
Red-bellied woodpecker	6×6	14	2	8–20
Red-headed woodpecker	6×6	14	2	8–20
Saw-whet owl	7×7	12	$2 \, ^1/_2$	8–20
Screech-owl	8×8	18	3	8–30
Titmice	4×4	12	$1 \, ^1/_2$	5–12
Tree swallow	5×5	10–12	$1 \, ^1/_2$	5–10
Violet-green swallow	5×5	10–12	$1 \, ^1/_2$	5–10
Western bluebird	5×5	12	$1 \, ^1/_2$–$1 \, ^9/_{16}$	5–6
White-breasted nuthatch	4×4	12	$1 \, ^1/_2$	5–12
Winter wren	4×4	6–8	1–$1 \, ^1/_4$	6–10
Wood duck	12×12	24	3×4	5–20

SOURCE: Adapted from S. Shalaway, *A Guide to Bird Homes*. (Marietta, OH: Bird Watcher's Digest, 1995)

Dimensions of Nesting Shelves

	Floor of Shelf (in.)	Depth of Shelf (in.)	Height Above Ground (ft.)
Eastern phoebe	6 × 6	6	8–12
American robin	6 × 8	8	6–15
Song sparrow	6 × 6	6	1–3
Barn swallow	6 × 6	6	8–12

Ten Tips for Installing a Purple Martin House

1. Select the right location, i.e. 30 feet (10 m) away from obstructions, but near your house; a water body within a mile or two (1.5 to 3 km) and the presence of wires for perching may be helpful.

2. Height above ground should be 12 to 20 feet (3 to 6 m); hole diameters 2 ¼ to 2 ½ inches (5 to 6 cm); cavity space 6 by 6 by 6 inches (15 by 15 by 15 cm) ; hole 1 inch (2.5 cm) above floor of cavity.

3. Choose light colors, preferably white, to reflect rays of hot sun.

4. Ensure plenty of ventilation with no chemical treatment on the inside.

5. The house should be rainproof and drain well.

6. Railings on ledges will prevent falling youngsters at fledging time.

7. Light interiors in compartments will discourage starlings.

8. Easy access (easy to raise and lower on a pole is best) should facilitate annual cleaning and removal of sparrow nests.

9. Both metal and wooden houses are suitable if they are durable; avoid sharp edges and splinters.

10. Predator guards should be installed to keep out snakes, raccoons, hawks, and owls.

Garden Flowers for North American Birds

Aster	Cornflower	Prince's plumes
Bachelor's button	Cosmos	Rock purslane
Basket flower	Dandelion	Royal sweet sultan
Bluebell	Dayflower	Silene
Calendula	Dusty miller	Sunflower
California poppy	Love-lies-bleeding	Sweet scabious
China aster	Marigold	Tarweed
Chrysanthemum	Phlox	Thistle
Coneflower	Portulaca	Verbena
Coreopsis	Prince's feather	Zinnia

Typical Characteristics of Flowers Pollinated by Hummingbirds

Flowering time:	diurnal
Flower shape:	weakly zygomorphic or radial
Blossom color:	vivid, often red
Odor:	none
Nectar:	very abundant in broad tubes
Flower position:	horizontal or hanging
Petal position:	often recurved

SOURCE: Adapted from P.A. Johnsgard, *The Hummingbirds of North America* (Washington, DC: Smithsonian Institution Press, 1983)

Flowering Plants for Hummingbirds*

Azalea	Dahlia	Indian paintbrush
Amaryllis	Daylily	Jacobiana
Bee balm	Delphinium	Japanese honeysuckle
Bergamot (wild, scarlet)	Evening primrose	Jewelweed
Blazing star	Firecracker vine	Lantana
Bleeding heart	Fire pink	Larkspur
Bugleweed	Fireweed	Limber honeysuckle
Butterfly bush	Flowering quince	Little cigar
Butterfly milkweed	Flowering tobacco	Lupine
Cannas	Four o'clocks	Madrone
Cardinal climber	Foxglove	Manzanitas
Cardinal flower	Fuschia	Mimosa tree
Citrus tree	Gayfeather	Morning glory
Clematis	Gladiolus	Nasturtium
Columbine	Hibiscus	Northern catalpa
Coral bells	Hollyhock	Red buckeye
Coralberry	Horse chestnut	Orange honeysuckle
Coral honeysuckle	Hosta	Paintbrush
Cypress vine	Impatiens	Penstemon

Petunia

Phlox

Red-hot poker

Salvia species

Scarlet gila

Scarlet runner bean

Scarlet sage

Shrimp plant

Siberian pea tree

Snapdragon

Spider flower

Sweet William

Tartarian honeysuckle

Tiger lily

Trumpet honeysuckle

Trumpet vine

Turk's cap

Weigela

Yucca

Zinnia

* Check local nursery for proper growing conditions

Shrubs and Trees for North American Birds

Northeast:

Highbush cranberry

Brambles

Eastern red cedar

Black cherry

Flowering crabapple

Virginia creeper

Flowering dogwood

Red-osier dogwood

American elder

Wild grape

Hawthorns

American holly

Amur honeysuckle

Tatarian honeysuckle

American mountain ash

Red mulberry

White oak

Cardinal autumn olive

Russian olive

Eastern white pine

Downy serviceberry

Staghorn sumac

Black tupelo

Southeast:

American beautyberry

Scarlet firethorn

Common greenbrier

Sugar hackberry

Shagbark hickory

Live oak

Cabbage palmetto

Common persimmon

Loblolly pine

Yaupon holly

Prairies and Plains:

Common chokecherry

Buffalo currant

Common hackberry

Amur maple

White mulberry

Burr oak

Ponderosa pine

Saskatoon serviceberry

Snowberry

Skunkbush

Mountains and Deserts:

Quaking aspen

Cascara buckthorn

Golden currant

Blueberry elder

Canyon grape

Grouseberry

Douglas hawthorn

Mesquite

Green mountain ash

Prickly pear cactus

Colorado blue spruce

Western thimbleberry

Pacific coast:

Holly-leaved buckthorn

Holly-leaved cherry

Pacific dogwood

Common fig

Tall red huckleberry

California live oak

California pepper tree

Shore pine

Four-wing saltbush

Pacific wax myrtle

Characteristics of Preferred Nesting Trees of Some North American Woodpeckers

Species	When Using Territory	Territory Size (hectares)	Minimum No. of Snags Used/Pair	Average DBH of Nest Trees (cm)	Average Height of Nest Trees (m)	Maximum Pairs Per 40 Hectares	Snags Needed per 40 Hectares to Maintain 100% of Cavity Nesters
Downy woodpecker	All year	4	4	20	6	10	400
Hairy woodpecker	All year	8	4	30	9	5	200
Pileated woodpecker	All year	70	4	56	18	0.6	24
Common flicker	Breeding	16	2	38	9	2.5	150
Red-bellied woodpecker	All year	6	4	46	12	6.7	270
Red-headed woodpecker	Breeding	4	2	50	12	10	200
Black-backed three-toed woodpecker	All year	30	4	38	9	1.3	52
Northern three-toed woodpecker	All year	30	4	35	9	1.3	52
Yellow-bellied sapsucker	Breeding	4	1	30	9	10	100

SOURCE: Adapted from K.E. Evans and R.N. Connor, U.S. Dept. Agriculture Forest Service publication GTR NC-51 (Washington, DC, 1979)

Feeding

Twenty Tips for Setting Up a Backyard Program

1. The bird table or platform feeder should have raised borders to prevent seed from blowing off, kept free of built-up droppings, and be well-drained.

2. Hanging feeders best keep seed clean, dry, and available in heavy snowfall.

3. Box-shaped hopper feeders set on a post and equipped with a seed catch tray or shelf perches are most attractive to ground-feeding birds.

4. Long, cylindrical tube feeders which are hung or placed on a pole and have multiple feeding ports each with a stick perch are preferred by finches, chickadees, and titmice; shelled peanuts in a porous metal tube feeder attract a wide variety of birds.

5. All feeders should be easily filled and cleaned and made of durable plastic or wood (weather-resistant cedar is best).

6. Birds will not freeze to the metal parts of feeders.

7. Feed year-round to enjoy the different varieties frequenting the neighborhood and watch parents bring their young to the feeder.

8. Locate your feeder near enough cover to provide shelter from weather, but not close enough to hide lurking predators like cats and hawks; feeders near windows should be installed close enough to prevent startled birds from striking the glass with serious impact.

9. While some consistency in feeding is recommended, birds do not become totally dependent on feeders, especially if there are others in the neighborhood.

10. The best ways to keep squirrels out of feeders include installing suitably sized conical or tubular baffles above or below, covering feeders in coated metal mesh, using a squirrel-proof hopper feeder with a weight-sensitive perch; using a durable metal tube feeder for peanuts as described in 4); offering the squirrels alternative food sources, or substituting safflower seed for sunflower seed; or only offering Nyjer (Niger) seed or plain suet. Applying hot pepper or capsaicin to bird foods is not recommended because it can be inhumane to squirrels and the impact on birds is not yet fully understood.

11. Buy fresh seeds that are well-filled and free of insects.

12. The best all-round seed accepted by the greatest variety of birds is black-oil sunflower with its thinner shell for easier access and more meat; the best all-round seed for small finches, siskins, and redpolls is Nyjer (Niger); shelled peanuts in a metal tube feeder is best for woodpeckers, nuthatches, and tits; the best all-round mix is black-oil sunflower seed, white millet and cracked corn.

13. To minimize feeding by pigeons, doves, and house sparrows, do not offer cracked corn or white millet; to dissuade grackles, use safflower instead of sunflower seed. Small tube feeders equipped with seed catchers or enclosing feeders in a cage made of large mesh will also dissuade pigeons.

14. Clean feeders regularly by removing old, moldy seed and by soaking in a light bleach solution (9 parts water to 1 part bleach).

15. Rendered beef or mutton suet or commercially available suet mixes offered year-round in a log drilled with wide holes, an onionskin bag, or wire cage will attract woodpeckers, nuthatches, and dozens of other backyard species.

16. Whether peanut butter offered in its pure form causes small birds to choke to death or leads to excessive salt intake is controversial.

17. Offering grit in the form of coarse builder's sand or chicken grit will help seed-eaters grind their digested seeds.

Feeding (Cont'd)

18. Crushed oyster shells or oven-baked, broken eggshells serve as calcium and mineral supplements for birds, especially laying females.

19. Halved oranges impaled on large spikes and sugar solutions are attractive to orioles and other nectar feeders.

20. Birds of prey that sometimes hunt feeder birds are protected by law and are a part of nature, generally capturing unfit individuals.

Feeder Preferences for North American Backyard Birds

	Ground Feeders	Raised Feeders (Low)	Raised Feeders (High)	Hanging Feeders	Suet Feeders
American goldfinch		X	X	X	
American tree sparrow	X	X			
Black-capped chickadee	X	X	X	X	X
Blue jay		X	X		
Common grackle	X	X			
Dark-eyed junco	X	X			
Evening grosbeak			X		
House finch		X	X	X	
House sparrow	X	X	X		
Mourning dove	X	X			
Northern cardinal		X	X		
Northern flicker	X	X			X
Northern mockingbird		X			
Pine siskin		X	X	X	
Purple finch		X	X		
Downy woodpecker		X	X		X
Red-bellied woodpecker	X	X			X
Red-breasted nuthatch	X	X			X
Red-headed woodpecker	X	X			X
Yellow-bellied sapsucker		X			X
Red-winged blackbird	X	X	X	X	
Song sparrow	X	X			
Starling	X	X		X	X
Tufted titmouse		X	X		
White-breasted nuthatch		X			X
White-crowned sparrow	X	X			
White-throated sparrow	X	X			

SOURCE: Adapted from K. Burke, *How to Attract Birds* (San Francisco: Ortho Books, 1983)

Most Widely Recommended Seed Types

(in rough order of popularity)

Black sunflower	Peanut hearts	Golden millet
Black striped sunflower	White millet	Canary seed
Gray striped sunflower	Cracked corn	Safflower
Hulled sunflower	Nyjer (Niger)	Rapeseed
Peanut kernels	Red millet	

Alternative Seed-Nut Offerings

Apple seeds	Alfalfa meal	Hulled oats
Pecan meats	Barley	Butternut
Cooked rice	Black walnut	Whole kernel corn
Melon seeds (ground)	Wheat	English walnut
Pumpkin seeds (ground)	Whole oats	Hickory nut
Squash seeds (broken)	Sorghum	Hempseed
Almonds (chopped)	Flaxseed	Rye

Most Widely Recommended Non-Seed Foods

American cheese	Cracker crumbs	Raisins
Baked apple	Cranberries	Strawberries
Raw apple	Cooked currants	Watermelon
Bananas	Cooked eggs	Cooked sweet potatoes
Bayberries	Crushed eggshells	Tomatoes
Blueberry	Grape jelly	Cooked potatoes
Biscuits	Grapes	Figs
Dog biscuits	Rolled oats	Salt
Baked goods	Mealworms	Beef suet
Cottage cheese	Meat scraps	Mutton suet
Cream cheese	Orange halves	Pokeberries
Cherries	Oyster shell	Peaches
Coconut	Pear halves	
Corn bread	Pie crust	

Food Preferences for Common Feeder Birds of North America

Species	Preferred Foods
Quail, pheasants	Cracked corn, millet, wheat milo
Pigeons, doves	Millet, cracked corn, wheat, milo, Nyjer, buckwheat, sunflower hearts and seed, baked goods
Roadrunner	Meat scraps, hamburger, suet
Hummingbirds	Plant nectar, small insects, sugar solution
Woodpeckers	Suet, meat scraps, sunflower hearts and seed, cracked corn, peanuts, fruits, sugar solution
Jays	Peanuts, sunflower, suet, meat scraps, cracked corn, baked goods
Crows, magpies, and nutcracker	Meat scraps, suet, cracked corn, peanuts, baked goods, leftovers, dog food
Titmice, chickadees	Peanut kernels, sunflower, suet, peanut butter
Nuthatches	Suet, suet mixes, sunflower hearts and seed, peanut kernels, peanut butter
Wrens, creepers	Suet, suet mixes, peanut butter, peanut kernels, bread, fruit, millet (wrens)
Mockingbirds, thrashers, catbirds	Halved apple, chopped fruits, baked goods, suet, nutmeats, millet (thrashers), soaked raisins, currants, sunflower hearts
Robins, bluebirds, other thrushes	Suet, suet mixes, mealworms, berries, baked goods, chopped fruits, soaked raisins, currants, nutmeats, sunflower hearts
Kinglets	Suet, suet mixes, baked goods
Waxwings	Berries, chopped fruits, canned peas, currants, raisins
Warblers	Suet, suet mixes, fruit, baked goods, sugar solution, chopped nutmeats
Tanagers	Suet, fruits, sugar solution, mealworms, baked goods
Cardinals, grosbeaks, pyrrhuloxias	Sunflower hearts, safflower, cracked corn, millet, fruit
Towhees, juncos	Millet, sunflower hearts, cracked corn, peanuts, baked goods, nutmeats
Sparrows, buntings	Millet, sunflower hearts, black-oil sunflower seeds, cracked corn, baked goods
Blackbirds, starlings	Cracked corn, milo, wheat, table scraps, baked goods, suet
Orioles	Halved oranges, apples, berries, sugar solution, grape jelly, suet, suet mixes, soaked raisins, and currants
Finches, siskins	Thistle (Nyjer), sunflower hearts, black-oil sunflower seed, millet, canary seed, fruits, peanut kernels, suet mixes

SOURCE: J. Zickefoose, *Enjoying Bird Feeding More* (Marietta, OH: Bird Watcher's Digest, 1994)

Feeding Tips for Common Feeder Birds in the U.K.

1. Tubular feeders are best for tits, chaffinches, greenfinches, siskins, robins, and blackbirds; bird tables are popular for starlings, blackbirds, robins, dunnocks, house sparrows, various finches woodpigeons, collared doves; and mesh feeders will attract tits, greenfinches, siskins, sparrows, nuthatches, woodpeckers. Filling the holes and cracks of an old log with fatty food, such as suet will bring in woodpeckers, tits, nuthatches, and starlings. For those without gardens, commercial feeders can be attached to windows by suction cups. Milk cartons and plastic bottles can be used as bird feeders.

2. The better mixtures of seeds to buy contain plenty of flaked maize, sunflower seeds, and broken peanuts. Only offer mixes with peanuts in the winter so as to avoid nestlings choking on them. Avoid seed mixtures that contain split peas, dried rice, lentils, or dog food because they can only be eaten in their dry form by large bird species. Wheat and barley grains are often included in seed mixtures, but they are really only suitable for pigeons, doves, and pheasants, which feed on the ground and rapidly increase their numbers, deter the smaller species, and upset neighbors.

3. Small seeds like millet are especially liked by house sparrows, dunnocks, finches, reed buntings and collared doves; flaked maize is readily eaten by blackbirds and dunnocks; tits and green finches favor peanuts and sunflower seeds. Pinhead oatmeal is excellent for many birds.

4. Peanuts are rich in fat and are popular with tits, greenfinches, house sparrows, nuthatches, great spotted woodpeckers, and siskins, although black sunflower seeds are now a preferred food in many gardens. You can buy peanut kernels (whole, broken, or sliced) for wild birds in bulk from dealers advertising in *Birds*. Peanut granules are also popular. Crushed or grated nuts attract robins, dunnocks, and even wrens. Nuthatches and coal tits may hoard peanuts and black sunflower seeds. Salted peanuts should not be used. Peanuts can be high in a natural toxin that can kill birds, so buy from a reputable dealer who will guarantee freedom from aflatoxin.

5. Fresh coconut in the shell is very popular with tits. Rinse out any residues of the sweet coconut water from the middle of the coconut before hanging it out to prevent the buildup of mildew. Desiccated coconut is unsuitable as bird food.

6. For insect-eating birds, mealworms are relished by robins and may attract pied wagtails. They can be obtained from advertised dealers in pet and wild bird food or raised easily at home. Waxworms are excellent but expensive. Ant pupae, insectivorous and softbill food available from bird food suppliers and pet shops can attract treecreepers and wrens.

7. Household foods suitable for garden birds include crumbled brown and white bread (moisten if very dry), cooked or uncooked pastry (especially made with real fats), cooked brown or white rice without added salt, and dry porridge oats and coarse oatmeal. Fat, including suet, is particularly welcomed by tits, great spotted woodpeckers, thrushes and wrens. Polyunsaturated fats are less desirable because they do not provide high levels of energy birds require in winter. Bacon rind (not too salty) can be chopped up finely for robins or suspended on strings for tits. Mild grated cheese is a favorite with robins, dunnocks, blackbirds, and song thrushes and will attract wrens if placed under hedgerows. Large bones with some fat or meat attached are good. Roast, baked (cold or opened up) or mashed potatoes with added real fats (not chips!) are all suitable, especially for wildfowl.

8. For fruit-eaters, dried fruits such as raisins, sultanas, and currents are particularly enjoyed by blackbirds, song thrushes, and robins. Apples, pears, and other fruit, including bruised and part-rotten ones, cut up, are very popular with all thrushes, tits, and starlings.

9. Whole hazelnuts (with the shell on) pushed into cracks in tree bark will please nuthatches and woodpeckers.

SOURCE: Royal Society for the Protection of Birds and the *Encyclopedia of Bird*care produced by Jacobi, Jayne & Company, U.K.

Ten Tips for Setting Up a Hummingbird Feeder

1. Choose a feeder that is attractive to hummingbirds (with some red parts), easy to clean (dishwasher-safe), functional on windy days, and equipped with insect guards.

2. Choose a feeder size that is large enough to prevent constant refilling but small enough to keep the solution from fermenting or going sour.

3. Hang your feeder near blossoming, bright flowers, especially red ones, out of direct sunlight and heavy wind, and close enough to enjoy the birds.

4. Feeders near windows should be hung close to the glass to prevent spooked hummingbirds from colliding at high speed.

5. To make a sugar solution, bring to a boil one part white sugar (do not use honey) and four parts water (perhaps three at first), let sit, and store in fridge.

6. Adding red food coloring is not necessary to attract the birds and may be harmful; tying a red ribbon or painting with red nail polish works just as well.

7. Hang the feeder with an easily visible (red is best) string or wire to prevent collisions.

8. Keep your feeder up as long as possible in the fall, as it will not keep hummingbirds from migrating and may provide food for stray migrants.

9. If there are several hummingbirds frequenting the yard, put up several feeders to minimize fighting.

10. Most important, wash the feeder with a warm, soapy solution every time it is filled.

Favorite Recipes for the Birds

1. Marvel Meal

1 cup	peanut butter
1 cup	vegetable shortening, melted beef suet, or bacon drippings
4 cups	cornmeal (yellow is higher in Vitamin A)
1 cup	white flour

This makes a soft, doughy food that can be offered in hardware cloth cages, smeared on the bark of trees, or pressed into holes in a suet log.

2. Miracle Meal

4 cups	yellow corn meal
1 cup	all-purpose flour
1 cup	lard or melted suet
1 teaspoon	corn oil

Plus sunflower hearts, peanut hearts, chopped soaked raisins

Melt lard and stir in other ingredients. Spike with sunflower hearts, peanut hearts, or chopped soaked raisins, as desired. Let set, cut into chunks, feed as suet. Mainly for bluebirds, but other birds like it too.

3. Bluebird Food

5 parts	oatmeal
1 part	corn syrup
1 part	peanut butter
1 part	bacon grease or lard

Mix well and push into holes in a feeder log. Other birds like it too.

4. Bird cake

Pour melted fat (suet or lard) onto a mixture of ingredients such as seeds, nuts, dried fruit, oatmeal, cheese, and cake. Use about one-third fat to two-thirds mixture. Stir well in a bowl and turn out onto the bird table or into an empty coconut shell when solid.

SOURCES:

Recipe 1: J.K. Terres in J. Zickefoose, *Enjoying Bird Feeding More* (Marietta, OH: Bird Watcher's Digest, 1986)

Recipe 2: J. Zickefoose, *Enjoying Bluebirds More* (Marietta, OH: Bird Watcher's Digest, 1993)

Recipe 3: O.W. Watkins in *Bird Watcher's Digest*, Jan./Feb. Issue (Marietta, OH: Bird Watcher's Digest, 1998)

Recipe 4: Royal Society for the Protection of Birds

Ten Tips for Installing a Bird Bath

1. Most commercially available, household, and natural receptacles will work as long as they are shallow, i.e. 1 to 2 inches (2.5 to 5 cm), and with a slight slope.

2. It should be placed reasonably close to perches for both drying off and for cover against sudden attack by cats, hawks, etc., but not so close as to facilitate ambush by them.

3. It should be within easy reach of a garden hose.

4. Clean it once a week for hygiene and prevention of mosquito breeding; a plastic scrub brush with a weak bleach solution (9 parts water and 1 part bleach) is best for cleaning.

5. Place the bath in the shade to help deter algae, but somewhere highly visible for your enjoyment

6. A rough bottom should facilitate birds' proper footing.

7. Overhanging branches should be trimmed to avoid contamination from birds perching above, as well as falling litter.

8. Addition of moving water like a drip or a spray to make noise will be more attractive.

9. Addition of hot water or use of submersible heaters to keep the bath open year-round should be used with caution in exceptionally cold weather; adding anti-freeze or glycerine is not recommended.

10. Hummingbirds and swallows like to fly through a fine mist.

Resources for Bird-Lovers

Ornithological and Bird-Watching Organizations

World

African Bird Club
c/o BirdLife International
Wellbrook Court, Girton Road
Cambridge UK CB3 0NA
E-mail: info@africanbirdclub.org
http://www.africanbirdclub.org/

BirdLife Americas Regional Office
BirdLife International
Vicente Cárdenas 120 y Japon, 3rd Floor
Quito
Ecuador
Postal address:
BirdLife International
Casilla 17-17-717
Quito
Ecuador
Tel. +593 2 453 645
E-mail: birdlife@birdlife.org.ec
http://www.geocities.com/RainForest/
Wetlands/6203

BirdLife Asia Regional Office
Jl. Jend. Ahmad Yani No. 11
Bogor 16161
Indonesia
Postal address:
PO Box 310/Boo
Bogor 16003
Indonesia
Tel. +62 251 333 234/+62 251 371 394
E-mail: birdlife@indo.net.id
http://www.kt.rim.or.jp/~birdinfo/indonesia

BirdLife Cambridge office
BirdLife International
Wellbrook Court
Girton Road
Cambridge, UK CB3 0NA
Tel. +44 1 223 277 318
E-mail: birdlife@birdlife.org.uk
http://www.birdlife.net

BirdLife European Regional Office
Droevendaalsesteeg 3a P.O. Box 127
NL-6700 AC
Wageningen
The Netherlands
Tel. +31 317 478831
E-mail: birdlife@birdlife.agro.nl

BirdLife Middle East Regional Office
BirdLife International
c/o Royal Society for the Conservation of Nature
(RSCN)
P.O. Box 6354
Amman 11183
Jordan
Tel: +962 6 535-5446
E-mail birdlife@nol.com.jo

European Community Office ECO
BirdLife International
Rue de la Loi 81A
B-1040 Brussels
Belgium
Tel. +32 2280 08 30
E-mail: bleco@birdlifeeco.net

The European Ornithologists' Union
c/o Elisabeth Wiprächtiger, Swiss Ornithological
Institute
CH-6204 Sempach, Switzerland
http://www.eou.at/

International Crane Foundation
E-11376 Shady Lane Rd. P.O. Box 447
Baraboo, WI 53913 USA
Tel: 608 356 9462
http://www.savingcranes.org/

The International Osprey Foundation
P.O. Box 250
Sanibel Island, FL 33957-0250 USA
http://www.ospreys.com/index.html

Neotropical Bird Club
C/o The Lodge, Sandy
Bedfordshire, UK SG19 2DL
http://www.neotropicalbirdclub.org/

World (Cont'd)

Oriental Bird Club
P.O.Box 324, Bedford
MK42 0WG
UK
mail@orientalbirdclub.org
http://www.orientalbirdclub.org/index.html

Ornithological Society of the Middle East
OSME, c/o 6 Mansion Drive, Tring
Hertfordshire, UK HP23 5BD
E-mail: secretary@osme.org
http://www.osme.org/index.html

Ornithological Society of the Middle East, the Caucasus, and Central Asia
c/o The Lodge
Sandy, Bedfordshire UK SG19 2DL
http://www.osme.org/

The Peregrine Fund
5668 West Flying Hawk Lane
Boise, ID 83709 USA
Tel: 208 362 3716
E-mail: tpf@peregrinefund.org
http://www.peregrinefund.org/

Raptor Research Foundation
http://biology.boisestate.edu/raptor/

The Waterbird Society
Upper Midwest Environmental Sciences Center
2630 Fanta Reed Rd., La Crosse
WI 54603 USA
Tel: 01 608 781 6247
E-mail: christine_custer@usgs.gov

World Owl Trust
The Owl Centre
Muncaster Castle, Ravenglass
Cumbria UK CA18 1RQ
Tel: +44 0 1229 717393
E-mail: admin@owls.org
http://www.owls.org/

World Pheasant Association
7-9 Shaftesbury Street, Fordingbridge, Hants, UK
SP6 1JF,
Tel. 01425 657129
E-mail: office@pheasant.org.uk
http://www.pheasant.org.uk/

World Working Group on Birds of Prey and Owls
P.O. Box 52, Towcester UK NN12 7ZW
Tel/Fax: +44 1604 86 23 31
E-mail: robin.chancellor@virgin.net
http://www.raptors-international.de/

Africa

MALAWI
Malawi Ornithologial Society
Department of Ornithology
Museum of Malawi
P.O. Box 30360
Chichiri, Blantyre 3
Malawi
E-mail: malawibirds@yahoo.com

NAMIBIA
Namibia Bird Club
P.O. Box 67
Windhoek, Namibia

GAMBIA
West Afrian Bird Study Association
Palm Grove Hol Banjul
The Gambia
E-mail: laminjobarteh2002@yahoo.com

ZIMBABWE
Ornithologial Association of Zimbabwe
P.O. Box CY 161
Causeway, Harare, Zimbabwe
E-mail: birds@harare.iafrica.com

BirdLife Zimbabwe
P.O. Box CY 161
Causeway, Harare, Zimbabwe
E-mail: birds@zol.co.zw

BOTSWANA
BirdLife Botswana
Private Bag 00300, Gaborone, Botswana
E-mail: blb@birdlifebotswana.org.bw
http://www.birdlifebotswana.org.bw

Africa (Cont'd)

BURUNDI
Association Burundaise Pour la Protection des Oiseaux
P.O. Box 7069, Bujumbura, Burundi
E-mail: aboburundi@yahoo.fr

TUNISIA
Association "les Amis des Oieaux
Avenue 18 Janvier 1952, Ariana Centre
App. C209, 2080 Ariana
Tunis, Tunisia
E-mail: aao.bird@planet.tn

SOUTH AFRICA
BirdLife South Africa
P.O. Box 515
Randburg 2125
Johannesburg, South Africa
Tel: +27 11 789 1122
E-mail: info@birdlife.org.za
http://www.birdlife.org.za/

Cape Bird Club (South Africa)
Tel: 021 439 3225
E-mail: info@capebirdclub.org
http://www.capebirdclub.org/

Wesvaal Bird Club
P. O. Box 2413
Potchefstroom 2520,
South Africa
http://www.geocities.com/RainForest/Vines/2022/

Vulture Study Group
Endangered Wildlife Trust
P.O. Box 72334
Parkview 2122
South Africa
Tel: 27 11 646 8617
E-mail: vsg@ewt.org.za

ZAMBIA
Zambian Ornithological Society
Box 33944
Lusaka 10101
Zambia
E-mail: zos@zamnet.zm
http://www.fisheagle.org/

Asia and the Middle East

BELARUS
APB-BirdLife Belarus
P.O.Box 306, Minsk, 220050 Belarus
E-mail: apb@tut.by
http://apb.iatp.by

CEYLON
Ceylon Bird Club
No. 39 Chatham Street
Colombo 1, Sri Lanka
E-mail: birdclub@usa.net

CYPRUS
BirdLife Cyprus
P.O. Box 28076, 2090 Lefkosia, Cyprus
E-mail: cos@cytanet.com.cy
http://www.birdlifecyprus.org

Cyprus Ornithological Society
4 Kanaris St.
Strovolos 154
Cyprus
Tel: +357 4 651002

HONG KONG
Hong Kong Bird Watching Society
G.P.O. Box 12460, Hong Kong
E-mail: hkbws@hkbws.org.hk
http://www.hkbws.org.hk/

INDIA
Bombay Natural History Society
Hornbill House
Shaheed Bhagat Singh Road
Mumbai 400 023
India
E-mail: bnhs@bom4.vsnl.net.in
http://www.bnhs.org
http://www.bnhs.org/

INDONESIA
BirdLife International-Indonesia Programme
P.O. Box 310/Boo, Bogor 16003 Indonesia
Tel: +62 251 357222
E-mail: prue@burug.org
http://www.english.birdlife.or.id/

Asia and the Middle East (Cont'd)

ISRAEL
Society for the Protection of Nature in Israel
Hashsela 4, Tel-Aviv 66103, Israel
E-mail: ioc@netvision.net.il
http://www.birds.org.il

Internation Birdwatching Centre
P.O. Box 774
Eilat 88106
Israel
http://www.arava.org/birds-eilat/about.html

Israel Ornithological centre
155 Herzl Street
Tel Aviv 68101
Israel
Tel: +972 3 6826802

JAPAN
Japan Alcid Society
E-mail: kojiono@gol.com
http://www2.gol.com/users/kojiono/

Japanese Society for the Preservation of Birds
3F, 54-5
Wada 3 chome
Suginame-ku
Tokyo 166-0012
Tel: +81 3 53785691
http://www.ask.ne.jp/~jspb

Ornithological Society of Japan
Laboratory of Biodiversity Science
School of Agriculture and Life Sciences
The University of Tokyo
Yayoi 1-1-1, Bunkyo-ku
Tokyo 113-8657, JAPAN
Tel: +81 3 5841 7541
E-mail: osj@lagopus.com
http://wwwsoc.nii.ac.jp/osj/

Wild Bird Society of Japan
2F Woody Nanpeidai
15-8 Nanpeidai-machi
Shibuya-ku

JORDAN
Royal Society for the Conservation of Nature
P.O. Box 6354, Jubeiha-Abu-Nusseir Circle
Amman 11183, Jordan
E-mail: adminrscn@rscn.org.jo
http://www.rscn.org.jo

LEBANON
Society for the Protection of Nature in
Lebanon
P.O. Box 11-5665, Riad-El-Solh
Beirut, Lebanon

MACEDONIA
Bird Study and Protection Society of
Macedonia
Institute of Biology
Faculty of Sciences
MAC-91000
Skopje, Macedonia
Tel: +389 91 117055
E-mail: brankom@iunona.pmf.ukim.edu.mk

MALTA
BirdLife Malta
57 Marina Court, Flat 28, Triq Abate Rigord
MT-Ta' Xbiex, MSD 12, Malta
Tel: 356 21347646
E-mail: info@birdlifemalta.org
http://www.birdlifemalta.org

NEPAL
Bird Conservation Nepal
P.O.Box 12465
Kathmandu,Nepal
Tel: +977 1 417805
http://www.birdlifenepal.org/index.asp

OMAN
Oman Bird Group
Oman Natural History Museum
P.O. Box 668
Muscat 113
Sultanate of Oman
Tel: +968 605400

PAKISTAN
Ornithologial Society of Pakistan
P.O. Box 73, 109/D, Dera Ghazi Khan, 32200
Pakistan
E-mail; osp@mul.paknet.com.pk

PALESTINIAN TERRITORY AUTHORITIES
Palestine Wildlife Society
Beit Sahour, P.O. Box 89
Palestine
E-mail: wildlife@palnet.com
http://www.wildlife-pal.org

Asia and the Middle East (Cont'd)

PHILLIPINES
Society for the Research of Golden Eagle (SRGE)
E-mail: srge@mbd.nifty.com
http://homepage1.nifty.com/srge/

The Philippine Eagle Foundation
E-mail: phileagl@info.com.ph
http://www.philippineagle.org/

RUSSIA
Russian Bird Conservation Union
Shosse Entuziastov 60, Building 1, Moscow
111123, Russia
E-mail: rbcu@online.ru
http://www.rbcu.ru/en_index.htm

SRI LANKA
Field Ornithology Group of Sri Lanka
Department of Zoology, University of Colombo
Colombo 03
Sri lanka
Tel: 075 342609
E-mail: fogsl@slt.lk

TAIWAN
Wild Bird Federation Taiwan
1F, No. 3, Lane 36 Chinglung Street
116 Taipei, Taiwan
E-mail: wbft@bird,org,tw

Wild Bird Society of Taipei
http://taipei.org.tw/English/redirect.asp

THAILAND
Bird Conservation Society of Thailand
69/12 Ramindra 24, Jarakhebua, Lardproa
Bangkok 10230, Thailand

Tel: 662 943 5965
http://www.bcst.org/ehome.asp

UNITED ARAB EMIRATES
Emirates Bird Group
P.O. Box 50394
Dubai, United Arab Emirates
Tel: +971 4 31378

The National Avian Research Center (NARC)
(Environmental Research & Wildlife
Development Agency)
P.O. Box 45553, Abu Dhabi
United Arab Emirates
Tel: 971 2 6817171
E-mail: ocombreau@erwda.gov.ae
http://www.erwda.com/../narc.asp

VIETNAM
BirdLife International in IndoChina
#4, Lane 209, Doi Can
Ba Dinh, Hanoi, Vietnam
Tel: 844 722 3864/20
E-mail: birdlife@birdlife,netnam.vn
http://www.wing-bsj.or.jp/~vietnam/index.htm

Bird Life International-Vietnam Programme
No. 11, Lane 167, Tay Son Street, Dong Da
Hanoi, Vietnam
E-mail: birdlife@birdlife.netnam.vn
http://www.birdlifevietnam.com

YEMAN
Yeman Ornithological Society
P.O. Box 2002, Sana'a
Republic of Yemen

Europe

ALBANIA
Albanian Society for the Protection of Birds
Museum of Natural Science
Rr. E. Kavajes 132, Tirana, Albania
E-mail: mns@albmail.com

AUSTRIA
BirdLife Österreich-Gesellschaft für
Vogelkunde
Museumsplatz 1/10/8, A-1070
Wien, Austria
E-mail: office@birdlife.at
http://www.birdlife.at

BELGIUM
Aves Société Ornithologique
Secrétariat AVES
Maison liégeoise de l'environnement
Rue Fusch, 3
4000 Liège
Tél: 04 250 95 90
http://www.aves.be/

BirdLife Belgium
Kardinaal Mercierplein 1, BE-2800
Mechelen, Belgium
E-mail: wim.vandenbossche@natuurpunt.be

Europe (Cont'd)

Brussels, Ornithological Working Group
E-mail: Erik.Toorman@bwk.kuleuven.ac.be
http://perswww.kuleuven.ac.be/~u0017670/avib.
html

Ligue Royal Belge pour la Protection des Oiseaux (LRBPO)
http://mrw.wallonie.be/dgrne/ong/refuges/lrbpo.
html

BULGARIA
Bulgarian Society for the Protection of Birds
The head office, Sofia
Tel/Fax: +359 2 722640
E-mail: bspb_hq@main.infotel.bg
http://plovdiv.techno-link.com/ClientsSites/
bspb_pd/bspb_new.htm

CROATIA
Hrvatsko Drustvo Za Zastitu Ptica I Prirode
Iiirski Trg 9, HR-10000
Zagreb, Croatia
Tel: 385 1 389 5445
E-mail: jasmina@mahazu.hazu.hr

CZECH REPUBLIC
Czech Society for Ornithology
Hornomecholupska 34, CZ-102 00
Praha 10, Czech Republic
E-mail: cso@birdlife.cz
http://www.birdlife.cz

DENMARK
Dansk Ornithologisk Forening (DOF)
Vesterbrogade 138-140
DK-1620 København V
Tel: 3331 4404
E-mail: dof@dof.dk
http://www.dof.dk/

ESTONIA
The Estonian Ornithological Society (EOS)
P.O. Box 227, Tartu 50002, Estonia
Tel: +3727 422195
E-mail: eoy@eoy.ee
http://www.eoy.ee/

FAROE ISLANDS
Faroese Ornithological Society
Postssmoga 1230, FR-110 Torshavn
Faroe Islands
E-mail: doreteb@ngs.fo

FINLAND
Birdlife Finland
BirdLife Suomi Finland ry
Mailing address: P.O.Box 1285, FIN-00101
Helsinki, Finland
Visiting address: Annankatu 29 A, FIN-00100
Helsinki, Finland
Tel: +358 9 4135 3300
E-mail: office@birdlife.fi
http://www.birdlife.fi/

The Finnish Ornithological Society
P.O. Box 17
FIN-00014 University of Helsinki
Finland
http://www.fmnh.helsinki.fi/users/sly/en/default
.htm

FRANCE
Ligue Pour la Protection des Oiseaux (LPO)
La Corderie Royale
BP 263
17305 Rochefort cedex
France
Tel: +33 05 46 82 12 34
E-mail: lpo@lpo-birdlife.asso.fr
http://www.lpo-birdlife.asso.fr/

Société d'Études Ornithologiques de France
Muséum National d'Histoire Naturelle
Laboratoire d'écologie générale
4, avenue du Petit Château—F-91800 Brunoy.
Tel: 01 47 30 24 48
E-mail: quetzalcom@libertysurf.fr
http://www.mnhn.fr/assoc/seof/accueil.htm

GERMANY
Dachverband Deutscher Avifaunisten
Tel: 0 48 34/ 6 04-0
E-mail: hhoetker@ftz-west.uni-kiel.de
http://www.der-gruene-
faden.de/inst/inst456.html

The German Ornithologists' Society (Deutsche Ornithologen-Gesellschaft)
Membership Office DO-G
c/o Institut für Vogelforschung
"Vogelwarte Helgoland"
An der Vogelwarte 21
D-26386 Wilhelmshaven
Germany
Tel: +49 4423 914148
E-mail: geschaeftsstelle@do-g.de
http://www.do-g.de/english/mainhtmlie.htm

Europe (Cont'd)

Institut für Ökologie und Naturschutz
Bergerstraße 108
16225 Eberswalde
Tel: 0 33 34-23 73-58 I Fax -59
E-mail: IfOeN@IfOeN.de

Kranich-Informationszentrum
Lindenstraße 27
18445 Groß Mohrdorf
Tel: 03 83 23-8 05-40 I Fax -41
E-mail: Gruidae@aol.com
http://www.Kraniche.de

Naturschutzbund Deutschland (NABU)
Herbert-Rabius-Str. 26, D-53225 Bonn, Germany
E-mail: NABU@NABU.de
http://www.NABU.de

GREECE
Hellenic Ornithological Society
Vas. Irakleiou 24
GR-10682, Athens, Greece
Tel/Fax: +30 210 8227937, +30 210 8228704
E-mail: birdlife-gr@ath.forthnet.gr
http://www.ornithologiki.gr/en/enmain.htm

HUNGARY
Hungarian Ornithological and Nature Conservation Society (MME)
Koltu u. 21, 391
H-1536
Budapest, Hungary
E-mail: mme@mme.hu
http://www.mme.hu

ICELAND
Icelandic Society for the Protection of Birds (ISPB)
P.O. Box 5069
125 Reykjavík, Iceland
Tel: 562 0477
E-mail: fuglavernd@fuglavernd.is
http://www.fuglavernd.is/enska/home.html

IRELAND
BirdWatch Ireland
Rockingham House, Newcastle, Co. Wicklow
Eire
Ireland
E-mail: info@birdwatchireland.org
http://www.birdwatchireland.ie

Northern Ireland Ornithologists' Club
E-mail: maurice.hughes@nioc.fsnet.co.uk
http://www.nioc.fsnet.co.uk/index.htm

ITALY
Centro Italiano Studi Onitologici-CISO
Francesco Mezzavilla
Via Malviste, 4—31057 Silea (TV) (Italy)
E-mail: f.mezza@libero.it.it
http://www.ciso-coi.org/

Comitato Italiano per la Protezione dei Rapaci (CIPR)
Via degli Estensi, 165
00164 Roma, Italy
E-mail: info@cipr.it
http://www.cipr.it/

Lega Italiana Protezione Uccelli (LIPU)
Via Trento, 49—1143100 Parma
Tel.: +39 0521 273043
E-mail: info@lipu.it
http://www.lipu.it/

LATVIA
Latvijas Ornitologijas Biedrib
P.O. Box 1010, Riga 1046, Latvia
E-mail: putni@lanet.lv
http://www.home.delfi.lv/putni

LITHUANIA
Lietuvos Ornitologu Draugija
Naugarduko St. 47-3, LT-2006
Vilnius, Lithuania
Tel: 8 5 213 04 98
E-mail: lod@birdlife.lt
http://www.birdlife.lt/

LUXEMBOURG
Ligue Luxembourgeoise pour la protection de la nature et des oiseaux
Haus vun der Natur
Kräizhaff, route de Luxembourg, L-1899
Kockelscheuer
Tel: 29 04 04, Fax: 29 05 04
E-mail: secretary@luxnatur.lu
http://www.luxnatur.lu

MOLDOVA
Moldova Ornithological and Herpetological Society
E-mail: zubcov@zoo.as.md

Europe (Cont'd)

THE NETHERLANDS

Dutch Birding Association
c/o Jeannette Admiraal
Iepenlaan 11
1901 ST Castricum
Netherlands
E-mail: dba@dutchbirding.nl
http://www.dutchbirding.nl/

Dutch Seabird Group/Nederlandse Zeevogelgroep (NZG)
Royal Netherlands Institute for Sea Research/
Koninklijk Nederlands Instituut voor Onderzoek der Zee (NIOZ)
P.O. Box 59, 1790 AB Den Burg
Texel, The Netherlands
Tel: + 31 222 369488
E-mail: camphuys@nioz.nl
E-mail: ned.zeevogelgroep@planet.nl
http://home.planet.nl/~camphuys/NZG.html

Netherlands Ornithologists' Union
Zoöligisch Museum
Postbus 94766
1090 GT Amsterdam
Tel: 020 525 6641
http://www.nioz.nl/en/deps/mee/ardea/com/htm

Vogelbescherming Nederland
Postbus 925
3700 AX Zeist
Tel: 030 6937700
E-mail: vogelinformatiecentrum@vogelbescherming.nl
http://www.vogelbescherming.nl

NORWAY

Norsk Ornitologisk Forening (NOF)
Sandgata 30 B,
7012 Trondheim
Tel: 73 52 60 40
E-mail: nof@birdlife.no
http://folk.uio.no/csteel/nof/

POLAND

Ogólnopolskie Towarzystwo Ochrony Ptaków
Ul. Hallera 4/2, PL-80-401
Gdansk, Poland
E-mail: office@otop.org.pl
http://www.otop.org.pl/

PORTUGAL

Associaçao Cientifica para a Conservaçao das Aves de Rapina
E-mail: bafari@visto.com
http://7mares.terravista.pt/bafari/

Sociedade Portuguesa para o Estudo das Aves
Rua de Vitória 53-3° Esq, PT-1100-618
Lisboa, Portugal
E-mail: Spea@spea.pt
http://www.spea.pt

ROMANIA

Romanian Ornithological Society
Str. Gheorghe Dima, 49/2, RO-3400
Cluj, Romania
E-mail: office@sor.ro
http://www.sor.ro

SLOVAKIA

Spolocnost Pre Ochranu Vtactva Na Slovensku
Mlynske Nivy 41, 821 09
Bratislava, Slovakia
E-mail: sovs@sovs.sk

SLOVENIA

Drusto Za Opazovanje in Proucevanje Ptic Slovenije (DOPPS)
Prvomajska 9, P.O. Box 2722, SI-1000
Ljubljana, Slovenia
E-mail: dopps@dopps-drustvo.si

SPAIN

Balearic Group of Ornithology and Defence of Nature
GOB Menorca
Camí des Castell, 59 07702 Maó (Spain)
Tel: +34 971 35 07
E-mail: info@gobmenorca.com
http://www.gobmenorca.com/e_index.htm

The Gibraltar Ornithological & Natural History Society
Gibraltar Natural History Field Centre
Jews' Gate
Upper Rock Nature Reserve
P. O. Box 843, Gibraltar
Tel: +350 72639
E-mail: enquiries@gonhs.org
http://www.gibnet.gi/~gonhs/

Europe (Cont'd)

Sociedad Española de Ornitología
Melquiades Biencinto 34, E-28053
Madrid, Spain
E-mail: seo@seo.org
http://www.seo.org

SWEDEN
Club 300
http://www.club300.se/

Göteborgs Ornitologiska Förening (GOF)
Box 166, 421 22 Västra Frölunda
Tel: 031 49 22 15
E-mail: gof@mbox301.swipnet.se
http://www.gof.nu/

Scandinavian Ornithological Society/Skånes
Ornitologiska Förening
Box 96
221 00 Lund, Sweden
E-mail: birds@skof.se
http://www.skof.se/eindex.html

Sveriges Ornitologiska Förening
Ekhagsvagen 3, S-104 03
Stockholm, Sweden
E-mail: birdlife@sofnet.org
http://www.sofnet.org

SWITZERLAND
ASPO BirdLife Suisse
Wiedingstr, 78, P.O. Bocx 8521, CH-8036
Zurich, Switzerland
E-mail: svs@birdlife.ch
http://www.birdlife.ch

UKRAINE
Ukrainske Tovaristvo Okhoroni Ptakhiv
P.O. Box 33
Kiev-01103, Ukraine
E-mail: utop@iptelecom.net.ua
http://www.utop.org.ua/

UNITED KINGDOM
Army Ornithological Society
The Secretary AOS
Headquarters Defence Logistics Organisation
Room 7261, MOD Main Building
Whitehall, London
SW1A 2HB
E-mail: ArmyOS@aol.com
http://armyos.tripod.com/

Aviornis UK
Cold Arbor Wildfowl, Tytherington Lane
Bollington, Cheshire, SK10 5AA, UK
Tel:+44 0 1625 573287
E-mail: Laurie@coldarbor.com
http://www.aviornis.co.uk/

The Barn Owl Trust
Waterleat, Ashburton, Devon
TQ13 7HU
Tel: 01364 653026
E-mail: info@barnowltrust.org.uk
http://www.barnowltrust.org.uk/

Bird Stamp Society
9 Cowley Drive
Worthy Down
Winchester
Hants, UK SO21 2QW
http://www.bird-stamps.org/bss.htm

The British Falconers' Club
Home Farm
Hints, Nr. Tamworth
Staffordshire, UK
B78 3DW
Tel: +44 01543 481737
http://www.britishfalconersclub.co.uk/

British Ornithologists' Club
Dene Cottage, West Harting, Nr. Petersfield
Hants GU31 5PA, UK
Tel/fax: +44 01730 825280
E-mail: mbcasement@aol.com
http://www.boc-online.org/

British Ornithologists' Union
The Natural History Museum, Tring
Hertfordshire UK HP23 6AP
Tel: 01442 890080
E-mail: bou@bou.org.uk
http://www.bou.org.uk/recgen.html

British Trust for Ornithology
BTO, The Nunnery, Thetford
Norfolk UK IP24 2PU
Tel: +44 01842 750050
E-mail: info@bto.org
http://www.bto.org/

Europe (Cont'd)

British Waterfowl Association
P. O. Box 163
Oxted UK
RH8 0WP
E-mail: info@waterfowl.org.uk
http://www.waterfowl.org.uk/bwa_pages/who.htm

Edward Grey Institute of Field Ornithology (EGI)
Department of Zoology, University of Oxford, South Parks Road, Oxford, UK OX1 3PS
Tel: +44 01865 271275
E-mail: lynne.bradley@zoology.oxford.ac.uk
E-mail: heather.green@zoology.oxford.ac.uk
http://egiwcruzool.zoo.ox.ac.uk/EGI/egihome.htm

Hawk and Owl Trust
The Membership Secretary
11 St Marys Close, Abbotskerswell, Newton Abbot, Devon UK TQ12 5QF
Tel/fax: +44 01626 334864
E-mail: hawkandowl@aol.com
http://www.hawkandowl.org/membership%202/membership.html

Knutsford Ornithological Society
E-mail: tony@10X50.com
http://www.10x50.com/

The National Birds of Prey Centre
Newent, Gloucestershire UK
GL18 1JJ
Tel: 0870 990 1992
http://www.nbpc.co.uk/

Royal Air Force Ornithological Society (RAFOS)
100 Moselle Drive
Churchdown
Gloucester, Glos UK
GL3 2TA
E-mail: wfrancis@dircon.co.uk
http://www.rafos.org.uk/

Royal Naval Birdwatching Society
Defence Estates
Blakemore Drive
Sutton Coldfield
West Midlands UK
B75 7RL

Tel: 0121 311 2140
E-mail: headoffice@de.mod.uk
http://www.defence-estates.mod.uk/conserva/sanct/rnbs.htm

Royal Society for the Protection of Birds (RSPB)
UK Headquarters
The Lodge
Sandy, Bedfordshire UK
SG19 2DL
Tel: 01767 680551
http://www.rspb.org.uk/

Scottish Ornithologists' Club (SOC)
Harbour Point
Newhailes Road
Musselburgh UK
EH21 6SJ
Tel: 0131 653 0653
E-mail: mail@the-soc.org.uk
http://www.the-soc.fsnet.co.uk/

Seabird Group
http://www.seabirdgroup.org.uk/index.htm

Sheffield Bird Study Group
http://www.sbsg.org/

UK400 Club
8 Sandycroft Road, Little Chalfont, Amersham, Buckinghamshire UK HP6 6QL
E-mail: lgre@uk400clubonline.co.uk
http://www.uk400clubonline.co.uk/

Wader Study Group
The National Centre for Ornithology
The Nunnery, Thetford
Norfolk UK JP24 2PU
http://web.uct.ac.za/depts/stats/adu/wsg/

Welsh Ornithological Society
http://members.aol.com/welshos/cac/index.html

Wildfowl & Wetlands Trust (WWT) Slimbridge, Glos GL2 7BT
Tel: 01453 891900
E-mail: info.slimbridge@wwt.org.uk
http://www.wwt.org.uk/index.asp

North America

CANADA

Avian Science and Conservation Centre
Macdonald Campus of McGill University
21,111 Lakeshore Road, Ste. Anne de Bellevue
QC H9X 3V9, Canada
Tel: 514 398 7760
E-mail: bird@nrs.mcgill.ca
http://www.nrs.mcgill.ca/ascc

Bird Studies Canada
P.O. Box 160, Port Rowan, ON N0E 1M0
Tel: 1 888 448 BIRD
E-mail: generalinfo@bsc-eoc.org
http://www.bsc-eoc.org/

British Columbia Field Ornithologists
P.O. Box 8059 Victoria, BC V8W 3R7
E-mail: ambuhler@coastnet.com
http://birding.bc.ca/bcfo/index.htm

Canadian World Parrot Trust
P.O. Box 29, Mount Hope, ON L0R 1W0
E-mail: cwparrot@sympatico.ca
http://www.canadianparrottrust.org/

Club des ornithologues de Québec Inc.
Domaine de Maizerets
2000 boul. Montmorency
Québec, QC G1J 5E7
Tel: 418 661 3544
E-mail: coq@coq.qc.ca
http://www.coq.qc.ca/

Ducks Unlimited Canada
P.O. Box 1160
Stonewall, MB R0C 2Z0
Tel: 1 800 665-DUCK (3825)
E-mail: webfoot@ducks.ca
http://www.ducks.ca/index.html

Edmonton Bird Club
Box 1111 Edmonton, AB T5J 2M1
http://ebc.fanweb.ca/

Étude des Populations d'Oiseaux du Québec
http://www.oiseauxqc.org/epoq.html

Greater Toronto Raptor Watch
http://www.gtrw.ca/

Manitoba Naturalists' Society
401-63 Albert Street
Winnipeg, MB R3B 1G4
Tel: 204 943 9029
E-mail: mns@escape.ca
http://www.manitobanature.ca/index.html

New Brunswick Federation of Naturalists
277 Douglas Avenue, Saint John, NB E2K 1E5
http://personal.nbnet.nb.ca/maryspt/NBFN.html

Nova Scotia Bird Society (NSBS)
c/o Nova Scotia Museum
1747 Summer Street
Halifax NS B3H 3A6
E-mail: ip-bird@chebucto.ca
http://www.chebucto.ns.ca/Recreation/
NS-BirdSoc/index.html

Ontario Field Ornithologists
Box 455, Station R
Toronto, ON M4G 4E1
E-mail: ofo@ofo.ca
http://www.ofo.ca/

**The Province of Quebec Society for the
Protection of Birds/La Société québécoise de
protection des oiseaux**
P.O.Box 43, Station B, Montreal QC H3B 3J5
E-mail: info@pqspb.org
http://www.pqspb.org/index.html

Toronto Ornithological Club
E-mail: info@torontobirding.ca
http://www.torontobirding.ca/

**Union Québécoise de réhabilitation des
oiseaux de proie (UQROP)**
C.P. 246
Saint-Hyacinthe QC J2S 7B6
Tel: 450 773 8521 (local 8545) *or*
     514 345-8521 (local 8545)
E-mail: info-uqrop@uqrop.qc.ca
http://www.uqrop.qc.ca/

Vancouver Island Birding
http://www.vancouverislandabound.com/
birding.htm

Yukon Bird Club
Box 31054
Whitehorse, YT Y1A 5P7
E-mail: YBC@yknet.yk.ca
http://www.yukonweb.com/community/ybc/

North America (Cont'd)

UNITED STATES

Alaska Raptor Center
P.O. Box 2984, 1000 Raptor Way, Sitka AK 99835
Tel: 907 747 8662
E-mail: birddoc.alaskaraptor@alaska.com
http://www.alaskraptor.org

American Bald Eagle Foundation
P.O. Box 49, 113 Haines Highway
AK 99827
Tel: 907 766 3094
E-mail: info@baldeagles.org
http://baldeagles.org/

American Bird Conservancy
P.O. Box 249
The Plains, VA 20198
Tel: 540 253 5780
E-mail: abc@abcbirds.org
http://www.abcbirds.org/

American Birding Association
P.O. Box 6599
Colorado Springs, CO 80934
Tel: 719 578 9703
E-mail: member@aba.org
http://www.americanbirding.org/

American Eagle Foundation
P.O. Box 333 Pigeon Forge TN 37868
Tel: 1 800 2EAGLES *or* 865 429 0157
E-mail: EagleMail@Eagles.org
http://www.eagles.org/

American Ornithologists' Union
Suite 402, 1313 Dolley Madison Blvd.
McLean, VA 22101
E-mail: AOU@BurkInc.com
http://www.aou.org/

Archbold Biological Station
P.O. Box 2057
Lake Placid, FL 33862
Tel: 863 465 2571
E-mail: archbold@archbold-station.org
http://www.archbold-station.org/

Association of Field Ornithologists
C/o Allen Press, P.O. Box 1897
Lawrence, KS 66044 1897
http://www.afonet.org/

The Brooks Bird Club, Inc.
P.O. Box 4077, Wheeling, WV 26003
http://www.brooksbirdclub.org

California Raptor Center
1 Shields Ave., School Of Veterinary Medicine
University of California, Davis CA 95616
http://www.vetmed.ucdavis.edu/ars/raptor.htm

Carolina Raptor Center
P.O. Box 16443, Charlotte, NC 28297
Tel: 704 875 6521
http://carolinaraptorcenter.org/

Center for the Study of Tropical Birds
218 Conway, San Antonio TX 78209-1716
Tel: 512 828 5306
E-mail: cstbinc1@aol.com
http://www.sctbinc.org/

The Cooper Ornithological Society
Ornithological Societies of North America
P.O. Box 1897
Lawrence, KS 66044-8897
http://www.cooper.org/

Cornell Lab of Ornithology
159 Sapsucker Woods Rd., Ithaca NY 14850
Tel: 1 800 843 2473
E-mail: cornellbirds@cornell.edu
http://birds.cornell.edu/

Delaware Valley Raptor Center
416 Cummins Hill Rd., Milford PA 18337
Tel: 570 296 6025
E-mail: dvraptors@yahoo.com
http://www.dvrconline.org/

Delta Waterfowl Foundation
P.O. Box 3128, Bismark ND 58502 *or*
P.O. Box 2800, Easton MD 21601
Tel: 888-987-3695
http://www.deltawaterfowl.org/

Ducks Unlimited, Inc.
One Waterfowl Way, Memphis TN 38120
Tel: 1 800 45DUCKS *or* 901 758 3825
http://www.ducks.org/

North America (Cont'd)

George Miksch Sutton Avian Research Center Inc.
P.O. Box 2007, Bartlesville OK 74005-2007
Tel: 918 336 BIRD
http://www.suttoncenter.org/

Hawk Migration Association of North America
164 1/2 Washington Street
Carbondale PA 18407-2483
E-mail: membership@hmana.org
http://www.hmana.org

Hawk Mountain Sanctuary Association
1700 Hawk Mountain Blvd., Kempton PA 19509
Tel: 610 756 6961
E-mail: info@hawkmountain.org
http://www.hawkmountain.org/default.shtml

Hawk Watch International, Inc.
1800 South West Temple, Suite 226
Salt Lake City, UT 84115
Tel: 801 484 6806
E-mail: hwi@hawkwatch.org
http://www.hawkwatch.org/

Hudson Valley Raptor Center
148 South Road, Stanforville NY 12581
Tel: 845 758 6957
E-mail: hvraptors@ulster.net
http://www.ulster.nct/-hrraptors/

The Illinois Raptor Center
5695 West Hill Road, Decatur IL 62522
Tel: 217 963 6909
E-mail: barnowl@illinoisraptorcenter.org
http://www.illinoisraptorcenter.org

Inland Bird Banding Association
http://www.aves.net/InlandBBA/
ibbamain.htm#write

The International Wild Waterfowl Association
P.O. Box 36, Scotland Neck NC 27874
Tel: 252 826 5038
http://www.wildwaterfowl.org/

Kansas Ornithological Society
http://www.ksbirds.org/kos/index.html?

National Audubon Society
Main Office: 700 Broadway, New York NY 10003
Tel: 212 979 3000
http://www.audubon.org/

National Bird-Feeding Society
P.O. Box 23, Northbrook IL 60065
Tel: 847 272 0135
http://www.birdfeeding.org/

National Flyway Council
C/o Joshua L. Slanot
Tawes State Office B.
580 Taylor Ave., Annapolis MD 21401
Tel: 410 260 8534
E-mail: jsondt@dnr.state.md.us

The National Wild Turkey Federation
P.O. Box 530, Edgefield SC 29824-1510
Tel: 1 800 THE NWTF
E-mail: jfelkins@nwt.net
http://www.nwtf.org/

Neotropical Migratory Bird Conservation
The National Fish and Wildlife Foundation
1120 Connecticut Avenue NW, Suite 900
Washington DC 20036
Tel: 202 857 0166
E-mail: canfield@NFWF.org
http://www.nfwf.org

Neotropical Ornithological Society
http://www.neotropicalornithology.org/

New Mexico Ornithological Society
University of New Mexico, Albuquerque
NM 87131
Tel: 505 277 0111
E-mail: bneville@unm.edu
http://biology-web.nmsu.edu/nmos/

North American Crane Working Group
341 W. Olympic Place, Seattle WA 98119
Tel: 308 384 4633
http://www.portup.com/~nacwg/home.htm

North American Falconers Association
E-mail: sokolinik@lycos.com
http://www.n-a-f-a.org/

North American Loon Fund
6 Lily Pond Rd., Gilford NH 032460
Tel: 989 772 9611
http://facstaff.uww.edu/wentzl/nalf/aNAFLhome
page.html

North America (Cont'd)

Oregon Raptor Center
P.O. Box 452, Mill City, OR 97360
E-mail: raptor@open.org
http://www.open.org/raptor/

Pacific Seabird Group
c/o Ron LeValley, Treasurer
Mad River Biologists
1497 Central Avenue, McKinleyville
CA 95519
E-mail: info@pacificseabirdgroup.org
http://www.pacificseabirdgroup.org/

Pheasants Forever, Inc.
1783 Buerkle Circle, St. Paul, MN 55110
Tel: 1 877 773 2070 *or* 651 773 2000
http://www.pheasantsforever.org/

Pilchuck Audubon Society
1803 Hewitt Ave. #108, Everett
WA 98201
Tel: 425 252 0926
http://www.pilchuckaudubon.org/morex.html

Platte River Whooping Crane Maintenance Trust, Inc.
6611 W Whooping Crane Dr, Wood River
NE 68883
Tel: 308 384 4633
E-mail: trust@whoopingcrane.org.

The Purple Martin Conservation Association
Edinboro University, Edinbohro PA 16444
Tel: 814 734 4420
E-mail: pmca@edinboro.edu
http://www.purplemartin.org/

Quail Unlimited
National Headquarters, P.O. Box 610
Edgefield, SC 29824
Tel: 803 637 5731
http://www.qu.org/

The Raptor Center
1920 Fitch Ave. St. Paul, MN 55108
Phone: 612 624 4745
E-mail: raptor@umn.edu
http://www.raptor.cvm.umn.edu/

The Raptor Center at Auburn University
1350 Raptor Road, Auburn
AL 36849-5523
Tel: 334 844-6025
E-mail: raptor@vetmed.auburn.edu
http://www.ocm.auburn.edu/serrc/index.html

Raptor Education Foundation
P.O. Box 200400 Denver, CO 80220
Tel: 303 680 8500
E-mail: raptor2@usaref.org

Raptor Society of Metropolitan Washington
11453 Heritage Commons Way Reston
VA 20194-1032
E-mail: panapier@tasc.com

Roger Tory Peterson Institute
311 Curtis Street, Jamestown NY 14701
http://www.rtpi.org/

The Ruffed Grouse Society, Inc.
451 McCormick Rd. Coraopolis, PA 15108
Tel: 412 262 4044 Toll Free: 1 888 564 6747
E-Mail: rgs@ruffedgrousesociety.org
http://www.ruffedgrousesociety.org/

Smithsonian Migratory Bird Center
Smithsonian Migratory Bird Center,
National Zoo, Washington DC 20008
http://www.nationalzoo.si.edu/ConservationAnd
Science/MigratoryBirds/default.cfm

Society for the Preservation of Raptors
P.O. Box 1462, Margaret River WA 6285
Tel: 08 945-6567
E-mail: raptorsociety@iinet.net.au
http://members.iinet.net.au/~spr/

The Santa Cruz Predatory Bird Research Group
Long Marine Lab, University of California
Santa Cruz CA 95060
Tel: 831 459 2466
E-mail: falconet@cats.ucsc.edu
http://www2.ucsc.edu/scpbrg

Texas Ornithological Society
Bert Frenz, 221 Rainbow Drive PMB 12190
Livingston TX 77399-2021
E-mail: bert@bafrenz.com
http://www.texasbirds.org/

North America (Cont'd)

The Trumpeter Swan Society
3800 County Road 24, Maple Plain
MN 55359
Tel: 763 476 4663
E-mail: ttss@threeriversparkdistrict.org
http://www.taiga.net/swans/contact_us.html

The Turkey Vulture Society
P.O. Box 50300, Reno NV 89513
E-mail: vulture@accutek.com.
http://www.accutek.com/vulture/

Western Field Ornithologists
http://www.wfo-cbrc.org/

Whooping Crane Conservation Association Inc.
http://www.whoopingcrane.com/

Wild Bird Feeding Institute
P.O. Box 763, Scottsbluff NE 69361
Tel: 1 888 839 1237
E-mail: info@wbfi.org
http://www.wbfi.org/

The Wildfowl Trust of North America
600 Discovery Lane, P.O. Box 519, Grasonville
MD 21638
Tel: 410 827 6694
http://www.wildfowltrust.org/index.htm

The Wilson Ornithological Society
Museum Of Zoology, University of Michigan
Ann Arbor MI 48109-1079
Tel: 202 357 1970
http://www.ummz.lsa.umich.edu/birds/wos.html

Women in Ornithology Resource Group
http://www.rci.rutgers.edu/~tsipoura/worg.html

World Bird Sanctuary
125 Bald Eagle Ridge Road, Valley Park
MO 63088
http://www.worldbirdsanctuary.org/

World Birding Center
Bentsen-Rio Grande Valley State Park
P.O. Box 988
Mission, Texas 78573
Tel: 956 519 6448
E-mail: Reynaldo.Ortiz@tpwd.state.tx.us
http://www.worldbirdingcenter.org

Australasia

The Australasian Wader Studies Group
Birds Australia, 415 Riversdale Rd.
Hawthorn East VIC 2123
http://www.tasweb.com.au/awsg/

Australian Raptor Association
P.O. Box A313, Sydney South NSW 1235
http://www.absa.asn.au

Bird Observers Club of Australia
P.O. Box 185, Nunawading VIC 3131
Tel: 613 3 9877 5342
E-mail: information@birdobservers.org.au
http://www.birdobservers.org.au

Birding NSW
P.O. Box Q277, QVB Post Office
Sydney NSW 1230
Tel: Sydney 02 9712 1180
Central Coast 02 4389 1390
E-mail: birdingnsw@yahoo.com.au
http://members.ozemail.com.au/~nswbirds/
index.html

Birds Australia
415 Riversdale Road
Hawthorn East, Victoria 3123
Tel: 03 9 882 2622
International callers: 61 3 9882 2622
E-mail: mail@birdsaustralia.com.au
http://www.birdsaustralia.com.au/

Birds Australia Parrot Association
Australian Bird Research Center
415 Riversdale Road, Hawthorn East VIC 3123
Tel: 03 9882 2622
E-mail: raou@raou.com.au
http://www.tasweb.com.au/bapa/

Canberra Ornithology Group
The Secretary, Canberra Ornithologists Group
Inc.
P.O. Box 631, Civic Square Act 2608
E-mail: cogoffice@ozemail.com.au
http://www.canberrabirds.dynamite.com.au/

Australasia (Cont'd)

Cumberland Bird Observers' Group
P.O. Box 550, Baulkham Hills 1755
http://www.cboc.org.au/default.html

Hunter Bird Observers Club
The Secretary, P.O. Box 24
New Lambton NSW 2305
E-mail: hboc@hunterlink.net.au
http://users.hunterlink.net.au/hboc/home.htm

Murrumbidgee Field Naturalist Inc.
E-mail: shabenbar@yahoo.com.au
http://www.angelfire.com/mn/fieldnats/

New South Wales Bird Atlassers
"Old Dromana" Moree 2400
New South Wales, Australia
Tel: 0267 533 242
http://www.bushwalking.org.au

Ornithological Society of New Zealand
P.O. Box 12397, Wellington, New Zealand
E-mail: OSNZ@xtra.co.nz
http://www.osnz.org.nz/

Queensland Wader Study Group
5 Stanmere Street, Carindale QLD 4152
E-mail: gouldian@ozemail.com.au
http://birdsqueensland.org.au/
waderstudygroup.html

Royal Forest and Bird Protection Society of New Zealand, Inc.
172 Taranaki Street, P.O. Box 631
Wellington, New Zealand
Tel: 04 385 7374
E-mail: office@wn.forest.bird.org.nz
http://www.forest.bird.org.nz/index.asp

Société Calédonienne d'Ornithologie
B.P. 3135, 98 846, Nouméa, Nouvelle-Calédonie
E-mail: barre@canl.nc

Société d'Ornithologie de Polynésie (MANU)
B.P. 21 098, Papeete
Tahiti, French Polynesia
E-mail: sop.manu@mail.pf

Society for the Preservation of Raptors
Avicultural Society of Western Australia
P.O. Box 1462, Margaret River WH 6255
E-mail: raptorsociety@iinet.net.au
http://members.iinet.net.au/~spr/

South Australian Ornithological Association
4 South Australian Museum North Terrace
Adelaide 5000
E-mail: birdssa@senet.com.au
http://www.birdssa.asn.au/

Southern Oceans Seabird Study Association
P.O. Box 142, Unandena NSW 2526
Tel: +61 02 4271 6004
E-mail: sossa@ozemail.com.au
http://members.ozemail.com.au/~sossa/

Sunshine Coast Ornithological Society
University of Sunshine Coast, Locked Bag 4
Maroochydore D.C. QLD 4558
E-mail: dglover@student.usc.edu.au
http://cwpp.slq.qld.gov.au/scos/contents.htm

Victorian Ornithological Research Group
133 Graydens Rd. Moorooduc VIC 3933
Tel: Spencer Unthank 03 5978 8340
http://www.vicnet.net.au/~vorg/lecvorg.htm

South and Central America, Caribbean

ARGENTINA
Asociacion Ornithilogica del Plata
25 de Mayo, 749-2 piso, oficina 6
C1002ABO Buenos Aires
Tel: +5411 4312 8958
http://www.avesargintinas.org.ar/

Aves Atgentinas/AOP
25 de May 749, 2° piso, oficina 6 1002ABO
Buenos Aires, Argentina
E-mail: info@avesargentinas.org.ar
http://www.avesargentinas.org.ar

BAHAMAS
The Bahamas National Trust
P.O. Box N-4105, Nassau, Bahamas
Tel: 809 393 1317
E-mail: bnt@bahamas.net.bs
http://www.bnt@bahamas.net.bs/environment/
origins.html

South and Central America, Caribbean (Cont'd)

BELIZE
Belize Audubon Society
12 Fort St., P.O. Box 1001, Belize City
Tel: +501 223 5004
E-mail: base@blt.net
http://www.belizeaudubon.org/

BERMUDA
Bermuda Audubon Society
http://www.audubon.bm/

BOLIVIA
Asociacion Armonía
400 Avenida Lomas de Arena, Casilla 3566
Santa Cruz, Bolivia
E-mail: armonia@scbbs-bo.com

BRAZIL
Brazilian Ornithological Society
Caixa Postal 238–868700-000 Ivaipora-
PR-Brasil
E-mail: ao@ao.com.br
http://www.ao.com.br/

CHILE
Union de Ornitologos de Chile
Casilla 13183, Santiago-21 Providencia 1108
Local 32-Stgo
Tel: 52 02 2368178
E-mail: unorch@unorch.cl
http://www.unorch.cl/

ECUADOR
Fundacion Ornitologica del Ecuador
La Tierra 203 y Av. de los Shyris
Casilla 17-17-906
E-mail: cecia@vio.satnet.net
http://cecia.org/

EL SALVADOR
Asociacion Audubon de El Salvador
P.O. Box 2166, Centro de Gobierno, la C.P.
Condominios Montemaria
Tel: +503 2980811
E-mail: harrouch@es.com.sv

FALKLANDS
Falklands Conservation
P.O. Box 26, Stanley Falkland Islands
Tel: +500 22247
E-mail: conservation@horizon.ca.fk
http://www.falklandislandsconservation.com/
index2.html

JAMAICA
BirdLife Jamaica
c/o Department of Life Sciences
University of the West Indies, Mona P.O.
Kingston 7, Jamaica, West Indies
E-mail: birdlifeja@yahoo.com

MEXICO
Consejo Internacional para la Preservación de les Aves—CIPAMEX
Mexico, D.F. 14091, Mexico
E-mail: cipamex@campus.iztacala.unam.mx
http://www.iztacala.unam.mx/wwwcampus/
cipamex/

PARAGUAY
Guyra Paraguay
Coronel Rafael Franco 381 c/Leandro Prieto
Casilla de Correos 1132
Asunción, Paraguay
E-mail: guyra@guyra.org.py
http://www.guyra.org.py/

PANAMA
Panama Audubon Society
Apartado 2026, Balboa, Panama
Tel: 507 224 9371
E-mail: info@panamaaudubon.org
http://www.panamaaudubon.org/

SURINAME
STINASU
P.O. Box 12252, Paramaribo, Suriname
Tel: 597 427102
http://www.stinasu.sr/

URUGUAY
Aves Uruguay—GUPECA
Canelones 1164—Montevideo—Uruguay
Casilla de Correo 6955
E-mail: info@avesuruguay.org.uy
http://www.avesuruguay.org.uy/

VENEZUELA
Sociedad Conservacionista Aububon de Venezuela
Apartado 80.450
Caracas 1080-A, Venezuela
E-mail: audubondevenezuela@audubonde-
venezuela.org
http://www.audubondevenezuela.org

Bird-Banding Organizations

Europe

GENERAL
EURING: The European Union for Bird Ringing
Netherlands Institute of Ecology
P.O. Box 40, NL-6666 ZG Heteren
E-mail: r.wasswnaare@nioo.know.nl
http://www.euring.org/

ALBANIA
Museum of Natural Sciences
Rr. e Kavajes 132, Tirana, Albania
Tel: +355 42 290 28
E-mail: mns@albmail.com

BELARUS
Belarus Ringing Center
Institute of Zoology Belarus,
National Academy of Sciences
Akademichnaya-27, Minsk 220072, Belarus
Tel: +375 17 284 25 04
E-mail: ring@biobel.bas-net.by

BELGIUM
Durme 5 Ringing Group, Belgium Ringing Scheme
E-mail: Kearsley.Lyndon@ping.be

Royal Belgian Institute of Natural Sciences
Vautierstraat 29, B-1000 Bruxelles, Belgium
Tel: +32 02 627 43 67
http://www.kbinirsnb.be/general/eng/main_e.htm

BULGARIA
Bulgarian Ornithological Centre
Institute of Zoology BAS
Boul. Tzar Osvoboditel 1, 1000 Sofia, Bulgaria
Tel: +359 88 51 15

CHANNEL ISLANDS
The Channel Islands Bird Ringing Scheme
Societe Jersaise
7 Pier Road, St. Helier, Jersey JE2 4XW
Channel Islands
Tel: +44 0 1534 583314
http://www.societe-jeriaise.org/pages/first.html

CROATIA
Hrvatska Akademija Zmanosti Umjetnosti
Zavod za Ornitologija
Ilirski trg broj 9/11, KR-41000 Zagreb, Croatia
Tel: +385 1 422 190
E-mail: zzo@hazu.hr

CYPRUS
Bird Ringing Center
P.O. Box 28076, Nicosia 2090, Cyprus
Tel: +357 26 62 29 69
E-mail: crabtree@cytanet.com.cy

CZECH AND SLOVAK REPUBLICS
Bird Ringing Center
Hornomecholupska 34, CZ-10200 Praha 10
Hostivar, Czech Republic
Tel: +42 2 71 96 12 56
E-mail: birdringczp@vol.cz

DENMARK
Copenhagen Bird Ringing Center
Zoological Museum
Universitetsparken 15, DK-2100
Copenhagen 0, Denmark
Tel: +45 35 32 10 29
E-mail: ringing@zmuc.ku.dk
http://www.zmuc.dk/verweb/ringing/

Danmarks Miljoundersogelser Kalo
NERI
Grenavej 12, Kalo, DK 8410 Ronde, Denmark
Tel: +45 89 20 17 00

ENGLAND
British Trust for Ornithology
The Nunnery
Thetford, Norfolk, UK IP24 2PU
Tel: +44 0 1842 750050
E-mail: ringing@bto.org
http://www.bto.org/

Dartford Ringing Group
E-mail: roger.taylor@tracegroup.com
http://www.dartford-ringing.co.uk

Durham Ringing Group
Robin M. Ward
E-mail: R.M.Ward@durham.ac.uk

East Yorkshire Ringing Group
E-mail: pjd@mail.infotrade.co.uk
http://www.eyrg.freeserve.co.uk

Gordano Valley Ringing Group
Lyndon Roberts
E-mail: lroberts@dircon.co.uk
http://www.bristol.digitalcity.org/members/
nature/bulletin/2002_09_413.htm/

Hudoleston & Jackson Bird Ringing Partnership
E-mail: steve@wheatear.biz
http://www.hjrg.org.uk/index.htm

Loganhurst Ringing Group
Dr. Steve Christmas
E-mail: sechris@liverpool.ac.uk

Morcambe Bay Wader Group
Jack Sheldon at Barrow
E-mail: Wes@cygnus.airtime.co.uk

North West Norfolk RG
John Middleton
E-mail: johnmiddleton@bmarket.freeserve.co.uk

North-West Swan Study
Wes Halton, 5 Westland Ave., Farnworth
Bolton, Lancs. UK BL4 9SR
Tel: 01204 709302
E-mail: Wes@cygnus.airtime.co.uk
http://www.sparc.airtime.co.uk/users/cygnus/
swanstud.htm

Rye Meads Ringing Group
Paul Roper, 1 Dewhurst Old School, Churchgate
Cheshunt Herts, UK EN8 9WB
Tel: 01992 640388
E-mail: rmrg@care4free.net
http://www.wildlifeweb.f9.co.uk/intro.html?
content.htm

Tees Ringing Group
Robin M. Ward
E-mail: R.M.Ward@durham.ac.uk

ESTONIA
Matsalu Bird Ringing Centre
EE 90305 Penijoe, Laanemaa, Estonia
Tel: +372 47 24221
E-mail: ring@matsalu.ee

FINLAND
Raasio Wader Ringing Station
http://www.jmp.fi/~pslty/raasio/index-en.html

Ringing Center; Finnish Museum of Natural History
Zoological Museum
P.O. Box 17, FIN-00014 Helsinki, Finland
Tel: +358 0 101 28847
E-mail: elmu_ren@cc.helsinki.fi
http://www.fmnh.helsinki.fi/N_default.asp

FRANCE
CRBPO
Museum National d'Histoire Naturelle
55 Rue Buffon, 75505 Paris, France
Tel: +33 1 40 79 30 78
E-mail: crbpo@mnhn.fr
http://www.mnhn.fr/mnhn/meo/crbpo/

GERMANY
Institut fur Vogelforschung
An der Vogelwarte 21, D-26386 Wilhelmshaven
Germany
Tel: +49 0 4421 96 89 0
E-mail: ifv@ifv.terramare.de
http://www.ifv.terramare.de/ifv_hp.htm

Beringungszentrale Hiddensee
Hiddensee Bird Ringing Center
An der Muehle 4, D-17493 Greifswald, Germany
Tel: +49 0 3834 830931
E-mail: beringung@hnm.de
http://hmn.de/uv/beringung/homepage.htm

Research Centre for Ornithology of the Max-Plank Society Andechs and Radolfzell
Vogelwarte Radolfzell
Bird Ringing Center, Schlossallee 2, Schloss
Moeggingen D-78315 Radolfzell, Germany
Tel: +49 0 7732 15 01 0
http://vowa.ornithol.mpg.de/~vwrado/

GREECE
Hellenic Bird Ringing Center
P.O. Box 4265, GR-10210 Athens, Greece
Tel: +30 0 251 36235
E-mail: takr@aegean.gr

HUNGARY
Hungarian Bird Ringing Center
Hungarian Ornithological and Nature
Conservation Society
Kolto 21, Budapest H-1121, Hungary
Tel: +36 1 275 62 47
E-mail: ringers@mme.hu

ICELAND
Icelandic Bird Ringing Scheme
Icelandic Institute of Natural History
Hlemmur 3, P.O. Box 5320, 125 Rejkjavik
Iceland
Tel: +354 562 9822

IRELAND
Cape Clear Bird Observatory
Clive Hutchison
E-mail: hutch@indigo.ie
http://www.informatique.iol.ie:8080/IrishBirds

ITALY
Dept. of Biology Ringing Group
(Univ. of Ferrara)
Contact: Stefano Volpini, Dept. of Biology, Univ.
of Ferrara, Via Borsari, 46, 44100 Ferrara, Italy
E-mail: col@dns.unife.it

Gruppo Inanellamento limicoli, Napoli
(Waders Ringing Group, Napoli)
Giancarlo Moschetti
E-mail: moschett@cds.unina.it

Isola della Cona
Paul Tout, 1 Dewhurst Old School, Churchgate
Cheshunt, Herts, UK EN8 9WB
Tel: 01992 640388
E-mail: tout@spin.it
http://home.xnet.it/tout/ENGCONA1.htm

Italian Ringing Center
Istituto Nazionale per la Fauna Selvatica
Via Ca'Fornacetta 9, I-40064 Ozzano Emilia
(BO), Italy
Tel: +39 051 65 12 111

KAZAKSTAN
Animal Marking Center
Institute of Zoology
Al-Farabi Ave., 93, Almaty 480060, Kazakstan
E-mail: InstZoo@nursat.kz

LATVIA
Bird Ringing Center
Institute of Biology
Miera Str 3, LV-2169 Salaspils, Latvia
Tel: +371 94 53 93
E-mail: ring@acad.latnet.lv

LITHUANIA
Lithuanian Bird Ringing Center
Zoological Museum
Laisves aleja 106, LT-3000 Kaunas, Lithuania
Tel: +370 7 205 870
E-mail: zcentras@takas.lt

MACEDONIA
BSPSM
Zoology Department, Institute of Biology
Faculty of Sciences
Skopje 91000, Macedonia
Tel: +389 91 117 055 ext. 614

MALTA
Bird Ringing Scheme
Malta Ornithological Society
P.O. Box 498, Valletta CMR 01, Malta
Tel: +356 23 06 84
E-mail: diomedea@waldonet.net.mt
http://www.zyworld.com/birding/vbrs.htm

NETHERLANDS
Vogel Ring Groep Schiermonnikoog
VRG Schiermonnikog, Langestreek 32, NL-9166
LC Schiermonnikog, The Netherlands
E-mail: holmer@worldonline.nl
http://www.geocities.com/RainForest/6549/vrgs.
htm

Vogelringstation Menork
De Bvorren 91 te 8408 HL, Lippenhuzen
Tel: 0513 465321
E-mail: Willem Bil—w.bil@hetnet.nl
http://www.vogelringstation.nl

Vogeltrekstation Arnhem
Centre for Terrestrial Ecology of the Netherlands
Institute of Ecology
P.O. Box 40, 6666 ZG Heteren, The Netherlands
Tel: +31 26 4791234
E-mail: vogeltrekstation@nioo.knaw.ntl
http://vogeltrekstation.nl

NORWAY
Bird Ringing Center
Stavanger Museum
Musegate 16, N-4005 Stavenger, Norway
Tel: +47 51 84 27 10

Jomfruland Bird Observatory
Kragero, S.E. Norway
http://www.hit.no/~u941436/jomfeng.htm

Lista Ringing Group
Boks 171, 4560 Vanse

Nord-Trondelag Ringing Group
c/o Knut Krogstad, Fletspatveien 10, 7500
Stjordal
http://home.inni.no/halvor/nof

Oslo & Akershus Ringing Group
Postboks 1050, Blindern 0316, Oslo
Tel: 0532 1444603
http://www.naturenett.org/nofoa/

POLAND
Ornithological Station of the Institute of Ecology
Polish Academy of Sciences
Nadwislanska 108, 80-680 Gdánsk 40, Poland
Tel: +351 0 58 308 07 59
E-mail: ring@stornit.gda.pl
http://www.stornit.gda.pl/

PORTUGAL
Bird Ringing Center/CEMPA
Instituto da Conservaçao da Naturaleza
Rua Filipe Folque, 46 3°/5°, 1050 Lisboa
Portugal
Tel: +351 0 1 352 30 18

ROMANIA
Centrala Ornitologica Romana
Institute for Plant Protection
Bld. Ion Ionescu dela Brad nr. 8, Sector I-71592
Bucharest, Romania
Tel: +40 0 1 222 30 36
E-mail: icpp@com.pcnet.ro

RUSSIA
Bird Ringing Center
Leninskiy prospect 86-310, Moscow 119313
Russia
Tel: +7 095 138 2231
E-mail: ring@bird.msk.ru

SCOTLAND
Aberdeen University Ringing Group
Andy Thorpe
E-mail: a.Thorpe@aberdeen.ac.uk

Grampian Ringing Group
R. Duncan, 86 Broadfold Drive, Bridge of Don
Aberdeen

Highland Ringing Group
Secretary, Bob Swain
14 St-Vincent Rd. Tain, Ross-shire
E-mail: highland.ringing.group@zetnet.co.uk
http://www.users.zetnet.co.uk.hrg/

Lothian Ringing Group
Clive Walton
E-mail: Walton@cwalton.freeserve.co.uk

SLOVENIJA
Bird Ringing Center
Slovene Museum of Natural History
Presernova 20, P.O. Box 290, SLO-1001
Ljubljana, Slovenjia
Tel: +386 0 61 21 16 70

SPAIN
Centro de Migracion de Aves
Miguel Dominguez Santaella
E-mail: domingue@samtyc.es
http://www.gurelur.org/centro%20migracion.htm

Grup d'Anellament del Grup Balear d'Ornitologia I Defensa de la Naturalesa (GOB)
Pere Garcás
E-mail: gob@ocea.es
http://www.gobmallorca.com/interinsolar.htm

Grup Catala d'Anellament, Catalan Group of Ringers
E-mail: qca.qca@supot.org
http://www.bcn.es/tjussana/gca/

Officina de Especies Migratorias
Dirección General de Conservación de la
Naturaleza
Ministerio de Medio Ambiente
Gran Via de San Francisco 4, E-28005 Madrid
Spain
Tel: +34 91 596 49 84
http://www.mma.es/conserv_nat/inventarios/
especies_migratorias/indice.htm

Sociedad de Ciencias Aranzadi
San Telmo Museoa
E-20012 Donostia, S. Sebastian, Spain
Tel: +34 0 43 42 29 45

SWEDEN
Bird Ringing Center
Swedish Museum of Natural History
P.O. Box 50 007, SE-104 05 Stockholm, Sweden
Tel: +46 0 8 5195 40 80
E-mail: bird.ringing@nrm.se
http://www.nrm.se/rc/

Bird Station Stora Fjaederaegg
Per Hansson
E-mail: Per.Hansson@ssko.slu.se

Takern Fieldstation
Takerns Faltstation, Box 204, 593 22, Mjolby
Tel: 0144-321 19
E-mail: lars.gezelius@e.lst.se
http://hem.fyristorg.com/takern/

SWITZERLAND
Bird Ringing Center
Schweizerische Vogelwarte
CH-6204 Sempach, Switzerland
Tel: +41 41 462 97 00
E-mail: ring@vogelwarte.ch
http://www.vogelwarte.ch/

TURKEY
National Ringing Scheme KAD
PK 311 Yenisehir, 06443 Ankara, Turkey
Tel: +90 312 434 1510
E-mail: ringing@kad.org.tr

UKRAINE
Ukrainian Ringing Centre
Institute of Zoology
B. Knmelnitsky St 15, 252601 Kyiv 30 GSP,
Ukraine
Tel: +380 44 2250112

YUGOSLAVIA
Centre for Animal Marking
Natural History Museum
Njegoseva 51, P.O. Box 401, 11000 Belgrade,
Federal Republic of Yugoslavia
Tel: +381 11 344 21 47
E-mail: animig@net.yu

Africa

Ringing Scheme of Eastern Africa
P.O. Box 15194, Langata 00509, Nairobi Kenya
Tel: 00 254 2891 419
E-mail: Graeme Backhurst—
graeme@wananchi.com

Safring
University of Cape Town, Rondebosch
South Africa 7701
Tel: 021 650 2421
E-mail: safring@adu.uct.ac.za
http://web.uct.ac.za/depts/stats/adu/
safring-index.htm

Middle East

Bird Migration Research Center
Japan
Tel: +81 4 7182 1107
E-mail: banding@ceres.ocn.ne.jp

Kibbutz Lotan Ringing Station
http://www.birdingisrael.com/birdsofisrael/
ringing/spring2000.htm

Israel Bird Ringing Centre
Atidim Industrial Park
P.O. Box 58020, Tel-Aviv, 61580, Israel
Tel: +972 3 6449622
E-mail: ibrc@netvision.net.il

Australia

The Australian Bird & Bat Banding Scheme
GPO Box 8, Canberra, Act 2601
Tel: 02 627 424 07
E-mail: abbbs@ea.gov.au
http://ea.gov.au/biodiversity/science/abbbs/

North America

GENERAL
Atlantic Bird Observatory
Phil Taylor
Dept. of Biology, Acadia University
Wolfville, NS B0P 1X0
Tel: 902 585 1313
E-mail: abo@acadiau.ca
http://landscape.acadiau.ca/abo/

Bird Banding Laboratory
National Biological Survey
12100 Beech Forest Rd., Laurel MD 20708-4037
Tel: 301 497 5790
E-mail: BBL@mail.fws.gov
For Bird Band Reports:
bandreports@patuxent.usgs.gov
http://www.pwrc.usgs.gov/bbl/

North American Banding Council
E-mail: Brenda.dale@ec.gc.ca
http://www.nabanding.net/nabanding/

CANADA
Beaverhill Bird Observatory (BBO)
P.O. Box 1418, Edmonton AB, T5J 2N5
Tel: 780 719 9803
E-mail: secretary—Geoffrey.holroyd@ec.gc.ca
http://www.beaverhillbirds.com/

Brier Island Bird Migration Research Station
Contact: Lance Laviolette
RR #1, Glen Robertson ON K0B 1H0
Tel: 613 874 2449
E-mail: lance.laviolette@lmco.com
http://www.bsc-eoc.org/national/bibs.html

Bruce Peninsula Bird Observatory
Contact: Audrey Heagy
General Delivery, Lion's Head ON
N0H 1W0
Tel: 519 372 8200
E-mail: aheagy@kwic.com

Calgary Bird Banding Society
Contact: Douglas M. Collister
3426 Lane Cr., Calgary AB T3E 5X2
Tel: 403 246 2697
E-mail: collies@telusplanet.net
http://www.bsc-eoc.org/national/ibs.html

Canadian Wildlife Service Bird Banding Office
National Wildlife Research Center, Canadian Wildlife Service
Hull, QC, K1A 0H3
Tel: 819 994 6176
http://www.ec.gc.ca/cws-scf/nwrc/bbo/index.html

Canadian Wildlife Service, Pacific Wildlife Research Center, Environment Canada
Contact: Wendy Easton
5421 Robertson Rd., RR 1, Delta BC
B4K 3N2
Tel: 604 940 4669
E-mail: wendy.Easton@ec.gc.ca

Delta Marsh Bird Observatory
Heidi den Haan
RR #2, P.O. Box 38, Portage la Prairie MB
R1N 3A2
Tel: 204 239 4287
E-mail: hdenhaan@cc.umanitoba.ca
http://www.dmbo.org/

Fundy Bird Observatory
P.O. Box 145, Castalia NB E0G 1L0
Tel: 506 662 8650
http://www.bsc-eoc.org/national/fbo.html

Haldimand Bird Observatory
Contact: John Miles
P.O. Box 25, Nanticoke ON N0A 1L0
Tel: 519 587 5223
E-mail: miles@kwic.com
http://geocities.com/haldimandbirdobservatory/

North America (Cont'd)

Holiday Beach Migration Observatory
E-mail: amazilia@juno.com
http://www.hbmo.org/

Innis Point Bird Observatory
Contact: William Petrie
P.O. Box 72137, Kanata North RPO, Kanata ON
K2K 2P4
Tel: 613 820 8434
E-mail: wfpetrie@magi.com
http://www.magi.com/~wfpetri/IPBO.html

Last Mountain Bird Observatory
Canadian Wildlife Service
Contact: Alan Smith
115 Perimeter Rd., Saskatoon SK S7N 0X4
Tel: 306 975 4091
E-mail: alan.smith@ec.gc.ca
http://www.naturesask.com/lmbo.html

Les Jeunes Explos Inc.
Contact: Jaques Ibarzabal
302 de la Riviere, Grands-Bergonnes
QC G0T 1G0
Tel: 418 232 6249
E-mail: jhawk.ibarzabal@sympatico.ca
http://www.bsc-eoc.org/national/odt.html

Lesser Slave Lake Bird Observatory
Box 1076, Slave Lake, AB T0G 2A0
Tel: 780 849 7117
E-mail: birds@lslbo.org
http://www.lslbo.org/

Long Point Bird Observatory
Tel: 519 586 2885
E-mail: generalinfo@bsc-eoc.org
http://www.bsc-eoc.org/lpbo/lpBirdo.html

Mackenzie Nature Observatory
Contact: Vi Lambie
Box 1598, Mackenzie BC V0J 2C0
Tel: 250 997 6876
E-mail: lambie@uniserve.com
http://www.bsc-eoc.org/national/mno.html

Mountsburg Banding Operation
Mountsburg Conservation Area
2259 Milborough Line, Campbellville
ON L0P 1B0
Tel: 905 854 2220
E-mail: buffalo@worldchat.com

Ontario Bird Banding Association
Secretary, Joanne Dewey
RR #8, 642 Elmbrook Rd., Picton
ON K0K 2T0
E-mail: dewey@reach.net
http://ontbanding.org/

Ontario Ministry of Natural Resources
P.O. Box 1749, Cornwall ON K6H 5V7
Tel: 613 933 1774

Prince Edward Point Bird Observatory
P.O. Box 2, Delhi ON N4B 2W8
Tel: 519 582 4738
E-mail: peptbo@rogers.com
http://www.peptbo.ca/

Rocky Point Bird Observatory
3370 Passage Way, Victoria BC V9C 4J6
Tel: 250 480 0493
E-mail: goshawk@telus.net
http://www.islandnet.com/~rpbo/

St. Andrews Banding Station
Contact: Tracey Dean
Huntsman Marine Science Center
1 Lower Campus Rd.
St. Andrews NB E5B 2V5
Tel: 506 529 1220
E-mail: tdean@huntsmanmarine.ca
http://www.huntsmanmarine.ca/home.html

Tadoussac Bird Observatory
Explos-Nature
C.P. 5070
Beauport, QC G1E 6B3
E-mail: jhawk.ibarzabal@sympatico.ca

Thunder Cape Bird Observatory
Contact: Nick Escott
133 South Hill Street, Thunder Bay ON P7B 3T9
Tel: 807 345 7122
E-mail: escott@norlink.net
http://www.tbfn.baynet.net/tcbotbfn.htm

Timiskaming Banding Group
RR #1, Coblat ON, P0J 1C0
Tel: 705 679 5030
E-mail: birdboy@ntl.sympatico.ca

North America (Cont'd)

Toronto Bird Observatory
Mary Boswell
807-70 Heath St. West, Toronto ON M4V 1T4
E-mail: mboswell@sympatico.ca
http://www.netrover.com/~nkhsin/tbopage/bohome.html

UNITED STATES

Alaska Bird Observatory
P.O. Box 80505, Fairbanks AK 99708
Tel: 907 451 7159
E-mail: birds@alaskabird.org
http://www.alaskabird.org/

Big Sur Ornithology Lab
HC 67, Box 99, Monterey CA 93940
Tel: 408 624 1202
E-mail: BSOLMAIL@aol.com

Black Swamp Bird Observatory
119 W. Water St., Oak Arbor OH 43449
Tel: 419 898 4070
E-mail: bsbobird@thirdplanet.net
http://www.bsbobird.org/

Braddock Bay Bird Observatory
P.O. Box 12876, Rochester NY 14612
Tel: 585 234 3525
E-mail: info@bbbo.org
http://www.bbbo.org/

California Department of Parks and Recreation
Contact: Christina Fabula
P.O. Box 440, Mendocino CA 95460
Tel: 707 937 5904
E-mail: cfabula@mcn.org

Cape Cod Museum of Natural History
Contact: Sue Finnegan
P.O. Box 1710, 869 Route 6A, Brewster MA 02631
Tel: 508 839 7016
E-mail: Sfinn8688@aol.com

Cape May Bird Observatory
P.O. Box 3, Cape May Point NJ 08210
Tel: 609 884 2736
http://www.covesoft.com/capemay/bird.html

Carnegie Museum of Natural History
Contact: Robert Mulvihill
HC 64, Box 453, Rector PA 15677-9605
Tel: 724 593 7521
E-mail: mulvipnr@westol.com
http://www.westol.com/~banding/

Center for the Study of Biodiversity
Contact: Dennis Meritt
De Paul University, Biological Sciences, 2325 North Clifton Ave., Chicago IL 60614-3207
Tel: 773 325 4937
E-mail: dmeritt@wppost.depaul.edu

Charleston Museum
360 Meeting St., Charleston SC 29403
Tel: 803 883 9325
E-mail: grackler@aol.com

Chipperwoods Bird Observatory, Inc.
10329 N. New Jersey St., Indianapolis IN 46280
Tel: 317 846 2616
E-mail: chipperwoods@worldnet.att.net
http://www.wbu.com/chipperwoods/

Coastal Virginia Wildlife Observatory
P.O. Box 11, Franktown VA 23354
Tel: 757 331 3870
E-mail: CVWO@worlnet.att.net
http://members.tripod.com/CVWO

Connecticut Audubon Coastal Center at Milford Park
Contact: Charlotte Weston
1 Milford Point Rd., Milford CT 06460
Tel: 203 877 2892
E-mail: charlotte.weston@snet.net

Coyote Creek Field Station
Contact: Al Jaramillo
P.O. Box 1027, Alviso CA 95002
Tel: 408 262 9204
E-mail: alvaro@sirius.com
http://www.sfbbo.org/

Eastern Bird Banding Association
Contact: Don Mease
2366 Springtown Hill Rd., Hellertown PA 18055
E-mail: measede@enter.net
http://www.pronetisp.net/~bpbird

North America (Cont'd)

Fernbank Forest
Fernbank Science Center,
156 Heaton Park Dr. NE, Atlanta GA 30307
Tel: 404 378 4314 ext. 322
E-mail: fernbank@fernbank.edu
http://fsc.fernbank.edu/

Florida Park Service
Kissimmee Prairie State Preserve, 33104 NW
192nd Ave., Okeechobee FL 34972
Tel: 863 462 5360
E-mail: kisspress@okeechobee.com

Golden Gate Raptor Observatory (GGRO)
Building 201, Fort Mason
San Francisco CA, 94123
Tel: 415 331 0730
E-mail: ggro@parkconservancy.org
http://www.ggro.org/

Hawk Ridge Nature Reserve
Contact: Dave Grosshuesch
5426 Juniata St., Duluth MN 55804
Tel: 218 525 7253
E-mail: sdgrossh@d.umn.edu

Hebron Banding Station
Contact: David Hauber
881 Whitney Creek Rd.
Coudersport, PA 16915
Tel: 814 274 8946
E-mail: haubers3@penn.com

Hilton Pond Center for Piedmont Natural History
Contact: Bill Hilton Jr.
1432 DeVinney Rd., York, SC 29745-2119
Tel: 803 684 5852
E-mail: hilton@hiltonpond.org
http://www.hiltonpond.org/

Hummer/Bird Study Group
P.O. Box 250, Clay AL 35048 0250
Tel: 205 681 2888
http://www.hummingbirdsplus.org

Idaho Bird Observatory
Dept. of Biology, Boise State University
1910 University Dr., Boise ID 83709
Tel: 208 377 1440
E-mail: gkalten@internetoutlet.net
http://www.idbsu.edu/biology/ibo

Inland Bird Banding Association
Contact: Tom Bartlett
1833 South Winfield Drive, Tiffin OH 44883
E-mail: Tom_Bartlett@Tiffin.k12.oh.us
http://www.aves.net/inlandbba/

Jug Bay Wetlands Sanctuary
1361 Wrighton Road, Lothian MD 207011
Tel: 410 741 9330
http://web.aacpl.lib.md.us/rp/parks/Jugbay

Kestrel Haven Avian Migratory Observatory
5373 Fitzgerald Rd., Burdett NY 14818-9626
Tel: 607 546 2169
E-mail: khmo@att.net
http://www.chemungvalleyaudubon.com/

LBJ Enterprises
1204 Freshwater Rd., Eureka CA 95503
Tel: 707 442 0339
E-mail: lbjent@humboldt1.com

Manomet Bird Observatory
P.O. Box 1770 Manomet, MA 02345
Tel: 508 224 6521
E-mail: tlloyd-evans@manomet.org
http://www.manomet.org/avian/resources/

Migratory Bird Banding: US Fish and Wildlife Service
E-mail: migratorybirds@fws.gov
http://www.migratorybirds.fws.gov/

Mitchell Lake Wetlands Society
Contact: Sumner Dana
1922 Oakline Dr., San Antonio TX 78232
Tel: 210 490 6802
E-mail: swdana@texas.net
http://sdana.home.texas.net/

Monitoring Avian Productivity and Survivorship (MAPS) Program
The Institute for Bird Populations
P.O. Box 1346, 11435 S.R. #1, Suite 23
Point Reyes Station CA 94956
http://www.birdpop.org/maps.htm

Old Myakka Bird Observatory
2210 Myakka Rd., Sarasota FL 34240
Tel: 941 322 8807
E-mail: OldmyakkaBO@cs.com

North America (Cont'd)

Oregon Bird Monitoring Sessions
Contact: Dennis Vroman
269 Shetland Dr., Grants Pass OR 97526
Tel: 541 479 4619
E-mail: dpvromen@cdsnet.net

The Point Reyes Bird Observatory
4490 Shoreline Highway
Stinson Beach CA 94970
Tel: 415 868 1221
http://www.prbo.org/cms/index.php

Rio Grande Bird Research, Inc.
4426 San Isidro NW, Albuquerque NM 87107
Tel: 505 345 2385
E-mail: swcox@flash.net

Rio Grande Valley Bird Observatory
P.O. Box 8125, Weslaco TX 78599
Tel: 956 969 2475
E-mail: rgvbo@geocities.com
http://www.geocities.com/RainForest/2240/

River Bend Nature Center
Contact: John Blackmer
1000 Rusdad Rd., P.O. Box 186 Fariault MN
55021
Tel: 507 332 7151
E-mail: blackmer@rbnc.org
http://www/rbnc.org/

Robbins Banding Center
7902 Brooklyn Bridge Rd.
Laurel, MD 20707-2822
Tel: 301 725 1176
E-mail: chan_robbins@usgs.gov

Rocky Mountain Bird Observatory
Contact: Tony Leukering
13401 Picadilly Rd., Brighton CO 80601
Tel: 303 659 4348
E-mail: tony.leukering@rmbo.org
http://www.rmbo.org/

Rouge River Bird Observatory
Natural Areas Dept.
University of Michigan-Dearborn
4901 Evergreen Rd., Dearborn MI 48128
Tel: 313 593 5338
E-mail: jcraves@umd.umich.edu
http://www.rrbo.org/

San Pedro Avian Research Center
San Pedro River, Hwy 90
Sierra Vista, AZ
E-mail: sanpedrobirds@earthlink.net

Santa Monica College
Life Sciences Department, Santa Monica College
1900 Pico Blvd., Santa Monica CA 90405-1628
Tel: 310 434 4704
E-mail: sakai_walter@smc.edu
http://homepage.smc.edu/sakai_walter/
ZUMA.HTM

Save the Dunes Conservation Fund
444 Barker Rd., Michigan City IN 46360
Tel: 219 879 3564
E-mail: sand@savedunes.org
http://www.savedunes.org/

Scioto Valley Bird and Nature Club
178 Church St., Chillicothe, OH 45601-2405
E-mail: coordinator@scops.org
http://www.scops.org/meeting.html

Southeastern Arizona Bird Observatory
P.O. Box 5521, Bisbee AZ 85603-5521
Tel: 520 432 1388
E-mail: sabo@sabo.org
http://www.sabo.org/

Starr Ranch Bird Observatory
Starr Ranch Sanctuary, 100 Bell Canyon Road
Trabuco Canyon CA 92679-3511
Tel: 949 858 3537
E-mail: dkamada@audubon.org
http://www.starrranch.org/

**Travis Audubon Society, Hornsby Bend Bird
Observatory**
P.O. Box 40787, Austin TX 78704-0014
Tel: 512 347 7572
E-mail: fergus@hornsbybend.org
http://www.hornsbybend.org/

Western Bird Banding Association
P.O. Box 716, Inverness CA 94937
E-mail: kmburton@svn.net
http://www.sfsu.edu/~sierra/western.htm

North America (Cont'd)

Whitefish Point Bird Observatory
16914 N. Whitefish Point Rd.
Paradise MI 49768
Tel: 906 492 3596
http://www.wpbo.org/

Wilson Creek MAPS Station
917 Sherman Ave., Janesville WI 53545
Tel: 608 741 9343
E-mail: catharus_thrush@yahoo.com
http://www.wilsoncreekmaps.com/

Zoological Society of Milwaukee
Contact: Vicki Piaskowski
1421 N. Water St., Milwaukee WI 53202
Tel: 414 276 0339
E-mail: vickip@execpc.com

Central and South America, Caribbean

Caribbean Conservation Corporation
USFS Redwood Sciences Laboratory
1700 Bayview Dr. Arcata CA 95521
Tel: 707 825 2992
E-mail: cjr2@axe.humboldt.edu
http://www.rsl.psw.fs.fed.us/

Estacion Ornitologica "La Mucuy"
IMPARQUES
Apartado Postal 229, Mérida Mountains, Sierra
Nevada National Park, Venezuela
Tel: 58 74 529102
E-mail: lamucuy@cantv.net
http://www.geocities.com/lamucuy2000/
english.html

Instituto de Ecologia A.C.
Contact: Fernando Gonzalez-Garcia
E-mail: gonzalez@sun.ieco.conacyt.mx

**Manantlan Institute for Ecology and
Biodiversity (IMECBIO)**
Contact: Eduardo Santana
E-mail: esantana@fisher.autlan.udg.mx

**Monte Verde, Costa Rica Bird Monitoring
Stations**
Contact: Dave McDonald
University of Wyoming
E-mail: dbmcd@uwyo.edu

Organization for Tropical Studies
La Selva Biological Station, Apdo 676-2050
San Pedros de Montes de Oca, Costa Rica
Tel: 506 710 1515 *or* 506 766 6565

**Ornithological Laboratory of the University
of Michoacan (UMSNH)**
Universidad Michoacana de San Nicolas de
Hidalfo, Facultad de Biologia
Laboratorio de Investigation en Ornitologia
Edificio B-4, Ciudad Universitia, Morelia, Mich.
58030, Mexico
Tel: 43 16 74 12
E-mail: fvgomez@zeus.ccu.umich.mx

Panama Audubon Society
E-mail: audupan@pananet.com

**Research Center for Wild Bird Conservation
Brazil**
Contact: Inex Nascimento
E-mail: ines@openline.com.br

**Sociedad Conservacionista Audubon de
Venezuela / EcoNatura**
Contact: Chris Sharpe
Apdo. 62826, Caracas 1060, Venezuela
Tel: +58 2 749701

Birding Hotlines

Canada

Alberta
Calgary: 403 237 8821
Northern Alberta Birding Hotline: 403 433 2473

British Columbia
Vancouver: 604 737 3074
Victoria: 250 592 3381

New Brunswick
Provincewide: 506 382 3825
Shediac/Moncton: 506 532 2873 {French}

Nova Scotia
Province wide: 902 582 7997
Cape Breton: Cathy Murrant 902 737 2684 *or*
Dave McCorquadale 902 794 2172

Ontario
Oshawa: 905 576 2738
Ottawa: 613 860 9000
Sault Ste. Marie: 705 256 2790
Toronto: 416 350 3000, ext. 2293
Windsor/Detroit: 810 477 1360
Barrie: 705 739 8585

Durham: 905 576 2738
Hamilton: 905 648 9537
Holiday Beach Migration Observatory:
519 252 2473
Kingston: 613 549 8023
London: 519 457 4593
Niagara Region/Buffalo: 716 896 1271
Point Pelee-Essex County: 519 322 2371
Sarnia: 519 337 9400
Simcoe: 705 739 8585

Quebec
Eastern Quebec: 418 660 9089
Sagueny/Lac St. Jean: 418 696 1868 {French}
Bas St. Laurent: 418 725 5118
Western Quebec: 819 778- 0737 {French}
Montreal: 514 989 5076 {English}
Montreal: 514 978 8849 {French}
Rive Sud: 418 990 1506

Saskatchewan
Provincewide: 306 949 2505

United States

North American Rare Bird Alert (NARB):
800 458 BIRD

Alabama
Statewide: 205 987 2730

Alaska
Statewide: 907 338 2473
Kachemak Bay: 907 235 7337
Seward: 907 224 2325
Fairbanks: 907 451 9213

Arizona
Phoenix: 602 832 8745
Tucson: 520 798 1005

Arkansas
Statewide: 501 753 5853

California
Arcata: 707 822 5666
Los Angeles: 213 874 1318
Monterey: 408 375 9122

Morro Bay: 805 528 7182
Northern CA: 415 681 7422
Orange County: 714 487 6869
Sacramento: 916 481 0118
San Bernadino: 909 793 5599
San Diego: 619 479 3400
San Joaquin/S. Sierra: 209 271 9420
Santa Barbara: 805 964 8240

Colorado
Statewide: 303 424 2144

Connecticut
Statewide 203 254 3665
Eastern (also statewide): 860 599 5159

Delaware
Statewide: 302 658 2747

District of Columbia
Voice of the Naturalist: 301 652 1088

Florida
Statewide: 561 340 0079
Miami: 305 667 7337
Lower Keys: 305 294 3438
Northern FL: 912 244 9190
Big Bend: 850 513 1771

Georgia
Statewide: 770 493 8862
Southern GA: 912 244 9190

Idaho
Northern: 208 882 6195
Southeast: 208 236 3337
Southwest: 208 368 6096

Illinois
Central Illinois: 217 785 1083
Chicago: 847 265 2118
DuPage: 630 406 8111
Northwestern IL: 815 965 3095

Indiana
Statewide: 317 259 0911

Iowa
Statewide: 319 338 9881

Kansas
Statewide: 913 372 5499
Kansas City: 913 342 2473
Wichita: 316 681 2266

Kentucky
Statewide: 502 894 9538

Louisiana
Baton Rouge: 504 768 9874
Southeast: 504 834 2473
Southwest: 318 988 9898

Maine
Statewide: 207 781 2332

Maryland
Statewide: 301 652 1088
Baltimore: 410 467 0653

Massachusetts
Boston: 617 259 8805
Cape Cod: 508 349 9464
Nantucket Island: 508 228 8818
Western MA: 413 253 2218

Michigan
Statewide: 616 471 4919
Southeast: 810 477 1360
Sault Ste. Marie: 705 256 2790

Minnesota
Statewide: 612 780 8890
Duluth: 218 525 5952

Missouri
Kansas City: 913 342 2473
Statewide: 573 445 9115
St. Louis: 314 935 8432

Montana
Statewide: 406 721 9799
Big Fork: 406 756 5595

Nebraska
Statewide: 402 292 5325

Nevada
Southern: 702 649 1516
Northwest: 702 324 2472

New Hampshire
Statewide: 603 224 9900

New Jersey
Cape May: 609 861 0466
Statewide: 908 766 2661

New Mexico
Statewide: 505 662 2101

New York
Albany: 518 439 8080
Buffalo: 716 896 1271
Finger Lakes, Ithaca: 607 254 2429
Lower Hudson: 914 666 6614
New York: 212 979 3070
Rochester: 716 425 4630
Syracuse: 315 668 8000

North Carolina
Statewide: 704 332 2473

North Dakota
Statewide: 701 250 4481

Ohio
Southwest OH, Cincinnati: 937 521 2847
Northeast OH, Cleveland: 216 526 2473
Central OH, Columbus: 614 221 9736
Blendon Woods, Columbus: 614 895 6222
Northwest OH, Toledo: 419 877 9640
West OH, Dayton: 513 277 6446
Youngstown: 330 742 6661

Oklahoma
Oklahoma City: 405 373 4531
Statewide: 918 669 6646

Oregon
Statewide: 503 292 0661
Klamath Basin: 541 850 3805
Northeastern: 208 882 6195

Pennsylvania
Allentown: 610 252 3455
Central PA: 717 255 1212, ext. 5761
Philadelphia: 215 567 2473
Reading/Bucks Co.: 610 376 6000, ext. 2473
Schuylkill County: 717 622 6013
Western PA: 412 963 0560
Wilkes-Barre: 717 825 2473

Rhode Island
Statewide: 401 949 3870
Reporting: 401 949 5454

South Carolina
Statewide: 704 332 2473

South Dakota
Statewide: 605 773 6460
Black Hills: 605 584 4141

Tennessee
Statewide: 615 356 7636
Chattanooga: 423 843 2822

Texas
Statewide: 713 964 5867
Abilene: 915 691 8981
Austin: 512 926 8751
Corpus Christi: 512 265 0377
Lubbock: 806 797 6690
Dallas-Ft. Worth (Northcentral): 817 329 1270
Northeast: 903 234 2473
Lower Rio Grande Valley: 210 308 6788
San Antonio: 210 733 8306
Waco (Central): 817 662 4390

Utah
Statewide: 801 538 4730

Vermont
Statewide: 802 457 2779

Virginia
Statewide: 757 238 2713

Washington
Statewide: 206 933 1831; (reporting 206)
454 2662
Southeastern: 208 882 6195
Lower Columbia Basin: 509 943 6957

West Virginia
Statewide: 304 736 3086

Wisconsin
Statewide: 414 352 3857
Madison: 608 255 2476
Northeast (Green Bay): 414 434 4207

Wyoming
Statewide: 307 265 2473

The World

Australia
Birdline NSW 02 +61 9439 9536
Birdline VIC +61 03 9882 2390
Canberra +61 02 6247 5530
Queensland +61 07 3283 4921

Belgium
Birdline—03 4880194—international code 0032

Denmark
Birdline—90 232400

England
InterBirdNet Rarities Update
0891 700 222, Birdline National
0891 700 249, Birdline Northwest
0891 700 246, Birdline Northeast
0891 700 247, Birdline Midlands
09068 700 245, Birdline East Anglia
0891 700 240, Birdline Southeast
0891 700 241, Birdline Southwest
0891 700 243, Birdline Scilly

France
Regional Birdlines:
+ CORA / Rhône-Alpes / 04 76 00 04 47
+ CORIF / Ile-de-France / 01 49 84 07 90
+ GNFC / Franche-Comté / 03 81 61 00 81
+ LPO Alsace / Alsace / 03 89 81 05 34
+ LPO Aquitaine / Aquitaine / 05 56 97 80 33
+ LPO Champagne Ardenne / Aubois lakes / 03 25 80 45 61
+ LPO-Maison de l'Oiseau / Champagne-Ardenne / 03 26 72 51 39
+ LPO 44 / Loire Atlantique-Vendée / 02 51 62 07 93
+ LPO Lorraine / Lorraine / 03 83 23 31 47
+ SEPOL / Limousin / 05 55 34 12 48

Ireland
Info Line Northern Ireland: 0891 700 800
Info Line: 1550 111 700 (Republic of Ireland only).

Netherlands
Birding Birdline (0900 20 321 28)

Norway
Norway Birdline 820 55050

Scotland
Birdline Scotland 0891 700234

Sweden
Swedish Birdline 071 268300

Wales
Birdline Wales 0891 700248
Birdline Northwest 0891 700249

For continual updates on hotline numbers, consult www.fatbirder.com, www.birding.com, American Birding Association, or Royal Society for the Protection of Birds

Government Organizations

North America

The North American Breeding Bird Survey
Keith Pardreck, USGS Patuxent Wildlife Research Center
12100 Beech Forest Rd., Laurel, MD 20708-4038
Tel: 301 497 5843
E-mail: Keith_Pardreck@usgs.gov
http://www.mp2-pwrc.usgs.gov/bbs/index.html

Partners in Flight
E-mail: terry_rich@fws.gov
http://www.partnersinflight.org/

United States Fish and Wildlife Service
E-mail: contact@fws.gov
http://www.fws.gov/

U.S. Geological Survey's Biological Resources Division
USGS National Center
12201 Sunrise Valley Dr., Reston VA 20192
Tel: 703 648 4000
E-mail: biologywebteam@usgs.gov
http://biology.usgs.gov/

Office of Migratory Bird Management
E-mail: migratorybirds@fws.gov
http://migratorybirds.fws.gov/

National Wildlife Refuge System
1010 Wisconsin Ave., NW, Suite 200
Washington, DC 20007
Tel: 202 333 9075 or 877 396 NWRA
E-mail: nwra@refugenet.org
http://www.refugenet.org/

Environment Canada Atlantic
45 Alderney Dr., Dartmouth, NS B2Y 2N6
E-mail: 15th.reception@ec.gc.ca
http://www.ns.ec.gc.ca/index_e.html

Environment Canada
Inquiry Center, 351 Joseph Boulevard
Hull, QC K1A 0H3
Tel: 819 997 2800 or 1 800 668 6767
E-mail: enviroinfo@ec.gc.ca
http://www.ec.gc.ca/

The Canadian Wildlife Service
Canadian Wildlife Service, Environment Canada, Ottawa, Ontario K1A 0H3
Tel: 819 997 1095
E-mail: cws-scf@ec.gc.ca
http://www.cws-scf.ec.gc.ca/index_e.cfm

U.S. Fish and Wildlife Service Migratory Bird Offices

Alaska Region
U.S. Fish and Wildlife Service
1011 E. Tudor Rd., Room 135
Anchorage, AK 99503
Tel: 907 786 3909
E-mail: chuck_young@fws.gov
http://alaska.fws.gov/mbm/index.html

Great Lakes-Big River Region
U.S. Fish and Wildlife Service
Box 45, Federal Bldg.
Ft. Snelling MN 55111-0045
Tel: 612 713 5458
http://midwest.fws.gov/midwestbird/

Mountain-Prairie Region
U.S. Fish and Wildlife Service
Denver Federal Center
P.O. Box 25486, Denver 80225
Tel: 303 236 8155
E-mail: MountainPrairie@fws.gov
http://mountain-prairie.fws.gov/birds/

Northeast Region
Migratory Birds and State Programs, Region 5
300 Westgate Center Dr., Hadley MA 01035
Tel: 413 253 8643
E-mail: northeastmigratorybirds@fws.gov
http://northeast.fws.gov/migratorybirds/

Pacific Region
U.S. Fish and Wildlife Service
911 N.E. 11th Avenue, Portland OR 97232
Tel: 503 231 6164
E-mail: Pacific_Birds@r1.fws.gov
http://migratorybirds.pacific.fws.gov/

Southeast Region
U.S. Fish and Wildlife Service
1875 Century Blvd., Suite 240, Atlanta GA
30345-3319
Tel: 404 679 7189
http://southeast.fws.gov/birds

Southwest Region
U.S. Fish and Wildlife Service
500 Gold Ave. SW, Alburquerque NM 87102
Tel: 505 248 6911
http://southwest.fws.gov/

United Kingdom

Countryside Agency
http://www.countryside.gov.uk/

Countryside Council for Wales
http://www.ccw.gov.uk

Department of the Environment for Northern Ireland
Environment and Heritage Service
Calvert House, High Street, Belfast BT
E-mail: press.office@doeni.gov.uk
http://www.doeni.gov.uk/

English Nature
Northminster House, Peterborough PE1 1UA
Tel: +44 01733 455000
E-mail: enquiries@english-nature.org.uk
http://www.english-nature.org.uk

Scottish Natural Heritage
12 Hope Terrace, Edinburgh, EH9 2AS
Tel: +44 0 131 447 4784
http://213.121.208.4/

Bird Journals and Magazines

Africa

Africa Birds and Birding
Freeport No CB0566
P.O. Box 44223
Claremont 7735
Cape Town, South Africa
Tel: 27 21 686 9001
E-mail: wildmags@iafrica.com

Afropavo
The Demographic Republic of Congo Birding
Association
c/o Tommy Pedersen, Havreveren 28, N-0680
Oslo, Norway
E-mail: stingray@online.ca

Babbler
BirdLife Botswana
Private Bag 00300
Gaborone, Botswana
E-mail: blb@birdlifebotswana.org.bw
http://www.birdlifebotswana.org.bw

Bulletin African Bird Club
c/o BirdLife International
Wellbrook Court
Girton Road
Cambridge UK CB3 0NA

Honeyguide
The Ornithological Association of Zimbabwe
OAZ, P.O. Box CY 161
Causeway, Harare
Zimbabwe
http://www.uq.edu.au/~anpwooda/pages/
oaz-z.html

Kenya Birds
Joint Publication of Dept. of Ornithology
National Museums of Kenya and Birdlife Kenya
Dr. L.A. Bennun, Dept. of Ornithology, National
Museums of Kenya, Box 40658, Nairobi, Kenya
Tel: 254 20 3742131 ext. 2421243
E-mail: KBIRDS@AFRICAONLINE.CO.KE

Malimbus
West African Ornithological Society
c/o Gérard Morel
1 route de Sallenelles
14860 Bréville-les-Monts, France
E-mail: gmore@mail.cpod.fr
http://www.malimbus.free.fr/members.htm

Marine Ornithology (formerly Cormorant)
http://www.marineornithology.org/

Scopus
Ornithological Sub-Committee of the East
Africa Natural History Society
G.C. Backhurst, Box 15194, Nairobi, Kenya
Tel: +254 2 7
E-mail: Graeme@ken.healthnet.org

Vulture News
Editor, Mark D. Anderson, Dept. of Agriculture
Land Reform, Environment and Conservation
Private Bag X5018, Kimberly 8300, S. Africa
Tel: +27 0 53 8420883
E-mail: manderson@grand.ncape.gov.za
http://www.ewt.org.za/working_groups.htm

Ostrich
BirdLife South Africa
P.O. Box 515
Randburg 2125
South Africa
Tel: +27 0 11 789 1122
Fax: +27 0 11 789 5188
E-mail: info@birdlife.org.za
http://www.inasp.org.uk/ajol/journals/ostrich

Australasia

Australian Field Ornithology
Bird Observers' Club of Australia
P.O. Box 185
Nunawading, Victoria 3131
Tel: 03 9877 5342
E-mail: information@birdobservers.org.au

Corella
Australian Bird Study Association Inc.
P.O. Box A313, Sydney South NSW 1235
E-mail: corella@absa.asn.au
http://www.absa.asn.au/corella.html

The Emu
Royal Australasian Ornithologists Union (RAOU)
415 Riversdale Road, Hawthorn East, VIC 3123
Australia
Tel: +61 3 9882 2622
E-mail: mail@birdsaustralia.com.au
http://www.publish.csiro.au/journals/emu/

Flightlines
Australian Bird and Bat Banding Scheme
Australian Nature Conservation Agency
GPO Box 8, Canberra, Act 2601
Tel: 02 62742407
E-mail: abbbs@ea.gov.au
http://www.ea.gov.au/biodiversity/science/abbbs/

Interpretive Birding Bulletin
P.O. Box 883, Cooroy QLD 4563 Australia
Tel: +7 5442 7274
http://www.ibirding.com

Journal of New Zealand Birds
New Zealand Birds
P.O. Box 744, Whakatane NZ
Tel: 64 07 312 5711
E-mail: narena@nzbirds.com
http://nzbirds.com/NZBirdsJournalCurrent.html

Notornis (Journal of the Ornithological Society
of New Zealand)
Editor: Murray Williams
P.O. Box 12397, Wellington
E-mail: mwilliams@doc.govt.nz

South Australian Ornithologist
c/o South Australian Museum
North Tee
Adelaide SA 5000
Australia
E-mail: horton.philippa@saugov.sa.gov.au

Southern Bird
Editor: Nick Allen
65 Allin Drive, Waikuku Beach
North Canterbury
Tel: 03 312 7183
E-mail: nick_allen@xtra.ca.nz

The Stilt
Australasian Wader Studies Group, Royal
Australasian Ornithologists Union (RAOU)
415 Riverdale Road, Hawthorn East, VIC 3123
Australia
http://www.tasweb.com.au/awsg/stilt/
stilt-00.htm

Wingspan
Royal Australasian Ornithologists Union (RAOU)
415 Riverdale Road, Hawthorn East, VIC 3123
Australia
Tel: +61 3 9882 2622
http://www.birdsaustralia.com.au/wingspan.html

Europe

BELGIUM
AVES—Contact
Secretariat Aves
Maison Liegeoise de L' Environnement
Rue Fusch 3, 4000 Liège
Tel: 04 250 95 90
http://www.aves.be/menudiff.htm

Bulletin Aves
Secretariat Aves
Maison Liegeoise de L' Environnement
Rue Fusch 3, 4000 Liège
Tel: 04 250 95 90
http://www.aves.be/menudiff.htm

Europe (Cont'd)

Bird Census News
European Bird Census Council
Anny Anselin, Institute of Nature Conservation
Kliniekstraat 25, B-1070, Brussels, Belgium
Tel: +32 2 558 18 26
E-mail: anny.anselin@instnat.be
http://zeus.nyf.hu/~szept/Bcncont.htm

L'Homme et L'oiseau
E-mail: protection.oiseaux@birdprotection.be
http://www.protectiondesoiseaux.be/

CZECH REPUBLIC
Buteo
Working Groups on Protection & Research of
Birds of Prey & Owls
Czech Society for Ornithology
Hornomech olupska 34, CZ-10200
Praha 10, Czech Republic
E-mail: cso@birdlife.cz
http://chkot.envi.cz/buteo_en.html

DENMARK
Dansk Ornithologisk ForeningsTidsskrift
Dansk Ornitologisk Foreng (Danish
Ornithological Society)
DOF: Vesterbrogade 140 DK1620 Kbh.v 331
4404
http://www.dof.dk/

Sylvia
Eeská spoleènost ornitologická
Hornomìchoupská 34
102 00 Praha 10-Hostivao
Czech Republic
Tel: 02 74866700
E-mail: cso@birdlife.cz

ESTONIA
Hirundo
Estonian Ornithological Society
P.O. Box 227, Veski St. 4, Tartu, Estonia
Tel: +372 7 422 195
E-mail: eoy@eoy.ee
http://www.loodus.ee/hirundo/English/

FINLAND
Alula
Eestinkallionte 16D, FIN-02280, Espoo, Finland
Tel: +358 9 803 6330
Mobile: +358 40 5063544
E-mail: antero.top@alula.fi
http://www.alula.fi

Aureola
The Ornithological Society of Northern
Ostrobotnia, Aureola, PL 388, 90101, Oulu
Finland
E-mail: teskelin@paju.oulu.fi

Ornis Fennica
The Finnish Ornithological Society, POB 17
(P. Rautatiekatu 13), FIN-00014, Helsinki
Finland
Tel: +358 8 5531 214
E-mail: esa.lammie@kolumbus.fi
luttp://www.tmnh/helsinki.fi/users/sly/en/
ornisfennica/default.htm

FRANCE
Alauda
Alauda-SEOF, MNHN, Laboratoire d' Ecologie
4 Ave. du Petit Chateau, F-91800 Brunoy
E-mail: quetzalcom@libertysurf.fr
http://www.mnhn.fr/assoc/seof/revue.htm

Le Bièvre
Centro Ornithologique Rhône-Alpes
Maison Rhodanienne de L' Environment
32 rue Ste-Helene, 69002, Lyon
Tel: 04 72 77 1984
E-mail: cora@worldnet.fr

Ornithos
Ligue pour la Protection des Oiseaux (LPO)
rue des Champs des Gardes, F-34230
Vendemian, France
Tel: +33 467 967 790
E-mail: duquet@club-internet.fr

Vivre Avec Les Oiseaux
Europeenne de Magazines, 44 ave. George V
75008, Paris, France
http://www.info-presse.fr/fiches/vivre-avec-
oiseaux_1572_gp.htm

GERMANY
Corax
Ornithologischen Arbeitgemeinshaft
http://www.ornithologie-schleswig-holstein.de

Der Falke
Das Journal für Vogelbeobachter
http://www.birdsnet.de/falke/fa-aktuell.htm

Europe (Cont'd)

Journal für ornithologie
c/o Institut fur Vogelforschung
Ander Vogelwarte 21, D-26386, Wilhelmshaven
Germany
Tel: +49 4423 914148
E-mail: geschaeftsstelle@do-g.de
http://www.blackwell.de/jo_e.htm

Ornithologische Jahresberichte Helgoland
Ornithologishe Arbeitsgemeinschaft
Helgoland, Postfach 869, 27498 Helgoland
Tel: FRG 0 47251338
E-mail: 047251339.0001@t-online.de

De Vogelwarte
c/o Institut fur Vogelforschung
Ander Vogelwarte 21, D-26386, Wilhelmshaven
Germany
Tel: +49 4423 914148
E-mail: geschaeftsstelle@do-g.de
http://www.blackwell.de/jo_e.htm

Die Vogelwelt
German Ornithologists' Society
Birdnet.de
http://www.birdnet.de/Vogelwelt/vw-aktuell.htm

HUNGARY

Aquila
Hungarian Institute of Ornithology
c/o Hungarian Natural History Museum
Baross u. 13, H-1088
Budapest, Hungary

Túzok
Journal of BirdLife Hungary
http://www.madartavlat.hu

ITALY

Avocetta
Journal of the Italian Center of Ornithological
Studies
Editors, c/o Dipartimento di Biologia
Animale e delli'Uomo, Universita degli Studi di
Torino, Via Accademia, Albertina 17-1-10123
Torino
http://www.unipv.it/webbio/ciso/avox.htm

Rivista Italiana di Ornithologia
Societa Italiana di Scienze Naturali
Corso Venezia, 55 20121, Milano
Tel: 02 79 59 65
E-mail: info@scienzenaturali.org

THE NETHERLANDS

Atlantic Seabirds
C.J. Camphuysen (NZG)
Ankerstraat 20
1794 BJ Oosterend, Texel
The Netherlands
Tel: +31 222 3186744
E-mail: kees.camphuysen@wxs.nl

Ardea
Netherlands Ornithologists Union (NOU)
P. Starmans, NOU, Oude Arnhemseweg 261
3705 BD Zeist
http://www.nioz.nl/en/deps/mee/ardea/
homepage.htm

Dutch Birding
P.O. Box 116, 2080 AC Santpoort-Zuid
The Netherlands
Tel: +31 23 5376749
E-mail: editors@dutchbirding.nl
http://www.dutchbirding.nl/

Sula
Dutch Seabird Group/Nedelandse Zeevogelgroep
(NZG)
P.O. Box 59, 1790 AB Den Burg, Texel
The Netherlands
Tel: +31.2223.69488
E-mail: camphuys@nioz.nl

NORWAY

Utsira Bird Observatory's Yearbook
Utsira Bird Observatory, Bjorn O. Tveit
Postboks 23, 5515 Utsira, Norway
E-mail: bjorn.tveit@gyldendal.no
http://home.sol.no/bhoeylan/utsira/e_start.html

POLAND

Acta Ornithologica
Museum and Institute of Zoology
Wilcza 64, PL-00-679, Warszawa, Poland
Tel: 4822 6293221
http://www.miiz.waw.pl/

The Ring
Bird Migration Research Station
University of Gdansk, Przebendowo, 84-210
Choczewo, Poland
Tel: +48 58 723315
E-mail: biopb@univ.gda.pl

Europe (Cont'd)

PORTUGAL
Pardela
The Portuguese Society for the Study of Birds
(SPEA)
Rua da Victoria, 53, 2-Dto, 1100 Lisboa, Portugal
Tel: +351 1 3431847

SPAIN
Ardeola
Sociedad Espanola de Ornitologia
C/Melquiades Biencinto 34, 28053, Madrid
Tel: (+34) 91 434 0910
E-mail: seo@seo.org
http://www.seo.org/infoseo.asp

Butlleti del Grup Catala d'Anellament
(Catalan Ringers Group Bulletin) Grup Catala
d'Anellament
Museu de Zoologia, P.O. Box 593, E-08080
Barcelona, Spain
E-mail: gca.gca@suport.org
http://www.terra.es/personal/gca.gca/
butgca15.htm

Cyanopsitta
Loro Parque Fundacion, Spain
http://www.darwin.bio.uci.edu/~sustain/bio65/
lec15/spix.html

El Escribano Digital
Sociedad Espanola de Ornitologia
C/Melquiades Biencinto 34, 28053, Madrid
Tel: +34 91 434 0910
E-mail: escribano-digital@seo.org
http://www.seo.org/infoseo.asp

L'Anuari d'Ornitologia de Catalunya
(Catalan Ringers Group Bulletin)
Grup Catala d'Anellament
Museu de Zoologia, P.O. Box 593, E-08080
Barcelona, Spain
E-mail: gca.gca@suport.org
http://www.terra.es/personal/gca.gca/proj2.htm

La Garcilla
Sociedad Espanola de Ornitologia
C/Melquiades Biencinto 34, 28053, Madrid
Tel: +34 91 434 0910
E-mail: seo@seo.org
http://www.seo.org/LaGarciIla.asp

La Revista de Anillamiento
(Catalan Ringers Group Bulletin) Grup Catala
d'Anellament
Museu de Zoologia, P.O. Box 593, E-08080
Barcelona, Spain
E-mail: gca.gca@suport.org
http://www.terra.es/personal/gca.gca/revani05.
htm

Revista de Anillamiento
Sociedad Espanola de Ornitologia
C/Melquiades Biencinto 34, 28053, Madrid
Tel: +34 91 434 0910
E-mail: seo@seo.org
http://www.seo.org/RevistadeAnillamiento.asp

SWEDEN
Anser
Skanes Ornitologiska Forening
Box 96, 22100 Lund
Tel: 046 14 66 08
E-mail: birds@skof.se
http://www.skof.se/anser/anser.htm

**Cinclus Scandinavicus (The International
Magazine about the Dipper)**
Texasgatan 5, SE-593 41 Vastervik
Tel: +46 0 11121682
E-mail: juhani.vuorinen@facere.se
http://www.torget.se/users/c/cinclus/Csinfo.htm

Faglar I Norrbotten
Norrbottens Ornitologiska Forening
Box 193, S-971 06 LULEAA, Sweden
Tel: +46 92047481
E-mail: TGN@on.mobile.telia.se

Faglar I Norrkopingstrakten
Fagelforeningen I Norrkoping
Juhani Vuorinen, Bergslagsgatan 37, SE-602 18
Norrkoping
E-mail: juhani.vuorinen@facere.se
http://www.torget.se/users/c/cinclus/finkinfo.
htm

Journal of Avian Biology
Scandinavian Ornithologists' Union
Dr. Roland Sandberg. Dept. of Ecology
Lund University, Ecology Building, SE-223 62
Lund, Sweden
Tel: +46 46 2223793
E-mail: JAB@ekol.lu.se
http://www.oikos.ekol.lu.se/JAB.jrnl.html

Europe (Cont'd)

Oikos
Dr. Pehr H. Enckell, Dept. of Ecology, Lund
University, Ecology Building, S-223 62 Lund
Sweden
Tel: +46 46 2223793
E-mail: Oikos@ekol.lu.se
http://oikos.ekol.lu.se/Oikos.jrnl.html

Ornis Svecica
Soren Svensson, Ekologihuset 22362 Lund,
Sweden
http://www.sofnet.org/index.asp?lev=116&typ=1

Svenska fageltidskriftspaketet
SOF/Juhani Vuorinen, Bergslagsgatan 37, SE-602
18 Norrkoping
Tel: +46 0 11 121682
E-mail: juhani.vuorinen@facere.se
http://www.torget.se/users/c/cinclus/svftpinfo.htm

Var Fagelvarld
Swedish Ornithological Society
Box 7006, 300 07, Halmstad
Tel: 035 37453
E-mail: anders.w@ornitologerna.se
http://www.sofnet.org/index.asp?lev=299&typ=1

SWITZERLAND
Avian Science
Journal of the European Ornithologists Union
C/o Elisabeth Wiprachtiger, Swiss Ornithological
Institute CH-6204 Sempach, Switzerland
E-mail: eou@bluewin.ch
http://www.eao.at/publ.html

Nos Oiseaux
La Société Romande pour L'étude et la protec-
tion des oiseaux
Claude Guex, rue des Eaux-Vives 78
CH-1207 Geneva, Switzerland

Ornis
BirdLife Suisse
Daniela Pauli and Stefan Bachmann
Tel: 01 463 72 71
E-mail: ornis@birdlife.ch

TURKEY
Yelkovan
Ornithological Journal of Turkey
http://erciyes.edu.tr/Yelkovan/OJT/
yelkovan-ojt.html

UKRAINE
Berkut (Ukrainian Journal of Ornithology
Dr. Vitaly Grishchenko, Kaniv Nature Reserve
19000 Kaniv, Ukraine
E-mail: vitaly@aquila.freenet.kiev.ua
http://www.geocities.com/berkut_ua/berkut.htm

Branta
The Azov-Black Sea Ornithological Station
Melitopol, Lenin Str., 20
Zaporizhzhya Region, Ukraine 72312
Tel: 06192 67305
E-mail: station@melitopol.net
http://ornitology.narod.ru/english/index.html

UNITED KINGDOM
Avian Pathology
Carfax Publishing Co.
Dr. L.N. Pavne., Institute for Animal Health
Compton Laboratory, Compton Newbury, Berks
RG16 0NN, England
http://bioline.bdt.org.br/ap

Bird Conservation International
Cambridge University Press, on behalf of
BirdLife International
Tel: +44 0 1223 326070
http://uk.cambridge.org/journals/bci/

Birding World
Stonerunner, Coast Road, Cley-next the Sea
Holt, Norfolk
NR25 7RY
E-mail: sales@birdingworld.co.uk
http://www.birdingworld.co.uk

Bird Study (Journal of the British Trust for
Ornithology)
British Trust for Ornithology, National Centre
for Ornithology
The Nunnery, Nunnery Place, Thetford, Norfolk
IP24 2PU
Tel: +44 0 1842 750050
E-mail: info@bto.org
http://www.bto.org/membership/birdstudy.htm

Bird Watching
Bretton Court
Bretton, Peterborough PE3 8DZ
Tel: 01733 264 666
E-mail: david.cromack@emap.com

Europe (Cont'd)

British Birds
The Banks, Mountfield, Roberts Bridge
East Sussex
TN32 5JY
Tel: +44 0 1580 882039
http://www.britishbirds.co.uk/

Birdwatch Magazine
Tel: 020 7704 9495
E-mail: editorial@birdwatch.co.uk
http://www.birdwatch.co.uk/

Bulletin of the British Ornithologist's Club
M.B. Casement, Dene Cottage
West Harding, Petersfield, Hants
GU31 5PA
E-mail: feare_wildwings@email.msn.com

Cotinga: The Journal of the Neotropical Bird Club
C/o The Lodge, Sandy, Bedfordshire
SG19 2DL
http://www.neotropicalbirdclub.org/cotinga/cotinga.html

The Ibis
BOU, c/o The Natural History Museum
Akeman St., Tring, Hertfordshire
HP23 6AP
Tel: 01442 890090
E-mail: bou@bou.org.uk
http://www.bou.org.uk/pubibis.html

Irish Birds
BirdWatch Ireland
Ruttledge House
8 Longford Place, Monkstown Co.
Dublin, Ireland
Tel: +353 1 402 2333
E-mail: bkavanagh@rcsi.ie
http://informatique.iol.ie:8080/IrishBirds/

The Magpie
Sheffield Bird Study Group, 4a Raven Road
Sheffield S7 1SB
E-mail: david.wood@sheffield.ac.uk
http://www.sbsg.org/

Peregrine
The Hawk and Owl Trust
The Corn Exchange
Baffins Lane
Chichester, West Sussex PO19 1GE
E-mail: bmh@mycenaedemon.co.uk

Ringing and Migration
British Trust for Ornithology, National Centre for Ornithology
The Nunnery, Nunnery Place, Thetford, Norfolk IP24 2PU
E-mail: m.hounsome@man.ac.uk

Scottish Bird Report
Scotland's Bird Club, Harbour Point
Newhailes Rd., Musselburgh EH21 6SJ
Tel: 0131 653 0653
E-mail: mail@the-soc.org,uk

Scottish Birds
Scotland's Bird Club, Harbour Point
Newhailes Rd., Musselburgh EH21 6SJ
Tel: 0131 653 0653
E-mail: mail@the-soc.org,uk

Waterbirds: The International Journal of Waterbird Biology
Ed. John C. Coulson, 29 St. Mary's Close
Shincliffe Village, Durham City, DH1 2ND
Tel: 44 0191 386 9107
E-mail: JohnCoulson1@compuserve.com

Wildfowl
The Wildfowl & Wetlands Trust
Slimbridge, Glos, GL2 7BT, England
Tel: 01453 891900
E-mail: info.slimbridge@wwt.org.uk
http://www.wwt.org.uk/

World Birdwatch
BirdLife International, Wellbrook Court
Girton Road, Cambridge CB3 0NA
Tel: +44 01223 277318
E-mail: howtohelp@birdlife.org

Asia and the Middle East

GENERAL

Falco
Middle Eastern Falcon Research Group
http://www.falcons.co.uk/MEFRG/

Forktail
Oriental Bird Club
P.O. Box 324
Bedford MK, MK42 0WG
E-mail: mail@orientalbirdclub.org
http://www.orientalbirdclub.org/publications/
forktail/index.html

OBC Bulletin
Oriental Bird Club
P.O. Box 324
Bedford MK, MK42 0WG
E-mail: mail@orientalbirdclub.org
http://www.orientalbirdclub.org/publications/
bulletin/index.html

RUSSIA
Avian Ecology and Behavior
Biological Station Rybachy, Rybachy 238535
Kaliningrad Region, Russia
E-mail: rybachy@bioryb.koenig.su
http://www.zin.ru/rybachy/journal.html

HONG KONG
Birds of Hong Kong
Geoff Carey, Flat 11D Block 3, Royal Ascot
Fo Tan, New Territories, Hong Kong
E-mail: gjc@netvigator.com

JAPAN
Strix
The Wild Bird Society of Japan
E-mail: koita@j-link.or.jp
http://www.j-link.or.jp/~kiota/stst14.html

Japanese Journal of Ornithology
Ornithological Society of Japan
Lab. of Biodiversity Science, School of
Agriculture and Life Sciences
University of Tokyo, 113-8657, Japan
Tel: +81 3 5841 7541
E-mail: osj@lagopus.com
http://www.soc.nii.ac.jp/osj/english/home_e.
html

**Journal of the Yamashina Institute for
Ornithology**
Bird Migration Research Center
Japan
Tel: +81 4 7182 1107
E-mail: banding@ceres.ocn.ne.jp

INDIA
**Journal of Indian Bird Records &
Conservation**
Harini Nature Conservation Foundation
E-mail: indianbirds@pritvi.com
http://www.angelfire.com/fl/indianbirds/

INDONESIA
Kukila
Bulletin of the Indonesian Ornithological
Society
http://www.pili.or.id/kukila/about.htm

ISRAEL
Israel Bird Ringing Center Newsletter
Israel Bird Ringing Center
155 Henzl Street
Te Aviv 86101 Israel
Tel: +972 2 6430111
E-mail: jshamoun@netmedia.net.il

Sandgrouse
Ornithological Society of the Middle East
C/o The Lodge, Sandy, Bedfordshire UK
SG19 2DL
E-mail: webmaster@osme.org
http://www.osme.org/index.html

North America

CANADA

Bird Trends
Judith Kennedy, Canadian Wildlife Service
Environment Canada
Ottawa, ON K1A 0H3
E-mail: Judith.Kennedy@ec.gc.ca
http://www.cws-scf.ec.gc.ca/birds/
news/index_e.cfm

Birder's Journal
701 Rossland Rd. East, Suite 393
Whitby, ON L1N 9K3
http://www.birdersjournal.com/HomePage.htm

Canadian IBA News
Canadian Nature Federation
1 Nicholas Street, Suite 606
Ottawa, ON K1N 7B7
Tel: 613 562 3447
E-mail: cchute@cnf.ca or cnf@cnf.ca
http://www.cnf.ca/bird/birds_news.html

Harmonies d'Oiseaux
Harmonies d'Oiseaux
573, 2ieme Rue, Suite 2
Laval, QC H7V 1H5
E-mail: glauz@total.net
http://www.total.net/~glauz/harmonies

L'Hirondelle
Association des Amateurs d'Hirondelles du
Quebec
1335 Chemin Bord-du-Lac
Dorval QC, H9S 2E5
Tel: 514 633 4000
http://132.204.160.212/~dcampbel/aahq/

OFO News
Ontario Field Ornithologists
Box 62014 Burlington Mall Postal Outlet
Burlington ON L7R 4K2
E-mail: ofo@ofa.ca
http://www.ofo.ca

Ontario Birds
Ontario Field Ornithologists
Box 62014 Burlington Mall Postal Outlet
Burlington ON L7R 4K2
E-mail: ofo@ofa.ca
http://www.ofo.ca

Picoides
Society of Canadian Ornithologists
c/o A.J. Erskine, Editor, Picoides
Canadian Wildlife Service
P.O. Box 1590
Sackville, NB E0A 3C0
Tel: 506 364 5035
http://www.nmnh.si.edu/BIRDNET/SocCanOrn/

Quebec Oiseaux
1251 rue Rachel Est.
Montreal QC H2J 2J9
E-mail: quebecoiseaux@aqgo.qc.ca
http://www.quebecoiseaux.qc.ca/

The Song Sparrow
Province of Quebec Society for the
Protection of Birds
P.O. Box 43, Station B
Montreal, QC H3B 3J5
Tel: 514 637 2141
E-mail: membership@pqspb.org
http://www.pqspb.org

Yukon Warbler
Box 31054
Whitehorse YT Y1A 5P7
http://www.yukonweb.com/community/ybc/

UNITED STATES

Alabama Birdlife
Alabama Ornithological Society
Dept. of Biology
University of North Alabama
Florence, AL 35632-0001

American Birds
National Audubon Society
700 Broadway, New York NY 10003
Tel: 212 979 3000

Audubon Magazine
National Audubon Society
700 Broadway, New York NY 10003
Tel: 212 979 3000
E-mail: editor@audubon.org
http://magazine.audubon.org/

The Auk
Dept. of Biological Sciences, Science and
Engineering 622
University of Arkansas, Fayetteville AR 72701
Tel: 479 575 4683
E-mail: auk@uark.edu
http://www.aou.org/aou/auk.html

North America (Cont'd)

Bird Behavior
David B. Miller, Department of Psychology
University of Connecticut, 406 Babbidge Road
U-20, Storrs, CT 06269-1020
E-mail: MILLERD@UCONNVM.UCONN.EDU
http://www.ucc.uconn.edu/~millerd/bbframes.
html

Bird Conservation
American Bird Conservancy
P.O. Box 249
The Plains, VA 20198
Tel: 540 253 5780
http://www.abcbirds.org

Bird Observer (The New England Birding
Journal)
P.O. Box 236, Arlington MA 02476-0003
E-mail: cmarsh@jocama.com
http://massbird.org/birdobserver/Default.htm

Bird Populations
The Institute for Bird Populations
P.O. Box 1346, 11435 S.R. #1, Suite 23
Point Reyes Station, CA 94956

BirdWatcher's Digest
P.O. Box 110, Marietta OH 45750
Tel: 1 800 879 2473
E-mail: bwd@birdwatchersdigest.com
http://www.birdwatchersdigest.com

Birder's World
Kalmbach Publishing Co.
21027 Crossroads Circle
Waukesha, WI 53186-4055
Postal: P.O. Box 1612, Waukesha WI 53187-1612
E-mail: kkammeraad@birdersworld.com
http://www.birdersworld.com

Birding
American Birding Association, Inc.
P.O. Box 6599, Colorado Spring, CO 80934
Tel: 719 578 9703
E-mail: member@aba.org
http://americanbirding.org/publications/bdggen.
htm

Birding Business
Longdown Management, Inc.
15 Forest Road
Hancock, NH 03449
Tel: 603 525 3803
E-mail: bdwatch@aol.com
http://www.birdwatchamerica.com

Birds and Blooms
P.O. Box 5359
Harlon IA 51593-0859
Tel: 1 800 344 6913

Birdscapes
US Fish and Wildlife Service and Canadian
Wildlife Service
Division of Bird Habitat Conservation
4401 North Fairfax Drive, Mailstop MBSP 4075
Arlington, Virginia 22203
Tel: 703 358 1784
E-mail: Jamie_j_coster-barringtonbutler@fws.gov
http://training.fws.gov/library/Birdscapes/
birdindex.htm

BirdScope
Cornell Laboratory of Ornithology
159 Sapsucker Woods Road
Ithaca, NY 14850-1999
Tel: 607 254 2473
E-mail: clomembership@ cornell.edu
http://www.birds.cornell.edu

Bluebird
North American Bluebird Society
The Wilderness Center
P.O. Box 244, Wilmot OH 44689-0244
Tel: 330 359 5511
http://www.media.nabluebirdsociety.org/blue-
bird_journal.htm

The Bluebird
The Audubon Society of Missouri
3867 Highway K, Shelbyville, MO 63469
Tel: 573 633 2628
E-mail: saxman@marktwain.net

The Bobolink
Holmes Area Birding Society
8918 C.R. 77
Fredericksburg, OH 44627
E-mail: bhglick@valkyrie.net

Colorado Birds
P.O. Box 481, Lyons CO 80540
Tel: 303 458 4802
E-mail: editor@cfo-link.org
http://www.cfo-link.org/leadpage.html

North America (Cont'd)

Colorado Birds
Colorado Field Ornithologists
c/o Doug Faulkner
6035 Parfet St.
Arvado, CO 80004
E-mail: editor@cfo-link.org
http://www.cfo-link.org/jounal.html

The Condor
Cooper Ornithological Society
Editor, David S. Dobkin
E-mail: dobkin@hderi.org
http://www.cooper.org

The Connecticut Warbler
Connecticut Ornithological Association
314 Unquowa Road
Fairfield, CT 06430
Tel: 860 658 5670
E-mail: CTWarbler@cs.com
http://www.ctbirding.org

Ducks Unlimited Magazine
1 Waterfowl Way, Memphis TN 38120
Tel: 901 758 3825
http://www.ducks.org/media/magazine/

Grus Americana
Whooping Crane Conservation Association
110 Wildwoods Lane
Lawrenceburg, TN 38464-6773
http://www.whoopingcrane.com

Guide
The Roger Tory Peterson Institute of Natural
History
311 Curtis Street
Jamestown, NY 14701-9629
http://www.rtpi.org

Hawk Chalk
North American Falconers' Association
6133 Belle Grove Drive
Baton Rouge, LA 70820

The Indiana Audubon Quarterly
901 Maplewood Dr.
New Castle, IN 47362-5255
Tel: 765 597 2459

Interpretive Birding Bulletin
1800 11th Ave. SE
St. Cloud MN 56304
Tel: 320 252 3909
http://www.ibirding.com

Journal of Field Ornithology
Association of Field Ornithologists
Dept. of Biological Sciences, University of Tulsa
Tulsa OK 74104-3189
http://www.afonet.org/english/journal.html

The Journal of Oregon Ornithology
P.O.Box 1467
Newport, Oregon 97365
http://www.orednet.org/~rbayer/j/joomenu.htm

The Journal of Raptor Research
Raptor Research Foundation Inc.
Carpenter Nature Center
12805 St. Croix Valley, Hastings MN 55033
E-mail: jim@carpenternaturecenter.org
http://biology.boisestate.edu/raptor/jrrcont.htm

The Kingbird
Federation of New York State Bird Clubs
c/o Emanuel Levine
585 Mead Terrace
South Terrace, NY 11550

The Kentucky Warbler
8207 Old Westport Road
Louisville, KY 40222-3913
http://www.biology.eku/kos.htm

La Tangara
Partners in Flight
Merrie Morrison, Managing Editor
Tel: 1 888 BIRD MAG
E-mail: mmorr@abcbirds.org
http://www.partnersinflight.org/pubs/
magnews.htm

Living Bird
Cornell Lab of Ornithology
159 Sapsucker Woods Rd.
Ithaca NY 14850
Tel: 1 800 843 BIRD
E-mail: cornellbirds@cornell.edu
http://birds.cornell.edu/publications/livingbird

The Loon/Minnesota Birding
The Minnesota Ornithologists' Union
J.F. Bell Museum of Natural History
University of Minnesota
10 Church St. Southeast
Minneapolis, MN 55455-0104
E-mail: mou@cbs,umn.edu
http://www.cbs.umn.edu/~mou

North America (Cont'd)

Maryland Birdlife
Maryland Ornithological Society
Cylburn Mansian, 4915 Greenspring Ave.
Baltimore MD 21209
Tel: 1 800 823 0050
http://www.mdbirds.org/publications/
birdlife.html

Meadowlark
Illinois Ornithological Society
P.O. Box 931, Lake Forest IL 60045
E-mail: meadowlark@illinoisbirds.org
http://www.illinoisbirds.org/meadowlark.html

The Migrant
Tennessee Ornithological Society
P.O. Box 198704
Nashville, TN 37219-8704
E-mail: treasurer@tnbirds.org
http://www.tnbirds.org/migrant.htm

NAFA Journal
North American Falconers' Association
Tel: 719 495 4506
E-mail: NAFAJournal@hotmail.com

Nature Society News
Nature Society
Purple Martin Junction, Griggsville IL 62340
E-mail: membership@naturesociety.org
http://www.naturesociety.org/news.html

The Nebraska Bird Review
Nebraska Ornithologists' Union
3745 Garfield
Lincoln, NE 68506-1028
E-mail: silcock@sidney.heartland.net
http://www.rip.physics.unk.edu/NOU/

North American Bird Bander
Inland Bird Banding Association
P.O. Box 832, Tiffin OH 44883
http://aves.net/InlandBBA/ibba-3.htm#2

North American Birds
American Birding Association
P.O. Box 6599, Colorado Springs CO 80934
Tel: 719 578 9703
E-mail: member@aba.org
http://americanbirding.org/publications/
nabgen.htm

Ohio Birds & Natural History
18722 Newell St., Floor 2
Shaker Hts., OH 44122
Tel: 877 411 0972
http://www.aves.net/magazine/

The Ohio Cardinal
c/o Edwin Pierce
2338 Harrington Road
Akron, OH 44319
E-mail: danielel@iwaynet.net

Oregon Birds
P.O. Box 10373
Eugene, OR 97440
http://www.oregonbirds.org

Ornithological Monographs
American Ornithologists' Union
Buteo Books: 3130 Laurel Rd.
Shipman VA, 22971
Tel: 1 800 722 2460
E-mail: allen@buteobooks.com
http://www.aou.org/aou/pubs.html#monographs

Ornithological Newsletter
Ornithological Societies of North America
Joyce Lancaster, Executive Director
OSNA
P.O. Box 1897
Lawrence, KS 66044
Tel: 1 800 627 0629 ext. 250
Fax 1 785 843 1274.
E-mail: osna@allenpress.com
http://www.birds.cornell.edu/osna/ornnews.html

Pennsylvania Birds
Pennsylania Society for Ornithology
Tel: 610 696 0687
E-mail: nickpul@bellatlantic.net
http://www.pabirds.org

The Praire Falcon
Northern Flint Hills Audubon Society
P.O. Box 1932
Manhattan, KS 66505-1932
http://www.ksu.edu/audubon/falcon.html

Purple Martin Update
Purple Martin Conservation Association
Edinboro University of Pennsylvania
Edinboro, PA 16444
Tel: 814 734 4420
E-mail: pmca@edinboro.edu
http://www.purplemartin.org

North America (Cont'd)

South Dakota Bird Notes
South Dakota Ornithologists' Union
NSU Box 740
Aberdeen, SD 57401
E:mail: Tallmand@nothern.edu

Texas Birds
Texas Ornithological Society
PMB# 189
6338 N. New Braunfels Ave.
San Antonio, TX 78209
E-mail: magazine@texasbirds.org
http://www.texasbirds.org/texas_birds/html

Utah Birds
Utah Ornithological Society
P.O.Box 1042
Cedar City, UT
84721-1042
http://www.netutah.com/uos/journal/htm

Waterbirds Journal
The Waterbirds Society
http://www.nmnh.si.edu/BIRDNET/cws

Western Birds
Western Field Ornithologists, Philip Unitt
San Diego Natural History Museum
P.O. Box 12390, San Diego CA 92112-1390
E-mail: birds@sdnhm.org
http://www.wfo-cbrc.org/

Wildbird
P.O. Box 52898
Boulder CO 80322-2898
Tel: 1 800 365 4421

Winging It
American Birding Association, Inc
P.O. Box 6599
Colorado Springs, CO 80934
Tel: 508 696 9359
E-mail: winging@aba.org

Wilson Bulletin
Wilson Ornithological Society
Museum of Zoology, University of Michigan
Ann Arbor MI 48109-1079
http://www.ummz.lsa umich.cdu/birds/
wilsonbull.html

Wings Over the Prairie
Illinois Ornithological Society
P.O. Box 931, Lake Forest IL 60045
E-mail: meadowlark@illinoisbirds.org
http://www.illinoisbirds.org/

The Yellowthroat
Maryland Ornithological Society
Cylburn Mansian, 4915 Greenspring Ave.
Baltimore MD 21209
Tel: 1 800 823 0050
http://www.mdbirds.org/publications/
birdlife.html

The Yellow Warbler
Dayton Audubon Society
1375 E. Siebenthaler Ave.
Dayton, OH 45414-5398
E-mail: audubon@dayton.net
http://www.dayton.net/Audubon/ywmay00.htm

Central and South America and the Caribbean

Ararajuba ~ Revista Brasileira de Ornitologia
Sociedade Brasileira de Ornitologia
Caixa Postal 2452
Brasilia DF 70849-970
E-mail: ararajuba@ieg.com.br
http://www.ararajuba.hpg.com.br or
http://www.ao.com.br/sbo.htm

Atualidades Ornitologicas
Caixa Postal 238 86870-000
Ivaipora PR, Brasil
E-mail: ao@ao.com.br

Boletim CEO
Centro de Estudos Ornitologicos
Caixa Postal 64532, 05402-970
Sao Paulo, SP, Brazil
E-mail: ceo@ib.usp.br
http://www.ib.usp.br/ceo/artig/boletim.htm

Boletin SAO
Sociedad Antioquena de Ornitologia
Cra 52, No. 73-298
Jardin Botanico JAU, Medellin Colombia
Tel: 4 211 5461
E-mail: sao@epm.net.co
http://araneus.humboldt.org.co/rnoa/sao/index.
htm

Central and South America and the Caribbean (Cont'd)

The Broadsheet
BirdLife Jamaica
93 Old Hope Road, Kingston 6
Jamaica W.I.
Tel: 876 978 5881
E-mail: mclevy@toj.com
http://www.jatoday.com.jm/gossebird.html

El Hornero
Aves Argentina
Asociación Ornitológica del Plata
25 de Mayo 749 2°6 (C1002ABO)
Buenos Aires, Argentina
Tel: +54 11 4312 1015 / 2284

Huitzil: Journal of Mexican Ornithology
Dr. Raul Ortiz-Pulido
CIB-UAEH, A.P. 69
Pachuca, Hidalgo 42001, Mexico
E-mail: editor@huitzil.net
http://www.huitzil.net/

On-line Magazines

@vesNews
http://www.surfnet.fi/birdlife/aves/index.html

African Bird Club
http://www.africanbirdclub.org/

Bali Bird Park Magazine
http://www.africanbirdclub.org/

Bird Observer
http://massbird.org/birdobserver/

Bird On!
http://www.birdcare.com/birdon/

Bird Watch
Tel: 020 7704-9495
E-mail: editorial@birdwatch.co.uk
http://www.birdwatch.co.uk/

East Coast Bird Magazine
E-mail: museum-info@gov.ns.ca
http://museum.gov.ns.ca/mnh/nature/nsbirds/
feature.htm

Essays on Nature and Birds
http://www.acsu.buffalo.edu/~insrisg/nature/
subject.html

InterBirdNet
E-mail: interbirdnet@birder.force9.net
http://www.birder.co.uk/

Interpretive Birding
http://www.ibirding.com/

Living Birds on the Web (Cornell)
http://birds.cornell.edu/Publications/livingbird/
index.html

Nature Illimitee
http://www.cam.org/~natil/

Neotropical Bird Club
http://www.neotropicalbirdclub.org/

Oriental Bird Club
http://www.orientalbirdclub.org/

Ornithological Newsletter On-Line
http://www.ornith.cornell.edu/OSNA/
ornnsewsl.htm

Ornithological Society of the Middle East
http://www.osme.org/

Ornithology.com
http://www.ornithology.com/

Peterson On-Line
http://www.petersononline.com/

The Dick E. Bird News
http://www.dickebird.com/

The NW Bird Watcher Magazine
http://thebirdgroup.com/

On-line Magazines (cont'd)

The Virtual Birder
http://www.virtualbirder.com/vbirder/

Ya Know You're a Birder
http://lightning.prohosting.com/~ees101/birds/comicindex.htm

Birding Links

American Birding Association's Links Page
http://www.americanbirding.org/abalinks/

Audubon Bird Links
http://www.audubon.org/bird/link/

Bird Forum
http://www.birdforum.net/

Bird Links
http://www.earthlife.net/birds/links.html

Bird Links on KWFN Web Site
http://www.sentex.net/~tntcomm/kwfn/Links.htm

Bird Links to the World
http://www.bsc-eoc.org/links/links.jsp

Birding.com
http://birding.com/

Birding B.C. & Birding Links
http://birdingbc.ca/links/index.php

Birding Hotspots Around the World
http://www.camacdonald.com/birding/birding.htm

Birding in Canada
http://www.web-nat.com/bic/

Birding in Quebec
http://www.virtualbirder.com/vbirder/realbirds/rbas/QC.html

Birding on the Web
http://www.birder.com/

BIRDNET
The Ornithological Council
http://www.nmnh.si.edu/BIRDNET

Birds
http://ces.iisc.ernet.in/hpg/cesmg/tvrbird.html

The Birdwatcher's Search Engine
http://birding.al-info.com

Birdwatching WWW Links
http://www.interlog.com/~gaillantg/birdlink.html

Birdweb
http://www.ummz.lsa.umich.edu/birds/

The Eagle Page
http://www.sky.net/~emily/eagle.html

Fat Birder Links Pages
http://www.fatbirder.com/links/signpost_and_discussion/mega_links_pages.html

Institute of African Ornithology: Links
http://web.uct.ac.za/depts/fitzpatrick/docs/websites.html

Net Vet Birds
http://netvet.wustl.edu/birds.htm#other

The Ornithology Website
http://birdwebsite.com/

The O.W.L. (The Ornithological Web Library)
http://aves.net/the-owl/

Tweeters
http://www.scn.org/earth/tweeters

Wildlife Web Site Directory
http://www.tc.umn.edu/~devo0028/sites.htm

Popular Field Guides for Worldwide Birding*

North America

The Sibley Guide to Birds, David Allen Sibley (New York: Alfred A. Knopf, 2000)

The Sibley Field Guide to Birds of Eastern North America, David Allen Sibley (New York: Alfred A. Knopf, 2003)

The Sibley Field Guide to Birds of Western North America, David Allen Sibley (New York: Alfred A. Knopf, 2003)

Field Guide to the Birds of North America, 4th edition (Washington, DC: National Geographic Society, 2002)

Birds of North America, Kenn Kaufman (New York: Houghton Mifflin, 2000)

All the Birds of North America, Jack L. Griggs (New York: Roundtable Press, 1997)

Stokes Field Guide to Birds: Eastern Region, Donald and Lillian Stokes (New York: Little Brown, 1996)

Stokes Field Guide to Birds: Western Region, Donald and Lillian Stokes (New York: Little Brown, 1996)

Peterson Field Guides: Western Birds, Roger Tory Peterson (Boston: Houghton Mifflin, 1990)

Peterson Field Guides Birds of Eastern and Central North American Birds, Roger Tory Peterson (Boston: Houghton Mifflin, 2002)

Birds of North America: A Guide to Field Identification, Chandler S. Robbins, Bertel Bruun, and Arthur B. Singer (New York: St. Martin's Press, 2001)

National Audubon Society Field Guide to North American Birds: Eastern Region, John Bull and John Farrand, Jr. (New York: Random House, 1994)

National Audubon Society Field Guide to North American Birds: Western Region, Miklas D. Udvardy and John Farrand, Jr. (New York: Random House, 1994)

A Field Guide to Advanced Birding, Kenn Kaufman (Boston: Houghton Mifflin, 1990)

A Guide to the Nests, Eggs, and Nestlings of North American Birds, Paul C. Baicich and Colin J. O. Harrison (Princeton, NJ: Princeton University Press, 1997)

A Field Guide to Western Birds' Nests, Hal H. Harrison (Boston: Houghton Mifflin, 1975)

Peterson Field Guides: Eastern Birds' Nests, Hal H. Harrison (Boston: Houghton Mifflin, 1975)

A Field Guide to Birds of the Desert Southwest, Barbara L. Davis (Houston: Gulf Publishing, 1997)

Central America

A Guide to Birds of Mexico and Northern Central America, Steve N.G. Howell and Sophie Webb, (New York: Oxford University Press, 1995)

Field Guide to Mexican Birds, Roger Tory Peterson (Boston: Houghton Mifflin, 1973)

A Field Guide to the Birds of Mexico and Adjacent Areas, 3rd Edition, Ernest Preston Edwards (Austin: University of Texas Press, 1998)

Caribbean

Guide to the Birds of Puerto Rico and the Virgin Islands, Revised Edition, Herbert A. Raffaele (Princeton, NJ: Princeton University Press, 1989)

Birds of Cuba, Orlando H. Garrido and Arturo Kirkconnell (Ithaca, NY: Cornell University Press, 2000)

A Guide to the Birds of West Indies, Herbert Raffaele, James Wiley, Orlando Garrido, Allan Keith, and Janis Raffaele (Princeton, NJ: Princeton University Press, 1998)

Field Guide to Birds of the West Indies, James Bond (Boston: Houghton Mifflin, 1993)

Birds of the West Indies, G. Michael Flieg and Allan Sander (Sanibel Island, FL: Ralph Curtis Books, 2000)

A Photographic Guide to Birds of the West Indies, Michael G. Flieg and Allan Sander (Sanibel Island, FL: Ralph Curtis Books 2000)

A Guide to the Birds of Bermuda, Eric J.R. Amos (Warwick, Bermuda: Corncrake, 1991)

Birds of the West Indies, Herbert Raffaele, James Wiley, Orlando Garrido, Allan Keith, and Janis Raffaele (Princeton, NJ: Princeton University Press, 2003)

Birds of Jamaica: A Photographic Field Guide, Audrey Downer and Robert L. Sutton (New York: Cambridge University Press, 1990)

South America

A Guide to the Birds of Costa Rica, F. Gary Stiles and Alexander F. Skutch (Ithaca, NY: Cornell University Press, 1989)

The Birds of Chile: A Field Guide, Braulio Araya and Sharon R. Chester (Santiago de Chile: LATOUR, 1993)

Birds of Belize, H. Lee Jones (Houston: University of Texas Press, 2004)

Birds of Chile, Alvaro Jaramillo (Princeton, NJ: Princeton University Press, 2003)

Birds of Patagonia, Tierra del Fuego, and Antarctic Peninsula, Enrique Couve and Claudio Vidal (Punta Arenas, Chile: Fantastico Sur, 2003)

A Guide to the Birds of Panama with Costa Rica, Nicaragua, and Honduras, Robert G. Ridgely and John A. Gwynne, Jr. (Princeton, NJ: Princeton University Press, 1989)

Guide to the Birds of Colombia, Steven L. Hilty and William L. Brown (Princeton, NJ: Princeton University Press, 1986)

Guide to the Birds of Venezuela, Steven L. Hilty (Princeton, NJ: Princeton University Press, 2003)

Guide to Birds of Trinidad and Tobago, Richard ffrench, (Ithaca, NY: Cornell University Press, 1991)

A Guide to the Birds of Peru, James F. Clements and Noam Shany, (Temecula, CA: Ibis Publishing, 2001)

All the Birds of Brazil: An Identification Guide, Deodato Souza (Editora DALL, 2002)

Birds of Southern South America and Antarctica, Martín Rodolfo de la Peña and Maurice Rumboll (Princeton, NJ: Princeton University Press, 1998)

A Guide to the Birds of the Galápagos Islands, Isabel Castro and Antonia Phillips (Princeton, NJ: Princeton University Press, 1997)

Europe

Peterson Field Guide to Birds of Britain and Europe, 6th edition, Roger Tory Peterson, Guy Mountfort, and P.A.D Hollom (Boston: Houghton Mifflin, 1993)

Collins Birds of Britain & Ireland, Dominic Couzens (Trafalgar Square Books, 1997)

Pocket Guide to the Birds of Britain and North-West Europe, Chris Kightley, Steve Madge, and Dave Nurney (New Haven, CT: Yale University Press, 1998)

Bird Nests, Eggs and Nestlings of Britain & Europe, Colin Harrison and Peter Castell (London: HarperCollins, 1998)

Pocket Guide to the Common Birds of Ireland, Eric Dempsey and Michael O'Clery (Dublin: Gill and Macmillan, 1995)

Birds of Britain and Europe, Jim Flegg and Martin Woodcock (London: New Holland, 2001)

A Photographic Guide to the Birds of the Britain and Europe, Paul Sterry and Jim Flegg, (London: Holland, 2001)

Hamlyn Guide to Birds of Britain and Europe, Bertel Brunn, Håkan Delin, Lars Svensson, Arthur Singer, and Dan Zetterström (New York: Hamlyn, 2001)

The Pocket Guide to Birds of Prey of Britain and Northern Europe, John Philip Burton (London: Dragon's World, 1991)

Birds of Europe, Lars Svenssen and Peter J. Grant (Princeton, NJ: Princeton University Press, 1999)

Les Oiseaux de France, Jean-Claude Chantelat and Pierre Nicolau-Gullaumet (Paris: Solar, 1993)

A Field Guide to Birds of Armenia, Marin S. Adamian and Daniel Klem (Yerevan, Armenia: University of Armenia, 1997)

Birds of Cyprus: A Concise, Simple and Fully Illustrated Guide, J.M.E. Took and Robin Reckitt (Nicosia: J. Philippides and Son, 1992)

Africa and Middle East

Birds of the Indian Ocean Islands: Madagascar, Mauritius, Réunion, Rodrigues, Seychelles and the Comoros, Ian Sinclair and Olivier Langrand (Cape Town/London: Struik/New Holland, 1998)

A Photographic Guide to Birds of Egypt and the Middle East, David Cottridge and R.F. Porter (London: New Holland, 2001)

The Macmillan Birder's Guide to European and Middle Eastern Birds: Including North Africa, Hadoram Shirihai and David Christie (London: Macmillan, 1996)

A Photographic Guide to Birds of Israel and the Middle East, David Cottridge and R.F. Porter (London: New Holland, 2000)

Field Guide to the Birds of the Middle East, R.F. Porter, S. Christensen, and P. Schiermacker-Hansen ((London: TA&D Poyser, 1996)

Birds of Israel and the Middle East, David M. Cottridge and Richard Porter (Sanibel Island, FL: Ralph Curtis Books, 2000)

Birds of Western and Central Africa, Ber van Perlo Grant (Princeton, NJ: Princeton University Press, 2002)

A Guide to the Birds of Western Africa, Nik Borrow and Ron Demey (Princeton, NJ: Princeton University Press, 2002)

A Field Guide to the Birds of Gambia and Senegal, Clive Barlow and Tim Wacher (New Haven, CT: Yale University Press, 1997)

Birds of Eastern Africa, Ber van Perlo (Princeton, NJ: Princeton University Press, 2001)

The Birds of East Africa, Terry Stevenson and John Fanshawe (Princeton, NJ: Princeton University Press, 2001)

Birds of Kenya and Northern Tanzania (Field Guide), Dale Zimmerman, Donald A. Turner, and David J. Pearson (Princeton, NJ: Princeton University Press, 1999)

Newman's Birds of Southern Africa, Kenneth Newman, (Johannesburg: Southern Book Publishers, 1999)

Southern Africa Birds: A Photographic Guide, Ian Sinclair (Sanibel Island, FL: Ralph Curtis Books, 2000)

SASOL: *The Larger Illustrated Guide to Birds of Southern Africa*, Ian Sinclair and Phil Hockey (Cape Town: Struik, 1996)

Birds of Southern Africa, Ber van Perlo (Princeton, NJ: SASOL: Princeton University Press, 2001)

A Photographic Guide to Birds of Prey of Southern, Central and East Africa, 2nd ed., D.G. Allan (Cape Town: Struik, 2000)

...of Madagascar: A Photographic Guide, Pete
...is and Frank Hawkins (New Haven, CT: Yale
...versity Press, 1998)

...ocket Guide to the Southern African Birds, 2nd ed.,
...urger Cillié, and Ulrick Oberprieler (Cape
Town: Sunbird, 2002)

Robert Birds of Southern Africa, 6th ed., Gordon
Lindsay Maclean, Trustees of the J. Voelcker Bird
Book Fund, 1993

The Collins Field Guide to the Birds of West Africa,
William Serle and Gerard J. Morel, (Lexington,
MA: S. Green, 1988)

Illustrated Guide to the Birds of Southern Africa, Ian
Sinclair, Phil Hockey, and William R. Tarboton
(Princeton, NJ: Princeton University Press, 1995)

_Field Guide to Nests and Eggs of Southern African
Birds_, William Tarboton, (Cape Town & London:
W. Struik, New Holland, 2001)

Green Guide: Birds of Botswana, Kenneth B.
Newman (Johannesburg: Southern Book
Publishers, 1998)

Birds of the Seychelles, Adrian Skerrett and Ian
Bullock (Princeton, NJ: Princeton University
Press, 2001)

Oiseaux de la Reunion, 2. ed., Nicolas Barre,
Christian H. Jouain, and Armand Barau
(Papeete, Tahiti: Editions du Pacifique, 1996)

Asia

A Field Guide to the Birds of China, John
Mackinnon and Karen Phillips (Oxford: Oxford
University Press, 2000)

_A Photographic Guide to Birds of China and Hong
Kong_, John Mackinnon and Nigel Hicks
(London: New Holland, 1996)

A Field Guide to the Birds of Taiwan, Wan-fu
Chang (T'ai-chung, Taiwan: T'ai-chung
University Press, 1980)

_A Photographic Guide to the Birds of India and the
Indian Subcontinent, Including Pakistan, Nepal,
Bhutan, Bangladesh, Sri Lanka, and the Maldives_,
Bikram Grewal (Princeton, NJ: Princeton
University Press, 2003)

Birds of India, Richard Grimmett, Carol Inskipp,
and Tim Inskipp (Princeton, NJ: Princeton
University Press, 1999)

A Field Guide to the Birds of Southwestern India,
R.J. Ranjit Daniels (Oxford: Oxford University
Press, 1997)

Birds of Nepal, Richard Grimmett, Carol Inskipp,
and Tim Inskipp, (Princeton, NJ: Princeton
University Press, 2000)

Field Guide to the Birds of Bhutan, Carol Inskipp
Tim Inskipp and Richard Grimmett, (London:
A&C Black, 1999)

A Field Guide to the Birds of Sri Lanka, John
Harrison (Oxford: Oxford University Press, 1999)

A Photographic Guide to the Birds of the Himalayas,
Bikram Grewal (London: New Holland, 1999)

Birds of Sri Lanka, Gehan de Silva, Deepal
Warakagoda and T.S.U. de Zylva (Sanibel Island,
FL: Ralph Curtis Books, 2000)

_A Photographic Guide to the Birds of Peninsular
Malaysia and Singapore_, G.W.D. Davidson and
Chew Yen Fook (Sanibel Island, FL: Ralph Curtis
Books, 1995)

The Birds of Singapore, Clive Briffet (Oxford:
Oxford University Press, 1993)

_A Field Guide to the Birds of West Malaysia and
Singapore_, Allen Jeyarajasingam and Alan Pearson
(Oxford: Oxford University Press, 1999)

Birds of Java, Sumatra and Bali, Tony Tilford
(Sanibel Island, FL: Ralph Curtis Books, 2000)

_A Field Guide to the Birds of Borneo, Sumatra, Java,
Bali_, John MacKinnon and Karen Phillipps
(Oxford: Oxford University Press, 1993)

Birds of the Phillipines, Tim Fisher and Nigel
Hicks, (Sanibel Island, FL: Ralph Curtis Books,
2000)

Guide to the Birds of the Phillippines, Robert S. Kennedy (Oxford: Oxford University Press, 2000)

Field Guide to the Birds of Korea, Woo-Shin Lee, Tae-How Koo, and Jin-Young Park, L.L. Evergreen Foundation, 2000

Birds of Thailand, Craig Robson, (Princeton, NJ: Princeton University Press, 2002)

Photographic Guide Birds of Thailand, Michael Webster and Chew Yen Fook (Sanibel Island, FL: Ralph Curtis Books, 1997)

Photographic Guide to the Birds of Southeast Asia: including the Phillippines and Borneo, Morten Strange (Princeton, NJ: Princeton University Press, 2000)

A Guide to the Birds of South-East Asia, Craig Robson (Princeton, NJ: Princeton University Press, 2000)

Field Guide to the Birds of the Solomons, Vanauta & New Caledonia, Chris Doughety, Nicolas Day, and Andrew Plant (London: A&C Black, 1999)

A Guide to the Birds of Thailand, Boonsong Lekhakun and Philip D. Round (Bangkok: Saha Karn Bhaet, 1991)

Birds of Northern India, Richard Grimmett and Tim Inskipp (Princeton, NJ: Princeton University Press, 2003)

Australasia

The Field Guide to the Birds of Australia, Grapham Pizzey and Frank Knight (Sydney: Angus and Robertson, 1999)

Field Guide to the Birds of Australia, 6th ed., Ken Simpson and Nicolas Day (Princeton, NJ: Princeton University Press, 1999)

Green Guide: Birds of Australia, Peter Rowland (London/Cape Town: New Holland/Struik, 2001)

A Field Guide to Nests and Eggs of Australian Birds, Gordon Beruldsen (Sydney: Rigby, 1980)

Field Guide to Australian Birds, Michael K. Morcombe (Archerfield, Australia: Steve Parish, 2000)

Field Guide to Tasmanian Birds, Dave Watts (London: New Holland, 1999)

Hand Guide to the Birds of New Zealand, Hugh Robertson and Barrie Heather (Oxford: Oxford University Press, 2001)

Birds of New Zealand and Outlying Islands, R.A. Falla, R.B. Sibson, and E.G. Turbott (London: HarperCollins, 1993)

The Field Guide to the Birds of New Zealand, Barrie D. Heather and Hugh A. Robertson (Oxford: Oxford University Press, 1997)

The Reed Field Guide to New Zealand Birds, Geoff Moon (Mechanicsburg, PA: Stackpole Books, 1992)

A Photographic Guide to Birds of New Zealand, Geoff Moon (London: New Holland, 2002)

Collins Guide to the Birds of New Zealand, Chloe Talbot-Kelly and Hermann Heinzel (London: Collins, 1993)

---

* Visit http://www.door.library.uiuc.edu/bix/fieldguides/birds.htm#asi for a more thorough, annotated list. For bird-finding guides, checklists, and species-oriented reference books, contact ABA Sales, American Birding Association, ph: 1 800 634 7736; www.americanbirding.org/abasales

Selected Video Recordings for Finding and Identifying Birds

North America

Audubon Society's Video Guide to Birds of North America
National Audubon Society
5 VHS videocassettes covering 505 species

Birding Hotspots in Texas
Karis and Don Herriott
1991; 74-minute VHS videotape

Birding Montana and the Big Sky Country
Karis and Don Herriott
1993; 62-minute VHS videotape

Birding Southeastern Arizona
Karis and Don Herriott
1995; 52-minute VHS videotape

Birds of Alaska
Karis and Don Herriott
1994; 105-minute VHS videotape

Nesting Seabirds of Machias Seal Island
Karis and Don Herriott
1989; 38-minute VHS videotape

Rare Birds of Sanibel
Karis and Don Herriott
1991; 110-minute VHS videotape

Spring Migration at the Dry Tortugas
Karis and Don Herriott
1990; 55-minute VHS videotape

Birding in Southeast Arizona
Terrie and Larry Gates
1993; VHS videotape covering 89 species

Hummingbirds of North America
Jon Dunn, Sheri Williamson, and John Vanderpoel
2003; 180-minute VHS videotape covering 24 species

Large Gulls of North America
John Vanderpoel
1997; 60-minutes, VHS videocassette covering 17 species

Small Gulls of North America
John Vanderpoel
1999; 180-minute VHS videotape covering 14 species

Shorebirds: A Guide to Shorebirds of Eastern North America
Richard K. Walton and Greg Dodge
70-minute VHS video covering 38 species

Shorebirds of North America in Action
Bob Hamblin
1991; VHS videotape covering 45 species

A.O.U. Checklist of Much Sought After Birds of North America
Bob Hamblin
2001; 2 VHS videotapes
Vol. 1: Least Grebe to Groove-billed Ani
Vol. 2: Flammulated Owl to Eurasian Tree Sparrow

Watching Warblers: A Video Guide to the Warblers of Eastern North America
Michael Male and Judy Fieth
1996; 60-minute VHS videotape

Watching Waders: A Video Guide to the Waders of North America
Michael Male and Judy Fieth
1999; 95-minute VHS videotape

Watching Sparrows
Michael Male and Judy Fieth
2002; 75-minute VHS videotape covering 46 species

Hawk Watch: A Video Guide to Eastern Raptors
Richard K. Walton and Greg Dodge
1998; 45-minute VHS video

Tyrant Flycatchers of North America in Action
Bob Hamblin
1994; VHS videotape

Sparrows and Other Members of the Finch Family in Action
Bob Hamblin
1993; 62-minute VHS videotape

Through the Seasons: An Introduction to the Seabirds and Marine Mammals of Monterey Bay
Les Lieurance and Debra Shearwater
1994; 36-minute VHS videotape covering 24 species

Birds of the Rainforest—The Native Forest Birds of Kaua'i
Jim Denny
2001; 26-minute VHS videotape covering 13 species

Video Guide to Identifying Florida Birds
Peter G. Merritt
2001; 2-hour VHS videotape covering over 200 species

Birding in Southeast Arizona
Terrie and Larry Gates
1993; VHS videotape covering 89 specie

Sea Birds of the Maine Coast
Down East
1998; 40-minute VHS videotape

Loons of the Northern Forest
Down East
1998; 45-minute VHS videotape

How to Start Watching Birds
Diane Porter
1994; 90-minute VHS videotape

Europe

Bill Oddie's Video Guide to British Birds
Paul Doherty—Bird Images
167-minute VHS videotape covering 280 species

BBC-RSPB Video Guide to British Garden Birds
BBC Video
David Attenborough
85 minutes

British Waders, Wildfowl And Gulls Series
Bill Oddie, 3-video set
1994; 164 minutes covering 91 species

Flamingoes / Flamants Roses (English Version)
Tour du Valat, France
23 minutes

The Video Guide to European Birds
J. Flegg
Series: THE VIDEO GUIDE TO EUROPEAN BIRDS
9-videocassette set covering 420 species

The Video Guide To North European Birds
J. Flegg
5-videocassette set covering 324 species

World

Birds of Costa Rica
Richard Kuehn and Dean Schuler
1997; VHS, 120-minutes covering 230 species

Shorebirds: A Video Guide to the Key Shorebirds of North America, Europe and Asia
Paul Doherty—Bird Images
2000; 230-minutes, 2 VHS videotapes

Watching Hummingbirds
Ark Media Group
1999; 30-minute VHS videotape

Where Eagles Fly and The Language of Birds
RSPB Films—BBC Video
Two films on one videocassette
53 minutes

Selected Audio Recordings for Identifying Birds

North America

to Bird Songs
ınal Geographic Society and the Cornell
oratory of Ornithology
85; 1 CD covering 180 species

Peterson Field Guides: Eastern/Central Bird Songs
Roger Tory Peterson, editor
2002; 2 cassettes or 1 CD covering 250 species

Peterson Field Guides: Western Bird Songs
Cornell/Interactive
1999; 2 CDs covering 500 species

Peterson Field Guides: Eastern/Central Birding by Ear
Richard K. Walton and Robert W. Lawson
2002; 3 CDs or 3 cassettes covering 85 species

Peterson Field Guides: Eastern and Central More Birding by Ear
Richard K. Walton and Robert W. Lawson
2002; 3 CDs or 3 cassettes

Peterson Field Guides: Western Birding by Ear
Richard K. Walton and Robert W. Lawson
1999; 3 CDs or 3 cassettes

Stokes Field Guide to Bird Song (Eastern)
Lang Elliott with Donald and Lillian Stokes
1997; 3 CDs or cassette set covering 372 species

Stokes Field Guide to Bird Song (Western)
Kevin J. Colver with Donald and Lillian Stokes
1999; 4 CDs or cassette set

Flight Calls of Migratory Birds
William R. Evans and Michael O'Brien
2002; CD-ROM covering 211 species

Bird Songs of California
Geoffrey A. Keller—Cornell Lab of Ornithology
2003; 3 CDs covering 220 species

Bird Songs of Florida
Geoffrey A. Keller
1997; CD or cassette covering 111 species

Songbirds of Yosemite and the Sierra Nevadas
Kevin J. Colver
1995; CD or cassette covering 76 species

Bird Songs of the Lower Rio Grande Valley and Southwestern Texas
Geoffrey A. Keller
2000; 74-minute CD covering 120 species

Bird Songs of Southeastern Arizona and Sonora Mexico
Geoffrey A. Keller
2001; 2-CDs covering 200 species

Songbirds of the Southwest Canyon County
Kevin J. Colver
1994; CD or cassette covering 66 species

Songbirds of Yellowstone and the High Rockies
Kevin J. Colver
1996; CD or cassette covering 78 species

Bird Songs of the Rocky Mountain States and Provinces
Robert Righter and Geoffrey A. Keller—Cornell Lab of Ornithology
1999; 3 CDs covering 250 species

Bird Songs of the Great Lakes
John Neville
2002; 1 CD covering 101 species

Hawaii Birds
Jim Denny
2003; 30-minute VHS or DVD-R covering 80 species

Bird Songs of Alaska
Leonard J. Peyton—Cornel Lab of Ornithology
1999; 2 CDs covering 260 species

Voices of Hawaii's Birds
Hawaii Audubon Society
1996; Two 60-minute cassettes covering 110 species

Bird Songs of Canada's West Coast
John Neville
1999; 1 CD covering 99 bird species

Bird Sounds of Canada
Monty Brigham
1994; 12 cassettes or 6 CDs
Vol. 1; Loons to Woodpeckers
Vol. 2: Flycatchers to Vireos
Vol. 3: Warblers to Sparrows

Bird Songs of the Kootenays
John Neville
1996; 1 CD

Birdsongs of the Pacific States
Thomas G. Sander
1995; 2 CDs or 2 cassettes covering 135 species

Bird Songs and Calls of Lake Tahoe
John V. Moore
1995; cassette covering 45 species

Songbirds of the Rocky Mountain Foothills
Kevin J. Colver
1994; CD or cassette covering 33 species

Sounds of Florida's Birds, 3rd Edition
John William Hardy
1996; cassette covering 98 species

Voices of Hawaii's Birds
Hawaii Audubon Society
1996; two 60-minute cassettes covering 110 species

Warblers of North America
Donald J. Borror and William W.H. Gunn—
Cornell Laboratory of Ornithology
1985; 2 cassettes covering 105 species

Central and South America

Birds of Eastern Ecuador
Peter H. English and Theodore A. Parker III
1992; cassette covering 99 species

Bird Songs of Belize, Guatemala and Mexico
Dale Delaney—Cornell Lab of Ornithology
1992; cassette covering 70 species

Bird Songs and Calls from Southeast Peru
Ben B. Coffey, Jr. and Lula C. Coffey
1993; cassette covering 85 species

Ecuador: More Bird Vocalizations From The Lowland Rainforest, Vol. 1
John V. Moore
1994; 58-minute cassette covering 105 species

Ecuador: More Bird Vocalizations from the Lowland Rain Forest, Vol. 2
John V. Moore
1996; 90-minute cassette covering 117 species

Ecuador: More Bird Vocalizations from the Lowland Rainforest, Vol. 3
John V. Moore
1997; 90-minute cassette covering 130 species

Songs of Argentine Birds
Roberto Stranek
4 cassettes covering over half the Argentine avifauna

Bird Songs of Belize, Guatemala, and Mexico
Dale Delaney
1992; cassette covering 70 species

Songs from a Belizean Rainforest
John Gilardi
1997; CD covering 100 species

A Bird Walk at Chan Chich
John V. Moore
1994; cassette covering 150 species

Voices of Costa Rican Birds: Caribbean Slope
David L. Ross, Jr. And Bret M. Whitney
1995; 2 cassettes or 2 CDs covering 220 species

Songs of Mexican Birds
Ben Coffey, Jr.
1990; 2 cassettes covering 246 species

The Birds of the Ecuadorian Highlands
Niels Krabbe, John V. Moore, Paul Coopmans,
Robert S. Ridgely, and Mitch Lysinger
2001; 3 CDs covering 240 species

Sounds of La Selva (Ecuador)
John V. Moore
1994; 80-minute cassette covering 120 species

Ecuador: More Bird Vocalizations from the Lowland Rain Forest
1994; Vol. 1—58 minute cassette covering 105 species
1996; Vol. 2—90 minute cassette covering 117 species
1997; Vo. 3—90 minute cassette covering 130 species

The Birds of Northwest Ecuador—Volume I: The Upper Foothills and Subtropics
John V. Moore, Paul Coopmans, Robert S. Ridgely, and Mitch Lysinger
1999; 3 CDs covering 190 species

The Birds of Northwest Ecuador—Volume II: The Lowlands and Lower Foothills
Olaf Jahn, John V. Moore, Patricio Mena Valenzuela, Niels Krabbe, Paul Coopmans, Mitch Lysinger and Robert S. Ridgely
2003; 2 CDs covering 253 species

The Birds of Cabanas San Isidro, Ecuador
John V. Moore and Mitch Lysinger
1997; 2 cassettes covering 154 species

Voices of Andean Birds—Volume 1: Birds of the Hill Forest of Southern Peru and Bolivia
Thomas S. Schulenberg—Cornell Lab of Ornithology
2000; 1 CD covering 99 species

Voices of Andean Birds—Volume 2: Birds of the Cloud Forest of Southern Peru and Bolivia
Thomas S. Schulenberg—Cornell Lab of Ornithology
2000; 1 CD covering 99 species

Voices of Amazonian Birds—Birds of the Rainforest of Southern Peru and Northern Bolivia—Volume 1: Tinamous (Tinamidea) through Barbets (Capitonidae)
Thomas Schulenbert, Curtis Marantz, and Peter H. English—Cornell Lab of Ornithology
2000; 1 CD

Voices of Amazonian Birds—Birds of the Rainforest of Southern Peru and Northern Bolivia—Volume 2: Toucans (Ramphastidae) through Antbirds (Thamnophilidae)
Thomas Schulenbert, Curtis Marantz, and Peter H. English—Cornell Lab of Ornithology
2000; 1 CD

Voices of Amazonian Birds—Birds of the Rainforest of Southern Peru and Northern Bolivia—Volume 3: Ground Antbirds (Formicariidae) through Jays (Corvidae)
Thomas Schulenbert, Curtis Marantz, and Peter H. English—Cornell Lab of Ornithology
2000; 1 CD

Voices of Birds of the Galapagos Islands
John William Hardy
1991; cassette covering 37 species

Voices of Costa Rican Birds: Caribbean Slope
David L. Ross, Jr. and Bret M. Whitney
1995; 2 cassettes or 2 CDs covering 220 species

Voices of Mexican Sparrows
J.W. Hardy and Larry L. Wolf
1993; cassette covering 8 species

Voices of Neotropical Birds
John William Hardy
1983; cassette covering 50 species

Voices of Neotropical Wood Warblers
J.W. Hardy, Ben B. Coffey, Jr., and George B. Reynard
1994; 76-minute cassette covering 63 species

A Sound Guide to the Birds of South East Peru
S. Grove
Cassette covering 93 species

Caribbean

Bird Songs in Jamaica
George B. Reynard and Robert L. Sutton-Cornell Lab of Ornithology
2000; 2 CDs covering 119 species

Bird Sounds of Trinidad and Tobago
William L. Murphy
1991; 28-minute cassette covering 39 species

Europe

Bird Songs of Britain and Europe
Jean C. Roché
1994; 4 CDs covering 396 species

Bird Sounds of Europe and Northwest Africa
Jean C. Roché and Jérome Chevereau
2002; 10 CDs (12 hours) covering 481 species

All the Bird Songs and Calls of Britain and Europe
Jean C. Roché
1994; 4 CDs or 4-cassette set covering 396 species
Volume 1—Falconidae
Volume 2: Tetraonidae—Columbidae
Volume 3: Cuculidae—Sylvidae
Volume 4: Sylvidae—Emberizidae

British Bird Sounds on CD
R Kettle and R Ranft—British Library
Boxed 2-CD set
152 minutes

Collins Field Guide: Bird Songs and Calls of Britain and Northern Europe
Geoff Sample
Cassette covering 160 species

Larks Ascending
J-C. Roché—France
65-minute cassette covering 7 lark species

Nocturnal and Diurnal Birds of Prey
J-C. Roché
Cassette covering 40 species

Our Favourite Garden Birds
J-C. Roché—France
75-minute cassette covering 99 garden bird species

Sounds of Migrant and Wintering Birds (Western European)
C. Chappuis
2 cassettes covering 147 species
106 minutes

Warbler Haunts
Richard Margoschis
Cassette covering 16 species
60 minutes

Africa

Southern Africa Bird Sounds
Guy Gibbon
1991 (tapes), 1995 (CDs)—6 cassettes or CDs covering 888 species

Bird Calls of the Kruger National Park, Volume 1
G.L. Maclean
99 species

Birds of the African Rainforests (Parts 1 and 2)
Stuart Keith
2 cassettes covering 92 species

Birds of the Gambia
R Thomas and S Thomas
60-minute cassette covering 46 species

Bird Recordings from Ethiopia
Steve Smith
1996; cassette covering 67 species

Bird Recordings from the Gambia
Steve Smith
1994; cassette covering 52 species

Birds of Southern Africa
Guy Gibbon—SA Birding, South Africa
100-minute cassette covering 300 species

Bird Songs of Zambia
Robert Stjernstedt
3 cassettes covering 415 species

Common Birds of Central Africa
Robert Stjernstedt
Cassette covering 104 species

LBJ's of Southern Africa
Guy Gibbon
Cassette covering 92 species

Moroccan Bird Songs and Calls
Mats Stromberg
90-minute cassette covering 76 species

...s of Zambia
...jernstedt
...e covering 95 species

Southern African Bird Calls
L Gillard
3-cassette set covering 541 species

Asia

...rdsongs of the Himalayas
...cott Connop
1995; cassette covering 70 species

Bird Songs of Korea
Lab of Ornithology, Dept. of Biology, Kyung-Hee
University
1996

Birdsongs of Nepal
Scott Connop
1993; cassette covering 66 species

**A Field Guide to the Bird Songs of South East
Asia**
T. White
National Sound Archive
2 cassettes totalling 110-minutes

Soviet Bird Songs
K. Mild
Two cassettes totalling 41 minutes and covering
122 species

Bird Recordings from Sri Lanka
Steve Smith
1995; cassette covering 46 species

Birds of Sulawesi
Steve Smith
1991; cassette covering 43 species

Birds of the South Pacific
R. Thomas and S. Thomas
Cassette covering 36 species

**Birds of Sabah, Sulawesi and the Lesser
Sundas**
R. Thomas and S. Thomas
Cassette covering 70 species

Indian Bird Calls
Bombay Natural History Society
2 cassettes covering 169 species

Wild Bird Songs of Japan
Hideo Ueda
1999; 3 CDs covering 283 species

**An Audio Guide to the Birds of South India,
Part 1**
P.S. Sivaprasad
1994; 90-minute cassette covering 66 species

Birds of Indonesia
D. Gibbs
1990; cassette covering 50 species

Birds of Irian Jaya
Steve Smith
1991: cassette covering 48 species

Birds of Irian Jaya and Halmahera
R. Thomas and S. Thomas
Cassette covering 40 species

Birds of Java, Bali and Sumatra
Steve Smith
1991; cassette covering 41 species

Birds of the Lesser Sundas
Steve Smith
1991; cassette covering 43 species

Birds of the Moluccas
Steve Smith
1991; cassette covering 42 species

Birds of Polynesia
Leslie McPherson
Cassette covering 56 species

Middle East

Bird Songs of Israel and the Middle East
Krister Mild
2 cassettes covering 15 species

Australasia

Australian Bird Calls Favourites
David Stewart—Nature Sound
2000; 1 CD covering 57 species

Australian Bird Sounds, Vols 1–3
David Stewart
1996; 3 cassettes
Vol. I, II, III, each covering 61 species

Bird Calls of Eastern Australia
Len Gillard
Cassette covering 152 species

Bird Calls of North Queensland Rainforests
A Griffin and RJ Swaby
Cassette covering 66 species

Bird Calls of Tropical Eastern Australia
A Griffin and RJ Swaby
Cassette covering 86 species

A Field Guide To Australian Birdsong
L. Gillard, R. Buckingham, L. Jackson
Series with 11 volumes
Vol. 1 Emu to Striated Heron
Vol. 2 Rufous Night Heron to Chestnut Rail
Vol. 3 Red-necked Crake to Black-naped Tern
Vol. 4 Sooty Tern to Superb Parrot
Vol. 5 Regent Parrot to Masked Owl

Vol. 6 Eastern Grass Owl to Ground
Cuckoo-shrike
Vol. 7 White-winged Triller to White-breasted
Whistler
Vol. 8 Little Shrike-thrush to Hall's Babbler
Vol. 9 Chestnut-crowned Babbler to Redthroat
Vol. 10 Calamanthus to Noisy Friarbird
Vol. 11 Little Friarbird to Scarlet Honeyeater

New Zealand Songbirds
B Gill, J Hawkins, and L McPherson
Cassette covering 25 species

Papua New Guinea Bird Calls: Non-Passerines
H. Crouch
Cassette covering 74 species

Papua New Guinea Bird Calls: Passerines
H. Crouch
Cassette covering 78 species

Song Birds of South Australia
H. Crouch and A. Crouch
Cassette covering 32 species

Songs and Calls of Tasmanian Birds
Kelsey Aves
Cassette covering 64 species

World—General

Voices of New World Owls
J.W. Hardy, B.B. Coffey, Jr., and G.B. Reynard
1999; cassette covering 61 species

Voices of the Woodcreepers
J.W. Hardy, T.A. Parker III, and Ben B. Coffey, Jr.
1995; cassette covering 46 species

A Sound Guide to Nightjars and Related Nightbirds
Richard Ranft
1998; CD covering 108 species

Voices of the Troupials, Blackbirds, and their Allies
J.W. Hardy, George B. Reynard, and Terry Taylor
1998; 2 cassettes covering 96 species

Voices of New World Parrots
Cornell Lab of Ornithology
2002; 3 CDs covering 140 species

Songs of the Antbirds
Cornell Lab of Ornithology
2002; 3 CDs covering 270 species

Voices of the Toucans
J.W. Hardy, T.A. Parker III, and Terry Taylor
1996; cassette covering 39 species

Voices of the New World Rails
J.W. Hardy, George B. Reynard, and Terry Taylor
1996; cassette covering 40 species

Songs of the Vireos and Their Allies
Jon C. Barlow and J.W. Hardy
1995; cassette almost all vireo species

Sounds of Nature: Finches
Donald J. Borror and William W.H. Gunn
Series: Sounds of Nature covering 226 species

s of All Mockingbirds, Thrashers, and
r Allies
. Hardy, John C. Barlow, and Ben B. Coffey,

987; cassette covering 34 species

**Voices of the New World Jays, Crows and
Their Allies**
John William Hardy
1990; cassette covering 48 species

Voices of New World Pigeons and Doves
J.W. Hardy, G.B. Reynard, and B.B. Coffey, Jr.
1989; cassette covering 59 species

Voices of New World Cuckoos and Trogons
J.W. Hardy, George B. Reynard, and Ben B.
Coffey, Jr.
1995; cassette covering 33 species

Voices of the New World Quails
J.W. Hardy and Ralph J. Raitt
1995; cassette covering 26 species

Voices of the New World Thrushes
John William Hardy and Theodore A. Parker III
1992; cassette covering 68 species

Voices of the Tinamous
J.W. Hardy, Jacques Vielliard, and Roberto
Straneck
1995; cassette covering 34 species

Voices of the Wrens, 3rd Edition
John William Hardy
1995; cassette covering almost wren species

Birding Software and CD-ROMs

Altaïr Productions Multimedia
9 Rue Alexandre Fleming
49066 ANGERS cedex 01
Tel: 0 825 454 825
Titles include:
Les oiseaux de nos jardins
Les oiseaux des montagnes et des forêts
Les oiseaux d'eau
E-mail: info@altair-pm.com
http://www.altair-multimedia.com/pages/
flash_cdroms.php3

Aviary Base
166 Jenner Road
Barry, South Glamorgan
UK CF62 7HR
E-mail: Support@aviarybase.co.uk
http://www.aviarybase.co.uk/

Aviary Manager
Company J&D Enterprises Pty. Ltd.
3 Wirilda Court, Doveton
Victoria, Australia 3177
Tel: +613 9791 1033 or 03 9791 1033
E-mail: sales@aviarymanager.com.au
http://www.aviarymanager.com.au/

AviSys Birding Software
PO Box 369
Placitas, NM 87043 USA
Tel: 1 800 354 7755
E-mail: support@avisys.net
http://www.avisys.net/

AviMate
Boundaries Unlimited, Inc.
P.O. Box 396
Gotha, FL 34734-0396
USA
Tel: 877 387 4452 within USA or 407 349 2080
outside USA
E-mail: sales@avimate.com
http://www.avimate.com

Axia International, Inc.
840—6 Avenue S.W., Suite 510, Atrium 2
Calgary, AB
Canada
T2P 3E5
Tel: 1 800 969 2942
Titles include:
Know Your Birds of Prey CD-ROM
Know Your Common Bird Songs CD-ROM
Know Your Owls CD-ROM
Know Your Waterfowl CD-ROM

The Bird-Book CD-ROM
Ken Simpson
Natural Learning Pty. Ltd., Australia
Tel: +44 01803 865913
E-mail: sales@nhbs.co.uk
http://www.nhbs.com/xbscripts/bkfsrch?search=
43989.

Bird Feeding Digest
National Bird-Feeding Society
P.O. Box 23
Northbrook, IL 60065
USA
Tel: 847 272 0135
E-mail: questions@birdfeeding.org
http://www.birdfeeding.org/digest.html

Bird in the Hand (Handheld)
Scarlet Owls, LLC
P.O. Box 5628
Charlottesville, VA 22905
USA
Tel: 434 977 6957
E-mail: Contact@ScarletOwls.com
http://www.scarletowls.com/

Bird Recorder (Handheld and PC)
Wildlife Computing-USA
P.O. Box 2845
Granite Bay, CA 95746
USA
Tel: 1 866 247 3810
E-mail: birder@surewest.net (US email) or
support@wildlife.co.uk (UK email)
http://home.surewest.net/bruwebb/
BirdRecorder32.htm (US site) or
http://www.wildlife.co.uk/testing/Default.htm
(UK site)

Bird Songs International
Wierengastraat 42
NL-9969 PD Westernieland
Netherlands
Tel: +31 595 528679
E-mail: info@birdsongs.com
www.birdsongs.com
Titles include:
Birds of Bolivia
Birds of Tropical Asia 2
Birds of Venezuela

Bird Song Master
Micro Wizard
5277 Forest Ave.
Columbus, OH 43214
USA
Tel: 614 846 1077
E-mail: microwizard@prodigy.net
http://www.microwizardsoftware.com/
bird_song_master_main.htm

Bird Tracker
Cabin Software
Tel: 208 772 1703
E-mail: cabinsoft@adelphia.net
http://www.cabinsoftware.biz/

Bird Watcher—The Interactive Birding Game
Wizard Works
http://www.wizardworks.com/

BirdBase and BirdArea
Santa Barbara Software Products
1400 Dover Road
Santa Barbara, CA 93103
USA
Tel: 805 963 4886
Published 2001
E-Mail: sbsp@aol.com
http://members.aol.com/sbsp/index.html

BirdBrain (Mac)
Ideaform Inc.
908 East Briggs
Fairfield, IA 52556
USA
Tel: 641 472 7256 *or* 1 800 779 7256 (from US
only)
Published 1999
E-mail: ideaform@birdwatching.com
http://www.birdwatching.com/software/
birdbrain/birdbrain.html

Birder (Life List)
Published 2001
E-mail: info@voguemechanics.com
http://voguemechanics.com/index.asp?Page=
birder

Birder's Notebook Birding Software
4 Different Editions
E-mail: ggsoftware@att.net
http://home.att.net/~ggsoftware/BNotebook.
html

...es Limited
...se, Ewden
...d, UK S36 4ZA
...00 919391
...il: birdguides@birdfood.co.uk
...://www.birdguides.com/
...les include:
...D-ROM Guide to Rarer British Birds
CD-ROM Guide to Garden Birds
CD-ROM Guide to All the Birds of Europe
CD-ROM Guide to British Birds
CD-ROM Concise Guide to British Birds
CD-ROM Guide to Eastern Birds
The Concise Guide to British Birds

Birding Database
Everett Associates Ltd
Longnor House
Gunthorpe-Melton Constable
Norfolk UK NR24 2NS
Tel: 01263 860035
E-mail: sales@birdsoftware.co.uk
http://www.birdsoftware.co.uk/

Birds: Cranes through Passerines
Fogware Publishing
E-mail: jcrsch@jcresearch.com
http://www.fog-ware.com/products/
jewelcase/birds.htm

Birds of Australia
Simpson & Day
Natural Learning Pty. Ltd., Australia
Tel: +44 01803 865913
Published 1999
E-mail: sales@nhbs.co.uk
http://www.nhbs.com/xbscripts/bkfsrch?search=
43989.

Birds of Britain and Europe
AA Multimedia
Stenhusa gård
380 62 Mörbylånga
Sweden
Tel: +45 485 44100
Published 1998
E-mail: info@naturbokhandeln.sofab.se
http://www.naturbokhandeln.com/bokinf/enst-
bok/4475.html

Birds of the Great Lakes
CyberNatural Software
Department of Zoology, University of Guelph
Guelph, ON Canada
N1G 2W1
Tel: 519 824 4120 ext. 6393
E-mail: cyber@uoguelph.ca
http://www.cybernatural.ca/products/birds.htm

Topics Entertainment
1600 SW 43rd Street
Renton, WA 98055
USA
Tel: 425 656 3621
E-mail: helpdesk@topics-ent.com
www.topics-ent.com
Titles include:
Birds of the World: The Ultimate Multimedia
Collection
The Ultimate Birder

BirdSong Identiflyer (Handheld)
Lanius Software
5055 Business Center Drive, Suite 108, #110
Fairfield, CA 94534
USA
Tel: 866 864 8279
E-mail: birdshrike@cs.com
http://www.onmymountain.com/v5/

BirdStar Identification Software
96 Craig Dr.
Kitchener, ON Canada
N2B 2J3
Published 2003
E-mail: lbond@birdstar.com
http://members.rogers.com/bond0308/order.htm

**British Birds: An Interactive Multimedia
CD-ROM**
British Library
Tel: +44 01803 865913
E-mail: sales@nhbs.co.uk
http://www.nhbs.com/xbscripts/bkfsrch?search=
24966

Bruce Flaig's Birds
Softdisk
Offer #BIRD96
P.O. Box 30008
Shreveport, LA 71130-0008
USA
Tel: 1 800 831 2694
Published 1996
http://www.softdisk.com/sd/birding/

The Complete Birds of the Western Palearctic on CD-Rom
Oxford University Press
Saxon Way West
Corby, Northants NN18 9ES UK
Published 1998
Tel: +44 0 1536 741727
E-mail: bookquery.uk@oup.com
http://www.oup.co.uk/academic/science/ornithology/bwp/cdrom/

Discover Birds with Ken Newman
Ken Newman
Tel: +44 01803 865913
E-mail: sales@nhbs.co.uk
http://www.nhbs.com/xbscripts/bkfsrch?search=66571

EMS Bird Databases
13 Manor Grove
Benton, Newcastle upon Tyne
UK NE7 7XQ
Tel: 0191 2920291
E-mail: emsdata@blueyonder.co.uk
http://www.environmental-entomology.co.uk/birddata.html

Expert Centre for Taxonomic Identification
http://www.eti.uva.nl/
Titles include:
Bird Remains Identification System
Birds of Europe

Eyewitness Virtual Reality: Birds
Dorling Kindersley Multimedia
95 Madison Avenue
New York, NY 10016
USA
Tel: 800 356 6575 *or* 212 213 4800
http://www.dk.com

John Gould's Birds of Australia CD-ROM
Protoavis Productions
RMB 4375
Seymour, Victoria
Australia 3660
E-mail: h@eck.net.au
http://www.protoavis.com.au/gould.htm

Lanius Excalibur (LifeList)
Lanius Software
5055 Business Center Drive, Suite 108, #110
Fairfield, CA 94534
USA
Tel: 866 864 8279
Published 2003
E-mail: birdshrike@cs.com
http://www.onmymountain.com/v5/

Map List
Flying Emu Software
Moraga, CA
USA
E-mail: emupilot@flyingemu.com
http://www.flyingemu.com/index.html

Mutimedia 2000, Inc.
2017 Eighth Avenue, 3rd Floor
Seattle, WA 98121
USA
Tel: 206 622 5530
E-mail: info@m-2k.com
http://www.m-2k.com/pages/HomePage.asp
Titles include:
Birds of the World
Webster's Millennium 2003 Birding Collection
The North American Bird Reference Guide

National Audubon Society Interactive CD-ROM Guide to North American Birds (Mac)
Published 1996
Random House, Alfred A. Knopf
http://www.randomhouse.com/knopf/catalog/display.pperl?isbn=0679760164

Natural Learning Complete Bird Encyclopedia
Software Solutions
4490 Chesswood Dr. #3
ON Canada
Tel: 416 638 4411
http://www.cdaccess.com/html/pc/nlbird.htm

New Zealand Birds and How to Photograph Them
Sunbreak Technologies/ProTech International Ltd
http://www.cdaccess.com/html/pc/nzbirds.htm

North American Bird Reference Book
Published 2003
Lanius Software
5055 Business Center Drive, Suite 108, #110
Fairfield, CA 94534
USA
Tel: 866 864 8279
E-mail: birdshrike@cs.com
http://www.onmymountain.com/v5/

Peterson Multimedia Guides: North American Birds
Simon & Schuster
100 Front Street
Riverside, NJ 08075
USA
Tel: 1 888 793 9972
E-mail: Consumer.CustomerService@simonand-schuster.com
http://www.simonsays.com/subs/book.cfm?areaid=58&isbn=0743503864

Raptors: Birds of Prey CD-ROM
Discerning Nature
http://www.cdaccess.com/html/shared/raptors.htm

Roberts' Multimedia Birds of Southern Africa
Published 2002
Southern African Birding cc
P.O.Box 1438
Westville, South Africa 3630
Tel: +27 031 2665948
E-mail: sales@sabirding.co.za
http://www.sabirding.co.za/

Thayer Birding Software
809 Walkerbilt Road, Suite 4
Naples, FL 34110-1511
USA
Tel: 1 800 865 2473 *or* 239 596 1637
E-mail: webmaster@thayerbirding.com
http://www.thayerbirding.com/
Titles include:
Guide to Birds of North America
Guide to Backyard Birds
Birder's Diary
Birds of My Area CD-ROMs

And Our Birds Series:
Ducks, Geese & Swans of North America
FeederWatcher's Guide to Backyard Birds
Hawks, Eagles and Owls of North America
Warblers of North America
Birds of My Region

Wings (Mac)
E-mail: wings_4d@mac.com
http://homepage.mac.com/wings_4d/

YardBirds Identification Software
Ramphastos
P.O. Box 2038
Haines City, FL 33845
USA
Tel: 1 888 221 BIRD
E-mail: pbunning@ramphastos.com
http://www.ramphastos.com/

Birding Festivals

U.S.

2003 Montana Audubon Bird Festival
Malta, Montana
Tel: 406 443 3949

A Celebration of Whooping Cranes
Port Arkansas, Texas
Tel: 1 800 45 COAST

Adirondack Raptor Celebration
Newcomb, New York
Tel: 518 582 2000

Adirondack Wildlife Festival
Paul Smiths, New York
Tel: 518 327 3000

Aiken Audubon Society Birdathon and Great Pikes Peak Birding Trail Festival II
Colorado Springs, Colorado
Tel: 970 897 2454

Alaska Bald Eagle Festival
Haines, Alaska
Tel: 907 766 2202

Alaska Birder's Summer Rendezvous
Bethel, Alaska
Tel: 907 543 5967

The Aleutian Goose Festival
Crescent City, California
Tel: 707 465 0888

The Allegany Nature Pilgrimage
Erie, Pennsylvania
Tel: 814 898 0284

Appalachian Discovery Birding & Heritage Trail Dedication Festival
Peebles, Ohio
Tel: 937 588 4411

Attwater's Prairie Chicken Festival
Eagle Lake, Texas
Tel: 979 234 3021

Audubon Country BirdFest
St. Francisville, Louisiana
Tel: 1 800 488 6502

Autumn Avian Affair
Bismarck, Arkansas
Tel: 501 865 2801

Autumn Weekend/The Bird Show
Cape May, New Jersey
Tel: 609 884 2736

Bald Eagle Appreciation Days
Keokuk, Iowa
Tel: 319 524 5599 *or* 1 800 383 1219

Bald Eagle Awareness Day
Pierre, South Dakota
Tel: 605 773 6503

Bald Eagle Days
Knoxville, Iowa
Tel: 641 828 7522

Bald Eagle Days Environmental Fair & Wildlife Art Show
Davenport, Iowa
Tel: 1 800 747 7800

Bald Eagle Watch
Davenport, Iowa
Tel: 1 800 747 7800

Balmorhea Birdfest
Balmorhea, Texas
Tel: 915 375 2325

Beaks & Bills, Feathers & Quills
Bismarck, Arkansas
Tel: 501 865 2801

Bethel Bunting Bash
Bethel, Alaska
Tel: 907 543 1015

Big "O" Birding Festival
Lake Okeechobee, Florida
Tel: 863 946 0300

Big Stone Bird Festival
Ortonville, Minnesota
Tel: 320 839 3284

Bigfork Birding Festival
Bigfork, Montana
Tel: 406 837 5888

Bird Fest
Ridgefield, Washington
Tel: 360 887 9495

Bird of Prey Week at Braddock Bay
Hilton, New York
Tel: 585 392 5685

Birdhouse Exhibit & Competition
Ogden, Utah
Tel: 801 621 7595

Birding and Crystal Festival
Jet, Oklahoma
Tel: 580 626 4794

Birding in the Big Thicket
Kountze, Texas
Tel: 866 456 8689

Birds & Blossoms A Weekend for Birders & Naturalists
Norfolk, Virginia
Tel: 757 441 5835

Blackwater Open House
Cambridge, Maryland
Tel: 410 228 2677

Bluebird Festival
Wills Point, Texas
Tel: 903 873 3111

...rd & Owl Weekend
...Marais, Minnesota
...3 388 2294

...kfast with the Birds
...veland, Ohio
...1: 216 321 5935

Bridger Raptor Festival
Bozeman, Montana
Tel: 406 585 1211

Buzzard Day
Hinckley, Ohio
Tel: 740 363 1257

California Duck Days
Davis, California
Tel: 530 297 1900

Celebration
Arizona
Tel: 520 432 1388

Celebration of Birds
Cherokee, Oklahoma
Tel: 580 596 3053

Centennial Celebration
Tok, Alaska
Tel: 907 883 5312

Clarksville Eagle Days
Jefferson City, Missouri
Tel: 660 785 2420

Coeur d'Alene Eagle Watch Week
Coeur d'Alene, Idaho
Tel: 208 769 5000

Connecticut River Eagle Festival
Fairfield, Connecticut
Tel: 1 800 714 7201

Copper River Delta Shorebird Festival
Cordova, Alaska
Tel: 907 424 7260

Cranefest 2003
Kearney, Nebraska
Tel: 308 237 1000

Delmarva Birding Weekend
Snow Hill, Maryland
Tel: 1 800 852 0335

Detroit Lakes Festival of Birds
Detroit Lakes, Minnesota
Tel: 1 800 542 3992

Eagle Awareness Days
Lake Guntersville State Park, Alabama
Tel: 256 571 5445.

Eagle Awareness Month
Little Rock, Arkansas
Tel: 501 371 7777

Eagle Awareness Week
Flippin, Arkansas
Tel: 1 800 775 6682

Eagle Days
Jefferson City, Missouri
Tel: 573 751 4115 ext. 3289

Eagle Days
Lawrence, Kansas
Tel: 785 842 0475

EagleFest
Emory, Texas
Tel: 903 473 3913

Eagle Watch
Jet, Oklahoma
Tel: 580 626 4794

Eagle Watch Weekend
Bloomington, Indiana
Tel: 812 837 9967

Eagles Et Cetera
Bismarck, Arkansas
Tel: 501 865 2801

Eastern Shore Birding Festival
Melfa, Virginia
Tel: 757 787 2460

Fall Birding Week on Little St. Simons Island
Little St. Simons Island, Georgia
Tel: 1 888 733 5774

Fall Migration Birding Festival on Lake Superior
Grand Marais, Minnesota
Tel: 218 387 9762

Feather & Foliage Festival
Kelleys Island, Ohio
Tel: 419 746 2258

Feliciana Hummingbird Celebration
St. Francisville, Louisiana
Tel: 225 635 6502

Festival
Port St. Joe, Florida
Tel: 850 229 9464

Festival Celebrating International Migratory Bird Day
Milton, Delaware
Tel: 302 684 8419

Festival of the Cranes
Socorro, New Mexico
Tel: 505 835 2077

Festival of Hummingbirds
Newark, Delaware
Tel: 1 800 529 3699

Fiesta de las Aves: A Spring Migration Winter Wings Weekend
Lake Village, Arkansas
Tel: 870 265 5480

Florida Birding & Nature Festival
St. Petersburg, Florida
Tel: 866 231 0586

Florida Keys Birding & Wildlife Festival
Marathon, Florida
Tel: 305 872 0774

Florida Panhandle Birding & Wildflower Florida Birding Festival & Nature Festival
Largo, Florida
Tel: 866 231 0586

Florida's First Coast Nature Festival
St. Augustine, Florida
Tel: 1 800 653 2489

Florida's Suwannee River Birdfest
Fanning, Florida
Tel: 352 493 6736

Galveston FeatherFest
Texas City, Texas
Tel: 409 945 6302

Garnet Festival
Wrangell, Alaska
Tel: 1 800 367 9745

Georgia's Colonial Coast Birding & Nature Festival
Jekyll Island, Georgia
Tel: 912 634 1322

Gila Bird and Nature Festival
Silver City, New Mexico
Tel: 1 800 548 9378

Godwit Days
Arcata, California
Tel: 800 908 WING

Grand Marais Boreal Birding Festival
Grand Marais, Minnesota
Tel: 1 888 387 9762

Grand Marais Fall Migration Birding Festival
Grand Marais, Minnesota
Tel: 1 888 387 9762

Grassland Songbird Tour
Malta, Montana
Tel: 406 654 2863

Grays Harbor Shorebird Festival
Hoquiam, Washington

The Great Adirondack Birding Festival
Paul Smiths, New York
Tel: 518 327 3000

Great Lakes Birding Festival & Road Rally
Belleville, Michigan
Tel: 734 697 0035

The Great Lakes Birding Festival: Wings Across the Water
St. Ignace, Michigan
Tel: 734 697 0035

The Great Louisiana BirdFest
Mandeville, Louisiana
Tel: 504 626 1238

Great River Birding Festival
Lake City, Minnesota
Tel: 877 525 3248

Salt Lake Bird Festival
Farmington, Utah
801 451 3286

The Great Texas Birding Classic
Austin, Texas
Tel: 1 888 892 4737

Hawkwatch Weekend
Harpers Ferry, Iowa
Tel: 563 873 1236

Havana Eagle Days Festival
Havana, Illinois
Tel: 309 543 6502

Horicon Marsh Bird Festival
Horicon, Wisconsin
Tel: 920 387 7860

Hummer/Bird Celebration
Rockport and Fulton, Texas
Tel: 1 800 242 0071

Hummingbird Celebration
Weldon, California
Tel: 760 378 3044

International Migratory Bird Day
Alviso, California
Tel: 408 262 5513

International Migratory Bird Day
Folkston, Georgia
Tel: 912 496 7836

International Migratory Bird Day
Laurel, Maryland
Tel: 301 497 5760

International Migratory Bird Day
Malta, Montana
Tel: 406 654 2863

International Migratory Bird Day
Powell, Ohio
Tel: 614 645 3448

International Migratory Bird Day
Chincoteague, Virginia

International Migratory Bird Day at Magee Marsh
Oak Harbor, Ohio
Tel: 419 898 0960

International Migratory Bird Day Celebration
Louisville, Kentucky
Tel: 502 458 1328

International Migratory Bird Day Festival
Rochester, New York
Tel: 585 482 2063

John Scharff Migratory Bird Festival
Burns, Oregon
Tel: 541 573 2636

Kachemak Bay Shorebird Festival
Homer, Alaska
Tel: 907 235 7740

Kern River Valley Turkey Vulture Festival
Weldon, California
Tel: 760 378 3044

Kettle Valley Songbird Festival
Republic, Washington
Tel: 509 775 0441

Kirtland's Warbler Festival
Roscommon, Michigan
Tel: 989 275 5000 ext. 266

Klamath Basin Bald Eagle Conference
Klamath Falls, Oregon
Tel: 541 882 1219

Lake Erie Wing Watch Weekend
Huron, Ohio
Tel: 419 625 2984

Lake Ozark Eagle Days
Jefferson City, Missouri
Tel: 573 526 5544

Leavenworth Spring Bird Fest
Leavenworth, Washington
Tel: 509 548 5807

Lower Rio Grand Valley Birding Festival
Springfield, Vermont

Midwest Birding Symposium
Green Bay, Wisconsin
Tel: 1 800 533 6644

Migratory Bird Festival
Smyrna, Delaware
Tel: 302 653 6872

Migration Celebration
Brazosport, Texas
Tel: 1 888 477 2505

Migration Celebration
Texas
Tel: 1 800 938 4853

Migration Celebration
Ghent, West Virginia
Tel: 304 466 4683

Migration Mania
Stevensville, Montana
Tel: 406 777 5552

Millwood Lake "Wings & Things" Nature Festival
Ashdown, Arkansas
Tel: 870 898 3343

Mingo Eagle Days
Jefferson City, Missouri
Tel: 573 290 5730

Mono Basin Bird Chautauqua
Lee Vining, California
Tel: 760 647 6386

Monte Vista Crane Festival
Colorado Springs, Colorado
Tel: 719 227 5221

Morro Bay Winter Bird Festival
Morro Bay, California
Tel: 805 772 4467 or 1 800 231 0592

Nature Quest 2003
Uvalde, Texas
Tel: 1 800 210 0380

Necedah Whooping Crane Festival
Necedah, Wisconsin
Tel: 608 565 2101

Nest with the Birds
Kelleys Island, Ohio
Tel: 440 461 1084

New Jersey Audubon Society Cape May Spring Weekend
Cape May, New Jersey
Tel: 609 884 2736

New Jersey Audubon Society Cape May Autumn Weekend/The Bird Show
Cape May, New Jersey
Tel: 609 884 2736

New Jersey Audubon Society World Series of Birding
Cape May, New Jersey
Tel: 609 884 2736

New River NeoTropical Festival
Oak Hill, West Virginia
Tel: 1 800 927 0263

Northern Shenandoah Valley Audubon Society Birding Festival
Winchester, Virginia
Tel: 540 667 6778

Old Chain of Rocks Bridge Eagle Days
Jefferson City, Missouri
Tel: 314 231 3803

Ontario Bird Festival
Mexico, New York
Tel: 1 800 248 4386

Oregon Shorebird Festival
Coos Bay, Oregon
Tel: 541 267 7208

Osprey Celebration
Kirkland, Washington
Tel: 425 576 8805

Othello Sandhill Crane Festival
Othello, Washington

Pelican Celebration Week
Jet, Oklahoma
Tel: 580 626 4794

Pelican Festival
Granger, Iowa
Tel: 515 323 5300

Pelican Week
Cherokee, Oklahoma
Tel: 580 596 3053

Pinewoods Bird Festival
Thomasville, Georgia
Tel: 229 226 2344

...lley Festival of Birds
...a, Wyoming
...7 326 8855

...oles & Prairie Birding Festival
...rington and Jamestown, North Dakota
...l: 1 888 921 2473

Pueblo Eagle Day
Colorado Springs, Colorado
Tel: 719 227 5221

Rio Grande Valley Birding Festival
Harlingen, Texas
Tel: 1 800 531 7346

Rivers & Bluffs Fall Birding Festival
Lansing, Iowa
Tel: 563 538 4991

The Salton Sea International Bird Festival
Imperial Valley, California
Tel: 760 344 5359

San Diego Bird Festival
San Diego, California
Tel: 619 516 0139

San Francisco Bay Flyway Festival
Mare Island Vallejo, California
Tel: 707 557 9816

Sandhill Crane Festival
Lodi, California
Tel: 209 367 7840

Shorebird Tour
Malta, Montana
Tel: 406 654 2863

Smithville Eagle Days
Jefferson City, Missouri
Tel: 816 532 0174

Space Coast Birding & Wildlife Festival
Titusville, Florida
Tel: 321 258 5224

Spring Birding Week on Little St. Simons Island
Little St. Simons Island, Georgia
Tel: 1 888 733 5774

Spring Birding Rendezvous
International Falls, Minnesota
Tel: 218 286 5258

Spring Wing Ding
Clay Center, Nebraska
Tel: 402 762 3518

Spring Wings Bird Festival
Fallon, Nevada
Tel: 775 428 6452

Springfield Eagle Days
Jefferson City, Missouri
Tel: 417 888 4237

Songbird Celebration
Portland, Oregon
Tel: 503 239 1820

South Texas Wildlife & Birding Festival
Kingsville, Texas
Tel: 1 800 333 5032

Southern Illinois Birding Weekend
Springfield, Illinois
Tel: 217 785 8774

Southwest Louisiana Migration Sensation
Arthur, Louisiana
Tel: 337 774 3675

Southwest Wings Birding & Nature Festival
Sierra Vista, Arizona
Tel: 520 378 0233

Sullys Hill Birding & Nature Festival
Devils Lake, North Dakota
Tel: 701 766 4272

Stork & Cork
Vicksburg, Mississippi
Tel: 601 279 6309

Swan Days
Hyde County, North Carolina
Tel: 252 926 4021

Texas Songbird Festival
Lago Vista, Texas
Tel: 512 267 7952

Tucson Bird Count
Tucson, Arizona
Tel: 520 622 5622

Upper Skagit Bald Eagle Festival
Concrete, Washington
Tel: 360 853 7283

Upper Tanana Migratory Bird Festival and Sandhill Crane Festival
Fairbanks, Alaska
Tel: 907 452 5162

Verde Valley Birding & Nature Festival
Cottonwood, Arizona
Tel: 928 282 2202

Walker Lake Loon Festival
Walker Lake, Nevada
Tel: 775 945 5896

Warblers and Wildflowers Festival
Bar Harbor, Maine
Contact: Bar Harbor Chamber of Commerce,
P.O. Box 158, Bar Harbor, ME 04609
Tel: 207 288 5103

Washington County Birding Event
Washington, Kansas
Tel: 785 325 2116

Waters of the Dancing Sky Wildlife Festival
Baudette, Minnesota
Tel: 218 634 1059

Waterfowl Week
Chincoteague Island, Virginia
Tel: 757 336 6122

Wild On Wetlands Weekend
Los Banos, California
Tel: 1 800 336 6354

Wings 'n Water Festival
Stone Harbor, New Jersey
Tel: 609 368 1211

Wings Over the Swamp
Folkston, Georgia
Tel: 912 496 7836

Wings Over Water Festival
Kill Devil Hills, North Carolina
Tel: 252 441 8144

Wings Over Willcox
Willcox, Arizona
Tel: 1 800 200 2272

Yuma Birding and Nature Festival
Yuma, Arizona
Tel: 1 800 293 0071

Canada

Annual Swan Festival
Saskatoon Island Provincial Park, Alberta
Tel: 780 766 2636

Beaverhill Lake Snow Goose Festival
Tofield, Alberta
Tel: 780 662 3269

Brant Festival
Qualicum Beach, British Columbia
Tel: 250 752 9171

Brant Winter Birding Festival
Cape Sable Island, Nova Scotia
Tel: 902 634 8844

Celebration of Swans
Whitehorse, Yukon
Tel: 867 667 8291

Creston Valley Osprey Festival
Creston Valley, British Columbia
Tel: 250 402 6900

Delta Marsh Birding Festival
Delta, Manitoba
Tel: 204 857 8637

Eagle Extravaganza
Goldstream Provincial Park, British Columbia
Tel: 250 478 9414

East Sooke HawkWatch
East Sooke Regional Park, British Columbia

Fall Migration Celebration
Tofield, Alberta
Tel: 780 662 3191

Festival of Birds
Leamington, Ontario
Tel: 519 322 2365

Festival of Hawks
Amherstburg, Ontario
Tel: 519 736 5209

Festival of Hawks
Essex, Ontario
Tel: 519 776 5209 ext. 308

Fraser Valley Bald Eagle Festival
Mission—Harrison, British Columbia
Tel: 604 826 6914

Golden Bear & Birding Festival
Golden, British Columbia
Tel: 1 800 622 4653

Huron Fringe Birding Festival
Port Elgin, Ontario
Tel: 519 389 6231

Lake George Marshfest
Echo Bay, Ontario
Tel: 705 949 1231

Manning Park Year Birding Blitz
Manning Provincial Park, British Columbia

Meadowlark Festival
Penticton, British Columbia
Tel: 250 492 5275

Point Pelee Festival of Birds
Point Pelee National Park, Ontario
Tel: 519 326 6173

Robson Bird Blitz
Mt. Robson Provincial Park, British Columbia
Tel: 250 614 9919

Salmon Arm Grebe Festival
Salmon Arm, British Columbia
Tel: 250 832 1389

Shorebirds and Friends Festival
Wadena, Saskatchewan
Tel: 306 338 2145

Snow Goose Festival
Delta, British Columbia
Tel: 604 946 6980

Southeast Yukon Warbler Festival
Watson Lake, Yukon
Tel: 867 536 2057

Warblers and Whimbrels Weekend
Presqu'ile Provincial Park, Ontario
Tel: 613 475 4324

Wings Over the Rockies
Invermere, British Columbia
Tel: 1 888 933 3311

Wye Marsh Festival
Midland, Ontario
Tel: 705 526 7809

U.K.

British Birdwatching Fair
Oakham, Rutland
Tel: 01572 771079

Lee Valley Birdwatching Fair
Fishers Green, Essex
Tel: 01922 702200

RSPB Members' Weekend
Sandy, Bedfordshire
Tel: 01767 680551

Worldwide

Birds a Plenty, Bay of Plenty Bird Festival
Whakatane, New Zealand
http://www.nzbirds.com/BirdFestival.html

National Bird Week
Darwin, Northwest Territories, Australia
http://www.urbanforest.on.ca.net/events.htm

Polish Bird Festival
Warsaw, Poland
Tel: (UK and Ireland only) 0117 9658333
(International) + 48 12 2921460

Thrung-Thrung Festival
Phobjikha, Bhutan

Tel: +975 2 327355

Tucacas Wings & Fins
Tucacas, Falcon, Venezuela
Tel: 058 414 341 2136

World Bird Festival
Barcelona, Spain
Tel: + 44 01223 277 318 or + 44 07779 018 332

Yucatan Bird Festival
Itzimna, Merida, Mexico
http://www.ecoyuc.com/toh.html

Tour Operators Specializing in Bird Tours

Africa

Beautiful Just Birding
Wakkerstroom, South Africa
http://www.birdtours.co.uk/
beautiful-just-birding/index.htm

Birding Ecotours
78 Somer Road
Eversdal, Durbanville
Western Cape, South Africa
7550
Tel +27 72 635 1501
E-mail: info@birdingecotours.co.za
http://www.birdingecotours.co.za

Hunyani Safaris
E-mail: DSBALM@lds.co.uk
http://www.lds.co.uk/bird-safari/

Indicator Birding
P.O. Box 11872
Vorna Valley
South Africa 1686
Tel: +27 0 12 653 2030
E-mail: info@birding.co.za *or*
etienne@birding.co.za
http://www.birding.co.za/indicator/
tours.htm

Lawson's Tours
P.O. Box 16849
West Acres, Nelspruit
South Africa
1211
Tel: +27 13 741 2458 or 2618
After Hours Tel: +27 13 741 3527
E-mail: lawsons@lawsons.co.za
http://www.lawsons.co.za/

Peter Ginn Birding Safaris
P.O. Box 44
Marondera
Zimbabwe
Tel: 263 79 23411
E-mail: pgbs@mango.zw
http://www.safari-tours.com/pgbs/

Asia

Birds Unlimited Camp
mpat
Khmandu, Nepal
el: 997 1 429515
-mail: aquabirds@info.com.np
http://www.aquabirds.com.np/index.htm

Canda Tours PVT Ltd.
330 Galle Road
Colombo 4, Sri Lanka
Tel: 94 1 555825
E-mail: canda@itmin.com
http://www.search.lk/canda/

KingBird Tours
Planetarium Station
P.O. Box 196
New York, NY 10024-0196
USA
Tel: 1 212 866 7923
E-mail: kingbirdtours@earthlink.net
http://www.kingbirdtours.com/

Kingfisher Tours
2 Villa Paloma
Shuen Wan, Tai Po
NT, Hong Kong
Tel: +852 2665 8506
E-mail: myrl@kthk.com.hk

Wild Bird Adventure Travels & Tours
5 Thazin Myaing Lane
Kyankhinsu Ward, Mingalardone Township
Yangon, Myanmar (Burma)
P.O Box 1136
Tel: 95+1 666 469
E-mail: wildbirdtt@mptmail.net.mm
http://wildmyanmar.com/

Europe

Bird Expeditions
Postjesweg 69
6706 BS Wageningen, The Netherlands
Tel: + 31 620 400 003
E-mail: info@birdexpeditions.nl
http://www.birdexpeditions.nl

Birdwatching Holidays
E-mail: rbtodd@todds9fsnet.co.uk
http://www.users.globalnet.co.uk/~rbtodd/todd.htm

Birding in Portugal
7665 880 Santa Clara a Velha
Portugal
Tel: +351 283 933065
E-mail: paradiseinportugal@mail.telepac.pt
http://www.birding-in-portugal.com/

Birds Poland
Aleksandrowice 46
32-084 Morawica
Kraków, Poland
Tel: 00 48 501 48 53 38
E-mail: bptourinfo@yahoo.co.uk or
lesgoddin@yahoo.com
http://birdspoland.prv.pl/

Donana Bird Tours
Donana National Park, Spain
Tel: 0034 955 755 460
E-mail: john@donanabirdtours.com
http://www.donanabirdtours.com/cgi-bin/web.asp?PageID=0

Ibis Excursions
Ganløseparken 46
Ganløse, 3660 Stenløse
Denmark
Tel: +45 48195940
E-mail: jeffprice@ibis-excursions.dk
www.ibis-excursions.dk

Kibbutz Lotan Centre for Birdwatching
Doar Na Hevel Eilot
Israel 88855
Tel: +972 8 6356888
E-mail: booking@birdingisrael.com
http://www.birdingisrael.com/toursBooking/index.htm

NatuurBeleven
Oostermeerkade 6
1184 TV Amstelveen
Tel: 31 20 4961620
E-mail: markui@globalxs.nl
http://www.globalxs.nl/home/m/markui/
Dutch_Birds.htm

The Bird ID Company
37 Westgate
Warham Road, Binham
Norfolk, England
NR21 0DQ
Tel: +44 0 1328 830617
E-mail: Paul.seethebird@Virgin.net
http://www.birdtour.co.uk/

Birding in Britain with Dominic Couzens
Tel: 01202 874330
E-mail: Dominic@birdwords.freeserve.co.uk
http://www.birdwords.co.uk

Focus on Birds
Ilex House, Basses Lane
Wells-Next-The-Sea, Norfolk UK
NR23 1DH
Tel: +44 0 1328 710556
E-mail: tommcjay@aol.com

Heatherlea
The Mountview Hotel
Nethybridge, Inverness-shire
Scotland
PH25 3EB
Tel: 01479 821248
E-mail: hleabirds@aol.com
http://www.heatherlea.co.uk/

Redwing Tours
Tel: +44 0 151 281 4410
E-mail: mark@redwing77.freeserve.co.uk
http://www.redwing77.freeserve.co.uk/

SpainBirds
E-mail: info@spainbirds.com

U.K.

Mercia Birding Tours
5 Arrow Drive
Albrighton, Wolverhampton
WV7 3PF
Tel: 01902 373 957
E-mail: info@merciatours.com
http://www.merciatours.com/
merciabirdingtours/

Merlin Bird Tours
Swn-y-Boda
Ffordd Y Briallu
Carmarthen, Carmarthenshire
Wales SA31 2JU
UK
Tel: 01267 220033
E-mail: enquiries@merlinbirdtours.co.uk
http://www.birdwatchingwales.co.uk/index.htm

North West Birds
Barn Close, Beetham
Cumbria, UK
LA7 7AL
Tel: 015395 63191
E-mail: nwbirds@nwbirds.co.uk
http://www.nwbirds.co.uk/

Raptor Rambles
Tan-y-Cefn
Nr. Rhayader—Powys
LD6 5PD
Tel: 01597 811 168
E-mail: info@raptor-rambles.co.uk
http://www.raptor-rambles.co.uk/

Australasia

...alian Ornithological Services Pty Ltd
...Box 385
...th Yarra, Victoria
...stralia
141
Tel: +61 3 9820 4223
E-mail: mahert@patash.com.au *or*
enquiries@philipmaher.com
http://www.philipmaher.com/main.htm

Birds & Bush Tours
P.O. Box 6037
Townsville, Queensland
Australia
4810
Tel: +61 07 4721 6489
E-mail: ian@birdsandbushtours.com.au
http://www.birdsandbushtours.com.au/

Broome Bird Observatory Tours
P.O. Box 1313, Broome, Western Australia 6725
Tel: +61 08 9193 5600
E-mail: bbo@birdsaustralia.com.au
http://home.it.net.au/~austecol/observatories/
broome.htm#Tours

Emu Tours Australia
P.O. Box 4
Jamberoo, NSW
Australia
2533
Tel: +61 2 42 360542
E-mail: emutours@ozemail.com.au
http://members.ozemail.com.au/~emutours/

Fine Feather Tours
P.O. Box 853
Mossman, North Queensland
Australia
4873
Tel: 61 07 4094 1199
E-mail: info@finefeathertours.com.au
http://www.finefeathertours.com.au/

Kimberley Birdwatching
P.O. Box 220
Broome, Western Australia
6725
Tel: 08 9192 1246
E-mail: kimbird@tpg.com.au
http://www.kimberleybirdwatching.com.au/

Kirrama Wildlife Tours
P.O. Box 1400
Innisfail, Queensland
Australia
4860
Tel: +61 7 4065 5181
E-mail: kirrama@znet.net.au
http://www.gspeak.com.au/kirrama/

Kiwi Wildlife Tours (New Zealand) Ltd
346 Cowan Bay Road, RD3
Warkworth, New Zealand
P.O. Box 88
Orewa, New Zealand
Tel: +64 9 422 2115
E-mail: info@kiwi-wildlife.co.nz
http://www.kiwi-wildlife.co.nz/index.php

Kapiti Bird Tours
160 Weggery Drive West
Waikanae
New Zealand
Tel: +64 4 905 1001
http://www.kapitibirdtours.co.nz/

Oceanwings Albatross Encounters
58 West End
Kaikoura, New Zealand
Tel: +64 3 319 6777
E-mail: info@oceanwings.co.nz
http://www.oceanwings.co.nz/

Sicklebill Safaris Ltd
38 Creake Road
Sculthorpe, Fakenham
Norfolk, UK
NR21 9NQ
Tel: +44 1328 856925
E-mail: ian@sicklebill.demon.co.uk
http://www.sicklebill.com/

Turnstone Nature Discovery
P.O. Box 3089
Broome, Western Australia
6725
Tel: 08 9192 8585
E-mail: turnstone@wn.com.au
http://www.turnstonenaturediscovery.com.au/

U.S.

Bird Treks
415 Peach Bottom Village
Peach Bottom, PA 17563-9716
USA
Tel: 717 548 3303
E-mail: info@birdtreks.com
http://www.birdtreks.com/

Florida Nature Tours
P.O. Box 618572
Orlando, FL 32861-8572
USA
Tel: 407 363 1360
E-mail: birds@floridanaturetours.com
http://www.floridanaturetours.com/

High Lonesome Ecotours, Inc.
570 S. Little Bear Trail
Sierra Vista, AZ 85635
USA
E-mail: hilone@hilonesome.com
Tel: 1 800 743 2668
http://www.hilonesome.com/index.html

Neotropical Journeys
3920 SE 14th Terrace
Gainesville, FL 32641
USA
Toll Free: 1 877 384 2589
Tel: 352 376 7110
E-mail: info@njourneys.com
http://www.njourneys.com/

Norita's World—Birding for Seniors
1160 S.E. Polk Circle
Camas, DC 98607
USA
E-mail: noritasworld@noritasworld.com
http://www.noritasworld.com/

South Florida Birding
P.O. Box 322244
Homestead, FL 33032
USA
Tel: 305 258 9607
E-mail: birderlm@bellsouth.net
http://www.southfloridabirding.com/

Wildside Birding Tours
14 Marchwood Road
Exton, PA 19341
USA
Toll Free: 888 875 9453
Tel: 610 363 3033
E-mail: tours@adventurecamera.com or
wildsident@aol.com
http://www.adventurecamera.com/birding/
index.html

South and Central America

AvesFoto
Brazil
E-mail: avesfoto@ig.com.br
http://www.avesfoto.com.br/index.html

AvesTravel
Ecuador
E-mail: avestrav@impsat.net.ec
http://www.angelfire.com/biz/Avestravel/

Avifauna Tours
17 Morne Haven Condominiums
Gilkes St., Morne Coco Rd.
Diego Martin, Trinidad
Tel: 868 633 5614
E-mail: avifauna@trinidad.net
http://www.trinidad.net/avifauna/

Bird Holidays
10 Ivegate
Yeadon, Leeds UK
LS19 7RE
Tel: 0113 3910510
E-mail: pjw.birdholidays@care4free.net or
phil@birdholidays.fsnet.co.uk
http://www.birdholidays.fsnet.co.uk/

Birding and More
5 Grogan's Park, Suite 102
The Woodlands TX 77380
USA
Toll Free: 1 800 451 8017
Tel: 281 367 3386
E-mail: adventure@tropicaltravel.com
http://www.birdingandmore.com/

...g Brazil Tours

...55 92 638 4540
...ail: info@birdingbraziltours.com
...tp://www.birdingbraziltours.com/

Birding Escapes
1641 NW 79th Avenue
Miami, FA 33126-1105
USA
Tel: +506 771 4582
E-mail: selvamar@racsa.co.cr
http://www.birdwatchingcostarica.com/

Birding Veracruz
Plaza Dona Marta #3
Tlacotalpan, Veracruz
Mexico
Tel: 011 52 288 884 2683
E-mail: birdingveracruz@yahoo.com
http://birdingveracruz.20m.com/index.html

Birdwatch Costa Rica
Apartado 7911
1000 San Jose
Costa Rica
Central America
Tel: +506-228-4768
E-mail: birdwatch@racsa.co.cr
http://www.birdwatchcostarica.com

Caligo Ventures, Inc.
156 Bedford Road
Armonk, NY 10504
USA
Toll Free: 1 800 426 7781 in the U.S. and
Canada
Tel: 914 273 6333
E-mail: info@caligo.com
http://www.caligo.com/

Costa Rica Gateway
P.O. Box 025216
Miami, FL 33102-5216
USA
Toll Free: 1 888 246 8513
Tel: 1 888 246 8513 *or* 011 506 297 4134
E-mail: sales@ranchonaturalista.com
http://www.ranchonaturalista.com/

Cotinga Tours
5762 Main St.
Elkridge, MD 21075
USA
Toll free: 1 888 205 6415
E-mail: cotingatours@msn.com
http://www.cotingatours.com/birding/

Falcon Tours Costa Rica
Viajes Halcon S.A.
P.O. Box 524
Guapiles, Costa Rica
7210
Tel: 506 710 4805
E-mail: freddymadrigal3@hotmail.com
http://www.falcontourscr.com/

Kestrel Nature Tours
224 Highbluffs Blvd.
Columbus, OH
USA 43235
Toll Free: 1 866 259 6519
Tel: 614 781 9426
E-mail: info@KestrelNatureTours.com
http://www.kestrelnaturetours.com/

Manu Expeditions
E-mail: Adventure@ManuExpeditions.com
http://www.birdinginperu.com/

Mindo Bird Tours
Casilla Postal 17-17-404
Quito, Ecuador
Tel: 593 2 2454304
E-mail: vperez@pi.pro.ec and jlyons@pi.pro.ec
http://www.mindobirds.com.ec/

Neblina Forest
Puembo—Ecuador
Quinta La Trinidad
Tel: 593 2 2140 015 593 2 2140 019
Toll Free: 1 800 538 2149 or 1 800 448 9140
http://www.neblinaforest.com/index.html
E-mail: info@neblinaforest.com or sales
@neblinaforest.com

Neotropical Birding Adventures
Costa Rica
Toll Free: 1 888 244 7119
E-mail: pamela@birdingadventures.com
http://www.birdingadventures.com/main.html

Safaris Corobici
Canas, Guanacaste
Costa Rica
Tel: 011 506 669 6191
E-mail: deanhouse@rmisp.com
http://www.nicoya.com/index.html

Serra dos Tucanos
Malands, Selsey Road
Sidlesham, Chichester
West Sussex, UK
PO20 7QX
Tel: +44 0 1243 641438
E-mail: serradostucanos@hotmail.com
http://www.serradostucanos.com.br/

Southern Bird Tours, LLC
Tel: 912 601 1090
E-mail: mwelford@gasou.edu
http://www2.gasou.edu/facstaff/mwelford/
Birds-Ecuador/Birding_Ecuador.htm

Swallows and Amazons
Rua Quintino Bocaiuva, 189
Andar 1, Sala 134
Manaus, Amazonas
Brazil
69005-110
Tel: 55 92 622 1246
E-mail: swallows@internext.com.br

Toucan Tours
49 Queen's Drive Fulwood
Preston, Lancs UK
PR2 9YL
Tel: 00 44 0 1772 787 862
E-mail: enquiries@toucantours.co.uk
http://www.toucantours.co.uk/

Trogon Travel
Bolkerhoeveweg 16
B-2520 Oelegem
Belgium
Tel: 0032 3 3852908
E-mail: trogon@wol.be
http://home.tiscali.be/fr018787/trogon/

Canada

BRITISH COLUMBIA
Avocet Tours
725 Richards Road
Kelowna, BC
Canada
V1X 2X5
Tel: 250 718 0335
E-mail: info@avocettours.com
http://www.avocettours.com/

ONTARIO
Birding with Brian
Tel: 905 854 3156
E-mail: brianwestland@hotmail.com
http://riron.freeyellow.com/newfile.html

NOVA SCOTIA
MacLeod Bird and Nature Travel Tours
15 Elizabeth Court
White's Lake, Nova Scotia
Canada
B3T 1Z2
Tel: 902 852 1228
E-mail: macleod.grayjay@ns.sympatico.ca
http://www3.ns.sympatico.ca/macleod.grayjay/
peter.htm

United States

ALASKA
Birdwatching Tours of Anchorage
4030 Galactica Drive
Anchorage, AK 99517
USA
Tel: 907 248 7282 *or* 1 888 334 7282
E-mail: dalefox@gci.net
http://www.anchoragebirding.com/

Wilderness Birding Adventures
5515 Wild Mountain Road
Eagle River, AK 99577
USA
Tel: 907 694 7442
E-mail: wildbird@alaska.net
http://www.wildernessbirding.com/index.html

ARIZONA
Stuart Healy
220 Stardust Street
Sierra Vista AZ 85635
USA
Tel: 520 458 7603
E-mail: stuarthealy@earthlink.net
http://www.aztrogon.com/

CALIFORNIA
Monterey Birding Adventures
P.O. Box 692
Moss Landing CA 95039
USA
Tel: 831 632 2473
E-mail: rimbirding@aol.com
http://www.montereybirdingadventures.com/

Shearwater Journeys
P.O. Box 190
Hollister, CA
USA 95024
Tel: 831 637 8527
E-mail: debiluv@earthlink.net
http://www.shearwaterjourneys.com/

FLORIDA
Swampland Bird Tours
National Audubon Society Wildlife Sanctuary
Lake Okeechobee FL
USA
Tel: 941 467 4411
E-mail: swamplan@okeechobee.com
http://www.geocities.com/CapeCanaveral/1020/
swampland.html

HAWAII
Hawaii Forest and Trails Birdwatching
Adventure
74–5035B Queen Kaahumanu Hwy.
Kailua-Kona HI 96740
USA
Toll Free: 1 800 464 1993
Tel: 81 08 331 8505
E-mail: info@hawaii-forest.com
http://hawaii-forest.com/otherbirds.html

MAINE
Puffin Tours of Machias Seal Island
8 Sea Street
Jonesport, ME 04649-9704
USA
Toll Free: 1 888 889 3222
Tel: 207 497 5933
E-mail: puffins@downeast.net
http://www.machiassealisland.com/

MICHIGAN
Dettling Tours
E-mail: Detman2@aol.com
http://www.geocities.com/amdettling/

NEW MEXICO
WingsWest Bird Watching Tours
2599 Camino Chueco
Santa Fe, NM 87505
USA
Tel: 505 473 2780
Toll Free: 1 800 583 6928
E-mail: wingswes@aol.com
http://www.collectorsguide.com/sf/a003.html

NEVADA
Lahontan Audubon Society
NV Important Bird Areas Program
511 West King St.
Carson City, NV 89703
USA
Tel: 775 841 5090
E-mail: dmcivor@audubon.org
http://www.nevadaaudubon.org/Field%20trips/
Birding%20tours.htm

NORTH CAROLINA
Seabirding Pelagic Tours
P.O. Box 772
Hatteras, NC 27943
USA
Tel: 252 986 1363
E-mail: brian@patteson.com
http://www.patteson.com/

Ventures Birding and Nature Tours
P.O Box 1095
Skyland, NC 28776
USA
Tel: 828 253 4247
E-mail: travel@birdventures.com
http://www.birdventures.com/

NORTH DAKOTA
Buffalo Commons Birding Safaris
2704 10th Avenue NW
Mandan, ND 58554
USA
Tel: 1 701 663 7142 or 1 701 228 5271
E-mail: barnhart@btinet.net or tgibson@ndak.net
http://webhost.btinet.net/~barnhart/index.html

TEXAS
Aransas Bay Birding Charters
P.O. Box 640
Fulton, TX 78358
USA
Tel: 361 727 2689
E-mail: craigt@dbstech.com
http://www.texasbirdingcentral.com/

Big Bend Birding Expeditions
P.O. Box 507
Terlingua, TX 79852
USA
Tel: 1 888 531 2223
E-mail: jim@bigbendbirding.com
http://www.bigbendbirding.com/index.html

Coastal Bend Birders Birding Tours
P.O. Box 160
Fulton, TX 78358
USA
Toll Free: 1 888 660 BIRD
Tel: 361 790 8884
E-mail: birders@intcomm.net
http://www.cybernet-ics.com/birders/

Oscar Carmona
P.O. Box 8160
Huntsville, TX 77340
USA
Tel: 936 730 8411
E-mail: hookbilledkite@hotmail.com
http://www.geocities.com/ringedkingfisher/
birdguide.html

VERMONT
Vermont Bird Tours
113 Bartlett Road
Plainfield, VT 05667
USA
Tel: 802 454 4640
E-mail: bryan@vermontbirdtours.com
http://www.vermontbirdtours.com/

WASHINGTON
Lopez Island Birding Tours
Tel: 360 468 3510
http://www.geocities.com/lopezbird/

Westport Seabirds Pelagic Trips
P.O. Box 665
Westport, WA 98595
USA
Tel: 360 268 5222
E-mail: pmand@reachone.com
http://www.westportseabirds.com/index.html

WISCONSIN
Blue Heron Tours
P.O. Box 6
311B Mill St.
Horicon, WI 53032-0006
USA
Tel: 920 485 4663
E-mail: blueheron@horiconmarsh.com
http://www.blueherontours.com/

Worldwide

AABirding
Box 7999
Cairns, Queensland
Australia
4870
Tel: 07 4031 8803
E-mail: tours@aabirding.com
http://aabirding.com

American Birding Association
P.O. Box 6599
Colorado Springs CO 80934
USA
Tel: 719 578 9703
E-mail: member@aba.org
http://www.americanbirding.org/convtours/
restours2.htm

Aves Tours
Von-Lüninckstr. 46
D-48151 Münster
Tel: 0049 0931/2919771
E-mail: contact@avestours.de
http://www.avestours.com/english/Birds/
startframeset.htm

Avian Adventures
49 Sandy Road, Norton
Stourbridge, UK
DY8 3AJ
Tel: +44 0 1384 372013
E-mail: aviantours@argonet.co.uk
http://www.avianadventures.co.uk/home.htm

Birdfinders
Westbank
Cheselbourne, Dorset UK
DT2 7NW
Tel (UK): 01258 839066
Tel (Overseas): +44 1258 839066
E-mail: birdfinders@compuserve.com
http://www.birdfinders.co.uk/

Birding Worldwide
Level 3, 818 Whitehorse Road
Box Hill 3128
VIC, Australia
Tel: +61 3 9899 9303
E-mail: enquiries@birdingworldwide.com.au
http://www.birdingworldwide.com.au/index.
html

Birdseekers
19 Crabtree Close
Marshmills
Plymouth, Devon UK
PL3 6EL
Tel: 01752 220947
E-mail: Bird@birdseekers.freeserve.co.uk
http://www.birdseekers.co.uk/

Birdquest, Ltd.
Two Jays, Kemple End
Birdy Brow, Lancashire UK
BB7 9QY
Tel: +44 01254 826317
E-mail: birders@birdquest.co.uk
http://www.birdquest.co.uk/

Birdwatching Breaks
Cygnus House
Gordons Mill, Balblair
Ross-shire
Scotland
IV7 8LQ
Tel: +44 0 1381 610495
E-mail: enquiries@birdwatchingbreaks.com
http://www.birdwatchingbreaks.com/

Borderland Tours
2550 W. Calle Padilla
Tucson, AZ 85745
USA
Toll Free: 1 800 525 7753
In Tucson: 520 882 7650
E-mail: rtaylor@borderland-tours.com
http://www.borderland-tours.com/

Celtic Bird Tours
84 Coity Road
Bridgend, South Wales
UK
CF31 1LT
Tel: 01656 645709
E-mail: Birds@celtictours.org.uk
http://www.celticbirdtours.com/

Clockwork Travel
5210 Pershing Avenue
Fort Worth, TX 76107
USA
Toll free: 1 800 752 6246
Tel: 817 735 4130
E-mail: kenneth@clockbird.com
http://www.birdtrips.com/Default2.htm

Eagle-Eye Tours
Tel (North America): 1 800 373 5678
Tel (UK): 0 800 328 1454
Tel: 604 948 9177
E-mail: birdtours@eagle-eye.com
http://www.eagle-eye.com/

Field Guides Inc.
9433 Bee Cave Road, Building 1, Suite 150
Austin, TX 78733
USA
Toll free: 1 800 728 4953
Tel: 512 263 7295
E-mail: fieldguides@fieldguides.com
http://www.fieldguides.com/

Flora and Fauna Field Tours
232 Belair Dr.
Bolton, ON L7E 1Z7
Canada
Tel: 905 857 2235
E-mail: flora_fauna_tours@hotmail.com or
nilsomdave@hotmail.com
http://members.rogers.com/milsomdave1/

Free-Living Holidays
E-mail: information@free-living.com
http://www.free-living.com

Ibisbill Tours
7 Holders Hill Gardens
London UK
NW4 1NP
Tel: +44 0 20 8203 4317
E-mail: ibisbill@talk21.com

InfoHub, Inc.
38764 Buckboard Common
Fremont, CA 94536
USA
E-mail: agent@infohub.com
http://www.infohub.com/TRAVEL/SIT/sit_pages/
Birdwatching.html

Island Holidays
Drummond Street
Comrie, Perthshire
Scotland PH6 2DS
Tel: 01764 670107
E-mail: enquiries@24islandholidays.com
http://www.24islandholidays.com/?net

Lifebirds Nature Tours
1433 West Cuyler Avenue, Suite 3
Chicago, IL 60613
USA
Tel: 773 244 2468
E-mail: info@lifebird.com
http://www.lifebird.com/fullmap.htm

Limosa Holidays
Suffield House, Northrepps
Norfolk UK
NR27 0LZ
Tel: +44 0 1263 578143
E-mail: limosaholidays@compuserve.com

New Horizons
Eastwood
Nottinghamshire UK
NG16 3DD
Tel: 00 44 01773 716550
E-mail: hallnewhorizons@nasuwt.net
http://www.newhorizonsonline.co.uk/

Ornitholidays
29, Straight Mile
Romsey, Hampshire UK
SO51 9BB
Tel: +44 0 1794 519445
E-mail: ornitholidays@compuserve.com
http://www.ornitholidays.co.uk/

Peregrine Bird Tours
2 Drysdale Place
Mooroolbark
Victoria, Australia
3138
Tel: +61 3 9726 8471 or +61 3 9727 3343
E-mail: birding@peregrinebirdtours.com
http://www.sub.net.au/~vwspbt01/

Raptours
P.O. Box 531467
Harlingen, TX 78553
USA
Tel: 956 364-0415
E-mail: raptours@tiagris.com

Sarus Bird Tours
12 Walton Drive
Walmersley, Bury
UK
BL9 5JU
Tel: +44 0 161 797 6243
E-mail: webenquiry@sarusbirdtours.co.uk
http://www.sarusbirdtours.co.uk/

Sawtelle Tours
2539 Vestal Parkway East
Vestal, NY 3850-2020
USA
Tel: 1 800 295 2222
E-mail: nature@sawtelletravel.com
http://www.birdcostarica.com/

Sunbird Tours
P.O. Box 76
Sandy, Beds UK
SG19 1DF
Tel: +44 01767 682969
E-mail: sunbird@sunbirdtours.co.uk
http://www.sunbirdtours.co.uk/

The Travelling Naturalist
P.O. Box 3141
Dorchester
Dorset UK
DT1 2XD
Tel: +44 01305 267994
E-mail: jamie@naturalist.co.uk
http://www.naturalist.co.uk/

Tropical Birding
Reina Victoria y La Pinta
Edficio Santiago 1, Dep. 501
Quito, Ecuador
Toll Free (US): 1 800 348 5941
Tel: +593 2 290 9753
E-mail: info@tropicalbirding.com
http://www.tropicalbirding.com/

Turaco Nature, Inc.
P.O. Box 54017
Oshawa, ON L1H 1A0
Canada
Toll-free: 1 877 295 1556
Tel: 905 725 1759
E-mail: turaco@sympatico.ca
http://www.turaco.com/

Victor Emanuel Nature Tours
2525 Wallingwood Drive, Suite 1003
Austin, TX 78746
USA
Toll free: 1 800 328 8368
Tel: 800 328 8368 or 512 328 5221
E-mail: info@ventbird.com
http://www.ventbird.com/

WildWings
577–579 Fishponds Road
Fishponds, Bristol
UK
BS16 3AF
Tel: 0117 9658 333
E-mail: wildinfo@wildwings.co.uk
http://www.wildwings.co.uk/bwintro.html

Wings Birding Tours
1643 N. Alvernon, Suite 109
Tucson, AZ 85712
USA
Toll Free: 1 888 293 6443
Tel: 520 320 9868
E-mail: wings@wingsbirds.com
http://www.wingsbirds.com/

Places to Go Birding

Top Twenty Countries for Species Numbers

eru
,800+ species in 68 families
04 endemics
0 speciality species
7 endangered species including 21 endemics

:olombia
,770 species in 67 families
0 endemics
7 speciality species
5 endangered species including 27 endemics

Srazil
,715 species in 72 families
82 endemics
0 speciality species
03 endangered species including 49 endemics

:cuador
,564 species in 67 families
+25 Galapagos endemics
0 + 10 speciality species
1 endangered species including 13 endemics

ndonesia
)ver 1,500 species
38 endemic species
36 endangered species

'enezuela
,383 species in 64 families
9 endemics
1 speciality species
:3 endangered species

:olivia
,374 species in 62 families
:0 endemics
7 speciality species
:8 endangered species including 6 endemics

:hina
,221 species in 75 families
8 endemic species plus 10 shared only with
ibet
10+ speciality species
6 endangered species

India
1,214 species in 81 families
34 endemic species plus 17 shared only with Sri
Lanka
113 speciality species
77 endangered species

Congo (formerly Zaire)
1,176 species in 73 families
14 endemic species
74 speciality species
25 endangered species

Kenya
1,137 species in 75 families
8 endemic species
76 speciality species
25 endangered species

Mexico
1,104 species in 69 families
213 of the 246 species endemic to North
America are represented here
97 endemic species

Tanzania
1,104 species in 75 families
21 endemic species
30 endangered species
76 speciality species

Uganda
1,073 species in 71 families
2 endemic species
43 speciality birds
12 endangered species

USA
1,043 species (including Hawaii) in 67 families
41 endemic species
78 endangered species

Argentina
988 species in 66 families
16 endemic species
44 specialities
41 endangered species including 2 endemics

Angola
971 species in 75 families
8 endemic species
8 speciality birds
16 endangered species

Cameroon
939 species in 76 families
7 endemic species
20 speciality species
18 endangered species

Panama
944 species in 59 families
11 endemics
64 endemics shared only with Costa Rica
9 endangered species

Sudan
938 species
1 endemic species
17 speciality birds
9 endangered species

SOURCE: www.camacdonald.com/birding

Sixty Top Birding Destinations in the World*

Crooked Tree Wildlife Sanctuary, Belize
Monteverde Cloud Forest Reserve, Costa Rica
Tikal National Park, Guatemala
Chiriqui Highlands, Panama
Panama Canal Rainforest Canopy Tower, Panama
Manu National Park, Peru
Falkland Islands
Iguazu National Park, Argentina
Itatiaia National Park, Brazil
Galapagos Islands, Ecuador
Buenaventura, Colombia
La Selva Lodge, Ecuador
Hato Pinero, Venezuela
Asa Wright Nature Centre, Trinidad
Siikalahti Conservation Area, Finland
Skagen, Denmark
Ottenby Bird Observatory, Sweden
Finnmark, Norway
Camargue, France
Coto Donana National Park, Spain
Straight of Gibraltar, Spain
Fuertaventura, Canary Islands
Danube Delta, Romania
Neusiedler See—Seewinkel National Park, Austria
Lauwersmeer, The Netherlands
Alpi Marittime, Italy
Lake Myvatn, Iceland
Eilat, Israel
Azraq Oasis, Jordan
Okovango Delta, Botswana

Samburu, Kenya
Kakamega National Forest, Kenya
Queen Elizabeth National Park, Uganda
Nyika National Park, Malawi
Luangwa Valley National Parks, Zambia
Victoria Falls, Zimbabwe
Capetown, South Africa
Kruger National Park, South Africa
Madagascar (Malagasy Republic)
The Seychelles
Black River Gorges National Park, Mauritius/Reunion
Keoladeo Ghanna Sanctuary, India
Vedanthangal Bird Sanctuary, India
Royal Chitwan National Park, Nepal
Fraser's Hill, Malaysia
Cat Tien National Park, Vietnam
Sinharaja Forest Reserve, Sri Lanka
Syunkunitai Wild Bird Sanctuary, Japan
Beidaihe, China
Kenting National Park, Taiwan
Mai Po Marshes, Hong Kong
South Georgia Island, Antarctica
Irian Jaya, Papua New Guinea
Melbourne/Victoria, Australia
Sydney, New South Wales, Australia
Brisbane, Queensland, Australia
Okarito Lagoon, New Zealand
Kaikoura, New Zealand
Bouma Forest Park, Fiji
New Caledonia

* North America and United Kingdom are given in separate lists

For more information, consult the American Birding Association, www.birding.com, www.fatbirder.com and/or www.camacdonald.com/birding/birding.htm

Twenty Top Birding Sites in the U.K.

Minsmere, Suffolk
Titchwell Marsh, Norfolk
Ouse Washes, Cambridgeshire
Dungeness, Kent
rne, Dorset
ortland Bill, Dorset
angstone Harbour, Hampshire
arne Islands, Northumberland
bernethy Forest, Loch Garten, Highland
umbergh Head, Mainland, Shetland
air Isle, Shetland

Isles of Scilly
Spurn Point, Yorkshire
Bempton Cliffs, Yorkshire
Hayle Estuary, Cornwall
Marazion Marsh, Cornwall
Valley Wetlands, Anglesey
South Stack Cliffs, Anglesey
Balranald, North Uist, Western Isles, Hebrides
Loch Druidibeg, South Uist, Western Isles,
Hebrides

or more information, contact the Royal Society for the Protection of Birds, www.birding.com,
www.fatbirder.com, and/or www.camacdonald.com/birding/birding.htm

Ninety Top Birding Spots in the U.S.

Alaska
Attu Island
Denali National Park (Mt. McKinley)
Pribilof Islands (St. Paul Island)
Nome
Resurrection Bay
Gambel

Alabama
Guntersville Lake
Audubon Bird Sanctuary, Dauphin Island

Arizona
Cave Creek/Portal/Chiricahua Mountains
Madera Canyon/Florida Wash/Santa Rita
Mountains
Ramsey Canyon/Huachuca Mountains
Rustler Park/Chiracahua Mountains
aguaro National Park (east unit)
Mogollon Rim, Flagstaff

Arkansas
Holla Bend National Wildlife Refuge
Lake Fayetteville

California
Elkhorn Slough/Moss Landing
oshua Tree/Big Morongo
Monterey Bay
Point Reyes/Bodega Bay

Salton Sea
Lower Klamath Refuges/Tule Lake
Mono Lake
Yosemite National Park

Colorado
Rocky Mountain Park/Golden Gate Canyon Park
Pawnee National Grasslands

Delaware
Delaware Bay/Bombay Hook National Wildlife
Refuge

Florida
Corkscrew Swamp Sanctuary
Dry Tortugas
Everglades National Park
Sanibel Island/Ding Darling National Wildlife
Refuge
Florida Keys
Merrit Island National Wildife Refuge

Georgia
Okefenokee Swamp
Little St. Simon's Island

Hawaii
Haleakala National Park
Haiwaii Volcanoes National Park

Idaho
Snake River Birds of Prey Natural Area

Illinois
Illinois Beach State Park

Indiana
Muscatatuck National Wildlife Refuge
Willow Slough State Fish and Wildlife Area
Jasper-Pulaski State Fish and Wildlife Area

Iowa
Cone Marsh Wildlife Area

Kansas
Quivira National Wildlife Refuge/Cheyenne
Bottoms

Maine
Acadia National Park
Machias Seal Island
Monhegan Island

Massachusetts
Plum Island/Newburyport

Minnesota
Duluth/Hawk Ridge Nature Reserve
Minnesota Valley National Wildlife Refuge

Montana
Bowdoin National Wildlife Refuge
Medicine Lake National Wildlife Refuge

Nebraska
Platte River

New Hampshire
Squam Lake
McCrillis Hill

New Jersey
Brigantine Division—Forsythe National Wildlife
Refuge
Cape May
Turkey Point
Parvin State Park

New Mexico
Bosque des Apache National Wildlife Refuge
Gila National Forest

New York
Central Park, New York City
Jamaica Bay National Wildlife Refuge
Niagara Falls

Hawthorn Orchard, East Ithaca
Lake Ontario lakefront, Rochester

North Carolina
Pea Island National Wildlife Refuge

Ohio
Crane Creek/Magee Marsh/Ottawa National
Wildlife Refuge

Oregon
Malheur National Wildlife Refuge
Waldo Lake

Pennsylvania
Hawk Mountain Sanctuary
Presque Isle State Park

Rhode Island
Block Island

South Carolina
Huntington Beach State Park

Tennessee
Reelfoot Lake

Texas
Aransas National Wildlife Reserve
Bentsen-Rio Grande Valley State Park
Big Bend National Park
Bolivar Flats
Falcon Dam/San Ygnacio
King Ranch
Padre Island National Seashore
Santa Ana National Wildlife Refuge

Utah
Bear River National Wildlife Refuge

Vermont
Dead Creek Wildlife Management Area

Virginia
Chincoteague National Wildlife Reserve
Monticello Park

Washington
Hoh Rainforest
Willapa Bay

Wyoming
Grand Teton National Park

For more information, consult the Cornell Laboratory of Ornithology, American Birding Association www.birding.com, www.fatbirder.com, and/or www.camacdonald.com/birding/birding.htm

Twenty-five Top Birding Spots in Canada

Alberta
Banff National Park/Lake Louise
Elk Island National Park
Beaverhill Lake

British Columbia
Vancouver/Reifel Bird Sanctuary and Victoria
Waterfront
Creston Valley
Queen Charlotte Islands

Manitoba
Churchill
Riding Mountain National Park
Delta Marsh

Newfoundland
Witless Bay Islands
Cape St. Mary's Bird Sanctuary

New Brunswick
Grand Manan
Fundy National Park

Nova Scotia
Cape Breton/French Mountain, Bird Island,
Ingonish

Ontario
Point Pelee National Park
Long Point, Port Rowan
Rondeau Provincial Park
Amherst Island

Prince Edward Island
Prince Edward Island National Park

Quebec
Bonaventure Island/Gaspe Peninsula
Mont Tremblant Provincial Park

Saskatchewan
Pelican Lake
Last Mountain Lake
Cyress Hills Provincial Park

Yukon
Dempster Highway

For more information, consult *A Bird-Finding Guide to Canada* by J. Cam Finlay, the American Birding Association, www.birding.com, www.fatbirder.com, and/or www.camacdonald.com/birding/birding.htm

Birding Trails in North America

Alabama
Alabama Coastal Birding Trail

Arizona
Southeast Arizona Birding Trail

California
Central Coast Birding Trail
Eastern Sierra Birding Trail

Colorado
Great Pikes Peak Birding Trail

Connecticut
The Connecticut Coastal Birding Trail

Florida
The Great Florida Trails

Georgia
Colonial Coast Birding Trail

Illinois
Great River Birding Trail

Iowa
Great River Birding Trail

Kansas
Kansas Birding and Prairie Flora Trails

Kentucky
John James Audubon Birding Trail

Louisiana
Grand Isle Birding Trail

Minnesota
Pine to Prairie Birding Trail
The Great River Birding Trail
Minnesota River Valley Birding Trail

Missouri
Great River Birding Trail

Montana
Great Montana Birding and Wildlife Trail

New Hampshire
The Connecticut River Birding Trail

New York
Audubon Niagara Birding Trail
The Lake Champlain Birding Trail

North Dakota
Steele Birding Drive

Ohio
Southern Ohio Birding and Heritage Trail

Oklahoma
Western Oklahoma Wildlife Heritage Train
Great Plains Trail of Oklahoma

Oregon
Oregon Cascades Birding Trail

Pennsylvania
Susquehanna River Birding and Wildlife Trail

Saskatchewan, Canada
The Saskatchewan Bird Trail

Texas
Great Texas Coastal Birding Trail
Upper Texas Coast
Central Texas Coast
Lower Texas Coast
Heart of Texas Wildlife Trail
Panhandle and Pineywoods Wildlife Trail

Utah
Great Salt Lakes Birding Trails

Vermont
The Connecticut River Birding Trail
The Lake Champlain Birding Trail

Virginia
Virginia Birding and Wildlife Trail

Wisconsin
Oak Leaf Birding Trail
Great Wisconsin Birding Trail

Washington
Great Washington Birding Trail (the Cascade Loop)

World Hawk-Watching Sites

Top Thirty Watch Sites with at Least 10,000 Migrant Raptors Annually

NORTH AMERICA
Canada
Beamer Conservation Area, ON
Hawk Cliff, ON
Holiday Beach, ON

United States
Braddock Bay, NY
Cape May Point, NJ
Derby Hill, NY
Golden Gate Observatory, CA
Goshute Mountains, NV
Hawk Mountain Sanctuary, PA
Hawk Ridge, MN
Montclair, NJ

CENTRAL AMERICA
Kekoldi (Talamanca), Costa Rica
Veracruz Coastal Plain, Mexico
Southern Panama Canal Zone, Panama

SOUTH AMERICA
Combeima Canyon, Colombia

EUROPE
Atanassovo Lake, Bulgaria
Organbidexka, France
Tarifa, Strait of Gibraltar, Spain
Gibraltar (UK), Spain
Falsterbo, Sweden
Bosphorus-Istanbul, Turkey

AFRICA
Bab-el-Mandeb, Djibouti
Cap Bon, Tunisia

ASIA
Bedaihe, China
Arava Valley, Israel
Elat, Israel
Chokpak Pass, Kazakstan
Belen Pass, Turkey

PACIFIC ISLANDS
Teluk Terima, Indonesia
Sheting, Taiwan

SOURCE: *Hawks Aloft Worldwide*—a Conservation Initiative of Hawk Mountain Sanctuary Association, 1700 Hawk Mountain Rd., Kempton PA 19529-9449, USA

Hawk Mountain Sanctuary Flight Statistics from 1934 to 2002

	Overall Annual Average	10-yr Annual Average (1992–2002)	Record Year (nos.)
Bald eagle	62	136	2002 (207)
Golden eagle	54	97	1998 (144)
Turkey vulture*	95	209	1999 (367)
Black vulture*	11	46	1999 (80)
Osprey	380	577	1990 (872)
American kestrel	396	618	1989 (839)
Merlin	46	127	2001 (176)
Peregrine falcon	26	44	2002 (62)
Red-shouldered hawk	274	295	1958 (468)
Broad-winged hawk	8,234	6,402	1978 (29,519)
Red-tailed hawk	3,313	3,742	1939 (6,208)
Rough-legged hawk	9	8	1961 (31)
Sharp-shinned hawk	4,355	4,949	1977 (10,612)
Cooper's hawk	342	742	1998 (1,118)
Northern goshawk	71	82	1972 (347)
Northern harrier	228	245	1980 (475)
Mississippi kite	0	0	2002 (1)
All raptors	18,021	18,502	1978 (40,698)

* counts only from 1990 to 2002

SOURCE: Hawk Mountain Sanctuary Association, 1700 Hawk Mountain Road, Kempton, PA 19529-944⁹ www.hawkmountain.org

Golden Gate Raptor Observatory Flight Statistics from 1989 to 2002

	Overall Annual Average	10-yr Annual Average (1992–2002)	Record Year
Bald eagle	0	3	1999 (7)
Golden eagle	14	19	1987 (39)
Turkey vulture	4,785	8,065	2002 (11,046)
Osprey	61	87	2000 (136)
American kestrel	467	603	1997 (758)
Merlin	95	145	1998 (250)
Peregrine falcon	66	114	1997 (225)
Prairie falcon	5	5	1988 (16)
Red-shouldered hawk	193	318	2002 (677)
Broad-winged hawk	180	112	1991 (249)
Red-tailed hawk	12,194	8,911	1999 (12,520)
Swainson's hawk	3	4	2002 (9)
Ferruginous hawk	16	21	1987/02 (34)
Rough-legged hawk	6	8	1988 (69)
Sharp-shinned hawk	3,467	4,122	1999 (6,348)
Cooper's hawk	1,819	2,389	1999 (3,015)
Northern goshawk	1	2	1988 (9)
Northern harrier	516	774	1999 (1,369)
White-tailed kite	32	53	2001 (86)
All raptors	19,238	25,732	2002 (35,288)

SOURCE: Golden Gate Raptor Observatory, Building 201, Fort Mason, San Francisco, CA 94123; Tel: 415 331 0730; www.ggro.org

Frequently Asked Questions (and Answers!)

1. **How many birds are there in the world?**
   James Fisher, a British ornithologist, gave an estimate of 100 billion. More recently, ornithological textbooks put it at 300 billion. The number is likely somewhere in between.

2. **How many different kinds of birds are there in the world?**
   This depends on what book and/or list one consults. According to BirdLife International, there are 9,797 species, of which 1,186 are threatened in some way.

3. **Why are bird species not listed alphabetically in field guides?**
   They are listed taxonomically with the most primitive first (e.g. ostriches, loons) and the most developed last (e.g. sparrows).

4. **Do bird species hybridize?**
   Some closely related species do interbreed, especially when geographical barriers are broken down by human activities.

5. **Are new bird species still being discovered?**
   Occasionally, but rarely, a new species is found in a remote region; more often a new species is created when sophisticated genetic techniques along with morphology and behavioral differences indicate that one species should be split into two or more.

6. **How long do birds live?**
   Generally, the larger the species, the longer it lives. Captive birds usually outlive wild ones. Most small songbirds do not make it past 2 to 4 years of age in the wild.

7. **Why am I seeing fewer birds than before?**
   Bird populations fluctuate over time due to weather patterns, disease outbreaks, and increased predator pressure. Local populations are affected by changing land uses; birds requiring specialized habitat are declining.

8. **Where do feathers come from?**
   Only birds have feathers, which originate from the skin and, once grown, become dead tissue; if a bird loses a grown feather, it will often grow a new one within weeks.

9. **What causes the color in birds?**
   While many colors are caused by pigments—some from arising heredity and some from diet—reflection and diffraction of light resulting from the structure of feathers is responsible for the colors in some birds.

10. **Are only the males more brightly colored?**
    In most species, the male is brightly colored to attract mates and defend the territory, but in a few species such as phalaropes, the males, which incubate the eggs and raise the young, are less brightly colored than the females.

11. **Are there albino birds?**
    Occasionally albinism, i.e. complete loss of pigmentation, can be seen in most melanistic species. Partial albinism or leucism resulting from partial loss of pigments is more common, being caused by poor diet, trauma to the affected area, or genetic defects.

12. **Why do some birds have bare areas on their heads?**
    The bare areas on the heads of some species become more brightly colored for courtship purposes; vultures and condors lack head feathers to minimize bacterial infection while sticking their heads into bloody carcasses.

13. **Can owls turn their heads 360 degrees?**
    A system of well-developed cervical vertebrae and neck muscles allow an owl to turn its head no more than 270 degrees.

14. **Are birds really "bird-brains"?**
Actually most birds are quite intelligent, with large brains relative to body size; they perform well in choice tests and some have incredible short-term memory capabilities to find stored food; corvids, e.g. crows, ravens, magpies, and jays, and many parrots are the most intelligent.

15. **How do birds breathe?**
It takes two inspirations and two expirations to oxygenate and remove carbon dioxide from the blood for each package of air; a combination of the lungs and several air sacs achieve this bellow-like action; there is no dead-end as there is in mammals' lungs.

16. **How do buoyant diving birds manage to dive underwater?**
They have many adaptations including non-hollow bones, removal of trapped air beneath the body feathers, swallowing stones, or filling hollow wing feathers with water.

17. **How are birds able to endure extremely cold temperatures?**
Non-shivering internal heat generation from intake of high-energy foods, behavioral modifications such as fluffing out feathers to trap heated air, avoiding wind chill by taking cover, huddling, etc., lowering body temperature and heart rate at night, slowing down blood flow to the extremities, and countercurrent heat transfer from arteries to veins are just some of the many adaptations.

18. **How can sea birds survive in such a salty environment?**
Sea birds as well as species in arid environments avoid salt overload by ejecting excess salt from special salt glands near their beaks controlled by hormones.

19. **How well can birds see?**
Due to several adaptations, their visual acuity is around three to four times better than that of humans; they may have greater sensitivity to movement; owls can see just as well during the day.

20. **How many eyelids do birds have?**
They have one upper and one lower, plus a third one called the nictitating membrane to cleanse and protect the eye.

21. **Do birds perceive color?**
Being so brightly colored, birds actually have four visual pigments, whereas humans only have three; owls can also perceive color, but less so due to their nocturnal lifestyle.

22. **Do birds smell?**
All birds have nostrils or nares, usually on their bills; while it is not their strongest sense, all birds can smell to some degree; the best "noses" are found in turkey vultures, kiwis, and petrels.

23. **How well do birds hear?**
Their ears are located under small stiff feathers on each side of the head; average hearing capability ranges from 5,000 hertz in songbirds to 30,000 hertz in some owls.

24. **Why do cagebirds act so erratically in their cages prior to impending extreme weather, floods, tidal waves, etc.?**
They are thought to be able to perceive infrasounds, i.e. extremely low-frequency sounds, produced by these phenomena.

25. **Do birds taste their food?**
Much better than we originally thought, but they have considerably fewer taste buds than mammals.

26. **Do all birds sing or call?**
Almost all do. Adult brown pelicans and magnificent frigatebirds are mute, while adult turkey vultures and double-crested cormorants only issue grunts. Virtually all baby birds can be noisy.

27. **Why do woodpeckers drum on metal roofs, chimney flashing, drainpipes, and TV antennas?**
Drumming is used to scare away intruding males and attract mates. Metal objects can maximize the volume.

28. **Do birds make noises other than with their voice-box or syrinx?**
A number of birds such as mourning doves and goldeneye ducks make whistling noises when they take off. Woodcocks make twittering musical sounds with stiff outer wing feathers and common snipe make a winnowing sound with rigid outer tail feathers. Owls clack their bills and grouse drum their wings.

29. **Why do small birds mob birds of prey?**
Small songbirds of various types flock together to harass hawks and owls to drive them out of the area; crows especially mob and chase owls in the daytime to ensure their safety while roosting at night.

30. **Where do birds go at night?**
Most birds roost or sleep in dense cover or cavities in trees and buildings; water birds, sometimes in mixed groups, roost in their element, but some roost in trees. Chicken-like birds sleep on the ground or in trees.

31. **Why do birds not fall over while sleeping on a perch?**
Their feet have tendons that lock them in a gripping position.

32. **Why do some birds flop about in the dirt?**
The dust helps to clean off parasites from their feathers.

33. **Why do some large birds spread their wings on sunny days?**
Vultures do this to gather the sun's rays for thermoregulation, but cormorants and similar water-birds lift their wings to drain the water from their hollow wing feathers.

34. **Why do some birds rub ants or mothballs or other odd materials on their feathers?**
Some songbirds do this to rid the plumage of ectoparasites.

35. **Do large birds like eagles or owls carry away human babies?**
There is absolutely no truth to this old person's tale. Raptors only attack humans to defend their nests.

36. **Do birds use tools?**
While gulls drop clams onto rocks and crows drop nuts onto paved surfaces to be crushed by vehicles, New Caledonia crows fashion hooked tools from leaves and twigs to extract grubs and larvae from cavities. The woodpecker finch of the Galapagos uses twigs, thorns, and cactus spines to flush prey from holes.

37. **Why do some birds ride on the backs of deer, rhinos, buffalo, and other large mammals?**
Sometimes it provides a convenient perch, but on most occasions, the birds are feeding on ticks and other insects in the fur.

38. **How do birds drink?**
Most dip their bills and tilt their heads back so that the water trickles down the throat; doves hold their bills in the water and suck up the water.

39. **Do birds drink in winter?**
Many songbirds do so if water is accessible. If not, they will eat snow.

40. **Do birds have teeth?**
No. They have hard cornified bills; some grazing or fish-eating waterfowl have lamellae to tear grass or hold slippery fish, respectively; all baby birds have an egg tooth for opening the shell, which is later lost. Falcons have a primitive tooth (previously thought to be used to sever cervical vertebrae of prey).

41. **Why do some birds eat stones or grit?**
Some use it in their stomachs to grind food (larks, doves, etc.) or remove grease (falcons). Some use stones as ballast for diving (penguins).

42. **Why do some birds eject pellets?**
Birds of prey, as well as other meat-eaters, form pellets of indigestible material, e.g. feathers, fur, bones, chitinous insect parts, and regurgitate them within 24 hours of a meal.

43. Do songbirds eat other birds?
Omnivorous corvids such as crows, ravens, magpies, and jays, kill and consume other birds, especially eggs and young; grackles kill sparrows and eat their brains.

44. Is bird-feeding bad for birds?
Yes and no. Some studies have shown increased reproductive performance with access to feeders; large numbers of birds combined with poor feeder hygiene can lead to disease outbreaks.

45. How do birds find my feeders?
They are highly mobile and use vocal and visual cues.

46. Why do birds remove fecal sacs from their nests and drop them into swimming pools?
They remove them from the babies to keep the nests clean and drop them into water bodies so as to avoid attracting predators to the nest area.

47. Do all birds mate for life?
Most birds return to the territory, not to a specific mate. Some larger species have very strong pair bonds that can last as long as both birds live, but a small portion do divorce one another.

48. Are all birds monogamous?
Socially, about 90 percent of all bird species are monogamous, but recent studies show a high percentage of infidelity in many different kinds of birds. Copulations with sneaky unmated males and neighboring males can lead to as much as 50 percent of the young being sired by them.

49. Who builds the nest?
The female plays the most important role in collecting the materials and weaving the nest, but in some species, the male helps too. Male crows, herons, and storks do most of the material collection.

50. Do all birds build nests?
Some birds like nighthawks, whip-poor-wills, and plovers simply deposit their eggs on the ground. Seabirds like auks and murres lay their eggs on cliffs without nesting material. Emperor penguins have no nests.

51. How do emperor penguins keep their eggs from freezing in the Antarctic?
They roll the egg onto their feet and a thick fold of skin drops down to keep it warm.

52. Why do birds place green leaves in their nests?
Aromatic compounds in the leaves facilitate nest cleaning and help reduce nest-dwelling parasites; green leaves could also indicate ownership of the nest.

53. Do birds use their nests in winter?
Most birds with woven structures do not use them for anything other than nesting. Some hole-nesting birds such as owls and tits do use nesting cavities for roosting.

54. Why do birds sing so much at dawn?
The dawn air results in the best transmission of songs to defend the territory and/or attract a mate; the poor light is also better for singing than feeding.

55. Do some songbirds sing at night?
Mockingbirds and nightingales are famous for this, especially with full moons or artificial light; sometimes unpaired birds do it to attract mates.

56. Why do members of a pair of birds touch each other's feathers and bills?
Allopreening or mutual grooming is a ritualized form of agonistic behavior that bridges the gap between aggressive attacks and sexual behavior.

57. Do birds ever lay unfertilized eggs?
Chickens without access to sperm do; occasionally but rarely, members of a wild pair of birds are not synchronized sexually, leading to infertile eggs.

58. Do birds have penes?
Only 3 percent of all birds have a penis, flightless birds and waterfowl among them; most have a grooved papilla-like organ down which the semen flows.

59. Do birds recognize their own eggs and young?
Most birds cannot recognize their own eggs. Parasitic layers like cowbirds and European cuckoos count on this inability. Gulls will even choose large, fake eggs to incubate over their own. Many birds accept any birds that hatch in their nests and raptors will accept fostered babies of another raptor species. Strange-looking young are often rejected by pheasants and ducks.

60. What happens to eggshells after birds hatch?
For precocial birds, they are left in the nest; for altricial birds, they are removed or eaten by the parents for calcium or crushed by the young.

61. Why do some birds fly in V-formations?
Some species like geese, cormorants, and pelicans apparently gain lift from the rising eddies of air currents whirling off the wingtips of the bird immediately ahead of them. This saves energy in the long run. Formation flying also prevents mid-air collisions among large birds.

62. Can birds fly backward?
Hummingbirds are masters at it, but other small songbirds, and even large herons, can flutter backward if pressed to do so.

63. Why do birds flying in tight, large flocks not bump into one another?
This is very difficult to study; possibly a combination of highly developed visual abilities, sensory receptors in the skin to detect vibrations from neighboring birds' wings, excellent motor coordinaton, and strong reflexes are responsible.

64. Do all birds migrate?
Most but not all bird species engage in north-south movements each spring and fall; grouse-like birds, owls, and woodpeckers are less likely to migrate; even within migratory species, some individuals stay north in winter, especially in mild winters with lots of food and cover.

65. How do birds know when to migrate?
Overall, the birds respond to internal annual clocks triggered by changing daylength, but weather conditions, e.g. prevailing winds, can modify the timing; ultimately the bird's hormones drive it to eat lots of food to accumulate enough body fat to migrate and become hyperactive.

66. Do small birds ever hitch rides on the backs of large birds?
There is no scientific evidence to indicate that migrating hummingbirds hitch rides on the backs of geese; occasionally a small bird defending its territory will alight briefly on the back of a large predatory bird.

67. Do migrating birds always use the same routes and return to the same localities?
Generally yes, but sometimes they get blown off course or lost in bad weather; generally most birds return to the same breeding ground each year.

68. Do parent birds show the young the migratory route?
In some species, the families migrate together, but young of many species find their own way without help.

69. How do birds navigate during migration?
Some combination of identifying physical landmarks, star patterns, and sun movements, detection of the earth's geomagnetic force by magnetic particles in the brain, and inherited memory is apparently responsible.

70. What should I do with a bird with a band on its leg?
Birds are banded mostly for scientific purposes, but sometimes for owner identification, e.g. racing pigeons. If the bird is dead, mail the band to the address on it; if the bird is alive; record the number and contact the local fish and game office or search on the Internet for your government bird-banding organization.

Resources for Ornithologists

Optical Equipment

Bresser Optics
Meade Instruments Europe GmbH & Co. KG
Siemensstr. 6 D-46325 Borken
Westf, Germany
Tel: 0 28 61 / 93 17 0
E-mail: info@meade.de
http://www.bresser.de/

Brunton
620 East Monroe Avenue
Riverton, WY 82501
USA
Tel: 307 856 6559
E-mail: info@brunton.com
http://www.brunton.com/

Brunton Canada
6-637 The Queensway
Peterborough, ON K9J7J6
Canada
Tel: 705 749 9327
E-mail: canada@brunton.com
http://www.brunton.com/

Burris Optics
331 East 8th Street
Greeley, CO 80631
USA
Tel: 970 356 1670
E-mail: customerservice@burrisoptics.com
http://www.burrisoptics.com/

Bushnell Corporation
9200 Cody
Overland Park, KS 66214-1734
USA
Tel: 913 752 3400
http://www.bushnell.com/birding/home.html

Bushnell Corporation of Canada
25A East Pearce St.
Richmond Hill, ON L4B 2M9
Canada
Toll Free: 1 800 361 5702
Tel: 905 771 2980
http://www.bushnell.com/

Bushnell Performance Optics Asia
2113 Hong Kong Plaza
369-375 Des Voeux Rd. West
Hong Kong
http://www.bushnell.com/

Bushnell Performance Optics Australia
3240 Fairchild Street
Heatherton VIC 3202
Australia
Tel: 61 385581000
http://www.bushnell.com/

Canon, Inc.
http://www.canon.com/index.html

Canon U.S.A., Inc.
One Canon Plaza
Lake Success, NY 11042
USA
Tel: 516 328 5000
http://www.usa.canon.com

Canon Canada, Inc.
6390 Dixie Road
Mississauga, ON L5T 1P7
Canada
Tel: 905 795 1111
http://www.canon.ca

Canon Mexicana, S. de R.L. de C.V.
Periferco Sur No. 4124, Col. ExRancho de
Anzaldo, C.P. 0100
Mexico D.F., Mexico
Tel: 52 5 490 2000
http://www.canon.com.mx

Canon Latin America, Inc.
703 Waterford Way, Suite 400
Miami, FL 33126
USA
Tel: 305 260 7400
http://www.canonlatinamerica.com

Carl Zeiss International
http://www.zeiss.com/
Birding
http://www.zeiss.de/C12567A80033F8E4?Open

Celestron International
2835 Columbia Street
Torrance, CA 90503
USA
Tel: 310 328 9560
E-mail: help@celestron.com
http://www.celestron.com/products.htm

Deutsche Optik
P.O. Box 601114
San Diego, CA 92160-1114
USA
Toll Free: 1 800 225 9407
Tel: 1 619 287 9860 *or* 619 287 9869
E-mail: info@deutscheoptik.com
http://www.deutscheoptik.com/

Docter-Optic
Analytik Jena AG
Niederlassung Eisfeld
Coburger Straße 72
D-98673 Eisfeld
Tel: +49 3686 371130
E-mail: b.fischer@docter-germany.com
http://www.docter-germany.com/

Eagle Optics
2120 W. Greenview Dr.
Middleton, WI 53562
USA
Tel: 1 800 289 1132
E-mail: webmaster@eagleoptics.com
http://www.eagleoptics.com/

Fuji Photo Optical Co., Ltd.
E-mail: sales@msv.fujinon.co.jp
http://www.fujinon.co.jp/en/index.htm

Fujinon, Inc. (USA)
10 High Point Drive
Wayne, NJ 07470
USA
Tel: 973 633 5600
http://www.fujinon.com/

Fujinon (Europe) GmbH
Halskestrasse 4, 47877 Willich
Germany
Tel: 49 2154 924 0
E-mail: fujinon@fujinon.de
http://www.fujinon.de/

Fujinon GmbH (France)
43, avenue des 3 Peuples
B. P. 45
F-78185 St. Quentin-en-Yvelines
Tel.: + 33 0 1/39 30 16 16
E-mail: fujinon@fujinon.fr
http://www.fujinon.de/

Gitzo S.A.
Créteil Parc
8/10 rue Sejourné
F-94044 Créteil
Tel: 33 014 513 1860
E-mail: helpdesk@gitzo.com
http://www.gitzo.com/

Guan Sheng Optical Co., Ltd.
No. 152, Huei An St, Chu Tung Town
Husinchu Hsien, Taiwan
R.O.C.
Tel: 886 3 595 1510
http://www.gs-telescope.com/

Hakuba USA
10621 Bloomfield Street, Suite 39
Los Alamitos, CA 90720
USA
Tel: 1 800 423 1623
E-mail: info@hakubausa.com
https://www.hakubausa.com/

KAHLES GesmbH
Zeillerg. 20-22, A-1170
Vienna, Austria
or
2 Slater Road
Cranston, RI 02920
USA
Tel: 866 606 8779
E-mail: info@kahlesoptik.com
http://www.kahlesoptik.com/

Kindermann (Canada) Inc.
Swarovski Optik
361 Steelcase Road West Unit #3
Markham, ON L3R 3V8
Canada
Tel: +001 905 940 9262

Kowa Optimed, Inc.
20001 S. Vermont Ave.
Torrance, CA 90502
USA
Tel: 1 800 966 5692
E-mail: scopekowa@kowa.com
http://www.kowascope.com/

Lamberts (Lancaster) Ltd.
5 Rosemary Lane
Lancaster, UK
Tel: +44 01524 37384
E-mail: lamberts@birdtours.co.uk
http://www.birdtours.co.uk/lamberts/

Leica Camera AG
Oskar-Barnack-Straße 11
D-35606 Solms
Tel: +490 6442 208 0
E-mail: info@leica-camera.com
http://www.leica-camera.com/index_e.html

Leica Camera Inc.
156 Ludlow Avenue
Northvale, NJ 07647
USA
Toll Free: 1 800 222 0118
Tel: 201 767 7500
E-mail: eileen.giunta@leicacamerausa.com
http://www.leica-camera.com/unternehmen/
international/usa/index_e.html

Leupold & Stevens, Inc.
P.O. Box 688
Beaverton, OR 97075-0688
USA
Tel: 503 526 1400
E-mail: productsales@leupold.com
http://www.leupold.com/

Manfrotto Trading
Via Livinallongo, 3—20139
Milano, Italy
Tel: 02 5660991
E-mail: trading@manfrotto.it
http://www.manfrottotrading.it/

Meade Instruments Europe
Siemensstraße 6
46325 Borken
Westfalen
Tel: +49 02861 9317 0
E-mail: info@meade.de
http://www.meade.de

Meopta Prerov, a.s.
Kabelikova 1, 750 02
Prerov, Czech Republic
Tel: +420 581 24 1111
E-mail: meopta@meopta.com
http://www.meopta.cz/

Minolta Corporation USA
101 Williams Drive
Ramsey, NJ 07446
USA
Tel: 201 825 4000
E-mail: shopcpg@minolta.com
http://www.minoltausa.com/eprise/main/
MinoltaUSA/MUSAContent/index.htm

MINOX GmbH
Walter-Zapp-Str. 4
35578 Wetzlar Germany
Tel. +49 0 6441 917 0
E-Mail: info@minox.com
http://www.minox.com

Mirador Optical Corp
4040-8 Del Rey Avenue
P.O. Box 11614
Marina del Rey, CA 90295-8854
USA
Toll Free: 1 800 748 5844
Tel: +1 310 821 5587

Nikon Corporation
Nikon Futaba Bldg., 3-25, Futaba 1-Chome
Shinagawa-Ku, Tokyo
Japan 142-0043
Tel: +81 3 3788 7697
http://www.nikon.co.jp/main/index_e.htm

Nikon Corporation Canada
1366 Aerowood Drive
Mississauga, ON L4W 1C1
Canada
Tel: 905 6259910
http://www.nikon.ca/default_2.asp

Nikon Corporation USA
1300 Walt Whitman Rd.
Melville, NY 11747-3064
USA
Tel: 631 547 4200
http://www.nikonusa.com/usa_home/home.jsp

Nikon U.K., Ltd.
380 Richmond Road, Kingston upon Thames
Surrey, UK
KT2 5PR
Tel: +44 20 8541 4440
http://www.nikon.co.uk/

Olympus Optical Co., Ltd.
E-mail: pr_dept@olympus.co.jp
http://www.olympus.co.jp/indexE.html

Olympus America, Inc.
2 Corporate Center Drive
Melville, NY 11747
USA
Tel: 1 800 622 6372
http://www.olympusamerica.com/

Olympus Optical Co. (Europa) GmbH
Wendenstrasse 14—18
20097 Hamburg
P.O. Box 10 49 08
Hamburg, Germany
20034
Tel: +49 40 23773 0
E-mail: info@olympus-europa.com
www.olympus-europa.com

OP/TECH USA
304 Andrea Drive, Belgrade, MT
USA 59714
Tel: 1 888 678 3244
E-mail: info@optechusa.com
http://www.optechusa.com/optech.
htm#WELCOME

Opticron
P.O Box 370, Unit 21, Titan Court, Laporte Way
Luton, Bedfordshire
UK
LU4 8YR
Tel: 01582 726522
International Tel: +44 1582 726522
E-mail: info@opticron.co.uk
http://www.opticron.co.uk/

Optolyth-Optik Walter Roth GmbH & Co. KG
Lehentalstr.1
D-91249 Weigendorf
Germany
Tel: 09154 4011
E-mail: service@optolyth.de
http://www.optolyth.de/

Pentax Canada Inc.
3131 Universal Drive
Mississauga, ON L4X 2E
Canada
Tel: 905 625 4930
E-mail: info@pentaxcanada.ca
http://www.pentaxcanada.ca

Pentax U.K. Ltd.
Pentax House, Heron Drive
Langley, Slough, Berks
UK
SL3 8PN
Tel: 44 1 753 79 27 92
E-mail: info@photo.pentax.co.uk
http://www.pentax.co.uk

Pentax USA
35 Inverness Drive East
Englewood, CO 80112
USA
Tel: 1 800 877 0155
http://www.pentaxusa.com/

Pioneer Research
97 Foster Road Suite 5
Moorestown, NJ 08057
USA
Tel: 1 800 257 7742
E-mail: info@pioneer-research.com
http://www.pioneer-research.com/

Redfield Optics
Meade Instruments Corporation
6001 Oak Canyon
Irvine, CA 92618
USA
Tel: 1 800 285 0689
http://www.redfieldoptics.com/

Sibir Optics Inc.
1315 FM 1187, Suite 107
Mansfield, TX 76063
USA
Tel: 817 453 9966
E-mail: sales@sibiroptics.com
http://www.sibiroptics.com/

Simmons Optics
Meade Instruments Corporation
6001 Oak Canyon
Irvine, CA 92618
USA
Tel: 1 800 285 0689
http://www.simmonsoptics.com/

Slik Corporation
Tokyo, Japan
http://www.slik.com/index.html

Steiner Optik GmbH
Dr.-Hans-Frisch-Straße 9
95448 Bayreuth
Germany
Tel: +49 0 921 / 78 79 16
E-mail: customer-service@steiner.de
http://www.steiner.de/home/index.html

Swarovski Optik North America
2 Slater Road
Cranston, RI 02920
USA
Tel: +001 401 734 1800
http://www.swarovskioptik.at/english/home/
index.asp

Swarovski Optik UK, Ltd.
Perrywood Business Park
Surrey, UK RH1 5JQ
Tel: +44 1737 856812
http://www.swarovskioptik.at/english/home/
index.asp

Swift Instruments, Inc.
952 Dorchester Avenue
Boston, MA 02125
USA
Tel: 1 800 446 1116
E-mail: info@swiftoptics.com
http://www.swift-optics.com/

Tasco
Bushnell Corporation
9200 Cody
Overland Park, KS 66214
USA
Tel: 1 800 423 3537
http://www.tasco.com/

Tele Vue Optics, Inc.
32 Elkay Dr.
Chester, NY 10918
USA
Tel: 845 469 4551
http://www.televue.com/home/default_2.asp

The Tiffen Company, LLC
90 Oser Avenue
Hauppauge, NY 11788-3886
USA
Tel: 631 273 2500
E-mail: techsupport@tiffen.com
http://www.tiffen.com/

Tiffen Europe Ltd.
Enterprise House
Weston Business Park
Weston on the Green
Oxford, Oxfordshire UK
OX6 8SY
Tel: +44 1869 343835
E-mail: tcarey@tiffen.com
http://www.tiffen.com/

THK Photo Products, Inc.
2360 Mira Mar Ave.
Long Beach, CA 90815
USA
Tel: 1 800 421 1141
E-mail: droberts@thkphoto.com
http://www.thkphoto.com/

Unitron, Inc.
120-C Wilbur Place
P.O Box 469
Bohemia, NY 11716-0469
USA
Tel: 631 589 6666
E-mail: info@unitronusa.com
http://www.unitronusa.com/

Velbon Tripod Co., Ltd.
6-1-5 Nogata Nakanoku
Tokyo, Japan
165-0027
Tel: 813 5327 6131
E-mail: info@velbon.com.au
http://www.velbon.com.au/

Vernonscope & Company
5 Ithaca Rd.
Candor, NY 13743
USA
Toll Free: 1 888 303 3526
Tel: 607 659 7000
E-mail: sales@VernonScope.com
http://www.vernonscope.com/

Vivitar USA
1280 Rancho Conejo Blvd
Newbury Park, CA 91320
USA
Tel: 805 498 7008
http://www.vivitar.com/

Vivitar (Europe) Ltd.
Suite 6, Cherry Orchard West
Kembrey Park
Swindon, Wiltshire, UK
SN2 8UP
Tel: 44 1793 554250
E-mail: vivitar.uk@virgin.net
http://www.vivitar.co.uk/

Vivitar (Asia) Limited
Units 1004-1005, 10th Floor
Conic Investment Building
13 Hok Yuen Street
Hunghom, Kowloon
Hong Kong
Tel: 852 2363 6313
E-mail: vgeneral@vivitarasia.com
http://www.vivitarasia.com/

Vivitar Canada Ltd.
90 Royal Crest Court
Markham, ON L3R 9X6
Canada
Tel: 905 513 7733

Vivitar France
48, rue Léonard de Vinci
BP 177
95691-Goussainville Cedex
France
Tel: 33 1 34 38 78 00
http://www.vivitar.co.uk/
E-mail: phrvivfr@aol.com

Vixen Co., Ltd.
5-17 Higashitokorozawa
Tokorozawa, Saitama
Japan
359-0021
Tel: +81 42 944 4141
http://www.vixen-global.com/index.html
E-mail: info@vixen.co.jp

Weaver Optics
Meade Instruments Corporation
6001 Oak Canyon
Irvine, CA 92618
USA
Tel: 949 451 1450
http://www.weaveroptics.com/

Bird Sound Recording and Amplification Devices

Marice Stith Recording Services
59 Autumn Ridge Circle
Ithaca, NY 14850
USA
Tel: 607 277 5920
E-mail: info@stithrecording.com
http://www.stithrecording.com/

Natural Technology Industries
P.O. Box 582
Youngstown, OH 44501
USA
Tel: 330 629 7583
E-mail: hearbirds@aol.com
http://natural-technology.com/

Saul Mineroff Electronics, Inc.
574 Meacham Avenue
Elmont, NY 11003
USA
Tel: 516 775 1370
E-mail TapeNixon@aol.com
http://www.mineroff.com/nature/index.htm

Sonic Technology Products
120 Richardson Street
Grass Valley, CA 95945
USA
Toll Free: 1 800 247 5548
Tel: 530 272 4607
E-mail: pestchaser@sonictechnology.com
http://www.sonictechnology.com/

UltraSound Gate
Raimund Specht
Hauptstr. 52
D-13158
Berlin, Germany
Tel: +49 30 916 37 58
E-mail: info@avisoft.info
http://www.ultrasoundgate.com/usg124.htm

Walker's Game Ear, Inc.
P.O. Box 1069
Media, PA 19063
USA
Toll Free: 1 800 424 1069
Tel: 610 565 8952
E-mail: Bob@walkersgameear.com
http://www.walkersgameear.com/

Bird Song Acoustic Analysis

Avisoft-SASLab
Raimund Specht
Hauptstr. 52
D-13158
Berlin, Germany
Tel: +49 30 916 37 58
E-mail: info@avisoft.info
http://www.avisoft-saslab.com/

Raven and Canary 1.2.4 (for Macintosh users)
Cornell Bioacoustics Research Program
159 Sapsucker Woods Rd
Ithaca, NY 14850
USA
Tel: 607 254 2408
E-mail: raven_orders@cornell.edu
http://www.birds.cornell.edu/brp/
Raven/Raven.html

Sound Ruler
The University of Texas, Section of Integrative
Biology
E-mail: mgpapp@users.sourceforge.net
http://soundruler.sourceforge.net/

Syrinx-PC
Cornell Bioacoustics Research Program
159 Sapsucker Woods Road
Ithaca, NY 14850
USA
E-mail: quill@bigfoot.com
http://syrinxpc.com/

Bird-Nest Monitoring Equipment

Sandpiper Technologies, Inc.
535 W. Yosemite Ave.
Manteca, CA 95337
USA
Tel: 209 239 7460
E-mail: Ann@Sandpipertech.com
http://www.peeperpeople.com

Netting for Capturing Wild Birds

Association of Field Ornithologists
c/o Manomet Center for Conservation Science
P.O. Box 1770
Manomet, MA 02345
USA
Tel: 508 224 6521
E-mail: afoband@manomet.org
http://www.afonet.org/english/mistnets.html

Australian Bird Study Association, Inc.
18 Lewis Drive, Medowie
NSW, Australia
2318
Tel: 02 4981 7846
E-mail: mistnets@absa.asn.au
http://www.absa.asn.au/mns.html

Avinet, Inc.
PO Box 1103, Dryden, NY 13053-1103
USA
Toll free: 1 888 284 6387
Tel: 607 844 3277
E-mail: info@avinet.com
http://www.avinet.com

British Trust for Ornithology
The National Centre for Ornithology
The Nunnery, Thetford
Norfolk, UK
IP24 2PU
Tel: 01842 750050
E-mail: rsales@bto.org
http://www.bto.org/ringing/ringsales/index.htm

Ecotone Ecological Analyses & Projects
ul. Slowackiego 12
81-871 Sopot, Poland
Tel: +48 58 552 33 73
E-mail: office@ecotone.pl
http://www.ecotone.pl/

SpiderTech Bird Nets
P.O. Box 6
Helsinki 00321
Tel: +358 9 5873066
E-mail: http://www.spidertech.fi/
www.spidertech.fi

Telemetry Gear for Tracking Birds

A1 Falconry UK Tracking Systems
UK
Tel: 07947 489656
E-mail: buyit@falconryuk.co.uk *or*
Findit@Wildlife-Tracking.co.uk
http://www.falconryuk.co.uk/

Advanced Telemetry Systems, Inc.
470 1st Avenue North, Box 398
Isanti, MN 55040
USA
Tel: 612 444 9267
E-mail: 70743.512@compuserve.com
http://www.biotelem.org/manufact.html#ats

Alpha Omega Computer Systems, Inc.
P.O. Box U
33815 Eastgate Circle
Corvallis, OR 97333
USA
Tel: 541 754 1911
E-mail: sales@ao.com
http://www.ao.com

Andreas Wagener Telemetrieanlagen
22 D—50672 Köln
Germany
Tel: +49 0 221 514966
E-mail: info@wagener-telemetrie.de
http://www.wagener-telemetrie.de

AVM Instrument Company, Ltd.
1213 South Auburn Street
Colfax, CA 95713-1898
USA
Tel: 530 346 6300
E-mail: sales@avminstrument.com *or*
design@avminstrument.com
http://www.avminstrument.com/

Ayama-Segutel Radio Tracking
133 Bajos, Camí Ral
Mataró 08301
Barcelona, Spain
Tel: +34 93 7905862
E-mail: ayama@ayama.com
http://www.ayama.com

Biotelemetrics, Inc.
6520 Contempo Lane
Boca Raton, FL 33433
USA
Tel: 561 394 0315
E-mail: biotran@ix.netcom.com
http://www.biotelemetrics.com

BioTrack
52 Furzebrook Rd.
Wareham, Dorset UK
BH20 5AX,
Tel: +44 0 1929 552 992
E-mail: info@biotrack.co.uk
http://www.biotrack.co.uk/

Communications Specialists Inc.
426 West Taft Ave.
Orange, CA 92865
USA
Tel: 1 800 854 0547
http://www.com-spec.com/

D & L Antenna Supply Co.
3410 Gibbs Rd
Kansas City, KS 66106-3308
USA
Tel: 913 677 8674
E-mail: dandl@birch.net
http://www.wavehunter.com/main.html

Falcon Telemetrics
The Parsonage, Llanrothal, Monmouth
NP NP25 5QJ
Tel: 01600 750300
E-mail: marcuss@euronet.nl
http://www.roofvogels.net/shop-telemetrics.html

Grant Systems Engineering
111 Manitou Drive
King City, ON L7B 1E7
Canada
Tel: 905 833 0061
E-mail: cgrant@grant.ca
http://www.grant.ca/

Global Tracking Systems, Inc.
Canada
Tel: 403 887 8866 or 403 563 5063
E-mail: gts-rjc@telusplanet.net *or*
gtsdmt@shaw.ca
http://www.gtstrack.com

H.A.B.I.T. Research
1-203 Harbour Rd.
Victoria, BC V9A 3S2
Canada
Tel: 250 381 9425
E-mail: info@habitresearch.com
http://www.habitresearch.com

Holohil Systems Ltd
112 John Cavanagh Road
Carp, ON K0A 1L0
Canada
Tel: 613 839 0676
E-mail: info@holohil.com
http://www.holohil.com/

Jescom Communications International, Inc.
90, 17Th Ave.
San Mateo, CA 94402
USA
Tel: 650 574 1421
E-mail: jescom@jescomusa.com
http://www.jescomusa.com/

Lotek Wireless Inc.
115 Pony Drive
Newmarket, ON L3Y 7B5
Canada
Tel: 905 836 6680
E-mail: telemetry@lotek.com or
service@lotek.com
http://www.lotek.com/avian.htm

Marshall Radio Telemetry
896 West 100 North
North Salt Lake City, UT 84054
USA
Tel: 801 936 9000
Toll Free: 1 800 729 7123
E-mail: info@marshallradio.com
http://www.marshallradio.com/
falconry/fhome.asp

Merlin Systems, Inc.
P.O. Box 190257
Boise, ID 83719
USA
Tel: 208 362 2254
E-Mail: info@merlin-systems.com
http://www.merlin-systems.com/

Microwave Telemetry Inc.
8835 Columbia 100 Parkway, Suites K and L
Columbia, MD 21045
USA
Tel: 410 715 5292
E-mail: inquiries@microwavetelemetry.com
http://www.microwavetelemetry.com/Birds.htm

North Star Science and Technology
Technology Center Building Room 4.036
1450 South Rolling Road
Baltimore, MD 21227
USA
E-mail: blakehenke@msn.com
http://www.northstarst.com/

Seimac Limited
271 Brownlow Avenue
Dartmouth, NS B3B 1W6
Canada
Tel: 877 772 3389
E-mail: dpenney@seimac.com
http://www.seimac.com/

Sirtrack Ltd
Private Bag 1403
Goddard Lane, Havelock North
New Zealand
Tel: +64 6 877 7736
E-mail: sirtrack@LandcareResearch.co.nz
http://sirtrack.landcareresearch.co.nz/index.asp

Sonotronics
3250 S. Dodge Blvd. Suite 6
Tucson, AZ 85713
USA
Tel: 520 746 3322
E-mail: sales@sonotronics.com
http://www.sonotronics.com/index.html

Telemetry Solutions
1130 Burnett Avenue, Suite J
Concord, CA 94520
USA
Tel: 925 798 2373
http://www.track-it.com/

Televit Internationl AB
Bandygatan 2, SE-71134 Lindesberg
Sweden
Tel: +46 581 17195
E-mail: info@televit.se
http://www.televilt.se/

Telonics Inc.
932 E. Impala Ave.
Mesa, AZ 85204-6699
USA
Tel: 480 892 4444
E-mail: info@telonics.com
http://www.telonics.com/

Titley Electronics Pty Ltd
P.O. Box 19
Ballina NSW
Australia 2478
Tel: 61 2 66 866617
E-mail: titley@nor.com.au
http://www.titley.com.au/index.html

Toyocom U.S.A., Inc.
617 East Golf Road, Suite 112
Arlington Heights, IL 60005
USA
Tel: 847 593 8780
http://www.toyocom.com/profile.html

Toyocom U.K.
7B Rosemary House, Lanwades Business Park
Kennet, Newmarket, Suffolk, UK
CB8 7PN
Tel: +44 1638 751803
http://www.toyocom.co.uk/

Toyocom Asia Pte, Ltd.
No.1 Tannery Road, #50-03
Cencon I, Singapore 347719
Tel: +65 841 6311
http://www.toyocom.co.jp/english/profile/
ub.html#asia

Toyocom
84, Tsukagoshi 3-chome, Saiwai-ku
Kawasaki-shi Kanagawa
Japan 212-8513
Tel: +81 44 542 5117
http://www.toyocom.co.jp/english/

TSE GmbH
Saalburgstraße 157
D-61350 Bad Homburg
Germany
Tel: +49 0 6172 789 285
E-mail: info@tse-systems.de
http://www.tse-systems.de/

Vemco Limited
100 Osprey Drive
Shad Bay, NS B3T 2C1
Canada
Tel: 902 852 3047
E-mail: sales@vemco.com
http://www.vemco.com

Wildlife Materials Inc.
1031 Autumn Ridge Road
Carbondale, IL 62901
USA
Tel: 618 549 6330
E-mail: info@wildlifematerials.com
http://www.wildlifematerials.com

Wildlife Tracking Inc.
5438 Betty Circle
Livermore, CA 94550
USA
Telephone: 925 294 9481
E-mail: sales@wildlifetrack.com
http://www.wildlifetrack.com

Wildlife Tracking Systems
Bush House
Muckley Farm
Bridgnorth, Shropshire
England
WV16 4RW
Tel: +44 0 1746 714062
E-mail: wildlifetracking@easynet.co.uk
http://www.wildlifetracking.co.uk

Satellite Tracking Centers for Birds

AvianRadar
3160 Airport Road, Suite 22A
Panama City, FL 32405
USA
Tel: 850 913 8003
E-mail: rMerritt@geo-marine.com
or aKelly@geo-marine.com
http://www.avianradar.com/

North Star Science and Technology
Technology Center Building Room 4.036
1450 South Rolling Road
Baltimore, MD 21227
USA
E-mail: blakehenke@msn.com
http://www.northstarst.com/

**NASA's Goddard Space Flight Center and
Patuxent Wildlife Research Center**
Satellite Tracking of Endangered Species
http://outside.gsfc.nasa.gov/ISTO/
satellite_tracking/

Service Argos, Inc.
1801 McCormick Drive, Suite 10
Largo, MD 20774
USA
Tel: 301 925 4411
E-mail: info@argosinc.com
http://www.argosinc.com/birds.htm

**The Migration Route Satellite-tracked by
ArgoSat NTT**
E-mail: wbc@wnn.or.jp
http://www.cls.fr/html/argos/documents/newslet
ter/nslan53/ntt_en.html
and http://www.wnn.or.jp/wnn-n/index.html
(Japanese)

Specialized Video Camera Recorders for Birds

BirdCam
7 Bellfield Drive
North Kessock, Inverness
Scotland
IV1 3XT
Tel: 01463 731525
E-mail: debbie@birdcam.co.uk
http://www.birdcam.co.uk/index.htm

Bird-Vu Birding Camera
Nature Vision, Inc.
213 NW 4th Street
Brainerd, MN 56401
USA
Tel: 218 825 0733
http://www.birdvu.com/

Ecowatch Camera
E-mail: sales@alanaecology.com
http://www.alanaecology.com/

DNA Sexing of Birds

AMR Laboratories
P.O. Box 656
Plymouth Meeting, PA 19462
USA
Tel: 877 424 1212
http://www.amrlabs.com/aviansexing.cfm

Avian Biotech International UK
P.O. Box 107
Truro, Cornwall, UK
TR1 2YR
Tel: 44 01872 262737
E-mail: contact@avianbiotech.com
http://www.avianbiotech.co.uk

Avian Biotech International USA
1336 Timberlane Road
Tallahassee, FL 32312-1766
USA
Toll Free: 1 800 514 9672
Tel (outside the U.S.): 850 386 1145
E-mail: contact@avianbiotech.com
http://www.avianbiotech.com

California Avian Laboratory
P.O. Box 5647, El Dorado Hills, CA 95762
USA
Toll Free (U.S.): 1 877 521 6004
Tel: 916 933 0898
E-mail: avianlab@surewest.net
http://www.californiaavianlab.com

DNA Solutions
P.O. Box 86, Houghton le Spring
UK
DH5 9UX
or
P.O. Box 22, Oakleigh
Australia
VIC 3166
Tel: (UK) 0845 1300 362
Tel: (Australia) 1800 000 362
E-mail: DNAtest@DNAsolutions.net
http://www.genescience.com.au/home.htm

Genetic Science Services
P.O. Box 115, Fitzroy
Victoria, Australia
3065
Tel: 03 8412 7077
E-mail: animal@genetype.com.au
http://www.geneticscienceservices.com/

HealthGene Corporation
2175 Keele St.
Toronto, ON M6M 3Z4
Canada
Toll Free: 1 877 371 1551
Tel: 416 658 2040
E-mail: info@healthgene.com
http://www.healthgene.com/vdl/breeders/avian/index.asp

GC Promochem
(Head Office)
Queens Road
Teddington, Middlesex
UK
TW11 0LY
Tel: +44 0 20 8943 7000
E-mail: info@lgc.co.uk
http://www.lgc.co.uk/business_sector.asp?strArea
No=40_5

Molecular Diagnostic Services, Ltd.
Box 903
Westville, 3630
South Africa
Tel: +27 31 267 1319
E-mail: mds@mdsafrica.net
http://mdsafrica.net/site/default.asp?dealer=4594

National Veterinary Diagnostic Services
23361 El Toro Road, Suite 218
Lake Forest, CA 92630-6921
USA
Tel: 949 859 3648
E-Mail: info@national-vet.com
http://www.national-vet.com/

Research Avian Laboratory, Inc.
14556 Midway Rd.
Dallas, TX 75244
USA
Tel: 972 960 2221
http://www.vetdna.com/

Vetark Professional
P.O. Box 60,Winchester
SO23 9XN
UK
Tel: 44 01962 880376
E-mail: info@vetark.co.uk
http://www.vetark.co.uk/birdDNApages.html#an
chor15576068

Vita-Tech Canada, Inc.
1345 Denison Street,
Markham, ON L3R 5V2
Canada
Toll Free in North America: 1 800 667 3411
E-mail: info@vita-tech.com
http://www.vita-tech.com/Avian/avsexing.htm

Vita-Tech U.S.A.
2316 Delaware Avenue, #333
Buffalo, New York 14216-2606
USA
Toll Free in North America: 1 800 667 3411
Tel: 416 798 4988
E-mail: info@vita-tech.com
http://www.vita-tech.com/Avian/avsexing.htm

Will-Tell Lab
P.O. Box 50 Jefferson, OR 97352
USA
Tel: 541 327 1783
E-mail: willtell@proaxis.com
http://www.proaxis.com/~willtell/

Zoogen Services, Inc.
1902 East 8th Street
Davis, CA 95616
USA
Toll Free: 1 800 995 2473
Tel: 530 750 5757
http://www.zoogen.biz/index.html
E-mail: customerservice@zoogen.biz

Bird Courses and Volunteer Opportunities Related to Birds

Bander Training Course
Braddock Bay Bird Observatory
P.O. Box 12876
Rochester, NY 14612
USA
E-mail: ebrooks@bbbo.org
http://www.bbbo.org/education/btc.html

Beginning Birdwatching and Birdwatching Improvers
BirdWatch Ireland
Ruttledge House
8 Longford Place, Monkstown
Co Dublin, Ireland
Tel: +353 1 2804322
E-mail: info@birdwatchireland.org
http://www.birdwatchireland.ie/

Biodiversity and Conservation of British Birds
University of Surrey
E-mail: I.Calder@surrey.ac.uk
http://www.surrey.ac.uk/Education/birds/

Bird Banding, Birding for Beginners and more
Eyre Bird Observatory
Cocklebiddy via Norseman WA
Western Australia 6443
Tel: 08 9039 3450
E-mail: eyrebirdobs@bigpond.com
http://home.it.net.au/~austecol/observatories/eyre.htm

Bird Course
Ithala Game Reserve
P.O. Box 314, Nottingham Road
South Africa 3280
Tel: 033 263 6113
Fax: 033 263 6970
E-Mail: info@sappibrett.com
http://www.kznwildlife.com/tree_bird.htm

Bird Identification Course
Quinte Conservation
2061 Old Highway #2,
R.R. #2, Belleville, ON K8N 4Z2
Canada
Tel: 613 968 3434
E-mail: quinteca@auracom.com
http://www.pec.on.ca/conservation/birdidentification.html#top

Bird Embroidery Class, Improving Observational Skills, Intro to Birding by Ear, Raptor Identification, Mountain Birding by Ear, Shorebird Identification
Sea & Sage Audubon Society
PO Box 5447, Irvine CA 92616
USA
Tel: 949 261 7963
http://shell.exo.com/~kenyon/birdclasses.htm

Birds and Birdwatching
Kingston Maurward College
Dorchester, Dorset
UK
DT2 8PY
Tel: 01305 215036
E-mail: tim.loasby@kmc.ac.uk
http://www.kmc.ac.uk/environ/birds_and_birdwatching.htm

Birds for Beginners, Winter Birdwatching, Intro to Falconry, Intro to Hawking, Intro to Bird Ringing, and more
FSC Environmental Education
Montford Bridge, Preston Montford
Shrewsbury, Shropshire
UK
SY4 1HW
Tel: 00 44 0 1743 852160
E-mail: fscee@hotmail.com
http://www.field-studies-council.org/leisurelearning2003/birdsandotheranimals/birds.asp#birds

Bird Sketching Workshop, Beginner's Birdwalk and Bird Banding Demonstrations
Maine Audubon Society
20 Gilsland Farm Road
Falmouth, ME 04105
USA
Tel: 207 781 2330 *or* 207 781 6180
E-mail: info@maineaudubon.org
http://www.maineaudubon.org/

Birdwatching Course
Nature Society (Singapore) Bird Group
Tel: 65 6741 2036
E-mail: alchia@singnet.com.sg *or*
kimseng@nss.org.sg
http://www.nss.org.sg/
wildbirdsingapore/page17.html

Field Ornithology I, I, III
City College of San Francisco and the Golden
Gate Audubon Society
USA
Tel: 415 561 1860
http://www.goldengateaudubon.org/
birding/birdingclasses.htm

Home Study Course in Bird Biology
Cornell Lab of Ornithology
159 Sapsucker Woods Road
Ithaca, NY 14850-1999
USA
Toll Free: 1 800 843 BIRD
Tel (outside the U.S.): 607 254 2452
E-mail: hstudy@cornell.edu
http://birds.cornell.edu/homestudy/

Institute for Field Ornithology Workshops
American Birding Association
ABA-IFO
P.O. Box 6599
Colorado Springs, CO 80934-6599
USA
Tel: 719 578 9703 ext. 235
E-mail: ifo@aba.org
http://www.americanbirding.org/
programs/eduifowksp.htm

**Intro to Birdwatching, Gull, Tern, and Skua
identification, Ducks and Geese, Backyard
Birdwatching, Birding by Ear, Endangered
Species Protocol, Point Counts and Bird
Banding, Shorebirds, Hawks, Sparrows**
Little Bird Jobs Enterprises and Humboldt State
University CA
USA
Tel: 707 442 0339 or 707 826 3357
E-mail: lbjent@humboldt1.com
http://www.humboldt1.com/~lbjent/
tours.htm

Know Your Birds
Online Bird Course for European Birds
http://www.knowyourbirds.com/vogelcursus/

**Landbird Monitoring Training Course and
Advanced Landbird Identification Workshops**
Point Reyes Bird Observatory
4990 Shoreline Hwy
Stinson Beach, CA 94970
USA
Tel: 415 868 0655, × 310
E-mail: djongsomjit@prbo.org
http://www.prbo.org/cms/index.php?
mid=217&module=browse

Ornithology Certificate
The Morton Arboretum
4100 Illinois Route 53
Lisle, IL 60532-1293
USA
Tel: 630 719 2468
E-mail: education@mortonarb.org.
http://www.mortonarb.org/
education/cert_ocp.htm

Spring Field Ornithology
Cornell Lab of Ornithology
159 Sapsucker Woods Rd.
Ithaca, NY 14850-1999
USA
Toll free (in the U.S.): 1 800 843 2473
Tel: 607 254 2452
E-mail: sfoclass@cornell.edu.
http://birds.cornell.edu/sfo/

Texas Birding Certificate Program
University of Houston Continuing Education
and Armand Bayou Nature Centre
102 HRM Bldg.
Houston, TX 77204-3027
USA
Toll free: 1 800 687 5465
Tel: 713 743 1060
http://www.uh.edu/academics/dce/bird.html

The Bird Course
Avian Science and Conservation Centre
McGill University
21, 111 Lakeshore Road
Ste. Anne-de-Bellevue, QC H9X 3V9
Canada
Tel: 514 398 7760
E-mail: bird@nrs.mcgill.ca
http://www.nrs.mcgill.ca/ascc/

The Identification & Natural History of Birds
Starr Ranch Audubon Sanctuary
100 Bell Canyon Road
Trabuco Canyon, CA 92679
USA
Tel: 541 937 3970 *or* 949 858 0309
E-mail: dbontra243@aol.com

Tropical Birding in Costa Rica: Introduction to Field Ornithology
P.O. Box 8-3870-1000
San Jose, Costa Rica
Tel (Office): +506 253 3267
Tel (Home): +506 231 1236 *or* +506 291 0862
E-mail: hjimenez@racsa.co.cr *or*
hjimenez@geocities.com
http://www.hjimenez.org/
description-birding.html

Training Course in Bird Taxidermy
Birds Only Wildlife Studio
Tel: 1 888 850 8822
E-mail gb@birdtaxidermist.com
http://www.birdtaxidermist.com/
training_courses.shtml

Volunteer Opportunities for Birders
American Birding Association
Online Directory: E-mail: execsec@aba.org
http://americanbirding.org/opps/

Longer Programs

Bird Biology Foundation Degree
Paradise Park Wildlife Sanctuary and Duchy College, Rosewarne
Camborne, Cornwall
UK
TR14 OAB
Tel: 01209 722100
E-mail: information@cornwall.ac.uk
http://www.cornwall.ac.uk/duchy/
rosewarne/Index.htm

Certificate in Desert or Field Ecology with Specialized Study Program in Field Ornithology
University of California Riverside Extension Centre
1200 University Avenue, Suite 336
Riverside, CA 92507-4596
USA
Tel: 909 787 5804
E-mail: sciences@ucx.ucr.edu
http://www.ucrextension.net/ns/birds/
default.html

Certificate or Diploma of Higher Education in Ornithology
The University of Birmingham with collaboration from The British Trust for Ornithology
United Kingdom
E-mail: g.r.martin@bham.ac.uk *or*
j.reynolds.2@bham.ac.uk
http://www.biosciences.bham.ac.uk/
tpd/ornithology.htm

Foundation Degree in Applied Ornithology
Bishop Burton College
Beverly, East Yorkshire
UK
HU17 8QG
Tel: 0800 731 82 81.16
http://www.bbc.ac.uk/sitefiles/
countrysidemanagement/
countrysidemanagement.html

Higher National Diploma in Ornithology
London School of Arboriculture, Countryside and the Environment
Capel Manor College
Bullsmoor Lane, Enfield
Middlesex UK
EN1 4RQ
Tel: 0208 366 4442
http://www.capel.ac.uk/Arb_mainpage.htm

Glossary

abdomen: undersurface of bird's body from the top of the sternum or breastbone to the cloaca

aberrant: abnormal or different from others of its kind

abrasion: wear on tips of feather vanes, perhaps changing the appearance of the plumage

accidental: species occurring in a particular place infrequently and irregularly (AKA vagrant)

accipiter: forest hawk with short, rounded wings and long tails, e.g. goshawk.

acclimation: process of adjusting to change in environment, usually temperature

acclimatization: physical adjustments to seasonal changes in temperature

acoustic meatus: short, curved tube with a circular or oval opening that collects sound waves for hearing.

adaptive coloration: modification of color to promote concealment or to enhance conspicuousness

adaptive radiation: branching out of one species into several to fit into newly available niches

addled: describes an egg wherein the developing embryo has died, usually in its early stage (AKA rotten)

adult: a bird in its final plumage and capable of breeding

adventitious color: feather color, e.g. soiling, caused by a chemical or other matter in a bird's environment

advertisement behavior: evolved communication through displays to increase the conspicuousness of an individual, say for territorial purposes

aerie: *see* eyrie

aerophaneric: coloration important in aerial display

aetiology: *see* etiology

afterfeather: miniature feather attached to the underside of a feather at its superior umbilicus

afferent: carrying impulses inward to nerve centers

after-hatching year (AHY): bird in at least its second calendar year of life

after-second year (ASY): bird in at least its third calendar year of life

after-third year (ATY): bird in at least its fourth calendar year of life

aftershaft: axis or shaft of an afterfeather

aggregation: a grouping of individual birds attracted to a commonly exploited environmental resource, e.g. food, wind currents, etc.

aggression: threatening and/or attack behavior by means of postures, movements and/or vocalizations

agonistic: describing aggressive behavior between individuals, e.g. attack, escape, etc.

air sacs: membranous sacs, usually eight, that fill with air and help with oxygen/carbon dioxide exchange and cooling

alarm: visual or vocal warning

albescence: abnormal condition of plumage associated with albinism and looseness or hairiness of feather structure

albinism: refers to a genetically based lack of pigments occurring in various degrees

albumen: the egg white surrounding and protecting the yolk

allantois: membranous sac that receives the waste products from and supplies oxygen to the embryo

Allen's Rule: body appendages tend to be longer in warmer parts of range and shorter in cooler ones

allometry: relationship between the rate of growth between different parts of an individual or between different groups or races

allopatric: mutually exclusive in a geographic sense

allopreening: preening of one bird by another, usually its mate

alternate plumage: plumage worn in breeding season in those species that have two plumages a year

altitudinal migration: vertical migration of individuals during different seasons

altitudinal distribution: distribution of bird species in accordance with height above sealevel in a given area

altricial: describes helpless, featherless nestlings dependent on adults for food and warmth for first few weeks of life

altruism: act of increasing the chance of survival on another individual, while decreasing one's own, e.g. warning call could attract attention of predator to caller

alula: small feathers projecting at the wrist of a bird's wing and functioning as a wing slot to prevent turbulence and stalling

ambivalence: behavioral term referring to the outcome of two or more conflicting tendencies, e.g. approach or avoidance

ambulatory: walking or running

amnion: fluid-filled sac enclosing the embryo inside the eggshell

amniotic closure: refers to protective sealing of eyes and ears during first few days of life in some birds

anal circlet: double row of feathers surrounding the cloaca

anatomy: body structure or the study of it

androgen: male hormone, e.g. testosterone, involved in reproduction

angulated: forming a distinct angle

ankylosis: stiffening or fixed union of a joint, occurring either naturally or pathologically

anosmatic: having no olfactory sense

antepisematic: coloration being used to threaten or dominate rivals

antebrachium: the wing between the elbow and the wrist

anthine: pipitlike

anthropomorphism: describing or interpreting actions of animals in terms of human actions and thoughts

anting: comfort behavior of certain passerine birds wherein the plumage is treated with body fluids of ants, e.g. formic acid, and other mostly pungent substances, likely for feather maintenance

antiphonal singing: alternate singing of members of a mated pair and not necessarily different songs

anvil: hard object, e.g. stone, used by some birds to smash snails

aposematic: describing protective adaptations, especially dealing with color or pattern

appendicular skeleton: the pectoral and pelvic girdles and the limbs of a bird's skeleton

apterium: area of skin devoid of contour feathers located between pterylae or feather tracts

aquiline: eaglelike

Archaeopteryx: believed to be the the earliest known fossil bird, described in 1861

area-sensitive species: species that respond negatively to decreasing habitat patch size

arena: *see* lek

areolae: small naked spaces between the scales of birds' feet

armchair tick: bird listing due in general to the taxonomic splitting of a species or reassessment of a record

arrested molt: interruption of molt within a feather tract, usually flight feathers

aspect ratio: proportion of wing length to breadth

assembly: collection of birds of same kind, e.g. flock, flight, party, raft, host, congregation, etc.

asymmetry: disproportion or disparity in size of body parts, e.g. skull, or internal organs

atlas: survey of a large geographical area that maps the occurrence or relative abundance of species, often restricted to a particular season e.g. Breeding Bird Atlas

attenuated: tapering to a narrow tip

auriculars: *see* ear coverts

austringer: falconer who trains and flies accipiter

autochthonous: refers to indigenous species

autolycism: refers to birds' use of humans and human-made objects, as well as other mammals, reptiles, fishes, and birds

autumnal recrudescence: reinitiation of nest building behavior after the mating season in the fall with reproductive hormone levels dropping from mating levels to premating levels

Aves: scientific name of Class of animals known as birds (plural of Latin *avis*)

aviary: enclosed area housing captive birds

aviculture: the keeping and breeding of non-domesticated birds in captivity

avifauna: the birdlife of an area

axial skeleton: skull, vertebral column, ribs, and sternum

axillaries: feathers in the axilla or armpits

B

band: distinctive broad bar of color or metal numbered ring placed on birds' legs for identification

banding: placing metal numbered rings on birds' legs for identification

banner-marks: conspicuous white areas shown during flight used to deflect predators' attack from vulnerable areas

barb: lateral branch of the rachis of a feather

barbicel: process on a barbule of a barb of a feather

barbule: lateral branch of a feather barb (AKA radius)

bare parts: area of body surface not covered with feathers, e.g. bill, eyes, legs, feet, etc.

basic plumage: plumage worn year-round in species with only one per year and in those with two, the dull plumage as opposed to the breeding plumage

bastard wing: *see* alula

Batesian mimicry: resemblance of a palatable to a distasteful species for a protective purpose

bating: falconry term referring to trained leashed raptor jumping off perch or fist

bazaar: Russian term for an association between nesting seabirds and various nesting predatory land birds, e.g. ravens, falcons, owls

eak: same as bill

eard: bristly appendage growing from breasts of turkeys

eau Geste Hypothesis: territorial male bird uses a repertoire of song variants to simulate the presence of many individuals to dissuade intruders

egging: behavior wherein both young and adult birds display to another to secure food

elly-soaking: wetting of the underside of an incubating bird to assist in heat loss and/or cool the eggs, generally seen in plovers and related species

elt: broad band across the breast or belly plumage

ergmann's Rule: body size tends to be larger in cool parts of a species' range and smaller in the warmer parts

ewit: a leather bracelet to hold bell onto the leg of a falconer's bird

ig Day: competition in which birders attempt to list as many species as possible in a 24-hour period

ilateral symmetry: refers to condition wherein external parts on the left and right side of the body are counterparts of one another

ill: projecting jaws of a bird, including upper and lower mandibles and their horny sheaths

illing: mated birds touching or caressing one another with the bill or beak

imaculation: occurrence of two spots in facial plumage of some duck species

inding to: seizing and holding the quarry by a falconer's bird

inocular vision: seeing an object with both eyes simultaneously to perceive depth

iochore: major ecological formation characterized by a general vegetation type, e.g. forest

iochromes: refers to pigment colors of birds as opposed to caused by feather structure

iodiversity: variety of life forms, their ecological roles, and their genetic diversity

iogeography: study of the distribution of living plant and animal life

iology: the study of life or animate nature

iomass: the total weight of organisms per unit area of land or the total weight of organisms of a particular kind, e.g. birds

iome: a major biotic community defined by certain environmental features, e.g. tundra, grassland

iometry: application of statistics to biology

iota: general term for flora and fauna

iotelemetry: using radiotransmitters to track movements of birds

biotic: describing an organic element in the environment

biotope: areas or regions fairly uniform in flora and fauna and other environmental features

biotype: population of same genotype

bipedal: two-footed, i.e. no use of forearms, for walking

bird calls: sounds made by humans, sometimes mechanically, to attract birds

bird strike: a collision between birds and aircraft

bird lime: sticky lime substance applied to perches or over live prey to capture birds, usually for catching migratory songbirds in Europe (*also see* guano)

bird city: large concentrations of colonially nesting birds

bird fancier: one who keeps and/or breeds birds (AKA aviculturist)

bird table: raised platform where food is put out to attract birds

Bird Race: competition in the United Kingdom in which birders try to see as many species as possible in 24 hours

bird's nest soup: Asian or Chinese soup made from saliva used by certain swiftlets to cement their nests

bird-watcher: general term to describe those who observe birds casually or otherwise

bird-watching: *see* bird-watcher

birdathon: fund-raising event whereupon sponsors pay money for each species seen by bird-watchers in a prescribed period

birder: general term to describe a more serious bird-watcher, eager to improve his or her skills and possibly maintaining a life list

birding: *see* birder

Birdline: United Kingdom telephone service that provides up-to-date information on rare bird sightings

birds of prey: generally refers to those birds that use hooked beaks and strong toes with sharp talons to eat their food, e.g. kites, falcons, eagles, hawks, owls, etc. (AKA raptors)

blastula: stage of cell division reached by the fertilized egg while in the shell gland.

blind: compact structure, e.g. small building, tent, or wall, from which bird-watchers and ornithologists view birds up close

bluebird trail: series or line of nesting boxes set up for bluebirds, often along country roads

bolus: mass or ball of food swallowed by a bird or, in the case of indigestible material, regurgitated

booming ground: term used in North America to describe social display ground of greater prairie chickens

booted: describes horny covering of the tarsus or referring to a feathered tarsus

brace: as in dead game, describes two birds of the same species

brachium: the wing between the trunk and the elbow

brailing: binding the manus to the forearm to prevent a wing from being unfolded and hence flight in captive birds

brancher: juvenile hawk out of the nest and perching on branches, but not yet fully independent

breastband: dark band of feathers across breast of bird

breeding season: time period during which members of a species mate, lay eggs, and raise their young

breeding cycle: complete sequence of reproduction from courtship to the independence of the young

breeding range: geographical area where species breeds

Breeding Bird Atlas: *see* atlas

Breeding Bird Survey: point counts of birds along roads during breeding season coordinated by the U.S. Fish and Wildlife and Canadian Wildlife Services

Breeding Bird Census: census of breeding birds using spot-mapping and coordinated by the National Audubon Societys

bridling: facial plumage marking resembling a bridle or a display seen in black noddies

bristle: feather with a shaft and no vane resembling a stiff hair

broad-front migration: movement of migrating birds across a broad geographical area

broken-wing trick: feigning a wing injury to draw a predator away from eggs or young, e.g. killdeer

brood: all young hatching from a single clutch of eggs

brood patch: heavily vascularized area of the skin on the belly put into contact with eggs during incubation

brood parasitism: exploitative deposition of eggs by one species into another species' nest, occurring in about 1% of all bird species

brood nest: a resting place for young, not necessarily where they hatched from, built by one or both of the parents

brood reduction: reducing the number of young in the nest to assure survival of the remaining nestlings

brooding: sitting on eggs, but mostly young, to protect them from hot sun, rain, or predators

bulla: bony sound chamber at the base of windpipe of a male duck

bursa of Fabricius: glandular sac in the upper wall of the cloaca of young birds believed to produce antibodies to fight disease

busking: aggressive display toward intruder by male mute swan paddling both feet in unison

butt: earthwork erected to conceal hunters waiting to shoot driven red grouse

butterfly flight: slow flapping flight used in aerial displays of many birds

C

cadge: a carrying device used by falconers to carry more than one falcon into the field

caecum: blind tube branching from junction of small and large intestine, usually paired but sometimes single or absent

cage bird: collective term for birds, mostly psittacine and passerine varieties, commonly kept in captivity and even domesticated

Cain and Abel Syndrome: based on Biblical story, refers to sibling aggression in raptors (mostly eagles), herons, seabirds, etc. leading to weaker one being killed and sometimes eaten

calamus: bare, basal part of a feather shaft.

call: short, distinctive vocalization

cannibalism: eating of one bird by another of the same species

cannon net: *see* rocket net

canopy feeding: behavior describing birds feeding in the crowns of trees or hunting method of black heron whereupon the wings are held forward over the head to create shade to attract fish

cap: darker area of feather coloration on top of head

capon: castrated domestic fowl

carinate: having a keel on the sternum

carnivorous: flesh-eating

carotenoid pigments: *see* lipochromes

carpal: the wrist joint on the wing forming the forward-pointing prominence

carpometacarpus: three fused bones of the manus

carpus: wrist or jointed part of the wing

carrier pigeon: homing or domestic pigeon

carrying capacity: maximum number of individuals that can use a given habitat without degrading it and leading to population reduction

caruncle: conspicuous unfeathered, fleshy growth on birds' heads

casque: enlargement on bill's upper surface or the front of the head in hornbills and on top of the head in cassowaries

...st: two or more trained hawks or falcons flown at the same time or to regurgitate a pellet

...sting: refers to regurgitating and ejecting a pellet of indigestible fur, feather, and bone by certain species, e.g. owls

...sual visitor: bird that infrequently visits a region

...atastrophe: event that causes a sudden, remarkable decrease in a population, even its elimination

...ensus: periodic count of the number of individuals in various bird species or the variety of species in a given geographical area

...ere: raised fleshy area at base of upper mandible in birds of prey

...erebellum: part of the hindbrain that controls muscular coordination

...erebral hemispheres: two halves of the forebrain that houses sensory perception, instinct, and behavior functions

...erebrum: *see* cerebral hemispheres

...erophagy: act of eating wax, e.g. honeyguides

...halaza: pair of twisted strands of albumen suspending the yolk as it proceeds down the oviduct

...haracter displacement: divergence of characters, e.g. bill size, plumage markings, etc., of closely related species in an area of geographical overlap

...hecklist: systematic and comprehensive list of species occurring in a specific geographical area or region

...hick: vague term given to nestling bird in altricial species and hatchlings up to a few days of age in precocial species

...hicken: general name for domestic barnyard fowl

...hoana: paired funnel-shaped olfactory passages or internal nares located inside upper mouth

...horion: membrane lining the inner shell wall of an egg

...horology: study of geographical distribution of organisms

...hristmas Bird Count: annual North American 24-hour censuses of areas 15 miles (24 km) in diameter by tens of thousands of bird-watchers between December 20 and January 2 begun in 1899

...humming: tossing putrid fish remains over the side of a boat to attract seabirds

...hurring: sustained low trill or reel, e.g. nightjar

...hyme: semi-fluid partly digested food passing from the gizzard to the duodenum

...iliary muscles: set of muscles at the base of the iris that focus the lens for accommodation

cinereous: ashen grey

cinnamomeous: yellowish or reddish brown color of cinnamon

circadian: refers to biological rhythm of roughly 24 hours

circannual: refers to biological rhythms of approximately one year

CITES: Convention on International Trade in Endangered Species signed by many countries to control trade in wildlife

clade: *see* cladistics

cladistics: method of biological classification using characters to define relationships among different taxonomic groups, e.g. species

class: a primary taxonomic category, e.g. Aves, Reptilia, Mammalia, etc.

classification: grouping of organisms into categories or taxa (*see* systematics)

clavicles: paired breast bones that form the furcula

claw: nail or talon at the end of the toe

cleidoic: refers to totally enclosed condition of birds' eggs representing a virtually sealed physiological system (except for pores for gaseous exchange)

cleptoparasitism: *see* kleptoparasitism

cline: a geographical gradient in a phenotypic character, e.g. egg size, plumage color, etc., within the range of a species

clipping: cutting the primary feathers of one wing to render a captive bird incapable of flight

cloaca: combined terminal opening of the alimentary (feces), excretory (urine), and reproductive (semen, eggs) systems

cloacal kiss: male reproductive organ contacting everted oviduct of female during copulatory act

close ringing: process of slipping an unbroken band or ring over a nestling bird's foot for permanent identification

club: term for a gathering of non-breeding seabirds on the edge of a breeding colony

clutch: a complete set of eggs laid by a female

clutch size: a discrete number of eggs laid within a nest

co-evolution: reciprocal evolutionary change in two or more interacting species wherein each species becomes adapted to the interaction, e.g. predator and prey

cob: male swan

cochlea: part of inner ear designed to transform sound vibrations into nerve impulses

cock: male bird

cock-fighting: sport of pitting male domestic fowl against one another in combat

cohort: term for a group of individuals of similar age within a population

coition: *see* copulation

cold-searching: finding nests by closely examining the likely habitat (*see* hot-searching)

collect: killing a bird as a specimen

coloniality: clumping of nests in a spatio-temporal fashion, sometimes with mixed species

colony: *see* coloniality

color phase: *see* morph

columella: slender bone stretching across the middle ear to connect the tympanic membrane to the inner ear

comb: fleshy, featherless, and sometimes brightly colored crest adorning the top of a head of some gallinaceous birds

comfort behavior: refers to a group of basic stereotyped maintenance activities, e.g. preening, bathing, dusting, stretching, etc.

commensalism: a relationship wherein one species benefits from another species which neither loses or gains

commissural point: point at the base of a bird's bill where the mandibles first come together

commissure: line along which the upper and lower mandibles close

Common Birds Census: censusing birds using the spot-mapping method and coordinated by the British Trust for Ornithology

community: a natural assemblage of species, usually within a defined habitat type

competition: interaction between two or more individuals of either the same or different species using a common resource

competitive exclusion: the exclusion of one species by another, usually in a particular habitat, when exploiting a common resource

compromise behavior: form of behavior in which two opposing drives are aroused simultaneously

cones: color-sensitive cells in the retina of birds that promote visual acuity

congeneric: species belonging to the same genus

conspecific: belong to the same species

constant-effort mist netting: capture method standardized over space and time used for counting numbers of birds caught in mist nets

contact call: noise made by an individual bird to keep in touch with the rest of the flock

contour feather: a main body feather, with vanes that are somewhat flat and firm

control: recovery and release of a bird already marked in some manner or a standard of comparison for checking inferences deduced from experiments

convergent evolution: structural and behavioral similarities in otherwise unrelated species or families of living organisms

cooperative breeding: non-breeding birds helping out at the nests of breeding members their species e.g. nest-building, incubatio feeding nestlings, etc.

copradeum: chamber in the cloaca into whic the large intestine empties

copulation: sexual act leading to the fertilizatic of the female's ova by the male's spermatozo (AKA coition)

coracoid: breastbone connecting the sternu with the pectoral girdle

cornea: transparent membrane protecting th lens and capable of changing its curvature f focusing

corniplume: tuft of feathers on head of a bir e.g. horned lark

corridor: a narrow front traditionally used b migrating birds, e.g. Pacific flyway

cosmopolitan: refers to species or even high taxa found in virtually all of the zoogeograph regions in the world, e.g. osprey

cot: shelter for domesticated birds, e.g. dovecot

countershading: contrast between dark uppe parts and light underparts of plumage to reduc shadowing effect as a form of camouflage

countersinging: singing in rivalry with anoth male within hearing (*see* duetting)

courtship feeding: feeding of one member of a adult pair by the other

courtship: describes a wide range of activitie related to attracting a mate and maintaining pair bond and leading to copulation and pa enting

covert: small feathers covering the bird's mai flight feathers on wings and tail

covey: group of gamebirds, especially quail

cranium: bony structure housing the brain

creance: light line or string attached to jesses of bird of prey when being trained to fly to the fis

creche: assemblage of still-dependent youn from several pairs of a species, e.g. mergansei eider

crepuscular: describes birds active at twilight

crest: tuft on feathers on the crown of a head which can be lowered or raised

crissum: undertail coverts distinctively colore from the rest of the undersurface of the bird

critical temperatures: minimum and maximun ambient temperatures delineating the ther moneutral zone in which metabolic hea production is at a minimum

cronism: actual or attempted swallowing of dea or sickly young by their parents

crop: enlargement of the esophagus to store foo and in some cases, digest food.

crop milk: milky secretion of the esophagus, usually the crop, regurgitated and fed to young in pigeons, flamingos, and penguins

cross-fostering: replacement of eggs or young of one species by those of another species

crowing area: territory defended by male pheasant

crown: top of the head from the forehead to the nape

crus: outermost segment of the leg between the knee and foot

cryptic: describing coloration or other characters that afford concealment or disguise for protection from enemies or capture of prey

culmen: ridge of upper mandible from base to tip

cursorial: adapted to running, e.g. roadrunner

cuticle: thin waxy layer apparently protecting the eggshell from water evaporation and microbial invasion

cyanic: bluish pigments of eggs highlighted by suppression of reddish-brown pigments

cygnet: a young swan

D

dancing bird: *see* lek

dark phase: melanistic morph within a species

Darwin's finches: group of finches on the Galapagos Islands used by Charles Darwin for his theory on the origin of species

dawn chorus: burst of spring song from many species in a rough order beginning before dawn and then dying away abruptly

decoy: live or constructed (often carved) forms, generally of waterfowl, to attract free-ranging birds

definitive plumage: final plumage worn by adults of a species that wore differing plumages previously

deme: a local population that may be considered separately from other populations of the same species

density-dependent: factors having an influence on individuals in a population related to the degree of crowding

density-independent: factors having an influence on individuals in a population not related to the degree of crowding

dermis: inner skin layer

dertrum: tip of upper mandible

determinate layer: a species whose number of eggs in its clutch cannot be altered by addition or removal of eggs

dewlap: fleshy growth on the lower head, e.g. wattle

delayed incubation: heating of the eggs taking place only after all eggs are laid

diaphragm: system of membranes that partially divide the thoraco-abdominal cavity into lungs and cervical air sacs above and the rest of the air sacs below

diastataxic: having an unusually large gap between the fourth and sixth secondary feathers due to a missing fifth, e.g. waders

diastema: gap in wing in a diastataxic bird

dichromatic: having two distinct types of coloration, either with the sexes or two color morphs of a species

differential migration: migration to different wintering areas by different individuals within a species due to size or sex

digit: toe or "finger"

digitigrade: standing on the toes with the heel in the air

dihedral: the angle at which the wing meets the body, e.g. raised in turkey vultures and harriers, flat in eagles

dimorphism: occurrence of two distinct forms such as size or plumage

directive marks: bright or contrasting markings inside the mouths of young birds to help parents feed them

disc: *see* facial disc

disjunct: refers to a discontinuous range or distribution of a species

dispersal: movements of non-breeding birds away from areas of high density, e.g. roost, breeding colony, birthplace, etc.

dispersion: spread of a species over all suitable habitats within its range

displacement activity: less relevant behavioral movements undertaken by an individual unable to perform a behavior of a higher priority

display: simple and elaborate behavioral activity by a bird to induce a desired behavior in other birds, e.g. feathers, flight, especially for courtship and territoriality

disruption: form of protective coloration wherein bold markings conceal an organism's anatomical shape, e.g. killdeer plover, or conspicuous features, e.g. eyes

distraction behavior: active anti-predator strategies used by an individual to deflect a predator or at least divert attention away from eggs or young

distress call: loud vocalization made by birds seized by a predator or human

distribution: geographic range of a species or other taxonomic categories

diurnal: active by day

divergent evolution: evolution of different anatomical structures in closely related birds e.g. Darwin's finches

diversity: relative abundance and composition of species within a given area

DNA fingerprinting: using drop of blood, feather pulp, or other cellular material containing DNA to determine the DNA sequence unique to each individual for testing paternity

DNA: stands for deoxyribonucleic acid, a double-stranded molecule, used as genetic material for sources of taxonomic data

DNA-DNA hybridization: modern biochemical technique using DNA that may be revolutionizing avian systematics

domestication: breeding and maintenance of a species continuously controlled by humans

dominance: refers to regular winner in aggressive encounters, including between members of a breeding pair

dominance hierarchy: order of dominance among individuals within a local flock (AKA pecking order)

double scratch: motion of jumping forward and backward in leaves and other debris to seek food, e.g. towhees, juncos

double-brooded: refers to a species laying a second clutch after raising one brood

down: feathers characterized by their fluffy vanes

drake: male duck

drift: displacement of a migrant off its flight track, usually by wind or choosing to fly downwind

droppings: waste products from excretory (urine) and alimentary systems (feces)

drumming: loud tapping on objects by woodpeckers to proclaim a territory or the beating of wings by a ruffed grouse to attract females

drunkenness: intoxication of birds eating fermented berries or nectar

Duck Stamp: special government stamp involuntarily purchased by duck hunters to raise money for waterfowl conservation

duckling: young duck not yet full-grown

ductus deferens: convoluted tubes running from the testes to the cloaca through which mature sperm pass

duetting: male and female of a pair singing or calling somewhat together in a responsive fashion

dummy nest: extra nests, often incomplete, built by male wrens, perhaps for sleeping or for exaggerated courtship

dump nesting: laying of eggs by more than one female of usually the same species in one nest, e.g. goldeneye

duodenum: part of small intestine between the gizzard and the ileum

dusky: dark brownish-black or blackish

dusting: behavioral application of fine earth or sand onto plumage, perhaps for feather maintenance

E

ear tuft: a bunch of long feathers found in pairs on the top of the head and used for behavioral communication, e.g. owls (AKA horns)

ear patch: area below the orbit

ear coverts: modified contour feathers that cover the outer ear openings

ecdysis: annual shedding of feathers

echolocation: ability to emit sounds and analyze echoes to detect presence of nearby objects, e.g. cave-dwelling oilbirds

eclipse molt: all flight feathers lost at the same time, mostly in waterfowl (see eclipse plumage)

eclipse plumage: dull post-nuptial plumage stage of short duration occurring in male birds undergoing wing feather renewal, notably in waterfowl

ecogeographical rules: rules relating geographical variation in size, body parts, color, etc., e.g. Gloger's, Allen's, Bergmann's

ecological release: increase in abundance of a species or broadening of a species' feeding habits in the absence of a competing species

ecological succession: changes in a habitat over time due to its modification by former colonists and the arrival of new species

ecological barrier: ecological factor that prevents range expansion of a species or that divides its range

ecology: study of plants and animals in relation to their environment

ecosystem: the sum of all the factors that make up a specific environment

ecotone: area of transition between adjacent plant associations and the animal communities related to them

ecotope: particular kind of habitat in a region

ecotype: locally adapted population or race with characters derived from selective pressures from its environment

ectoparasite: parasites inhabiting the exterior of its host's body, e.g. mites, lice, ticks

edaphic: describes environmental factors dependent on conditions of soil or substratum

edge effect: increase in diversity of flora and fauna in a transition area between two habitats or community types

edge species: species preferring habitat in a transition area between two habitat or community types

dible nests: *see* bird's nest soup

fferent: carrying impulses outward from nerve centers

gg recognition: ability of some species to recognize their own eggs, especially in colonially-nesting birds, e.g. guillemots

gg mimicry: form of nest parasitism wherein the color of the parasite's eggs resemble those of the host, e.g. cuckoos

gg: end-product of the development of the female reproductive cell or ovum consisting of yolk, albumen, membranes, and outer shell

gg-bound: unable to lay an egg present in the oviduct due to obstruction or malformation of the egg

gg covering: covering of eggs by adult temporarily departing the nest, e.g. grebes, tits

gg tooth: small, sharp (often hook-like) projection on the tip of the upper mandible used by a full-term embryo to chip open the eggshell during hatching

gg retrieval: behavior wherein scrape-nesting species, e.g. terns, gulls, retrieve eggs accidentally ejected from the nest, but close by

gg Rule: average clutch size within a species tends to increase the more northerly the latitude

gg-eating: consumption of other birds' eggs by adult birds and their young

gger: person who collects eggs of rare birds

ggshell thinning: the laying of abnormally thin-shelled eggs by poor nutrition, disease, age, stress, and, notably, organochlorine pesticides such as DDT

lbow: angle or joint on the wing closest to the body

lectrophoresis: a laboratory process to characterize the different proteins in a mixture by their net charge, size, shape, or isoelectric charges to determine genetic relationships

margination: notched or forked appearance of a tail (or a primary feather) due to narrowing of the shape of the feather(s)

mbryo: young bird from the beginning of development in the egg until hatching

mbryology: study of embryo development

migration: movement of individuals from an area

ndangered: category assigned to a species whose numbers have declined to a some critically low level

ndemic: restricted to or only found in a particular geographic area

ndogamy: mating within the group

ndoparasite: parasites that inhabit the interior of a host's body

endornithocory: the dispersal of seeds in the environment by means of a bird's feces or pellets

endysis: developing a new coat of feathers

energetics: term to describe the intake and utilization of energy

epididymis: body of convoluted tubules lying aside each testes where spermatozoa accumulate before passing down the vas deferens

epigamic: describes characters or actions, usually a display, to promote synchronized reproductive behavior

episematic: describes an appearance, e.g. color, or behavior that aids in recognition

epithema: horny growth on the bill

epizootic: epidemic-like disease that kills large numbers of organisms

erythrism: obvious presence of reddish pigments in the plumage

escape distance: distance upon which a bird will depart upon the approach of a human or predator

escapee: a formerly captive bird that has escaped into the wild

estrogens: female sex hormones responsible for reproduction

ethology: study of behavior

etiology: the study of causation of disease

euryoecious: ability to exist in a wide variety of habitats

euryphagous: ecologically tolerant of a wide range of foods

eusyanthropic: living in or on houses of humans, e.g. phoebes

eutaxic: refers to wings with a full complement of secondary feathers

evolution: theory describing the origin of today's diversity of organisms from a lesser diversity by a process of gradual change from generation to generation

exanthropic: living apart from humans

excrement: *see* droppings

exotic: describes a species that is alien to a particular area

extinct: describes a species or subspecies no longer existing

extinction: the complete disappearance of a species from the earth or from an island

extirpate: exterminate, eradicate, or eliminate

extirpation: the elimination of a species from an island, local area, or region

extralimital: describes species occurring outside the boundaries of a given area

eyass: a nestling falcon or hawk

eye ring: area of contrasting feathers or skin encircling an eye

eye line: pale mark running above the eye or dark eye running through the eye

eye stripe: *see* eye line

eyelash: bristle that resembles a human eyelash, e.g. seen in hornbills, cuckoos, ostrich, secretary bird

eyelid: one of two folds of skin above and below the eye to cover it (*see also* nictitating membrane)

eyespot: *see* ocella

eyrie: nest of a bird of prey

F

facial disc: well-defined, flat, roundish feature of some bird's faces, e.g. owls, harriers, to act as a parabola to collect sound waves

facultative brood parasite: a species that lays eggs in the nest of a host species but is not dependent on doing so to raise young

falcated: hooked, sickle-shaped

falconry: use of trained birds of prey to capture game

fall: sudden presence of birds, usually during migration and along a coast, caused by an interruption of migration by inclement weather (AKA rush)

false crop: expansion of crop as a storage place for seeds, e.g. redpoll

false wing: *see* alula

Family: primary taxonomic category indicating a grouping of genera, e.g. falconiformes

fasciated: striped or banded

fault bar: conspicuous streaks in tail feathers caused by poor nutrition leading to improper growth of feather hooks

fauna: total animal life of a region or area

feather cortex: lightweight, spongy material with the feather shaft

feather sheath: protective tissue surrounding the developing feather tissue

feather tract: *see* pteryla

feather: a unit of plumage that is unique to birds

feather comb: pectinated (comb-like) claw on the middle toes of certain birds, e.g. nightjars

fecal sac: white, gelatinous package of excrement from nestlings removed by parents, presumably for nest sanitation

femur: thighbone

feral: describes populations of domesticated species that have reverted to a free-ranging existence

ferruginous: iron- or rusty-colored

fertilization: union of a male gamete, i.e. spermatozoon, with a female gamete, i.e. ovum, in the female's upper oviduct

fibula: small thin bone below the knee and running parallel to the tibiotarsus

field character: a distinctive feature or trait used to identify a species in the wild

field mark: characteristic, e.g. color, shape, etc used to identify a wild bird

field guide: a pocket-sized book composed of illustrations and accompanying information used to identify birds in the wild

filoplume: a type of feather resembling a fine thin hair

filtration feeding: using the tongue to press mud and water against a filter of stiff hairs and lamellae inside the mandibles, e.g flamingos

first-year bird: bird in its first 12–16 months

fitness: the number of offspring left by an individual of a particular kind of organism

fixation: an abnormal behavioral attachment of one individual to another of a different species

flammulated: describes plumage tinged with rufous

flank: fleshy part of the side above the proximal end of the leg

fledging success: percent of hatchings that fledge or average number of young fledged

fledging: acquisition of first true feathers by young bird

fledgling: young bird that has just left the nest

flight year: year in which some northerly species, general non-migratory, head south in large numbers to seek food resources

flight: a form of locomotion achieved in birds by use of flight feathers and lightness

flight feathers: primary and secondary feathers of the wing

flight song: habitual singing during flight to pronounce territory in birds nesting in open habitats, e.g. grassland, tundra

flight muscles: collectively the breast muscles to lift and lower the wings

flight pattern: distinctive outline or silhouette of certain flying birds, e.g. raptors, ducks

flightlessness: having a reduced or absent flight apparatus such that flight is impossible, e.g. ostriches, some grebes

flipper: modified wing of penguins

floater: unpaired bird during the breeding season capable of breeding

floating birds: reserve of non-breeding or non-territorial birds present in breeding or territorial populations

flock: *see* assembly

flocking: joining of individuals of same or different species into groups for social purposes

flora: total plant life of an area or region

flyway: broad-front band or pathway used by migrating birds often over prominent geographic features, e,g, coastlines, mountain ranges, etc.

follicle: highly vascularized layers of tissue that surround the ovum until the latter is released or the growth structure from which a feather develops

food pass: aerial food pass from a male to a female raptor during breeding season

food chain: successional flow of energy from one trophic level to another, e.g. seed eaten by a mouse, mouse eaten by a hawk, etc.

foot-paddling: quick trembling motions of the foot by some shorebirds to stir up invertebrate prey

foot-stirring: raking movements of the foot by herons and egrets to flush out small prey in mud flats, shallow water, and meadows

foot-trembling: *see* foot-paddling

footedness: physiological dominance of one foot over another in some birds, e.g. pigeons, raptors, parrots

foramen magnum: opening through which the spinal cord emerges from the skull

forearm: antebrachium

forebrain: front section of the brain responsible for complex behavioral instincts and instructions, e.g. nest-building.

forest fragmentation: development of forests, e.g. logging, that leaves the remaining forest stands in varying sizes and degrees of isolation

form: a taxonomic term referring to a group of birds below the sub-specific level (AKA variety)

fossil: preserved remains of members of Class *Aves*

fossorial: habit of digging as in burrowing to make a nest

founder population: founders of a new population or breeding colony containing only a proportion of the genetic variation of the original parent population

fovea: a point on the retina of the eye facilitating sharper focus

fratricide: *see* Cain and Abel Syndrome

freezing: motionless behavior to escape detection

fright molt: sudden partial molt that occurs outside of the normal molt period, often caused by fear

frontal: pertaining to the forehead

frugivorous: fruit-eating

fulvous: tawny or brownish-yellow

furcula: bony structure formed by fusion of right and left clavicles (AKA wishbone)

G

gall bladder: reservoir for bile in some birds, but not all

gallinaceous: resembling a domestic fowl

game bird: quarry species, notably grouse, pheasants, turkeys, snipe, woodcock, bustards, hunted by humans

gamete: a germ cell, i.e. spermatozoon, ovum

gamosematic: describes appearance or behavior that helps pair members find one another

gander: male goose

gape: wide open mouth (AKA commissure)

gaping: panting with mouth open to shed heat or nestling birds opening their mouths widely to stimulate parents to feed them

Gause's Rule: ecological rule wherein two species with identical ecological requirements cannot coexist in the same environment

gene flow: exchange of genetic traits between populations

gene: unit of inheritance within a chromosome

genetic drift: change in the frequency of a gene complex in a population, usually as a result of isolation of a small segment from its main population

genetic swamping: one species successfully hybridizing with another and eventually incorporating its gene pool into its own, e.g. mallard and black duck

genetics: study of heredity, i.e. the passing of characters from parents to offspring

genome: full set of chromosomes

genotype: group in which an individual falls due to its genetic makeup

genus: taxomomic category representing a group of species

Geographic Information System (GIS): set of computer software and hardware for analyzing and displaying spatially referenced features with non-geographic attributes, e.g. species

geographical speciation: gradual formation of a new species caused by geographical isolation from the parent species

germ-cell: *see* gamete

germinal spot: area on the yolk sac that develops into the blastula and eventually the embryo

gestalt: term referring to the sense of the whole being greater than the sum of the parts in identifying a bird; *see* GIS, GISS

GIS: a descriptive acronym for a bird seen, referring to General Impression and Shape pronounced as "jizz"

GISS: similar to above, referring to General Information on Size and Shape

gizzard: the grinding muscular stomach present in most birds (AKA ventriculus)

glaucous: bluish- or silvery-grey

gleaning: foraging for insects or similar food from leafy or bark surfaces

Gloger's Rule: races of a given species in warm, humid areas are likely to be more heavily pigmented than those in cool and dry areas

glottis: slit-like entrance to the trachea located in the rear of the mouth

gobbling ground: North American term for social display ground of lesser prairie chicken

gonad: refers to primary sex organs, i.e. testes in males, ovaries in females

gonys: prominent ridge formed by the junction of the two halves of the lower jaw towards the tip, e.g. gulls

gorget: band of color on throat or upper breast in hummingbirds

gosling: young goose

grallatorial: pertaining to wading

graminivorous: grass-eating

granivorous: seed-eating

gregariousness: *see* flocking

grin line: plumage marking along the lower mandible that gives a bird the appearance of smiling, e.g. trumpeter swan

grit: coarse, small matter, e.g. stones, sand, diatoms, shells, etc., ingested by some birds to acquire minerals and to aid in digestion

grooming: maintenance of feathers, i.e. orientation, cleanliness, oiling, and waterproofing

guano: excreta or droppings of seabirds dried into a rough lime-like powder often collected by humans for fertilizer

guild: two or more species' populations exploiting the same type of resources in similar ways

gular fluttering: rapid oscillation of floor of mouth and upper throat, generally for cooling, e.g. as in owls

gular pouch: enlarged skin sac in the upper throat for panting (cooling), for storage of fish, e.g. pelicans, or for display, e.g. frigatebird

gular sac: *see* gular pouch

gullet: anterior part of esophagus

gynandromorphism: genetic aberration wherein one part of an animal's body is female and another part is male

H

habitat: particular environment, i.e. flora, fauna, soil, climate, in which a particular organism lives

habituation: learned behavior where an organism does not respond to recurring stimuli

hacking: a procedure used by falconers to release raptors back into the wild

hackle: long, slender feather on the neck, e.g. Galliformes

haggard: raptor caught as an adult and trained by a falconer

hallux: the first or hind toe, usually pointing backward and sometimes reduced in size

hamulus: a hooked barbicel

hand quill: primary feather

handedness: footedness in parrots where the feet are used to handle food

Harderian glands: secretory glands found in the eyes of birds for protective purposes

hatching success: percentage of (fertile) eggs that hatch

hatching year (HY): a bird in first basic plumage in its first calendar year

hatching: emergence of developed chick from an incubated egg

hatchling: a newly hatched bird

hawking: catching insects while in flight or *see* falconry

head-scratching: use of feet to respond to irritations in areas unreachable with the bill

heading: direction in which a bird is flying

Heligoland trap: long funnel-like wire-netting cage with a wide opening at one end and a windowed catching-box at the other end to trap birds

helmet: ornament, usually feather-like, on top of some birds' heads, e.g. helmet-shrikes

helpers: *see* cooperative breeding

hen: a female bird

herbivorous: plant-eating

Herbst's corpuscle: ovoid masses of nerve endings that receive tactile information

heritability: proportion of total variation with a genetic basis within a population

hermaphrodite: animal with both male and female sex organs

heronry: nesting colony of herons

Hesse's Rule: forms of warm-blooded animals living in cold regions have relatively higher heart weights than those in warm regions

heterochroism: abnormal color differences

heterogynism: taxonomic characters that distinguish closely related species being more strongly marked in females than males

hibernation: rare in birds, but see torpidity

hill: display ground of the ruff

hindbrain: rear section of the brain linking spinal cord and peripheral nervous system

histology: study of minute structure of tissues

hoary: frosty-grey or silver

holding: using the feet to hold food and other objects, e.g. parrots

home range: area occupied by an individual, a pair, or group of birds *or* an area (that may or may not be defended) to which an individual restricts most of its usual activities

homing: using various directional cues, e.g. landscape, celestial, geomagnetic, to return to a location, e.g. nest, loft

homogenous: of the same character or nature

homosexuality: pairing of same-sex birds, occurring in populations where the sex ratio is strongly skewed

homothermous: warm-blooded

hood: area of distinctive color covering large part of head as in plumage or leather cap or helmet fitted for the head of a trained raptor to exclude light and vision to induce calming

hooklet: smallest unit of barb structure that helps hold feather shape

hooting: refers to distinctive call of some birds, e.g. owls

hopping: locomotion of most perching birds when on the ground

hot-searching: finding nests by attempting to flush sitting birds from the vegetation

Hotline: *see* Rare Bird Alert

hovering: remaining stationary in mid-air while beating the wings rapidly, e.g. hummingbird, kestrel

humerus: upper wing bone

hunger trace: *see* fault bar

hybrid: individual produced from a cross of two individuals of dissimilar genetic background, often morphologically different

hybridization: *see* hybrid

hyoid apparatus: bones of the tongue

hyoptile: supplemental small feather originating from the base of a contour feather

hyperphagia: overeating by migrants to store energy

hypophysis: pituitary gland

hyporachis: shaft of hyoptile

hyporadius: barb of hyoptile

hypotarsus: protrusion on back of tarsometatarsus

hypothalamus: part of the forebrain

I

ileum: posterior part of the small intestine

image-fighting: territorial attacks of a bird on its own reflection in a window, mirror, etc.

immature: young fully feathered bird not in adult plumage but capable of breeding

impervious: refers to closed nostrils, e.g. gannet

imping: falconry technique for repairing broken feathers

imprinting: an often irreversible behavioral phenomenon where a young bird develops an attachment to its parent and hence, species recognition

incubation: the transfer of heat from a bird's body (or in some megapodes, decaying organic matter) to an egg to facilitate embryonic development

incubation patch: *see* brood patch

indeterminate layer: species in which the number of eggs in a clutch can be altered by addition or removal of eggs

indicator species: those species whose presence, due to their ecological requirements, demonstrate the existence of certain environmental conditions

indigenous: describes species native to an area

individual distance: minimum distance at which one individual will tolerate the presence of another

information centre: theoretically a communal roost wherein birds gathering pass on information about good feeding sites to one another

infrasound: very low frequency sounds detected by birds but not humans, perhaps used in homing

infundibulum: top of the oviduct that receives the released ovum and where fertilization takes place

ingluvies: *see* crop

inheritance: *see* genetics

injury feigning: behavior of adult wherein it pretends to be injured to draw predator or intruder away from nest

innate behavior: behavior that an individual is born with and not learned

insectivorous: insect-eating

instinct: *see* innate behavior

insurance egg: extra egg laid by a species that normally only raises one nestling

integument: skin and organs comprising the protective covering of an organism, e.g. plumage

integumentary structures: outgrowths from the skin, e.g. feathers, spurs, combs, wattles, sacs, pouches

intention movements: incomplete initial pha of a behavior pattern

interbreeding: mating between two memb different species resulting in hybrid offsp

interference: optical process responsible for iridescence in feathers by waves of light either reinforcing or canceling one another

interference competition: competition in which one species prevents another from having access to a limited resource

intergradation: cross-breeding of different subspecies within a single species

intermewed: refers to a hawk that has undergone a molt in captivity

interspaces: *see* areolae

interspecific competition: competition between individuals of different species

interspecific: refers to an interaction or relationship between two species

intraspecific: refers to an interaction or relationship between members of the same species

intraspecific competition: competition between individuals of the same species

introduced species: species found outside its natural range due to inadvertent or deliberate introduction by humans, e.g. house sparrow

introgression: gene flow between genetically divergent populations or occurring only between species

invasion: expansion of a species' range into a new area (*but also see* irruption)

iridiscence: display of spectral colors in feathers during repositioning in the sun, e.g. grackles

iris: pigmented part of the eye surrounding the pupil

irruption: irregular mass movement of birds post-breeding to areas beyond normal range, usually caused by a sudden superabundance of food, e.g. crossbills, raptors

Isabelline: greyish-yellow or brown tinged with reddish-yellow

island biogeography: theory in which the number of species on an island results from an equilibrium between immigration and extinction

isochronal lines: lines drawn on a map between locations reached by migrants of a given species on the same date

isolating mechanism: a difference between species or populations thereof that helps to prevent interbreeding and maintain reproductive isolation

isthmus: part of the oviduct where the two shell membranes are laid down on the egg

ɔum: part of the small intestine

: leather straps worn on the legs of a trained ﹐r for restraining purposes

jizz: combination of characteristics which identify a bird (or other animal) in the field (*see* GI and GISS)

jugging: sleeping place of partridge

jugulum: lower part of the exterior throat

juvenal: describes the first post-natal plumage o a young bird

juvenile: young bird that has not yet reache breeding maturity

K

keel: narrow median process or carina of the ster num for the attachment of breast muscles

Kelso's Rule: ear openings and skin flaps covering them are larger among northern-nesting populations of owls and smaller in southern ones

keratin: main structural protein making up horny parts of skin, scales, feathers, and bills

kettle: used to describe a flock of migrating raptors sharing a rising thermal

keystone species: species whose abundance impacts upon the structure and dynamics of an ecosystem

kin selection: a mechanism whereby natural selection works indirectly on related individuals who share a proportion of their genes

kleptoparasitism: interspecific and intraspecific food-stealing behavior widespread in birds

knee: femoro-tibial leg joint

koilin: interior lining of the gizzard that can be periodically shed or moulted

kronism: *see* cronism

L

labyrinth: semicircular canals in inner ear that facilitate equilibrium

lachrymal glands: glands secreting substances that help moisten the eye

lamellae: fine, hair-like structures lining bills of some species to facilitate filter-feeding of small particles

laparotomy: minor surgical process for assessment of internal organs, generally to determine sex

lappet: drooping folds of skin on the head or neck, e.g. turkey, vulture

larder: collection of prey items, e.g. mice, birds, etc., impaled on thorns or barbed wire by shrikes and other birds

larynx: uppermost part of the trachea below the glottis

laying: act of deposition of an egg (AKA oviposition)

LBJ's: bird-watcher's term that refers to "little

brown jobs," i.e. small brownish birds hard to identify

leading edge: the forward or front lifting edge of the wing

leap-frog migration: movement of a northern breeding population to wintering grounds lying further south than those occupied by a southern breeding population of the same species, as well as the reverse

learning: production of adaptive changes in individual behavior resulting from experience

lek: communal display ground where males of a given species congregate to attract and court females

leucism: abnormal paleness in the plumage due to environmental factors, e.g. abnormal diet

life list: record of birds seen by a birder in his or her lifetime

life zone: an area defined in terms of humidity and temperature

life expectancy: number of years an individual might survive in the wild

life bird: bird species observed by a birder for the first time

lifer: *see* life bird

light phase: pale-colored morph within a species

Lincoln Index: an equation or formula referring to a mark-recapture method to determine populations of vertebrates

lipochromes: naturally occurring pigments, i.e. yellows, oranges, and reds, in the feathers and skin

lister: birder who is willing to travel great distances to record new bird species

listing: competitive birding for the greatest number of species within a given area or time period

long-distance migration: migratory pattern in which a species flies from its breeding area in Arctic or temperate latitudes to tropical or subtropical latitudes where it winters

longevity: number of years an individual might survive under any conditions, i.e. wild or captivity

loomery: breeding colony of guillemots

loop migration: circular pattern of migration where the fall pathway differs from the one used in the spring

lore: small area on each side of a bird's face

lumper: someone who prefers to combine apparently distinct forms into one, e.g. subspecies into species

lure: imitation prey swung by falconers to recover their birds

M

magnum: part of oviduct where albumen is added to the ovum

malar stripe: plumage marking on the cheek of a bird

Malpighian layer: epidermal cells which grow into the structure of the feather proper

mandible: upper and lower half of a bird's bill

mantle: feathers of the back, scapulars, and upper wing coverts

manus: bones, i.e. carpometacarpus and phalanges, representing the "hand"

marbled: irregular marking of plumage with spots, speckles, blotches, or streaks

marginal coverts: small feathers overlying the secondary coverts on the shoulder of the wing

marking: refers to banding, ringing, or otherwise altering a bird for identification

mating: *see* copulation

mating system: the relationship between the sexes within the social organization, e.g. monogamy

maturity: attainment of an age whereupon a bird is capable of breeding

maxilla: upper half of the bill or paired facial bones that support the bill

Mayfield method: method of calculating the rate of nesting success based on the number of days a nest was observed

Mayr's Rule: races in cooler climates often more strongly migratory than those in more southerly, warmer ones

mechanical sounds: non-vocal sounds made by bills, tail, or wings

medulla oblongata: lower part of hindbrain

melanism: excessive amounts of black or dark brown pigments in plumage or eggs

merrythought: *see* furcula

mesoptile: second of two nestling down plumages

metacarpus: *see* carpometacarpus

metapopulation: set of populations living in unconnected habitat patches but linked by movement of individuals between them

metatarsus: fused bones of the foot (*see* tarsometatarsus)

mews: holding facilities for molting or breeding raptors trained by falconers

microsmatic: poorly developed olfactory powers

midbrain: middle section of the brain regulating vision, muscular coordination, and balance, and physiological controls

migration: movements of bird populations at predictable times of year, generally fall and spring, to exploit new resources

migratory restlessness: unsettled or active behavior of birds just prior to departing on migration

mimicry: resemblance of one species to another for either mutual or one-sided benefit, but rare in birds (*but see* vocal mimicry)

mirror: white spot on black wing tip of some gulls

mist net: a finely woven, almost invisible net hung from poles used to catch flying birds for purposes of measurement and affixing leg bands

mobbing: noisy flocking of birds, often of several species, to drive off a predator

molt: periodic shedding and replacement of worn plumage and even epidermal structures like tarsal scales

molt migration: regular movement by some birds to and from an area where they molt

Monitoring Avian Productivity and Survivorship program (MAPS): program coordinated by the Institute for Bird Populations that involves constant-effort mist netting, banding, and intensive point counts during the breeding season at a continent-wide network of stations

monogamy: mating with one partner only

monophagous: restricting the diet to one type of food

monotypic: taxonomic category that has a single representative of the next lowest category, e.g. montypic order has only one family

moon-watching: practice of recording birds flying across the moon

morph: variation of color, size, or other characteristic of a species; also referred to a phase

morphology: study of form or shape, including color and anatomy

moustachial stripe: a streak running back from the base of a bill, as in plumage

mule: cross between a canary and another species of finch

multi-brooded: producing more than one clutch or brood per season

Murphy's Rule: island birds have larger bills than related mainland birds

mutes: raptor droppings

mutual preening: *see* allopreening

mycosis: disease caused by fungus

myology: study of muscles

N

nail: horny structure found at the tip of the upper mandible of all wildfowl species or horny tip of a bird claw

ape: back part of the neck

res: paired openings comprising the nasal cavities

narial feathers: long feathers at the base of the upper bill that partly cover the nares

natal down: initial coat of feathers worn by a nestling bird

natal dispersal: movement from natal site to first breeding or potential breeding site

natatorial: pertaining to swimming

natural selection: those ecological factors or processes that lead to individuals of a species passing on advantageous traits to offspring to perpetuate their genotype

naturalized birds: species that have been introduced directly or indirectly by humans and now breeding regularly as wild birds

navigation: the use of landmarks, geomagnetism, position of sun and/or stars, etc. to follow a migration route

nectar-feeders: birds that feed on sugary fluid in flowers or fruit juices

nectarivorous: *see* nectar-feeders

neontology: study of geologically recent forms of life

neossology: study of young birds

neossoptile: refers to natal down plumage

neotropical migrant: migratory bird in the Neotropical fauna region

nest: structure made or adopted by a bird in which to lay and incubate its eggs

nest parasitism: rare phenomenon wherein one species of bird takes over the nest of another for its own use, e.g. black-billed cuckoo

nest-building: behavior associated with excavating or constructing a nest

nest-robbing: eating of eggs or young nestlings by other birds, e.g. magpies

nest-sharing: using of a common nest by two females, sometimes of different species

nestbox: artificial nest, i.e. made by humans

nesting association: group nesting involving two or more bird species or a bird and non-avian species

nestling: a young bird still in the nest and dependent on its parents for some resource

niche expansion: increases in places where a species feeds or breeds or in type of foods it eats

niche: position or role an organism plays in its community

nictitating membrane: a third eyelid, usually transparent, for protection and/or lubrication of the avian eye

nidicolous: young birds that remain in the nest after hatching

nidification: building of a nest

nidifugous: young birds that leave the nest immediately upon hatching

nocturnal: active at night

nomadism: movements of species that do not revisit breeding or non-breeding areas

nomenclature: scientific naming of species, sub-species, genera, families, etc. for classification purposes

nominate: the first officially documented species in a genus

non-breeder: individual that does not breed in a given reproductive season

nostrils: *see* nares

nuptial: describes plumage or display in breeding season

O

obligate brood parasite: a bird species that cannot attain full development independent of a host species

observatory: an establishment often strategically located to promote study of bird migration by observation and/or banding

occiput: back part of the head just above the nape

oceanic: describing birds capable of feeding long distances offshore

ocella: eye-like pattern on plumage, e.g. American kestrel head

oil gland: *see* uropygial gland

olfactory bulbs: parts of forebrain dedicated to processing olfactory data

oligotokous: producing few eggs

olivaceous: brownish-green to greenish-brown

omnivorous: eating both plant and animal food

ontogeny: developmental history of an individual

oocyte: cell stage in the formation of an ovum

oology: study of birds' eggs

operculum: flap covering the nares or the acoustic meatus

optic lobes: parts of brain dedicated to processing visual data

orbit: cavity in the skull that houses the eyeball or the circular area around the eye on the head

ornithichnite: fossilized footprint of a bird

ornitholite: bird fossil

ornithologist: person, professional or amateur, who studies birds

ornithology: the study of birds

ornithomancy: predicting the future by observing bird behavior

ornithophilous: describes plants fertilized with birds serving as intermediates

ornithosis: *see* psittacosis

ortstreue: German term referring to the tendency of migrants to return to a previous breeding or wintering area

ossification: formation of bone

osteology: study of bones and bone structure

ostium: *see* infundibulum

ovary: female gonad

overshooting: movement of birds migrating in the right direction but beyond their normal destination

oviduct: tube through which the ovum passes and undergoes development into a hard-shelled egg

oviparity: refers to the universal practice of birds laying eggs in which embryos develop outside the female's body

oviposition: *see* laying

ovotestis: pertains to the fusion of germ cells of the ovum and testis in the event of the loss of the left ovary

ovulation: release of the ovum from a ruptured follicle in the ovary

ovum: female germ-cell

owlet: nestling owl

P

pair formation: establishment of a pair through an exchange of social signals and responses for the purpose of reproduction

pair: two adult birds apparently mated

pair bond: relationship between members of a breeding couple from courtship through fledging young from the nest

palaeontology: *see* paleontology

palaeospecies: *see* paleospecies

palate: roof of the mouth

paleontology: study of fossilized remains of plants and animals

paleospecies: species only known from fossil remains

pancreas: lobulated endocrine gland located in the upper intestine and secreting digestive enzymes as well as two hormones for metabolism regulation

panting: rapid breathing to dissipate excessive body heat

parasematic: describes an appearance or behavior that distracts the attention of a predator away from the more vulnerable body part or individual to one less vulnerable

paratrepsis: term encompassing all forms of distraction display

parental care: protection, feeding, and care young from hatching to independence by or both parents

parthenogenesis: production of an ind' from an egg not fertilized by a male e.g. turkey

partial migrant: species in which some members of its population migrate and some do not

Partners-In-Flight: a conservation program for neotropical migrants of the Western Hemisphere endorsed by government and non-government organizations

passage hawk: one-year old hawk or falcon trapped during migration by a falconer for training

passage migrant: migrating birds that pass through an area without remaining in summer or winter

passerine: member of the order Passeriformes, i.e. perching songbirds

patagium: fold of skin in a wing running from the upper arm to the forearm

patristic: resemblances among species or other taxa attributed to a common ancestry rather than due to convergent evolution

pecking order: dominance hierarchy among social birds derived from domestic poultry

pecten: comb-like nutritional organ feeding the avascular retina of a eye

pectoral: pertaining to the breast

peep: refers to look-alike shorebirds

pelagic: describes birds dwelling near ocean or open sea

pellet: bolus of undigested portions of food, e.g. fur, feather, bones, regurgitated by some birds, especially birds of prey

pelvic: describes the combination of bones at the base of the spinal column that give support to the legs.

pen: female swan

penis: male copulatory organ found in some birds, e.g. ducks

pennae: contour feather with the barbs forming a coherent vane

perching bird: *see* passerine

perforate: refers to incomplete septum of some birds, e.g. turkey vulture

peritoneum: membrane lining the abdominal cavity and coating the internal organs

permanent resident: individual or species that breeds and winters in the same region

pervious: open nares as opposed to closed ones

pessulus: bony structure within the syrinx employed to make sound

pesticide: chemical agent of synthetic or natural origin used by humans to control nuisance organisms, e.g. insecticides, herbicides, fungicides, rodenticidies

nx: digit bones

ric: refers to coloration or other characters purpose is to be conspicuous as opposed ic

pharynx: throat cavity leading to the esophagus and trachea

phase: *see* morph

phenology: study of visible appearances in relation to season or climate, e.g. first arrival of a migratory species

phenotype: sum of organism's external characteristics, i.e. appearance, as opposed to genotype

philopatry: fidelity to a home area (*see* orstreue)

phoresy: passive transport of one organism by another without involving parasitism

photoperiodism: daily light-dark cycle used as a source of predictive information for annual events, e.g. breeding, migration

phylogeny: evolutionary history of a taxon

physiology: study of bodily function

pigeon's milk: *see* crop milk

pigmentary colors: pigments widely found in the bill, soft parts, and feathers of birds, e.g. melanin, carotenoids, hemoglobin, porphyrins

pigmentation abnormality: change in the amount and distribution of pigments, particularly the melanins and lipochromes

pileated: crested or capped shape of feathers on a bird's crown

pileum: entire top of the head from forehead to nape

pinfeather: newly growing feather still in its sheath

pinion: outer portion of a bird's wing from which the flight feathers arise, or a single flight feather, or collectively, the flight feathers

pinioning: cutting one wing at the carpal joint to prevent the primary feathers from growing, permanently prohibiting flight in captive birds

pipping: the act of chipping a hole in the airspace and eggshell by the embryo in preparation for hatching

piracy: *see* kleptoparasitism

piscivorous: fish-eating

pishing: "shshshsh" sound preceded with a "p" made by humans to attract songbirds in close

pitch: height from which a falcon begins its stoop

play: activity performed by mostly young, but also adult birds of a wide variety of species

pluma: contour feather where the barbs are free and do not form a coherent vane

plumage abnormality: abnormal colors, changes in feather patterning, changes in feather structure due to changes in the amount and distribution of pigments or chemical changes in the pigments themselves

plumage: feather covering of a bird or feathered appearance of a bird in various stages of immaturity in its lifetime plumbeous: lead-colored

plume: a long display feather, e.g. pheasant tail

plumula: down feather

plumule: *see* plumula

plunge-diving: behavior wherein a flying bird dives into the water from the air

pneumatization: the invasion of air sacs into the hollow bones in birds' skeletons

podotheca: horny covering of the unfeathered areas of legs and feet

pogonium: web of a feather

pollex: thumb or first digit of the hand of the wing

polyandry: mating system wherein a female regularly mates with two or more males

polychromatism: refers to variations in plumage colors worn by individuals within a species, e.g. gyrfalcon

polygamy: mating system wherein a bird has more than one mate

polygyny: mating system wherein a male regularly mates with two or more females

polymorphism: coexistence within an interbreeding population of two or more genetically determined forms or morphs

polytokous: producing many eggs

polytypic: taxon with more than one unit in the next lowest category, e.g. genus with several species

population: total number of individuals in a given area

poryphyrin pigments: pigments related to hemoglobin and bile and common in red and brown feathers of some bird

postfledging mortality: death rate of young after leaving the nest

postjuvenal molt: renewal of feathers from juvenal plumage to first winter plumage

postnuptial molt: renewal of feathers from breeding plumage to winter plumage

poult: domestic chicken

poultry: refers to birds of domesticated species to be eaten by humans

powder down: feathers that produce a fine powder for water resistance

precocial: refers to young birds that are active and not nestbound right after hatching

predation: killing of one species by another for food

preen gland: *see* uropygial gland

preening: act of grasping feathers in the bill to remove oil, dirt, and ectoparasites

preening invitation: bowing of head and ruffling of feathers by one species to induce another to preen it, e.g. cowbirds

prejuvenal molt: first complete change of feathers from natal down to juvenal plumage

prenuptial molt: renewal of feathers from winter plumage to breeding plumage

primary: flight feathers borne on the manus

proaposematic: refers to markings that warn predators of undesirability, e.g. egg patterns or colors

proepisematic: refers to plumage markings that serve to facilitate recognition and help maintain contact among members of family or feeding groups, e.g. waders

prolactin: hormone secreted by the pituitary gland and involved with broodiness, formation of a brood patch, production of crop milk, and other forms of sexual behavior

promiscuity: indiscriminate, casual sexual relationships, often brief in nature

pronating: rotation of the wing's leading edge downward to increase lift

protoptile: first of two nestling down plumages

proventriculus: the glandular or chemical stomach preceding the gizzard

psilopedic: refers to young bird with little or no down when hatched

psittacine: member of the parrot family

psittacosis: virus disease affecting parrots and some other birds and communicable to humans

pteryla: discrete tract of skin bearing contour feathers

pterylography: study of arrangement of feathers on the skin

pterylosis: arrangement of contour feathers into orderly groups or tracts

ptilopedic: refers to young bird wearing down when hatched

ptilopody: refers to feathered toes and legs

ptilosis: *see* plumage

puffinosis: disease of the manx shearwater similar to psittacosis

pullet: immature female domestic fowl

pullus: age-class name for nestling or chick prior to fledging used by scientists

pupil: round opening in the eyeball that contracts or expands to allow the entry of light

pygostyle: caudal end bone of the vertebral column

pyloric stomach: specialized chamber between the gizzard and small intestine with various functions in different bird species

pylorus: opening of the gizzard into the duodenum

Q

quasi-social: referring to behavioral adaptations that facilitate aggregation behavior

quill: calamus of a feather or a feather in general

R

race: *see* subspecies

rachis: shaft of a feather

racing pigeon: domesticated pigeon bred for its flying ability

racket: terminal broadening of a feather vane

racquet: *see* racket

radiation: geographical spread of a species or group of related species from a geographical region where they originally evolved or divergence of forms of common ancestry

radiotracking: *see* biotelemetry

radius: slender of two bones comprising the forearm of the wing

raft: dense flock of birds, e.g. waterfowl, on the water

rain-posture: special stance taken by certain birds in regions of seasonal downpours to shed water while perching

ramus: barb of a feather or one of two lateral halves of the lower mandible

range: geographic area in which a species is found

rapacious: subsisting on prey taken by violent means, e.g. raptorial birds

raptor, raptorial: *see* bird of prey

Rare Bird Alert: telephone service facilitating exchange of information on rare bird sightings among North American birders

rarity: a bird uncommon in a given area, but perhaps common elsewhere

ratite: refers to flightless birds not having a keel, e.g. kiwi

recovery team: group of specialists assigned to produce and implement a recovery plan in North America

recovery plan: government plan or program set up to restore endangered species in North America

recruitment: addition of new individuals to a population by reproduction

rectrices: main tail feathers

rectrix: *see* rectrices

redirection: directing a behavioral response at something other than what an observer would expect, e.g. hungry bird pecking at inanimate objects

reeve: a female ruff

refuge: land set aside for protection of wildlife

regurgitation: act of casting up or vomiting partly digested food for nestlings or undigestible parts

of prey, i.e. fur, feather, and bone, or stomach oil in some young seabirds

releaser: behavioral for a stimulus that signals another organism to perform an appropriate action

relic population: isolated population that once had a much wider distribution

remex: *see* remiges

remicle: small feather found on the wing in some birds

remiges: main flight feather, i.e. primaries, secondaries

Rensch's Rule: stomach, intestine, and caeca of birds on a mixed diet are relatively smaller in tropical than temperate zone races or wings of races living in a cold climate or high altitudes are relatively longer than those in warmer climates or low altitudes

reproductive isolation: refers to those factors that prevent interbreeding between closely related species

reserve: land set aside for wildlife and with restricted use by people

resident: individual, populations, subspecies, or species that remains in a given area throughout the year

resident: non-migratory or sedentary individual inhabiting a given area year-round

restoration ecology: study of re-creating a natural or self-sustaining community or ecosystem

retromigration: migratory movement of birds misled by a geographical feature, e.g. coastline, into taking a direction divergent or even opposite to their normal desired one

reverse migration: migratory movement of birds in the opposite direction to which they are expected

rhamphotheca: covering of the bill that is horny in most birds but soft and leathery in some shorebirds and waterfowl

rhodopsin: light-sensitive substance found in the rods of the retina

rictal bristles: thin, stiff feathers growing around the beak in some insectivorous birds

rictus: soft, fleshy part of a bird's bill at the angle of the mouth

ring: leg band

ringing up: upward circling flight of hunting falcon to get above its avian prey

ringing: *see* banding

rocket net: large mesh nets propelled by projectiles shot from cannons to catch large numbers of feeding birds at one time

rod: light-sensitive cells in the retina of birds, e.g. more plentiful in nocturnal species roding: territorial twilight flights of male Eurasian woodcock

rookery: refers to nesting colony of rooks as well as other birds

roost: place for flocking species, e.g. blackbirds, gather to sleep

roosting: sleep or resting behavior in a bird

rostrum: bill or beak

Roundup: bird-watching event whereupon a given area is covered as thoroughly as possible by birding teams

rufescent: somewhat tinged with reddish

ruff: male sandpiper

rufous: appearing orangy-brown to reddish-brown

rump: area between lower back and the base of the tail

ruptive: refers to patterns or bold markings, e.g. stripes, spots, that serve to break up the body outline

rush: *see* fall

S

saddle: unbroken continuation of color on upper surface of bird's wings

salt gland: specialized glands in the orbital area to secrete excess salt, e.g. seabirds

saltatory: pertaining to leaping

sanctuary: area of land of any size with restricted use by people

sap-feeding: using the tongue to eat sap oozing from a hole drilled in the bark of a tree, e.g. sapsucker

scansorial: pertaining to climbing on tree trunks

scapula: paired shoulder blade

scapulars: feathers above the shoulder

scapus: whole feather stem

scaring: refers to using a stimulus to move birds away from an area where they might cause damage

scavenger: bird that feeds upon dead animals, garbage, and sewage

schizochroism: color abnormality whereby a pigment or several pigments normally in the plumage are missing

sclera: ring of overlapping bony plates that protect the eye

scrape: a slightly hollowed out depression in a nest substrate, sometimes lined with material, in which a bird lays its eggs or European term for an artificially constructed shallow pool to attract wading birds

scutella: overlapping horny scales arranged vertically on the tarsus

search image: fixation on an abundant food source that is learned from past experience

second-year (SY): bird in its second calendar year of life

secondary: flight feather arising on the forearm or ulna

sedentary: *see* resident

seed dispersal: the incidental spreading of seeds by plants via birds, especially frugivores which void intact seeds

sematic: describes a color or behavior that serves as a signal for warning or attraction

semi-altricial: refers to a hatchling borne with its eyes open and a coat of down, but remains in the nest to be cared for by the parents until fledging

semi-precocial: same as semi-altricial except that it leaves the nest when it can walk while still fed by the parents

semi-species: forms that are closely related but totally isolated geographically

semicircular canals: specialized organ within the inner ear that serve to maintain a bird's equilibrium

semiplume: type of feather intermediate between a contour feather and down

set: *see* clutch

setose: having bristles

sex role reversal: refers to a species wherein the female courts the male and the male incubates the eggs, e.g. phalarope

sexual selection: refers to competition among members of one sex for mating opportunities with the opposite sex

sexual dimorphism: differences in the appearance of the male and female of a species

shaft: midrib of a feather

shank: refers to all or part of the leg (AKA tarsus)

sharming: refers to grunts and squeals of a water rail

shell gland: uterus of an oviduct where eggshell is laid down

short-distance migration: migratory pattern in which a species moves within rather between temperate or tropical zones

siblicide: *see* Cain and Abel Syndrome

sibling species: two or more closely related species that look like one another but do not interbreed

sickles: elongated central tail feathers in some species

sight record: eye-witness recording of a bird species in a given area that was not confirmed by a collected specimen, photograph, or t recording

sign stimulus: phenomenon, usually vis which organisms can be expected to r predictably

sinciput: area on head comprising the forehead and crown

singing assembly: group of two or more territorial males localized in a lek or arena for courtship and singing

single-brooded: raising only one family of young in a breeding season

sink population: population that occupies sink habitat and that requires emigration of individuals to sustain itself

sink habitat: habitat in which reproduction is not sufficient to balance with mortality to maintain population levels

sinuated: describes a feather with one edge cut away in a wavy fashion

site tenacity: attachment of birds and their succeeding generations to a nesting site

skin: study specimen consisting of a dead bird, i.e. preserved skin, feathers, legs, skull, and beak

smoke-bathing: comfort behavior wherein a bird exposes itself to smoke, steam, or the heat of flames to discourage ectoparasites

soaring: sustained flight without wing-flapping and aided by air movements

sociobiology: study of the biological basis of behavior

soft parts: *see* bare parts

solferino: bluish-red

sonagram: written reproduction of a recorded bird song

sonagraph: machine that employs a stylus to transfer pattern of pitch and frequency from recordings of bird song

song period: time of year in which a particular species sings

source habitat: habitat that is capable of exporting individuals

source population: population that occupies source habitat in which the output of offspring exceeds the carrying capacity

spark or spark bird: the first bird to begin one's interest in bird-watching

specialist: species with narrow food and/or habitat preferences

speciation: process wherein new species are formed as a result of reproductive isolation

species: group of interbreeding natural populations that are reproductively isolated from other populations

ᴄies pair: two very closely related and similar-ᴋing species

s diversity index: mathematical index ᵈescribes the numbers and relative abun-ᵒf bird species in a given area

species group: refers to a collection of closely related species

species-specific: referring to one particular species

speculum: distinctive wing patch on the secondaries, especially seen in waterfowl plumage

spermatozoa: male germ cells

spermatozoid: male germ cell in the free-swimming stage

spermatozoon: male germ cell

spishing: *see* pishing

spleen: reddish-brown, round organ involved in immune response

splitter: someone who prefers to separate bird forms into smaller taxonomic units, e.g. subspecies

spot-mapping method: census in which individuals seen or heard during a specified period are plotted on a map to estimate territories or home ranges

spur: sharp, horny growth on the back of the tarsus, e.g. pheasant

squab: unfledged nestling, usually a pigeon or dove

squeaking: making mouse-like noises puckering one's lips or sucking on the back of one's hand to attract songbirds

stenoecious: able to exist in one or a few habitats

stenophagous: restricted to eating only certain foods

sternum: breast-bone or keel to which flight muscles are anchored

stipule: newly emerging feather

stomach oil: foul-smelling liquid regurgitated by some seabirds in self-defense, e.g. fulmar

stooping: steep diving generally by birds of prey pursuing quarry

stragulum: *see* mantle

striated: streaked

structural coloration: color produced when feather structure interferes with light waves to absorb parts of the spectrum and reflect others, e.g. blue

strutting ground: refers to the social display of the sage grouse

stupefying baits: chemicals placed in food to render organisms comatose, e.g. alpha chloralose

sub-adult: bird not yet in its full adult plumage

subclass: secondary taxonomic category between class and order

subfamily: secondary taxonomic category between family and genus

subgenus: secondary taxonomic occasionally interposed between genus and order

suborder: secondary taxonomic category between order and family

subsong: song differing from the main characteristic song of a species

subspecies: population that is morphologically, physiologically, or behaviorally distinct from members of other populations of its species, but can interbreed when contact is made

summer resident: species that breeds in a given area but spends the winter elsewhere

summer visitor: species that spends the warmer months of the year in a given area but breeds elsewhere

sunbathing: *see* sunning

sunning: comfort behavior wherein a bird orientates itself or adopts a special posture to capture the sun's warmth

superciliary: refers to plumage marking above the eye, e.g. stripe, line

superfamily: secondary taxonomic category between suborder and family

superorder: secondary taxonomic category between subclass and order

superspecies: species ranked below a genus, but having no nomenclatural status

supinating: rotating leading edge of the wing upward to promote braking

supraorbital gland: *see* salt gland

surface-diving: behavior wherein a bird on the surface of the water submerges itself

symbiosis: relationship between two organisms that is beneficial to one another

sympatric: occurring in the same geographical area

synanthropic: preferring human-altered habitat

synaposematic: refers to a warning signal shared with other species

synchronous hatching: refers to the simultaneous emergence of young from a clutch of eggs

synsacrum: bone resulting fusion of thoracic, lumbar, and sacral vertebrae

syrinx: (*pl.* syringes): organ of voice or song

systematics: refers to the use of nomenclature to classify organisms taxonomically

T

tail: collectively refers to the feathers or retrices and their respective coverts used for flight, display and courtship

talon: sharp, pointed claw on the toe of a raptor

tape lure: pre-recorded calls used to attract birds

tarsal scale: horny, keratinous material covering the exterior of the foot and/or leg sometimes in overlapping fashion

tarsometatarsus: bone of a bird's leg between the ankle and the toes

tarsus: bird's leg between the ankle and the toes

tawny: golden-brown

taxa: plural of taxon

taxis: movement toward or away from a stimulus

taxon: category used for classifying and naming biological entities, e.g. kingdom, phylum, class, order, etc.

taxonomy: science of classification or using nomenclature to name plants and animals

tectrices: plural for tectrix

tectrix: *see* covert

telemetry: *see* biotelemetry

teleology: study of adaptation

teleoptiles: various feathers of an adult bird

teratism: morphological or anatomical abnormality

tercel: *see* tiercel

territory: area defended by one or more individuals against other individuals of the same or different species

tertiaries: feathers arising from the humerus that function as additional flight feathers instead of just coverts

testes: paired male gonads

thermal: column of warm air rising from the earth

third-year (TY): bird in its third calendar year

thoracic: pertaining to the thorax

thorax: chest cavity housing heart and lungs

tibotarsus: leg bone between the knee and the ankle

tick: new species added to a birder's list

ticker: *see* lister

tiercel: male falcon

tippet: elongated facial feathers of typical grebes

tobogganing: use of body by penguins to slide down an icy surface, generally to enter the water

tomia: *see* tomium

tomial tooth: toothlike projection on mandible of falcons and shrikes

tomium: cutting edge of a mandible on a beak

tool-using: using external objects as extensions of the body to attain a goal, e.g. woodpecker finch using a cactus spine to probe for insects

topography: external areas and features of a bird's plumage and bare parts

torpidity: state of dormancy and lowered body temperature undertaken to conserve energy during a period of energy shortage, e.g. poorwills

trachea: windpipe arising from glottis and subdividing into two bronchi leading to the lungs

track: flight path of a bird relative to the earth' surface

train: long tail of a peacock or the tail of a ' coner's bird

transient: refers to migrating birds that are passing through an area, but neither breeds or overwinters there

traplining: behavior of hummingbirds wherein they visit a variety of flowers over a regularly traveled route

trash bird: bird-watcher's term that refers to birds undesirable for a bird list, e.g. feral pigeon or another locally abundant species

treading: act of a male bird copulating with a female

trill: rapid succession of notes

trituration: muscular action of gizzard to grind or crush into fine particles

triumph ceremony: display given by a pair of birds following a successful aggressive encounter

trophic level: position in the food chain based on the number of energy-transfer steps above or below it, e.g. herbivore

trophic: pertaining to food or nutrition

tropism: tendency to react to a given stimulus in a certain manner

tubenose: marine birds like albatrosses, petrels, and shearwaters that pump out excess salt from special glands via a tube on their beak

tunic: one of three membrane layers enclosing the eyeball

turacin: copper-based red pigment in feathers

turning down: releasing captive-bred birds into the wild

turnover ratio: number of species enter and disappearing from a community

twitcher: *see* lister

tympanum: eardrum

typaniform membrane: syringeal membranes that vibrate to produce sound

U

ulna: thicker of two bones comprising the forearm of the wing

umbilicus: opening in a feather shaft allowing for nutrition of a growing feather

uncinate process: hook-like projections on birds' ribs for tendon attachments

unguis: nail at the tip of the upper mandible of waterfowl

uniparous: laying only one egg, e.g. auk

urates: insoluble part of the nitrogenous wastes of a bird

uric acid: collective term for nitrogenous wastes excreted by birds

ᴜrine: water portion of the nitrogenous wastes of a bird

ᴜodeum: chamber of the cloaca where the uric ᴜd is stored prior to release

uropygial gland: secretory gland just above the base of the tail feathers that provides oil for preening

uropygium: *see* rump

uterus: *see* shell gland

V

vagina: region of the oviduct where the egg is held prior to oviposition

vagrant: a bird that accidentally or purposely wanders beyond its normal range

vane: series of barbs on each side of a rachis of a feather

variegated: with spots or patches of different colors

variety: *see* form

vas deferens: *see* ductus deferens

vector: an animal carrier of parasites or infections transmissable to other organisms

vent: opening of the cloaca

ventral: describing the belly side or the lower surface of the body

ventriculus: *see* gizzard

vermiculated: plumage covered with a dense pattern of irregular fine lines

vernacular name: common, popular, or local name for a bird

vertex: *see* crown

vexillum: *see* vane

vibrissae: small, bristle-like feathers found at the base of the bill or around the eyes and sensitive to the touch

vinaceous: wine-colored

visitor: refers to birds present in a given area at a certain time of the year, e.g. summer, winter

visual acuity: sharpness of vision or ability to perceive fine detail

vitelline membrane: outside layer that encloses the yolk of an egg

vitellus: egg yolk

vocal mimicry: imitation by birds of sounds other than their own vocalizations

vocalization: sound produced by the syrinx

volant: capable of flight

W

wader: shorebird

water dance: courtship display on or under water by alcids, loons, and grebes

waterfowl: wild aquatic birds

wattle: *see* lappet

wave: refers to an abundance of migrant land birds of many species arriving simultaneously in a given area

web: fleshy membrane between the toes, usually in waterbirds, or vane or vexillum

wildfowl: quarry species of birds other than gamebirds

window: seemingly translucent patch on the underside of wings used as an identifying feature in some birds, e.g. red-shouldered hawk

window-fighting: *see* image-fighting

wing clapping: producing a loud crack by striking raised wings together

wing formula: mathematical description of the shape of the outer portion of a bird's wing

wing-loading: mathematical formula between a bird's wing area and body weight

wingbar: one or two contrasting lines running across a bird's folded wing

wingspan: measurement from one wing-tip to the other when wings are fully extended

winnowing: wavering sound produced by snipe during courtship flight

Winter Bird Population Study: census coordinated by the National Audubon Society in the U S, wherein wintering birds are counted and mapped

wishbone: *see* furcula

world birder: birder intent on seeing birds all over the world

wreck: refers to large number of pelagic birds incapacitated on land by strong onshore winds during migration

wrist: joint of the forearm and the manus

X

xanthochromism: abnormal dominance of yellow coloration due to absence of normal amounts of darker pigments

xerophilous: adapted to living in a dry climate

Y

yarak: falconry term that refers to a readiness to hunt in raptors

Year List: an attempt to *see* as many species as possible in a selected geographical area in one year

yolk sac: membranous pouch containing the egg yolk that is provided as food to the developing embryo

yolk: yellow-orange mass of protein and fat granules enclosed by a thin transparent membrane

Z

zone: distinctive broad band of color encircling the body

zoogeography: study of the distribution of flora and fauna over large geographic areas

zoology: study of animals

zoonosis: disease transmitted naturally from animals to humans

zugscheide: German term referring to a line or zone whereupon the birds living on either side migrate in different directions, e.g. white stork

zugunruhe: *see* migratory restlessness

zwischenzug: German term referring to nomadic movements by birds between the breeding season and migration

zygomatic arch: facial bones

Taxonomy

American and British Equivalencies in Names of Birds

American	Latin	British
Arctic loon	*Gavia arctica*	Black-throated diver
Atlantic puffin	*Fratercula arctica*	Puffin
Bank swallow	*Riparia riparia*	Sand martin
Barn swallow	*Hirundo rustica*	Swallow
Black scoter	*Melanitta nigra*	Common scoter
Black-bellied plover	*Pluvialis squatarola*	Grey plover
Black-billed magpie	*Pica pica*	Magpie
Black-crowned night heron	*Nycticorax nycticorax*	Night heron
Black-legged kittiwake	*Rissa tridactyla*	Kittiwake
Bohemian waxwing	*Bombycilla garrulus*	Waxwing
Boreal owl	*Aegolius funereus*	Tengmalm's owl
Brant	*Branta bernicla*	Brent goose
Chickadee	*Parus spp.*	Tit
Common goldeneye	*Bucephala clangula*	Goldeneye
Common loon	*Gavia immer*	Great northern diver
Common merganser	*Mergus merganser*	Goosander
Common moorhen	*Gallinula chloropus*	Moorhen
Common murre	*Uria aalge*	Guillemot
Common raven	*Corvus corax*	Raven
Common redpoll	*Carduelis flammea*	Redpoll
Dovekie	*Alle alle*	Little auk
Eared grebe	*Podiceps nigricollis*	Black-necked grebe
Eurasian coot	*Fulica atra*	Coot
European golden-plover	*Pluvialis apricaria*	Golden plover
Gray partridge	*Perdix perdix*	Partridge
Great cormorant	*Phalacrocorax carbo*	Cormorant
Greater scaup	*Aythya marila*	Scaup
Green-winged teal	*Anas crecca*	Teal
Hawk	*Buteo spp.*	Buzzard
Hoary redpoll	*Carduelis hornemanni*	Arctic redpoll
Horned grebe	*Podiceps auritus*	Slavonian grebe
Horned lark	*Eremophila alpestris*	Shore lark
Kinglets	*Regulus spp.*	Goldcrest, Firecrest

American	Latin	British
Lapland longspur	*Calcarius lapponicus*	Lapland bunting
Long-tailed jaeger	*Stercorarius longicaudus*	Long-tailed skua
Mew gull	*Larus canus*	Common gull
Northern harrier	*Circus cyaneus*	Hen harrier
Northern lapwing	*Vanellus vanellus*	Lapwing
Northern shoveler	*Anas clypeata*	Shoveler
Northern shrike	*Lanius excubitor*	Great grey shrike
Oldsquaw	*Clangula hyemalis*	Long-tailed duck
Parasitic jaeger	*Stercorarius parasiticus*	Arctic skua
Pomarine jaeger	*Stercorarius pomarinus*	Pomarine skua
Red crossbill	*Loxia curvirostra*	Crossbill
Red knot	*Calidris canutus*	Knot
Red phalarope	*Phalaropus fulicaria*	Grey phalarope
Red-throated loon	*Gavia stellata*	Red-throated diver
Ring-necked pheasant	*Phasianus colchicus*	Pheasant
Rock ptarmigan	*Lagopus mutus*	Ptarmigan
Ruddy turnstone	*Arenaria interpres*	Turnstone
Snowy plover	*Charadrius alexandrinus*	Kentish plover
Thick-billed murre	*Uria lomia*	Brünnich's guillemot
White-winged scoter	*Melanitta fusca*	Velvet scoter
White-winged crossbill	*Loxia leucoptera*	Two-barred crossbill
Willow ptarmigan	*Lagopus lagopus*	Red/Willow grouse
Winter wren	*Troglodytes troglodytes*	Wren
Yellow-billed loon	*Gavia adamsii*	White-billed diver

Classification of the Class Aves (Traditional)

ORDER	FAMILY	
STRUTHIONIFORMES	STRUTHIONIDAE	Ostrich (1)
	RHEIDAE	Rheas (2)
	CASUARIIDAE	Cassowaries (3)
	DROMAIIDAE	Emu (1)
	APTERYGIDAE	Kiwis (3)
TINAMIFORMES	TINAMIDAE	Tinamous (47)
SPHENISCIFORMES	SPHENISCIDAE	Penguins (17)
GAVIIFORMES	GAVIIDAE	Divers (4)
PODICIPEDIFORMES	PODICIPEDIDAE	Grebes (22)
PROCELLARIIFORMES	DIOMEDEIDAE	Albatrosses (14)
	PROCELLARIIDAE	Petrels, shearwaters (70)
	HYDROBATIDAE	Storm-petrels (20)
	PELECANOIIDIDAE	Diving-petrels (4)
PELECANIFORMES	PHAETHONTIDAE	Tropicbirds (3)
	PELECANIDAE	Pelicans (7)
	SULIDAE	Gannets, boobies (9)
	PHALACROCORACIDAE	Cormorants (39)
	ANHINGIDAE	Darters (2)
	FREGATIDAE	Frigatebirds (5)
CICONIFORMES	ARDEIDAE	Herons (60)
	SCOPIDAE	Hamerkop (1)
	CICONIIDAE	Storks (19)
	BALAENCIPITIDAE	Shoebill (1)
	THRESKIORNITHIDAE	Ibises, spoonbills (32)
PHOENICOPTERIFORMES	PHOENICOPTERIDAE	Flamingos (5)
ANSERIFORMES	ANHIMIDAE	Screamers (3)
	ANATIDAE	Ducks, geese, swans (147)
FALCONIFORMES	CATHARTIDAE	New World vultures (7)
	PANDIONIDAE	Osprey (1)
	ACCIPITRIDAE	Hawks, eagles (217)
	SAGITTARIIDAE	Secretarybird (1)
	FALCONIDAE	Caracaras, falcons (61)
GALLIFORMES	MEGAPODIIDAE	Megapodes (12)
	CRACIDAE	Guans, chachalacas, curassows (44)
	PHASIANDIAE	Pheasants, grouse (213)
	OPISTHOCOMIDAE	Hoatzin (1)
GRUIFORMES	MESITORNITHIDAE	Mesites (3)
	TURNICIDAE	Buttonquail (14)
	PEDIONOMIDAE	Plains-wanderer (1)

ORDER	FAMILY	
	GRUIDAE	Cranes (15)
	ARAMIDAE	Limpkin (1)
	PSOPHIIDAE	Trumpeters (3)
	RALLIDAE	Rais, coots (133)
	HELIORNITHIDAE	Finfoots (3)
	RHYNOCHETIDAE	Kagu (1)
	EURYPYGIDAE	Sunbittern (1)
	CARIAMIDAE	Seriemas (2)
	OTIDIDAE	Bustards (24)
CHARADRIIFORMES	JACANIDAE	Jacanas (8)
	ROSTRATULIDAE	Painted snipes (2)
	DROMADIDAE	Crab plover (1)
	HAEMATOPODIDAE	Oystercatchers (7)
	IBIDORHYNCHIDAE	Ibisbill (1)
	RECURVIROSTRIDAE	Avocets, stilts (13)
	BURHINIDAE	Thick-knees (9)
	GLAREOLIDAE	Coursers, pratincoles (16)
	CHARADRIIDAE	Plovers (64)
	SCOLOPACIDAE	Sandpipers, snipes (86)
	THINOCORIDAE	Seedsnipes (4)
	CHIONIDIDAE	Sheathbills (2)
	STERCORARIIDAE	Skuas (5)
	LARIDAE	Gulls, terns (90)
	RYNCHOPIDAE	Skimmers (3)
	ALCIDAE	Auks (23)
COLUMBIFORMES	PTEROCLIDIDAE	Sandgrouse (16)
	COLUMBIDAE	Pigeons, doves (283)
PSITTACHIFORMES	LORIIDAE	Lories (55)
	CACATUIDAE	Cockatoos (18)
	PSITTACIDAE	Parrots (271)
CUCULIFORMES	MUSOPHAGIDAE	Turacos (19)
	CUCULIDAE	Cuckoos (130)
STRIGIFORMES	TYTONIDAE	Barn owls (12)
	STRIGIDAE	Typical owls (134)
CAPRIMULGIFORMES	STEATORNITHIDAE	Oilbird (1)
	PODARGIDAE	Frogmouths (13)
	NYCTIBIIDAE	Potoos (5)
	AEGOTHELIDAE	Owlet-nightjars (8)
	CAPRIMULGIDAE	Nightjars (76)
APODIFORMES	APODIDAE	Swifts (82)
	HEMIPROCNIDAE	Tree-swifts (4)
	TROCHILIDAE	Hummingbirds (338)

ORDER	FAMILY	
COLIFORMES	COLIIDAE	Mousebirds (6)
TROGONIFORMES	TROGONIDAE	Trogons (37)
CORACIIFORMES	ALCEDINIDAE	Kingfishers (90)
	TODIDAE	Todies (5)
	MOMOTIDAE	Motmots (9)
	MEROPIDAE	Bee-eaters (21)
	CORACIIDAE	Rollers (11)
	BRACHYPTERACIIDAE	Ground-rollers (5)
	LEPTOSOMATIDAE	Cuckoo-roller (1)
	UPUPIDAE	Hoopoe (1)
	PHOENICULIDAE	Woodhoopoes (8)
	BUCEROTIDAE	Hornbills (44)
PICIFORMES	GALBULIDAE	Jacamars (17)
	BUCCONIDAE	Puffbirds (34)
	CAPITONIDAE	Barbets (81)
	INDICATORIDAE	Honeyguides (14)
	RAMPHASTIDAE	Toucans (33)
	PICIDAE	Woodpeckers (204)
PASSERIFORMES	EURYLAIMIDAE	Broadbills (14)
	DENDROCOCLAPTIDAE	Woodcreepers (52)
	FURNARIIDAE	Ovenbirds (218)
	FORMICARIIDAE	Antbirds (228)
	CONOPOPHAGIDAE	Gnateaters (11)
	RHINOCRYPTIDAE	Tapaculos (33)
	COTINGIDAE	Cotingas (79)
	PIPRIDAE	Manakins (57)
	TYRANNIDAE	Tyrant flycatchers (374)
	OXYRUNCIDAE	Sharpbill (1)
	PHYTOTOMIDAE	Plantcutters (3)
	PITTIDAE	Pittas (24)
	XENICIDAE	New Zealand wrens (4)
	PHILEPITTIDAE	Asities (4)
	MENURIDAE	Lyrebirds (2)
	ATRICHORNITHIDAE	Scrub-birds (2)
	ALAUDIDAE	Larks (77)
	HIRUNDINIDAE	Swallows, martins (80)
	MOTACILLIDAE	Wagtails, pipits (54)
	CAMPEPHAGIDAE	Cuckooshrikes (70)
	PYCNONOTIDAE	Bulbuls (123)
	IRENIDAE	Leafbirds, ioras, Fairy-bluebirds (14)
	LANIIDAE	Shrikes (74)
	VANGIDAE	Vanga shrikes (13)

ORDER	FAMILY	
PASSERIFORMES	BOMBYCILLIDAE	Waxwings (8)
	DULIDAE	Palmchat (1)
	CINCLIDAE	Dippers (5)
	TROGLODYTIDAE	Wrens (59)
	MIMIDAE	Mockingbirds, thrashers (31)
	PRUNELLIDAE	Accentors (12)
	MUSCICAPIDAE	Thrushes, chats, logrunners, babblers, parrot bills, rockfowl, gnatwrens, Old World warblers, Australasian wrens, Old World fly catchers, wattle-eyes, batises, monarchs, fantails, whistlers (1,423)
	AEGITHALIDAE	Long-tailed tits (8)
	REMIZIDAE	Penduline tits (10)
	PARIDAE	Tits, chickadees (47)
	SITTIDAE	Nuthatches (25)
	CERTHIIDAE	Treecreepers (6)
	RHABDORNITHIDAE	Philippine creepers (2)
	CLIMACTERIDAE	Australian creepers (6)
	DICAEIDAE	Flowerpeckers (58)
	NECTARINIIDAE	Sunbirds (116)
	ZOSTEROPIDAE	White-eyes (83)
	MELIPHAGIDAE	Honeyeaters (171)
	EMBERIZIDAE	Buntings, cardinals, tanagers (558)
	PARULIDAE	New World warblers (126)
	DREPANIDIDAE	Hawaiian honeycreepers (23)
	VIREONIDAE	Vireos (43)
	ICTERIDAE	New World blackbirds (95)
	FRINGILLIDAE	Finches (122)
	ESTRILDIDAE	Waxbills (127)
	PLOCEIDAE	Weavers, sparrows 143)
	STURNIDAE	Starlings (111)
	ORIOLIDAE	Orioles (28)
	DICRURIDAE	Drongos (20)
	CALLAEIDAE	Wattlebirds (3)
	GRALLINIDAE	Magpie-larks (4)
	ARTAMIDAE	Woodswallows (10)
	CRACTICIDAE	Butcherbirds (8)
	PTILONORHYNCHIDAE	Bowerbirds (18)
	PARADISAEIDAE	Birds of paradise (42)
	CORVIDAE	Crows, jays (105)

SOURCE: J. del Hoyo, J.A. Elliott, and J. Sargatal, eds. *Handbook of the Birds of the World*, Vol. 1 (Barcelona: Lynx Edicions, 1992)

Classification of the Class Aves (DNA-DNA Hybridization)

ORDER	FAMILY	
STRUTHIONIFORMES	STRUTHIONIDAE	Ostrich (1)
	RHEIDAE	Rheas (2)
	CASUARIIDAE	Cassowaries, emus (4)
	APTERYGIDAE	Kiwis (3)
TINAMIFORMES	TINAMIDAE	Tinamous (47)
CRACIFORMES	CRACIDAE	Guans, chachalacas, curassows (50)
	MEGAPODIIDAE	Megapodes (19)
GALLIFORMES	PHASIANIDAE	Grouse, turkeys, pheasants, partridges, etc. (177)
	NUMIDIDAE	Guineafowl (6)
	ODONTOPHORIDAE	New World quail (31)
ANSERIFORMES	ANHIMIDAE	Screamers (3)
	ANSERANATIDAE	Magpie goose (1)
	DENDROCYGNIDAE	Whistling-ducks (9)
	ANATIDAE	Stiff-tailed ducks, freckled ducks, swans, geese, typical ducks (148)
TURNICIFORMES	TURNICIDAE	Buttonquails (17)
PICIFORMES	INDICATORIDAE	Honeyguides (17)
	PICIDAE	Woodpeckers, wrynecks (215)
	MEGALAIMIDAE	Asian barbets (26)
	LYBIIDAE	African barbets (42)
	RAMPHASTIDAE	New World barbets, toucans (55)
GALBULIFORMES	GALBULIDAE	Jacamars (18)
	BUCCONIDAE	Puffbirds (33)
BUCEROTIFORMES	BUCEROTIDAE	Typical hornbills (54)
	BUCORVIDAE	Ground-hornbills (2)
UPUPIFORMES	UPUPIDAE	Hoopoes (2)
	PHOENICULIDAE	Woodhoopoes (5)
	RHINOPOMASTIDAE	scimitarbills (3)
TROGONIFORMES	TROGONIDAE	African trogons, New World trogons, Asian trogons (39)
CORACIIFORMES	CORACIIDAE	Typical rollers (12)
	BRACHYPTERACIIDAE	Ground-rollers (5)
	LEPTOSOMIDAE	Cuckoo-roller (1)
CORACIIFORMES	MOMOTIDAE	Motmots (9)

ORDER	FAMILY	
CORACIIFORMES	TODIDAE	Todies (5)
	ALCEDINIDAE	Alcedinid kingfishers (24)
	DACELONIDAE	Dacelonid kingfishers (61)
	CERYLIDAE	Cerylid kingfishers (9)
	MEROPIDAE	Bee-eaters (26)
COLIIFORMES	COLIIDAE	Typical mousebirds, long-tailed mousebirds (6)
CUCULIFORMES	CUCULIDAE	Old World cuckoos (79)
	CENTROPODIDAE	Coucals (30)
	COCCYZIDAE	American cuckoos (18)
	OPISTHOCOMIDAE	Hoatzin (1)
	CROTOPHAGIDAE	Anis, Guira cuckoo (4)
	NEOMORPHIDAE	Roadrunners, ground-cuckoos (11)
PSITTACIFORMES	PSITTACIDAE	Parrots and allies (358)
APODIFORMES	APODIDAE	Typical swifts (99)
	HEMIPROCNIDAE	Tree-swifts (4)
TROCHILIFORMES	TROCHILIDAE	Hermits, typical hummingbirds (319)
MUSOPHAGIFORMES	MUSOPHAGIDAE	Turacos/plantain-eaters (23)
STRIGIFORMES	TYTONIDAE	Barn and grass owls (17)
	STRIGIDAE	Typical owls (161)
	AEGOTHELIDAE	Owlet-nightjars (8)
	PODARGIDAE	Australian frogmouths (3)
	BATRACHOSTOMIDAE	Asian frogmouths (11)
	STEATORNITHIDAE	Oilbird (1)
	NYCTIBIIDAE	Potoos (7)
	EUROSTOPODIDAE	Eared-nightjars (7)
	CAPRIMULGIDAE	Nighthawks, nightjars (76)
COLUMBIFORMES	COLUMBIDAE	Pigeons, doves (310)
GRUIFORMES	EURYPYGIDAE	Sunbittern (1)
	OTIDIDAE	Bustards (25)
	GRUIDAE	Crowned-cranes, typical cranes (15)
	HELIORNITHIDAE	Limpkin, finfoots (4)
	PSOPHIIDAE	Trumpeters (3)
GRUIFORMES	CARIAMIDAE	Seriemas (2)
	RYHYNOCHETIDAE	Kagu (1)
	RALLIDAE	Rails, gallinules, coots (142)
	MESITORNITHIDAE	Mesites (3)
CICONIIFORMES	PTEROCLIDAE	Sandgrouse (16)
	THINOCORIDAE	Seedsnipes (4)
	PEDIONOMIDAE	Plains-wanderer (1)

ORDER	FAMILY	
CICONIIFORMES	SCOLOPACIDAE	Woodcock, snipes, sandpipers, curlews, phalaropes (88)
	ROSTRATULIDAE	Painted-snipes (2)
	JACANIDAE	Jacanas (8)
	CJOPMODODAE	Sheathbills (2)
	BIRJOMODAE	Thick-knees (9)
	CJARADROODAE	Oystercatchers, avocets, stilts, plovers, lapwings (89)
	GLAREOLIDAE	Crab Plover/pratincoles, coursers (18)
	LARIDAE	Skuas, jaegers, skimmers, gulls, terns, auks, murres, puffins (129)
	ACCIPITRIDAE	Osprey/hawks, eagles (240)
	SAGITTARIIDAE	Secretarybird (1)
	FALCONIDAE	Caracaras, falcons (63)
	PODICIPEDIDAE	Grebes (21)
	PHAETHONTIDAE	Tropicbirds (3)
	SULIDAE	Gannets, boobies (9)
	ANHINGIDAE	Darters (4)
	PHALACROCORACIDAE	Cormorants (38)
	ARDEIDAE	Herons (65)
	SCOPIDAE	Hamerkop (1)
	PHOENICOPTERIDAE	Flamingos (5)
	THRESKIORNITHIDAE	Ibises, spoonbills (34)
	PELECANIDAE	Shoebills, pelicans (9)
	CICONIIDAE	New World vultures, storks (26)
	FREGATIDAE	Frigatebirds (5)
	SPHENISCIDAE	Penguins (17)
	GAVIIDAE	Divers (5)
	PROCELLARIIDAE	Petrels, shearwaters, diving-petrels, albatrosses, storm-petrels (115)
PASSERIFORMES	ACANTHISITTIDAE	New Zealand wrens (4)
	PITTIDAE	Pittas (31)
	EURYLAIMIDAE	Broadbills (14)
	PHILEPITTIDAE	Asities (4)
	Incertae sedis	Broad-billed sapayoa (1)
	TYRANNIDAE	Mionectine flycatchers, antpipits, tyrant flycatchers, schiffornises, tityras, becards, cotingas, plantcutters, sharpbills, manakins (537)

ORDER	FAMILY	
ASSERIFORMES	THAMNOPHILIDAE	Typical antbirds (188)
	FURNARIIDAE	Ovenbirds, woodcreepers (280)
	FORMICARIIDAE	Ground antbirds (56)
	CONOPOPHAGIDAE	Gnateaters (8)
	RHINOCRYPTIDAE	Tapaculos (28)
	CLIMACTERIDAE	Australo-Papuan treecreepers (7)
	MENURIDAE	Lyrebirds, scrub-birds (4)
	PTILONORHYNCHIDAE	Bowerbirds (20)
	MALURIDAE	Fairywrens, emuwrens, grasswrens (26)
	MELIPHAGIDAE	Honeyeaters, Australian chats (182)
	PARDALOTIDAE	Pardalotes, bristlebirds, scrubwrens, thornbills, whitefaces, etc. (68)
	EOPSALTRIIDAE	Australo-Papuan robins, scrub-robins (46)
	IRENIDAE	Fairy-bluebirds, leafbirds (10)
	ORTHONYCHIDAE	logrunners, chowchillas (2)
	POMATOSTOMIDAE	Australo-Papuan babblers (5)
	LANIIDAE	True shrikes (30)
	VIREONIDAE	Vireos, peppershrikes, etc. (51)
	CORVIDAE	Quail-thrushes, whipbirds, Australian chough, apostlebirds, sittellas, *Mohoua*, shrike-tits, crested bellbirds, mottled whistlers, whistlers, shrike-thrushes, crows, magpies, jays, nutcrackers, birds of paradise, melampittas, currawongs, woodswallows, peltops, Bornean bristleheads, orioles, cuckooshrikes, fantails, drongos, monarchs, magpie-larks, ioras, bush-shrikes, helmet-shrikes, vangas, batises, wattle-eyes ((647)
	CALLAEATIDAE	New Zealand wattlebirds (3)
	PICATHARTIDAE	Rock-jumpers, rockfowl (4)
	BOMBYCILLIDAE	Palmchar, silky flycatchers, waxwings (8)
	CINCLIDAE	Dippers (5)

ORDER	FAMILY	
PASSERIFORMES	MUSCICAPIDAE	True thrushes, black-breasted fruit-hunters, shortwings, alethes, Old World flycatchers, chats (449)
	STURNIDAE	Starlings, mynas, mockingbirds, thrashers, catbirds (148)
	SITTIDAE	Nuthatches, wallcreepers (25)
	CERTHIDAE	Northern creepers, Spotted creepers, wrens, gnatchatchers, verdins, gnatwrens (97)
	PARIDAE	Penduline tits, tits, chickadees (65)
	AEGITHALIDAE	Long-tailed tits, bushtits (8)
	HIRUNDINIDAE	River martins, swallows, martins (89)
	REGULIDAE	Kinglets (6)
	PYCNONOTIDAE	Bulbuls (137)
	HYPOCOLIIDAE	Grey hypocolius (1)
	CISTICOLIDAE	African warblers (119)
	ZOSTEROPIDAE	White-eyes (96)
	SYLVIIDAE	Leaf-warblers, grass-warblers, laughingthrushes, babblers, rhabdornises, wrentits, *Sylvia* warblers (552)
	ALAUDIDAE	Larks (91)
	NECTARINIIDAE	Sugarbirds, flowerpeckers, sunbirds, spiderhunters (169)
	MELANOCHARITIDAE	*Melanocharis* berrypeckers, longbills (10)
	PARAMYTHIIDAE	Tit berrypeckers, crested berrypeckers (2)
	PASSERIDAE	Sparrows, rock-sparrows, wagtails, pipits, accentors, weavers, estrildine finches, whydahs (386)
	FRINGILLIDAE	Olive warblers, chaffinches, brambling, goldfinches, crossbills, Hawaiian honeycreepers, buntings, longspurs, towhees, wood-warblers, tanagers, neotropical honeycreepers, seedeaters, flowerpiercers, cardinals, troupials, meadowlarks, New World blackbirds (993)

SOURCE: J. del Hoyo, J.A. Elliott, and J. Sargatal, eds. *Handbook of the Birds of the World*, Vol. 1 (Barcelona: Lynx Edicions, 1992)

Indexed Checklist of the World's Birds*

R   Limited Recognition of Full-Species
       Status
       Extinct
18   Extinct 18th Century
19   Extinct 19th Century
20   Extinct 20th Century
GT   Globally Threatened
PGT   Possibility Global Threatened
PE   Possibility Extinct
PH   Possible Hybrid
GD   Genetically Diluted

* this list was the latest available in the summer of 2003; it is being constantly updated by the Nomenclature Committee of the American Ornithologists' Union

SOURCE: Taxonomic list provided by Mr. M.G. Wells and Wordlist and Thayer Birding Software, L.L.C. An electronic version is available at www.ThayerBirding. com as Cornell Laboratory of Ornithology's Birder's Diary version 3.

STRUTHIONIFORMES

Struthionidae

  Southern Ostrich *Struthio camelus*
  Somali Ostrich *Struthio molybdophanes* LR

RHEIFORMES

Rheidae

  Greater Rhea *Rhea americana* GT
  Lesser Rhea *Rhea pennata* GT

CASUARIIFORMES

Casuariidae

  Southern Cassowary *Casuarius casuarius* GT
  Dwarf Cassowary *Casuarius bennetti* GT
  Northern Cassowary *Casuarius unappendiculatus* GT

Dromaiidae

  Spotted Emu *Dromaius novaehollandiae*
  King Island Emu *Dromaius ater* E19
  Kangaroo Island Emu *Dromaius baudinianus* E19

DINORNITHIFORMES

Apterygidae

  Tokoeka *Apteryx australis* GT
  Brown Kiwi *Apteryx mantelli* GT, LR
  Little Spotted Kiwi *Apteryx owenii* GT
  Great Spotted Kiwi *Apteryx haastii* GT

TINAMIFORMES

Tinamidae

  Grey Tinamou *Tinamus tao*
  Solitary Tinamou *Tinamus solitarius* GT
  Black Tinamou *Tinamus osgoodi* GT
  Great Tinamou *Tinamus major*

  White-throated Tinamou *Tinamus guttatus*
  Highland Tinamou *Nothocercus bonapartei*
  Tawny-breasted Tinamou *Nothocercus julius*
  Hooded Tinamou *Nothocercus nigrocapillus*
  Cinereous Tinamou *Crypturellus cinereus*
  Berlepsch's Tinamou *Crypturellus berlepschi* LR
  Little Tinamou *Crypturellus soui*
  Tepuí Tinamou *Crypturellus ptaritepui* GT
  Brown Tinamou *Crypturellus obsoletus*
  Undulated Tinamou *Crypturellus undulatus*
  Pale-browed Tinamou *Crypturellus transfasciatus* GT
  Brazilian Tinamou *Crypturellus strigulosus*
  Grey-legged Tinamou *Crypturellus duidae*
  Red-footed Tinamou *Crypturellus erythropus* LR
  Yellow-legged Tinamou *Crypturellus noctivagus* GT
  Black-capped Tinamou *Crypturellus atrocapillus*
  Thicket Tinamou *Crypturellus cinnamomeus*
  Slaty-breasted Tinamou *Crypturellus boucardi*
  Chocó Tinamou *Crypturellus kerriae* GT
  Variegated Tinamou *Crypturellus variegatus*
  Rusty Tinamou *Crypturellus brevirostris*
  Bartlett's Tinamou *Crypturellus bartletti* LR
  Small-billed Tinamou *Crypturellus parvirostris*
  Barred Tinamou *Crypturellus casiquiare*
  Tataupa Tinamou *Crypturellus tataupa*
  Red-winged Tinamou *Rhynchotus rufescens*
  Taczanowski's Tinamou *Nothoprocta taczanowskii* GT
  Kalinowski's Tinamou *Nothoprocta kalinowskii* GT

Ornate Tinamou *Nothoprocta ornata*
Chilian Tinamou *Nothoprocta perdicaria*
Brushland Tinamou *Nothoprocta cinerascens*
Andean Tinamou *Nothoprocta pentlandii*
Curve-billed Tinamou *Nothoprocta curvirostris*
White-bellied Nothura *Nothura boraquira*
Lesser Nothura *Nothura minor* GT
Darwin's Nothura *Nothura darwinii*
Spotted Nothura *Nothura maculosa*
Chaco Nothura *Nothura chacoensis* LR
Dwarf Tinamou *Taoniscus nanus* GT
Elegant Crested Tinamou *Eudromia elegans*
Quebracho Crested Tinamou *Eudromia formosa* LR
Puna Tinamou *Tinamotis pentlandii*
Patagonian Tinamou *Tinamotis ingoufi*

SPHENISCIFORMES
Spheniscidae

King Penguin *Aptenodytes patagonicus*
Emperor Penguin *Aptenodytes forsteri*
Gentoo Penguin *Pygoscelis papua* GT
Adélie Penguin *Pygoscelis adeliae*
Chinstrap Penguin *Pygoscelis antarctica*
Fiordland Crested Penguin *Eudyptes pachyrhynchus* GT
Snares Crested Penguin *Eudyptes robustus* GT, LR
Erect-crested Penguin *Eudyptes sclateri* GT
Rockhopper Penguin *Eudyptes chrysocome* GT
Royal Penguin *Eudyptes schlegeli* GT, LR
Macaroni Penguin *Eudyptes chrysolophus* GT
Yellow-eyed Penguin *Megadyptes antipodes* GT
Little Penguin *Eudyptula minor*
Jackass Penguin *Spheniscus demersus* GT
Humboldt Penguin *Spheniscus humboldti* GT
Magellanic Penguin *Spheniscus magellanicus* GT
Galápagos Penguin *Spheniscus mendiculus* GT

ANSERIFORMES
Anhimidae

Horned Screamer *Anhima cornuta*
Southern Screamer *Chauna torquata*
Northern Screamer *Chauna chavaria* GT
Anseranatidae

Magpie Goose *Anseranas semipalmata*

Dendrocygnidae

Spotted Whistling-Duck *Dendrocygna guttata*
Plumed Whistling-Duck *Dendrocygna eytoni*
Fulvous Whistling-Duck *Dendrocygna bicolor*
Wandering Whistling-Duck *Dendrocygna arcuata*
Lesser Whistling-Duck *Dendrocygna javanica*
White-faced Whistling-Duck *Dendrocygna viduata*
West Indian Whistling-Duck *Dendrocygna arborea* GT
Black-bellied Whistling-Duck *Dendrocygna autumnalis*
White-backed Duck *Thalassornis leuconotus*
Anatidae

Mute Swan *Cygnus olor*
Black Swan *Cygnus atratus*
Black-necked Swan *Cygnus melanocorypha*
Whooper Swan *Cygnus cygnus*
Trumpeter Swan *Cygnus buccinator* LR
Tundra Swan *Cygnus columbianus* LR
Coscoroba Swan *Coscoroba coscoroba*
Freckled Duck *Stictonetta naevosa* GT
Masked Duck *Nomonyx dominica*
Ruddy Duck *Oxyura jamaicensis*
White-headed Duck *Oxyura leucocephala* GT
Andean Ruddy Duck *Oxyura ferruginea* LR
Maccoa Duck *Oxyura maccoa*
Argentine Blue-billed Duck *Oxyura vittata*
Australian Blue-billed Duck *Oxyura australis*
Musk Duck *Biziura lobata*
Black-headed Duck *Heteronetta atricapilla*
Swan Goose *Anser cygnoides* GT
Forest Bean Goose *Anser fabalis*
Tundra Bean Goose *Anser serrirostris* LR
Pink-footed Goose *Anser brachyrhynchus*
Greater White-fronted Goose *Anser albifrons*
Lesser White-fronted Goose *Anser erythropus* GT
Greylag Goose *Anser anser*
Bar-headed Goose *Anser indicus*
Lesser Snow Goose *Chen caerulescens*
Ross's Goose *Chen rossii*
Emperor Goose *Chen canagica* GT
Hawaiian Goose *Branta sandvicensis* GT
Canada Goose *Branta canadensis*

Tundra Goose *Branta hutchinsii* LR

Barnacle Goose *Branta leucopsis*

Brent Goose *Branta bernicla*

Black Brant *Branta nigricans*

Red-breasted Goose *Branta ruficollis* GT

Cape Barren Goose *Cereopsis novaehollandiae*

Blue-winged Goose *Cyanochen cyanopterus* GT

Andean Goose *Chloephaga melanoptera*

Upland Goose *Chloephaga picta*

Kelp Goose *Chloephaga hybrida*

Ashy-headed Goose *Chloephaga poliocephala*

Ruddy-headed Goose *Chloephaga rubidiceps*

Orinoco Goose *Neochen jubata* GT

Egyptian Goose *Alopochen aegyptiacus*

Ruddy Shelduck *Tadorna ferruginea*

South African Shelduck *Tadorna cana*

Paradise Shelduck *Tadorna variegata*

Australian Shelduck *Tadorna tadornoides*

Common Shelduck *Tadorna tadorna*

White-headed Shelduck *Tadorna radjah*

Crested Shelduck *Tadorna cristata* PE

Magellanic Flightless Steamerduck *Tachyeres pteneres*

Flying Steamerduck *Tachyeres patachonicus*

Falkland Flightless Steamerduck *Tachyeres brachypterus*

White-headed Steamerduck *Tachyeres leucocephalus* GT

Spur-winged Goose *Plectropterus gambensis*

Muscovy Duck *Cairina moschata*

White-winged Duck *Cairina scutulata* GT

Knob-billed Duck *Sarkidiornis melanotos*

Hartlaub's Duck *Pteronetta hartlaubii* GT

Green Pygmy-Goose *Nettapus pulchellus*

Cotton Pygmy-Goose *Nettapus coromandelianus*

African Pygmy-Goose *Nettapus auritus*

Ringed Teal *Callonetta leucophrys*

American Wood Duck *Aix sponsa*

Mandarin Duck *Aix galericulata*

Maned Duck *Chenonetta jubata*

Brazilian Teal *Amazonetta brasiliensis*

Blue Duck *Hymenolaimus malachorhynchos* GT

Torrent Duck *Merganetta armata*

Salvadori's Teal *Salvadorina waigiuensis* GT

Eurasian Wigeon *Anas penelope*

American Wigeon *Anas americana*

Chiloe Wigeon *Anas sibilatrix*

Amsterdam Island Wigeon *Anas marecula* E

Falcated Duck *Anas falcata*

Gadwall *Anas strepera*

Baikal Teal *Anas formosa* GT

Eurasian Teal *Anas crecca*

Green-winged Teal *Anas carolinensis* LR

Speckled Teal *Anas flavirostris*

Andean Teal *Anas andium* LR

Cape Teal *Anas capensis*

Sunda Teal *Anas gibberifrons*

Andaman Teal *Anas albogularis* LR

Grey Teal *Anas gracilis* LR

Madagascar Teal *Anas bernieri* GT

Chestnut Teal *Anas castanea*

Auckland Island Teal *Anas aucklandica* GT

Brown Teal *Anas chlorotis* GT, LR

Campbell Island Teal *Anas nesiotis* GT, LR

Mallard *Anas platyrhynchos*

Hawaiian Duck *Anas wyvilliana* GT, LR

Laysan Duck *Anas laysanensis* GT, LR

Mottled Duck *Anas fulvigula* LR

American Black Duck *Anas rubripes*

Yellow-billed Duck *Anas undulata*

Spot-billed Duck *Anas poecilorhyncha*

Pacific Black Duck *Anas superciliosa* LR

African Black Duck *Anas sparsa* LR

Meller's Duck *Anas melleri* GT, LR

Philippine Duck *Anas luzonica* GT

Spectacled Duck *Anas specularis* GT

Crested Duck *Anas specularioides*

Northern Pintail *Anas acuta*

Eaton's Pintail *Anas eatoni* GT, LR

Crozet Pintail *Anas drygalskii* LR

South Georgian Teal *Anas georgica*

White-cheeked Pintail *Anas bahamensis*

Red-billed Duck *Anas erythrorhyncha*

Silver Teal *Anas versicolor*

Puna Teal *Anas puna* LR

Hottentot Teal *Anas hottentota* LR

Garganey *Anas querquedula*

Blue-winged Teal *Anas discors*

Cinnamon Teal *Anas cyanoptera*

Red Shoveler *Anas platalea*

Cape Shoveler *Anas smithii*

Australasian Shoveler *Anas rhynchotis*

Northern Shoveler *Anas clypeata*

Pink-eared Duck *Malacorhynchus membranaceus*

Marbled Duck *Marmaronetta angustirostris* GT

Pink-headed Duck *Rhodonessa caryophyllacea* PE

Red-crested Pochard *Netta rufina*

Southern Pochard *Netta erythrophthalma*

Rosy-billed Pochard *Netta peposaca*

Canvasback *Aythya valisineria*

Common Pochard *Aythya ferina*

Redhead *Aythya americana*

Ring-necked Duck *Aythya collaris*

Hardhead *Aythya australis*

Baer's Pochard *Aythya baeri* GT

Ferruginous Duck *Aythya nyroca* GT

Madagascar Pochard *Aythya innotata* GT

New Zealand Scaup *Aythya novaeseelandiae*

Tufted Duck *Aythya fuligula*

Greater Scaup *Aythya marila*

Lesser Scaup *Aythya affinis*

Common Eider *Somateria mollissima*

King Eider *Somateria spectabilis*

Spectacled Eider *Somateria fischeri* GT

Steller's Eider *Polysticta stelleri* GT

Labrador Duck *Camptorhynchus labradorius* E

Harlequin Duck *Histrionicus histrionicus*

Long-tailed Duck *Clangula hyemalis*

Common Scoter *Melanitta nigra*

Surf Scoter *Melanitta perspicillata*

Velvet Scoter *Melanitta fusca*

Bufflehead *Bucephala albeola*

Barrow's Goldeneye *Bucephala islandica*

Common Goldeneye *Bucephala clangula*

Hooded Merganser *Lophodytes cucullatus*

Smew *Mergellus albellus*

Brazilian Merganser *Mergus octosetaceus* GT

Red-breasted Merganser *Mergus serrator*

Scaly-sided Merganser *Mergus squamatus* GT

Common Merganser *Mergus merganser*

Auckland Islands Merganser *Mergus australis* E20

GALLIFORMES
Megapodiidae

Nicobar Scrubfowl *Megapodius nicobariensis* GT, LR

Philippine Scrubfowl *Megapodius cumingii* LR

Sula Scrubfowl *Megapodius bernsteinii* GT, LR

Forsten's Scrubfowl *Megapodius forstenii* LR

Tanimbar Scrubfowl *Megapodius tenimberensis* LR

New Guinea Scrubfowl *Megapodius affinis* LR

Orange-footed Scrubfowl *Megapodius reinwardt* LR

Melanesian Scrubfowl *Megapodius eremita* LR

Dusky Scrubfowl *Megapodius freycinet* LR

Biak Megapode *Megapodius geelvinkianus* GT, LR

Vanuatu Scrubfowl *Megapodius layardi* GT, LR

Micronesian Scrubfowl *Megapodius laperouse* GT

Polynesian Scrubfowl *Megapodius pritchardii* GT

Moluccan Scrubfowl *Eulipoa wallacei* GT

Malleefowl *Leipoa ocellata* GT

Australian Brush-Turkey *Alectura lathami*

Red-billed Brush-Turkey *Talegalla cuvieri*

Black-billed Brush-Turkey *Talegalla fuscirostris*

Brown Collared Brush-Turkey *Talegalla jobiensis*

Wattled Brush-Turkey *Aepypodius arfakianus*

Bruijn's Brush-Turkey *Aepypodius bruijnii* GT

Maleofowl *Macrocephalon maleo* GT

Cracidae

Plain Chachalaca *Ortalis vetula*

Grey-headed Chachalaca *Ortalis cinereiceps* LR

Chestnut-winged Chachalaca *Ortalis garrula*

Rufous-vented Chachalaca *Ortalis ruficauda*

Rufous-headed Chachalaca *Ortalis erythroptera* GT

Rufous-bellied Chachalaca *Ortalis wagleri* LR

West Mexican Chachalaca *Ortalis poliocephala* LR

Chaco Chachalaca *Ortalis canicollis*

White-bellied Chachalaca *Ortalis leucogastra* LR

Speckled Chachalaca *Ortalis guttata* LR

Colombian Chachalaca *Ortalis columbiana* LR

Little Chachalaca *Ortalis motmot*

Buff-browed Chachalaca *Ortalis superciliaris* GT, LR

Band-tailed Guan *Penelope argyrotis*

Bearded Guan *Penelope barbata* GT, LR

Andean Guan *Penelope montagnii*

Baudó Guan *Penelope ortoni* GT, LR

Marail Guan *Penelope marail*

Rusty-margined Guan *Penelope superciliaris*

Red-faced Guan *Penelope dabbenei*

Dusky-legged Guan *Penelope obscura*

Spix's Guan *Penelope jacquacu* LR

White-winged Guan *Penelope albipennis* GT

Cauca Guan *Penelope perspicax* GT, LR

Crested Guan *Penelope purpurascens*

White-browed Guan *Penelope jacucaca* GT, LR

Chestnut-bellied Guan *Penelope ochrogaster* GT

White-crested Guan *Penelope pileata* GT

Trinidad Piping-Guan *Pipile pipile* GT

Blue-throated Piping-Guan *Pipile cumanensis* LR

Red-throated Piping-Guan *Pipile cujubi* LR

Black-fronted Piping-Guan *Pipile jacutinga* GT

Wattled Piping-Guan *Aburria aburri* PGT

Black Guan *Chamaepetes unicolor* GT

Sickle-winged Guan *Chamaepetes goudotii*

Highland Guan *Penelopina nigra* GT

Horned Guan *Oreophasis derbianus* GT

Nocturnal Curassow *Nothocrax urumutum*

Crestless Curassow *Mitu tomentosa*

Salvin's Curassow *Mitu salvini*

Amazonian Razor-billed-Curassow *Mitu tuberosa* LR

Alagoas Curassow *Mitu mitu* GT

Helmeted Curassow *Pauxi pauxi* GT

Horned Curassow *Pauxi unicornis* GT

Great Curassow *Crax rubra* GT

Blue-billed Curassow *Crax alberti* GT

Yellow-knobbed Curassow *Crax daubentoni* GT

Black Curassow *Crax alector*

Wattled Curassow *Crax globulosa* GT

Bare-faced Curassow *Crax fasciolata*

Red-billed Curassow *Crax blumenbachii* GT

Odontophoridae

Bearded Tree-Quail *Dendrortyx barbatus* GT

Long-tailed Tree-Quail *Dendrortyx macroura*

Buffy-crowned Tree-Quail *Dendrortyx leucophrys*

Mountain Quail *Oreortyx pictus*

Scaled Quail *Callipepla squamata*

California Quail *Lophortyx californicus*

Gambel's Quail *Lophortyx gambelii* LR

Elegant Quail *Lophortyx douglasii*

Barred Quail *Philortyx fasciatus*

Northern Bobwhite *Colinus virginianus*

Black-throated Bobwhite *Colinus nigrogularis* LR

Crested Bobwhite *Colinus cristatus*

Spot-bellied Bobwhite *Colinus leucopogon* LR

Marbled Woodquail *Odontophorus gujanensis*

Spot-winged Woodquail *Odontophorus capueira*

Rufous-fronted Woodquail *Odontophorus erythrops*

Black-fronted Woodquail *Odontophorus atrifrons* GT

Dark-backed Woodquail *Odontophorus melanonotus* GT

Chestnut Woodquail *Odontophorus hyperythrus* GT

Rufous-breasted Woodquail *Odontophorus speciosus*

Gorgeted Woodquail *Odontophorus strophium* GT

Tacarcuna Woodquail *Odontophorus dialeucos* GT

Venezuelan Woodquail *Odontophorus columbianus* GT

Black-breasted Woodquail *Odontophorus leucolaemus*

Stripe-faced Woodquail *Odontophorus balliviani*

Starred Woodquail *Odontophorus stellatus*

Spotted Woodquail *Odontophorus guttatus*

Singing Quail *Dactylortyx thoracicus*

Montezuma Quail *Cyrtonyx montezumae*

Salle's Quail *Cyrtonyx sallei* LR

Ocellated Quail *Cyrtonyx ocellatus* GT, LR

Tawny-faced *Quail Rhynchortyx cinctus*

Melagrididae

Wild Turkey *Meleagris gallopavo*

Ocellated Turkey *Meleagris ocellata* GT

Tetraonidae

Siberian Grouse *Falcipennis falcipennis* GT

Spruce Grouse *Falcipennis canadensis*

Blue Grouse *Dendragapus obscurus*

Willow Ptarmigan *Lagopus lagopus*

Rock Ptarmigan *Lagopus mutus*

White-tailed Ptarmigan *Lagopus leucurus*

Caucasian Black Grouse *Tetrao mlokosiewiczi* PGT

Eurasian Black Grouse *Tetrao tetrix*

Black-billed Capercaillie *Tetrao parvirostris* LR

Western Capercaillie *Tetrao urogallus*

Severtzov's Hazel Grouse *Bonasa sewerzowi* GT

Hazel Grouse *Bonasa bonasia*

Ruffed Grouse *Bonasa umbellus* LR

Greater Sage-Grouse *Centrocercus urophasianus*

Gunnison Sage-Grouse *Centrocercus minimus* GT, LR

Sharp-tailed Grouse *Tympanuchus phasianellus*

Greater Prairie Chicken *Tympanuchus cupido*

Lesser Prairie Chicken *Tympanuchus pallidicinctus* GT, LR

Phasianidae

Snow Partridge *Lerwa lerwa*

See-see Partridge *Ammoperdix griseogularis*

Sand Partridge *Ammoperdix heyi*

Caucasian Snowcock *Tetraogallus caucasicus*

Caspian Snowcock *Tetraogallus caspius*

Tibetan Snowcock *Tetraogallus tibetanus*

Altai Snowcock *Tetraogallus altaicus*

Himalayan Snowcock *Tetraogallus himalayensis*

Verreaux's Monal-Partridge *Tetraophasis obscurus*

Széchenyi's Monal-Partridge *Tetraophasis szechenyii* LR

Rock Partridge *Alectoris graeca*

Chukar *Alectoris chukar* LR

Rusty-necklaced Partridge *Alectoris magna* LR

Philby's Partridge *Alectoris philbyi*

Barbary Partridge *Alectoris barbara*

Red-legged Partridge *Alectoris rufa*

Arabian Partridge *Alectoris melanocephala*

Snow Mountain Quail *Anurophasis monorthonyx* GT

Black Francolin *Francolinus francolinus*

Painted Francolin *Francolinus pictus*

Chinese Francolin *Francolinus pintadeanus*

Red-necked Francolin *Francolinus afer*

Swainson's Francolin *Francolinus swainsonii*

Grey-breasted Francolin *Francolinus rufopictus*

Yellow-necked Francolin *Francolinus leucoscepus*

Erckel's Francolin *Francolinus erckelii*

Pale-bellied Francolin *Francolinus ochropectus* GT

Chestnut-naped Francolin *Francolinus castaneicollis*

Jackson's Francolin *Francolinus jacksoni*

Handsome Francolin *Francolinus nobilis*

Mount Cameroon Francolin *Francolinus camerunensis* GT

Swierstra's Francolin *Francolinus swierstrai* GT

Ahanta Francolin *Francolinus ahantensis*

Scaly Francolin *Francolinus squamatus*

Grey-striped Francolin *Francolinus griseostriatus* GT

Double-spurred Francolin *Francolinus bicalcaratus*

Heuglin's Francolin *Francolinus icterorhynchus*

Clapperton's Francolin *Francolinus clappertoni*

Hildebrandt's Francolin *Francolinus hildebrandti*

Natal Francolin *Francolinus natalensis*

Hartlaub's Francolin *Francolinus hartlaubi*

Harwood's Francolin *Francolinus harwoodi* GT

Red-billed Francolin *Francolinus adspersus*

Cape Francolin *Francolinus capensis*

Crested Francolin *Francolinus sephaena*

Ring-necked Francolin *Francolinus streptophorus*

Moorland Francolin *Francolinus psilolaemus*

Kirk's Francolin *Francolinus rovuma* LR

Shelley's Francolin *Francolinus shelleyi*

Grey-winged Francolin *Francolinus africanus*

Orange River Francolin *Francolinus levaillantoides*

Red-winged Francolin *Francolinus levaillantii*

Finsch's Francolin *Francolinus finschi*

Coqui Francolin *Francolinus coqui*

White-throated Francolin *Francolinus albogularis*

Schlegel's Francolin *Francolinus schlegelii*

Latham's Francolin *Francolinus lathami*

Nahan's Francolin *Francolinus nahani* PGT

Indian Grey Francolin *Francolinus pondicerianus*

Swamp Francolin *Francolinus gularis* GT

Grey Partridge *Perdix perdix*

Daurian Partridge *Perdix dauurica*

Tibetan Partridge *Perdix hodgsoniae*

Long-billed Partridge *Rhizothera longirostris* GT

Madagascar Partridge *Margaroperdix madagarensis*

Black Wood-Partridge *Melanoperdix nigra* GT

Common Quail *Coturnix coturnix*

Japanese Quail *Coturnix japonica* LR

Rain Quail *Coturnix coromandelica*

Harlequin Quail *Coturnix delegorguei*

Stubble Quail *Coturnix pectoralis* LR

New Zealand Quail *Coturnix novaezelandiae* E

Brown Quail *Coturnix australis* LR

Swamp Quail *Coturnix ypsilophora*

African Blue Quail *Coturnix adansonii* LR

Blue-breasted Quail *Coturnix chinensis*

Jungle Bush-Quail *Perdicula asiatica* LR

Rock Bush-Quail *Perdicula argoondah* LR

Painted Bush-Quail *Perdicula erythrorhyncha*

Manipur Bush-Quail *Perdicula manipurensis* GT

Common Hill-Partridge *Arborophila torqueola*

Rufous-throated Hill-Partridge *Arborophila rufogularis*

White-cheeked Hill-Partridge *Arborophila atrogularis* GT

Taiwan Hill-Partridge *Arborophila crudigularis* GT

Chestnut-breasted Hill-Partridge *Arborophila mandellii* GT

Barred Hill-Partridge *Arborophila brunneopectus* LR

Sichuan Hill-Partridge *Arborophila rufipectus* GT

White-necklaced Partridge *Arborophila gingica* GT

Orange-necked Hill-Partridge *Arborophila davidi* GT

Chestnut-headed Tree-Partridge *Arborophila cambodiana* GT

Grey-breasted Hill-Partridge *Arborophila orientalis* GT, LR

Malaysian Hill-Partridge *Arborophila campbelli* LR

Chestnut-bellied Tree-Partridge *Arborophila javanica*

Red-billed Hill-Partridge *Arborophila rubrirostris*

Red-breasted Tree-Partridge *Arborophila hyperythra*

Hainan Hill-Partridge *Arborophila ardens* GT

Chestnut-necklaced Hill-Partridge *Arborophila charltonii* GT

Scaly-breasted Partridge *Arborophila chloropus* LR

Annam Hill-Partridge *Arborophila merlini* PGT, LR

Ferruginous Partridge *Caloperdix oculea* GT

Crimson-headed Wood-Partridge *Haematortyx sanguiniceps*

Crested Partridge *Rollulus rouloul* GT

Stone Partridge *Ptilopachus petrosus*

Udzungwa Forest-Partridge *Xenoperdix udzungwensis* GT, LR

Mountain Bamboo-Partridge *Bambusicola fytchii*

Chinese Bamboo-Partridge *Bambusicola thoracica*

Red Spurfowl *Galloperdix spadicea*

Painted Spurfowl *Galloperdix lunulata*

Sri Lanka Spurfowl *Galloperdix bicalcarata*

Himalayan Mountain Quail *Ophrysia superciliosa* PE

Blood Pheasant *Ithaginis cruentus*

Western Horned Tragopan *Tragopan melanocephalus* GT

Satyr Tragopan *Tragopan satyra* GT

Blyth's Tragopan *Tragopan blythii* GT

Temminck's Tragopan *Tragopan temminckii*

Cabot's Tragopan *Tragopan caboti* GT

Koklass Pheasant *Pucrasia macrolopha*

Himalayan Monal *Lophophorus impejanus*

Sclater's Monal *Lophophorus sclateri* GT

Chinese Monal *Lophophorus lhuysii* GT

Red Junglefowl *Gallus gallus*

Sri Lanka Junglefowl *Gallus lafayetii*

Grey Junglefowl *Gallus sonneratii*

Green Junglefowl *Gallus varius*

Kalij Pheasant *Lophura leucomelanos*

Silver Pheasant *Lophura nycthemera*

Imperial Pheasant *Lophura imperialis* PGT

Edwards's Pheasant *Lophura edwardsi* GT

Vietnamese Pheasant *Lophura hatinhensis* GT, LR

Swinhoe's Pheasant *Lophura swinhoii* GT

Hoogerwerf's Pheasant *Lophura hoogerwerfi* GT, LR

Salvadori's Pheasant *Lophura inornata* GT

Crestless Fireback *Lophura erythrophthalma* GT

Crested Fireback *Lophura ignita* GT

Siamese Fireback *Lophura diardi* GT

Bulwer's Pheasant *Lophura bulweri* GT, LR

Tibetan Eared-Pheasant *Crossoptilon harmani* GT, LR

White Eared-Pheasant *Crossoptilon crossoptilon* GT

Brown Eared-Pheasant *Crossoptilon mantchuricum* GT

Blue Eared-Pheasant *Crossoptilon auritum*

Cheer Pheasant *Catreus wallichi* GT

Elliot's Pheasant *Syrmaticus ellioti* GT

Mrs Hume's Pheasant *Syrmaticus humiae* GT

Mikado Pheasant *Syrmaticus mikado* GT

Copper Pheasant *Syrmaticus soemmerringii* GT

Reeves' Pheasant *Syrmaticus reevesii* GT

Common Pheasant *Phasianus colchicus*

Green Pheasant *Phasianus versicolor* LR

Golden Pheasant *Chrysolophus pictus*

Lady Amhurst's Pheasant *Chrysolophus amherstiae*

Bronze-tailed Peacock-Pheasant *Polyplectron chalcurum*

Mountain Peacock-Pheasant *Polyplectron inopinatum* GT

Germain's Peacock-Pheasant *Polyplectron germaini* GT

Grey Peacock-Pheasant *Polyplectron bicalcaratum*

Malaysian Peacock-Pheasant *Polyplectron malacense* GT

Bornean Peacock-Pheasant *Polyplectron schleiermacheri* GT, LR

Palawan Peacock-Pheasant *Polyplectron emphanum* GT

Crested Argus *Rheinardia ocellata* GT

Great Argus *Argusianus argus* GT

Indian Peafowl *Pavo cristatus*

Green Peafowl *Pavo muticus* GT

Congo Peafowl *Afropavo congensis* GT

Numididae

Black Guineafowl *Phasidus niger*

White-breasted Guineafowl *Agelastes meleagrides* GT

Helmeted Guineafowl *Numida meleagris*

Plumed Guineafowl *Guttera plumifera*

Crested Guineafowl *Guttera pucherani*

Vulturine Guineafowl *Acryllium vulturinum*

GAVIIFORMES
Gaviidae

Red-throated Loon *Gavia stellata*

Arctic Loon *Gavia arctica*

Pacific Loon *Gavia pacifica* LR

Common Loon *Gavia immer*

Yellow-billed Loon *Gavia adamsii* LR

PODICIPEDIFORMES
Podicipedidae

Red-throated Little Grebe *Tachybaptus ruficollis*

Australasian Little Grebe *Tachybaptus novaehollandiae* LR

Madagascar Little Grebe *Tachybaptus pelzelnii* GT

Delacour's Little Grebe *Tachybaptus rufolavatus* GT

Pied-billed Grebe *Podilymbus podiceps*

Atitlán Grebe *Podilymbus gigas* E20

White-tufted Grebe *Rollandia rolland*

Short-winged Grebe *Rollandia microptera*

Hoary-headed Grebe *Poliocephalus poliocephalus*

New Zealand Grebe *Poliocephalus rufopectus* GT

Least Grebe *Poliocephalus dominicus*

Great Grebe *Podiceps major*

Red-necked Grebe *Podiceps grisegena*

Great Crested Grebe *Podiceps cristatus*

Horned Grebe *Podiceps auritus*

Black-necked Grebe *Podiceps nigricollis*

Colombian Grebe *Podiceps andinus* E20

Silvery Grebe *Podiceps occipitalis*

Puna Grebe *Podiceps taczanowskii* GT

Hooded Grebe *Podiceps gallardoi* GT, LR

Western Grebe *Aechmophorus occidentalis*

Clark's Grebe *Aechmophorus clarkii* LR

PROCELLARIIFORMES
Diomedeidae

Southern Royal Albatross *Diomedea epomophora* GT

Northern Royal Albatross *Diomedea sanfordi* GT, LR

Antipodean Albatross *Diomedea antipodensis* GT, LR

Snowy Albatross *Diomedea chionoptera* GT, LR

Tristan Albatross *Diomedea dabbenena* GT, LR

Wandering Albatross *Diomedea exulans* GT

Laysan Albatross *Phoebastria immutabilis*

Black-footed Albatross *Phoebastria nigripes* GT

Waved Albatross *Phoebastria irrorata* GT

Short-tailed Albatross *Phoebastria albatrus* GT

Sooty Mollymawk *Phoebetria fusca* GT

Light-mantled Mollymawk *Phoebetria palpebrata* GT

Yellow-nosed Mollymawk *Thalassarche chlororhynchos* GT

Indian Yellow-nosed Mollymawk *Thalassarche carteri* GT, LR

Grey-headed Mollymawk *Thalassarche chrysostoma* GT

Buller's Mollymawk *Thalassarche bulleri* GT

Shy Mollymawk *Thalassarche cauta* GT

White-capped Mollymawk *Thalassarche steadi* LR

Salvin's Mollymawk *Thalassarche salvini* GT, LR

Chatham Islands Mollymawk *Thalassarche eremita* GT, LR

Black-browed Mollymawk *Thalassarche melanophris* GT

Campbell Islands Mollymawk *Thalassarche impavida* PGT, LR

Procellariidae

Southern Giant Petrel *Macronectes giganteus* GT

Northern Giant Petrel *Macronectes halli* GT, LR

Northern Fulmar *Fulmarus glacialis*

Southern Fulmar *Fulmarus glacialoides*

Antarctic Petrel *Thalassoica antarctica*

Cape Petrel *Daption capense*

Snow Petrel *Pagodroma nivea*

Greater Snow Petrel *Pagodroma confusa* LR

Kerguelen Petrel *Aphrodroma brevirostris*

Great-winged Petrel *Pterodroma macroptera*

Mascarene Petrel *Pterodroma aterrima* GT, LR

White-headed Petrel *Pterodroma lessonii*

Black-capped Petrel *Pterodroma hasitata* GT

Jamaican Petrel *Pterodroma caribbaea* GT, LR

Bermuda Petrel *Pterodroma cahow* GT, LR

Atlantic Petrel *Pterodroma incerta* GT

Beck's Petrel *Pterodroma becki* GT, LR

Herald Petrel *Pterodroma heraldica* LR

Henderson Petrel *Pterodroma atrata* GT, LR

Phoenix Petrel *Pterodroma alba* GT

Mottled Petrel *Pterodroma inexpectata* GT

Providence Petrel *Pterodroma solandri* GT

Murphy's Petrel *Pterodroma ultima* GT

Kermadec Petrel *Pterodroma neglecta*

Magenta Petrel *Pterodroma magentae* GT, LR

Trindade Island Petrel *Pterodroma arminjoniana* GT

Soft-plumaged Petrel *Pterodroma mollis*

Fea's Petrel *Pterodroma feae* GT, LR

Zino's Petrel *Pterodroma madeira* GT, LR

Barau's Petrel *Pterodroma baraui* GT

Hawaiian Petrel *Pterodroma sandwichensis* GT, LR

Galápagos Petrel *Pterodroma phaeopygia* GT

Juan Fernández Petrel *Pterodroma externa* GT, LR

White-necked Petrel *Pterodroma cervicalis* GT, LR

Cook's Petrel *Pterodroma cookii* GT

De Filippi's Petrel *Pterodroma defilippiana* GT, LR

Gould's Petrel *Pterodroma leucoptera* GT

Collared Petrel *Pterodroma brevipes* LR

Bonin Petrel *Pterodroma hypoleuca* LR

Black-winged Petrel *Pterodroma nigripennis* LR

Chatham Islands Petrel *Pterodroma axillaris* GT

Stejneger's Petrel *Pterodroma longirostris* GT

Pycroft's Petrel *Pterodroma pycrofti* GT, LR

Fiji Petrel *Pseudobulweria macgillivrayi* GT, LR

Tahiti Petrel *Pseudobulweria rostrata* GT

Blue Petrel *Halobaena caerulea*

Broad-billed Prion *Pachyptila vittata*

Salvin's Prion *Pachyptila salvini* LR

Antarctic Prion *Pachyptila desolata* LR

Slender-billed Prion *Pachyptila belcheri*

Fairy Prion *Pachyptila turtur*

Fulmar Prion *Pachyptila crassirostris* LR

Bulwer's Petrel *Bulweria bulwerii*

Jouanin's Petrel *Bulweria fallax* GT, LR

Grey Petrel *Procellaria cinerea* GT

White-chinned Petrel *Procellaria aequinoctialis* GT

Spectacled Petrel *Procellaria conspicillata* GT, LR

Parkinson's Petrel *Procellaria parkinsoni* GT, LR

Westland Petrel *Procellaria westlandica* GT, LR

Streaked Shearwater *Calonectris leucomelas* LR

Cory's Shearwater *Calonectris diomedea*

Cape Verde Islands Shearwater *Calonectris edwardsii* LR

Pink-footed Shearwater *Puffinus creatopus* GT

Flesh-footed Shearwater *Puffinus carneipes*

Great Shearwater *Puffinus gravis*

Wedge-tailed Shearwater *Puffinus pacificus*

Buller's Shearwater *Puffinus bulleri* GT

Sooty Shearwater *Puffinus griseus*

Short-tailed Shearwater *Puffinus tenuirostris*

Heinroth's Shearwater *Puffinus heinrothi* GT, LR

Christmas Island Shearwater *Puffinus nativitatis*

Manx Shearwater *Puffinus puffinus*

Yelkouan Shearwater *Puffinus yelkouan* LR

Balearic Shearwater *Puffinus mauretanicus* GT, LR

Canarian Shearwater *Puffinus holeae* E

Olson's Shearwater *Puffinus olsoni* E

Fluttering Shearwater *Puffinus gavia* LR

Hutton's Shearwater *Puffinus huttoni* GT, LR

Black-vented Shearwater *Puffinus opisthomelas* GT, LR

Townsend's Shearwater *Puffinus auricularis* GT, LR

Newell's Shearwater *Puffinus newelli* GT, LR

Little Shearwater *Puffinus assimilis*

Persian Shearwater *Puffinus persicus* GT, LR

Bannerman's Shearwater *Puffinus bannermani* LR

Audubon's Shearwater *Puffinus lherminieri*

Pelecanoididae

Peruvian Diving-Petrel *Pelecanoides garnotii* GT

Magellanic Diving-Petrel *Pelecanoides magellani*

South Georgian Diving-Petrel *Pelecanoides georgicus*

Common Diving-Petrel *Pelecanoides urinatrix*

Hydrobatidae

Wilson's Storm-Petrel *Oceanites oceanicus*

Elliot's Storm-Petrel *Oceanites gracilis* PGT

Grey-backed Storm-Petrel *Garrodia nereis*

White-faced Storm-Petrel *Pelagodroma marina*

White-bellied Storm-Petrel *Fregetta grallaria*

Black-bellied Storm-Petrel *Fregetta tropica* LR

White-throated Storm-Petrel *Nesofregetta fuliginosa* GT

European Storm-Petrel *Hydrobates pelagicus*

Least Storm-Petrel *Halocyptena microsoma*

Wedge-rumped Storm-Petrel *Oceanodroma tethys*

Madeiran Storm-Petrel *Oceanodroma castro*

Leach's Storm-Petrel *Oceanodroma leucorhoa*

Markham's Storm-Petrel *Oceanodroma markhami* PGT

Matsudaira's Storm-Petrel *Oceanodroma matsudairae* PGT, LR

Guadalupe Storm-Petrel *Oceanodroma macrodactyla* GT

Tristram's Storm-Petrel *Oceanodroma tristrami* GT, LR

Swinhoe's Storm-Petrel *Oceanodroma monorhis*

Ashy Storm-Petrel *Oceanodroma homochroa* GT, LR

Hornby's Storm-Petrel *Oceanodroma hornbyi* PGT

Fork-tailed Storm-Petrel *Oceanodroma furcata*

Black Storm-Petrel *Oceanodroma melania*

PELECANIFORMES

Phaethontidae

Red-billed Tropicbird *Phaethon aethereus*

Red-tailed Tropicbird *Phaethon rubricauda*

White-tailed Tropicbird *Phaethon lepturus*

Sulidae

Abbott's Booby *Papasula abbotti* GT

Northern Gannet *Morus bassanus*

Cape Gannet *Morus capensis* GT, LR

Australasian Gannet *Morus serrator* LR

Blue-footed Booby *Sula nebouxii*

Peruvian Booby *Sula variegata*

Masked Booby *Sula dactylatra*

Nazca Booby *Sula granti* LR

Tasmanian Booby *Sula tasmani* E

Red-footed Booby *Sula sula*

Brown Booby *Sula leucogaster*

Anhingidae

African Darter *Anhinga rufa* LR

Oriental Darter *Anhinga melanogaster* GT, LR
Australian Darter *Anhinga novaehollandiae* LR
American Darter *Anhinga anhinga*

Phalacrocoracidae

Double-crested Cormorant P*halacrocorax auritus*
Neotropical Cormorant P*halacrocorax olivaceus* LR
Little Black Cormorant *Phalacrocorax sulcirostris*
Great Cormorant *Phalacrocorax carbo*
White-breasted Cormorant *Phalacrocorax lucidus* LR
Indian Cormorant *Phalacrocorax fuscicollis*
Cape Cormorant *Phalacrocorax capensis* GT
Socotra Cormorant *Phalacrocorax nigrogularis* GT
Bank Cormorant *Phalacrocorax neglectus* GT
Japanese Cormorant *Phalacrocorax capillatus*
Brandt's Cormorant *Phalacrocorax penicillatus*
European Shag *Phalacrocorax aristotelis*
Pelagic Cormorant *Phalacrocorax pelagicus*
Red-faced Cormorant *Phalacrocorax urile*
Rock Shag *Phalacrocorax magellanicus*
Guanay Shag *Phalacrocorax bougainvillii*
Chatham Islands Shag *Phalacrocorax onslowi* GT, LR
Pitt Island Shag *Phalacrocorax featherstoni* GT
Auckland Islands Shag *Phalacrocorax colensoi* GT
Bounty Islands Shag *Phalacrocorax ranfurlyi* GT
Pied Cormorant *Phalacrocorax varius*
Black-faced Cormorant *Phalacrocorax fuscescens*
Rough-faced Cormorant *Phalacrocorax carunculatus* GT
Bronze Shag *Phalacrocorax chalconotus* GT, LR
Campbell Island Shag *Phalacrocorax campbelli* GT
Kerguelen Shag *Phalacrocorax verrucosus* LR
Red-legged Shag *Phalacrocorax gaimardi* GT
Spotted Shag *Phalacrocorax punctatus*
Imperial Shag *Phalacrocorax atriceps*
King Cormorant *Phalacrocorax albiventer*
Macquarie Shag *Phalacrocorax purpurescens* LR
Heard Shag *Phalacrocorax nivalis* LR
Antarctic Shag *Phalacrocorax bransfieldensis* LR

South Georgia Shag *Phalacrocorax georgianus* LR
Crozet Shag *Phalacrocorax melanogenis* LR
Little Pied Cormorant *Phalacrocorax melanoleucos*
Pallas's Cormorant *Phalacrocorax perspicillatus* E
Long-tailed Cormorant *Phalacrocorax africanus*
Crowned Cormorant *Phalacrocorax coronatus* GT, LR
Little Cormorant *Phalacrocorax niger* LR
Pygmy Cormorant *Phalacrocorax pygmeus* GT
Galápagos Cormorant *Phalacrocorax harrisi* GT

Balaenicipitidae

Shoebill *Balaeniceps rex* GT

Pelecanidae

Great White Pelican *Pelecanus onocrotalus* LR
Pink-backed Pelican *Pelecanus rufescens*
Spot-billed Pelican *Pelecanus philippensis* GT
Dalmatian Pelican *Pelecanus crispus* GT, LR
Australian Pelican *Pelecanus conspicillatus*
American White Pelican *Pelecanus erythrorhynchos*
Brown Pelican *Pelecanus occidentalis*
Peruvian Pelican *Pelecanus thagus* LR

Fregatidae

Ascension Island Frigatebird *Fregata aquila* GT
Christmas Island Frigatebird *Fregata andrewsi* GT, LR
Magnificent Frigatebird *Fregata magnificens* LR
Greater Frigatebird *Fregata minor* LR
Lesser Frigatebird *Fregata ariel*

CICONIIFORMES

Ardeidae

Whistling Heron *Syrigma sibilatrix*
Capped Heron *Pilherodius pileatus*
Grey Heron *Ardea cinerea*
Great Blue Heron *Ardea herodias* LR
Cocoi Heron *Ardea cocoi*
Pacific Heron *Ardea pacifica*
Black-headed Heron *Ardea melanocephala*
Humblot's Heron *Ardea humbloti* GT
White-bellied Heron *Ardea insignis* GT
Great-billed Heron *Ardea sumatrana*
Goliath Heron *Ardea goliath*
Purple Heron *Ardea purpurea*

Pied Heron *Ardea picata*
Cattle Egret *Bubulcus ibis*
Great Egret *Casmerodius albus*
Intermediate Egret *Mesophoyx intermedia*
Reddish Egret *Egretta rufescens*
Slaty Egret *Egretta vinaceigula* GT, LR
Black Heron *Egretta ardesiaca*
Tricolored Heron *Egretta tricolor*
White-faced Egret *Egretta novaehollandiae*
Little Blue Heron *Egretta caerulea*
Snowy Egret *Egretta thula*
Little Egret *Egretta garzetta*
Chinese Egret *Egretta eulophotes* GT, LR
Pacific Reef-Egret *Egretta sacra*
Western Reef-Egret *Egretta gularis* LR
Dimorphic Egret *Egretta dimorpha* LR
Squacco Heron *Ardeola ralloides*
Indian Pond-Heron *Ardeola grayii*
Chinese Pond-Heron *Ardeola bacchus*
Javan Pond-Heron *Ardeola speciosa*
Madagascar Squacco Heron *Ardeola idae* GT
Rufous-bellied Heron *Ardeola rufiventris*
Striated Heron *Butorides striatus* LR
Green Heron *Butorides virescens* LR
Galápagos Heron *Butorides sundevalli* LR
Chestnut-bellied Heron *Agamia agami*
Yellow-crowned Night-Heron *Nyctanassa violacea*
Black-crowned Night-Heron *Nycticorax nycticorax*
Rufous Night-Heron *Nycticorax caledonicus*
White-backed Night-Heron *Gorsachius leuconotus*
White-eared Night-Heron *Gorsachius magnificus* GT
Japanese Night-Heron *Gorsachius goisagi* GT
Malaysian Night-Heron *Gorsachius melanolophus*
Boat-billed Heron *Cochlearius cochlearius*
Bare-throated Tiger-Heron *Tigrisoma mexicanum*
Fasciated Tiger-Heron *Tigrisoma fasciatum*
Rufescent Tiger-Heron *Tigrisoma lineatum*
Forest Bittern *Zonerodius heliosylus* GT
White-crested Tiger-Heron *Tigriornis leucolophus* PGT
Zigzag Heron *Zebrilus undulatus*

Stripe-backed Bittern *Ixobrychus involucris*
Least Bittern *Ixobrychus exilis*
Little Bittern *Ixobrychus minutus*
Black-backed Bittern *Ixobrychus novaezelandiae* E, LR
Yellow Bittern *Ixobrychus sinensis*
Von Schrenck's Bittern *Ixobrychus eurhythmus*
Cinnamon Bittern *Ixobrychus cinnamomeus*
African Dwarf Bittern *Ixobrychus sturmii*
Black Bittern *Dupetor flavicollis*
Pinnated Bittern *Botaurus pinnatus*
American Bittern *Botaurus lentiginosus*
Great Bittern *Botaurus stellaris*
Australasian Bittern *Botaurus poiciloptilus* GT

Scopidae
Hamerkop *Scopus umbretta*

Ciconiidae
Wood Stork *Mycteria americana*
Milky Stork *Mycteria cinerea* GT
Yellow-billed Stork *Mycteria ibis*
Painted Stork *Mycteria leucocephala* GT
Asian Openbill *Anastomus oscitans*
African Openbill *Anastomus lamelligerus*
Black Stork *Ciconia nigra*
Abdim's Stork *Ciconia abdimii*
Woolly-necked Stork *Ciconia episcopus*
Storm's Stork *Ciconia stormi* GT, LR
Maguari Stork *Ciconia maguari*
European White Stork *Ciconia ciconia*
Oriental White Stork *Ciconia boyciana* GT, LR
Black-necked Stork *Ephippiorhynchus asiaticus* GT
Saddle-billed Stork *Ephippiorhynchus senegalensis*
Jabiru *Jabiru mycteria* GT
Lesser Adjutant *Leptoptilos javanicus* GT
Greater Adjutant *Leptoptilos dubius* GT
Marabou *Leptoptilos crumeniferus*

Threskiornithidae
Sacred Ibis *Threskiornis aethiopicus*
Madagascar Sacred Ibis *Threskiornis bernieri* LR
Black-headed Ibis *Threskiornis melanocephalus* GT, LR
Australian White Ibis *Threskiornis molucca* LR
Straw-necked Ibis *Threskiornis spinicollis*
Black Ibis *Pseudibis papillosa*

White-shouldered Ibis *Pseudibis davisoni* GT, LR

Giant Ibis *Pseudibis gigantea* GT

Northern Bald Ibis *Geronticus eremita* GT

Southern Bald Ibis *Geronticus calvus* GT

Crested Ibis *Nipponia nippon* GT

Olive Ibis *Bostrychia olivacea*

Dwarf Olive Ibis *Bostrychia bocagei* GT, LR

Spot-breasted Ibis *Bostrychia rara*

Hadada Ibis *Bostrychia hagedash*

Wattled Ibis *Bostrychia carunculata*

Plumbeous Ibis *Harpiprion caerulescens*

Buff-necked Ibis *Theristicus caudatus*

Andean Ibis *Theristicus branickii* LR

Black-faced Ibis *Theristicus melanopis*

Sharp-tailed Ibis *Cercibis oxycerca*

Green Ibis *Mesembrinibis cayennensis*

Whispering Ibis *Phimosus infuscatus*

American White Ibis *Eudocimus albus* LR

Scarlet Ibis *Eudocimus ruber*

Glossy Ibis *Plegadis falcinellus*

White-faced Ibis *Plegadis chihi* LR

Puna Ibis *Plegadis ridgwayi*

Madagascar Crested Ibis *Lophotibis cristata* GT

Eurasian Spoonbill *Platalea leucorodia*

Black-faced Spoonbill *Platalea minor* GT

African Spoonbill *Platalea alba*

Royal Spoonbill *Platalea regia* LR

Yellow-billed Spoonbill *Platalea flavipes*

Roseate Spoonbill *Platalea ajaja*

Cathartidae

Turkey Vulture *Cathartes aura*

Lesser Yellow-headed Vulture *Cathartes burrovianus*

Greater Yellow-headed Vulture *Cathartes melambrotus*

American Black Vulture *Coragyps atratus*

American King Vulture *Sarcoramphus papa*

Californian Condor *Gymnogyps californianus* GT

Andean Condor *Vultur gryphus* GT

PHOENICOPTERIFORMES

Phoenicopteridae

Caribbean Flamingo *Phoenicopterus ruber*

Greater Flamingo *Phoenicopterus roseus* LR

Chilean Flamingo *Phoenicopterus chilensis* GT

Lesser Flamingo *Phoeniconaias minor* GT, LR

Andean Flamingo *Phoenicoparrus andinus* GT

Puna Flamingo *Phoenicoparrus jamesi* GT

FALCONIFORMES

Pandionidae

Osprey *Pandion haliaetus*

Accipitridae

African Baza *Aviceda cuculoides*

Madagascar Baza *Aviceda madagascariensis*

Jerdon's Baza *Aviceda jerdoni*

Pacific Baza *Aviceda subcristata*

Black Baza *Aviceda leuphotes*

Grey-headed Kite *Leptodon cayanensis*

White-collared Kite *Leptodon forbesi* GT, LR

Hook-billed Kite *Chondrohierax uncinatus*

Long-tailed Honey-Buzzard *Henicopernis longicauda*

Black Honey-Buzzard *Henicopernis infuscatus* GT, LR

European Honey-Buzzard *Pernis apivorus*

Oriental Honey-Buzzard *Pernis ptilorhyncus* LR

Barred Honey-Buzzard *Pernis celebensis* LR

American Swallow-tailed Kite *Elanoides forficatus*

Bat Hawk *Macheiramphus alcinus*

Pearl Kite *Gampsonyx swainsonii*

White-tailed Kite *Elanus leucurus* LR

Black-shouldered Kite *Elanus caeruleus*

Australian Black-shouldered Kite *Elanus axillaris* LR

Letter-winged Kite *Elanus scriptus*

African Swallow-tailed Kite *Chelictinia riocourii*

Snail Kite *Rostrhamus sociabilis*

Slender-billed Kite *Rostrhamus hamatus*

Double-toothed Kite *Harpagus bidentatus*

Rufous-thighed Kite *Harpagus diodon*

Plumbeous Kite *Ictinia plumbea* LR

Mississippi Kite *Ictinia mississippiensis*

Square-tailed Kite *Lophoictinia isura* GT

Black-breasted Kite *Hamirostra melanosternon*

Black Kite *Milvus migrans*

Yellow-billed Kite *Milvus aegyptius* LR

Black-eared Kite *Milvus lineatus* LR

Red Kite *Milvus milvus*

Whistling Kite *Haliastur sphenurus*

Brahminy Kite *Haliastur indus*

White-bellied Sea-Eagle *Haliaeetus leucogaster*

Sanford's Sea-Eagle *Haliaeetus sanfordi* GT, LR

African Fish-Eagle *Haliaeetus vocifer*

Madagascar Fish-Eagle *Haliaeetus vociferoides* GT

Pallas's Fish-Eagle *Haliaeetus leucoryphus* GT

Bald Eagle *Haliaeetus leucocephalus*

White-tailed Eagle *Haliaeetus albicilla* GT

Steller's Sea-Eagle *Haliaeetus pelagicus* GT

Lesser Fish-Eagle *Ichthyophaga humilis* GT

Grey-headed Fish-Eagle *Ichthyophaga ichthyaetus* GT

Monk Vulture *Aegypius monachus* GT

Lappet-faced Vulture *Torgos tracheliotus* GT

White-headed Vulture *Trigonoceps occipitalis*

Red-headed Vulture *Sarcogyps calvus* GT

Hooded Vulture *Necrosyrtes monachus*

Eurasian Griffon *Gyps fulvus*

Long-billed Griffon *Gyps indicus* GT

Himalayan Griffon *Gyps himalayensis* LR

Rüppell's Griffon *Gyps rueppellii*

Cape Griffon *Gyps coprotheres* GT

Indian White-rumped Vulture *Gyps bengalensis* GT

African White-backed Vulture *Gyps africanus*

Egyptian Vulture *Neophron percnopterus*

Lammergeier *Gypaetus barbatus*

Palm-nut Vulture *Gypohierax angolensis*

Short-toed Eagle *Circaetus gallicus*

Beaudouin's Snake-Eagle *Circaetus beaudouini* LR

Black-chested Snake-Eagle *Circaetus pectoralis* LR

Brown Snake-Eagle *Circaetus cinereus*

Southern Banded Snake-Eagle *Circaetus fasciolatus* GT

Smaller Banded Snake-Eagle *Circaetus cinerascens*

Bateleur *Terathopius ecaudatus*

Crested Serpent-Eagle *Spilornis cheela*

Philippine Serpent-Eagle *Spilornis holospilus* LR

Sulawesi Serpent-Eagle *Spilornis rufipectus* LR

Mountain Serpent-Eagle *Spilornis kinabaluensis* GT, LR

Nicobar Serpent-Eagle *Spilornis minimus* GT, LR

Great Nicobar Serpent-Eagle *Spilornis klossi* LR

Andaman Serpent-Eagle *Spilornis elgini* GT, LR

Congo Serpent-Eagle *Dryotriorchis spectabilis*

Madagascar Serpent-Eagle *Eutriorchis astur* GT

Dark Chanting-Goshawk *Melierax metabates*

Pale Chanting-Goshawk *Melierax canorus*

Eastern Chanting-Goshawk *Melierax poliopterus* LR

Gabar Goshawk *Melierax gabar*

African Harrier-Hawk *Polyboroides typus* LR

Madagascar Harrier-Hawk *Polyboroides radiatus*

Lizard Buzzard *Kaupifalco monogrammicus*

Grasshopper Buzzard *Butastur rufipennis*

Rufous-winged Buzzard *Butastur liventer*

White-eyed Buzzard *Butastur teesa*

Grey-faced Buzzard *Butastur indicus*

Spotted Harrier *Circus assimilis*

Black Harrier *Circus maurus* GT

Hen Harrier *Circus cyaneus*

Cinereous Harrier *Circus cinereus*

Pallid Harrier *Circus macrourus* GT

Pied Harrier *Circus melanoleucos*

Montagu's Harrier *Circus pygargus*

Eurasian Marsh Harrier *Circus aeruginosus*

Eastern Marsh Harrier *Circus spilonotus* LR

Papuan Harrier *Circus spilothorax* LR

Swamp Marsh Harrier *Circus approximans* LR

African Marsh Harrier *Circus ranivorus* LR

Réunion Harrier *Circus maillardi* GT, LR

Madagascar Harrier *Circus macrosceles* GT, LR

Long-winged Harrier *Circus buffoni*

Grey-bellied Goshawk *Accipiter poliogaster*

Crested Goshawk *Accipiter trivirgatus*

Sulawesi Crested Goshawk *Accipiter griseiceps*

Red-chested Goshawk *Accipiter toussenelii*

African Goshawk *Accipiter tachiro*

Chestnut-flanked Sparrowhawk *Accipiter castanilius*

Levant Sparrowhawk *Accipiter brevipes* LR

Shikra *Accipiter badius*

Nicobar Sparrowhawk *Accipiter butleri* GT, LR

Chinese Sparrowhawk *Accipiter soloensis*

Frances' Sparrowhawk *Accipiter francesii*

Spot-tailed Sparrowhawk *Accipiter trinotatus*

Brown Goshawk *Accipiter fasciatus*

Variable Goshawk *Accipiter hiogaster* LR

Grey Goshawk *Accipiter novaehollandiae*

Black-mantled Goshawk *Accipiter melanochlamys*

Pied Goshawk *Accipiter albogularis*

Fiji Goshawk *Accipiter rufitorques* LR

New Caledonia Sparrowhawk *Accipiter haplochrous* GT

Moluccan Goshawk *Accipiter henicogrammus* LR

Blue-and-grey Sparrowhawk *Accipiter luteoschistaceus* GT

Imitator Sparrowhawk *Accipiter imitator* GT

Grey-headed Goshawk *Accipiter poliocephalus*

New Britain Goshawk *Accipiter princeps* GT, LR

Tiny Hawk *Accipiter superciliosus*

Semicollared Hawk *Accipiter collaris* GT

Red-thighed Sparrowhawk *Accipiter erythropus* LR

African Little Sparrowhawk *Accipiter minullus*

Japanese Sparrowhawk *Accipiter gularis* LR

Besra *Accipiter virgatus*

Small Sparrowhawk *Accipiter nanus* GT, LR

Australian Collared Sparrowhawk *Accipiter cirrocephalus*

New Britain Collared Sparrowhawk *Accipiter brachyurus* GT

Rufous-necked Sparrowhawk *Accipiter erythrauchen*

Vinous-breasted Sparrowhawk *Accipiter rhodogaster*

Madagascar Sparrowhawk *Accipiter madagascariensis* GT

Ovampo Sparrowhawk *Accipiter ovampensis*

Eurasian Sparrowhawk *Accipiter nisus*

Rufous-breasted Sparrowhawk *Accipiter rufiventris* LR

Sharp-shinned Hawk *Accipiter striatus*

White-breasted Hawk *Accipiter chionogaster* LR

Plain-breasted Hawk *Accipiter ventralis* LR

Rufous-thighed Hawk *Accipiter erythronemius*

Cooper's Hawk *Accipiter cooperii*

Gundlach's Hawk *Accipiter gundlachi* GT

Bicolored Hawk *Accipiter bicolor*

Chilean Hawk *Accipiter chilensis* LR

Great Sparrowhawk *Accipiter melanoleucus*

Henst's Goshawk *Accipiter henstii* GT

Northern Goshawk *Accipiter gentilis*

Meyer's Goshawk *Accipiter meyerianus* LR

Chestnut-shouldered Goshawk *Erythrotriorchis buergersi* PGT

Red Goshawk *Erythrotriorchis radiatus* GT

Doria's Hawk *Megatriorchis doriae* GT

African Long-tailed Hawk *Urotriorchis macrourus*

Crane Hawk *Geranospiza caerulescens*

Barred Hawk *Leucopternis princeps*

Black-faced Hawk *Leucopternis melanops*

White-browed Hawk *Leucopternis kuhli*

White-necked Hawk *Leucopternis lacernulata* GT

Semiplumbeous Hawk *Leucopternis semiplumbea*

White Hawk *Leucopternis albicollis*

Grey-backed Hawk *Leucopternis occidentalis* GT

Mantled Hawk *Leucopternis polionota* PGT

Plumbeous Hawk *Leucopternis plumbea* GT, LR

Slate-colored Hawk *Leucopternis schistacea*

Common Black-Hawk *Buteogallus anthracinus*

Mangrove Black-Hawk *Buteogallus subtilis* LR

Rufous Crab Hawk *Buteogallus aequinoctialis*

Great Black-Hawk *Buteogallus urubitinga*

Savannah Hawk *Buteogallus meridionalis*

Black Solitary Eagle *Harpyhaliaetus solitarius* PGT, LR

Crowned Solitary Eagle *Harpyhaliaetus coronatus* GT

Black-collared Hawk *Busarellus nigricollis*

Black-chested Buzzard-Eagle *Geranouetus melanoleucus*

Harris' Hawk *Parabuteo unicinctus*

Grey Hawk *Asturina nitida*

Roadside Hawk *Buteo magnirostris*

White-rumped Hawk *Buteo leucorrhous*

Ridgway's Hawk *Buteo ridgwayi* GT

Red-shouldered Hawk *Buteo lineatus*

Broad-winged Hawk *Buteo platypterus*

Short-tailed Hawk *Buteo brachyurus*

White-throated Hawk *Buteo albigula* LR

Swainson's Hawk *Buteo swainsoni*

Galápagos Hawk *Buteo galapagoensis* GT

White-tailed Hawk *Buteo albicaudatus*

Red-backed Hawk *Buteo polyosoma*

Puna Hawk *Buteo poecilochrous* LR

Zone-tailed Hawk *Buteo albonotatus*

Hawaiian Hawk *Buteo solitarius* GT

Rufous-tailed Hawk *Buteo ventralis* LR
Red-tailed Hawk *Buteo jamaicensis*
Common Buzzard *Buteo buteo*
African Mountain Buzzard *Buteo oreophilus* LR
Madagascar Buzzard *Buteo brachypterus*
Long-legged Buzzard *Buteo rufinus*
Rough-legged Buzzard *Buteo lagopus*
Upland Buzzard *Buteo hemilasius* LR
Ferruginous Hawk *Buteo regalis* GT
African Red-tailed Buzzard *Buteo auguralis*
Archer's Buzzard *Buteo archeri* LR
Augur Buzzard *Buteo augur* LR
Jackal Buzzard *Buteo rufofuscus*
Guiana Crested Eagle *Morphnus guianensis* GT
Harpy Eagle *Harpia harpyja* GT
New Guinea Eagle *Harpyopsis novaeguineae* GT
Great Philippine Eagle *Pithecophaga jefferyi* GT
Asian Black Eagle *Ictinaetus malayensis*
Lesser Spotted Eagle *Aquila pomarina*
Greater Spotted Eagle *Aquila clanga* GT
Tawny Eagle *Aquila rapax*
Steppe Eagle *Aquila nipalensis* LR
Spanish Imperial Eagle *Aquila adalberti* GT, LR
Eastern Imperial Eagle *Aquila heliaca* GT
Gurney's Eagle *Aquila gurneyi* GT
Golden Eagle *Aquila chrysaetos*
Wedge-tailed Eagle *Aquila audax*
Verreaux's Eagle *Aquila verreauxii*
Wahlberg's Eagle *Aquila wahlbergi*
Bonelli's Eagle *Hieraaetus fasciatus*
African Hawk-Eagle *Hieraaetus spilogaster*
Booted Eagle *Hieraaetus pennatus*
Little Eagle *Hieraaetus morphnoides*
Ayres's Hawk-Eagle *Hieraaetus ayresii*
Rufous-bellied Hawk-Eagle *Hieraaetus kienerii*
Martial Eagle *Polemaetus bellicosus*
Long-crested Eagle *Lophaetus occipitalis*
Black-and-white Hawk-Eagle *Spizastur melanoleucus*
Cassin's Hawk-Eagle *Spizaetus africanus*
Changeable Hawk-Eagle *Spizaetus cirrhatus*
Mountain Hawk-Eagle *Spizaetus nipalensis*
Javan Hawk-Eagle *Spizaetus bartelsi* GT, LR
Sulawesi Hawk-Eagle *Spizaetus lanceolatus* LR
Philippine Hawk-Eagle *Spizaetus philippensis* GT, LR

Blyth's Hawk-Eagle *Spizaetus alboniger* LR
Wallace's Hawk-Eagle *Spizaetus nanus* GT, LR
Black Hawk-Eagle *Spizaetus tyrannus*
Ornate Hawk-Eagle *Spizaetus ornatus*
Crowned Hawk-Eagle *Stephanoaetus coronatus*
Black-and-chestnut Eagle *Oroaetus isidori*

Sagittariidae

Secretarybird *Sagittarius serpentarius*

Falconidae

Black Caracara *Daptrius ater*
Red-throated Caracara *Ibycter americanus*
Carunculated Caracara *Phalcoboenus carunculatus* LR
Mountain Caracara *Phalcoboenus megalopterus*
White-throated Caracara *Phalcoboenus albogularis* LR
Striated Caracara *Phalcoboenus australis* GT
Southern Crested Caracara *Caracara plancus*
Guadaloupe Caracara *Caracara lutosa* E
Northern Crested Caracara *Caracara cheriway* LR
Chimango Caracara *Milvago chimango*
Yellow-headed Caracara *Milvago chimachima*
Laughing Falcon *Herpetotheres cachinnans*
Barred Forest-Falcon *Micrastur ruficollis*
Plumbeous Forest-Falcon *Micrastur plumbeus* GT, LR
Lined Forest-Falcon *Micrastur gilvicollis* LR
Slaty-backed Forest-Falcon *Micrastur mirandollei*
Collared Forest-Falcon *Micrastur semitorquatus*
Buckley's Forest-Falcon *Micrastur buckleyi*
Spot-winged Falconet *Spiziapteryx circumcinctus*
African Pygmy Falcon *Polihierax semitorquatus*
White-rumped Falcon *Polihierax insignis* GT
Collared Falconet *Microhierax caerulescens*
Black-thighed Falconet *Microhierax fringillarius*
White-fronted Falconet *Microhierax latifrons* GT
Philippine Falconet *Microhierax erythrogenys*
Pied Falconet *Microhierax melanoleucos*
Lesser Kestrel *Falco naumanni* GT
Greater Kestrel *Falco rupicoloides*
Fox Kestrel *Falco alopex*
American Kestrel *Falco sparverius*
Eurasian Kestrel *Falco tinnunculus*

Madagascar Kestrel *Falco newtoni*
Mauritius Kestrel *Falco punctatus* GT
Seychelles Kestrel *Falco araea* GT
Spotted Kestrel *Falco moluccensis*
Nankeen Kestrel *Falco cenchroides*
Grey Kestrel *Falco ardosiaceus*
Dickinson's Kestrel *Falco dickinsoni*
Madagascar Banded Kestrel *Falco zoniventris*
Red-footed Falcon *Falco vespertinus*
Amur Falcon *Falco amurensis* LR
Red-necked Falcon *Falco chicquera*
Merlin *Falco columbarius*
Brown Falcon *Falco berigora*
New Zealand Falcon *Falco novaeseelandiae* GT
Eurasian Hobby *Falco subbuteo*
African Hobby *Falco cuvierii* LR
Oriental Hobby *Falco severus*
Australian Hobby *Falco longipennis*
Eleonora's Falcon *Falco eleonorae*
Sooty Falcon *Falco concolor*
Bat Falcon *Falco rufigularis* LR
Aplomado Falcon *Falco femoralis*
Grey Falcon *Falco hypoleucos* GT
Black Falcon *Falco subniger*
Lanner Falcon *Falco biarmicus*
Prairie Falcon *Falco mexicanus*
Laggar Falcon *Falco jugger* LR
Saker Falcon *Falco cherrug*
Gyrfalcon *Falco rusticolus*
Orange-breasted Falcon *Falco deiroleucus*
Taita Falcon *Falco fasciinucha* GT
Peregrine Falcon *Falco peregrinus*
Barbary Falcon *Falco pelegrinoides* LR

GRUIFORMES
Turnicidae
Small Buttonquail *Turnix sylvatica*
Red-backed Buttonquail *Turnix maculosa* LR
Sumba Buttonquail *Turnix everetti* GT, LR
Black-rumped Buttonquail *Turnix nana* LR
Luzon Buttonquail *Turnix worcesteri* PGT, LR
Hottentot Buttonquail *Turnix hottentotta*
Yellow-legged Buttonquail *Turnix tanki*
Barred Buttonquail *Turnix suscitator*
Madagascar Buttonquail *Turnix nigricollis*
Spotted Buttonquail *Turnix ocellata*

Black-breasted Buttonquail *Turnix melanogaster* GT
Painted Buttonquail *Turnix varia*
Chestnut-backed Buttonquail *Turnix castanota* GT
Buff-breasted Buttonquail *Turnix olivii* GT, LR
Red-chested Buttonquail *Turnix pyrrhothorax*
Little Buttonquail *Turnix velox*
Quail-Plover *Ortyxelos meiffrenii*

Gruidae
Common Crane *Grus grus*
Black-necked Crane *Grus nigricollis* GT
Hooded Crane *Grus monacha* GT
Sandhill Crane *Grus canadensis*
Red-crowned Crane *Grus japonensis* GT
Whooping Crane *Grus americana* GT
Japanese White-naped Crane *Grus vipio* GT
Sarus Crane *Grus antigone* GT
Brolga *Grus rubicunda*
Siberian White Crane *Grus leucogeranus* GT
Wattled Crane *Bugeranus carunculatus* GT
Demoiselle Crane *Anthropoides virgo*
Stanley Crane *Anthropoides paradisea* GT
Black Crowned Crane *Balearica pavonina* GT
Grey Crowned Crane *Balearica regulorum*

Aramidae
Limpkin *Aramus guarauna*

Psophiidae
Common Trumpeter *Psophia crepitans*
White-winged Trumpeter *Psophia leucoptera*
Green-winged Trumpeter *Psophia viridis*

Mesitornithidae
White-breasted Mesite *Mesitornis variegata* GT
Brown Mesite *Mesitornis unicolor* GT
Bensch's Monia *Monias benschi* GT

Rallidae
Nkulengu Rail *Himantornis haematopus*
Grey-throated Rail *Canirallus oculeus*
Madagascar Grey-throated Rail *Canirallus kioloides*
Chestnut-bellied Rail *Eulabeornis castaneoventris*
Bare-eyed Rail *Gymnocrex plumbeiventris*
Talaud Rail *Gymnocrex talaudensis* GT, LR
Blue-faced Rail *Gymnocrex rosenbergii* GT
Red-winged Woodrail *Aramides calopterus*

Slaty-breasted Woodrail *Aramides saracura*

Giant Woodrail *Aramides ypecaha*

Brown Woodrail *Aramides wolfi* GT

Little Woodrail *Aramides mangle*

Grey-necked Woodrail *Aramides cajanea*

Rufous-necked Woodrail *Aramides axillaris*

Uniform Crake *Amaurolimnas concolor*

Snoring Rail *Aramidopsis plateni* GT

Bar-winged Rail *Nesoclopeus poecilopterus* E, LR

Woodford's Rail *Nesoclopeus woodfordi* GT

Weka *Gallirallus australis* GT

New Caledonian Rail *Gallirallus lafresnayanus* PE

Lord Howe Island Rail *Gallirallus sylvestris* GT

Okinawa Rail *Gallirallus okinawae* GT

Barred Rail *Gallirallus torquatus*

New Britain Rail *Gallirallus insignis* GT

Buff-banded Rail *Gallirallus philippensis*

Roviana Rail *Gallirallus rovianae* GT, LR

Guam Rail *Gallirallus owstoni* GT

Wake Island Rail *Gallirallus wakensis* E

Tahitian Rail *Gallirallus pacificus* E

Dieffenbach's Rail *Gallirallus dieffenbachii* E

Chatham Islands Rail *Gallirallus modestus* E

Sharpe's Rail *Gallirallus sharpei* E

Slaty-breasted Rail *Gallirallus striatus*

Plumbeous Rail *Pardirallus sanguinolentus*

Blackish Rail *Pardirallus nigricans*

Spotted Rail *Pardirallus maculatus*

Madagascar White-throated Rail *Dryolimnas cuvieri*

Aldabra Rail *Dryolimnas aldabranus* LR

Luzon Rail *Lewinia mirificus* PGT, LR

Auckland Islands Rail *Lewinia muelleri* GT, LR

Lewin's Rail *Lewinia pectoralis*

African Water Rail *Rallus caerulescens*

Madagascar Rail *Rallus madagascariensis*

Water Rail *Rallus aquaticus*

Bogotá Rail *Rallus semiplumbeus* GT

King Rail *Rallus elegans* LR

Clapper Rail *Rallus longirostris*

Plain-flanked Rail *Rallus wetmorei* GT

Virginia Rail *Rallus limicola*

Ecuadorian Rail *Rallus aequatorialis* LR

Austral Rail *Rallus antarcticus* GT, LR

Inaccessible Island Rail *Atlantisia rogersi* GT

Rouget's Rail *Rougetius rougetii* GT

Zapata Rail *Cyanolimnas cerverai* GT

Chestnut Forest Rail *Rallina rubra*

White-striped Forest Rail *Rallina leucospila* GT

Forbes's Forest Rail *Rallina forbesi*

Mayr's Forest Rail *Rallina mayri* PGT

Red-necked Crake *Rallina tricolor*

Andaman Banded Crake *Rallina canningi* PGT

Red-legged Banded Crake *Rallina fasciata*

Slaty-legged Banded Crake *Rallina eurizonoides*

Red-chested Flufftail *Sarothrura rufa*

White-spotted Flufftail *Sarothrura pulchra*

Chestnut-headed Flufftail *Sarothrura lugens*

Streaky-breasted Flufftail *Sarothrura boehmi*

Buff-spotted Flufftail *Sarothrura elegans*

Striped Flufftail *Sarothrura affinis*

Madagascar Flufftail *Sarothrura insularis*

Slender-billed Flufftail *Sarothrura watersi* GT

White-winged Flufftail *Sarothrura ayresi* GT

Ocellated Crake *Micropygia schomburgkii*

Darwin's Rail *Coturnicops notatus*

Swinhoe's Yellow Crake *Coturnicops exquisitus* GT, LR

Yellow Rail *Coturnicops noveboracensis*

Chestnut-headed Crake *Anurolimnas castaneiceps*

Russet-crowned Crake *Anurolimnas viridis*

Black-banded Crake *Anurolimnas fasciatus*

Rusty-flanked Crake *Laterallus levraudi* GT

Ruddy Crake *Laterallus ruber*

Grey-breasted Crake *Laterallus exilis*

Galápagos Rail *Laterallus spilonotus* GT

Rufous-sided Crake *Laterallus melanophaius*

White-throated Crake *Laterallus albigularis* LR

Red-and-white Crake *Laterallus leucopyrrhus*

Black Rail *Laterallus jamaicensis* GT

Junín Rail *Laterallus tuerosi* GT, LR

Rufous-faced Crake *Laterallus xenopterus* GT

Corn Crake *Crex crex* GT

African Crake *Crecopsis egregia*

Yellow-breasted Crake *Poliolimnas flaviventer*

White-browed Crake *Poliolimnas cinereus*

Dot-winged Crake *Porzana spiloptera* GT

Ash-throated Crake *Porzana albicollis*

Hawaiian Crake *Porzana sandwichensis* E

Spotless Crake *Porzana tabuensis*

Kosrae Crake *Porzana monasa* E
Henderson Island Crake *Porzana atra* GT
Miller's Crake *Porzana nigra* E
Little Crake *Porzana parva*
Baillon's Crake *Porzana pusilla*
Laysan Crake *Porzana palmeri* E
Australian Spotted Crake *Porzana fluminea*
Eurasian Spotted Crake *Porzana porzana*
Sora *Porzana carolina*
Ruddy-breasted Crake *Porzana fusca*
Band-bellied Crake *Porzana paykullii* GT
Paint-billed Crake *Neocrex erythrops*
Colombian Crake *Neocrex colombianus* PGT, LR
Striped Crake *Aenigmatolimnas marginalis*
Plain Bushhen *Amaurornis olivaceus*
Moluccan Rufous-tailed Moorhen *Amaurornis moluccanus* LR
Talaud Bushhen *Amaurornis magnirostris* LR
Isabelline Bushhen *Amaurornis isabellinus*
African Black Crake *Amaurornis flavirostra*
Brown Crake *Amaurornis akool*
Olivier's Rail *Amaurornis olivieri* GT
Black-tailed Crake *Amaurornis bicolor*
White-breasted Waterhen *Amaurornis phoenicurus*
Drummer Rail *Habroptila wallacii* GT
New Guinea Flightless Rail *Habroptila inepta* GT
Watercock *Gallicrex cinerea*
Black-tailed Native-hen *Gallinula ventralis*
Tasmanian Native-hen *Gallinula mortierii*
Samoan Woodrail *Gallinula pacifica* PE
San Cristobal Mountain Rail *Gallinula silvestris* GT
Tristan Moorhen *Gallinula nesiotis* E
Dusky Moorhen *Gallinula tenebrosa*
Common Moorhen *Gallinula chloropus*
Lesser Moorhen *Gallinula angulata*
Spot-flanked Gallinule *Gallinula melanops*
Azure Gallinule *Porphyrio flavirostris*
Allen's Gallinule *Porphyrio alleni*
American Purple Gallinule *Porphyrio martinica*
Purple Swamphen *Porphyrio porphyrio*
White Gallinule *Porphyrio albus* E
Takahe *Porphyrio mantelli* GT
Red-gartered Coot *Fulica armillata*

White-winged Coot *Fulica leucoptera*
Red-fronted Coot *Fulica rufifrons*
Giant Coot *Fulica gigantea*
Horned Coot *Fulica cornuta* GT
Caribbean Coot *Fulica caribaea* GT, LR
Hawaiian Coot *Fulica alai* GT, LR
Andean Coot *Fulica ardesiaca* LR
American Coot *Fulica americana*
Eurasian Coot *Fulica atra*
Red-knobbed Coot *Fulica cristata*

Heliornithidae

African Finfoot *Podica senegalensis*
Masked Finfoot *Heliopais personata* GT
Sungrebe *Heliornis fulica*

Rhynochetidae

Kagu *Rhynochetos jubatus* GT

Eurypygidae

Sunbittern *Eurypyga helias*

Cariamidae

Red-legged Seriema *Cariama cristata*
Black-legged Seriema *Chunga burmeisteri*

Otididae

Little Bustard *Tetrax tetrax* GT
Denham's Bustard *Neotis denhami* GT
Ludwig's Bustard *Neotis ludwigii*
Nubian Bustard *Neotis nuba* GT
Heuglin's Bustard *Neotis heuglinii*
Houbara Bustard *Chlamydotis undulata* GT
Macqueen's Bustard *Chlamydotis macqueenii* GT, LR
Arabian Bustard *Ardeotis arabs*
Kori Bustard *Ardeotis kori*
Indian Bustard *Ardeotis nigriceps* GT
Australian Bustard *Ardeotis australis*
Great Bustard *Otis tarda* GT
Buff-crested Bustard *Lophotis gindiana* LR
Savile's Bustard *Lophotis savilei* LR
Red-crested Bustard *Lophitis ruficrista*
White-quilled Bustard *Afrotis afraoides* LR
Black Bustard *Afrotis afra*
Vigors's Bustard *Heterotetrax vigorsii*
Rüppell's Bustard *Heterotetrax rueppellii*
Little Brown Bustard *Heterotetrax humilis* GT
Blue Bustard *Eupodotis caerulescens* GT
White-bellied Bustard *Eupodotis senegalensis*
Black-bellied Bustard *Lissotis melanogaster*

Hartlaub's Bustard *Lissotis hartlaubii*

Bengal Florican *Houbaropsis bengalensis* GT

Lesser Florican *Sypheotides indica* GT

CHARADRIIFORMES
Pedionomidae

Plains-wanderer *Pedionomus torquatus* GT

Jacanidae

Lesser African Jacana *Microparra capensis*

Greater African Jacana *Actophilornis africanus*

Madagascar Jacana *Actophilornis albinucha*

Comb-crested Jacana *Irediparra gallinacea*

Pheasant-tailed Jacana *Hydrophasianus chirurgus*

Bronze-winged Jacana *Metopidius indicus*

Northern Jacana *Jacana spinosa*

Wattled Jacana *Jacana jacana* LR

Rostratulidae

Greater Painted-Snipe *Rostratula benghalensis*

American Painted-Snipe *Nycticryphes semicollaris*

Dromadidae

Crab-Plover *Dromas ardeola*

Haematopodidae

Eurasian Oystercatcher *Haematopus ostralegus*

Canary Island Oystercatcher *Haematopus niger* E

American Oystercatcher *Haematopus palliatus* LR

Australian Pied Oystercatcher *Haematopus longirostris* LR

South Island Oystercatcher *Haematopus finschi* LR

American Black Oystercatcher *Haematopus bachmani*

African Black Oystercatcher *Haematopus moquini* GT, LR

Variable Oystercatcher *Haematopus unicolor*

Chatham Islands Oystercatcher *Haematopus chathamensis* GT, LR

Magellanic Oystercatcher *Haematopus leucopodus*

Blackish Oystercatcher *Haematopus ater*

Sooty Oystercatcher *Haematopus fuliginosus*

Ibidorhynchidae

Ibisbill *Ibidorhyncha struthersii*

Recurvirostridae

Black-winged Stilt *Himantopus himantopus*

White-headed Stilt *Himantopus leucocephalus* LR

Black-tailed Stilt *Himantopus melanurus* LR

Black-necked Stilt *Himantopus mexicanus* LR

Hawaiian Stilt *Himantopus knudseni* LR

Black Stilt *Himantopus novaezelandiae* GT, LR

Banded Stilt *Cladorhynchus leucocephalus* LR

Eurasian Avocet *Recurvirostra avosetta*

American Avocet *Recurvirostra americana*

Red-necked Avocet *Recurvirostra novaehollandiae*

Andean Avocet *Recurvirostra andina*

Burhinididae

Eurasian Stone-Curlew *Burhinus oedicnemus*

Senegal Thick-knee *Burhinus senegalensis*

Water Thick-knee *Burhinus vermiculatus*

Spotted Thick-knee *Burhinus capensis*

Double-striped Thick-knee *Burhinus bistriatus*

Peruvian Thick-knee *Burhinus superciliaris*

Bush Thick-knee *Burhinus grallarius* GT, LR

Great Thick-knee *Esacus recurvirostris* LR

Great Australian Stone-Curlew *Esacus magnirostris* GT

Glareolidae

Egyptian Plover *Pluvianus aegyptius*

Cream-colored Courser *Cursorius cursor*

Somali Courser *Cursorius somalensis* LR

Burchell's Courser *Cursorius rufus*

Indian Courser *Cursorius coromandelicus*

Temminck's Courser *Cursorius temminckii* LR

Two-banded Courser *Smutsornis africanus*

Heuglin's Courser *Rhinoptilus cinctus*

Violet-tipped Courser *Rhinoptilus chalcopterus*

Jerdon's Courser *Rhinoptilus bitorquatus* GT

Australian Pratincole *Stiltia isabella*

Collared Pratincole *Glareola pratincola*

Oriental Pratincole *Glareola maldivarum* LR

Black-winged Pratincole *Glareola nordmanni* PGT

Madagascar Pratincole *Glareola ocularis*

Rock Pratincole *Glareola nuchalis*

Grey Pratincole *Glareola cinerea*

Small Pratincole *Glareola lactea*

Charadriidae

Northern Lapwing *Vanellus vanellus*

Long-toed Lapwing *Vanellus crassirostris*

Spur-winged Lapwing *Vanellus spinosus*

River Lapwing *Vanellus duvaucelii* LR

Black-headed Lapwing *Vanellus tectus*

Yellow-wattled Lapwing *Vanellus malabaricus*

White-headed Lapwing *Vanellus albiceps*

Senegal Lapwing *Vanellus lugubris*

Black-winged Lapwing *Vanellus melanopterus*

Crowned Lapwing *Vanellus coronatus*

Senegal Wattled Lapwing *Vanellus senegallus*

Spot-breasted Lapwing *Vanellus melanocephalus*

Brown-chested Lapwing *Vanellus superciliosus*

Sociable Lapwing *Vanellus gregarius* GT

White-tailed Lapwing *Vanellus leucurus*

Southern Lapwing *Vanellus chilensis*

Andean Lapwing *Vanellus resplendens*

Grey-headed Lapwing *Vanellus cinereus*

Red-wattled Lapwing *Vanellus indicus* LR

Javanese Lapwing *Vanellus macropterus* PE

Banded Lapwing *Vanellus tricolor* LR

Masked Lapwing *Vanellus miles*

Pied Lapwing *Hoploxypterus cayanus*

Blacksmith Plover *Anitibyx armatus*

European Golden-Plover *Pluvialis apricaria*

American Golden-Plover *Pluvialis dominica* LR

Pacific Golden-Plover *Pluvialis fulva* LR

Grey Plover *Pluvialis squatarola*

Red-breasted Plover *Charadrius obscurus* GT

Greater Ringed Plover *Charadrius hiaticula*

Semipalmated Plover *Charadrius semipalmatus* LR

Long-billed Plover *Charadrius placidus* LR

Little Ringed Plover *Charadrius dubius*

Wilson's Plover *Charadrius wilsonia*

Killdeer *Charadrius vociferus*

Piping Plover *Charadrius melodus* GT

Black-banded Sandplover *Charadrius thoracicus* GT

Kittlitz's Sandplover *Charadrius pecuarius*

St. Helena Sandplover *Charadrius sanctaehelenae* GT, LR

Forbes's Banded Plover *Charadrius forbesi*

Three-banded Plover *Charadrius tricollaris*

Kentish Plover *Charadrius alexandrinus*

White-fronted Plover *Charadrius marginatus* LR

Peruvian Plover *Charadrius occidentalis* LR

Red-capped Plover *Charadrius ruficapillus* LR

Malaysian Sandplover *Charadrius peronii* GT

Javan Plover *Charadrius javanicus* GT, LR

Chestnut-banded Plover *Charadrius pallidus*

Collared Plover *Charadrius collaris*

Double-banded Plover *Charadrius bicinctus*

Two-banded Plover *Charadrius falklandicus*

Puna Plover *Charadrius alticola* LR

Lesser Sandplover *Charadrius mongolus*

Greater Sandplover *Charadrius leschenaultii*

Caspian Plover *Charadrius asiaticus*

Oriental Plover *Charadrius veredus* LR

Rufous-chested Plover *Charadrius modestus*

Mountain Plover *Charadrius montanus* GT

Hooded Plover *Thinornis rubricollis* GT

New Zealand Shore Plover *Thinornis novaeseelandiae* GT

Black-fronted Dotterel *Elseyornis melanops*

Red-kneed Dotterel *Erythrogonys cinctus*

Mountain Dotterel *Eudromias morinellus*

Wrybill *Anarhynchus frontalis* GT

Diademed Sandpiper-Plover *Phegornis mitchellii* GT

Inland Dotterel *Peltohyas australis*

Tawny-throated Dotterel *Oreopholus ruficollis*

Magellanic Plover *Pluvianellus socialis* GT

Scolopacidae

Black-tailed Godwit *Limosa limosa*

Hudsonian Godwit *Limosa haemastica* LR

Bar-tailed Godwit *Limosa lapponica*

Marbled Godwit *Limosa fedoa*

Little Curlew *Numenius minutus* LR

Eskimo Curlew *Numenius borealis* GT

Eurasian Whimbrel *Numenius phaeopus*

Bristle-thighed Curlew *Numenius tahitiensis* GT

Slender-billed Curlew *Numenius tenuirostris* GT

Eurasian Curlew *Numenius arquata*

Far-eastern Curlew *Numenius madagascariensis* GT

Long-billed Curlew *Numenius americanus* GT, LR

Upland Sandpiper *Bartramia longicauda*

Spotted Redshank *Tringa erythropus*

Common Redshank *Tringa totanus*

Marsh Sandpiper *Tringa stagnatilis*

Common Greenshank *Tringa nebularia*

Nordmann's Greenshank *Tringa guttifer* GT

Greater Yellowlegs *Tringa melanoleuca*

Lesser Yellowlegs *Tringa flavipes*

Green Sandpiper *Tringa ochropus*

Solitary Sandpiper *Tringa solitaria*

Wood Sandpiper *Tringa glareola*

Common Sandpiper *Actitis hypoleucos*

Spotted Sandpiper *Actitis macularia* LR

Grey-tailed Tattler *Heteroscelus brevipes* LR

Wandering Tattler *Heteroscelus incanus*

Terek Sandpiper *Xenus cinereus*

Willet *Catoptrophorus semipalmatus*

Tuamotu Sandpiper *Prosobonia cancellata* GT

White-winged Sandpiper *Prosobonia leucoptera* E

Ellis's Sandpiper *Prosobonia ellisi* E

Ruddy Turnstone *Arenaria interpres*

Black Turnstone *Arenaria melanocephala*

Wilson's Phalarope *Steganopus tricolor*

Red-necked Phalarope *Phalaropus lobatus*

Red Phalarope *Phalaropus fulicarius*

Eurasian Woodcock *Scolopax rusticola*

Bukidnon Woodcock *Scolopax bukidnonensis* LR

Amami Woodcock *Scolopax mira* GT, LR

Dusky Woodcock *Scolopax saturata*

Rosenberg's Woodcock *Scolopax rosenbergii* LR

Sulawesi Woodcock *Scolopax celebensis* GT, LR

Moluccan Woodcock *Scolopax rochussenii* GT

American Woodcock *Scolopax minor*

Chatham Islands Snipe *Coenocorypha pusilla* GT

New Zealand Snipe *Coenocorypha aucklandica* GT

Solitary Snipe *Gallinago solitaria*

Latham's Snipe *Gallinago hardwickii* PGT

Wood Snipe *Gallinago nemoricola* GT, LR

Pintailed Snipe *Gallinago stenura*

Swinhoe's Snipe *Gallinago megala*

African Snipe *Gallinago nigripennis*

Madagascar Snipe *Gallinago macrodactyla* GT

Great Snipe *Gallinago media* GT

Common Snipe *Gallinago gallinago*

Wilson's Snipe *Gallinago delicata*

Magellan Snipe *Gallinago paraguaiae*

Puna Snipe *Gallinago andina* LR

Noble Snipe *Gallinago nobilis*

Giant Snipe *Gallinago undulata*

Cordilleran Snipe *Gallinago stricklandii* GT

Andean Snipe *Gallinago jamesoni*

Imperial Snipe *Gallinago imperialis* GT

Jack Snipe *Lymnocryptes minimus*

Short-billed Dowitcher *Limnodromus griseus*

Long-billed Dowitcher *Limnodromus scolopaceus* LR

Asian Dowitcher *Limnodromus semipalmatus* GT, LR

Surfbird *Aphriza virgata*

Red Knot *Calidris canutus*

Great Knot *Calidris tenuirostris*

Sanderling *Calidris alba*

Semipalmated Sandpiper *Calidris pusilla*

Western Sandpiper *Calidris mauri*

Red-necked Stint *Calidris ruficollis* LR

Little Stint *Calidris minuta*

Temminck's Stint *Calidris temminckii*

Long-toed Stint *Calidris subminuta* LR

Least Sandpiper *Calidris minutilla*

White-rumped Sandpiper *Calidris fuscicollis*

Baird's Sandpiper *Calidris bairdii*

Pectoral Sandpiper *Calidris melanotos*

Sharp-tailed Sandpiper *Calidris acuminata*

Purple Sandpiper *Calidris maritima*

Rock Sandpiper *Calidris ptilocnemis*

Dunlin *Calidris alpina*

Curlew Sandpiper *Calidris ferruginea*

Spoon-billed Sandpiper *Eurynorhynchus pygmeus* GT

Broad-billed Sandpiper *Limicola falcinellus*

Stilt Sandpiper *Micropalama himantopus*

Buff-breasted Sandpiper *Tryngites subruficollis* GT

Ruff *Philomachus pugnax*

Thinocoridae

Rufous-bellied Seedsnipe *Attagis gayi*

White-bellied Seedsnipe *Attagis malouinus*

Grey-breasted Seedsnipe *Thinocorus orbignyianus*

Least Seedsnipe *Thinocorus rumicivorus*

Chionididae

American Sheathbill *Chionis alba*

Black-faced Sheathbill *Chionis minor*

Stercorariidae

Great Skua *Stercorarius skua*
Chilean Skua *Stercorarius chilensis*
South Polar Skua *Stercorarius maccormicki* LR
Antarctic Skua *Stercorarius antarcticus* LR
Brown Skua *Stercorarius lonnbergi* LR
Pomarine Jaeger *Stercorarius pomarinus*
Parasitic Jaeger *Stercorarius parasiticus*
Long-tailed Jaeger *Stercorarius longicaudus*

Laridae

Magellan Gull *Gabianus scoresbii*
Pacific Gull *Gabianus pacificus*
Ivory Gull *Pagophila eburnea*
Lava Gull *Larus fuliginosus* GT
Grey Gull *Larus modestus*
Heermann's Gull *Larus heermanni* GT
White-eyed Gull *Larus leucophthalmus* GT
Sooty Gull *Larus hemprichii*
Belcher's Gull *Larus belcheri*
Olrog's Gull *Larus atlanticus* GT, LR
Black tailed Gull *Larus crassirostris*
Audouin's Gull *Larus audouinii* GT
Ring-billed Gull *Larus delawarensis*
Californian Gull *Larus californicus*
Mew Gull *Larus canus*
Herring Gull *Larus argentatus*
Heuglin's Gull *Larus heuglini* LR
Vega Gull *Larus vegae* LR
Caspian Gull *Larus cachinnans* LR
Armenian Gull *Larus armenicus* LR
Thayer's Gull *Larus thayeri* LR
Lesser Black-backed Gull *Larus fuscus*
Western Gull *Larus occidentalis*
Yellow-footed Gull *Larus livens* LR
Kelp Gull *Larus dominicanus*
Slaty-backed Gull *Larus schistisagus* LR
Greater Black-backed Gull *Larus marinus*
Glaucous-winged Gull *Larus glaucescens* LR
Glaucous Gull *Larus hyperboreus*
Iceland Gull *Larus glaucoides*
Great Black-headed Gull *Larus ichthyaetus*
Laughing Gull *Larus atricilla*
Franklin's Gull *Larus pipixcan*
Indian Black-headed Gull *Larus brunnicephalus* LR

Grey-headed Gull *Larus cirrocephalus*
Andean Gull *Larus serranus*
Silver Gull *Larus novaehollandiae*
Red-billed Gull *Larus scopulinus* LR
Hartlaub's Gull *Larus hartlaubii* LR
Mediterranean Gull *Larus melanocephalus*
Relict Gull *Larus relictus* GT, LR
Black-billed Gull *Larus bulleri* GT
Brown-hooded Gull *Larus maculipennis* LR
Common Black-headed Gull *Larus ridibundus*
Slender-billed Gull *Larus genei*
Bonaparte's Gull *Larus philadelphia*
Saunders's Gull *Larus saundersi* GT
Little Gull *Larus minutus*
Swallow-tailed Gull *Creagrus furcatus*
Sabine's Gull *Xema sabini*
Ross's Gull *Rhodostethia rosea*
Black-legged Kittiwake *Rissa tridactyla*
Red-legged Kittiwake *Rissa brevirostris* GT

Sternidae

Whiskered Tern *Chlidonias hybrida*
White-winged Black Tern *Chlidonias leucopterus*
Black Tern *Chlidonias niger*
Large-billed Tern *Phaetusa simplex*
Gull-billed Tern *Gelochelidon nilotica*
Caspian Tern *Hydroprogne caspia*
Greater Crested Tern *Thalasseus bergii*
Royal Tern *Thalasseus maximus*
Lesser Crested Tern *Thalasseus bengalensis*
Chinese Crested Tern *Thalasseus bernsteini* GT
Elegant Tern *Thalasseus elegans* GT
Sandwich Tern *Thalasseus sandvicensis*
River Tern *Sterna aurantia*
South American Tern *Sterna hirundinacea*
Common Tern *Sterna hirundo*
Arctic Tern *Sterna paradisaea*
Antarctic Tern *Sterna vittata*
Kerguelen Tern *Sterna virgata* GT
Forster's Tern *Sterna forsteri*
Trudeau's Tern *Sterna trudeaui*
Roseate Tern *Sterna dougallii*
White-fronted Tern *Sterna striata*
White-cheeked Tern *Sterna repressa*
Black-naped Tern *Sterna sumatrana*
Black-bellied Tern *Sterna acuticauda* GT

Grey-backed Tern *Sterna lunata*
Aleutian Tern *Sterna aleutica*
Bridled Tern *Sterna anaethetus*
Sooty Tern *Sterna fuscata*
Australian Fairy Tern *Sterna nereis* GT
Black-fronted Tern *Sterna albostriata* GT
Amazon Tern *Sterna superciliaris* LR
Damara Tern *Sterna balaenarum* GT
Chilean Tern *Sterna lorata* GT, LR
Little Tern *Sterna albifrons*
Least Tern *Sterna antillarum* LR
Saunders's Tern *Sterna saundersi* LR
Inca Tern *Larosterna inca*
Blue Noddy *Procelsterna cerulea*
Grey Noddy *Procelsterna albivitta* LR
Brown Noddy *Anous stolidus*
Black Noddy *Anous minutus* LR
Lesser Noddy *Anous tenuirostris*
Common White Tern *Gygis alba*
Little White Tern *Gygis microrhyncha* LR

Rynchopidae

Black Skimmer *Rynchops niger*
African Skimmer *Rynchops flavirostris* GT, LR
Indian Skimmer *Rynchops albicollis* GT, LR

Alcidae

Little Auk *Alle alle*
Razorbill *Alca torda*
Great Auk *Pinguinus impennis* E
Thick-billed Murre *Uria lomvia*
Common Murre *Uria aalge*
Black Guillemot *Cepphus grylle*
Pigeon Guillemot *Cepphus columba*
Spectacled Guillemot *Cepphus carbo*
Marbled Murrelet *Brachyramphus marmoratus* GT
Long-billed Murrelet *Brachyramphus perdix* LR
Kittlitz's Murrelet *Brachyramphus brevirostris*
Xantus's Murrelet *Synthliboramphus hypoleucus* GT, LR
Craveri's Murrelet *Synthliboramphus craveri* GT, LR
Ancient Murrelet *Synthliboramphus antiquus*
Crested Murrelet *Synthliboramphus wumizusume* GT
Cassin's Auklet *Ptychoramphus aleuticus*
Parakeet Auklet *Cyclorrhynchus psittacula*

Crested Auklet *Aethia cristatella*
Least Auklet *Aethia pusilla*
Whiskered Auklet *Aethia pygmaea*
Rhinoceros Auklet *Cerorhinca monocerata*
Atlantic Puffin *Fratercula arctica*
Horned Puffin *Fratercula corniculata*
Tufted Puffin *Fratercula cirrhata*

PTEROCLIFORMES
Pteroclididae

Tibetan Sandgrouse *Syrrhaptes tibetanus*
Pallas's Sandgrouse *Syrrhaptes paradoxus*
Pin-tailed Sandgrouse *Pterocles alchata*
Namaqua Sandgrouse *Pterocles namaqua*
Chestnut-bellied Sandgrouse *Pterocles exustus*
Spotted Sandgrouse *Pterocles senegallus*
Black-bellied Sandgrouse *Pterocles orientalis*
Crowned Sandgrouse *Pterocles coronatus*
Yellow-throated Sandgrouse *Pterocles gutturalis*
Variegated Sandgrouse *Pterocles burchelli*
Madagascar Sandgrouse *Pterocles personatus*
Black-faced Sandgrouse *Pterocles decoratus*
Lichtenstein's Sandgrouse *Pterocles lichtensteinii* LR
Double-banded Sandgrouse *Pterocles bicinctus*
Painted Sandgrouse *Pterocles indicus*
Four-banded Sandgrouse *Pterocles quadricinctus*

COLUMBIFORMES
Raphidae

Dodo *Raphus cucullatus* E
Réunion Solitaire *Raphus solitarius* E
Rodrigues Solitaire *Pezophaps solitaria* E

Columbidae

Rock-Pigeon *Columba livia*
Blue Hill Pigeon *Columba rupestris*
Snow Pigeon *Columba leuconota*
Speckled Pigeon *Columba guinea*
White-collared Pigeon *Columba albitorques*
Stock-Pigeon *Columba oenas*
Yellow-eyed Pigeon *Columba eversmanni* GT
Somali Pigeon *Columba oliviae* PGT, LR
Common Wood-Pigeon *Columba palumbus*
Trocaz Pigeon *Columba trocaz* GT
Bolle's Pigeon *Columba bollii* GT
African Wood-Pigeon *Columba unicincta*
Laurel Pigeon *Columba junoniae* GT

Cameroon Olive Pigeon *Columba sjostedti* LR

African Olive Pigeon *Columba arquatrix*

São Tomé Olive Pigeon *Columba thomensis* GT, LR

Comoro Olive Pigeon *Columba pollenii* GT, LR

Speckled Wood-Pigeon *Columba hodgsonii*

White-naped Pigeon *Columba albinucha* GT, LR

Ashy Wood-Pigeon *Columba pulchricollis*

Nilgiri Wood-Pigeon *Columba elphinstonii* GT

Sri Lanka Wood-Pigeon *Columba torringtoni* GT

Pale-capped Pigeon *Columba punicea* GT

Silvery Pigeon *Columba argentina* GT

Andaman Wood-Pigeon *Columba palumboides* GT

Japanese Wood-Pigeon *Columba janthina* GT

White-throated Pigeon *Columba vitiensis*

White-headed Pigeon *Columba leucomela*

Bonin Wood-Pigeon *Columba versicolor* E

Ryukyu Wood-Pigeon *Columba jouyi* E

Yellow-legged Pigeon *Columba pallidiceps* GT

White-crowned Pigeon *Patagioenas leucocephala*

Scaly-naped Pigeon *Columba squamosa* LR

Scaled Pigeon *Columba speciosa*

Picazuro Pigeon *Columba picazuro*

Bare-eyed Pigeon *Columba corensis*

American Spotted Pigeon *Columba maculosa*

Band-tailed Pigeon *Patagioenas fasciata*

Chilean Pigeon *Columba araucana*

Jamaican Band-tailed Pigeon *Columba caribaea* GT

Rufous Pigeon *Columba cayennensis*

Red-billed Pigeon *Patagioenas flavirostris*

Salvin's Pigeon *Columba oenops* GT

Plain Pigeon *Columba inornata* GT

Plumbeous Pigeon *Columba plumbea*

Ruddy Pigeon *Columba subvinacea*

Short-billed Pigeon *Columba nigrirostris*

Dusky Pigeon *Columba goodsoni* LR

Eastern Bronze-naped Pigeon *Columba delegorguei*

Madagascar Turtle-Dove *Columba picturata*

Bronze-naped Pigeon *Columba iriditorques*

São Tomé Bronze-naped Pigeon *Columba malherbii*

Mauritius Pink Pigeon *Columba mayeri* GT

European Turtle-Dove *Streptopelia turtur*

Dusky Turtle-Dove *Streptopelia lugens*

Pink-bellied Turtle-Dove *Streptopelia hypopyrrha* LR

Oriental Turtle-Dove *Streptopelia orientalis*

Island Collared-Dove *Streptopelia bitorquata* LR

Eurasian Collared-Dove *Streptopelia decaocto*

African Collared-Dove *Streptopelia roseogrisea* LR

Ringed Turtle-Dove *Streptopelia risoria* LR

African White-winged Dove *Streptopelia reichenowi* GT, LR

Mourning Collared-Dove *Streptopelia decipiens*

Red-eyed Dove *Streptopelia semitorquata*

Ring-necked Dove *Streptopelia capicola*

Vinaceous Turtle-Dove *Streptopelia vinacea*

Red Collared-Dove *Streptopelia tranquebarica*

Spotted Turtle-Dove *Streptopelia chinensis*

Laughing Turtle-Dove *Streptopelia senegalensis*

African Lemon Dove *Aplopelia larvata*

São Tomé Lemon Dove *Aplopelia simplex* LR

Barred Cuckoo-Dove *Macropygia unchall*

Brown Cuckoo-Dove *Macropygia amboinensis*

Philippine Cuckoo-Dove *Macropygia tenuirostris* LR

Large Brown Cuckoo-Dove *Macropygia phasianella* LR

Enggano Cuckoo-Dove *Macropygia cinnamomea* LR

Ruddy Cuckoo-Dove *Macropygia emiliana* LR

Dusky Cuckoo-Dove *Macropygia magna* LR

Andamans Cuckoo-Dove *Macropygia rufipennis* GT

Mackinlay's Cuckoo-Dove *Macropygia mackinlayi* LR

Little Cuckoo-Dove *Macropygia ruficeps*

Black-billed Cuckoo-Dove *Macropygia nigrirostris* LR

Great Cuckoo-Dove *Reinwardtoena reinwardtii*

Pied Cuckoo-Dove *Reinwardtoena browni*

Crested Cuckoo-Dove *Reinwardtoena crassirostris* GT

White-faced Cuckoo-Dove *Turacoena manadensis*

Black Cuckoo-Dove *Turacoena modesta* GT

Emerald-spotted Wood-Dove *Turtur chalcospilos*

Black-billed Wood-Dove *Turtur abyssinicus*

Blue-spotted Wood-Dove *Turtur afer*

White-breasted Wood-Dove *Turtur tympanistria*

Blue-headed Wood-Dove *Turtur brehmeri*

Namaqua Dove *Oena capensis*

Common Emerald Dove *Chalcophaps indica*

Stephan's Ground-Dove *Chalcophaps stephani*

New Guinea Black Bronzewing *Henicophaps albifrons*

New Britain Bronzewing *Henicophaps foersteri* GT

Common Bronzewing *Phaps chalcoptera*

Brush Bronzewing *Phaps elegans*

Flock Bronzewing *Phaps histrionica*

Crested Pigeon *Geophaps lophotes*

Spinifex Pigeon *Geophaps plumifera*

Red-plumed Pigeon *Geophaps ferruginea* LR

Squatter Pigeon *Geophaps scripta*

Partridge Pigeon *Geophaps smithii* GT, LR

Chestnut-quilled Rock-Pigeon *Petrophassa rufipennis*

White-quilled Rock-Pigeon *Petrophassa albipennis*

Diamond Dove *Geopelia cuneata*

Zebra Ground-Dove *Geopelia striata*

Barred Dove *Geopelia maugeus* LR

Peaceful Dove Geopelia placida LR

Bar-shouldered Dove *Geopelia humeralis*

Wonga Pigeon *Leucosarcia melanoleuca*

Passenger Pigeon *Ectopistes migratorius* E

Mourning Dove *Zenaida macroura*

Socorro Dove *Zenaida graysoni* GT, LR

Eared Dove *Zenaida auriculata* LR

Zenaida Dove *Zenaida aurita*

Galápagos Dove *Zenaida galapagoensis*

White-winged Dove *Zenaida asiatica*

West Peruvian Dove *Zenaida meloda* LR

Common Ground-Dove *Columbina passerina*

Plain-breasted Ground-Dove *Columbina minuta*

Ecuadorian Ground-Dove *Columbina buckleyi* LR

Ruddy Ground-Dove *Columbina talpacoti*

Picui Ground-Dove *Columbina picui*

Gold-billed Ground-Dove *Columbina cruziana*

Blue-eyed Ground-Dove *Columbina cyanopis* GT

Inca Dove *Scardafella inca* LR

Scaly Dove *Scardafella squammata*

Blue Ground-Dove *Claravis pretiosa*

Purple-barred Ground-Dove *Claravis godefrida* GT

Purple-breasted Ground-Dove *Claravis mondetoura*

Bare-faced Ground-Dove *Metriopelia ceciliae*

Bare-eyed Ground-Dove *Metriopelia morenoi*

Black-winged Ground-Dove *Metriopelia melanoptera*

Bronze-winged Ground-Dove *Metriopelia aymara*

Long-tailed Ground-Dove *Uropelia campestris*

White-tipped Dove *Leptotila verreauxi*

White-faced Dove *Leptotila megalura* LR

Grey-fronted Dove *Leptotila rufaxilla* LR

Grey-headed Dove *Leptotila plumbeiceps* LR

Brown-backed Dove *Leptotila battyi* GT, LR

Pallid Dove *Leptotila pallida*

Grenada Dove *Leptotila wellsi* GT, LR

White-bellied Dove *Leptotila jamaicensis*

Cassin's Dove *Leptotila cassini*

Buff-bellied Dove *Leptotila ochraceiventris* GT

Tolima Dove *Leptotila conoveri* GT

Veracruz Quail-Dove *Geotrygon carrikeri* GT, LR

Lawrence's Quail-Dove *Geotrygon lawrencii*

Costa Rican Quail-Dove *Geotrygon costaricensis*

Russet-crowned Quail-Dove *Geotrygon goldmani* GT, LR

Saphire Quail-Dove *Geotrygon saphirina*

Purple-crowned Quail-Dove *Geotrygon purpurata* LR

Grey-faced Quail-Dove *Geotrygon caniceps* GT

Crested Quail-Dove *Geotrygon versicolor* GT

Olive-backed Quail-Dove *Geotrygon veraguensis*

White-faced Quail-Dove *Geotrygon albifacies* LR

Rufous-breasted Quail-Dove *Geotrygon chiriquensis* LR

Lined Quail-Dove *Geotrygon linearis*

White-throated Quail-Dove *Geotrygon frenata*

Key West Quail-Dove *Geotrygon chrysia* LR

Bridled Quail-Dove *Geotrygon mystacea*

Violaceous Quail-Dove *Geotrygon violacea*

Ruddy Quail-Dove *Geotrygon montana*

Blue-headed Quail-Dove *Starnoenas cyanocephala* GT

Nicobar Pigeon *Caloenas nicobarica* GT

Spotted Green-Pigeon *Caloenas maculata* E18

Luzon Bleeding-heart *Gallicolumba luzonica* GT

Mindanao Bleeding-heart *Gallicolumba criniger* GT, LR

Mindoro Bleeding-heart *Gallicolumba platenae* GT, LR

Negros Bleeding-heart *Gallicolumba keayi* GT, LR

Sulu Bleeding-heart *Gallicolumba menagei* GT, LR

Cinnamon Ground-Dove *Gallicolumba rufigula*

Norfolk Island Dove *Gallicolumba norfolciensis* E

Sulawesi Ground-Dove *Gallicolumba tristigmata*

White-breasted Ground-Dove *Gallicolumba jobiensis*

Truk Island Ground-Dove *Gallicolumba kubaryi* GT, LR

Society Islands Ground-Dove *Gallicolumba erythroptera* GT

White-throated Ground-Dove *Gallicolumba xanthonura* GT

Friendly Quail-Dove *Gallicolumba stairi* GT

Santa Cruz Ground-Dove *Gallicolumba sanctaecrucis* GT

Tanna Ground-Dove *Gallicolumba ferruginea* E

Thick-billed Ground-Dove *Gallicolumba salamonis* GT

Marquesan Ground-Dove *Gallicolumba rubescens* GT

Grey-breasted Quail-Dove *Gallicolumba beccarii*

Palau Ground-Dove *Gallicolumba canifrons* GT

Wetar Island Ground-Dove *Gallicolumba hoedtii* GT

Thick-billed Ground-Pigeon *Trugon terrestris*

Solomon Islands Crowned-Pigeon *Microgoura meeki* E

Pheasant Pigeon *Otidiphaps nobilis*

Western Crowned-Pigeon *Goura cristata* GT

Maroon-breasted Crowned-Pigeon *Goura scheepmakeri* GT

Victoria Crowned-Pigeon *Goura victoria* GT

Tooth-billed Pigeon *Didunculus strigirostris* GT

White-eared Brown-Dove *Phapitreron leucotis*

Amethyst Brown-Dove *Phapitreron amethystina*

Tawitawi Brown-Dove *Phapitreron cinereiceps* GT, LR

Mindanao Brown-Dove *Phapitreron brunneiceps* GT

Cinnamon-headed Green-Pigeon *Treron fulvicollis* GT

Little Green-Pigeon *Treron olax*

Pink-necked Green-Pigeon *Treron vernans*

Orange-breasted Green-Pigeon *Treron bicincta*

Pompadour Green-Pigeon *Treron pompadora*

Thick-billed Green-Pigeon *Treron curvirostra*

Grey-cheeked Green-Pigeon *Treron griseicauda* LR

Sumba Green-Pigeon *Treron teysmannii* GT, LR

Flores Green-Pigeon *Treron floris* GT, LR

Timor Green-Pigeon *Treron psittacea* GT, LR

Large Green-Pigeon *Treron capellei* GT

Yellow-footed Green-Pigeon *Treron phoenicoptera*

Bruce's Green-Pigeon *Treron waalia*

Madagascar Green-Pigeon *Treron australis*

African Green-Pigeon *Treron calva* LR

Comoro Green-Pigeon *Treron griveaudi* LR

Pemba Green-Pigeon *Treron pembaensis* LR

São Tomé Green-Pigeon *Treron sanctithomae* LR

Pintailed Green-Pigeon *Treron apicauda*

Sumatran Green-Pigeon *Treron oxyura* GT

Yellow-vented Green-Pigeon *Treron seimundi*

Wedge-tailed Green-Pigeon *Treron sphenura*

White-bellied Green-Pigeon *Treron sieboldii*

Whistling Green-Pigeon *Treron formosae* GT

Black-backed Fruit-Dove *Ptilinopus cinctus*

Black-banded Fruit-Dove *Ptilinopus alligator* LR

Red-naped Fruit-Dove *Ptilinopus dohertyi* GT, LR

Pink-headed Fruit-Dove *Ptilinopus porphyreus* LR

Flame-breasted Fruit-Dove *Ptilinopus marchei* GT

Cream-bellied Fruit-Dove *Ptilinopus merrilli* GT

Yellow-breasted Fruit-Dove *Ptilinopus occipitalis*

Red-eared Fruit-Dove *Ptilinopus fischeri* LR

Jambu Fruit-Dove *Ptilinopus jambu* GT

Maroon-chinned Fruit-Dove *Ptilinopus subgularis* GT, LR

Black-chinned Fruit-Dove *Ptilinopus leclancheri*

Scarlet-breasted Fruit-Dove *Ptilinopus bernsteinii*

Wompoo Fruit-Dove *Ptilinopus magnificus*

Pink-spotted Fruit-Dove *Ptilinopus perlatus*

Ornate Fruit-Dove *Ptilinopus ornatus*

Silver-shouldered Fruit-Dove *Ptilinopus tannensis* GT

Orange-fronted Fruit-Dove *Ptilinopus aurantiifrons*

Wallace's Fruit-Dove *Ptilinopus wallacii*

Superb Fruit-Dove *Ptilinopus superbus*

Many-colored Fruit-Dove *Ptilinopus perousii* LR

Purple-capped Fruit-Dove *Ptilinopus porphyraceus*

Palau Fruit-Dove *Ptilinopus pelewensis*

Rarotonga Fruit-Dove *Ptilinopus rarotongensis* GT

Marianas Fruit-Dove *Ptilinopus roseicapilla* GT

Rose-crowned Fruit-Dove *Ptilinopus regina*

Silver-capped Fruit-Dove *Ptilinopus richardsii*

Grey-green Fruit-Dove *Ptilinopus purpuratus*

Mahatea Fruit-Dove *Ptilinopus chalcurus* GT, LR

Atoll Fruit-Dove *Ptilinopus coralensis* GT, LR

Grey's Fruit-Dove *Ptilinopus greyii*

Rapa Island Fruit-Dove *Ptilinopus huttoni* GT

White-capped Fruit-Dove *Ptilinopus dupetithouarsii*

Moustached Fruit-Dove *Ptilinopus mercierii* E

Henderson Island Fruit-Dove *Ptilinopus insularis* GT

Lilac-capped Fruit-Dove *Ptilinopus coronulatus*

Crimson-capped Fruit-Dove *Ptilinopus pulchellus*

Blue-capped Fruit-Dove *Ptilinopus monacha* GT

White-bibbed Fruit-Dove *Ptilinopus rivoli*

Yellow-bibbed Fruit-Dove *Ptilinopus solomonensis* LR

Claret-breasted Fruit-Dove *Ptilinopus viridis*

White-headed Fruit-Dove *Ptilinopus eugeniae* GT, LR

Orange-bellied Fruit-Dove *Ptilinopus iozonus* LR

Knob-billed Fruit-Dove *Ptilinopus insolitus* LR

Grey-headed Fruit-Dove *Ptilinopus hyogastra*

Carunculated Fruit-Dove *Ptilinopus granulifrons* GT

Black-naped Fruit-Dove *Ptilinopus melanospila*

Dwarf Fruit-Dove *Ptilinopus naina*

Negros Fruit-Dove *Ptilinopus arcanus* GT

Orange Dove *Ptilinopus victor* LR

Golden Dove *Ptilinopus luteovirens*

Yellow-headed Fruit-Dove *Ptilinopus layardi* GT, LR

Cloven-feathered Dove *Drepanoptila holosericea* GT

Mauritius Blue-Pigeon *Alectroenas nitidissima*

Madagascar Blue-Pigeon *Alectroenas madagascariensis*

Comoro Blue-Pigeon *Alectroenas sganzini*

Seychelles Blue-Pigeon *Alectroenas pulcherrima*

Pink-bellied Imperial-Pigeon *Ducula poliocephala* GT

White-bellied Imperial-Pigeon *Ducula forsteni* LR

Mindoro Imperial-Pigeon *Ducula mindorensis* GT, LR

Grey-headed Imperial-Pigeon *Ducula radiata*

Spotted Imperial-Pigeon *Ducula carola* GT

Green Imperial-Pigeon *Ducula aenea*

White-spectacled Imperial-Pigeon *Ducula perspicillata*

Elegant Imperial-Pigeon *Ducula concinna*

Pacific Imperial-Pigeon *Ducula pacifica*

Micronesian Imperial-Pigeon *Ducula oceanica*

Polynesian Imperial-Pigeon *Ducula aurorae* GT

Nukuhiva Imperial-Pigeon *Ducula galeata* GT

Red-knobbed Imperial-Pigeon *Ducula rubricera*

Spice Imperial-Pigeon *Ducula myristicivora*

Purple-tailed Imperial-Pigeon *Ducula rufigaster*

Cinnamon-bellied Imperial-Pigeon *Ducula basilica* LR

Finsch's Imperial-Pigeon *Ducula finschii* LR

Shining Imperial-Pigeon *Ducula chalconota*

Island Imperial-Pigeon *Ducula pistrinaria*

Pink-headed Imperial-Pigeon *Ducula rosacea* GT

Christmas Island Imperial-Pigeon *Ducula whartoni* GT, LR

Grey Imperial-Pigeon *Ducula pickeringii* GT

Peale's Imperial-Pigeon *Ducula latrans*

Chestnut-bellied Imperial-Pigeon *Ducula brenchleyi* GT

Baker's Imperial-Pigeon *Ducula bakeri* GT

New Caledonian Imperial-Pigeon *Ducula goliath* GT

Pinon Imperial-Pigeon *Ducula pinon*

Black Imperial-Pigeon *Ducula melanochroa*

Collared Imperial-Pigeon *Ducula mullerii*

Banded Imperial-Pigeon *Ducula zoeae*

Mountain Imperial-Pigeon *Ducula badia*

Dark-backed Imperial-Pigeon *Ducula lacernulata*

Timor Imperial-Pigeon *Ducula cineracea* GT

Pied Imperial-Pigeon *Ducula bicolor* LR

Silver-tipped Imperial-Pigeon *Ducula luctuosa* LR

Australian Pied Imperial-Pigeon *Ducula spilorrhoa* LR

Yellow-tinted Imperial-Pigeon *Ducula subflavescens* GT, LR

Topknot Pigeon *Lopholaimus antarcticus*

New Zealand Fruit-Pigeon *Hemiphaga novaeseelandiae* GT

Sombre Pigeon *Cryptophaps poecilorrhoa*

Papuan Mountain-Pigeon *Gymnophaps albertisii*

Long-tailed Mountain-Pigeon *Gymnophaps mada*

Pale Mountain-Pigeon *Gymnophaps solomonensis*

SITTACIFORMES

Loridae

Black Lory *Chalcopsitta atra*

Rajah Lory *Chalcopsitta insignis* LR

Duyvenbode's Lory *Chalcopsitta duivenbodei* LR

Yellow-streaked Lory *Chalcopsitta sintillata*

Cardinal Lory *Chalcopsitta cardinalis*

Black-winged Lory *Eos cyanogenia* GT, LR

Violet-necked Lory *Eos squamata* LR

Blue-streaked Lory *Eos reticulata* GT, LR

Red-and-blue Lory *Eos histrio* GT

Red Lory *Eos bornea*

Blue-eared Lory *Eos semilarvata* LR

Dusky Lory *Pseudeos fuscata*

Ornate Lorikeet *Trichoglossus ornatus* LR

Rainbow Lorikeet *Trichoglossus haematodus*

Red-collared Lorikeet *Trichoglossus rubritorquis* LR

Pohnpei Lorikeet *Trichoglossus rubiginosus* LR

Mindanao Lorikeet *Trichoglossus johnstoniae* GT, LR

Yellow-and-green Lorikeet *Trichoglossus flavoviridis* LR

Scaly-breasted Lorikeet *Trichoglossus chlorolepidotus*

Perfect Lorikeet *Trichoglossus euteles* LR

Goldie's Lorikeet *Trichoglossus goldiei*

Varied Lorikeet *Psitteuteles versicolor*

Iris Lorikeet *Psitteuteles iris* GT

Purple-bellied Lory *Lorius hypoinochrous* LR

Western Black-capped Lory *Lorius lory*

White-naped Lory *Lorius albidinuchus* GT

Yellow-bibbed Lory *Lorius chlorocercus*

Purple-naped Lory *Lorius domicella* GT, LR

Chattering Lory *Lorius garrulus* GT, LR

Collared Lory *Phigys solitarius*

Blue-crowned Lory *Vini australis*

Kuhl's Lory *Vini kuhlii* GT

Stephen's Lory *Vini stepheni* GT

Tahitian Lory *Vini peruviana* GT

Ultramarine Lory *Vini ultramarina* GT

Musk Lorikeet *Glossopsitta concinna*

Little Lorikeet *Glossopsitta pusilla*

Purple-crowned Lorikeet *Glossopsitta porphyrocephala*

Palm Lorikeet *Charmosyna palmarum* GT

Red-chinned Lorikeet *Charmosyna rubrigularis*

Meek's Lorikeet *Charmosyna meeki* GT

Blue-fronted Lorikeet *Charmosyna toxopei* GT

Striated Lorikeet *Charmosyna multistriata* GT

Wilhelmina's Lorikeet *Charmosyna wilhelminae*

Red-spotted Lorikeet *Charmosyna rubronotata*

Red-flanked Lorikeet *Charmosyna placentis*

New Caledonian Lorikeet *Charmosyna diadema* PE

Red-throated Lorikeet *Charmosyna amabilis* GT

Duchess Lorikeet *Charmosyna margarethae* GT

Fairy Lorikeet *Charmosyna pulchella*

Josephine's Lorikeet *Charmosyna josefinae*

Papuan Lorikeet *Charmosyna papou*

Whiskered Lorikeet *Oreopsittacus arfaki*

Musschenbroek's Lorikeet *Neopsittacus musschenbroekii*

Emerald Lorikeet *Neopsittacus pullicauda*

Cacatuidae

Palm Cockatoo *Probosciger aterrimus*

Long-billed Black-Cockatoo *Calyptorhynchus baudinii* GT, LR

Short-billed Black-Cockatoo *Calyptorhynchus latirostris* GT, LR

Yellow-tailed Black-Cockatoo *Calyptorhynchus funereus*

Red-tailed Black-Cockatoo *Calyptorhynchus banksii*

Glossy Black-Cockatoo *Calyptorhynchus lathami* GT

Gang-gang Cockatoo *Callocephalon fimbriatum*

Galah *Eolophus roseicapillus*

Major Mitchell's Cockatoo *Cacatua leadbeateri*

Yellow-crested Cockatoo *Cacatua sulphurea* GT

Sulphur-crested Cockatoo *Cacatua galerita* LR

Blue-eyed Cockatoo *Cacatua ophthalmica* LR

Salmon-crested Cockatoo *Cacatua moluccensis* GT, LR

Great White Cockatoo *Cacatua alba* GT

Philippine Islands Cockatoo *Cacatua haematuropygia* GT

Tanimbar Cockatoo *Cacatua goffini* GT, LR

Little Corella *Cacatua sanguinea*

Eastern Long-billed Corella *Cacatua tenuirostris*

Western Long-billed Corella *Cacatua pastinator*

Ducorps's Cockatoo *Cacatua ducorpsii*

Cockatiel *Nymphicus hollandicus*

Psittacidae

Norfolk Island Kaka *Nestor productus* E

New Zealand Kaka *Nestor meridionalis* GT

Kea *Nestor notabilis* GT

Buff-faced Pygmy-Parrot *Micropsitta pusio*

Yellow-capped Pygmy-Parrot *Micropsitta keiensis* LR

Geelvink Pygmy-Parrot *Micropsitta geelvinkiana* GT, LR

Meek's Pygmy-Parrot *Micropsitta meeki*

Finsch's Pygmy-Parrot *Micropsitta finschii*

Red-breasted Pygmy-Parrot *Micropsitta bruijnii*

Orange-breasted Fig-Parrot *Opopsitta gulielmitertii*

Double-eyed Fig-Parrot *Opopsitta diophthalma*

Large Fig-Parrot *Psittaculirostris desmarestii*

Edwards's Fig-Parrot *Psittaculirostris edwardsii*

Salvadori's Fig-Parrot *Psittaculirostris salvadorii* GT

Guaiabero *Bolbopsittacus lunulatus*

Blue-rumped Parrot *Psittinus cyanurus* GT

Brehm's Tiger-Parrot *Psittacella brehmii*

Painted Tiger-Parrot *Psittacella picta*

Modest Tiger-Parrot *Psittacella modesta*

Madarasz's Tiger-Parrot *Psittacella madaraszi*

Red-cheeked Parrot *Geoffroyus geoffroyi*

Blue-collared Parrot *Geoffroyus simplex*

Singing Parrot *Geoffroyus heteroclitus*

Green Racquet-tail *Prioniturus luconensis* GT, LR

Blue-crowned Racquet-tail *Prioniturus discurus*

Palawan Racquet-tail *Prioniturus platenae* GT, LR

Blue-winged Racquet-tail *Prioniturus verticalis* GT, LR

Mindanao Racquet-tail *Prioniturus waterstradti* GT, LR

Montane Racquet-tail *Prioniturus montanus* GT, LR

Yellowish-breasted Racquet-tail *Prioniturus flavicans* GT, LR

Golden-mantled Racquet-tail *Prioniturus platurus*

Buru Racquet-tail *Prioniturus mada* LR

Great-billed Parrot *Tanygnathus megalorhynchos*

Blue-naped Parrot *Tanygnathus lucionensis* GT

Müller's Parrot *Tanygnathus sumatranus*

Rufous-tailed Parrot *Tanygnathus heterurus* LR

Black-lored Parrot *Tanygnathus gramineus* GT

Eclectus Parrot *Eclectus roratus*

Pesquet's Parrot *Psittrichas fulgidus* GT

Red Shining-Parrot *Prosopeia tabuensis*

Kandavu Shining-Parrot *Prosopeia splendens* GT

Masked Shining-Parrot *Prosopeia personata* GT

Australian King Parrot *Alisterus scapularis*

Green-winged King Parrot *Alisterus chloropterus* LR

Moluccan King Parrot *Alisterus amboinensis* PGT

Red-winged Parrot *Aprosmictus erythropterus*

Olive-shouldered Parrot *Aprosmictus jonquillaceus* GT, LR

Superb Parrot *Polytelis swainsonii* GT

Regent Parrot *Polytelis anthopeplus*

Alexandra's Parrot *Polytelis alexandrae* GT

Red-capped Parrot *Purpureicephalus spurius*

Mallee Ringneck *Barnardius barnardi* LR

Australian Ringneck *Barnardius zonarius*

Green Rosella *Platycercus caledonicus*

Crimson Rosella *Platycercus elegans*

Yellow Rosella *Platycercus flaveolus* LR

Adelaide Rosella *Platycercus adelaidae* LR

Eastern Rosella *Platycercus eximius*

Pale-headed Rosella *Platycercus adscitus*

Northern Rosella *Platycercus venustus* LR

Western Rosella *Platycercus icterotis*

Red-rumped Parrot *Psephotus haematonotus*

Mulga Parrot *Psephotus varius*

Golden-shouldered Parrot *Psephotus chrysopterygius* GT

Hooded Parrot *Psephotus dissimilis* GT, LR

Paradise Parrot *Psephotus pulcherrimus* E

Bluebonnet *Northiella haemogaster*

Antipodes Green Parrot *Cyanoramphus unicolor* GT

Red-fronted Parakeet *Cyanoramphus novaezelandiae*

New Caledonian Parrot *Cyanoramphus saisseti* LR

Norfolk Island Parrot *Cyanoramphus cookii* GT, LR

Yellow-fronted Parakeet *Cyanoramphus auriceps* GT

Chatham Islands Parakeet *Cyanoramphus forbesi* GT, LR

Malherbe's Parrot *Cyanoramphus malherbi* GT, LR

Black-fronted Parakeet *Cyanoramphus zealandicus* E

Raiatea Parakeet *Cyanoramphus ulietanus* E

Horned Parakeet *Eunymphicus cornutus* GT

Ouvea Parakeet *Eunymphicus uvaeensis* GT, LR

Bourke's Parrot *Neopsephotus bourkii*

Blue-winged Parrot *Neophema chrysostoma*

Elegant Parrot *Neophema elegans*

Rock Parrot *Neophema petrophila*

Orange-bellied Parrot *Neophema chrysogaster* GT

Turquoise Parrot *Neophema pulchella*

Scarlet-chested Parrot *Neophema splendida* GT

Swift Parrot *Lathamus discolor* GT

Budgerigar *Melopsittacus undulatus*

Ground Parrot *Pezoporus wallicus*

Night Parrot *Geopsittacus occidentalis* GT

Kakapo *Strigops habroptilus* GT

Mascarene Parrot *Mascarinus mascarinus* E

Vasa Parrot *Coracopsis vasa*

Black Parrot *Coracopsis nigra*

African Grey Parrot *Psittacus erithacus*

Brown-necked Parrot *Poicephalus robustus*

Red-fronted Parrot *Poicephalus gulielmi*

Brown-headed Parrot *Poicephalus cryptoxanthus*

Niam-Niam Parrot *Poicephalus crassus* LR

Senegal Parrot *Poicephalus senegalus* LR

Red-bellied Parrot *Poicephalus rufiventris* LR

Brown Parrot *Poicephalus meyeri*

Rüppell's Parrot *Poicephalus rueppellii* LR

Yellow-fronted Parrot *Poicephalus flavifrons* LR

Grey-headed Lovebird *Agapornis canus*

Red-headed Lovebird *Agapornis pullarius*

Black-winged Lovebird *Agapornis taranta*

Black-collared Lovebird *Agapornis swindernianus*

Rosy-faced Lovebird *Agapornis roseicollis*

Fischer's Lovebird *Agapornis fischeri* GT

Yellow-collared Lovebird *Agapornis personatus*

Lilian's Lovebird *Agapornis lilianae*

Black-cheeked Lovebird *Agapornis nigrigenis* GT

Vernal Hanging-Parrot *Loriculus vernalis* LR

Sri Lanka Hanging-Parrot *Loriculus beryllinus*

Philippine Hanging-Parrot *Loriculus philippensis* LR

Black-billed Hanging-Parrot *Loriculus bonapartei* LR

Blue-crowned Hanging-Parrot *Loriculus galgulus*

Sulawesi Hanging-Parrot *Loriculus stigmatus*

Sangihe Hanging-Parrot *Loriculus catamene* GT, LR

Moluccan Hanging-Parrot *Loriculus amabilis* LR

Sula Hanging-Parrot *Loriculus sclateri* LR

Green Hanging-Parrot *Loriculus exilis* GT, LR

Wallace's Hanging-Parrot *Loriculus flosculus* GT

Yellow-throated Hanging-Parrot *Loriculus pusillus* GT, LR

Orange-fronted Hanging-Parrot *Loriculus aurantiifrons*

Green-fronted Hanging-Parrot *Loriculus tener* GT

Alexandrine Parakeet *Psittacula eupatria*

Seychelles Parakeet *Psittacula wardi* E

Rose-ringed Parakeet *Psittacula krameri*

Mauritius Parakeet *Psittacula echo* GT, LR

Newton's Parakeet *Psittacula exsul* E

Himalayan Slaty-headed Parakeet *Psittacula himalayana*

Grey-headed Parakeet *Psittacula finschii* LR

Plum-headed Parakeet *Psittacula cyanocephala*

Blossom-headed Parakeet *Psittacula roseata* LR

Malabar Parakeet *Psittacula columboides*

Layard's Parakeet *Psittacula calthropae*

Derbyan Parakeet *Psittacula derbiana*

Indian Red-breasted Parakeet *Psittacula alexandri*

Nicobar Parakeet *Psittacula caniceps* GT

Long-tailed Parakeet *Psittacula longicauda* GT

Hyacinthine Macaw *Anodorhynchus hyacinthinus* GT

Indigo Macaw *Anodorhynchus leari* GT, LR

Glaucous Macaw *Anodorhynchus glaucus* PE

Little Blue Macaw *Cyanopsitta spixii* GT

Blue-and-yellow Macaw *Ara ararauna*

Blue-throated Macaw *Ara glaucogularis* GT

Military Macaw *Ara militaris* GT

Great Green Macaw *Ara ambigua* GT, LR

Scarlet Macaw *Ara macao*

Red-and-green Macaw *Ara chloroptera*

Cuban Macaw *Ara tricolor* E

Jamaican Macaw *Ara gossei* E

Red-fronted Macaw *Ara rubrogenys* GT

Chestnut-fronted Macaw *Ara severa*

Red-bellied Macaw *Orthopsittaca manilata*

Golden-collared Macaw *Propyrrhura auricollis*

Blue-winged Macaw *Propyrrhura maracana* GT

Blue-headed Macaw *Propyrrhura couloni*

Red-shouldered Macaw *Diopsittaca nobilis*

Blue-crowned Conure *Aratinga acuticaudata*

Golden Conure *Aratinga guarouba* GT

Green Conure *Aratinga holochlora*

Pacific Conure *Aratinga strenua* LR

Socorro Conure *Aratinga brevipes* GT, LR

Red-throated Conure *Aratinga rubritorquis* LR

Finsch's Conure *Aratinga finschi* LR

Red-fronted Conure *Aratinga wagleri*

Mitred Conure *Aratinga mitrata*

Red-masked Conure *Aratinga erythrogenys* GT

White-eyed Conure *Aratinga leucophthalmus*

Hispaniolan Conure *Aratinga chloroptera* GT, LR

Cuban Conure *Aratinga euops* GT

Golden-capped Conure *Aratinga auricapilla* GT, LR

Jandaya Conure *Aratinga jandaya* LR

Sun Conure *Aratinga solstitialis*

Dusky-headed Conure *Aratinga weddellii*

Olive-throated Conure *Aratinga nana*

Aztec Conure *Aratinga astec* LR

Orange-fronted Conure *Aratinga canicularis*

Brown-throated Conure *Aratinga pertinax*

Cactus Conure *Aratinga cactorum* LR

Peach-fronted Conure *Aratinga aurea*

Nanday Conure *Nandayus nenday*

Golden-plumed Parakeet *Leptosittaca branickii* GT

Yellow-eared Parakeet *Ognorhynchus icterotis* GT

Thick-billed Parrot *Rhynchopsitta pachyrhyncha* GT

Maroon-fronted Parrot *Rhynchopsitta terrisi* GT, LR

Carolina Parakeet *Conuropsis carolinensis* E

Patagonian Burrowing Parrot *Cyanoliseus patagonus*

Blue-throated Conure *Pyrrhura cruentata* GT

Blaze-winged Parakeet *Pyrrhura devillei* LR

Maroon-bellied Conure *Pyrrhura frontalis*

Crimson-bellied Conure *Pyrrhura perlata*

Pearly Conure *Pyrrhura lepida* GT, LR

Green-cheeked Conure *Pyrrhura molinae*

Maroon-faced Conure *Pyrrhura leucotis* LR

Painted Conure *Pyrrhura picta*

Santa Marta Parakeet *Pyrrhura viridicata* GT

Fiery-shouldered Conure *Pyrrhura egregia*

Maroon-tailed Conure *Pyrrhura melanura*

El Oro Conure *Pyrrhura orcesi* GT, LR

Rock Conure *Pyrrhura rupicola*

White-breasted Conure *Pyrrhura albipectus* GT

Flame-winged Conure *Pyrrhura calliptera* GT

Blood-eared Conure *Pyrrhura hoematotis*

Rose-headed Parakeet *Pyrrhura rhodocephala*

Sulphur-winged Conure *Pyrrhura hoffmanni*

Austral Parakeet *Enicognathus ferrugineus*

Slender-billed Parakeet *Enicognathus leptorhynchus*

Monk Parakeet *Myiopsitta monachus*

Cliff Parakeet *Myiopsitta luchsi* LR

Grey-hooded Parakeet *Psilopsiagon aymara*

Mountain Parakeet *Psilopsiagon aurifrons*

Barred Parakeet *Bolborhynchus lineola*

Andean Parakeet *Bolborhynchus orbygnesius*

Rufous-fronted Parakeet *Bolborhynchus ferrugineifrons* GT

Mexican Parrotlet *Forpus cyanopygius*

Green-rumped Parrotlet *Forpus passerinus*

Blue-winged Parrotlet *Forpus xanthopterygius* LR

Spectacled Parrotlet *Forpus conspicillatus*

Dusky-billed Parrotlet *Forpus sclateri*

Pacific Parrotlet *Forpus coelestis*

Yellow-faced Parrotlet *Forpus xanthops* GT

Plain Parakeet *Brotogeris tirica*

Canary-winged Parakeet *Brotogeris versicolurus*

Yellow-chevroned Parakeet *Brotogeris chiriri* LR

Grey-cheeked Parakeet *Brotogeris pyrrhopterus* GT

Orange-chinned Parakeet *Brotogeris jugularis* LR

Cobalt-winged Parakeet *Brotogeris cyanoptera* LR

Golden-winged Parakeet *Brotogeris chrysopterus*

Tui Parakeet *Brotogeris sanctithomae*

Tepui Parrotlet *Nannopsittaca panychlora*

Amazonian Parrotlet *Nannopsittaca dachilleae* GT, LR

Lilac-tailed Parrotlet *Touit batavica*

Red-fronted Parrotlet *Touit costaricensis* PGT, LR

Scarlet-shouldered Parrotlet *Touit huetii*

Blue-fronted Parrotlet *Touit dilectissima*

Sapphire-rumped Parrotlet *Touit purpurata*

Brown-backed Parrotlet *Touit melanonotus* GT

Golden-tailed Parrotlet *Touit surda* GT

Spot-winged Parrotlet *Touit stictoptera* GT

Black-headed Parrot *Pionites melanocephala*

White-bellied Parrot *Pionites leucogaster*

Pileated Parrot *Pionopsitta pileata*

Brown-hooded Parrot *Pionopsitta haematotis*

Rose-faced Parrot *Pionopsitta pulchra* LR

Orange-cheeked Parrot *Pionopsitta barrabandi*

Saffron-headed Parrot *Pionopsitta pyrilia* GT

Caica Parrot *Pionopsitta caica*

Vulturine Parrot *Gypopsitta vulturina*

Black-eared Parrot *Hapalopsittaca melanotis*

Rusty-faced Parrot *Hapalopsittaca amazonina* GT

Indigo-winged Parrot *Hapalopsittaca fuertesi* GT, LR

Red-faced Parrot *Hapalopsittaca pyrrhops* GT, LR

Short-tailed Parrot *Graydidascalus brachyurus*

Blue-headed Parrot *Pionus menstruus*

Red-billed Parrot *Pionus sordidus*

Scaly-headed Parrot *Pionus maximiliani*

Plum-crowned Parrot *Pionus tumultuosus*

White-capped Parrot *Pionus seniloides* LR

White-crowned Parrot *Pionus senilis*

Bronze-winged Parrot *Pionus chalcopterus*

Dusky Parrot *Pionus fuscus*

Yellow-billed Amazon *Amazona collaria* PGT, LR

Cuban Amazon *Amazona leucocephala* GT

Hispaniolan Amazon *Amazona ventralis* PGT, LR

White-fronted Amazon *Amazona albifrons*

Yellow-lored Amazon *Amazona xantholora*

Black-billed Amazon *Amazona agilis* GT

Puerto Rican Amazon *Amazona vittata* GT

Tucuman Amazon *Amazona tucumana* LR

Red-spectacled Amazon *Amazona pretrei* GT

Red-crowned Amazon *Amazona viridigenalis* GT

Lilac-crowned Amazon *Amazona finschi* LR

Red-lored Amazon *Amazona autumnalis*

Red-tailed Amazon *Amazona brasiliensis* GT

Blue-cheeked Amazon *Amazona dufresniana* GT, LR

Red-browed Amazon *Amazona rhodocorytha* GT, LR

Festive Amazon *Amazona festiva*

Yellow-faced Amazon *Amazona xanthops* GT

Yellow-shouldered Amazon *Amazona barbadensis* GT

Blue-fronted Amazon *Amazona aestiva*

Yellow-naped Amazon *Amazona auropalliata* LR

Yellow-crowned Amazon *Amazona ochrocephala*

Yellow-headed Amazon *Amazona oratrix* GT, LR

Kawall's Amazon *Amazona kawalli* LR

Orange-winged Amazon *Amazona amazonica*

Scaly-naped Amazon *Amazona mercenaria*

Mealy Amazon *Amazona farinosa*

Vinaceous Amazon *Amazona vinacea* GT

St. Lucia Amazon *Amazona versicolor* GT

Red-necked Amazon *Amazona arausiaca* GT

St. Vincent Amazon *Amazona guildingii* GT

Imperial Amazon *Amazona imperialis* GT

Red-fan Parrot *Deroptyus accipitrinus*

Blue-bellied Parrot *Triclaria malachitacea* GT

MUSOPHAGIFORMES
Musophagidae

Great Blue Turaco *Corythaeola cristata*

Western Grey Plantain-eater *Crinifer piscator* LR

Eastern Grey Plantain-eater *Crinifer zonurus*

Grey Go-away-bird *Corythaixoides concolor* LR

Bare-faced Go-away-bird *Corythaixoides personata*

White-bellied Go-away-bird *Criniferoides leucogaster*

Violet Turaco *Musophaga violacea*

Lady Ross's Turaco *Musophaga rossae* LR

Ruwenzori Turaco *Ruwenzorornis johnstoni* LR

Purple-crested Turaco *Tauraco porphyreolophus*

Green Turaco *Tauraco persa*

Schalow's Turaco *Tauraco schalowi* LR

Livingstone's Turaco *Tauraco livingstonii* LR

Knysna Turaco *Tauraco corythaix* LR

Black-billed Turaco *Tauraco schuettii* LR

Fischer's Turaco *Tauraco fischeri* GT, LR

Red-crested Turaco *Tauraco erythrolophus*

Bannerman's Turaco *Tauraco bannermani* GT

Yellow-billed Turaco *Tauraco macrorhynchus*

Hartlaub's Turaco *Tauraco hartlaubi*

White-cheeked Turaco *Tauraco leucotis* LR

Ruspoli's Turaco *Tauraco ruspolii* GT, LR

White-crested Turaco *Tauraco leucolophus*

CUCULIFORMES
Opisthocomidae

Hoatzin *Opisthocomus hoazin*

Cuculidae

Great Spotted Cuckoo *Clamator glandarius*

Chestnut-winged Cuckoo *Clamator coromandus*

Jacobin Cuckoo *Oxylophus jacobinus*

Levaillant's Cuckoo *Oxylophus levaillantii*

Thick-billed Cuckoo *Pachycoccyx audeberti*

Sulawesi Hawk-Cuckoo *Cuculus crassirostris*

Large Hawk-Cuckoo *Cuculus sparverioides*

Common Hawk-Cuckoo *Cuculus varius*

Small Hawk-Cuckoo *Cuculus vagans* GT

Hodgson's Hawk-Cuckoo *Cuculus fugax*

Philippine Hawk-Cuckoo *Cuculus pectoralis* LR

Red-chested Cuckoo *Cuculus solitarius*

Black Cuckoo *Cuculus clamosus*

Indian Cuckoo *Cuculus micropterus*

Common Cuckoo *Cuculus canorus*

African Cuckoo *Cuculus gularis* LR

Oriental Cuckoo *Cuculus saturatus*

Horsfield's Cuckoo *Cuculus horsfieldi* LR

Lesser Cuckoo *Cuculus poliocephalus*

Madagascar Cuckoo *Cuculus rochii* LR

Pallid Cuckoo *Cuculus pallidus*

Dusky Long-tailed Cuckoo *Cercococcyx mechowi*

Olive Long-tailed Cuckoo *Cercococcyx olivinus*

Barred Long-tailed Cuckoo *Cercococcyx montanus* LR

Banded Bay Cuckoo *Penthoceryx sonneratii*

Grey-bellied Cuckoo *Cacomantis passerinus* LR

Plaintive Cuckoo *Cacomantis merulinus*

Brush-Cuckoo *Cacomantis variolosus*

Rusty-breasted Cuckoo *Cacomantis sepulcralis* LR

Chestnut-breasted Cuckoo *Cacomantis castaneiventris*

Moluccan Cuckoo *Cacomantis heinrichi* GT

Fan-tailed Brush-Cuckoo *Cacomantis flabelliformis*

Little Long-billed Cuckoo *Rhamphomantis megarhynchus*

African Emerald Cuckoo *Chrysococcyx cupreus*

Yellow-throated Cuckoo *Chrysococcyx flavigularis*

Klaas's Cuckoo *Chrysococcyx klaas*

Diederik Cuckoo *Chrysococcyx caprius*

Black-eared Cuckoo *Misocalius osculans*

Asian Emerald Cuckoo *Chalcites maculatus*

Violet Cuckoo *Chalcites xanthorhynchus*

Horsfield's Bronze-Cuckoo *Chalcites basalis*

Shining Bronze-Cuckoo *Chalcites lucidus*

New Guinea Bronze-Cuckoo *Chalcites poecilurus* LR

Gould's Bronze-Cuckoo *Chalcites russatus* LR

Green-cheeked Bronze-Cuckoo *Chalcites rufomerus* LR

Little Bronze-Cuckoo *Chalcites minutillus*

Pied Bronze-Cuckoo *Chalcites crassirostris* LR

Rufous-throated Bronze-Cuckoo *Chalcites ruficollis*

White-eared Bronze-Cuckoo *Chalcites meyeri*

White-crowned Koel *Caliechthrus leucolophus*

Asian Drongo-Cuckoo *Surniculus lugubris*

Philippine Drongo-Cuckoo *Surniculus velutinus* LR

Dwarf Koel *Microdynamis parva*

Asian Koel *Eudynamys scolopacea*

Black-billed Koel *Eudynamys melanorhyncha* LR

Australian Koel *Eudynamys cyanocephala* LR

Long-tailed Koel *Urodynamis taitensis*

Channel-billed Cuckoo *Scythrops novaehollandiae*

Yellowbill *Ceuthmochares aereus*

Black-bellied Malkoha *Rhopodytes diardi* GT

Chestnut-bellied Malkoha *Rhopodytes sumatranus* GT

Large Green-billed Malkoha *Rhopodytes tristis*

Blue-faced Malkoha *Rhopodytes viridirostris*

Sirkeer Malkoha *Taccocua leschenaultii*

Raffles Malkoha *Rhinortha chlorophaea*

Red-billed Malkoha *Zanclostomus javanicus*

Yellow-billed Malkoha *Rhamphococcyx calyorhynchus*

Chestnut-breasted Malkoha *Rhamphococcyx* curvirostris

Red-faced Malkoha *Phaenicophaeus pyrrhocephalus* GT

Red-crested Malkoha *Dasylophus superciliosus*

Scale-feathered Malkoha *Lepidogrammus cumingi*

Bornean Ground-Cuckoo *Carpococcyx radiatus* GT

Sumatran Ground-Cuckoo *Carpococcyx viridis* GT, LR

Coral-billed Ground-Cuckoo *Carpococcyx renauldi* PGT

Snail-eating Coua *Coua delalandei* E

Giant Coua *Coua gigas*

Coquerel's Coua *Coua coquereli*

Red-breasted Coua *Coua serriana*

Red-fronted Coua *Coua reynaudii*

Running Coua *Coua cursor*

Red-capped Coua *Coua ruficeps*

Olive-capped Coua *Coua olivaceiceps* LR

Crested Coua *Coua cristata*

Verreaux's Coua *Coua verreauxi* GT

Blue Coua *Coua caerulea*

Crotophagidae

Greater Ani *Crotophaga major*

Smooth-billed Ani *Crotophaga ani*

Groove-billed Ani *Crotophaga sulcirostris*

Guira Cuckoo *Guira guira*

Neomorphidae

Striped Ground-Cuckoo *Tapera naevia*

Lesser Ground-Cuckoo *Morococcyx erythropygus*

Pheasant Cuckoo *Dromococcyx phasianellus*

Pavonine Cuckoo *Dromococcyx pavoninus*

Greater Roadrunner *Geococcyx californianus*

Lesser Roadrunner *Geococcyx velox*

Rufous-vented Ground-Cuckoo *Neomorphus geoffroyi*

Scaled Ground-Cuckoo *Neomorphus squamiger* GT, LR

Banded Ground-Cuckoo *Neomorphus radiolosus* GT

Rufous-winged Ground-Cuckoo *Neomorphus rufipennis*

Red-billed Ground-Cuckoo *Neomorphus pucheranii*

Coccyzidae

Dwarf Cuckoo *Coccyzus pumilus* LR

Ash-colored Cuckoo *Coccyzus cinereus*

Black-billed Cuckoo *Coccyzus erythropthalmus*

Yellow-billed Cuckoo *Coccyzus americanus*

Pearly-breasted Cuckoo *Coccyzus euleri* LR

Mangrove Cuckoo *Coccyzus minor*

Cocos Island Cuckoo *Coccyzus ferrugineus* GT, LR

Dark-billed Cuckoo *Coccyzus melacoryphus* LR

Grey-capped Cuckoo *Coccyzus lansbergi*

Bay-breasted Cuckoo *Hyetornis rufigularis* GT

Chestnut-bellied Cuckoo *Hyetornis pluvialis*

Squirrel Cuckoo *Piaya cayana*

Black-bellied Cuckoo *Piaya melanogaster*

Little Cuckoo *Piaya minuta*

Great Lizard-Cuckoo *Saurothera merlini*

Jamaican Lizard-Cuckoo *Saurothera vetula*

Hispaniolan Lizard-Cuckoo *Saurothera longirostris*

Puerto Rican Lizard-Cuckoo *Saurothera vieilloti*

Centropodidae

Buff-headed Coucal *Centropus milo*

Goliath Coucal *Centropus goliath*

Violet Coucal *Centropus violaceus*

Greater Black Coucal *Centropus menbeki*

New Britain Coucal *Centropus ateralbus*

Biak Island Coucal *Centropus chalybeus* GT, LR

Pheasant Coucal *Centropus phasianinus*

Kai Coucal *Centropus spilopterus* LR

Bernstein's Coucal *Centropus bernsteini* LR

Green-billed Coucal *Centropus chlororhynchus* GT

Short-toed Coucal *Centropus rectunguis* GT

Black-hooded Coucal *Centropus steerii* GT

Greater Coucal *Centropus sinensis*

Brown Coucal *Centropus andamanensis* LR

Sunda Coucal *Centropus nigrorufus* GT

Philippine Coucal *Centropus viridis*

Madagascar Coucal *Centropus toulou*

Black-chested Coucal *Centropus grillii* LR

Lesser Coucal *Centropus bengalensis* LR

Black-throated Coucal *Centropus leucogaster*

Smaller Black-throated Coucal *Centropus neumanni*

Gabon Coucal *Centropus anselli* LR

Blue-headed Coucal *Centropus monachus*

Coppery-tailed Coucal *Centropus cupreicaudus* LR

Senegal Coucal *Centropus senegalensis*

White-browed Coucal *Centropus superciliosus*

Burchell's Coucal *Centropus burchelli* LR

Black-faced Coucal *Centropus melanops*

Bay Coucal *Centropus celebensis*

Rufous Coucal *Centropus unirufus* GT, LR

STRIGIFORMES
Tytonidae

Madagascar Red Owl *Tyto soumagnei* GT

Common Barn-Owl *Tyto alba*

Australian Barn-Owl *Tyto delicatula* LR

Galápagos Barn-Owl *Tyto punctatissima* LR

Ashy-faced Barn-Owl *Tyto glaucops* LR

Sulawesi Masked-Owl *Tyto rosenbergi*

Taliabu Masked-Owl *Tyto nigrobrunnea* PE

Minahassa Masked-Owl *Tyto inexpectata* GT, LR

Lesser Masked-Owl *Tyto sororcula* PGT, LR

Manus Masked-Owl *Tyto manusi* PGT, LR

Australian Masked-Owl *Tyto novaehollandiae*

Tasmanian Masked-Owl *Tyto castanops* LR

New Britain Masked-Owl *Tyto aurantia* PGT

Greater Sooty Owl *Tyto tenebricosa*

Lesser Sooty Owl *Tyto multipunctata*

African Grass-Owl *Tyto capensis*

Australasian Grass-Owl *Tyto longimembris* LR

Oriental Bay-Owl *Phodilus badius*

Congo Bay-Owl *Phodilus prigoginei* GT

Strigidae

Northern White-faced Owl *Ptilopsis leucotis*

Southern White-faced Owl *Ptilopsis granti* LR

Flammulated Owl *Otus flammeolus*

White-fronted Scops-Owl *Megascops sagittatus* GT

Reddish Scops-Owl *Megascops rufescens* GT

Cinnamon Scops-Owl *Megascops icterorhynchus*

Sokoke Scops-Owl *Megascops ireneae* GT

Mountain Scops-Owl *Megascops spilocephalus* LR

Andaman Scops-Owl *Megascops balli* GT, LR

Mindanao Scops-Owl *Megascops mirus* GT, LR

Sulawesi Scops-Owl *Megascops manadensis*

Sangihe Scops-Owl *Megascops collari* LR

Nicobar Scops-Owl *Megascops alius* PGT, LR

Javan Scops-Owl *Megascops angelinae* GT, LR

Simeulue Scops-Owl *Megascops umbra* GT

Engaño Scops-Owl *Megascops enganensis* GT, LR

São Tomé Scops-Owl *Megascops hartlaubi* GT, LR

Luzon Scops-Owl *Megascops longicornis* GT, LR

Mindoro Scops-Owl *Megascops mindorensis* GT

Striated Scops-Owl *Megascops brucei*

African Scops-Owl *Megascops senegalensis* LR

Eurasian Scops-Owl *Megascops scops*

Oriental Scops-Owl *Megascops sunia* LR

Elegant Scops-Owl *Megascops elegans* GT, LR

Mantanani Scops-Owl *Megascops mantananensis* GT

Moluccan Scops-Owl *Megascops magicus* LR

Siau Scops-Owl *Megascops siaoensis* GT, LR

Flores Scops-Owl *Megascops alfredi* GT, LR

Anjouan Scops-Owl *Megascops capnodes* GT, LR

Madagascar Scops-Owl *Megascops rutilus*

Torotoroka Scops-Owl *Megascops madagascariensis* LR

Mohéli Scops-Owl *Megascops moheliensis* GT

Grand Comoro Scops-Owl *Megascops pauliani* GT, LR

Pemba Scops-Owl *Megascops pembaensis* LR

Rajah Scops-Owl *Megascops brookii*

Indian Scops-Owl *Megascops bakkamoena*

Collared Scops-Owl *Megascops lettia* LR

Sunda Scops-Owl *Megascops lempiji* LR

Japanese Scops-Owl *Megascops semitorques* LR

Philippine Scops-Owl *Megascops megalotis* LR

Palawan Scops-Owl *Megascops fuliginosus* GT, LR

Mentawai Scops-Owl *Megascops mentawi* GT, LR

Wallace's Scops-Owl *Megascops silvicola*

Biak Island Scops-Owl *Megascops beccarii* GT

Bare-legged Scops-Owl *Megascops insularis* GT

Eastern Screech-Owl *Megascops asio*

Western Screech-Owl *Megascops kennicottii* LR

Balsas Screech-Owl *Megascops seductus* GT, LR

Pacific Screech-Owl *Megascops cooperi* LR

Whiskered Screech-Owl *Megascops trichopsis*

Tropical Screech-Owl *Megascops choliba*

Long-tufted Screech-Owl *Megascops sanctaecatarinae* LR

West Peruvian Screech-Owl *Megascops roboratus* LR

Maria Koepcke's Screech-Owl *Megascops koepckeae*

Bare-shanked Screech-Owl *Megascops clarkii*

Bearded Screech-Owl *Megascops barbarus* GT

Cloud-forest Screech-Owl *Megascops marshalli* GT

Rufescent Screech-Owl *Megascops ingens*

Colombian Screech-Owl *Megascops colombianus* GT, LR

Cinnamon Screech-Owl *Megascops petersoni* LR

Tawny-bellied Screech-Owl *Megascops watsonii*

Black-capped Screech-Owl *Megascops atricapillus*

Hoy's Screech-Owl *Megascops hoyi* LR

Vermiculated Screech-Owl *Megascops vermiculatus*

Foothill Screech-Owl *Megascops roraimae* LR

Guatemalan Screech-Owl *Megascops guatemalae* LR

Chocó Screech-Owl *Megascops centralis* LR

Rio Napo Screech-Owl *Megascops napensis* LR

Puerto Rican Screech-Owl *Megascops nudipes*

White-throated Screech-Owl *Megascops albogularis*

Bare-legged Screech-Owl *Gymnoglaux lawrencii*

Palau Owl *Pyrroglaux podarginus*

Giant Scops-Owl *Mimizuku gurneyi* GT

Great Horned-Owl *Bubo virginianus*

Magellanic Horned-Owl *Bubo magellanicus* LR

Eurasian Eagle-Owl *Bubo bubo*

Pharaoh Eagle-Owl *Bubo ascalaphus* LR

Indian Eagle-Owl *Bubo bengalensis* LR

Cape Eagle-Owl *Bubo capensis*

Spotted Eagle-Owl *Bubo africanus*

Vermiculated Eagle-Owl *Bubo cinerascens* LR

Fraser's Eagle-Owl *Bubo poensis*

Spot-bellied Eagle-Owl *Bubo nipalensis*

Usambara Eagle-Owl *Bubo vosseleri* GT, LR

Barred Eagle-Owl *Bubo sumatranus*

Shelley's Eagle-Owl *Bubo shelleyi*

Verreaux's Eagle-Owl *Bubo lacteus*

Dusky Eagle-Owl *Bubo coromandus*

Akun Eagle-Owl *Bubo leucostictus*

Philippine Eagle-Owl *Bubo philippensis* GT

Blakiston's Eagle-Owl *Bubo blakistoni* GT

Snowy Owl *Bubo scandiaca*

Brown Fish-Owl *Ketupa zeylonensis*

Tawny Fish-Owl *Ketupa flavipes*

Buffy Fish-Owl *Ketupa ketupu*

Pel's Fishing-Owl *Scotopelia peli*

Rufous Fishing-Owl *Scotopelia ussheri* GT

Vermiculated Fishing-Owl *Scotopelia bouvieri*

Maned Owl *Jubula lettii*

Crested Owl *Lophostrix cristata*

Spectacled Owl *Pulsatrix perspicillata*

Tawny-browed Owl *Pulsatrix koeniswaldiana* LR

Band-bellied Owl *Pulsatrix melanota*

Spotted Wood-Owl *Strix seloputo*

Mottled Wood-Owl *Strix ocellata*

Brown Wood-Owl *Strix leptogrammica*

Bartels's Wood-Owl *Strix bartelsi* LR

Eurasian Tawny Owl *Strix aluco*

Hume's Tawny Owl *Strix butleri*

Northern Barred Owl *Strix varia*

Fulvous Owl *Strix fulvescens* LR

Californian Spotted Owl *Strix occidentalis* GT

Ural Owl *Strix uralensis*

Great Grey Owl *Strix nebulosa*

Sichuan Wood-Owl *Strix davidi* GT, LR

Rusty-barred Owl *Strix hylophila*

Rufous-legged Owl *Strix rufipes*

Chaco Owl *Strix chacoensis* LR

African Wood-Owl *Ciccaba woodfordii*

Mottled Owl *Ciccaba virgata*

Black-and-white Owl *Ciccaba nigrolineata* LR

Black-banded Owl *Ciccaba huhula*

Rufous-banded Owl *Ciccaba albitarsis* LR

Northern Hawk-Owl *Surnia ulula*

Collared Owlet *Glaucidium brodiei*

Eurasian Pygmy-Owl *Glaucidium passerinum*

Pearl-spotted Owlet *Glaucidium perlatum*

Mountain Pygmy-Owl *Glaucidium gnoma*

Baja Pygmy-Owl *Glaucidium hoskinsii* LR

Guatemalan Pygmy-Owl *Glaucidium cobanense* LR

Costa Rican Pygmy-Owl *Glaucidium costaricanum* LR

Cloud-forest Pygmy-Owl *Glaucidium nubicola* GT, LR

Californian Pygmy-Owl *Glaucidium californicum* LR

Least Pygmy-Owl *Glaucidium minutissimum*

Colima Pygmy-Owl *Glaucidium palmarum* LR

Tamaulipas Pygmy-Owl *Glaucidium sanchezi* LR

Central American Pygmy-Owl *Glaucidium griseiceps* LR

Subtropical Pygmy-Owl *Glaucidium parkeri* LR

Ferruginous Pygmy-Owl *Glaucidium brasilianum*

Ridgway's Pygmy-Owl *Glaucidium ridgwayi* LR

Tucuman Pygmy-Owl *Glaucidium tucumanum* LR

Austral Pygmy-Owl *Glaucidium nanum* LR

Andean Pygmy-Owl *Glaucidium jardinii*

Hardy's Pygmy-Owl *Glaucidium hardyi* LR

Peruvian Pygmy-Owl *Glaucidium peruanum* LR

Yungas Pygmy-Owl *Glaucidium bolivianum* LR

Cuban Pygmy-Owl *Glaucidium siju*

Red-chested Owlet *Glaucidium tephronotum*

Sjöstedt's Barred Owlet *Glaucidium sjostedti* LR

Jungle Owlet *Glaucidium radiatum*

Chestnut-backed Owlet *Glaucidium castanonotum* GT, LR

Asian Barred Owlet *Glaucidium cuculoides*

Javan Barred Owlet *Glaucidium castanopterum* LR

African Barred Owlet *Glaucidium capense*

Ngami Owlet *Glaucidium ngamiense* LR

Chestnut Barred Owlet *Glaucidium castaneum*

Prigogine's Owlet *Glaucidium albertinum* GT

Eastern Barred Owlet *Glaucidium scheffleri* LR

Long-whiskered Owlet *Xenoglaux loweryi* GT

Elf Owl *Micrathene whitneyi*

Little Owl *Athene noctua*

Spotted Owlet *Athene brama*

Forest Owlet *Athene blewitti* GT

Burrowing Owl *Athene cunicularia*

Boreal Owl *Aegolius funereus*

Northern Saw-whet Owl *Aegolius acadicus*

Unspotted Saw-whet Owl *Aegolius ridgwayi* LR

Buff-fronted Owl *Aegolius harrisii*

Papuan Hawk-Owl *Uroglaux dimorpha* PGT

Rufous Hawk-Owl *Ninox rufa* LR

Powerful Owl *Ninox strenua* GT

Barking Hawk-Owl *Ninox connivens*

Southern Boobook *Ninox boobook* LR

Morepork *Ninox novaeseelandiae*

Sumba Boobook *Ninox rudolfi* GT, LR

Brown Hawk-Owl *Ninox scutulata*

Andaman Hawk-Owl *Ninox affinis* GT

White-browed Hawk-Owl *Ninox superciliaris*

Philippine Hawk-Owl *Ninox philippensis*

Ochre-bellied Hawk-Owl *Ninox ochracea* GT

Cinnabar Hawk-Owl *Ninox ios* GT, LR

Moluccan Hawk-Owl *Ninox squamipila*

Christmas Island Hawk-Owl *Ninox natalis* GT, LR

Jungle Hawk-Owl *Ninox theomacha*

Manus Hawk-Owl *Ninox meeki*

Speckled Hawk-Owl *Ninox punctulata*

Bismarck Hawk-Owl *Ninox variegata*

New Britain Hawk-Owl *Ninox odiosa*

Solomon Islands Hawk-Owl *Ninox jacquinoti*

White-faced Owl *Sceloglaux albifacies* E20

Striped Owl *Pseudoscops clamator*

Jamaican Owl *Pseudoscops grammicus*

Northern Long-eared Owl *Asio otus*

Stygian Owl *Asio stygius*

African Long-eared Owl *Asio abyssinicus* LR

Madagascar Long-eared Owl *Asio madagascariensis* LR

Short-eared Owl *Asio flammeus*

African Marsh Owl *Asio capensis*

Fearful Owl *Nesasio solomonensis* GT

CAPRIMULGIFORMES

Steatornithidae

Oilbird *Steatornis caripensis*

Podargidae

Tawny Frogmouth *Podargus strigoides*

Great Papuan Frogmouth *Podargus papuensis*

Marbled Frogmouth *Podargus ocellatus*

Large Frogmouth *Batrachostomus auritus* GT

Dulit Frogmouth *Batrachostomus harterti* GT

Philippine Frogmouth *Batrachostomus septimus*

Gould's Frogmouth *Batrachostomus stellatus* GT

Sri Lanka Frogmouth *Batrachostomus moniliger*

Hodgson's Frogmouth *Batrachostomus hodgsoni*

Short-tailed Frogmouth *Batrachostomus poliolophus* GT

Sharpe's Frogmouth *Batrachostomus mixtus* GT, LR

Javan Frogmouth *Batrachostomus javensis*

Blyth's Frogmouth *Batrachostomus affinis* LR

Sunda Frogmouth *Batrachostomus cornutus* LR

Nyctibiidae

Great Potoo *Nyctibius grandis*

Long-tailed Potoo *Nyctibius aethereus*

Common Potoo *Nyctibius jamaicensis* LR

Grey Potoo *Nyctibius griseus*

Andean Potoo *Nyctibius maculosus* LR

White-winged Potoo *Nyctibius leucopterus*

Rufous Potoo *Nyctibius bracteatus*

Aegothelidae

Moluccan Owlet-Nightjar *Aegotheles crinifrons*

Large Owlet-Nightjar *Aegotheles insignis*

Spangled Owlet-Nightjar *Aegotheles tatei* PGT, LR

Australian Owlet-Nightjar *Aegotheles cristatus*

New Caledonian Owlet-Nightjar *Aegotheles savesi* GT

Barred Owlet-Nightjar *Aegotheles bennettii*

Wallace's Owlet-Nightjar *Aegotheles wallacii* PGT

Mountain Owlet-Nightjar *Aegotheles albertisi*

Archbold's Owlet-Nightjar *Aegotheles archboldi*

Eurostopodidae

Spotted Eared-Nightjar *Eurostopodus argus*

White-throated Eared-Nightjar *Eurostopodus mystacalis*

Sulawesi Eared Nightjar *Eurostopodus diabolicus* GT

Papuan Eared-Nightjar *Eurostopodus papuensis*

Archbold's Eared-Nightjar *Eurostopodus archboldi*

Malaysian Eared-Nightjar *Eurostopodus temminckii*

Great Eared-Nightjar *Eurostopodus macrotis*

Caprimulgidae

Semi-collared Nighthawk *Lurocalis semitorquatus*

Rufous-bellied Nighthawk *Lurocalis rufiventris* LR

Least Nighthawk *Chordeiles pusillus*

Sand-colored Nighthawk *Chordeiles rupestris*

Lesser Nighthawk *Chordeiles acutipennis*

Common Nighthawk *Chordeiles minor*

Antillean Nighthawk *Chordeiles gundlachii* LR

Bahian Nighthawk *Nyctiprogne vielliardi* GT, LR

Band-tailed Nighthawk *Nyctiprogne leucopyga*

Nacunda Nighthawk *Podager nacunda*

Brown Nightjar *Veles binotatus*

Pauraque *Nyctidromus albicollis*

Common Poorwill *Phalaenoptilus nuttallii*

Jamaican Poorwill *Siphonorhis americanus* PE

Least Pauraque *Siphonorhis brewsteri* PGT, LR

Eared Poorwill *Nyctiphrynus mcleodii*

Yucatan Poorwill *Nyctiphrynus yucatanicus*

Ocellated Poorwill *Nyctiphrynus ocellatus*

Chocó Poorwill *Nyctiphrynus rosenbergi* GT, LR

Chuck-will's-widow *Caprimulgus carolinensis*

Rufous Nightjar *Caprimulgus rufus*

Cuban Nightjar *Caprimulgus cubanensis*

Hispaniolan Nightjar *Caprimulgus ekmani* LR

Silky-tailed Nightjar *Caprimulgus sericocaudatus*

Tawny-collared Nightjar *Caprimulgus salvini* LR

Yucatan Nightjar *Caprimulgus badius* LR

Buff-collared Nightjar *Caprimulgus ridgwayi*

Whip-poor-will *Caprimulgus vociferus*

Puerto Rican Nightjar *Caprimulgus noctitherus* GT, LR

Dusky Nightjar *Caprimulgus saturatus*

Band-winged Nightjar *Caprimulgus longirostris*

White-tailed Nightjar *Caprimulgus cayennensis*

White-winged Nightjar *Caprimulgus candicans* GT, LR

Spot-tailed Nightjar *Caprimulgus maculicaudus*

Scrub Nightjar *Caprimulgus anthonyi* LR

Little Nightjar *Caprimulgus parvulus*

Cayenne Nightjar *Caprimulgus maculosus* PGT

Blackish Nightjar *Caprimulgus nigrescens*

Roraiman Nightjar *Caprimulgus whitelyi* LR

Pygmy Nightjar *Caprimulgus hirundinaceus*

Red-necked Nightjar *Caprimulgus ruficollis*

Jungle Nightjar *Caprimulgus indicus*

Eurasian Nightjar *Caprimulgus europaeus*

Sombre Nightjar *Caprimulgus fraenatus* LR

Sykes's Nightjar *Caprimulgus mahrattensis*

Vaurie's Nightjar *Caprimulgus centralasicus* PGT

Nubian Nightjar *Caprimulgus nubicus*

Egyptian Nightjar *Caprimulgus aegyptius*

Golden Nightjar *Caprimulgus eximius*

Jerdon's Nightjar *Caprimulgus atripennis* LR

Large-tailed Nightjar *Caprimulgus macrurus*

Sulawesi Nightjar *Caprimulgus celebensis* LR

Philippine Nightjar *Caprimulgus manillensis* LR

Fiery-necked Nightjar *Caprimulgus pectoralis*

Black-shouldered Nightjar *Caprimulgus nigriscapularis* LR

Rufous-cheeked Nightjar *Caprimulgus rufigena*

Donaldson-Smith's Nightjar *Caprimulgus donaldsoni*

Abyssinian Nightjar *Caprimulgus poliocephalus*

Ruwenzori Nightjar *Caprimulgus ruwenzorii* LR

Madagascar Nightjar *Caprimulgus madagascariensis*

Indian Nightjar *Caprimulgus asiaticus*

African White-tailed Nightjar *Caprimulgus natalensis*

Plain Nightjar *Caprimulgus inornatus*

Star-spotted Nightjar *Caprimulgus stellatus*

Franklin's Nightjar *Caprimulgus monticolus* LR

Savannah Nightjar *Caprimulgus affinis*

Freckled Nightjar *Caprimulgus tristigma*

Bonaparte's Nightjar *Caprimulgus concretus* GT

Salvadori's Nightjar *Caprimulgus pulchellus* GT

Collared Nightjar *Caprimulgus enarratus*

Bates's Nightjar *Caprimulgus batesi*

Itombwe Nightjar *Caprimulgus prigoginei* GT

Gabon Nightjar *Scotornis fossii* LR

Long-tailed Nightjar *Scotornis climacurus*

Slender-tailed Nightjar *Scotornis clarus* LR

Standard-winged Nightjar *Macrodipteryx longipennis*

Pennant-winged Nightjar *Macrodipteryx vexillarius*

Ladder-tailed Nightjar *Hydropsalis climacocerca*

Scissor-tailed Nightjar *Hydropsalis brasiliana*

Swallow-tailed Nightjar *Uropsalis segmentata*

Lyre-tailed Nightjar *Uropsalis lyra*

Long-trained Nightjar *Macropsalis forcipata*

Sickle-winged Nightjar *Macropsalis anomalus* GT

APODIFORMES

Apodidae

Sooty Swift *Cypseloides fumigatus*

Spot-fronted Swift *Cypseloides cherriei* PGT

White-fronted Swift *Cypseloides storeri* PGT, LR

White-chinned Swift *Cypseloides cryptus*

White-chested Swift *Cypseloides lemosi* GT

Great Swift *Cypseloides rothschildi* GT, LR

Tepui Swift *Cypseloides phelpsi*

Chestnut-collared Swift *Cypseloides rutilus*

Black Swift *Nephoecetes niger*

Great Dusky Swift *Aerornis senex*

White-collared Swift *Streptoprocne zonaris*

Biscutate Swift *Streptoprocne biscutata*

White-naped Swift *Streptoprocne semicollaris*

Waterfall Swift *Hydrochous gigas* GT

Moluccan Swiftlet *Aerodramus infuscatus* LR

Australian Swiftlet *Aerodramus terraereginae* LR

Pacific White-rumped Swiftlet *Aerodramus spodiopygius*

Mountain Swiftlet *Aerodramus hirundinaceus*

Edible-nest Swiftlet *Aerodramus fuciphagus*

Oustalet's Swiftlet *Aerodramus germani* LR

Grey-rumped Swiftlet *Aerodramus francicus* GT

Grey Swiftlet *Aerodramus amelis* LR

Uniform Swiftlet *Aerodramus vanikorensis*

Palawan Swiftlet *Aerodramus palawanensis* LR

Whitehead's Swiftlet *Aerodramus whiteheadi* PGT, LR

Mossy-nest Swiftlet *Aerodramus salangana* LR

Caroline Islands Swiftlet *Aerodramus inquietus*

Mariana Swiftlet *Aerodramus bartschi* GT, LR

Palau Swiftlet *Aerodramus pelewensis* LR

Brown-rumped Swiftlet *Aerodramus mearnsi*

Mayr's Swiftlet *Aerodramus orientalis* PGT

Papuan Swiftlet *Aerodramus papuensis* PGT

Bare-legged Swiftlet *Aerodramus nuditarsus*

Himalayan Swiftlet *Aerodramus brevirostris*

Black-nest Swiftlet *Aerodramus maximus*

Volcano Swiftlet *Aerodramus vulcanorum* GT, LR

Indochinese Swiftlet *Aerodramus rogersi* LR

Seychelles Swiftlet *Aerodramus elaphrus* GT

Indian Swiftlet *Aerodramus unicolor* LR

Tahitian Swiftlet *Aerodramus leucophaeus* GT

Marquesas Swiftlet *Aerodramus ocistus* LR

Cook Islands Swiftlet *Aerodramus sawtelli* GT

Glossy Swiftlet *Collocalia esculenta*

Philippine Swiftlet *Collocalia marginata* LR

Pygmy Swiftlet *Collocalia troglodytes*

Linchi Swiftlet *Collocalia linchi* LR

Scarce Swift *Schoutedenapus myoptilus* LR

Schouteden's Swift *Schoutedenapus schoutedeni* GT

Philippine Needletail *Mearnsia picina* GT

Papuan Needletail *Mearnsia novaeguineae*

Malagasy Spinetail *Zoonavena grandidieri*

São Tomé Spinetail *Zoonavena thomensis*

Indian White-rumped Spinetail *Zoonavena sylvatica*

Mottled Spinetail *Telacanthura ussheri*

Black Spinetail *Telacanthura melanopygia*

Silver-rumped Spinetail *Rhaphidura leucopygialis*

Sabine's Spinetail *Rhaphidura sabini*

Cassin's Spinetail *Neafrapus cassini*

Böhm's Spinetail *Neafrapus boehmi*

White-throated Needletail *Hirundapus caudacutus*

Silver-backed Needletail *Hirundapus cochinchinensis* LR

Brown-backed Needletail *Hirundapus giganteus*

Purple Needletail *Hirundapus celebensis* LR

Band-rumped Swift *Chaetura spinicauda*

Costa Rican Swift *Chaetura fumosa*

Lesser Antillean Swift *Chaetura martinica*

Grey-rumped Swift *Chaetura cinereiventris*

Pale-rumped Swift *Chaetura egregia* LR

Chimney Swift *Chaetura pelagica*

Vaux's Swift *Chaetura vauxi*

Chapman's Swift *Chaetura chapmani*

Amazonian Swift *Chaetura viridipennis* LR

Ashy-tailed Swift *Chaetura andrei*

Short-tailed Swift *Chaetura brachyura*

Tumbes Swift *Chaetura ocypetes* LR

White-throated Swift *Aeronautes saxatalis*

White-tipped Swift *Aeronautes montivagus*

Andean Swift *Aeronautes andecolus*

Antillean Palm-Swift *Tachornis phoenicobia*

Pygmy Swift *Tachornis furcata*

Fork-tailed Swift *Tachornis squamata*

Great Swallow-tailed Swift *Panyptila sanctihieronymi*

Lesser Swallow-tailed Swift *Panyptila cayennensis*

Asian Palm-Swift *Cypsiurus balasiensis* LR

African Palm-Swift *Cypsiurus parvus*

Alpine Swift *Tachymarptis melba*

Mottled Swift *Tachymarptis aequatorialis*

Cape Verde Swift *Apus alexandri*
African Black Swift *Apus barbatus*
Madagascar Black Swift *Apus balstoni* LR
Forbes-Watson's Swift *Apus berliozi*
Bradfield's Swift *Apus bradfieldi*
Nyanza Swift *Apus niansae* LR
Pallid Swift *Apus pallidus*
Common Swift *Apus apus*
Plain Swift *Apus unicolor* LR
Dark-rumped Swift *Apus acuticauda* GT
Pacific Swift *Apus pacificus*
Little Swift *Apus affinis*
House Swift *Apus nipalensis* LR
Horus Swift *Apus horus*
Loanda Swift *Apus toulsoni* LR
African White-rumped Swift *Apus caffer*
Bates's Black Swift *Apus batesi*

Hemiprocnidae

Crested Treeswift *Hemiprocne coronata* LR
Grey-rumped Treeswift *Hemiprocne longipennis*
Moustached Treeswift *Hemiprocne mystacea*
Whiskered Treeswift *Hemiprocne comata*

TROCHILIFORMES

Trochilidae

Hook-billed Hermit *Ramphodon dohrnii* GT, LR
Saw-billed Hermit *Ramphodon naevius* GT
Bronze Hermit *Glaucis aenea*
Rufous-breasted Hermit *Glaucis hirsuta*
Pale-tailed Barbthroat *Threnetes niger*
Band-tailed Barbthroat *Threnetes ruckeri*
White-whiskered Hermit *Phaethornis yaruqui*
Green Hermit *Phaethornis guy*
Tawny-bellied Hermit *Phaethornis syrmatophorus*
Eastern Long-tailed Hermit *Phaethornis superciliosus*
Baron's Hermit *Phaethornis baroni* LR
Western Long-tailed Hermit *Phaethornis longirostris* LR
Great-billed Hermit *Phaethornis malaris*
Scale-throated Hermit *Phaethornis eurynome*
Black-billed Hermit *Phaethornis nigrirostris* LR
White-bearded Hermit *Phaethornis hispidus* LR,PH
Pale-bellied Hermit *Phaethornis anthophilus*
Koepcke's Hermit *Phaethornis koepckeae* GT, LR

Straight-billed Hermit *Phaethornis bourcieri*
Needle-billed Hermit *Phaethornis philippii*
Dusky-throated Hermit *Phaethornis squalidus* PH
Sooty-capped Hermit *Phaethornis augusti*
Planalto Hermit *Phaethornis pretrei*
Buff-bellied Hermit *Phaethornis subochraceus*
Cinnamon-throated Hermit *Phaethornis nattereri*
Reddish Hermit *Phaethornis ruber*
Black-throated Hermit *Phaethornis atrimentalis* LR
White-browed Hermit *Phaethornis stuarti* LR
Grey-chinned Hermit *Phaethornis griseogularis*
Little Hermit Phaethornis *longuemareus*
Streak-throated Hermit *Phaethornis rupurumii* LR
Stripe-throated Hermit *Phaethornis striigularis* LR
Minute Hermit *Phaethornis idaliae* LR
Broad-tipped Hermit *Anopetia gounellei*
White-tipped Sicklebill *Eutoxeres aquila*
Buff-tailed Sicklebill *Eutoxeres condamini*
Blue-fronted Lancebill *Doryfera johannae*
Green-fronted Lancebill *Doryfera ludovicae*
Tooth-billed Hummingbird *Androdon aequatorialis*
Scaly-breasted Hummingbird *Phaeochroa cuvierii*
Wedge-tailed Sabrewing *Campylopterus curvipennis*
Long-tailed Sabrewing *Campylopterus excellens* GT, LR
Grey-breasted Sabrewing *Campylopterus largipennis*
Rufous Sabrewing *Campylopterus rufus*
Rufous-breasted Sabrewing *Campylopterus hyperythrus*
Buff-breasted Sabrewing *Campylopterus duidae* LR
Violet Sabrewing *Campylopterus hemileucurus*
White-tailed Sabrewing *Campylopterus ensipennis* GT
Lazuline Sabrewing *Campylopterus falcatus*
Santa Marta Sabrewing *Campylopterus phainopeplus* GT
Napo Sabrewing *Campylopterus villaviscensio* GT

Sombre Hummingbird *Campylopterus cirrochloris*

Swallow-tailed Hummingbird *Campylopterus macrourus*

White-necked Jacobin *Florisuga mellivora*

Black Jacobin *Florisuga fuscus*

Brown Violetear *Colibri delphinae*

Green Violetear *Colibri thalassinus*

Sparkling Violetear *Colibri coruscans*

White-vented Violetear *Colibri serrirostris*

Green-throated Mango *Anthracothorax viridigula*

Green-breasted Mango *Anthracothorax prevostii*

Veraguan Mango *Anthracothorax veraguensis* LR

Black-throated Mango *Anthracothorax nigricollis*

Antillean Mango *Anthracothorax dominicus*

Green Mango *Anthracothorax viridis*

Jamaican Mango *Anthracothorax mango*

Fiery-tailed Awlbill *Avocettula recurvirostris*

Purple-throated Carib *Eulampis jugularis*

Green-throated Carib *Eulampis holosericeus*

Ruby-topaz Hummingbird *Chrysolampis mosquitus*

Antillean Crested Hummingbird *Orthorhyncus cristatus*

Violet-headed Hummingbird *Klais guimeti*

Emerald-chinned Hummingbird *Abeillia abeillei*

Black-breasted Plovercrest *Stephanoxis lalandi*

Tufted Coquette *Lophornis ornatus*

Dot-eared Coquette *Lophornis gouldii*

Frilled Coquette *Lophornis magnificus*

Short-crested Coquette *Lophornis brachylopha* GT, LR

Rufous-crested Coquette *Lophornis delattrei*

Spangled Coquette *Lophornis stictolophus*

Festive Coquette *Lophornis chalybeus*

Peacock Coquette *Lophornis pavoninus*

Black-crested Coquette *Paphosia helenae*

White-crested Coquette *Paphosia adorabilis*

Wire-crested Thorntail *Discosura popelairii*

Black-bellied Thorntail *Discosura langsdorffi*

Coppery Thorntail *Discosura letitiae* PGT

Green Thorntail *Discosura conversii*

Racquet-tailed Coquette *Discosura longicauda*

Blue-chinned Sapphire *Chlorostilbon notatus*

Blue-tailed Emerald *Chlorostilbon mellisugus*

Western Emerald *Chlorostilbon melanorhynchus* LR

Chirbiquete Emerald *Chlorostilbon olivaresi* LR

Simon's Emerald *Chlorostilbon vitticeps* LR

Glittering-bellied Emerald *Chlorostilbon aureoventris*

Canivet's Emerald *Chlorostilbon canivetii* LR

Golden-crowned Emerald *Chlorostilbon auriceps* LR

Cozumel Emerald *Chlorostilbon forficatus* LR

Garden Emerald *Chlorostilbon assimilis* LR

Brace's Emerald *Chlorostilbon bracei* E

Cuban Emerald *Chlorostilbon ricordii*

Hispaniolan Emerald *Chlorostilbon swainsonii*

Puerto Rican Emerald *Chlorostilbon maugaeus*

Red-billed Emerald *Chlorostilbon gibsoni* LR

Coppery Emerald *Chlorostilbon russatus*

Narrow-tailed Emerald *Chlorostilbon stenura*

Green-tailed Emerald *Chlorostilbon alice*

Short-tailed Emerald *Chlorostilbon poortmani*

Dusky Hummingbird *Cynanthus sordidus*

Broad-billed Hummingbird *Cynanthus latirostris*

Blue-headed Hummingbird *Cyanophaia bicolor*

Mexican Woodnymph *Thalurania ridgwayi* GT, LR

Purple-crowned Woodnymph *Thalurania colombica* LR

Green-crowned Woodnymph *Thalurania fannyi* LR

Emerald-bellied Woodnymph *Thalurania hypochlora* LR

Fork-tailed Woodnymph *Thalurania furcata*

Long-tailed Woodnymph *Thalurania watertonii*

Violet-capped Woodnymph *Thalurania glaucopis*

Fiery-throated Hummingbird *Panterpe insignis* LR

Violet-bellied Hummingbird *Damophila julie*

Sapphire-throated Hummingbird *Lepidopyga coeruleogularis*

Sapphire-bellied Hummingbird *Lepidopyga lilliae* GT

Shining-green Hummingbird *Lepidopyga goudoti*

Xantus's Hummingbird *Basilinna xantusii*

White-eared Hummingbird *Basilinna leucotis* LR

Blue-throated Goldentail *Hylocharis eliciae*

Rufous-throated Sapphire *Hylocharis sapphirina*

White-chinned Sapphire *Hylocharis cyanus*

Flame-rumped Sapphire *Hylocharis pyropygia*

Gilded Sapphire *Hylocharis chrysura*

Blue-headed Sapphire *Hylocharis grayi*

Humboldt's Sapphire *Hylocharis humboldtii* LR

Golden-tailed Sapphire *Chrysuronia oenone*

Violet-capped Hummingbird *Goldmania violiceps*

Pirre Hummingbird *Goethalsia bella* GT

Red-billed Streamertail *Trochilus polytmus*

Black-billed Streamertail *Trochilus scitulus* LR

White-throated Hummingbird *Leucochloris albicollis*

White-tailed Goldenthroat *Polytmus guainumbi*

Tepui Goldenthroat *Polytmus milleri*

Green-tailed Goldenthroat *Polytmus theresiae*

Many-spotted Hummingbird *Taphrospilus hypostictus*

Buffy Hummingbird *Leucippus fallax*

Tumbes Hummingbird *Leucippus baeri*

Spot-throated Hummingbird *Leucippus taczanowskii*

Olive-spotted Hummingbird *Leucippus chlorocercus*

White-bellied Hummingbird *Leucippus chionogaster*

Green-and-white Hummingbird *Leucippus viricauda*

White-bellied Emerald *Agyrtria candida*

White-chested Emerald *Agyrtria brevirostris*

Versicolored Emerald *Agyrtria versicolor*

Blue-fronted Emerald *Agyrtria rondoniae* LR

Andean Emerald *Agyrtria franciae*

Plain-bellied Emerald *Agyrtria leucogaster*

Red-billed Azurecrown *Agyrtria cyanocephala*

Green-fronted Hummingbird *Agyrtria viridifrons* LR

Violet-crowned Hummingbird *Agyrtria violiceps*

Honduran Emerald *Polyerata luciae* GT

Glittering-throated Emerald *Polyerata fimbriata*

Sapphire-spangled Emerald *Polyerata lactea*

Charming Hummingbird *Polyerata decora* LR

Blue-chested Hummingbird *Polyerata amabilis*

Purple-chested Hummingbird *Polyerata rosenbergi*

Mangrove Hummingbird *Polyerata boucardi* GT

Indigo-capped Hummingbird *Saucerottia cyanifrons*

Berylline Hummingbird *Saucerottia beryllina*

Blue-tailed Hummingbird *Saucerottia cyanura*

Steely-vented Hummingbird *Saucerottia saucerrottei*

Copper-rumped Hummingbird *Saucerottia tobaci*

Green-bellied Hummingbird *Saucerottia viridigaster*

Copper-tailed Hummingbird *Saucerottia cupreicauda* LR

Snowy-breasted Hummingbird *Saucerottia edward*

Cinnamon Hummingbird *Amazilia rutila*

Buff-bellied Hummingbird *Amazilia yucatanensis*

Rufous-tailed Hummingbird *Amazilia tzacatl*

Chestnut-bellied Hummingbird *Amazilia castaneiventris* GT

Amazilia Hummingbird *Amazilia amazilia*

Loja Hummingbird *Amazilia alticola* LR

White-tailed Hummingbird *Eupherusa poliocerca* GT, LR

Stripe-tailed Hummingbird *Eupherusa eximia*

Blue-capped Hummingbird *Eupherusa cyanophrys* GT, LR

Black-bellied Hummingbird *Eupherusa nigriventris*

White-tailed Emerald *Elvira chionura*

Coppery-headed Emerald *Elvira cupreiceps*

Snowcap *Microchera albocoronata*

White-vented Plumeleteer *Chalybura buffonii*

Bronze-tailed Plumeleteer *Chalybura urochrysia*

Blue-throated Hummingbird *Lampornis clemenciae*

Amethyst-throated Hummingbird *Lampornis amethystinus*

Green-throated Mountain-Gem *Lampornis viridipallens*

Green-breasted Mountain-Gem *Lampornis sybillae* LR

White-bellied Mountain-Gem *Lampornis hemileucus*

White-throated Mountain-Gem *Lampornis castaneoventris*

Purple-throated Mountain-Gem *Lampornis calolaema* LR

Grey-tailed Mountain-Gem *Lampornis cinereicauda* LR

Garnet-throated Hummingbird *Lamprolaima rhami*

Speckled Hummingbird *Adelomyia melanogenys*

Blossomcrown *Anthocephala floriceps* GT

Purple-bibbed Whitetip *Urosticte benjamini*

Rufous-vented Whitetip *Urosticte ruficrissa* LR

Ecuadorean Piedtail *Phlogophilus hemileucurus* GT

Peruvian Piedtail *Phlogophilus harterti* GT

Brazilian Ruby *Clytolaema rubricauda*

Gould's Jewelfront *Heliodoxa aurescens*

Fawn-breasted Brilliant *Heliodoxa rubinoides*

Violet-fronted Brilliant *Heliodoxa leadbeateri*

Green-crowned Brilliant *Heliodoxa jacula*

Velvet-browed Brilliant *Heliodoxa xanthogonys*

Black-throated Brilliant *Heliodoxa schreibersii*

Pink-throated Brilliant *Heliodoxa gularis* GT

Rufous-webbed Brilliant *Heliodoxa branickii*

Empress Brilliant *Heliodoxa imperatrix*

Magnificent Hummingbird *Eugenes fulgens*

Admirable Hummingbird *Eugenes spectabilis* LR

Scissor-tailed Hummingbird *Hylonympha macrocerca* GT

Violet-chested Hummingbird *Sternoclyta cyanopectus*

Crimson Topaz *Topaza pella*

Fiery Topaz *Topaza pyra* LR

Black-breasted Hillstar *Oreotrochilus melanogaster*

Ecuadorian Hillstar *Oreotrochilus chimborazo* LR

Andean Hillstar *Oreotrochilus estella*

Green-headed Hillstar *Oreotrochilus stolzmanni* LR

White-sided Hillstar *Oreotrochilus leucopleurus* LR

Wedge-tailed Hillstar *Oreotrochilus adela* GT

White-tailed Hillstar *Urochroa bougueri*

Giant Hummingbird *Patagona gigas*

Shining Sunbeam *Aglaeactis cupripennis*

Purple-backed Sunbeam *Aglaeactis aliciae* GT

White-tufted Sunbeam *Aglaeactis castelnaudii*

Black-hooded Sunbeam *Aglaeactis pamela*

Mountain Velvetbreast *Lafresnaya lafresnayi*

Great Sapphirewing *Pterophanes cyanopterus*

Bronzy Inca *Coeligena coeligena*

Brown Inca *Coeligena wilsoni*

Black Inca *Coeligena prunellei* GT

Collared Inca *Coeligena torquata*

Gould's Inca *Coeligena inca* LR

White-tailed Starfrontlet *Coeligena phalerata*

Golden-bellied Starfrontlet *Coeligena bonapartei*

Golden Starfrontlet *Coeligena eos* LR

Blue-throated Starfrontlet *Coeligena helianthea*

Buff-winged Starfrontlet *Coeligena lutetiae*

Violet-throated Starfrontlet *Coeligena violifer*

Rainbow Starfrontlet *Coeligena iris*

Sword-billed Hummingbird *Ensifera ensifera*

Green-backed Firecrown *Sephanoides sephaniodes*

Juan Fernández Firecrown *Sephanoides fernandensis* GT

Buff-tailed Coronet *Boissonneaua flavescens*

Chestnut-breasted Coronet *Boissonneaua matthewsii*

Velvet-purple Coronet *Boissonneaua jardini*

Orange-throated Sunangel *Heliangelus mavors*

Longuemare's Sunangel *Heliangelus clarissae* LR

Amethyst-throated Sunangel *Heliangelus amethysticollis*

Gorgeted Sunangel *Heliangelus strophianus*

Royal Sunangel *Heliangelus regalis* GT

Bogotá Sunangel *Heliangelus zusii* PE

Tourmaline Sunangel *Heliangelus exortis*

Flame-throated Sunangel *Heliangelus micraster* LR

Purple-throated Sunangel *Heliangelus viola*

Black-breasted Puffleg *Eriocnemis nigrivestis* GT

Söderström's Puffleg *Eriocnemis soderstromi* LR, PH

Glowing Puffleg *Eriocnemis vestitus*

Tuquoise-throated Puffleg *Eriocnemis godini* GT

Coppery-bellied Puffleg *Eriocnemis cupreoventris* GT

Sapphire-vented Puffleg *Eriocnemis luciani*

Coppery-naped Puffleg *Eriocnemis sapphiropygia* LR

Golden-breasted Puffleg *Eriocnemis mosquera*

Blue-capped Puffleg *Eriocnemis glaucopoides*

Colorful Puffleg *Eriocnemis mirabilis* GT

Emerald-bellied Puffleg *Eriocnemis alinae*

Black-thighed Puffleg *Eriocnemis derbyi* GT

Greenish Puffleg *Haplophaedia aureliae*

Buff-thighed Puffleg *Haplophaedia assimilis* LR

Hoary Puffleg *Haplophaedia lugens* GT

Booted Racquet-tail *Ocreatus underwoodii*

Black-tailed Trainbearer *Lesbia victoriae*

Green-tailed Trainbearer *Lesbia nuna*

Red-tailed Comet *Sappho sparganura*

Bronze-tailed Comet *Polyonymus caroli*

Purple-backed Thornbill *Ramphomicron microrhynchum*

Black-backed Thornbill *Ramphomicron dorsale*

Black Metaltail *Metallura phoebe*

Coppery Metaltail *Metallura theresiae*

Scaled Metaltail *Metallura aeneocauda*

Violet-throated Metaltail *Metallura baroni* GT

Fire-throated Metaltail *Metallura eupogon*

Neblina Metaltail *Metallura odomae* GT

Viridian Metaltail *Metallura williami*

Tyrian Metaltail *Metallura tyrianthina*

Perija Metaltail *Metallura iracunda* GT

Rufous-capped Thornbill *Chalcostigma ruficeps*

Olivaceous Thornbill *Chalcostigma olivaceum*

Blue-mantled Thornbill *Chalcostigma stanleyi*

Bronze-tailed Thornbill *Chalcostigma heteropogon*

Rainbow-bearded Thornbill *Chalcostigma herrani*

Bearded Helmetcrest *Oxypogon guerinii*

Mountain Avocetbill *Opisthoprora euryptera*

Grey-bellied Comet *Taphrolesbia griseiventris* GT

Long-tailed Sylph *Aglaiocercus kingi*

Venezuelan Sylph *Aglaiocercus berlepschi* LR

Violet-tailed Sylph *Aglaiocercus coelestis*

Bearded Mountaineer *Oreonympha nobilis*

Hyacinth Visorbearer *Augastes scutatus* GT

Hooded Visorbearer *Augastes lumachellus* GT

Wedge-billed Hummingbird *Schistes geoffroyi*

Purple-crowned Fairy *Heliothryx barroti* LR

Black-eared Fairy *Heliothryx aurita*

Horned Sungem *Heliactin bilopha*

Marvellous Spatuletail *Loddigesia mirabilis* GT

Plain-capped Starthroat *Heliomaster constantii*

Long-billed Starthroat *Heliomaster longirostris*

Stripe-breasted Starthroat *Heliomaster squamosus*

Blue-tufted Starthroat *Heliomaster furcifer*

Oasis Hummingbird *Rhodopis vesper*

Peruvian Sheartail *Thaumastura cora*

Amethyst Woodstar *Calliphlox amethystina*

Bahama Woodstar *Philodice evelynae*

Magenta-throated Woodstar *Philodice bryantae*

Purple-throated Woodstar *Philodice mitchellii*

Slender Sheartail *Doricha enicura*

Mexican Sheartail *Doricha eliza*

Sparkling-tailed Hummingbird *Tilmatura dupontii*

Slender-tailed Woodstar *Microstilbon burmeisteri*

Lucifer Hummingbird *Calothorax lucifer*

Beautiful Hummingbird *Calothorax pulcher*

Ruby-throated Hummingbird *Archilochus colubris*

Black-chinned Hummingbird *Archilochus alexandri*

Vervain Hummingbird *Mellisuga minima*

Bee Hummingbird *Mellisuga helenae* GT

Anna's Hummingbird *Calypte anna*

Costa's Hummingbird *Calypte costae*

Calliope Hummingbird *Stellula calliope*

Bumblebee Hummingbird *Atthis heloisa*

Wine-throated Hummingbird *Atthis ellioti* LR

Purple-collared Woodstar *Myrtis fanny*

Chilean Woodstar *Eulidia yarrellii* GT

Short-tailed Woodstar *Myrmia micrura*

White-bellied Woodstar *Chaetocercus mulsant*

Little Woodstar *Chaetocercus bombus* GT

Gorgeted Woodstar *Chaetocercus heliodor*

Colombian Woodstar *Chaetocercus astreans*

Esmeraldas Woodstar *Chaetocercus berlepschi* GT

Rufous-shafted Woodstar *Chaetocercus jourdanii*

Broad-tailed Hummingbird *Selasphorus platycercus*

Rufous Hummingbird *Selasphorus rufus*

Allen's Hummingbird *Selasphorus sasin*

Volcano Hummingbird *Selasphorus flammula*

Glow-throated Hummingbird *Selasphorus ardens* GT

Scintillant Hummingbird *Selasphorus scintilla*

COLIIFORMES

Coliidae

Speckled Mousebird *Colius striatus*

Red-backed Mousebird *Colius castanotus*

White-headed Mousebird *Colius leucocephalus*

White-backed Mousebird *Colius colius*

Red-faced Mousebird *Urocolius indicus*

Blue-naped Mousebird *Urocolius macrourus*

TROGONIFORMES

Trogonidae

Resplendent Quetzal *Pharomachrus mocinno* GT

Crested Quetzal *Pharomachrus antisianus* LR

White-tipped Quetzal *Pharomachrus fulgidus*

Golden-headed Quetzal *Pharomachrus auriceps* LR

Pavonine Quetzal *Pharomachrus pavoninus*

Eared Quetzal *Euptilotis neoxenus* GT

Cuban Trogon *Priotelus temnurus*

Hispaniolan Trogon *Temnotrogon roseigaster* GT

Slaty-tailed Trogon *Trogon massena*

Lattice-tailed Trogon *Trogon clathratus*

Black-tailed Trogon *Trogon melanurus*

Ecuadorian Trogon *Trogon mesurus* LR

Chocó Trogon *Trogon comptus* LR

Baird's Trogon *Trogon bairdii* GT, LR

Amazonian White-tailed Trogon *Trogon viridis*

Western White-tailed Trogon *Trogon chionurus* LR

Citreoline Trogon *Trogon citreolus*

Black-headed Trogon *Trogon melanocephalus* LR

Mountain Trogon *Trogon mexicanus*

Elegant Trogon *Trogon elegans*

Collared Trogon *Trogon collaris*

Orange-bellied Trogon *Trogon aurantiiventris* LR

Masked Trogon *Trogon personatus*

Black-throated Trogon *Trogon rufus*

Surucua Trogon *Trogon surrucura*

Blue-crowned Trogon *Trogon curucui*

Amazonian Violaceous Trogon *Trogon violaceus*

Northern Violaceous Trogon *Trogon caligatus* LR

Narina Trogon *Apaloderma narina*

Bare-cheeked Trogon *Apaloderma aequatoriale*

Bar-tailed Trogon *Apaloderma vittatum*

Javan Trogon *Apalharpactes reinwardtii*

Sumatran Trogon *Apalharpactes mackloti* LR

Malabar Trogon *Harpactes fasciatus*

Red-naped Trogon *Harpactes kasumba* GT

Diard's Trogon *Harpactes diardii* GT

Philippine Trogon *Harpactes ardens*

Whitehead's Trogon *Harpactes whiteheadi* GT

Cinnamon-rumped Trogon *Harpactes orrhophaeus* GT

Scarlet-rumped Trogon *Harpactes duvaucelii* GT

Orange-breasted Trogon *Harpactes oreskios*

Red-headed Trogon *Harpactes erythrocephalus*

Ward's Trogon *Harpactes wardi* GT

CORACIIFORMES

Cerylidae

Crested Kingfisher *Megaceryle lugubris*

Giant Kingfisher *Megaceryle maxima*

Ringed Kingfisher *Megaceryle torquata*

Belted Kingfisher *Megaceryle alcyon*

Lesser Pied Kingfisher *Ceryle rudis*

Amazon Kingfisher *Chloroceryle amazona*

Green Kingfisher *Chloroceryle americana*

Green-and-rufous Kingfisher *Chloroceryle inda*

American Pygmy Kingfisher *Chloroceryle aenea*

Alcedinidae

Blyth's Kingfisher *Alcedo hercules* GT

Common Kingfisher *Alcedo atthis*

Half-collared Kingfisher *Alcedo semitorquata* LR

Blue-eared Kingfisher *Alcedo meninting*

Shining-blue Kingfisher *Alcedo quadribrachys*

Blue-banded Kingfisher *Alcedo euryzona* GT

Caerulean Kingfisher *Alcedo coerulescens*

Little Kingfisher *Alcedo pusilla*

Azure Kingfisher *Alcedo azurea*

Bismarck Kingfisher *Alcedo websteri* GT, LR

Madagascar Kingfisher *Alcedo vintsioides* LR

Silvery Kingfisher *Alcedo argentata* GT, LR

Indigo-banded Kingfisher *Alcedo cyanopecta*

Variable Dwarf-Kingfisher *Alcedo lepida*

Malachite Kingfisher *Alcedo cristata*

São Tomé Kingfisher *Alcedo thomensis* LR

Goodfellow's Kingfisher *Alcedo goodfellowi* LR

White-bellied Kingfisher *Alcedo leucogaster*

Príncipe Kingfisher *Alcedo nais* LR

African Dwarf-Kingfisher *Ispidina lecontei*

African Pygmy-Kingfisher *Ispidina picta*

Madagascar Pygmy-Kingfisher *Ispidina madagascariensis*

Oriental Dwarf-Kingfisher *Ceyx erithaca*

Rufous-backed Dwarf-Kingfisher *Ceyx rufidorsa* LR

Philippine Dwarf-Kingfisher *Ceyx melanurus* GT

Sulawesi Dwarf-Kingfisher *Ceyx fallax* GT

Dacelonidae

Banded Kingfisher *Lacedo pulchella*

Laughing Kookaburra *Dacelo novaeguineae*

Blue-winged Kookaburra *Dacelo leachii*

Spangled Kookaburra *Dacelo tyro*

Rufous-bellied Kookaburra *Dacelo gaudichaud*

Shovel-billed Kingfisher *Clytoceyx rex*

Hook-billed Kingfisher *Melidora macrorrhina*

Lilac-cheeked Kingfisher *Cittura cyanotis* GT

Brown-winged Stork-billed-Kingfisher *Pelargopsis amauroptera* GT

Brown-headed Stork-billed-Kingfisher *Pelargopsis capensis*

Celebes Stork-billed Kingfisher *Pelargopsis melanorhyncha*

Ruddy Kingfisher *Halcyon coromanda*

Chocolate-backed Kingfisher *Halcyon badia*

White-breasted Kingfisher *Halcyon smyrnensis*

Black-capped Kingfisher *Halcyon pileata*

Javan Kingfisher *Halcyon cyanoventris*

Grey-headed Kingfisher *Halcyon leucocephala*

Woodland Kingfisher *Halcyon senegalensis*

African Mangrove Kingfisher *Halcyon senegaloides*

Blue-breasted Kingfisher *Halcyon malimbica*

Brown-hooded Kingfisher *Halcyon albiventris*

Striped Kingfisher *Halcyon chelicuti*

Lesser Yellow-billed Kingfisher *Syma torotoro*

Mountain Yellow-billed Kingfisher *Syma megarhyncha*

Black-sided Kingfisher *Todiramphus nigrocyaneus* PGT

Winchell's Kingfisher *Todiramphus winchelli* GT, LR

Moluccan Kingfisher *Todiramphus diops*

Lazuli Kingfisher *Todiramphus lazuli* GT, LR

Forest Kingfisher *Todiramphus macleayii* LR

New Britain Kingfisher *Todiramphus albonotatus* GT

Ultramarine Kingfisher *Todiramphus leucopygius*

Chestnut-bellied Kingfisher *Todiramphus farquhari* GT

Red-backed Kingfisher *Todiramphus pyrrhopygia*

Timor Kingfisher *Todiramphus australasia* GT

Sacred Kingfisher *Todiramphus sanctus*

Micronesian Kingfisher *Todiramphus cinnamominus*

Sombre Kingfisher *Todiramphus funebris* GT

Mangrove Kingfisher *Todiramphus chloris*

Obscure Kingfisher *Todiramphus enigma* GT, LR

Beach Kingfisher *Todiramphus saurophaga*

Flat-billed Kingfisher *Todiramphus recurvirostris*

Tahiti Kingfisher *Todiramphus veneratus*

Pacific Kingfisher *Todiramphus tuta*

Mangaia Kingfisher *Todiramphus ruficollaris* GT, LR

Niau Kingfisher *Todiramphus gertrudae* LR

Mangareva Kingfisher *Todiramphus gambieri* E20, LR

Marquesas Kingfisher *Todiramphus godeffroyi* GT

White-rumped Kingfisher *Caridonax fulgidus*

Moustached Kingfisher *Actenoides bougainvillei* GT

Rufous-collared Kingfisher *Actenoides concretus* GT

Spotted Kingfisher *Actenoides lindsayi*

Blue-capped Kingfisher *Actenoides hombroni* GT, LR

Green-backed Kingfisher *Actenoides monachus* GT

Scaly-breasted Kingfisher *Actenoides princeps*

Aru Paradise-Kingfisher *Tanysiptera hydrocharis* PGT

Common Paradise-Kingfisher *Tanysiptera galatea*

Biak Paradise-Kingfisher *Tanysiptera riedelii* GT, LR

Numfor Paradise-Kingfisher *Tanysiptera carolinae* GT

Kofiau Paradise-Kingfisher *Tanysiptera ellioti* PGT, LR

Red-breasted Paradise-Kingfisher *Tanysiptera nympha*

Brown-headed Paradise-Kingfisher *Tanysiptera danae*

White-tailed Paradise-Kingfisher *Tanysiptera sylvia*

Black-headed Paradise-Kingfisher *Tanysiptera nigriceps* LR

Todidae

Cuban Tody *Todus multicolor*

Narrow-billed Tody *Todus angustirostris*

Jamaican Tody *Todus todus*

Puerto Rican Tody *Todus mexicanus*

Broad-billed Tody *Todus subulatus*

Motmotidae

Tody Motmot *Hylomanes momotula*

Blue-throated Motmot *Aspatha gularis*

Broad-billed Motmot *Electron platyrhynchum*

Keel-billed Motmot *Electron carinatum* GT

Turquoise-browed Motmot *Eumomota superciliosa*

Rufous-capped Motmot *Baryphthengus ruficapillus*

Rufous Motmot *Baryphthengus martii* LR

Russet-crowned Motmot *Momotus mexicanus*

Blue-crowned Motmot *Momotus momota*

Highland Motmot *Momotus aequatorialis* LR

Meropidae

Red-bearded Bee-eater *Nyctyornis amictus*

Blue-bearded Bee-eater *Nyctyornis athertoni*

Purple-bearded Bee-eater *Meropogon forsteni*

Black Bee-eater *Merops gularis*

Blue-headed Bee-eater *Merops muelleri*

Red-throated Bee-eater *Merops bulocki*

White-fronted Bee-eater *Merops bullockoides* LR

Little Bee-eater *Merops pusillus*

Blue-breasted Bee-eater *Merops variegatus*

Cinnamon-chested Bee-eater *Merops oreobates*

Swallow-tailed Bee-eater *Merops hirundineus*

Black-headed Bee-eater *Merops breweri*

Somali Bee-eater *Merops revoilii*

White-throated Bee-eater *Merops albicollis*

Little Green Bee-eater *Merops orientalis*

Böhm's Bee-eater *Merops boehmi*

Blue-throated Bee-eater *Merops viridis* LR

Blue-cheeked Bee-eater *Merops persicus* LR

Madagascar Bee-eater *Merops superciliosus*

Blue-tailed Bee-eater *Merops philippinus* LR

Rainbow Bee-eater *Merops ornatus*

European Bee-eater *Merops apiaster*

Bay-headed Bee-eater *Merops leschenaulti* LR

Rosy Bee-eater *Merops malimbicus*

Carmine Bee-eater *Merops nubicus*

Southern Carmine Bee-eater *Merops nubicoides* LR

Coraciidae

European Roller *Coracias garrulus*

Abyssinian Roller *Coracias abyssinica*

Lilac-breasted Roller *Coracias caudata*

Racquet-tailed Roller *Coracias spatulata*

Rufous-crowned Roller *Coracias noevia*

Indian Roller *Coracias benghalensis*

Purple-winged Roller *Coracias temminckii*

Blue-bellied Roller *Coracias cyanogaster*

African Broad-billed Roller *Eurystomus glaucurus*

Blue-throated Roller *Eurystomus gularis*

Dollarbird *Eurystomus orientalis*

Azure Roller *Eurystomus azureus* GT, LR

Brachypteraciidae

Short-legged Ground-Roller *Brachypteracias leptosomus* GT

Scaly Ground-Roller *Brachypteracias squamigera* GT

Pitta-like Ground-Roller *Atelornis pittoides*

Crossley's Ground-Roller *Atelornis crossleyi* GT

Long-tailed Ground-Roller *Uratelornis chimaera* GT

Leptosomatidae

Madagascar Cuckoo-Roller *Leptosomus discolor*

Comoro Cuckoo-Roller *Leptosomus gracilis* LR

Upupidae

Eurasian Hoopoe *Upupa epops*

African Hoopoe *Upupa africana* LR

Madagascar Hoopoe *Upupa marginata* LR

Phoeniculidae

Green Woodhoopoe *Phoeniculus purpureus*

Black-billed Woodhoopoe *Phoeniculus somaliensis*

Violet Woodhoopoe *Phoeniculus damarensis*

White-headed Woodhoopoe *Phoeniculus bollei*

Forest Woodhoopoe *Phoeniculus castaneiceps*

Black Scimitarbill *Rhinopomastus aterrimus* LR

Common Scimitarbill *Rhinopomastus cyanomelas*

Abyssinian Scimitarbill *Rhinopomastus minor*

Bucerotidae

African Pied Hornbill *Tockus fasciatus*

Crowned Hornbill *Tockus alboterminatus*

Bradfield's Hornbill *Tockus bradfieldi*

Pale-billed Hornbill *Tockus pallidirostris*

African Grey Hornbill *Tockus nasutus*

Hemprich's Hornbill *Tockus hemprichii*

Monteiro's Hornbill *Tockus monteiri*

Black Dwarf Hornbill *Tockus hartlaubi*

Red-billed Dwarf Hornbill *Tockus camurus*

African Red-billed Hornbill *Tockus erythrorhynchus*

Eastern Yellow-billed Hornbill *Tockus flavirostris*

Southern Yellow-billed Hornbill *Tockus leucomelas* LR

Von der Decken's Hornbill *Tockus deckeni*

Jackson's Hornbill *Tockus jacksoni* LR

Indian Grey Hornbill *Ocyceros birostris*

Malabar Grey Hornbill *Ocyceros griseus*

Sri Lankan Grey Hornbill *Ocyceros gingalensis* LR

African White-crested Hornbill *Tropicranus albocristatus*

Austen's Brown Hornbill *Anorrhinus austeni* LR

Tickell's Brown Hornbill *Anorrhinus tickelli* GT

Bushy-crested Hornbill *Anorrhinus galeritus*

Luzon Hornbill *Penelopides manillae* LR

Mindoro Hornbill *Penelopides mindorensis* GT, LR

Visayan Tarictic Hornbill *Penelopides panini* GT

Samar Hornbill *Penelopides samarensis* LR

Mindanao Hornbill *Penelopides affinis* LR

Sulawesi Tarictic Hornbill *Penelopides exarhatus* LR

Long-crested Hornbill *Berenicornis comatus* GT

Rufous-necked Hornbill *Aceros nipalensis* GT

Wrinkled Hornbill *Aceros corrugatus* GT, LR

Rufous-headed Hornbill *Aceros waldeni* GT, LR

Writhed Hornbill *Aceros leucocephalus* GT

Red-knobbed Hornbill *Aceros cassidix* LR

Wreathed Hornbill *Rhyticeros undulatus*

Plain-pouched Hornbill *Rhyticeros subruficollis* GT, LR

Papuan Wreathed Hornbill *Rhyticeros plicatus*

Sumba Wreathed Hornbill *Rhyticeros everetti* GT

Narcondam Wreathed Hornbill *Rhyticeros narcondami* GT, LR

Asian Black Hornbill *Anthracoceros malayanus* GT

Malabar Pied Hornbill *Anthracoceros coronatus* GT

Oriental Pied Hornbill *Anthracoceros albirostris* LR

Sulu Hornbill *Anthracoceros montani* GT

Palawan Hornbill *Anthracoceros marchei* GT

Piping Hornbill *Bycanistes fistulator*

Trumpeter Hornbill *Bycanistes bucinator*

Brown-cheeked Hornbill *Bycanistes cylindricus* GT

White-thighed Hornbill *Bycanistes albotibialis* LR

Black-and-white-casqued Hornbill *Bycanistes subcylindricus*

Silvery-cheeked Hornbill *Bycanistes brevis*

Black-casqued Hornbill *Ceratogymna atrata*

Yellow-casqued Hornbill *Ceratogymna elata* GT

Rhinoceros Hornbill *Buceros rhinoceros* GT

Great Pied Hornbill *Buceros bicornis* GT

Rufous Hornbill *Buceros hydrocorax* GT

Helmeted Hornbill *Rhinoplax vigil* GT

Northern Ground-Hornbill *Bucorvus abyssinicus*

Southern Ground-Hornbill *Bucorvus leadbeateri*

PICIFORMES

Galbulidae

Chestnut Jacamar *Galbalcyrhynchus leucotis*

Purus Jacamar *Galbalcyrhynchus purusianus* LR

White-throated Jacamar *Brachygalba albogularis*

Brown Jacamar *Brachygalba lugubris*

Pale-headed Jacamar *Brachygalba goeringi*

Dusky-backed Jacamar *Brachygalba salmoni*

Three-toed Jacamar *Jacamaralcyon tridactyla* GT

Yellow-billed Jacamar *Galbula albirostris*

Purple-necked Jacamar *Galbula cyanicollis* LR

Green-tailed Jacamar *Galbula galbula*

Rufous-tailed Jacamar *Galbula ruficauda*

Black-chinned Jacamar *Galbula melanogenia* LR

White-chinned Jacamar *Galbula tombacea* LR

Bluish-fronted Jacamar *Galbula cyanescens*

Coppery-chested Jacamar *Galbula pastazae* GT

Purplish Jacamar *Galbula chalcothorax* LR

Bronzy Jacamar *Galbula leucogastra*

Paradise Jacamar *Galbula dea*

Great Jacamar *Jacamerops aureus*

Bucconidae

White-necked Puffbird *Notharchus macrorhynchos*

Black-breasted Puffbird *Notharchus pectoralis*

Brown-banded Puffbird *Notharchus ordii*

Pied Puffbird *Notharchus tectus*

Chestnut-capped Puffbird *Bucco macrodactylus*

Spotted Puffbird *Bucco tamatia*

Sooty-capped Puffbird *Bucco noanamae* GT

Collared Puffbird *Bucco capensis*

Barred Puffbird *Nystalus radiatus*

White-eared Puffbird *Nystalus chacuru*

Striolated Puffbird *Nystalus striolatus*

Spot-backed Puffbird *Nystalus maculatus*

Russet-throated Puffbird *Hypnelus ruficollis*

Crescent-chested Puffbird *Malacoptila striata*

White-chested Puffbird *Malacoptila fusca*

Semicollared Puffbird *Malacoptila semicincta*

Black-streaked Puffbird *Malacoptila fulvogularis*

Rufous-necked Puffbird *Malacoptila rufa*

White-whiskered Puffbird *Malacoptila panamensis*

Moustached Puffbird *Malacoptila mystacalis*

Lanceolated Monklet *Micromonacha lanceolata*

Rusty-breasted Nunlet *Nonnula rubecula*

Fulvous-chinned Nunlet *Nonnula sclateri*

Brown Nunlet *Nonnula brunnea*

Grey-cheeked Nunlet *Nonnula frontalis* LR

Rufous-capped Nunlet *Nonnula ruficapilla*

Chestnut-headed Nunlet *Nonnula amaurocephala*

White-faced Nunbird *Hapaloptila castanea*

Black Nunbird *Monasa atra*

Black-fronted Nunbird *Monasa nigrifrons*

White-fronted Nunbird *Monasa morphoeus*

Yellow-billed Nunbird *Monasa flavirostris*

Swallow-winged Puffbird *Chelidoptera tenebrosa*

Megalaimidae

Fire-tufted Barbet *Psilopogon pyrolophus*

Great Barbet *Megalaima virens*

Red-vented Barbet *Megalaima lagrandieri*

Brown-headed Barbet *Megalaima zeylanica*

Lineated Barbet *Megalaima lineata* LR

White-cheeked Barbet *Megalaima viridis*

Green-eared Barbet *Megalaima faiostricta*

Brown-throated Barbet *Megalaima corvina*

Gold-whiskered Barbet *Megalaima chrysopogon*

Red-crowned Barbet *Megalaima rafflesii* GT

Red-throated Barbet *Megalaima mystacophanos* GT

Black-banded Barbet *Megalaima javensis* GT

Sri Lanka Yellow-fronted Barbet *Megalaima flavifrons*

Golden-throated Barbet *Megalaima franklinii*

Black-browed Barbet *Megalaima oorti*

Blue-throated Barbet *Megalaima asiatica*

Mountain Barbet *Megalaima monticola* LR

Moustached Barbet *Megalaima incognita*

Yellow-crowned Barbet *Megalaima henricii* GT

Flame-fronted Barbet *Megalaima armillaris*

Golden-naped Barbet *Megalaima pulcherrima*

Blue-eared Barbet *Megalaima australis*

Bornean Barbet *Megalaima eximia*

Crimson-fronted Barbet *Megalaima rubricapilla*

Coppersmith Barbet *Megalaima haemacephala*

Brown Barbet *Calorhamphus fuliginosus*

Lybiidae

Naked-faced Barbet *Gymnobucco calvus*

Bristle-nosed Barbet *Gymnobucco peli*

Sladen's Barbet *Gymnobucco sladeni* LR

Grey-throated Barbet *Gymnobucco bonapartei*

White-eared Barbet *Smilorhis leucotis*

Green Barbet *Cryptolybia olivacea*

Woodward's Barbet *Cryptolybia woodwardii* LR

Anchieta's Barbet *Stactolaema anchietae*

Whyte's Barbet *Stactolaema whytii*

Yellow-spotted Barbet *Buccanodon duchaillui*

Speckled Tinkerbird *Pogoniulus scolopaceus*

Moustached Green Tinkerbird *Pogoniulus leucomystax*

Eastern Green Tinkerbird *Pogoniulus simplex*

Western Green Tinkerbird *Pogoniulus coryphaeus*

Red-fronted Tinkerbird *Pogoniulus pusillus*

Yellow-fronted Tinkerbird *Pogoniulus chrysoconus*

Yellow-rumped Tinkerbird *Pogoniulus bilineatus*

White-chested Tinkerbird *Pogoniulus makawai* PGT, LR

Yellow-throated Tinkerbird *Pogoniulus subsulphureus*

Red-rumped Tinkerbird *Pogoniulus atroflavus*

Spot-flanked Barbet *Tricholaema lacrymosa*

Pied Barbet *Tricholaema leucomelas*

Red-fronted Barbet *Tricholaema diademata*

Miombo Barbet *Tricholaema frontata*

African Black-throated Barbet *Tricholaema melanocephala*

Hairy-breasted Barbet *Tricholaema hirsuta*

Banded Barbet *Lybius undatus*

Vieillot's Barbet *Lybius vieilloti*

Black-collared Barbet *Lybius torquatus*

Black-billed Barbet *Lybius guifsobalito*

Red-faced Barbet *Lybius rubrifacies* GT

Chaplin's Barbet *Lybius chaplini* GT

White-headed Barbet *Lybius leucocephalus*

Black-backed Barbet *Lybius minor*

Brown-breasted Barbet *Lybius melanopterus*

Double-toothed Barbet *Lybius bidentatus*

Bearded Barbet *Lybius dubius*

Black-breasted Barbet *Lybius rolleti*

Yellow-billed Barbet *Trachyphonus purpuratus*

Crested Barbet *Trachyphonus vaillantii*

Red-and-yellow Barbet *Trachyphonus erythrocephalus*

D' Arnaud's Barbet *Trachyphonus darnaudii*

Usambiro Barbet *Trachyphonus usambiro* LR

Yellow-breasted Barbet *Trachyphonus margaritatus*

Capitonidae

Scarlet-crowned Barbet *Capito aurovirens*

Scarlet-banded Barbet *Capito wallacei* LR

Spot-crowned Barbet *Capito maculicoronatus*

Orange-fronted Barbet *Capito squamatus* GT

White-mantled Barbet *Capito hypoleucus* GT

Black-girdled Barbet *Capito dayi*

Five-colored Barbet *Capito quinticolor* GT

Black-spotted Barbet *Capito niger*

Gilded Barbet *Capito auratus* LR

Brown-chested Barbet *Capito brunneipectus* LR

Lemon-throated Barbet *Eubucco richardsoni*

Red-headed Barbet *Eubucco bourcierii*

Scarlet-hooded Barbet *Eubucco tucinkae*

Versicolored Barbet *Eubucco versicolor*

Prong-billed Barbet *Semnornis frantzii*

Toucan Barbet *Semnornis ramphastinus* GT

Ramphastidae

Emerald Toucanet *Aulacorhynchus prasinus*

Groove-billed Toucanet *Aulacorhynchus sulcatus*

Chestnut-tipped Toucanet *Aulacorhynchus derbianus*

Crimson-rumped Toucanet *Aulacorhynchus haematopygus*

Yellow-browed Toucanet *Aulacorhynchus huallagae* GT

Blue-banded Toucanet *Aulacorhynchus coeruleicinctis*

Green Araçari *Pteroglossus viridis*

Lettered Araçari *Pteroglossus inscriptus* LR

Red-necked Araçari *Pteroglossus bitorquatus*

Ivory-billed Araçari *Pteroglossus azara*

Brown-mandibled Araçari *Pteroglossus mariae* LR

Black-necked Araçari *Pteroglossus aracari*

Chestnut-eared Araçari *Pteroglossus castanotis*

Many-banded Araçari *Pteroglossus pluricinctus*

Collared Araçari *Pteroglossus torquatus*

Fiery-billed Araçari *Pteroglossus frantzii* LR

Stripe-billed Araçari *Pteroglossus sanguineus*

Pale-mandibled Araçari *Pteroglossus erythropygius* LR

Curl-crested Araçari *Pteroglossus beauharnaesii*

Spot-billed Toucanet *Selenidera maculirostris*

Gould's Toucanet *Selenidera gouldii*

Golden-collared Toucanet *Selenidera reinwardtii*

Tawny-tufted Toucanet *Selenidera nattereri*

Guianan Toucanet *Selenidera culik*

Yellow-eared Toucanet *Selenidera spectabilis*

Saffron Toucanet *Baillonius bailloni* GT

Grey-breasted Mountain-Toucan *Andigena hypoglauca* GT

Plate-billed Mountain-Toucan *Andigena laminirostris* GT

Hooded Mountain-Toucan *Andigena cucullata*

Black-billed Mountain-Toucan *Andigena nigrirostris*

Red-breasted Toucan *Ramphastos dicolorus*

Yellow-ridged Toucan *Ramphastos culminatus* LR

Citron-throated Toucan *Ramphastos citreolaemus* LR

Channel-billed Toucan *Ramphastos vitellinus*

Chocó Toucan *Ramphastos brevis*

Keel-billed Toucan *Ramphastos sulfuratus*

Toco Toucan *Ramphastos toco*

Red-billed Toucan *Ramphastos tucanus*

Cuvier's Toucan *Ramphastos cuvieri* LR

Chestnut-mandibled Toucan *Ramphastos swainsonii* LR

Black-mandibled Toucan *Ramphastos ambiguus*

Indicatoridae

Cassin's Honeybird *Prodotiscus insignis*

Eastern Green-backed Honeybird *Prodotiscus zambesiae*

Wahlberg's Honeybird *Prodotiscus regulus*

Zenker's Honeyguide *Melignomon zenkeri*

Yellow-footed Honeyguide *Melignomon eisentrauti* PGT

Spotted Honeyguide *Indicator maculatus*

Scaly-throated Honeyguide *Indicator variegatus*

Greater Honeyguide *Indicator indicator*

Lesser Honeyguide *Indicator minor*

Thick-billed Honeyguide *Indicator conirostris*

Least Honeyguide *Indicator exilis*

Willcocks's Honeyguide *Indicator willcocksi*

Pallid Honeyguide *Indicator meliphilus*

Dwarf Honeyguide *Indicator pumilio* GT

Yellow-rumped Honeyguide *Indicator xanthonotus* GT

Malaysian Honeyguide *Indicator archipelagicus* GT

Lyre-tailed Honeyguide *Melichneutes robustus*

Picidae

Eurasian Wryneck *Jynx torquilla*

Red-throated Wryneck *Jynx ruficollis*

Speckled Piculet *Picumnus innominatus*

Bar-breasted Piculet *Picumnus aurifrons*

Orinoco Piculet *Picumnus pumilus* LR

Lafresnaye's Piculet *Picumnus lafresnayi* LR

Golden-spangled Piculet *Picumnus exilis*

Ecuadorian Piculet *Picumnus sclateri*

Scaled Piculet *Picumnus squamulatus*

White-bellied Piculet *Picumnus spilogaster*

Guianan Piculet *Picumnus minutissimus*

Spotted Piculet *Picumnus pygmaeus*

Speckle-chested Piculet *Picumnus steindachneri* GT

Varzea Piculet *Picumnus varzeae*

White-barred Piculet *Picumnus cirratus*

Ocellated Piculet *Picumnus dorbygnianus* LR

Ochre-collared Piculet *Picumnus temminckii* LR

White-wedged Piculet *Picumnus albosquamatus*

Rusty-necked Piculet *Picumnus fuscus* GT

Rufous-breasted Piculet *Picumnus rufiventris*

Tawny Piculet *Picumnus fulvescens* GT, LR

Ochraceous Piculet *Picumnus limae* GT

Mottled Piculet *Picumnus nebulosus* GT

Plain-breasted Piculet *Picumnus castelnau*

Fine-barred Piculet *Picumnus subtilis*

Olivaceous Piculet *Picumnus olivaceus*

Greyish Piculet *Picumnus granadensis*

Chestnut Piculet *Picumnus cinnamomeus*

African Piculet *Sasia africana*

Rufous Piculet *Sasia abnormis*

White-browed Piculet *Sasia ochracea*

Antillean Piculet *Nesoctites micromegas*

White Woodpecker *Melanerpes candidus*

Lewis' Woodpecker *Melanerpes lewis*

Guadeloupe Woodpecker *Melanerpes herminieri* GT

Puerto Rican Woodpecker *Melanerpes portoricensis*

Red-headed Woodpecker *Melanerpes erythrocephalus*

Acorn Woodpecker *Melanerpes formicivorus*

Yellow-tufted Woodpecker *Melanerpes cruentatus*

Yellow-fronted Woodpecker *Melanerpes flavifrons*

Golden-naped Woodpecker *Melanerpes chrysauchen*

Black-cheeked Woodpecker *Melanerpes pucherani*

White-fronted Woodpecker *Melanerpes cactorum*

Hispaniolan Woodpecker *Melanerpes striatus*

Jamaican Woodpecker *Melanerpes radiolatus*

Golden-cheeked Woodpecker *Melanerpes chrysogenys*

Grey-breasted Woodpecker *Melanerpes hypopolius*

Yucatan Woodpecker *Melanerpes pygmaeus* LR

Red-crowned Woodpecker *Melanerpes rubricapillus*

Hoffmann's Woodpecker *Melanerpes hoffmannii* LR

Gila Woodpecker *Melanerpes uropygialis*

Golden-fronted Woodpecker *Melanerpes aurifrons*

Red-bellied Woodpecker *Melanerpes carolinus*

Great Red-bellied Woodpecker *Melanerpes superciliaris*

Yellow-bellied Sapsucker *Sphyrapicus varius*

Red-naped Sapsucker *Sphyrapicus nuchalis* LR

Red-breasted Sapsucker *Sphyrapicus ruber* LR

Williamson's Sapsucker *Sphyrapicus thyroideus*

Cuban Green Woodpecker *Xiphidiopicus percussus*

Fine-spotted Woodpecker *Campethera punctuligera*

Bennett's Woodpecker *Campethera bennettii*

Nubian Woodpecker *Campethera nubica*

Reichenow's Woodpecker *Campethera scriptoricauda* LR

Golden-tailed Woodpecker *Campethera abingoni*

Mombasa Woodpecker *Campethera mombassica* LR

Knysna Woodpecker *Campethera notata* GT

Green-backed Woodpecker *Campethera cailliautii*

Little Green Woodpecker *Campethera maculosa*

Fine-banded Woodpecker *Campethera tullbergi*

Buff-spotted Woodpecker *Campethera nivosa*

Brown-eared Woodpecker *Campethera caroli*

Ground Woodpecker *Geocolaptes olivaceus*

Little Grey Woodpecker *Dendropicos elachus*

Speckle-breasted Woodpecker *Dendropicos poecilolaemus*

Abyssinian Golden-backed Woodpecker *Dendropicos abyssinicus*

Cardinal Woodpecker *Dendropicos fuscescens*

Melancholy Woodpecker *Dendropicos lugubris* LR

Gabon Woodpecker *Dendropicos gabonensis*

Stierling's Woodpecker *Dendropicos stierlingi*

Bearded Woodpecker *Dendropicos namaquus*

Yellow-crested Woodpecker *Dendropicos xantholophus*

Fire-bellied Woodpecker *Dendropicos pyrrhogaster*

Elliot's Woodpecker *Dendropicos elliotii*

Grey Woodpecker *Dendropicos goertae*

Grey-headed Woodpecker *Dendropicos spodocephalus* LR

Olive Woodpecker *Dendropicos griseocephalus* LR

Sulawesi Pygmy-Woodpecker *Picoides temminckii*

Sulu Woodpecker *Picoides ramsayi* GT, LR

Philippine Woodpecker *Picoides maculatus*

Brown-capped Woodpecker *Picoides nanus* LR

Sunda Pygmy-Woodpecker *Picoides moluccensis* LR

Brown-backed Woodpecker *Picoides obsoletus*

Pygmy-Woodpecker *Picoides kizuki*

Grey-capped Woodpecker *Picoides canicapillus* LR

Lesser Spotted Woodpecker *Picoides minor*

Fulvous-breasted Woodpecker *Picoides macei*

Stripe-breasted Woodpecker *Picoides atratus*

Brown-fronted Woodpecker *Picoides auriceps*

Yellow-crowned Woodpecker *Picoides mahrattensis*

Arabian Woodpecker *Picoides dorae* GT

Rufous-bellied Woodpecker *Picoides hyperythrus*

Crimson-breasted Woodpecker *Picoides cathpharius*

Darjeeling Pied Woodpecker *Picoides darjellensis*

Middle Spotted Woodpecker *Picoides medius*

White-backed Woodpecker *Picoides leucotos*

Himalayan Woodpecker *Picoides himalayensis*

Sind Woodpecker *Picoides assimilis*

Syrian Woodpecker *Picoides syriacus*

White-winged Woodpecker *Picoides leucopterus*

Great Spotted Woodpecker *Picoides major*

Chequered Woodpecker *Picoides mixtus*

Striped Woodpecker *Picoides lignarius*

Ladder-backed Woodpecker *Picoides scalaris*

Nuttall's Woodpecker *Picoides nuttallii*

Downy Woodpecker *Picoides pubescens*

Red-cockaded Woodpecker *Picoides borealis* GT

Strickland's Woodpecker *Picoides stricklandi*

Arizona Woodpecker *Picoides arizonae* LR

Hairy Woodpecker *Picoides villosus*

White-headed Woodpecker *Picoides albolarvatus*

Eurasian Three-toed Woodpecker *Picoides tridactylus*

American Three-toed Woodpecker *Picoides dorsalis*

Black-backed Three-toed Woodpecker *Picoides arcticus*

Scarlet-backed Woodpecker *Veniliornis callonotus*

Yellow-vented Woodpecker *Veniliornis dignus*

Bar-bellied Woodpecker *Veniliornis nigriceps*

Smoky-brown Woodpecker *Veniliornis fumigatus*

Little Woodpecker *Veniliornis passerinus*

Dot-fronted Woodpecker *Veniliornis frontalis*

White-spotted Woodpecker *Veniliornis spilogaster*

Blood-colored Woodpecker *Veniliornis sanguineus*

Yellow-eared Woodpecker *Veniliornis maculifrons*

Chocó Woodpecker *Veniliornis chocoensis* GT, LR

Red-stained Woodpecker *Veniliornis affinis*

Golden-collared Woodpecker *Veniliornis cassini* LR

Red-rumped Woodpecker *Veniliornis kirkii*

Rufous-winged Woodpecker *Piculus simplex* LR

Stripe-cheeked Woodpecker *Piculus callopterus* LR

Lita Woodpecker *Piculus litae* LR

White-throated Woodpecker *Piculus leucolaemus*

Yellow-throated Woodpecker *Piculus flavigula*

Golden-green Woodpecker *Piculus chrysochloros*

White-browed Woodpecker *Piculus aurulentus* GT

Golden-olive Woodpecker *Piculus rubiginosus*

Grey-crowned Woodpecker *Piculus auricularis* LR

Crimson-mantled Woodpecker *Piculus rivolii*

Black-necked Woodpecker *Chrysoptilus atricollis*

Spot-breasted Woodpecker *Chrysoptilus punctigula*

Green-barred Woodpecker *Chrysoptilus melanochloros*

Golden-breasted Woodpecker *Chrysoptilus melanolaimus* LR

Northern Flicker *Colaptes auratus*

Gilded Flicker *Colaptes chrysoides* LR

Fernandina's Flicker *Colaptes fernandinae* GT

Chilean Flicker *Colaptes pitius*

Andean Flicker *Colaptes rupicola*

Campo Flicker *Colaptes campestris*

Field Flicker *Colaptes campestroides* LR

Rufous Woodpecker *Celeus brachyurus*

Cinnamon Woodpecker *Celeus loricatus*

Waved Woodpecker *Celeus undatus*

Scaly-breasted Woodpecker *Celeus grammicus*

Chestnut-colored Woodpecker *Celeus castaneus*

Chestnut Woodpecker *Celeus elegans*

Pale-crested Woodpecker *Celeus lugubris*

Blond-crested Woodpecker *Celeus flavescens*

Cream-colored Woodpecker *Celeus flavus*

Rufous-headed Woodpecker *Celeus spectabilis*

Ringed Woodpecker *Celeus torquatus*

Helmeted Woodpecker *Dryocopus galeatus* GT

Black-bodied Woodpecker *Dryocopus schulzi* GT

Lineated Woodpecker *Dryocopus lineatus*

Pileated Woodpecker *Dryocopus pileatus*

Andaman Woodpecker *Dryocopus hodgei* GT, LR

White-bellied Woodpecker *Dryocopus javensis*

Black Woodpecker *Dryocopus martius*

Powerful Woodpecker *Campephilus pollens*

Crimson-bellied Woodpecker *Campephilus haematogaster*

Red-necked Woodpecker *Campephilus rubricollis*

Robust Woodpecker *Campephilus robustus*

Pale-billed Woodpecker *Campephilus guatemalensis*

Crimson-crested Woodpecker *Campephilus melanoleucos*

Guayaquil Woodpecker *Campephilus gayaquilensis* GT

Cream-backed Woodpecker *Campephilus leucopogon*

Magellanic Woodpecker *Campephilus magellanicus*

Ivory-billed Woodpecker *Campephilus principalis* GT

Imperial Woodpecker *Campephilus imperialis* PE

Banded Woodpecker *Picus mineaceus*

Crimson-winged Woodpecker *Picus puniceus*

Lesser Yellownape *Picus chlorolophus*

Chequer-throated Woodpecker *Picus mentalis*

Greater Yellownape *Picus flavinucha*

Laced Woodpecker *Picus vittatus*

Streak-breasted Woodpecker *Picus viridanus* LR

Streak-throated Green Woodpecker *Picus xanthopygaeus*

Common Scaly-bellied Woodpecker *Picus squamatus*

Japanese Green Woodpecker *Picus awokera*

Eurasian Green Woodpecker *Picus viridis*

Levaillant's Green Woodpecker *Picus vaillantii* LR

Red-collared Woodpecker *Picus rabieri* GT

Black-headed Woodpecker *Picus erythropygius*

Grey-headed Green Woodpecker *Picus canus*

Olive-backed Woodpecker *Dinopium rafflesii* GT

Himalayan Flameback *Dinopium shorii*

Common Goldenback *Dinopium javanense*

Black-rumped Flameback *Dinopium benghalense*

Greater Flameback *Chrysocolaptes lucidus*

White-naped Woodpecker *Chrysocolaptes festivus*

Pale-headed Woodpecker *Gecinulus grantia*

Bamboo Woodpecker *Gecinulus viridis* LR

Okinawan Woodpecker *Sapheopipo noguchii* GT

Maroon Woodpecker *Blythipicus rubiginosus*

Bay Woodpecker *Blythipicus pyrrhotis*

Orange-backed Woodpecker *Reinwardtipicus validus*

Buff-rumped Woodpecker *Meiglyptes tristis*

Black-and-buff Woodpecker *Meiglyptes jugularis*

Buff-necked Woodpecker *Meiglyptes tukki* GT

Grey-and-buff Woodpecker *Hemicircus concretus*

Heart-spotted Woodpecker *Hemicircus canente*

Ashy Woodpecker *Mulleripicus fulvus*

Sooty Woodpecker *Mulleripicus funebris*

Great Slaty Woodpecker *Mulleripicus pulverulentus*

PASSERIFORMES

Dendrocolaptidae

Tyrannine Woodcreeper *Dendrocincla tyrannina*

Thrush-like Woodcreeper *Dendrocincla turdina* LR

Plain-brown Woodcreeper *Dendrocincla fuliginosa*

Tawny-winged Woodcreeper *Dendrocincla anabatina*

White-chinned Woodcreeper *Dendrocincla merula*

Ruddy Woodcreeper *Dendrocincla homochroa*

Long-tailed Woodcreeper *Deconychura longicauda*

Spot-throated Woodcreeper *Deconychura stictolaema*

Olivaceous Woodcreeper *Sittasomus griseicapillus*

Wedge-billed Woodcreeper *Glyphorynchus spirurus*

Scimitar-billed Woodcreeper *Drymornis bridgesii*

Long-billed Woodcreeper *Nasica longirostris*

Cinnamon-throated Woodcreeper *Dendrexetastes rufigula*

Red-billed Woodcreeper *Hylexetastes perrotii*

Uniform Woodcreeper *Hylexetastes uniformis* LR

Brigida's Woodcreeper *Hylexetastes brigidai*

Bar-bellied Woodcreeper *Hylexetastes stresemanni*

Strong-billed Woodcreeper *Xiphocolaptes promeropirhynchus*

Great-billed Woodcreeper *Xiphocolaptes orenocensis* LR

White-throated Woodcreeper *Xiphocolaptes albicollis*

Vila Nova Woodcreeper *Xiphocolaptes villanovae* LR

Moustached Woodcreeper *Xiphocolaptes falcirostris* GT

Great Rufous Woodcreeper *Xiphocolaptes major*

Amazon Barred Woodcreeper *Dendrocolaptes certhia*

Northern Barred Woodcreeper *Dendrocolaptes sanctithomae* LR

Hoffmanns's Woodcreeper *Dendrocolaptes hoffmannsi*

Black-banded Woodcreeper *Dendrocolaptes picumnus*

Planalto Woodcreeper *Dendrocolaptes platyrostris*

Straight-billed Woodcreeper *Xiphorhynchus picus*

Zimmer's Woodcreeper *Xiphorhynchus necopinus*

Striped Woodcreeper *Xiphorhynchus obsoletus*

Ocellated Woodcreeper *Xiphorhynchus ocellatus*

Spix's Woodcreeper *Xiphorhynchus spixii*

Elegant Woodcreeper *Xiphorhynchus elegans*

Chestnut-rumped Woodcreeper *Xiphorhynchus pardalotus*

Buff-throated Woodcreeper *Xiphorhynchus guttatus*

Cocoa Woodcreeper *Xiphorhynchus susurrans* LR

Dusky-billed Woodcreeper *Xiphorhynchus eytoni* LR

Ivory-billed Woodcreeper *Xiphorhynchus flavigaster*

Black-striped Woodcreeper *Xiphorhynchus lachrymosus*

Spotted Woodcreeper *Xiphorhynchus erythropygius* LR

Olive-backed Woodcreeper *Xiphorhynchus triangularis*

White-striped Woodcreeper *Lepidocolaptes leucogaster*

Streak-headed Woodcreeper *Lepidocolaptes souleyetii*

Narrow-billed Woodcreeper *Lepidocolaptes angustirostris*

Spot-crowned Woodcreeper *Lepidocolaptes affinis* LR

Montane Woodcreeper *Lepidocolaptes lacrymiger* LR

Scaled Woodcreeper *Lepidocolaptes squamatus*

Lesser Woodcreeper *Lepidocolaptes fuscus*

Lineated Woodcreeper *Lepidocolaptes albolineatus*

Greater Scythebill *Campylorhamphus pucherani* GT

Red-billed Scythebill *Campylorhamphus trochilirostris*

Black-billed Scythebill *Campylorhamphus falcularius* LR

Brown-billed Scythebill *Campylorhamphus pusillus*

Curve-billed Scythebill *Campylorhamphus procurvoides*

Furnariidae

Campo Miner *Geobates poecilopterus* GT

Common Miner *Geositta cunicularia*

Greyish Miner *Geositta maritima*

Coastal Miner *Geositta peruviana*

Puna Miner *Geositta punensis*

Dark-winged Miner *Geositta saxicolina*

Creamy-rumped Miner *Geositta isabellina*

Short-billed Miner *Geositta antarctica*

Rufous-banded Miner *Geositta rufipennis*

Thick-billed Miner *Geositta crassirostris*

Slender-billed Miner *Geositta tenuirostris*

Chaco Earthcreeper *Upucerthia certhioides*

Bolivian Earthcreeper *Upucerthia harterti* LR

Straight-billed Earthcreeper *Upucerthia ruficauda*

Rock Earthcreeper *Upucerthia andaecola*

White-throated Earthcreeper *Upucerthia albigula*

Striated Earthcreeper *Upucerthia serrana*

Scale-throated Earthcreeper *Upucerthia dumetaria*

Buff-breasted Earthcreeper *Upucerthia validirostris* LR

Plain-breasted Earthcreeper *Upucerthia jelskii*

Bar-winged Cinclodes *Cinclodes fuscus*

Stout-billed Cinclodes *Cinclodes excelsior*

Royal Cinclodes *Cinclodes aricomae* GT, LR

Olrog's Cinclodes *Cinclodes olrogi* LR

Cordoba Cinclodes *Cinclodes comechingonus* LR

Long-tailed Cinclodes *Cinclodes pabsti*

White-winged Cinclodes *Cinclodes atacamensis*

White-bellied Cinclodes *Cinclodes palliatus* GT

Grey-flanked Cinclodes *Cinclodes oustaleti*

Dark-bellied Cinclodes *Cinclodes patagonicus*

Chilean Seaside Cinclodes *Cinclodes nigrofumosus*

Peruvian Seaside Cinclodes *Cinclodes taczanowskii*

Blackish Cinclodes *Cinclodes antarcticus*

Crag Chilia *Chilia melanura*

Lesser Hornero *Furnarius minor*

Tail-banded Hornero *Furnarius figulus*

Tricolored Hornero *Furnarius tricolor* LR

Pale-legged Hornero *Furnarius leucopus*

Pacific Hornero *Furnarius cinnamomeus* LR

Pale-billed Hornero *Furnarius torridus* LR

Rufous Hornero *Furnarius rufus*

Crested Hornero *Furnarius cristatus*

Des Murs's Wiretail *Sylviorthorhynchus desmursii*

Thorn-tailed Rayadito *Aphrastura spinicauda*

Mas Afuera Rayadito *Aphrastura masafuerae* GT

Brown-capped Tit-Spinetail *Leptasthenura fuliginiceps*

Tawny Tit-Spinetail *Leptasthenura yanacensis* GT

Tufted Tit-Spinetail *Leptasthenura platensis*

Plain-mantled Tit-Spinetail *Leptasthenura aegithaloides*

Araucaria Tit-Spinetail *Leptasthenura setaria* GT

Streaked Tit-Spinetail *Leptasthenura striata*

Striolated Tit-Spinetail *Leptasthenura striolata*

Rusty-crowned Tit-Spinetail *Leptasthenura pileata*

White-browed Tit-Spinetail *Leptasthenura xenothorax* GT, LR

Andean Tit-Spinetail *Leptasthenura andicola*

Perijá Thistletail *Schizoeaca perijana* GT, LR

White-chinned Spinetail *Schizoeaca fuliginosa*

Mouse-colored Thistletail *Schizoeaca griseomurina*

Ochre-browed Thistletail *Schizoeaca coryi*

Vilcabamba Thistletail *Schizoeaca vilcabambae* LR

Eye-ringed Thistletail *Schizoeaca palpebralis*

Itatiaia Spinetail *Schizoeaca moreirae*

Puna Thistletail *Schizoeaca helleri* LR

Black-throated Thistletail *Schizoeaca harterti* LR

Chotoy Spinetail *Schoeniophylax phryganophila*

Rufous-capped Spinetail *Synallaxis ruficapilla*

Bahia Spinetail *Synallaxis whitneyi* GT, LR

Buff-browed Spinetail *Synallaxis superciliosa* LR

Sooty-fronted Spinetail *Synallaxis frontalis*

Azara's Spinetail *Synallaxis azarae*

Dark-breasted Spinetail *Synallaxis albigularis*

Pale-breasted Spinetail *Synallaxis albescens*

Chicli Spinetail *Synallaxis spixi*

Cinereous-breasted Spinetail *Synallaxis hypospodia*

Pinto's Spinetail *Synallaxis infuscata* GT, LR

Slaty Spinetail *Synallaxis brachyura*

Apurimac Spinetail *Synallaxis courseni* GT

Dusky Spinetail *Synallaxis moesta*

Cabanis' Spinetail *Synallaxis cabanisi* LR

MacConnell's Spinetail *Synallaxis macconnelli*

Silvery-throated Spinetail *Synallaxis subpudica*

Blackish-headed Spinetail *Synallaxis tithys* GT

Grey-bellied Spinetail *Synallaxis cinerascens*

White-bellied Spinetail *Synallaxis propinqua*

Red-shouldered Spinetail *Synallaxis hellmayri* GT

Plain-crowned Spinetail *Synallaxis gujanensis*

Marañón Spinetail *Synallaxis maranonica* GT, LR

White-lored Spinetail *Synallaxis albilora* LR

Ruddy Spinetail *Synallaxis rutilans*

Chestnut-throated Spinetail *Synallaxis cherriei* GT

Rufous Spinetail *Synallaxis unirufa*

Black-throated Spinetail *Synallaxis castanea* LR

Rusty-headed Spinetail *Synallaxis fuscorufa* GT

Russet-bellied Spinetail *Synallaxis zimmeri* GT

Rufous-breasted Spinetail *Synallaxis erythrothorax*

Stripe-breasted Spinetail *Synallaxis cinnamomea*

Necklaced Spinetail *Synallaxis stictothorax*

Chinchipe Spinetail *Synallaxis chinchipensis* LR

White-whiskered Spinetail *Poecilurus candei*

Hoary-throated Spinetail *Poecilurus kollari* GT

Ochre-cheeked Spinetail *Poecilurus scutatus*

White-browed Spinetail *Hellmayrea gularis*

Red-faced Spinetail *Cranioleuca erythrops*

Line-cheeked Spinetail *Cranioleuca antisiensis*

Bolivian Spinetail *Cranioleuca henricae* GT, LR

Baron's Spinetail *Cranioleuca baroni* LR

Pallid Spinetail *Cranioleuca pallida*

Ash-browed Spinetail *Cranioleuca curtata*

Tepui Spinetail *Cranioleuca demissa*

Olive Spinetail *Cranioleuca obsoleta*

Streak-capped Spinetail *Cranioleuca hellmayeri*

Crested Spinetail *Cranioleuca subcristata*

Stripe-crowned Spinetail *Cranioleuca pyrrhophia*

Marcapata Spinetail *Cranioleuca marcapatae*

Light-crowned Spinetail *Cranioleuca albiceps*

Grey-headed Spinetail *Cranioleuca semicinerea*

Creamy-crested Spinetail *Cranioleuca albicapilla*

Coiba Spinetail *Cranioleuca dissita* GT, LR

Rusty-backed Spinetail *Cranioleuca vulpina*

Parker's Spinetail *Cranioleuca vulpecula* LR

Scaled Spinetail *Cranioleuca muelleri*

Speckled Spinetail *Cranioleuca gutturata*

Sulphur-bearded Spinetail *Cranioleuca sulphurifera*

Pink-legged Graveteiro *Acrobatornis fonsecai* GT

Yellow-chinned Spinetail *Certhiaxis cinnamomea*

Red-and-white Spinetail *Certhiaxis mustelina*

Lesser Canastero *Asthenes pyrrholeuca*

Short-billed Canastero *Asthenes baeri*

Canyon Canastero *Asthenes pudibunda*

Rusty-fronted Canastero *Asthenes ottonis*

Iquico Canastero *Asthenes heterura* GT

Cordilleran Canastero *Asthenes modesta*

Cactus Canastero *Asthenes cactorum* LR

Cipó Canastero *Asthenes luizae* GT, LR

Creamy-breasted Canastero *Asthenes dorbignyi*

Dark-winged Canastero *Asthenes arequipae* LR

Pale-tailed Canastero *Asthenes huancavelicae* GT, LR

White-tailed Canastero *Asthenes usheri* LR

Berlepsch's Canastero *Asthenes berlepschi* GT

Chestnut Canastero *Asthenes steinbachi* GT

Dusky-tailed Canastero *Asthenes humicola*

Patagonian Canastero *Asthenes patagonica*

Streak-throated Canastero *Asthenes humilis*

Austral Canastero *Asthenes anthoides* GT

Streak-backed Canastero *Asthenes wyatti*

Cordoba Canastero *Asthenes sclateri* LR

Puna Canastero *Asthenes punensis* LR

Line-fronted Canastero *Asthenes urubambensis* GT

Junin Canastero *Asthenes virgata* LR

Many-striped Canastero *Asthenes flammulata*

Scribble-tailed Canastero *Asthenes maculicauda*

Hudson's Canastero *Asthenes hudsoni*

Great Spinetail *Siptornopsis hypochondriacus* GT

Orinoco Softtail *Thripophaga cherriei* GT

Striated Softtail *Thripophaga macroura* GT

Plain Softtail *Thripophaga fusciceps*

Russet-mantled Softtail *Thripophaga berlepschi* GT

Common Thornbird *Phacellodomus rufifrons*

Little Thornbird *Phacellodomus sibilatrix*

Streak-fronted Thornbird *Phacellodomus striaticeps*

Red-eyed Thornbird *Phacellodomus erythrophthalmus*

Spot-breasted Thornbird *Phacellodomus maculipectus* LR

Freckle-breasted Thornbird *Phacellodomus striaticollis*

Chestnut-backed Thornbird *Phacellodomus dorsalis* PGT

Greater Thornbird *Phacellodomus ruber*

Canebrake Groundcreeper *Clibanornis dendrocolaptoides* GT

Bay-capped Wren Spinetail *Spartonoica maluroides* GT

Wren-like Rushbird *Phleocryptes melanops*

Curve-billed Reedhaunter *Limnornis curvirostris*

Straight-billed Reedhaunter *Limnornis rectirostris* GT

Firewood-gatherer *Anumbius annumbi*

Lark-like Brushrunner *Coryphistera alaudina*

Band-tailed Earthcreeper *Eremobius phoenicurus*

Spectacled Prickletail *Siptornis striaticollis*

Orange-fronted Plushcrown *Metopothrix aurantiacus*

Double-banded Greytail *Xenerpestes minlosi*

Equatorial Greytail *Xenerpestes singularis* GT

Rusty-winged Barbtail *Premnornis guttuligera*

Spotted Barbtail *Premnoplex brunnescens*

White-throated Barbtail *Premnoplex tatei* GT

Roraiman Barbtail *Roraimia adusta*

Ruddy Treerunner *Margarornis rubiginosus*

Star-chested Treerunner *Margarornis stellatus* GT

Beautiful Treerunner *Margarornis bellulus* GT, LR

Pearled Treerunner *Margarornis squamiger*

Sharp-tailed Streamcreeper *Lochmias nematura*

Rufous Cacholote *Pseudoseisura cristata*

Brown Cacholote *Pseudoseisura lophotes*

White-throated Cacholote *Pseudoseisura gutturalis*

Buffy Tuftedcheek *Pseudocolaptes lawrencii* LR

Pacific Tuftedcheek *Pseudocolaptes johnsoni* LR

Streaked Tuftedcheek *Pseudocolaptes boissonneautii*

Point-tailed Palmcreeper *Berlepschia rikeri*

Chestnut-winged Hookbill *Ancistrops strigilatus*

Eastern Woodhaunter *Hyloctistes subulatus*

Western Woodhaunter *Hyloctistes virgatus* LR

Guttulated Foliage-gleaner *Syndactyla guttulata*

Lineated Foliage-gleaner *Syndactyla subalaris*

Buff-browed Foliage-gleaner *Syndactyla rufosuperciliata*

Rufous-necked Foliage-gleaner *Syndactyla ruficollis* GT

Montane Foliage-gleaner *Anabacerthia striaticollis*

Scaly-throated Foliage-gleaner *Anabacerthia variegaticeps* LR

White-browed Foliage-gleaner *Philydor amaurotis* GT

Rufous-tailed Foliage-gleaner *Philydor ruficaudatus*

Rufous-rumped Foliage-gleaner *Philydor erythrocercus*

Slaty-winged Foliage-gleaner *Philydor fuscipennis* LR

Ochre-bellied Foliage-gleaner *Philydor ochrogaster* LR

Chestnut-winged Foliage-gleaner *Philydor erythropterus*

Ochre-breasted Foliage-gleaner *Philydor lichtensteini*

Rufous-backed Foliage-gleaner *Philydor erythronotus* LR

Alagoas Foliage-gleaner *Philydor novaesi* GT

Black-capped Foliage-gleaner *Philydor atricapillus*

Buff-fronted Foliage-gleaner *Philydor rufus*

Cinnamon-rumped Foliage-gleaner *Philydor pyrrhodes*

Russet-mantled Foliage-gleaner *Philydor dimidiatus*

Peruvian Recurvebill *Simoxenops ucayalae* GT

Bolivian Recurvebill *Simoxenops striatus* GT

Pale-browed Treehunter *Cichlocolaptes leucophrus*

Uniform Treehunter *Thripadectes ignobilis*

Streak-breasted Treehunter *Thripadectes rufobrunneus*

Black-billed Treehunter *Thripadectes melanorhynchus*

Striped Treehunter *Thripadectes holostictus*

Streak-capped Treehunter *Thripadectes virgaticeps*

Buff-throated Treehunter *Thripadectes scrutator*

Flammulated Treehunter *Thripadectes flammulatus*

Buff-throated Foliage-gleaner *Automolus ochrolaemus*

Olive-backed Foliage-gleaner *Automolus infuscatus*

White-eyed Foliage-gleaner *Automolus leucophthalmus*

Brown-rumped Foliage-gleaner *Automolus melanopezus*

White-throated Foliage-gleaner *Automolus roraimae*

Ruddy Foliage-gleaner *Automolus rubiginosus*

Chestnut-crowned Foliage-gleaner *Automolus rufipileatus*

White-collared Foliage-gleaner *Anabazenops fuscus*

Bamboo Foliage-gleaner *Anabazenops dorsalis*

Chestnut-capped Foliage-gleaner *Hylocryptus rectirostris*

Henna-hooded Foliage-gleaner *Hylocryptus erythrocephalus* GT

Tawny-throated Leaftosser *Sclerurus mexicanus*

Short-billed Leaftosser *Sclerurus rufigularis*

Grey-throated Leaftosser *Sclerurus albigularis*

Black-tailed Leaftosser *Sclerurus caudacutus*

Rufous-breasted Leaftosser *Sclerurus scansor*

Scaly-throated Leaftosser *Sclerurus guatemalensis*

Sharp-billed Xenops *Heliobletus contaminatus*

Rufous-tailed Xenops *Xenops milleri*

Slender-billed Xenops *Xenops tenuirostris*

Plain Xenops *Xenops minutus*

Streaked Xenops *Xenops rutilans*

Great Xenops *Megaxenops parnaguae* GT

White-throated Treerunner *Pygarrhichas albogularis*

Thamnophilidae

Fasciated Antshrike *Cymbilaimus lineatus*

Bamboo Antshrike *Cymbilaimus sanctaemariae* LR

Spot-backed Antshrike *Hypoedaleus guttatus*

Giant Antshrike *Batara cinerea*

Large-tailed Antshrike *Mackenziaena leachii*

Tufted Antshrike *Mackenziaena severa*

Black-throated Antshrike *Frederickena viridis*

Undulated Antshrike *Frederickena unduligera*

Great Antshrike *Taraba major*

Black-crested Antshrike *Sakesphorus canadensis*

Silvery-cheeked Antshrike *Sakesphorus cristatus*

Collared Antshrike *Sakesphorus bernardi*

Black-backed Antshrike *Sakesphorus melanonotus*

Band-tailed Antshrike *Sakesphorus melanothorax*

Glossy Antshrike *Sakesphorus luctuosus*

White-bearded Antshrike *Biatas nigropectus* GT

Barred Antshrike *Thamnophilus doliatus*

Chapman's Antshrike *Thamnophilus zarumae* LR

Bar-crested Antshrike *Thamnophilus multistriatus*

Chestnut-backed Antshrike *Thamnophilus palliatus*

Lined Antshrike *Thamnophilus tenuepunctatus* LR

Black-hooded Antshrike *Thamnophilus bridgesi*

Black Antshrike *Thamnophilus nigriceps*

Cocha Antshrike *Thamnophilus praecox* GT, LR

Blackish-grey Antshrike *Thamnophilus nigrocinereus*

Castelnau's Antshrike *Thamnophilus cryptoleucus* LR

White-shouldered Antshrike *Thamnophilus aethiops*

Uniform Antshrike *Thamnophilus unicolor*

Plain-winged Antshrike *Thamnophilus schistaceus*

Mouse-colored Antshrike *Thamnophilus murinus*

Upland Antshrike *Thamnophilus aroyae*

Western Slaty Antshrike *Thamnophilus atrinucha* LR

Guianan Slaty Antshrike *Thamnophilus punctatus*

Peruvian Slaty Antshrike *Thamnophilus leucogaster* LR

Natterer's Slaty Antshrike *Thamnophilus stictocephalus* LR

Bolivian Slaty Antshrike *Thamnophilus sticturus* LR

Planalto Slaty Antshrike *Thamnophilus pelzelni* LR

Sooretama Slaty Antshrike *Thamnophilus ambiguus* LR

Streak-backed Antshrike *Thamnophilus insignis*

Amazonian Antshrike *Thamnophilus amazonicus*

Variable Antshrike *Thamnophilus caerulescens*

Rufous-winged Antshrike *Thamnophilus torquatus*

Rufous-capped Antshrike *Thamnophilus ruficapillus*

Spot-winged Antshrike *Pygiptila stellaris*

Pearly Antshrike *Megastictus margaritatus*

Black Bushbird *Neoctantes niger*

Recurve-billed Bushbird *Clytoctantes alixii* GT

Rondônia Bushbird *Clytoctantes atrogularis* GT

Speckled Antshrike *Xenornis setifrons* GT

Russet Antshrike *Thamnistes anabatinus*

Spot-breasted Antvireo *Dysithamnus stictothorax* GT

Plain Antvireo *Dysithamnus mentalis*

Streak-crowned Antvireo *Dysithamnus striaticeps*

Spot-crowned Antvireo *Dysithamnus puncticeps*

Rufous-backed Antvireo *Dysithamnus xanthopterus*

Bicolored Antvireo *Dysithamnus occidentalis* GT

White-streaked Antvireo *Dysithamnus leucostictus* LR

Plumbeous Antvireo *Dysithamnus plumbeus* GT

Dusky-throated Antshrike *Thamnomanes ardesiacus*

Saturnine Antshrike *Thamnomanes saturninus* LR

Cinereous Antshrike *Thamnomanes caesius*

Bluish-slate Antshrike *Thamnomanes schistogynus*

Pygmy Antwren *Myrmotherula brachyura*

Griscom's Antwren *Myrmotherula ignota* LR

Short-billed Antwren *Myrmotherula obscura*

Sclater's Antwren *Myrmotherula sclateri*

Klages's Antwren *Myrmotherula klagesi* GT

Guianan Streaked Antwren *Myrmotherula surinamensis*

Pacific Streaked Antwren *Myrmotherula pacifica* LR

Amazonian Streaked Antwren *Myrmotherula multostriata* LR

Yellow-throated Antwren *Myrmotherula ambigua*

Cherrie's Antwren *Myrmotherula cherriei*

Rufous-bellied Antwren *Myrmotherula guttata*

Stripe-chested Antwren *Myrmotherula longicauda*

Plain-throated Antwren *Myrmotherula hauxwelli*

Star-throated Antwren *Myrmotherula gularis*

Brown-bellied Antwren *Myrmotherula gutturalis*

Checker-throated Antwren *Myrmotherula fulviventris*

White-eyed Antwren *Myrmotherula leucophthalma*

Alagoas Antwren *Myrmotherula snowi* GT

Yasuní Antwren *Myrmotherula fjeldsaai* LR

Foothills Antwren *Myrmotherula spodionota* LR

Stipple-throated Antwren *Myrmotherula haematonota*

Ornate Antwren *Myrmotherula ornata*

Rufous-tailed Antwren *Myrmotherula erythrura*

White-flanked Antwren *Myrmotherula axillaris*

Slaty Antwren *Myrmotherula schisticolor*

Río Suno Antwren *Myrmotherula sunensis*

Long-winged Antwren *Myrmotherula longipennis*

Salvadori's Antwren *Myrmotherula minor* GT

Ihering's Antwren *Myrmotherula iheringi*

Rio de Janeiro Antwren *Myrmotherula fluminensis* GT, LR, PH

Ashy Antwren *Myrmotherula grisea* GT

Unicolored Antwren *Myrmotherula unicolor* GT

Plain-winged Antwren *Myrmotherula behni*

Band-tailed Antwren *Myrmotherula urosticta* GT

Grey Antwren *Myrmotherula menetriesii*

Leaden Antwren *Myrmotherula assimilis*

Banded Antwren *Dichrozona cincta*

Stripe-backed Antbird *Myrmorchilus strigilatus*

Ash-throated Antwren *Herpsilochmus parkeri* GT, LR

Black-capped Antwren *Herpsilochmus atricapillus* LR

Pileated Antwren *Herpsilochmus pileatus* GT

Creamy-bellied Antwren *Herpsilochmus motacilloides* LR

Spot-tailed Antwren *Herpsilochmus sticturus*

Colombian Antwren *Herpsilochmus dugandi* LR

Todd's Antwren *Herpsilochmus stictocephalus*

Ancient Antwren *Herpsilochmus gentryi* GT

Spot-backed Antwren *Herpsilochmus dorsimaculatus*

Roraiman Antwren *Herpsilochmus roraimae*

Pectoral Antwren *Herpsilochmus pectoralis* GT

Large-billed Antwren *Herpsilochmus longirostris*

Yellow-breasted Antwren *Herpsilochmus axillaris*

Rufous-winged Antwren *Herpsilochmus rufimarginatus*

Dot-winged Antwren *Microrhopias quixensis*

Black-hooded Antwren *Formicivora erythronotos* GT, LR

Narrow-billed Antwren *Formicivora iheringi* GT

White-fringed Antwren *Formicivora grisea*

Serra Antwren *Formicivora serrana* LR

Restinga Antwren *Formicivora littoralis* GT

Black-bellied Antwren *Formicivora melanogaster*

Rusty-backed Antwren *Formicivora rufa*

Paraná Antwren *Stymphalornis acutirostris* GT

Ferruginous Antbird *Drymophila ferruginea*

Bertoni's Antwren *Drymophila rubricollis*

Rufous-tailed Antbird *Drymophila genei* GT

Ochre-rumped Antbird *Drymophila ochropyga* GT

Striated Antbird *Drymophila devillei*

Long-tailed Antbird *Drymophila caudata*

Dusky-tailed Antbird *Drymophila malura*

Scaled Antbird *Drymophila squamata*

Streak-capped Antwren *Terenura maculata*

Orange-bellied Antwren *Terenura sicki* GT

Rufous-rumped Antwren *Terenura callinota*

Perija Antwren *Terenura venezuelana* LR

Chestnut-shouldered Antwren *Terenura humeralis*

Yellow-rumped Antwren *Terenura sharpei* GT

Ash-winged Antwren *Terenura spodioptila*

Grey Antbird *Cercomacra cinerascens*

Rio de Janeiro Antbird *Cercomacra brasiliana* GT

Dusky Antbird *Cercomacra tyrannina*

Willis's Antbird *Cercomacra laeta* LR

Parker's Antbird *Cercomacra parkeri*

Blackish Antbird *Cercomacra nigrescens*

Black Antbird *Cercomacra serva*

Jet Antbird *Cercomacra nigricans*

Rio Branco Antbird *Cercomacra carbonaria* GT

Manu Antbird *Cercomacra manu* LR

Mato Grosso Antbird *Cercomacra melanaria*

Bananal Antbird *Cercomacra ferdinandi*

White-backed Fire-eye *Pyriglena leuconota*

Fringe-backed Fire-eye *Pyriglena atra* GT

White-shouldered Fire-eye *Pyriglena leucoptera*

Slender Antbird *Rhopornis ardesiaca* GT

White-browed Antbird *Myrmoborus leucophrys*

Ash-breasted Antbird *Myrmoborus lugubris*

Black-faced Antbird *Myrmoborus myotherinus*

Black-tailed Antcreeper *Myrmoborus melanurus* GT

Warbling Antbird *Hypocnemis cantator*

Yellow-browed Antbird *Hypocnemis hypoxantha*

Black-chinned Antbird *Hypocnemoides melanopogon*

Band-tailed Antbird *Hypocnemoides maculicauda*

Black-and-white Antbird *Myrmochanes hemileucus*

Bare-crowned Antbird *Gymnocichla nudiceps*

Silvered Antbird *Sclateria naevia*

Black-headed Antbird *Percnostola rufifrons*

Allpahuayo Antbird *Percnostola arenarum* LR

Slate-colored Antbird *Percnostola schistacea*

Spot-winged Antbird *Percnostola leucostigma*

Caura Antbird *Percnostola caurensis*

White-lined Antbird *Percnostola lophotes*

White-bellied Antbird *Myrmeciza longipes*

Chestnut-backed Antbird *Myrmeciza exsul*

Ferruginous-backed Antbird *Myrmeciza ferruginea*

Scalloped Antbird *Myrmeciza ruficauda* GT

White-bibbed Antbird *Myrmeciza loricata*

Squamate Antbird *Myrmeciza squamosa*

Grey-bellied Antbird *Myrmeciza pelzelni*

Chestnut-tailed Antbird *Myrmeciza hemimelaena*

Grey-headed Antbird *Myrmeciza griseiceps* GT

Dull-mantled Antbird *Myrmeciza laemosticta*

Esmeraldas Antbird *Myrmeciza nigricauda* LR

Stub-tailed Antbird *Myrmeciza berlepschi* LR

Yapacana Antbird *Myrmeciza disjuncta*

Plumbeous Antbird *Myrmeciza hyperythra*

Goeldi's Antbird *Myrmeciza goeldii*

White-shouldered Antbird *Myrmeciza melanoceps*

Sooty Antbird *Myrmeciza fortis*

Immaculate Antbird *Myrmeciza immaculata*

Black-throated Antbird *Myrmeciza atrothorax*

White-plumed Antbird *Pithys albifrons*

White-masked Antbird *Pithys castanea* PGT, PH

Rufous-throated Antbird *Gymnopithys rufigula*

White-throated Antbird *Gymnopithys salvini*

Lunulated Antbird *Gymnopithys lunulata*
Bicolored Antbird *Gymnopithys bicolor* LR
White-cheeked Antbird *Gymnopithys leucaspis*
Wing-banded Antbird *Myrmornis torquata*
Bare-eyed Antbird *Rhegmatorhina gymnops*
Harlequin Antbird *Rhegmatorhina berlepschi*
Chestnut-crested Antcatcher *Rhegmatorhina cristata*
White-breasted Antcatcher *Rhegmatorhina hoffmannsi*
Hairy-crested Antcatcher *Rhegmatorhina melanosticta*
Spotted Antbird *Hylophylax naevioides*
Spot-backed Antbird *Hylophylax naevia*
Dot-backed Antbird *Hylophylax punctulata*
Scale-backed Antbird *Hylophylax poecilinota*
Black-spotted Bare-eye *Phlegopsis nigromaculata*
Reddish-winged Bare-eye *Phlegopsis erythroptera*
Pale-faced Antbird *Skutchia borbae*
Ocellated Antbird *Phaenostictus mcleannani*

Formicariidae

Rufous-capped Antthrush *Formicarius colma*
Black-faced Antthrush *Formicarius analis*
Mexican Antthrush *Formicarius moniliger* LR
Rufous-fronted Antthrush *Formicarius rufifrons* GT
Black-headed Antthrush *Formicarius nigricapillus*
Rufous-breasted Antthrush *Formicarius rufipectus*
Such's Antthrush *Chamaeza meruloides* LR
Scalloped Antthrush *Chamaeza turdina* LR
Short-tailed Antthrush *Chamaeza campanisona*
Striated Antthrush *Chamaeza nobilis*
Brazilian Antthrush *Chamaeza ruficauda*
Barred Antthrush *Chamaeza mollissima*
Black-crowned Antpitta *Pittasoma michleri*
Rufous-crowned Antpitta *Pittasoma rufopileatum* GT
Undulated Antpitta *Grallaria squamigera*
Giant Antpitta *Grallaria gigantea* GT
Great Antpitta *Grallaria excelsa* GT
Variegated Antpitta *Grallaria varia*
Moustached Antpitta *Grallaria alleni* GT, LR
Scaled Antpitta *Grallaria guatimalensis*

Cundinamarca Antpitta *Grallaria kaestneri* GT LR
Táchira Antpitta *Grallaria chthonia* GT
Plain-backed Antpitta *Grallaria haplonota*
Ochre-striped Antpitta *Grallaria dignissima*
Elusive Antpitta *Grallaria eludens* GT
Chestnut-crowned Antpitta *Grallaria ruficapilla*
Watkins's Antpitta *Grallaria watkinsi* LR
Santa Marta Antpitta *Grallaria bangsi* GT
Stripe-headed Antpitta *Grallaria andicola*
Puna Antpitta *Grallaria punensis* LR
Pale-billed Antpitta *Grallaria carrikeri*
Bicolored Antpitta *Grallaria rufocinerea* GT
Chestnut-naped Antpitta *Grallaria nuchalis*
Chestnut Antpitta *Grallaria blakei* GT
White-throated Antpitta *Grallaria albigula*
Red-and-white Antpitta *Grallaria erythroleuca*
Yellow-breasted Antpitta *Grallaria flavotincta* LR
White-bellied Antpitta *Grallaria hypoleuca*
Jocotoco Antpitta *Grallaria ridgelyi* GT
Rusty-tinged Antpitta *Grallaria przewalskii* LR
Bay Antpitta *Grallaria capitalis* LR
Grey-naped Antpitta *Grallaria griseonucha*
Rufous Antpitta *Grallaria rufula*
Rufous-faced Antpitta *Grallaria erythrotis*
Tawny Antpitta *Grallaria quitensis*
Brown-banded Antpitta *Grallaria milleri* GT
Streak-chested Antpitta *Hylopezus perspicillatus*
Spotted Antpitta *Hylopezus macularius*
Masked Antpitta *Hylopezus auricularis* GT, LR
Fulvous-bellied Antpitta *Hylopezus dives* LR
White-lored Antpitta *Hylopezus fulviventris*
Amazonian Antpitta *Hylopezus berlepschi*
White-browed Antpitta *Hylopezus ochroleucus* GT
Speckle-breasted Antpitta *Hylopezus nattereri* LR
Thrush-like Antpitta *Myrmothera campanisona*
Tepui Antpitta *Myrmothera simplex*
Ochre-breasted Antpitta *Grallaricula flavirostris*
Rusty-breasted Antpitta *Grallaricula ferrugineipectus*
Slate-crowned Antpitta *Grallaricula nana*
Scallop-breasted Antpitta *Grallaricula loricata* GT

Peruvian Antpitta *Grallaricula peruviana* GT

Crescent-faced Antpitta *Grallaricula lineifrons* GT

Ochre-fronted Antpitta *Grallaricula ochraceifrons* GT

Hooded Antpitta *Grallaricula cucullata* GT

onopophagidae

Rufous Gnateater *Conopophaga lineata*

Chestnut-belted Gnateater *Conopophaga aurita*

Hooded Gnateater *Conopophaga roberti*

Ash-throated Gnateater *Conopophaga peruviana*

Slaty Gnateater *Conopophaga ardesiaca*

Chestnut-crowned Gnateater *Conopophaga castaneiceps*

Black-cheeked Gnateater *Conopophaga melanops*

Black-bellied Gnateater *Conopophaga melanogaster*

hinocryptidae

Chestnut-throated Huet-huet *Pteroptochos castaneus* LR

Black-throated Huet-huet *Pteroptochos tarnii*

Moustached Turca *Pteroptochos megapodius*

White-throated Tapaculo *Scelorchilus albicollis*

Chucao Tapaculo *Scelorchilus rubecula*

Crested Gallito *Rhinocrypta lanceolata*

Sandy Gallito *Teledromas fuscus*

Rusty-belted Tapaculo *Liosceles thoracicus*

Collared Crescentchest *Melanopareia torquata*

Olive-crowned Crescentchest *Melanopareia maximiliani*

Maranón Crescentchest *Melanopareia maranonica* GT, LR

Elegant Crescentchest *Melanopareia elegans*

Spotted Bamboowren *Psilorhamphus guttatus* GT

Slaty Bristlefront *Merulaxis ater* GT

Stresemann's Bristlefront *Merulaxis stresemanni* GT

Ochre-flanked Tapaculo *Eugralla paradoxa*

Ash-colored Tapaculo *Myornis senilis*

Unicolored Tapaculo *Scytalopus unicolor*

Blackish Tapaculo *Scytalopus latrans* LR

Grey Tapaculo *Scytalopus parvirostris* LR

Equatorial Rufous-vented Tapaculo *Scytalopus micropterus* LR

Colombian Tapaculo *Scytalopus infasciatus* LR

Southern White-crowned Tapaculo *Scytalopus bolivianus* LR

Santa Marta Tapaculo *Scytalopus sanctaemartae* LR

Northern White-crowned Tapaculo *Scytalopus atratus* LR

Perija Tapaculo *Scytalopus nigricans* LR

Large-footed Tapaculo *Scytalopus macropus*

Peruvian Rufous-vented Tapaculo *Scytalopus femoralis*

Tacarcuna Tapaculo *Scytalopus panamensis* GT

Narino Tapaculo *Scytalopus vicinior* LR

Mérida Tapaculo *Scytalopus meridanus* LR

Caracas Tapaculo *Scytalopus caracae* LR

Spillmann's Tapaculo *Scytalopus spillmanni* LR

Zimmer's Tapaculo *Scytalopus zimmeri* LR

Andean Tapaculo *Scytalopus simonsi* LR

Cuzco Tapaculo *Scytalopus urubambae* LR

Sharp-billed Tapaculo *Scytalopus acutirostris* LR

Silvery-fronted Tapaculo *Scytalopus argentifrons*

Brown-rumped Tapaculo *Scytalopus latebricola*

Dusky Tapaculo *Scytalopus fuscus* LR

Magellanic Tapaculo *Scytalopus magellanicus*

Elfin Forest Tapaculo *Scytalopus altirostris* LR

Ancash Tapaculo *Scytalopus affinis* LR

Páramo Tapaculo *Scytalopus canus* LR

Rufous-rumped Tapaculo *Scytalopus griseicollis* LR

White-browed Tapaculo *Scytalopus superciliaris* LR

Mouse-colored Tapaculo *Scytalopus speluncae*

Tall-grass Wetland Tapaculo *Scytalopus iraiensis* GT

Brasília Tapaculo *Scytalopus novacapitalis* GT, LR

Bahia Tapaculo *Scytalopus psychopompus* GT, LR

White-breasted Tapaculo *Scytalopus indigoticus* GT

Chocó Tapaculo *Scytalopus chocoensis* LR

Ecuadorian Tapaculo *Scytalopus robbinsi*

Chusquea Tapaculo *Scytalopus parkeri*

Diademed Tapaculo *Scytalopus schulenbergi*

Ocellated Tapaculo *Acropternis orthonyx*

Tyrannidae

Planato Tyrannulet *Phyllomyias fasciatus*

Zeledoni's Tyrannulet *Phyllomyias zeledoni* LR

Rough-legged Tyrannulet *Phyllomyias burmeisteri*

Greenish Tyrannulet *Phyllomyias virescens*

Reiser's Tyrannulet *Phyllomyias reiseri* LR

Urich's Tyrannulet *Phyllomyias urichi* GT, LR

Sclater's Tyrannulet *Phyllomyias sclateri*

Grey-capped Tyrannulet *Phyllomyias griseocapilla* GT

Plumbeous-crowned Tyrannulet *Phyllomyias plumbeiceps*

Sooty-headed Tyrannulet *Phyllomyias griseiceps*

Black-capped Tyrannulet *Phyllomyias nigrocapillus*

Ashy-headed Tyrannulet *Phyllomyias cinereiceps*

Tawny-rumped Tyrannulet *Phyllomyias uropygialis*

Paltry Tyrannulet *Zimmerius vilissimus*

Venezuelan Tyrannulet *Zimmerius improbus* LR

Bolivian Tyrannulet *Zimmerius bolivianus*

Red-billed Tyrannulet *Zimmerius cinereicapillus* LR

Mishana Tyrannulet *Zimmerius villarejoi* LR

Slender-footed Tyrannulet *Zimmerius gracilipes*

Golden-faced Tyrannulet *Zimmerius chrysops* LR

Loja Tyrannulet *Zimmerius flavidifrons* LR

Peruvian Tyrannulet *Zimmerius viridiflavus*

White-lored Tyrannulet *Ornithion inerme*

Yellow-bellied Tyrannulet *Ornithion semiflavum* LR

Brown-capped Tyrannulet *Ornithion brunneicapillum*

Southern Beardless Tyrannulet *Camptostoma obsoletum* LR

Northern Beardless Tyrannulet *Camptostoma imberbe*

Mouse-colored Tyrannulet *Phaeomyias murina*

Tumbes Tyrannulet *Phaeomyias tumbezana* LR

Northern Scrub-Flycatcher *Sublegatus arenarum* LR

Southern Scrub-Flycatcher *Sublegatus modestus*

Dusky Flycatcher *Sublegatus obscurior* LR

Campo Suiriri Flycatcher *Suiriri affinis* LR

Chaco Suiriri Flycatcher *Suiriri suiriri*

Chapada Flycatcher *Suiriri islerorum*

Yellow-crowned Tyrannulet *Tyrannulus elatus*

Forest Elaenia *Myiopagis gaimardii*

Grey Elaenia *Myiopagis caniceps*

Foothill Elaenia *Myiopagis olallai* LR

Pacific Elaenia *Myiopagis subplacens*

Yellow-crowned Elaenia *Myiopagis flavivertex*

Greenish Elaenia *Myiopagis viridicata*

Jamaican Elaenia *Myiopagis cotta*

Grey-and-white Tyrannulet *Pseudelaenia leucospodia*

Caribbean Elaenia *Elaenia martinica*

Yellow-bellied Elaenia *Elaenia flavogaster*

Large Elaenia *Elaenia spectabilis* LR

Noronha Elaenia *Elaenia ridleyana* GT, LR

White-crested Elaenia *Elaenia albiceps*

Small-billed Elaenia *Elaenia parvirostris*

Olivaceous Elaenia *Elaenia mesoleuca*

Slaty Elaenia *Elaenia strepera*

Mottle-backed Elaenia *Elaenia gigas*

Brownish Elaenia *Elaenia pelzelni*

Plain-crested Elaenia *Elaenia cristata*

Lesser Elaenia *Elaenia chiriquensis*

Rufous-crowned Elaenia *Elaenia ruficeps*

Mountain Elaenia *Elaenia frantzii* LR

Highland Elaenia *Elaenia obscura*

Great Elaenia *Elaenia dayi*

Sierran Elaenia *Elaenia pallatangae*

Greater Antillian Elaenia *Elaenia fallax*

White-throated Tyrannulet *Mecocerculus leucophrys*

White-tailed Tyrannulet *Mecocerculus poecilocercus*

Buff-banded Tyrannulet *Mecocerculus hellmayri*

Rufous-winged Tyrannulet *Mecocerculus calopterus*

Sulphur-bellied Tyrannulet *Mecocerculus minor*

White-banded Tyrannulet *Mecocerculus stictopterus*

Torrent Tyrannulet *Serpophaga cinerea*

River Tyrannulet *Serpophaga hypoleuca*

Sooty Tyrannulet *Serpophaga nigricans*

White-crested Tyrannulet *Serpophaga subcristata*

White-bellied Tyrannulet *Serpophaga munda* LR

Slender-billed Inezia *Inezia tenuirostris*

Plain Inezia *Inezia inornata*

Amazonian Inezia *Inezia subflava*

Pale-tipped Inezia *Inezia caudata* LR

Lesser Wagtail-Tyrant *Stigmatura napensis* LR

Greater Wagtail-Tyrant *Stigmatura budytoides*

Agile Tit-Tyrant *Uromyias agilis*

Unstreaked Tit-Tyrant *Uromyias agraphia*

Ash-breasted Tit-Tyrant *Anairetes alpinus* GT

Marañón Tit-Tyrant *Anairetes nigrocristatus* LR

Pied-crested Tit-Tyrant *Anairetes reguloides*

Yellow-billed Tit-Tyrant *Anairetes flavirostris*

Tufted Tit-Tyrant *Anairetes parulus*

Juan Fernandez Tit-Tyrant *Anairetes fernandezianus* GT

Many-colored Rush Tyrant *Tachuris rubrigastra*

Sharp-tailed Tyrant *Culicivora caudacuta* GT

Grey-backed Tachuri *Polystictus superciliaris* GT

Bearded Tachuri *Polystictus pectoralis* GT

Dinelli's Doradito *Pseudocolopteryx dinellianus* GT

Crested Doradito *Pseudocolopteryx sclateri*

Subtropical Doradito *Pseudocolopteryx acutipennis*

Warbling Doradito *Pseudocolopteryx flaviventris*

Tawny-crowned Pygmy-Tyrant *Euscarthmus meloryphus*

Rufous-sided Pygmy-Tyrant *Euscarthmus rufomarginatus* GT

Streak-necked Flycatcher *Mionectes striaticollis*

Olive-striped Flycatcher *Mionectes olivaceus*

Ochre-bellied Flycatcher *Mionectes oleagineus*

MacConnell's Flycatcher *Mionectes macconnelli*

Grey-hooded Flycatcher *Mionectes rufiventris*

Rufous-breasted Leptopogon *Leptopogon rufipectus*

Inca Leptopogon *Leptopogon taczanowskii*

Sepia-capped Leptopogon *Leptopogon amaurocephalus*

Slaty-capped Leptopogon *Leptopogon superciliaris*

Yellow Tyrannulet *Capsiempis flaveola* LR

Black-fronted Tyrannulet *Phylloscartes nigrifrons*

Chapman's Bristle-Tyrant *Phylloscartes chapmani*

Variegated Bristle-Tyrant *Phylloscartes poecilotis*

Marbled-faced Bristle-Tyrant *Phylloscartes ophthalmicus*

Southern Bristle-Tyrant *Phylloscartes eximius* GT

Ecuadorean Tyrannulet *Phylloscartes gualaquizae*

Rufous-lored Tyrannulet *Phylloscartes flaviventris*

Cinnamon-faced Tyrannulet *Phylloscartes parkeri*

Venezuelan Bristle-Tyrant *Phylloscartes venezuelanus* GT

Spectacled Bristle-Tyrant *Phylloscartes orbitalis*

Antioquia Bristle-Tyrant *Phylloscartes lanyoni* GT

Minas Gerais Tyrannulet *Phylloscartes roquettei* GT

Mottle-cheeked Tyrannulet *Phylloscartes ventralis*

Bahia Tyrannulet *Phylloscartes beckeri* GT

São Paulo Tyrannulet *Phylloscartes paulistus* GT

Restinga Tyrannulet *Phylloscartes kronei* GT

Oustalet's Tyrannulet *Phylloscartes oustaleti* GT

Serra do Mar Tyrannulet *Phylloscartes difficilis* GT

Alagoas Tyrannulet *Phylloscartes ceciliae* GT, LR

Yellow-green Tyrannulet *Phylloscartes flavovirens*

Olive-green Tyrannulet *Phylloscartes virescens*

Rufous-browed Tyrannulet *Phylloscartes superciliaris*

Bay-ringed Tyrannulet *Phylloscartes sylviolus* GT

Bronze-olive Pygmy-Tyrant *Pseudotriccus pelzelni*

Hazel-fronted Pygmy-Tyrant *Pseudotriccus simplex*

Rufous-headed Pygmy-Tyrant *Pseudotriccus ruficeps*

Southern Antpipit *Corythopis delalandi*

Ringed Antpipit *Corythopis torquata*

Eared Pygmy-Tyrant *Myiornis auricularis*

White-bellied Pygmy-Tyrant *Myiornis albiventris* PGT

Short-tailed Pygmy-Tyrant *Myiornis ecaudatus*

Black-capped Pygmy-Tyrant *Myiornis atricapillus*

Scale-crested Pygmy-Tyrant *Lophotriccus pileatus*

Long-crested Pygmy-Tyrant *Lophotriccus eulophotes*

Double-banded Pygmy-Tyrant *Lophotriccus vitiosus*

Helmeted Pygmy-Tyrant *Lophotriccus galeatus*

Pale-eyed Pygmy-Tyrant *Lophotriccus pilaris*

Black-chested Tyrant *Taeniotriccus andrei*

Rufous-crowned Tody-Tyrant *Poecilotriccus ruficeps*

Lulu's Tody-Tyrant *Poecilotriccus luluae*

Black-and-white Tody-Tyrant *Poecilotriccus capitalis*

White-cheeked Tody-Tyrant *Poecilotriccus albifacies* LR

Slaty Tody-Flycatcher *Poecilotriccus sylvius*

Southern Bentbill *Oncostoma olivaceum* LR

Northern Bentbill *Oncostoma cinereigulare*

Snethlage's Tody-Tyrant *Hemitriccus minor*

Boat-billed Tody-Tyrant *Hemitriccus josephinae*

Drab-breasted Bamboo Tyrant *Hemitriccus diops*

Brown-breasted Bamboo Tyrant *Hemitriccus obsoletus*

Flammulated Bamboo Tyrant *Hemitriccus flammulatus*

White-eyed Tody-Tyrant *Hemitriccus zosterops*

White-bellied Tody-Tyrant *Hemitriccus griseipectus* LR

Zimmer's Tody-Tyrant *Hemitriccus aenigma*

Eye-ringed Tody-Tyrant *Hemitriccus orbitatus* GT

Johannes' Tody-Tyrant *Hemitriccus iohannis* LR

Stripe-necked Tody-Tyrant *Hemitriccus striaticollis*

Hangnest Tody-Tyrant *Hemitriccus nidipendulus*

Yungas Tody-Tyrant *Hemitriccus spodiops*

Pearly-vented Tody-Tyrant *Hemitriccus margaritaceiventer*

Pelzeln's Tody-Tyrant *Hemitriccus inornatus* LR

Black-throated Tody-Tyrant *Hemitriccus granadensis*

Buff-breasted Tody-Tyrant *Hemitriccus mirandae* GT

Cinnamon-breasted Tody-Tyrant *Hemitriccus cinnamomeipectus* GT, LR

Buff-throated Tody-Tyrant *Hemitriccus rufigularis* GT

Kaempfer's Tody-Tyrant *Hemitriccus kaempferi* GT

Fork-tailed Tody-Tyrant *Hemitriccus furcatus* GT

Buff-cheeked Tody-Flycatcher *Todirostrum senex*

Ruddy Tody-Flycatcher *Todirostrum russatum*

Ochre-faced Tody-Flycatcher *Todirostrum plumbeiceps*

Smoky-fronted Tody-Flycatcher *Todirostrum fumifrons*

Rusty-fronted Tody-Flycatcher *Todirostrum latirostre*

Spotted Tody-Flycatcher *Todirostrum maculatum*

Yellow-lored Tody-Flycatcher *Todirostrum poliocephalum*

Common Tody-Flycatcher *Todirostrum cinereum*

Short-tailed Tody-Flycatcher *Todirostrum viridanum* GT

Painted Tody-Flycatcher *Todirostrum pictum* LR

Yellow-browed Tody-Flycatcher *Todirostrum chrysocrotaphum*

Black-headed Tody-Flycatcher *Todirostrum nigriceps* LR

Golden-winged Tody-Flycatcher *Todirostrum calopterum*

Black-backed Tody-Flycatcher *Todirostrum pulchellum* LR

Brownish Flycatcher *Cnipodectes subbrunneus*

Large-headed Flatbill *Ramphotrigon megacephala*

Rufous-tailed Flatbill *Ramphotrigon ruficauda*

Dusky-tailed Flatbill *Ramphotrigon fuscicauda*

Eye-ringed Flatbill *Rhynchocyclus brevirostris*

Pacific Flatbill *Rhynchocyclus pacificus* LR

Olivaceous Flatbill *Rhynchocyclus olivaceus*

Fulvous-breasted Flatbill *Rhynchocyclus fulvipectus*

Yellow-olive Flatbill *Tolmomyias sulphurescens*

Orange-eyed Flatbill *Tolmomyias traylori*

Zimmer's Flatbill *Tolmomyias assimilis*

Yellow-margined Flatbill *Tolmomyias flavotectus* LR

Grey-crowned Flatbill *Tolmomyias poliocephalus*

Ochre-lored Flatbill *Tolmomyias flaviventris*

Olive-faced Flatbill *Tolmomyias viridiceps* LR

Cinnamon-crested Spadebill *Platyrinchus saturatus*

Stub-tailed Spadebill *Platyrinchus cancrominus* LR

White-throated Spadebill *Platyrinchus mystaceus*

Golden-crowned Spadebill *Platyrinchus coronatus*

Yellow-throated Spadebill *Platyrinchus flavigularis*

White-crested Spadebill *Platyrinchus platyrhynchos*

Russet-winged Spadebill *Platyrinchus leucoryphus* GT

Amazonian Royal-Flycatcher *Onychorhynchus coronatus*

Northern Royal-Flycatcher *Onychorhynchus mexicanus* LR

Pacific Royal-Flycatcher *Onychorhynchus occidentalis* GT, LR

Atlantic Royal-Flycatcher *Onychorhynchus swainsoni* GT, LR

Ornate Flycatcher *Myiotriccus ornatus*

Ruddy-tailed Flycatcher *Terenotriccus erythrurus*

Tawny-breasted Flycatcher *Myiobius villosus*

Bearded Flycatcher *Myiobius barbatus*

Whiskered Flycatcher *Myiobius mastacalis* LR

Sulphur-rumped Flycatcher *Myiobius sulphureipygius* LR

Black-tailed Flycatcher *Myiobius atricaudus*

Flavescent Flycatcher *Myiophobus flavicans*

Orange-crested Flycatcher *Myiophobus phoenicomitra*

Unadorned Flycatcher *Myiophobus inornatus*

Roraiman Flycatcher *Myiophobus roraimae*

Orange-banded Flycatcher *Myiophobus lintoni* GT

Handsome Flycatcher *Myiophobus pulcher*

Olive-chested Flycatcher *Myiophobus cryptoxanthus*

Ochraceous-breasted Flycatcher *Myiophobus ochraceiventris*

Bran-colored Flycatcher *Myiophobus fasciatus*

Euler's Flycatcher *Lathrotriccus euleri*

Grey-breasted Flycatcher *Lathrotriccus griseipectus* GT

Tawny-chested Flycatcher *Aphanotriccus capitalis* GT

Black-billed Flycatcher *Aphanotriccus audax* GT

Belted Flycatcher *Xenotriccus callizonus* GT

Pileated Flycatcher *Xenotriccus mexicanus* GT

Cinnamon Flycatcher *Pyrrhomyias cinnamomea*

Northern Tufted-Flycatcher *Mitrephanes phaeocercus*

Olive Tufted-Flycatcher *Mitrephanes olivaceus*

Olive-sided Flycatcher *Contopus cooperi*

Greater Pewee *Contopus pertinax* LR

Dark Pewee *Contopus lugubris* LR

Smoke-colored Pewee *Contopus fumigatus*

Ochraceous Pewee *Contopus ochraceus*

Western Wood Pewee *Contopus sordidulus*

Eastern Wood Pewee *Contopus virens*

Tropical Pewee *Contopus cinereus*

Tumbes Pewee *Contopus punensis* LR

Blackish Pewee *Contopus nigrescens*

White-throated Pewee *Contopus albogularis*

Cuban Pewee *Contopus caribaeus*

Jamaican Pewee *Contopus pallidus* LR

Hispaniolan Pewee *Contopus hispaniolensis* LR

Lesser Antillean Pewee *Contopus latirostris*

Yellow-bellied Flycatcher *Empidonax flaviventris*

Acadian Flycatcher *Empidonax virescens*

Willow Flycatcher *Empidonax traillii*

Alder Flycatcher *Empidonax alnorum* LR

White-throated Flycatcher *Empidonax albigularis*

Least Flycatcher *Empidonax minimus*

Hammond's Flycatcher *Empidonax hammondii*

American Dusky Flycatcher *Empidonax oberholseri*

Grey Flycatcher *Empidonax wrightii*

Pine Flycatcher *Empidonax affinis*

Pacific-slope Flycatcher *Empidonax difficilis*

Cordilleran Flycatcher *Empidonax occidentalis* LR

Yellowish Flycatcher *Empidonax flavescens* LR

Buff-breasted Flycatcher *Empidonax fulvifrons*

Black-capped Flycatcher *Empidonax atriceps*

Cocos Island Flycatcher *Nesotriccus ridgwayi* GT

Fuscous Flycatcher *Cnemotriccus fuscatus*

Eastern Phoebe *Sayornis phoebe*

Black Phoebe *Sayornis nigricans*

Say's Phoebe *Sayornis saya* LR

Vermilion Flycatcher *Pyrocephalus rubinus*

Crowned Chat-Tyrant *Silvicultrix frontalis*

Jelski's Chat-Tyrant *Silvicultrix jelskii* LR

Yellow-bellied Chat-Tyrant *Silvicultrix diadema*

Golden-browed Chat-Tyrant *Silvicultrix pulchella*

Slaty-backed Chat-Tyrant *Ochthoeca cinnamomeiventris*

Rufous-breasted Chat-Tyrant *Ochthoeca rufipectoralis*

Brown-backed Chat-Tyrant *Ochthoeca fumicolor*

D' Orbigny's Chat-Tyrant *Ochthoeca oenanthoides*

White-browed Chat-Tyrant *Ochthoeca leucophrys*

Piura Chat-Tyrant *Ochthoeca piurae* GT, LR

Tumbes Tyrant *Ochthoeca salvini* GT

Drab Water-Tyrant *Ochthornis littoralis*

Patagonian Tyrant *Colorhamphus parvirostris*

Red-rumped Bush-Tyrant *Cnemarchus erythropygius*

Streak-throated Bush-Tyrant *Myiotheretes striaticollis*

Santa Marta Bush-Tyrant *Myiotheretes pernix* GT

Smoky Bush-Tyrant *Myiotheretes fumigatus*

Rufous-bellied Bush-Tyrant *Myiotheretes fuscorufus*

Rufous-webbed Bush-Tyrant *Polioxolmis rufipennis*

Fire-eyed Diucon *Xolmis pyrope*

Grey Monjita *Xolmis cinerea*

Black-crowned Monjita *Xolmis coronata*

White-rumped Monjita *Xolmis velata*

White Monjita *Xolmis irupero*

Rusty-backed Monjita *Xolmis rubetra*

Salinas Monjita *Xolmis salinarum* GT, LR

Black-and-white Monjita *Heteroxolmis dominicana* GT

Chocolate-vented Tyrant *Neoxolmis rufiventris*

Lesser Shrike-Tyrant *Agriornis murina*

Black-billed Shrike-Tyrant *Agriornis montana*

White-tailed Shrike-Tyrant *Agriornis andicola* GT

Great Shrike-Tyrant *Agriornis livida*

Grey-bellied Shrike-Tyrant *Agriornis microptera*

Spot-billed Ground-Tyrant *Muscisaxicola maculirostris*

Dark-faced Ground-Tyrant *Muscisaxicola macloviana*

Little Ground-Tyrant *Muscisaxicola fluviatilis*

Cinnamon-bellied Ground-Tyrant *Muscisaxicola capistrata*

Rufous-naped Ground-Tyrant *Muscisaxicola rufivertex*

White-browed Ground-Tyrant *Muscisaxicola albilora*

Puna Ground-Tyrant *Muscisaxicola juninensis*

Paramo Ground-Tyrant *Muscisaxicola alpina*

Plain-capped Ground-Tyrant *Muscisaxicola grisea* LR

Cinereous Ground-Tyrant *Muscisaxicola cinerea* LR

White-fronted Ground-Tyrant *Muscisaxicola albifrons*

Ochre-naped Ground-Tyrant *Muscisaxicola flavinucha*

Black-fronted Ground-Tyrant *Muscisaxicola frontalis*

Short-tailed Field-Tyrant *Muscigralla brevicauda*

Patagonian Negrito *Lessonia rufa*

Andean Negrito *Lessonia oreas*

Cinereous Tyrant *Knipolegus striaticeps*

Hudson's Black Tyrant *Knipolegus hudsoni*

Amazonian Black Tyrant *Knipolegus poecilocercus*

Andean Tyrant *Knipolegus signatus*

Plumbeous Tyrant *Knipolegus cabanisi* LR

Blue-billed Black-Tyrant *Knipolegus cyanirostris*

Rufous-tailed Tyrant *Knipolegus poecilurus*

Riverside Tyrant *Knipolegus orenocensis*

White-winged Black-Tyrant *Knipolegus aterrimus*

Crested Black-Tyrant *Knipolegus lophotes*

Velvety Black-Tyrant *Knipolegus nigerrimus*

Spectacled Tyrant *Hymenops perspicillatus*

Pied Water-Tyrant *Fluvicola pica*

Black-backed Water-Tyrant *Fluvicola albiventer* LR

Masked Water-Tyrant *Fluvicola nengeta*

White-headed Marsh-Tyrant *Arundinicola leucocephala*

Long-tailed Tyrant *Colonia colonus*

Cock-tailed Tyrant *Alectrurus tricolor* GT

Strange-tailed Tyrant *Alectrurus risora* GT

Streamer-tailed Tyrant *Gubernetes yetapa*
Yellow-browed Tyrant *Satrapa icterophrys*
Cliff Flycatcher *Hirundinea ferruginea*
Swallow Flycatcher *Hirundinea bellicosa* LR
Cattle Tyrant *Machetornis rixosus*
Shear-tailed Grey Tyrant *Muscipipra vetula*
Rufous-tailed Attila *Attila phoenicurus*
Cinnamon Attila *Attila cinnamomeus*
Ochraceous Attila *Attila torridus* GT
Citron-bellied Attila *Attila citriniventris*
White-eyed Attila *Attila bolivianus*
Grey-hooded Attila *Attila rufus*
Bright-rumped Attila *Attila spadiceus*
Rufous Casiornis *Casiornis rufa*
Ash-throated Casiornis *Casiornis fusca* LR
Greyish Mourner *Rhytipterna simplex*
Pale-bellied Mourner *Rhytipterna immunda*
Rufous Mourner *Rhytipterna holerythra*
Eastern Sirystes *Sirystes sibilator*
Western Sirystes *Sirystes albogriseus* LR
Rufous Flycatcher *Myiarchus semirufus*
Yucatan Flycatcher *Myiarchus yucatanensis*
Sad Flycatcher *Myiarchus barbirostris*
Dusky-capped Flycatcher *Myiarchus tuberculifer*
Swainson's Flycatcher *Myiarchus swainsoni*
Venezuelan Flycatcher *Myiarchus venezuelensis* LR
Panama Flycatcher *Myiarchus panamensis* LR
Short-crested-Flycatcher *Myiarchus ferox*
Apical Flycatcher *Myiarchus apicalis*
Pale-edged Flycatcher *Myiarchus cephalotes*
Sooty-crowned Flycatcher *Myiarchus phaeocephalus*
Ash-throated Flycatcher *Myiarchus cinerascens*
Nutting's Flycatcher *Myiarchus nuttingi*
Great Crested-Flycatcher *Myiarchus crinitus*
Brown-crested Flycatcher *Myiarchus tyrannulus*
Galápagos Flycatcher *Myiarchus magnirostris*
Grenada Flycatcher *Myiarchus nugator*
Rufous-tailed Flycatcher *Myiarchus validus*
Puerto Rican Flycatcher *Myiarchus antillarum*
La Sagra's Flycatcher *Myiarchus sagrae* LR
Stolid Flycatcher *Myiarchus stolidus*
Lesser Antillian Flycatcher *Myiarchus oberi* LR
Flammulated Flycatcher *Deltarhynchus flammulatus*

Greater Kiskadee *Pitangus sulphuratus*
Lesser Kiskadee *Philohydor lictor*
Boat-billed Flycatcher *Megarynchus pitangua*
Rusty-margined Flycatcher *Myiozetetes cayanensis*
Social Flycatcher *Myiozetetes similis*
Grey-capped Flycatcher *Myiozetetes granadensis*
Dusky-chested Flycatcher *Myiozetetes luteiventris*
White-bearded Flycatcher *Phelpsia inornata*
White-ringed Flycatcher *Conopias albovittata*
Yellow-throated Flycatcher *Conopias parva* LR
Three-striped Flycatcher *Conopias trivirgata*
Lemon-browed Flycatcher *Conopias cinchoneti*
Golden-crowned Flycatcher *Myiodynastes chrysocephalus*
Golden-bellied Flycatcher *Myiodynastes hemichrysus* LR
Streaked Flycatcher *Myiodynastes maculatus*
Sulphur-bellied Flycatcher *Myiodynastes luteiventris*
Baird's Flycatcher *Mylodynastes bairdii*
Piratic Flycatcher *Legatus leucophaius*
Variagated Flycatcher *Empidonomus varius*
Crowned Slaty Flycatcher *Griseotyrannus aurantioatrocristatus*
Sulphury Flycatcher *Tyrannopsis sulphurea*
Snowy-throated Kingbird *Tyrannus niveigularis*
White-throated Kingbird *Tyrannus albogularis*
Tropical Kingbird *Tyrannus melancholicus* LR
Couch's Kingbird *Tyrannus couchii* LR
Cassin's Kingbird *Tyrannus vociferans*
Thick-billed Kingbird *Tyrannus crassirostris*
Western Kingbird *Tyrannus verticalis*
Scissor-tailed Flycatcher *Tyrannus forficatus*
Fork-tailed Flycatcher *Tyrannus savana*
Eastern Kingbird *Tyrannus tyrannus*
Grey Kingbird *Tyrannus dominicensis*
Loggerhead Kingbird *Tyrannus caudifasciatus*
Giant Kingbird *Tyrannus cubensis* GT
White-naped Xenopsaris *Xenopsaris albinucha*
Green-backed Becard *Pachyramphus viridis*
Yellow-cheeked Becard *Pachyramphus xanthogenys* LR
Barred Becard *Pachyramphus versicolor*
Slaty Becard *Pachyramphus spodiurus* GT, LR
Cinereous Becard *Pachyramphus rufus*

Chestnut-crowned Becard *Pachyramphus castaneus*

Cinnamon Becard *Pachyramphus cinnamomeus* LR

White-winged Becard *Pachyramphus polychopterus*

Black-capped Becard *Pachyramphus marginatus*

Black-and-white Becard *Pachyramphus albogriseus*

Grey-collared Becard *Pachyramphus major* LR

Glossy-backed Becard *Pachyramphus surinamus*

Rose-throated Becard *Pachyramphus aglaiae*

One-colored Becard *Pachyramphus homochrous*

Pink-throated Becard *Pachyramphus minor*

Crested Becard *Pachyramphus validus*

Jamaican Becard *Pachyramphus niger*

Black-tailed Tityra *Tityra cayana*

Masked Tityra *Tityra semifasciata*

Black-crowned Tityra *Tityra inquisitor*

Pipridae

Várzea Schiffornis *Schiffornis major*

Greenish Schiffornis *Schiffornis virescens*

Thrush-like Schiffornis *Schiffornis turdinus*

Broad-billed Sapayoa *Sapayoa aenigma*

Cinnamon Neopipo *Neopipo cinnamomea*

Yellow-headed Manakin *Chloropipo flavicapilla* GT

Green Manakin *Chloropipo holochlora*

Olive Manakin *Chloropipo uniformis*

Jet Manakin *Chloropipo unicolor*

Helmeted Manakin *Antilophia galeata*

Araripe Manakin *Antilophia bokermanni* GT

White-collared Manakin *Manacus candei* LR

Orange-collared Manakin *Manacus aurantiacus* LR

Golden-collared Manakin *Manacus vitellinus* LR

White-bearded Manakin *Manacus manacus*

White-bibbed Manakin *Corapipo leucorrhoa*

White-ruffed Manakin *Corapipo altera* LR

White-throated Manakin *Corapipo gutturalis*

Long-tailed Manakin *Chiroxiphia linearis* LR

Lance-tailed Manakin *Chiroxiphia lanceolata* LR

Blue-backed Manakin *Chiroxiphia pareola*

Yungas Manakin *Chiroxiphia boliviana* LR

Swallow-tailed Manakin *Chiroxiphia caudata* LR

White-crowned Manakin *Dixiphia pipra*

Blue-crowned Manakin *Lepidothrix coronata*

Blue-rumped Manakin *Lepidothrix isidorei*

Cerulean-capped Manakin *Pipra coeruleocapilla*

Snow-capped Manakin *Pipra nattereri*

Golden-crowned Manakin *Pipra vilasboasi* GT

Opal-crowned Manakin *Pipra iris*

Crimson-hooded Manakin *Pipra aureola*

Band-tailed Manakin *Pipra fasciicauda*

Wire-tailed Manakin *Pipra filicauda*

Red-capped Manakin *Pipra mentalis*

Golden-headed Manakin *Pipra erythrocephala*

Red-headed Manakin *Pipra rubrocapilla*

Round-tailed Manakin *Pipra chloromeros*

Scarlet-horned Manakin *Pipra cornuta*

White-fronted Manakin *Lepidothrix serena*

Orange-bellied Manakin *Lepidothrix suavissima* LR

Golden-winged Manakin *Masius chrysopterus*

Pin-tailed Manakin *Ilicura militaris*

Striped Manakin *Machaeropterus regulus*

Fiery-capped Manakin *Machaeropterus pyrocephalus*

Club-winged Manakin *Machaeropterus deliciosus*

Black Manakin *Xenopipo atronitens*

Orange-crested Manakin *Heterocercus aurantiivertex* LR

Yellow-crested Manakin *Heterocercus flavivertex*

Flame-crested Manakin *Heterocercus linteatus* LR

Pale-bellied Tyrant-Manakin *Neopelma pallescens*

Saffron-crested Tyrant-Manakin *Neopelma chrysocephalum*

Wied's Tyrant-Manakin *Neopelma aurifrons* GT

Sulphur-bellied Tyrant-Manakin *Neopelma sulphureiventer*

Dwarf Tyrant-Manakin *Tyranneutes stolzmanni*

Tiny Tyrant-Manakin *Tyranneutes virescens*

Grey-headed Piprites *Piprites griseiceps*

Wing-barred Piprites *Piprites chloris*

Black-capped Piprites *Piprites pileatus* GT

Cotingidae

Guianian Red-Cotinga *Phoenicircus carnifex*

Black-necked Red-Cotinga *Phoenicircus nigricollis*

Shrike-like Cotinga *Laniisoma elegans* GT

Andean Laniisoma *Laniisoma buckleyi* LR

Cinereous Cotinga *Laniocera hypopyrra*

Speckled Cotinga *Laniocera rufescens*

Swallow-tailed Cotinga *Phibalura flavirostris* GT

Black-and-gold Cotinga *Tijuca atra* GT

Grey-winged Cotinga *Tijuca condita* GT

Hooded Berryeater *Carpornis cucullatus* GT

Black-headed Berryeater *Carpornis melanocephalus* GT

Red-crested Cotinga *Ampelion rubrocristata*

Chestnut-crested Cotinga *Ampelion rufaxilla*

Bay-vented Cotinga *Doliornis sclateri*

Chestnut-bellied Cotinga *Doliornis remseni* GT

White-cheeked Cotinga *Zaratornis stresemanni* GT

Green-and-black Fruiteater *Pipreola riefferii*

Band-tailed Fruiteater *Pipreola intermedia*

Barred Fruiteater *Pipreola arcuata*

Golden-breasted Fruiteater *Pipreola aureopectus*

Black-chested Fruiteater *Pipreola lubomirskii* LR

Orange-breasted Fruiteater *Pipreola jucunda* LR

Masked Fruiteater *Pipreola pulchra* LR

Scarlet-breasted Fruiteater *Pipreola frontalis*

Fiery-throated Fruiteater *Pipreola chlorolepidota* GT

Handsome Fruiteater *Pipreola formosa*

Red-banded Fruiteater *Pipreola whitelyi*

Scaled Fruiteater *Ampelioides tschudii*

Buff-throated Purpletuft *Iodopleura pipra* GT

Dusky Purpletuft *Iodopleura fusca*

White-browed Purpletuft *Iodopleura isabellae*

Kinglet Calyptura *Calyptura cristata* GT

Grey-tailed Piha *Lathria subalaris*

Olivaceous Piha *Lathria cryptolophus*

Dusky Piha *Lipaugus fuscocinereus*

Chestnut-capped Piha *Lipaugus weberi* LR

Screaming Piha *Lipaugus vociferans*

Rufous Piha *Lipaugus unirufus*

Cinnamon-vented Piha *Lipaugus lanioides* GT

Rose-collared Piha *Lipaugus streptophorus*

Scimitar-winged Piha *Chirocylla uropygialis*

Purple-throated Cotinga *Porphyrolaema porphyrolaema*

Lovely Cotinga *Cotinga amabilis* LR

Turquoise Cotinga *Cotinga ridgwayi* GT, LR

Blue Cotinga *Cotinga nattererii* LR

Plum-throated Cotinga *Cotinga maynana* LR

Banded Cotinga *Cotinga maculata* GT, LR

Purple-breasted Cotinga *Cotinga cotinga*

Spangled Cotinga *Cotinga cayana*

Pompadour Cotinga *Xipholena punicea*

White-tailed Cotinga *Xipholena lamellipennis*

White-winged Cotinga *Xipholena atropurpurea* GT

Black-tipped Cotinga *Carpodectes hopkei*

Snowy Cotinga *Carpodectes nitidus* LR

Yellow-billed Cotinga *Carpodectes antoniae* GT

Black-faced Cotinga *Conioptilon mcilhennyi*

Bare-necked Fruitcrow *Gymnoderus foetidus*

Crimson Fruitcrow *Haematoderus militaris*

Purple-throated Fruitcrow *Querula purpurata*

Red-ruffed Fruitcrow *Pyroderus scutatus*

Bare-necked Umbrellabird *Cephalopterus glabricollis* GT, LR

Amazonian Umbrellabird *Cephalopterus ornatus*

Long-wattled Umbrellabird *Cephalopterus penduliger* GT, LR

Capuchinbird *Perissocephalus tricolor*

Three-wattled Bellbird *Procnias tricarunculata* GT

White Bellbird *Procnias alba*

Bearded Bellbird *Procnias averano*

Bare-throated Bellbird *Procnias nudicollis* GT

Guianan Cock-of-the-rock *Rupicola rupicola*

Andean Cock-of-the-rock *Rupicola peruviana*

Oxyruncidae

Sharpbill *Oxyruncus cristatus*

Phytotomidae

Rufous-tailed Plantcutter *Phytotoma rara*

White-tipped Plantcutter *Phytotoma rutila*

Peruvian Plantcutter *Phytotoma raimondii* GT

Eurylaimidae

African Broadbill *Smithornis capensis*

Rufous-sided Broadbill *Smithornis rufolateralis*

Grey-headed Broadbill *Smithornis sharpei*

African Green Broadbill *Pseudocalyptomena graueri* GT

Dusky Broadbill *Corydon sumatranus*

Black-and-red Broadbill *Cymbirhynchus macrorhynchos*

Banded Broadbill *Eurylaimus javanicus*

Black-and-yellow Broadbill *Eurylaimus ochromalus* GT

Wattled Broadbill *Eurylaimus steerii* GT

Visayan Wattled Broadbill *Eurylaimus samarensis* GT, LR

Silver-breasted Broadbill *Serilophus lunatus*

Long-tailed Broadbill *Psarisomus dalhousiae*

Lesser Green Broadbill *Calyptomena viridis* GT

Hose's Broadbill *Calyptomena hosii* GT

Whitehead's Broadbill *Calyptomena whiteheadi*

Pittidae

Eared Pitta *Pitta phayrei*

Blue-naped Pitta *Pitta nipalensis*

Blue-rumped Pitta *Pitta soror*

Rusty-naped Pitta *Pitta oatesi*

Schneider's Pitta *Pitta schneideri* GT

Giant Pitta *Pitta caerulea* GT

Whiskered Pitta *Pitta kochi* GT

Red-bellied Pitta *Pitta erythrogaster*

Sula Pitta *Pitta dohertyi* GT, LR

Blue-banded Pitta *Pitta arquata*

Garnet Pitta *Pitta granatina* GT

Graceful Pitta *Pitta venusta* GT, LR

Blue Pitta *Pitta cyanea*

Banded Pitta *Pitta guajana*

Bar-bellied Pitta *Pitta elliotii*

Gurney's Pitta *Pitta gurneyi* GT

Blue-headed Pitta *Pitta baudii* GT

Hooded Pitta *Pitta sordida*

Superb Pitta *Pitta superba* GT, LR

Ivory-breasted Pitta *Pitta maxima* LR

Indian Pitta *Pitta brachyura*

Fairy Pitta *Pitta nympha* GT, LR

Blue-winged Pitta *Pitta moluccensis* LR

African Pitta *Pitta angolensis*

Green-breasted Pitta *Pitta reichenowi* LR

Black-and-crimson Pitta *Pitta ussheri* LR

Azure-breasted Pitta *Pitta steerii* GT, LR

Mangrove Pitta *Pitta megarhyncha* GT, LR

Noisy Pitta *Pitta versicolor*

Elegant Pitta *Pitta elegans* LR

Rainbow Pitta *Pitta iris* LR

Black-faced Pitta *Pitta anerythra* GT

Philepittidae

Velvet Asity *Philepitta castanea*

Schlegel's Asity *Philepitta schlegeli* GT

Common Sunbird Asity *Neodrepanis coruscans*

Yellow-bellied Sunbird Asity *Neodrepanis hypoxantha* GT

Xenicidae

Rifleman *Acanthisitta chloris*

Bush Wren *Xenicus longipes* E20

Rock Wren *Xenicus gilviventris* GT

Stephens Island Wren *Traversia lyalli* E

Alaudidae

Western Singing Bushlark *Mirafra cantillans* LR

Eastern Singing Bushlark *Mirafra juvanica*

Hova Lark *Mirafra hova*

Monotonous Lark *Mirafra passerina* LR

Northern White-tailed Lark *Mirafra albicauda*

Melodious Lark *Mirafra cheniana* GT

Kordofan Lark *Mirafra cordofanica* LR

Williams's Lark *Mirafra williamsi* PGT

Friedmann's Lark *Mirafra pulpa* PGT

Rufous-naped Lark *Mirafra africana*

Red Somali Lark *Mirafra sharpii* LR

Red-winged Lark *Mirafra hypermetra*

Somali Long-billed Lark *Mirafra somalica*

Ash's Lark *Mirafra ashi* GT

Angolan Lark *Mirafra angolensis*

Flappet Lark *Mirafra rufocinnamomea*

Clapper Lark *Mirafra apiata*

Collared Lark *Mirafra collaris* LR

Fawn-colored Lark *Mirafra africanoides*

Abyssinian Lark *Mirafra alopex* LR

Rufous-winged Bushlark *Mirafra assamica*

Indian Bushlark *Mirafra erythroptera*

Rusty Bushlark *Mirafra rufa*

Gillett's Lark *Mirafra gilletti*

Degodi Lark *Mirafra degodiensis* GT

Bradfield's Lark *Mirafra naevia* LR

Pink-breasted Lark *Mirafra poecilosterna*

Sabota Lark *Mirafra sabota*

Karoo Long-billed Lark *Mirafra subcoronata* LR

Rudd's Lark *Heteromirafra ruddi* GT

Archer's Long-clawed Lark *Heteromirafra archeri* GT

Sidamo Lark *Heteromirafra sidamoensis* GT

Cape Long-billed Lark *Certhilauda curvirostris*

Angulhas Long-billed Lark *Certhilauda brevirostris* GT, LR

Eastern Long-billed Lark *Certhilauda semitorquata* LR

Damara Long-billed Lark *Certhilauda damarensis* LR

Benguela Long-billed Lark *Certhilauda benguelensis* LR

Short-clawed Lark *Certhilauda chuana*

Karoo Lark *Certhilauda albescens*

Barlow's Lark *Certhilauda barlowi* LR

Dune Lark *Certhilauda erythrochlamys* LR

Ferruginous Lark *Certhilauda burra* GT

Dusky Lark *Pinarocorys nigricans*

Rufous-rumped Lark *Pinarocorys erythropygia* LR

Spike-heeled Lark *Chersomanes albofasciata*

Greater Hoopoe-Lark *Alaemon alaudipes*

Lesser Hoopoe-Lark *Alaemon hamertoni*

Thick-billed Lark *Ramphocoris clotbey*

Calandra Lark *Melanocorypha calandra*

Bimaculated Lark *Melanocorypha bimaculata*

Long-billed Calandra Lark *Melanocorypha maxima*

Mongolian Lark *Melanocorypha mongolica*

White-winged Lark *Melanocorypha leucoptera*

Black Lark *Melanocorypha yeltoniensis*

Bar-tailed Lark *Ammomanes cincturus*

Rufous-tailed Lark *Ammomanes phoenicurus*

Desert Lark *Ammomanes deserti*

Gray's Lark *Ammomanes grayi*

Greater Short-toed Lark *Calandrella brachydactyla* LR

Erlanger's Short-toed Lark *Calandrella erlangeri* LR

Red-capped Lark *Calandrella cinerea*

Blanford's Lark *Calandrella blanfordi* LR

Hume's Short-toed Lark *Calandrella acutirostris*

Sandlark *Calandrella raytal*

Lesser Short-toed Lark *Calandrella rufescens*

Somali Short-toed Lark *Calandrella somalica* LR

Athi Short-toed Lark *Calandrella athensis* LR

Asian Short-toed Lark *Calandrella cheleensis*

Pink-billed Lark *Spizocorys conirostris*

Sclater's Lark *Spizocorys sclateri* GT

Obbia Lark *Spizocorys obbiensis* PGT

Masked Lark *Spizocorys personata*

Botha's Lark *Botha fringillaris* GT

Dunn's Lark *Eremalauda dunni*

Stark's Lark *Eremalauda starki*

DuPont's Lark *Chersophilus duponti*

Short-tailed Lark *Pseudalaemon fremantlii*

Crested Lark *Galerida cristata*

Thekla Lark *Galerida theklae* LR

Malabar Crested Lark *Galerida malabarica* LR

Sykes Lark *Galerida deva*

Sun Lark *Galerida modesta*

Large-billed Lark *Calendula magnirostris*

Woodlark *Lullula arborea*

Eurasian Skylark *Alauda arvensis*

Japanese Skylark *Alauda japonica* LR

Oriental Skylark *Alauda gulgula*

Razo Lark *Alauda razae* GT

Black-eared Sparrow-Lark *Eremopterix australis*

Chestnut-backed Sparrow-Lark *Eremopterix leucotis*

Chestnut-headed Sparrow-Lark *Eremopterix signata*

Grey-backed Sparrow-Lark *Eremopterix verticalis*

Black-crowned Sparrow-Lark *Eremopterix nigriceps*

Ashy-crowned Sparrow-Lark *Eremopterix grisea*

Fischer's Sparrow Lark *Eremopterix leucopareia*

Horned-Lark *Eremophila alpestris*

Temminck's Horned-Lark *Eremophila bilopha* LR

Hirundinidae

African River-Martin *Pseudochelidon eurystomina* PGT

White-eyed River-Martin *Pseudochelidon sirintarae* GT

Tree Swallow *Tachycineta bicolor*

Mangrove Swallow *Tachycineta albilinea*

Tumbes Swallow *Tachycineta stolzmanni* LR

White-winged Swallow *Tachycineta albiventer* LR

White-rumped Swallow *Tachycineta leucorrhoa*

Chilean Swallow *Tachycineta meyeni*

Violet-green Swallow *Tachycineta thalassina*

Bahama Swallow *Tachycineta cyaneoviridis* GT

Golden Swallow *Tachycineta euchrysea* GT

Brown-chested Martin *Progne tapera*

Purple Martin *Progne subis*
Grey-breasted Martin *Progne chalybea* LR
Cuban Martin *Progne cryptoleuca* LR
Caribbean Martin *Progne dominicensis* LR
Sinaloa Martin *Progne sinaloae* PGT, LR
Galápagos Martin *Progne modesta*
Southern Martin *Progne elegans* LR
Peruvian Martin *Progne murphyi* LR
Brown-bellied Swallow *Notiochelidon murina*
Blue-and-white Swallow *Notiochelidon cyanoleuca*
Pale-footed Swallow *Notiochelidon flavipes*
Black-capped Swallow *Notiochelidon pileata*
White-banded Swallow *Atticora fasciata*
Black-collared Swallow *Atticora melanoleuca*
White-thighed Swallow *Neochelidon tibialis*
Tawny-headed Swallow *Stelgidopteryx fucata*
Northern Rough-winged Swallow *Stelgidopteryx serripennis* LR
Ridgeway's Rough-winged Swallow *Stelgidopteryx ridgwayi* LR
Southern Rough-winged Swallow *Stelgidopteryx ruficollis*
White-backed Swallow *Cheramoeca leucosternus*
Brown-throated Sand-Martin *Riparia paludicola*
Congo Sand-Martin *Riparia congica*
Common Sand-Martin *Riparia riparia*
Pale Sand-Martin *Riparia diluta* LR
Banded Sand-Martin *Riparia cincta*
Mascarene Martin *Phedina borbonica*
Congo Martin *Phedina brazzae* PGT
Grey-rumped Swallow *Pseudhirundo griseopyga*
Eurasian Crag Martin *Hirundo rupestris*
Pale Crag Martin *Hirundo obsoleta* LR
Rock Martin *Hirundo fuligula* LR
Dusky Crag Martin *Hirundo concolor*
Barn Swallow *Hirundo rustica*
Red-chested Swallow *Hirundo lucida* LR
Angolan Swallow *Hirundo angolensis* LR
White-throated Swallow *Hirundo albigularis* LR
Ethiopian Swallow *Hirundo aethiopica* LR
Pacific Swallow *Hirundo tahitica* LR
Hill Swallow *Hirundo domicola* LR
Welcome Swallow *Hirundo neoxena* LR
Wire-tailed Swallow *Hirundo smithii*

Blue Swallow *Hirundo atrocaerulea* GT
Black-and-rufous Swallow *Hirundo nigrorufa*
White-throated Blue Swallow *Hirundo nigrita*
Pied-winged Swallow *Hirundo leucosoma*
White-tailed Swallow *Hirundo megaensis* GT
Pearl-breasted Swallow *Hirundo dimidiata*
Greater Striped Swallow *Hirundo cucullata*
Lesser Striped Swallow *Hirundo abyssinica*
Rufous-chested Swallow *Hirundo semirufa*
Mosque Swallow *Hirundo senegalensis*
Red-rumped Swallow *Hirundo daurica*
Striated Swallow *Hirundo striolata* LR
West African Swallow *Hirundo domicella* LR
Angolan Cliff Swallow *Petrochelidon rufigula* LR
Preuss's Swallow *Petrochelidon preussi*
Andean Swallow *Petrochelidon andecola*
Red Sea Swallow *Petrochelidon perdita* PGT, LR
Tree Martin *Petrochelidon nigricans*
South African Cliff Swallow *Petrochelidon spilodera*
American Cliff Swallow *Petrochelidon pyrrhonota*
West Indian Cave Swallow *Petrochelidon pallida*
Mexican Cave Swallow *Petrochelidon pelodoma* LR
Chestnut-collared Swallow *Petrochelidon rufocollaris* LR
Streak-throated Swallow *Petrochelidon fluvicola*
Fairy Martin *Petrochelidon ariel*
Forest Cliff Swallow *Petrochelidon fuliginosa*
Common House-Martin *Delichon urbica*
Asian House-Martin *Delichon dasypus* LR
Nepal House-Martin *Delichon nipalensis*
Square-tailed Sawwing *Psalidoprocne nitens*
Cameroon Mountain Sawwing *Psalidoprocne fuliginosa* PGT
White-headed Sawwing *Psalidoprocne albiceps*
Blue Sawwing *Psalidoprocne pristoptera*
Black Sawwing *Psalidoprocne holomelas* LR
Ethiopian Sawwing *Psalidoprocne oleaginea* LR
Brown Sawwing *Psalidoprocne antinorii* LR
Petit's Sawwing *Psalidoprocne petiti*
Mangbettu Sawwing *Psalidoprocne mangbettorum* LR
Shari Sawwing *Psalidoprocne chalybea* LR

Eastern Sawwing *Psalidoprocne orientalis* LR
Fanti Sawwing *Psalidoprocne obscura*

Motacillidae

Forest Wagtail *Dendronanthus indicus*
Yellow Wagtail *Motacilla flava*
Yellow-headed Wagtail *Motacilla lutea* LR
Black-headed Wagtail *Motacilla feldegg* LR
Green-headed Wagtail *Motacilla taivana* LR
Citrine Wagtail *Motacilla citreola*
Grey Wagtail *Motacilla cinerea*
Mountain Wagtail *Motacilla clara*
White Wagtail *Motacilla alba*
Mekong Wagtail *Motacilla samveasnae* LR
Black-backed Wagtail *Motacilla lugens* LR
Japanese Pied Wagtail *Motacilla grandis* LR
White-browed Wagtail *Motacilla madaraspatensis* LR
African Pied Wagtail *Motacilla aguimp* LR
Cape Wagtail *Motacilla capensis*
Madagascar Wagtail *Motacilla flaviventris* LR
Golden Pipit *Tmetothylacus tenellus*
Orange-throated Longclaw *Macronyx capensis*
Yellow-throated Longclaw *Macronyx croceus*
Fülleborn's Longclaw *Macronyx fuellebornii*
Ethiopian Longclaw *Macronyx flavicollis* GT
Pangani Longclaw *Macronyx aurantiigula*
Rosy-breasted Longclaw *Macronyx ameliae*
Grimwood's Longclaw *Macronyx grimwoodi* PGT
Sharpe's Longclaw *Hemimacronyx sharpei* GT
Yellow-breasted Pipit *Hemimacronyx chloris* GT
Grassland Pipit *Anthus cinnamomeus* LR
Cameroon Pipit *Anthus camaroonensis* LR
Richard's Pipit *Anthus richardi* LR
Paddyfield Pipit *Anthus rufulus* LR
New Zealand Pipit *Anthus novaeseelandiae*
Australian Pipit *Anthus australis* LR
Mountain Pipit *Anthus hoeschi*
Blyth's Pipit *Anthus godlewskii* LR
Tawny Pipit *Anthus campestris*
Bannerman's Pipit *Anthus bannermani* LR
Long-billed Pipit *Anthus similis*
Woodland Pipit *Anthus nyassae*
Buffy Pipit *Anthus vaalensis*
Long-tailed Pipit *Anthus longicaudatus* PGT, LR
Plain-backed Pipit *Anthus leucophrys*

Long-legged Pipit *Anthus pallidiventris*
Malindi Pipit *Anthus melindae* GT
Meadow Pipit *Anthus pratensis*
Eurasian Tree Pipit *Anthus trivialis*
Olive-backed Pipit *Anthus hodgsoni*
Rosy Pipit *Anthus roseatus*
Red-throated Pipit *Anthus cervinus*
Pechora Pipit *Anthus gustavi*
Menzbier's Pipit *Anthus menzbieri* LR
Buff-bellied Pipit *Anthus rubescens* LR
Water Pipit *Anthus spinoletta*
Rock Pipit *Anthus petrosus* LR
Nilgiri Pipit *Anthus nilghiriensis* GT
Upland Pipit *Anthus sylvanus*
Berthelot's Pipit *Anthus berthelotii*
African Rock Pipit *Anthus crenatus*
Striped Pipit *Anthus lineiventris*
Short-tailed Pipit *Anthus brachyurus*
Bush Pipit *Anthus caffer*
Sokoke Pipit *Anthus sokokensis* GT
Jackson's Pipit *Anthus latistriatus* LR
New Guinea Pipit *Anthus gutturalis*
Sprague's Pipit *Anthus spragueii* GT, LR
Short-billed Pipit *Anthus furcatus*
Yellowish Pipit *Anthus lutescens*
Chaco Pipit *Anthus chacoensis*
Correndera Pipit *Anthus correndera*
South Georgia Pipit *Anthus antarcticus* GT, LR
Ochre-breasted Pipit *Anthus nattereri* GT
Hellmayr's Pipit *Anthus hellmayri*
Paramo Pipit *Anthus bogotensis*

Campephagidae

Ground Cuckooshrike *Pteropodocys maxima*
Large Cuckooshrike *Coracina macei* LR
Javan Cuckooshrike *Coracina javensis* LR
Black-faced Cuckooshrike *Coracina novaehollandiae*
Wallacean Cuckooshrike *Coracina personata* LR
Buru Island Cuckooshrike *Coracina fortis* GT
Moluccan Cuckooshrike *Coracina atriceps*
Slaty Cuckooshrike *Coracina schistacea* LR
Melanesian Cuckooshrike *Coracina caledonica*
Stout-billed Cuckooshrike *Coracina caeruleogrisea*
Caerulean Cuckooshrike *Coracina temminckii*
Sunda Cuckooshrike *Coracina larvata*

Bar-bellied Cuckooshrike *Coracina striata*
Pied Cuckooshrike *Coracina bicolor* GT
Yellow-eyed Cuckooshrike *Coracina lineata*
White-lored Cuckooshrike *Coracina boyeri*
White-rumped Cuckooshrike *Coracina leucopygia*
White-bellied Cuckooshrike *Coracina papuensis*
Little Cuckooshrike *Coracina robusta* LR
Hooded Cuckooshrike *Coracina longicauda*
Halmahera Cuckooshrike *Coracina parvula*
Pygmy Cuckooshrike *Coracina abbotti*
New Caledonian Cuckooshrike *Coracina analis*
Grey Cuckooshrike *Coracina caesia*
White-breasted Cuckooshrike *Coracina pectoralis*
Grauer's Cuckooshrike *Coracina graueri* GT
Madagascar Cuckooshrike *Coracina cinerea*
Comoro Cuckooshrike *Coracina cucullata* LR
Blue Cuckooshrike *Coracina azurea*
Mauritius Cuckooshrike *Coracina typica* GT
Réunion Cuckooshrike *Coracina newtoni* GT
Blackish Cuckooshrike *Coracina coerulescens*
Sumba Cicadabird *Coracina dohertyi*
Kai Cicadabird *Coracina dispar* GT, LR
Slender-billed Greybird *Coracina tenuirostris*
Sula Cicadabird *Coracina sula* LR
Sulawesi Cicadabird *Coracina morio*
Pale Cicadabird *Coracina ceramensis* LR
Papuan Cicadabird *Coracina incerta*
Black-bibbed Cicadabird *Coracina mindanensis* GT, LR
White-winged Cuckooshrike *Coracina ostenta* GT
Grey-headed Cuckooshrike *Coracina schisticeps*
New Guinea Cuckooshrike *Coracina melas*
Black-bellied Greybird *Coracina montana*
Solomon Islands Cuckooshrike *Coracina holopolia* GT
McGregor's Cuckooshrike *Coracina mcgregori* GT
Indochinese Cuckooshrike *Coracina polioptera*
Black-winged Cuckooshrike *Coracina melaschistos*
Lesser Cuckooshrike *Coracina fimbriata*
Black-headed Cuckooshrike *Coracina melanoptera*

Orange Cuckooshrike *Campochaera sloetii*
Black-and-white Triller *Lalage melanoleuca*
Pied Triller *Lalage nigra*
White-rumped Triller *Lalage leucopygialis* LR
White-shouldered Triller *Lalage sueurii*
Australian Triller *Lalage tricolor* LR
Rufous-bellied Triller *Lalage aurea*
Tanimbar Triller *Lalage moesta* LR
Black-browed Triller *Lalage atrovirens* LR
Varied Triller *Lalage leucomela* LR
Polynesian Triller *Lalage maculosa*
Samoan Triller *Lalage sharpei* GT
Long-tailed Triller *Lalage leucopyga* E,LR
African Black Cuckooshrike *Campephaga flava*
Red-shouldered Cuckooshrike *Campephaga phoenicea*
Petit's Cuckooshrike *Campephaga petiti*
Purple-throated Cuckooshrike *Campephaga quiscalina*
Western Cuckooshrike *Campephaga lobata* GT
Eastern Cuckooshrike *Campephaga oriolina* PGT, LR
Rosy Minivet *Pericrocotus roseus*
Swinhoe's Minivet *Pericrocotus cantonensis* LR
Ashy Minivet *Pericrocotus divaricatus* LR
Ryukyu Minivet *Pericrocotus tegimae* LR
Small Minivet *Pericrocotus cinnamomeus* LR
Fiery Minivet *Pericrocotus igneus* GT, LR
Flores Minivet *Pericrocotus lansbergei*
White-bellied Minivet *Pericrocotus erythropygius*
Grey-chinned Minivet *Pericrocotus solaris*
Long-tailed Minivet *Pericrocotus ethologus*
Short-billed Minivet *Pericrocotus brevirostris*
Sunda Minivet *Pericrocotus miniatus*
Scarlet Minivet *Pericrocotus flammeus*
Bar-winged Flycatcher-Shrike *Hemipus picatus*
Black-winged Flycatcher-Shrike *Hemipus hirundinaceus*
Large Woodshrike *Tephrodornis gularis*
Common Woodshrike *Tephrodornis pondicerianus*

Pycnonotidae

Crested Finchbill *Spizixos canifrons*
Collared Finchbill *Spizixos semitorques*
Straw-headed Bulbul *Pycnonotus zeylanicus* GT
Striated Bulbul *Pycnonotus striatus*

Cream-striped Bulbul *Pycnonotus leucogrammicus*

Spot-necked Bulbul *Pycnonotus tympanistrigus* GT

Black-and-white Bulbul *Pycnonotus melanoleucus* GT

Grey-headed Bulbul *Pycnonotus priocephalus*

Black-headed Bulbul *Pycnonotus atriceps*

Black-crested Bulbul *Pycnonotus melanicterus*

Scaly-breasted Bulbul *Pycnonotus squamatus* GT

Grey-bellied Bulbul *Pycnonotus cyaniventris* GT

Red-whiskered Bulbul *Pycnonotus jocosus*

Brown-breasted Bulbul *Pycnonotus xanthorrhous*

Light-vented Bulbul *Pycnonotus sinensis*

Styan's Bulbul *Pycnonotus taivanus* PGT

White-eared Bulbul *Pycnonotus leucotis* LR

White-cheeked Bulbul *Pycnonotus leucogenys*

Red-vented Bulbul *Pycnonotus cafer*

Sooty-headed Bulbul *Pycnonotus aurigaster* LR

White-spectacled Bulbul *Pycnonotus xanthopygos*

African Red-eyed Bulbul *Pycnonotus nigricans*

Cape Bulbul *Pycnonotus capensis*

Garden Bulbul *Pycnonotus barbatus*

Somali Bulbul *Pycnonotus somaliensis* LR

African White-eared Bulbul *Pycnonotus dodsoni* LR

Dark-capped Bulbul *Pycnonotus tricolor* LR

Puff-backed Bulbul *Pycnonotus eutilotus* GT

Blue Wattled Bulbul *Pycnonotus nieuwenhuisii*

Yellow-wattled Bulbul *Pycnonotus urostictus*

Orange-spotted Bulbul *Pycnonotus bimaculatus*

Stripe-throated Bulbul *Pycnonotus finlaysoni*

Yellow-throated Bulbul *Pycnonotus xantholaemus* GT

Yellow-eared Bulbul *Pycnonotus penicillatus* GT

Flavescent Bulbul *Pycnonotus flavescens*

Yellow-vented Bulbul *Pycnonotus goiavier*

White-browed Bulbul *Pycnonotus luteolus*

Olive-winged Bulbul *Pycnonotus plumosus*

Streak-eared Bulbul *Pycnonotus blanfordi*

Cream-vented Bulbul *Pycnonotus simplex*

Red-eyed Bulbul *Pycnonotus brunneus*

Spectacled Bulbul *Pycnonotus erythropthalmos*

Kakamega Bulbul *Pycnonotus kakamegae* LR

Shelley's Greenbul *Andropadus masukuensis* LR

Cameroon Mountain Greenbul *Andropadus montanus* GT

Little Greenbul *Andropadus virens*

Mrs Hall's Greenbul *Andropadus hallae*

Grey Greenbul *Andropadus gracilis*

Ansorge's Greenbul *Andropadus ansorgei*

Plain Greenbul *Andropadus curvirostris*

Zanzibar Sombre Greenbul *Andropadus importunus*

Yellow-whiskered Greenbul *Andropadus latirostris*

Slender-billed Greenbul *Andropadus gracilirostris*

Grey-throated Greenbul *Andropadus tephrolaemus*

Mountain Greenbul *Andropadus nigriceps* LR

Green-throated Greenbul *Andropadus chlorigula* LR

Olive-headed Greenbul *Andropadus olivaceiceps* LR

Stripe-cheeked Greenbul *Andropadus milanjensis*

Golden Greenbul *Calyptocichla serina*

Honeyguide Greenbul *Baeopogon indicator*

Sjöstedt's Honeyguide Greenbul *Baeopogon clamans*

Spotted Greenbul *Ixonotus guttatus*

Simple Greenbul *Chlorocichla simplex*

Yellow-throated Greenbul *Chlorocichla flavicollis*

Yellow-bellied Greenbul *Chlorocichla flaviventris*

Yellow-necked Greenbul *Chlorocichla falkensteini* LR

Joyful Greenbul *Chlorocichla laetissima*

Prigogine's Greenbul *Chlorocichla prigoginei* GT

Swamp Palm Bulbul *Thescelocichla leucopleura*

Terrestrial Brownbul *Phyllastrephus terrestris*

Northern Brownbul *Phyllastrephus strepitans*

Grey-olive Greenbul *Phyllastrephus cerviniventris* LR

Pale-olive Greenbul *Phyllastrephus fulviventris*

Cameroon Olive Greenbul *Phyllastrephus poensis*

Toro Olive Greenbul *Phyllastrephus hypochloris*

Baumann's Olive Greenbul *Phyllastrephus baumanni* PGT

Grey-headed Greenbul *Phyllastrephus poliocephalus* GT

Malawi Greenbul *Phyllastrephus alfredi* LR

Yellow-streaked Greenbul *Phyllastrephus flavirostriatus*

Tiny Greenbul *Phyllastrephus debilis*

Sassi's Olive Greenbul *Phyllastrephus lorenzi* GT

Common Leaflove *Phyllastrephus scandens*

Fischer's Greenbul *Phyllastrephus fischeri*

Cabanis' Greenbul *Phyllastrephus cabanisi*

Olive Mountain Greenbul *Phyllastrephus placidus* LR

White-throated Greenbul *Phyllastrephus albigularis*

Icterine Greenbul *Phyllastrephus icterinus*

Xavier's Greenbul *Phyllastrephus xavieri*

Liberian Greenbul *Phyllastrephus leucolepis* GT

Common Tetraka *Bernieria madagascariensis*

Short-billed Tetraka *Bernieria zosterops*

Appert's Tetraka *Bernieria apperti* GT

Dusky Tetraka *Bernieria tenebrosa* GT

Grey-crowned Tetraka *Bernieria cinereiceps* GT

Common Bristlebill *Bleda syndactyla*

Green-tailed Bristlebill *Bleda eximia* GT

Grey-headed Bristlebill *Bleda canicapilla*

Western Bearded Greenbul *Criniger barbatus*

Eastern Bearded Greenbul *Criniger chloronotus* LR

Red-tailed Greenbul *Criniger calurus*

White-bearded Greenbul *Criniger ndussumensis* LR

Yellow-bearded Greenbul *Criniger olivaceus* GT

Finsch's Bearded Bulbul *Alophoixus finschii* GT

White-throated Bulbul *Alophoixus flaveolus*

Puff-throated Bulbul *Alophoixus pallidus*

Ochraceous Bulbul *Alophoixus ochraceus*

Grey-cheeked Bearded Bulbul *Alophoixus bres*

Yellow-bellied Bulbul *Alophoixus phaeocephalus*

Golden Bulbul *Alophoixus affinis*

Hook-billed Bulbul *Setornis criniger* GT

Hairy-backed Bulbul *Tricholestes criniger*

Olive Bulbul *Iole virescens* LR

Grey-eyed Bulbul *Iole propinqua*

Buff-vented Bulbul *Iole olivacea* GT, LR

Sulphur-bellied Bulbul *Ixos palawanensis* LR

Yellow-browed Bulbul *Iole indica*

Philippine Bulbul *Ixos philippinus*

Zamboanga Bulbul *Ixos rufigularis* GT, LR

Streak-breasted Bulbul *Ixos siquijorensis* GT

Asian Brown-eared Bulbul *Ixos amaurotis*

Yellowish Bulbul *Ixos everetti*

Streaked Bulbul *Ixos malaccensis* GT, LR

Ashy Bulbul *Hemixos flavala*

Chestnut Bulbul *Hemixos castanonotus* LR

Mountain Bulbul *Hypsipetes mcclellandii* LR

Sunda Bulbul *Hypsipetes virescens*

Madagascar Black Bulbul *Hypsipetes madagascariensis*

Seychelles Bulbul *Hypsipetes crassirostris*

Comoros Black Bulbul *Hypsipetes parvirostris* LR

Réunion Bulbul *Hypsipetes borbonicus*

Mauritius Bulbul *Hypsipetes olivaceus* GT

Black Bulbul *Hypsipetes leucocephalus* LR

Nicobar Bulbul *Hypsipetes nicobariensis* GT

White-headed Bulbul *Hypsipetes thompsoni*

Malia *Malia grata*

Black-collared Bulbul *Neolestes torquatus*

Aegithinidae

Common Iora *Aegithina tiphia*

Marshall's Iora *Aegithina nigrolutea* LR

Green Iora *Aegithina viridissima* GT

Great Iora *Aegithina lafresnayei*

Chloropseidae

Philippine Leafbird *Chloropsis flavipennis* GT

Yellow-throated Leafbird *Chloropsis palawanensis*

Greater Green Leafbird *Chloropsis sonnerati*

Lesser Green Leafbird *Chloropsis cyanopogon* GT

Blue-winged Leafbird *Chloropsis cochinchinensis*

Golden-fronted Leafbird *Chloropsis aurifrons*

Orange-bellied Leafbird *Chloropsis hardwickii*

Blue-masked Leafbird *Chloropsis venusta* GT

Irenidae

Asian Fairy-Bluebird *Irena puella*

Philippine Fairy-Bluebird *Irena cyanogaster*

Laniidae

Northern White-crowned Shrike *Eurocephalus rueppelli*

Southern White-crowned Shrike *Eurocephalus anguitimens*

White Helmetshrike *Prionops plumatus*

Grey-crested Helmetshrike *Prionops poliolophus* GT

Red-billed Helmetshrike *Prionops caniceps*

Yellow-crested Helmetshrike *Prionops alberti* GT

Gabon Helmetshrike *Prionops rufiventris* LR

Retz's Helmetshrike *Prionops retzii*

Angola Helmetshrike *Prionops gabela* GT

Chestnut-fronted Helmetshrike *Prionops scopifrons*

White-tailed Shrike *Lanioturdus torquatus*

Brubru *Nilaus afer*

Pringle's Puffback *Dryoscopus pringlii*

Northern Puffback *Dryoscopus gambensis*

Black-backed Puffback *Dryoscopus cubla*

Red-eyed Puffback *Dryoscopus senegalensis*

Pink-footed Puffback *Dryoscopus angolensis*

Sabine's Puffback *Dryoscopus sabini*

Marsh Tchagra *Tchagra minuta*

Anchieta's Tchagra *Tchagra anchietae* LR

Black-crowned Tchagra *Tchagra senegala*

Southern Tchagra *Tchagra tchagra*

Brown-crowned Tchagra *Tchagra australis*

Three-streaked Tchagra *Tchagra jamesi*

Red-naped Bushshrike *Laniarius ruficeps*

Lühder's Bushshrike *Laniarius luehderi*

Orange-breasted Bushshrike *Laniarius brauni* GT, LR

Amboim Bushshrike *Laniarius amboimensis* GT, LR

Bulo Burti Boubou *Laniarius liberatus* GT, LR

Turati's Boubou *Laniarius turatii* LR

Tropical Boubou *Laniarius aethiopicus* LR

Gabon Boubou *Laniarius bicolor* LR

Southern Boubou *Laniarius ferrugineus*

Yellow-crowned Gonolek *Laniarius barbarus*

Black-headed Gonolek *Laniarius erythrogaster* LR

Crimson-breasted Gonolek *Laniarius atrococcineus* LR

Papyrus Gonolek *Laniarius mufumbiri* GT

Yellow-breasted Boubou *Laniarius atroflavus*

Fülleborn's Black Boubou *Laniarius fuelleborni*

Mountain Sooty Boubou *Laniarius poensis* LR

Slate-colored Boubou *Laniarius funebris*

Sooty Boubou *Laniarius leucorhynchus*

Rosy-patched Bushshrike *Rhodophoneus cruentus*

Tsavo Bushshrike *Rhodophoneus cathemagmenus* LR

Grey-green Bushshrike *Telophorus bocagei*

Sulphur-breasted Bushshrike *Telophorus sulfureopectus*

Rufous-breasted Bushshrike *Telophorus olivaceus*

Black-fronted Bushshrike *Telophorus nigrifrons* LR

Many-colored Bushshrike *Telophorus multicolor*

Mount Kupé Bushshrike *Telophorus kupeensis* GT

Bokmakierie Bushshrike *Telophorus zeylonus*

Perrin's Bushshrike *Telophorus viridis*

Four-colored Bushshrike *Telophorus quadricolor* LR

Doherty's Bushshrike *Telophorus dohertyi*

Fiery-breasted Bushshrike *Malaconotus cruentus*

Lagden's Bushshrike *Malaconotus lagdeni* GT

Green-breasted Bushshrike *Malaconotus gladiator* GT

Grey-headed Bushshrike *Malaconotus blanchoti*

Monteiro's Bushshrike *Malaconotus monteiri* PGT

Uluguru Bushshrike *Malaconotus alius* GT

Western Nicator *Nicator chloris*

Eastern Nicator *Nicator gularis* LR

Yellow-throated Nicator *Nicator vireo*

Yellow-billed Shrike *Corvinella corvina*

Magpie Shrike *Corvinella melanoleuca*

Tiger Shrike *Lanius tigrinus*

Souza's Shrike *Lanius souzae*

Brown Shrike *Lanius cristatus*

Red-backed Shrike *Lanius collurio* LR

Isabelline Shrike *Lanius isabellinus* LR

Burmese Shrike *Lanius collurioides*

Bull-headed Shrike *Lanius bucephalus*

Emin's Shrike *Lanius gubernator*

Bay-backed Shrike *Lanius vittatus*

Long-tailed Shrike *Lanius schach*

Grey-backed Shrike *Lanius tephronotus* LR

Mountain Shrike *Lanius validirostris* GT

Mackinnon's Shrike *Lanius mackinnoni*

Lesser Grey Shrike *Lanius minor*

Loggerhead Shrike *Lanius ludovicianus*

Great Grey Shrike *Lanius excubitor*
Southern Grey Shrike *Lanius meridionalis* LR
Grey-backed Fiscal *Lanius excubitoroides*
Long-tailed Fiscal *Lanius cabanisi*
Chinese Grey Shrike *Lanius sphenocercus*
Taita Fiscal *Lanius dorsalis*
Somali Fiscal *Lanius somalicus*
Common Fiscal *Lanius collaris*
Uhehe Fiscal *Lanius marwitzi* LR
Newton's Fiscal *Lanius newtoni* GT
Masked Shrike *Lanius nubicus*
Woodchat Shrike *Lanius senator*

Vangidae

Red-tailed Vanga *Calicalicus madagascariensis*
Red-shouldered Vanga *Calicalicus rufocarpalis* LR
Rufous Vanga *Schetba rufa*
Hook-billed Vanga *Vanga curvirostris*
Lafresnaye's Vanga *Xenopirostris xenopirostris*
Van Dam's Vanga *Xenopirostris damii* GT
Pollen's Vanga *Xenopirostris polleni* GT
Sickle-billed Vanga *Falculea palliata*
White-headed Vanga *Artamella viridis*
Chabert Vanga *Leptopterus chabert*
Madagascar Blue Vanga *Cyanolanius madagascarinus*
Comoro Blue Vanga *Cyanolanius comorensis* LR
Bernièr's Vanga *Oriolia bernieri* GT
Helmet Vanga *Euryceros prevostii* GT
Tylas Vanga *Tylas eduardi*
Nuthatch Vanga *Hypositta corallirostris*
Short-toed Nuthatch Vanga *Hypositta perdita* PGT

Bombycillidae

Bohemian Waxwing *Bombycilla garrulus*
Japanese Waxwing *Bombycilla japonica* GT
Cedar Waxwing *Bombycilla cedrorum*
Grey Silky-Flycatcher *Ptilogonys cinereus*
Long-tailed Silky-Flycatcher *Ptilogonys caudatus*
Phainopepla *Phainopepla nitens*
Black-and-yellow Silky-Flycatcher *Phainoptila melanoxantha*
Hypocolius *Hypocolius ampelinus*

Dulidae

Palmchat *Dulus dominicus*

Cinclidae

White-throated Dipper *Cinclus cinclus*
Brown Dipper *Cinclus pallasii*
American Dipper *Cinclus mexicanus*
White-capped Dipper *Cinclus leucocephalus*
Rufous-throated Dipper *Cinclus schulzi* GT

Troglodytidae

Donacobius *Donacobius atricapilla*
Boucard's Cactus-Wren *Campylorhynchus jocosus*
Spotted Cactus-Wren *Campylorhynchus gularis*
Yucatan Cactus-Wren *Campylorhynchus yucatanicus*
Northern Cactus-Wren *Campylorhynchus brunneicapillus*
Giant Cactus-Wren *Campylorhynchus chiapensis* LR
Bicolored Cactus-Wren *Campylorhynchus griseus*
Rufous-naped Cactus-Wren *Campylorhynchus rufinucha*
Thrush-like Cactus-Wren *Campylorhynchus turdinus*
White-headed Cactus-Wren *Campylorhynchus albobrunneus* LR
Stripe-backed Cactus-Wren *Campylorhynchus nuchalis*
Fasciated Cactus-Wren *Campylorhynchus fasciatus*
Band-backed Cactus-Wren *Campylorhynchus zonatus*
Grey-barred Cactus-Wren *Campylorhynchus megalopterus*
Tooth-billed Wren *Odontorchilus cinereus*
Grey-mantled Wren *Odontorchilus branickii* LR
American Rock Wren *Salpinctes obsoletus*
Canyon Wren *Catherpes mexicanus*
Sumichrast's Wren *Hylorchilus sumichrasti* GT
Nava's Wren *Hylorchilus navai* GT, LR
Rufous Wren *Cinnycerthia unirufa*
Peruvian Wren *Cinnycerthia peruana*
Sharpe's Wren *Cinnycerthia olivascens* LR
Fulvous Wren *Cinnycerthia fulva* LR
Short-billed Marsh-Wren *Cistothorus platensis*
Paramo Wren *Cistothorus meridae*
Apolinar's Marsh-Wren *Cistothorus apolinari* GT
Marsh-Wren *Cistothorus palustris*

Western Marsh-Wren *Cistothorus paludicola* LR

Zapata Wren *Ferminia cerverai* GT

Black-throated Wren *Thryothorus atrogularis*

Sooty-headed Wren *Thryothorus spadix* LR

Black-bellied Wren *Thryothorus fasciatoventris*

Plain-tailed Wren *Thryothorus euophrys*

Inca Wren *Thryothorus eisenmanni*

Whiskered Wren *Thryothorus mystacalis* LR

Moustached Wren *Thryothorus genibarbis*

Coraya Wren *Thryothorus coraya*

Happy Wren *Thryothorus felix*

Spot-breasted Wren *Thryothorus maculipectus* LR

Rufous-breasted Wren *Thryothorus rutilus*

Speckle-breasted Wren *Thryothorus sclateri* LR

Riverside Wren *Thryothorus semibadius*

Black-capped Wren *Thryothorus nigricapillus*

Stripe-breasted Wren *Thryothorus thoracicus*

Stripe-throated Wren *Thryothorus leucopogon* LR

Banded Wren *Thryothorus pleurostictus*

Carolina Wren *Thryothorus ludovicianus*

Rufous-and-white Wren *Thryothorus rufalbus*

Nicéforo's Wren *Thryothorus nicefori* GT, LR

Sinaloa Wren *Thryothorus sinaloa* LR

Plain Wren *Thryothorus modestus*

Buff-breasted Wren *Thryothorus leucotis*

Superciliated Wren *Thryothorus superciliaris*

Fawn-breasted Wren *Thryothorus guarayanus*

Long-billed Wren *Thryothorus longirostris*

Grey Wren *Thryothorus griseus*

Bewick's Wren *Thryomanes bewickii*

Socorro Wren *Thryomanes sissonii* GT

Northern Wren *Troglodytes troglodytes*

Clarión Island Wren *Troglodytes tanneri* GT

House Wren *Troglodytes aedon*

Cobb's Wren *Troglodytes cobbi* GT, LR

Rufous-browed Wren *Troglodytes rufociliatus* LR

Ochraceous Wren *Troglodytes ochraceus* LR

Santa Marta Wren *Troglodytes monticola* LR

Mountain Wren *Troglodytes solstitialis*

Tepui Wren *Troglodytes rufulus*

Timberline Wren *Thryorchilus browni*

White-bellied Wren *Uropsila leucogastra*

White-breasted Wood-Wren *Henicorhina leucosticta*

Grey-breasted Wood-Wren *Henicorhina leucophrys*

Bar-winged Wood-Wren *Henicorhina leucoptera* GT

Northern Nightingale Wren *Microcerculus philomela* LR

Southern Nightingale Wren *Microcerculus marginatus*

Flutist Wren *Microcerculus ustulatus*

Wing-banded Wren *Microcerculus bambla*

Song Wren *Cyphorhinus phaeocephalus* LR

Chestnut-breasted Wren *Cyphorhinus thoracicus*

Musician Wren *Cyphorhinus aradus*

Mimidae

Grey Catbird *Dumetella carolinensis*

Black Catbird *Dumetella glabrirostris* GT

Blue Mockingbird *Melanotis caerulescens*

Blue-and-white Mockingbird *Melanotis hypoleucus* LR

Northern Mockingbird *Mimus polyglottos*

Tropical Mockingbird *Mimus gilvus* LR

Bahaman Mockingbird *Mimus gundlachii*

Chilean Mockingbird *Mimus thenca*

Long-tailed Mockingbird *Mimus longicaudatus*

Chalk-browed Mockingbird *Mimus saturninus*

Patagonian Mockingbird *Mimus patagonicus*

White-banded Mockingbird *Mimus triurus*

Brown-backed Mockingbird *Mimus dorsalis*

Galapogos Mockingbird *Nesomimus parvulus* LR

Charles Mockingbird *Nesomimus trifasciatus* GT

Hood Mockingbird *Nesomimus macdonaldi* GT, LR

San Cristobal Mockingbird *Nesomimus melanotis* LR

Socorro Thrasher *Mimodes graysoni* GT

Sage Thrasher *Oreoscoptes montanus*

Brown Thrasher *Toxostoma rufum*

Long-billed Thrasher *Toxostoma longirostre*

Cozumel Thrasher *Toxostoma guttatum* GT

Grey Thrasher *Toxostoma cinereum*

Bendire's Thrasher *Toxostoma bendirei*

Ocellated Thrasher *Toxostoma ocellatum*

Curve-billed Thrasher *Toxostoma curvirostre*

Le Conte's Thrasher *Toxostoma lecontei*

Vizcaino Thrasher *Toxostoma arenicola* LR

California Thrasher *Toxostoma redivivum*

Crissal Thrasher *Toxostoma crissale*

Brown Trembler *Cinclocerthia ruficauda*

Grey Trembler *Cinclocerthia gutturalis* LR

White-breasted Trembler *Ramphocinclus brachyurus* GT

Scaly-breasted Thrasher *Allenia fusca*

Pearly-eyed Thrasher *Margarops fuscatus*

Prunellidae

Alpine Accentor *Prunella collaris*

Altai Accentor *Prunella himalayana*

Robin Accentor *Prunella rubeculoides*

Rufous-breasted Accentor *Prunella strophiata*

Siberian Accentor *Prunella montanella*

Brown Accentor *Prunella fulvescens*

Radde's Accentor *Prunella ocularis* LR

Yemen Accentor *Prunella fagani* GT, LR

Black-throated Accentor *Prunella atrogularis*

Mongolian Accentor *Prunella koslowi*

Hedge Accentor *Prunella modularis*

Japanese Accentor *Prunella rubida*

Maroon-backed Accentor *Prunella immaculata*

Turdidae

Gould's Shortwing *Brachypteryx stellata*

Rusty-bellied Shortwing *Brachypteryx hyperythra* GT

White-bellied Shortwing *Brachypteryx major* GT

Lesser Shortwing *Brachypteryx leucophrys*

White-browed Shortwing *Brachypteryx montana*

Greater Shortwing *Heinrichia calligyna*

White-tailed Alethe *Alethe diademata*

Fire-crested Alethe *Alethe castanea* LR

Red-throated Alethe *Alethe poliophrys*

Brown-chested Alethe *Alethe poliocephala*

White-chested Alethe *Alethe fuelleborni*

Cholo Mountain Alethe *Alethe choloensis* GT

Red-tailed Antthrush *Neocossyphus rufus*

White-tailed Antthrush *Neocossyphus poensis*

Rufous Flycatcher-Thrush *Neocossyphus fraseri*

Finsch's Flycatcher-Thrush *Neocossyphus finschii*

Cape Rockjumper *Chaetops frenatus*

Orange-breasted Rockjumper *Chaetops aurantius* LR

Eastern Bluebird *Sialia sialis*

Western Bluebird *Sialia mexicana*

Mountain Bluebird *Sialia currucoides*

Omao *Myadestes obscurus* GT

Kama'o *Myadestes myadestinus* GT

Amaui *Myadestes woahensis* E

Oloma'o *Myadestes lanaiensis* GT

Puaiohi *Myadestes palmeri* GT

Townsend's Solitaire *Myadestes townsendi*

Brown-backed Solitaire *Myadestes occidentalis*

Cuban Solitaire *Myadestes elisabeth* GT

Rufous-throated Solitaire *Myadestes genibarbis*

Black-faced Solitaire *Myadestes melanops* LR

Varied Solitaire *Myadestes coloratus* LR

Andean Solitaire *Myadestes ralloides*

Slate-colored Solitaire *Myadestes unicolor*

Rufous-brown Solitaire *Cichlopsis leucogenys* LR

White-eared Solitaire *Entomodestes leucotis*

Black Solitaire *Entomodestes coracinus*

Indian Robin *Saxicoloides fulicata*

Littoral Rock-Thrush *Pseudocossyphus imerinus*

Forest Rock-Thrush *Pseudocossyphus sharpei* LR

Amber Mountain Rock-Thrush *Pseudocossyphus erythronotus*

Benson's Rock-Thrush *Pseudocossyphus bensoni* GT, LR

Cape Rock-Thrush *Monticola rupestris*

Sentinel Rock-Thrush *Monticola explorator*

Short-toed Rock-Thrush *Monticola brevipes*

Transvaal Rock-Thrush *Monticola pretoriae* LR

Miombo Rock-Thrush *Monticola angolensis*

Rufous-tailed Rock-Thrush *Monticola saxatilis*

Blue-capped Rock-Thrush *Monticola cinclorhynchus*

White-throated Rock-Thrush *Monticola gularis* LR

Little Rock-Thrush *Monticola rufocinereus*

Chestnut-bellied Rock-Thrush *Monticola rufiventris*

Blue Rock-Thrush *Monticola solitarius*

Sri Lanka Whistling-Thrush *Myophonus blighi* GT

Shiny Whistling-Thrush *Myophonus melanurus*

Sunda Whistling-Thrush *Myophonus glaucinus*

Brown-winged Whistling-Thrush *Myophonus castaneus* LR

Malaysian Whistling-Thrush *Myophonus robinsoni* GT

Malabar Whistling-Thrush *Myophonus horsfieldii*

Taiwan Whistling-Thrush *Myophonus insularis* LR

Blue Whistling-Thrush *Myophonus caeruleus*

Large Whistling-Thrush *Myophonus flavirostris* LR

Geomalia *Geomalia heinrichi* GT

Slaty-backed Ground-Thrush *Zoothera schistacea* GT

Moluccan Ground-Thrush *Zoothera dumasi* GT

Chestnut-capped Ground-Thrush *Zoothera interpres*

Red-backed Ground-Thrush *Zoothera erythronota* GT

Chestnut-backed Ground-Thrush *Zoothera dohertyi* GT, LR

Ashy Ground-Thrush *Zoothera cinerea* GT

Orange-sided Thrush *Zoothera peronii* GT

Pied Ground-Thrush *Zoothera wardii*

Orange-headed Ground-Thrush *Zoothera citrina*

Everett's Ground-Thrush *Zoothera everetti* GT

Siberian Ground-Thrush *Zoothera sibirica*

Abyssinian Ground-Thrush *Zoothera piaggiae*

Kivu Ground-Thrush *Zoothera tanganjicae* GT, LR

Crossley's Ground-Thrush *Zoothera crossleyi* GT

Orange Ground-Thrush *Zoothera gurneyi*

Oberlaender's Ground-Thrush *Zoothera oberlaenderi* GT

Black-eared Ground-Thrush *Zoothera cameronensis*

Prigogine's Ground-Thrush *Zoothera kibalensis* LR

Grey Ground-Thrush *Zoothera princei*

Spotted Ground-Thrush *Zoothera guttata* GT

Spot-winged Ground-Thrush *Zoothera spiloptera* GT

Sunda Ground-Thrush *Zoothera andromedae*

Plain-backed Thrush *Zoothera mollissima*

Long-tailed Thrush *Zoothera dixoni*

White's Ground-Thrush *Zoothera dauma*

Amami Thrush *Zoothera major* GT, LR

Horsfield's Thrush *Zoothera horsfieldi* LR

Fawn-breasted Thrush *Zoothera machiki* GT, LR

Russet-tailed Thrush *Zoothera heinei* LR

Bassian Thrush *Zoothera lunulata* LR

Northern Melanesian Ground-Thrush *Zoothera talaseae* GT

San Cristobal Ground-Thrush *Zoothera margaretae* PGT, LR

Guadalcanal Ground-Thrush *Zoothera turipavae* PGT, LR

Long-billed Thrush *Zoothera monticola*

Dark-sided Thrush *Zoothera marginata*

Bonin Islands Thrush *Zoothera terrestris* E

Varied Thrush *Ixoreus naevius*

Aztec Thrush *Ridgwayia pinicola*

Sulawesi Mountain Thrush *Cataponera turdoides*

Tristan Thrush *Nesocichla eremita* GT

Forest Thrush *Cichlherminia lherminieri* GT

Black-billed Nightingale-Thrush *Catharus gracilirostris*

Orange-billed Nightingale-Thrush *Catharus aurantiirostris*

Slaty-backed Nightingale-Thrush *Catharus fuscater*

Russet Nightingale-Thrush *Catharus occidentalis*

Ruddy-capped Nightingale-Thrush *Catharus frantzii*

Black-headed Nightingale-Thrush *Catharus mexicanus*

Spotted Nightingale-Thrush *Catharus dryas*

Veery *Catharus fuscescens*

Grey-cheeked Thrush *Catharus minimus*

Bicknell's Thrush *Catharus bicknelli* GT, LR

Swainson's Thrush *Catharus ustulatus*

Hermit Thrush *Catharus guttatus*

Wood Thrush *Hylocichla mustelina*

Yellow-legged Thrush *Platycichla flavipes*

Pale-eyed Thrush *Platycichla leucops*

Groundscraper Thrush *Psophocichla litsipsirupa*

Olivaceous Thrush *Turdus olivaceofuscus* GT

Kurrichane Thrush *Turdus libonyanus*

African Bare-eyed Thrush *Turdus tephronotus*

Yemen Thrush *Turdus menachensis* GT
Comoros Thrush *Turdus bewsheri*
Olive Thrush *Turdus olivaceus*
African Thrush *Turdus pelios* LR
Somali Thrush *Turdus ludoviciae* GT, LR
Abyssinian Thrush *Turdus abyssinicus* LR
Taita Thrush *Turdus helleri* GT, LR
Black-breasted Thrush *Turdus dissimilis*
Grey-backed Thrush *Turdus hortulorum* LR
Tickell's Thrush *Turdus unicolor*
Japanese Grey Thrush *Turdus cardis*
White-collared Blackbird *Turdus albocinctus*
Ring Ouzel *Turdus torquatus*
Grey-winged Blackbird *Turdus boulboul*
Common Blackbird *Turdus merula*
Island Thrush *Turdus poliocephalus*
Brown-headed Thrush *Turdus chrysolaus* LR
Izu Islands Thrush *Turdus celaenops* GT
Chestnut Thrush *Turdus rubrocanus*
Kessler's Thrush *Turdus kessleri*
Grey-sided Thrush *Turdus feae* GT
Pale Thrush *Turdus pallidus*
Eyebrowed Thrush *Turdus obscurus* LR
Dark-throated Thrush *Turdus ruficollis*
Dusky Thrush *Turdus naumanni*
Fieldfare *Turdus pilaris*
Redwing *Turdus iliacus*
Common Song Thrush *Turdus philomelos*
Chinese Song Thrush *Turdus mupinensis*
Mistle Thrush *Turdus viscivorus*
Grand Cayman Thrush *Turdus ravidus* E
Red-legged Thrush *Turdus plumbeus*
Chiguanco Thrush *Turdus chiguanco*
Sooty Thrush *Turdus nigrescens*
Great Thrush *Turdus fuscater*
Black Thrush *Turdus infuscatus*
Glossy-black Thrush *Turdus serranus*
Andean Slaty Thrush *Turdus nigriceps*
Eastern Slaty Thrush *Turdus subalaris* LR
Plumbeous-backed Thrush *Turdus reevei*
Black-hooded Thrush *Turdus olivater*
Marañón Thrush *Turdus maranonicus*
Chestnut-bellied Thrush *Turdus fulviventris*
Rufous-bellied Thrush *Turdus rufiventris*
Austral Thrush *Turdus falcklandii*

Pale-breasted Thrush *Turdus leucomelas*
Creamy-bellied Thrush *Turdus amaurochalinus*
American Mountain Thrush *Turdus plebejus*
Black-billed Thrush *Turdus ignobilis*
Lawrence's Thrush *Turdus lawrencii*
Cocoa Thrush *Turdus fumigatus*
Lesser Antillean Thrush *Turdus personus* LR
Pale-vented Thrush *Turdus obsoletus*
Hauxwell's Thrush *Turdus hauxwelli* LR
Unicolored Thrush *Turdus haplochrous* GT
Clay-colored Thrush *Turdus grayi*
American Bare-eyed Thrush *Turdus nudigenis*
Ecuadorean Thrush *Turdus maculirostris* LR
White-eyed Thrush *Turdus jamaicensis*
White-throated Thrush *Turdus assimilis* LR
Dagua Thrush *Turdus daguae* LR
White-necked Thrush *Turdus albicollis*
Rufous-backed Thrush *Turdus rufopalliatus*
Grayson's Thrush *Turdus graysoni* LR
White-chinned Thrush *Turdus aurantius*
La Selle Thrush *Turdus swalesi* GT
Rufous-collared Thrush *Turdus rufitorques*
American Robin *Turdus migratorius*
Black-breasted Fruithunter *Chlamydochaera jefferyi*

Saxicoliidae

White-starred Bush-Robin *Pogonocichla stellata*
Swynnerton's Bush-Robin *Swynnertonia swynnertoni* GT
Forest-Robin *Stiphrornis erythrothorax*
Sangha Forest-Robin *Stiphrornis sanghensis* PGT, LR
Alexander's Akalat *Sheppardia poensis* LR
Grey-winged Akalat *Sheppardia polioptera* LR
Bocage's Akalat *Sheppardia bocagei*
Whiskered Akalat *Sheppardia cyornithopsis*
Equatorial Akalat *Sheppardia aequatorialis*
Sharpe's Akalat *Sheppardia sharpei*
East Coast Akalat *Sheppardia gunningi* GT
Gabela Akalat *Sheppardia gabela* GT
Usambara Akalat *Sheppardia montana* GT
Iringa Akalat *Sheppardia lowei* GT
European Robin *Erithacus rubecula*
Japanese Robin *Erithacus akahige*
Ryukyu Robin *Erithacus komadori*
Rufous-tailed Robin *Luscinia sibilans*

Siberian Rubythroat *Luscinia calliope*

White-tailed Rubythroat *Luscinia pectoralis*

Rufous-headed Robin *Luscinia ruficeps* GT

Blackthroat *Luscinia obscura* GT

Firethroat *Luscinia pectardens* GT, LR

Indian Blue Robin *Luscinia brunnea*

Siberian Blue Robin *Luscinia cyane*

Thrush Nightingale *Luscinia luscinia*

Rufous Nightingale *Luscinia megarhynchos*

Bluethroat *Luscinia svecica*

White-browed Bush-Robin *Tarsiger indicus*

Rufous-breasted Bush-Robin *Tarsiger hyperythrus*

Collared Bush-Robin *Tarsiger johnstoniae*

Red-flanked Bluetail *Tarsiger cyanurus*

Golden Bush-Robin *Tarsiger chrysaeus*

Oriental Magpie-Robin *Copsychus saularis*

Seychelles Magpie-Robin *Copsychus sechellarum* GT

Madagascar Magpie-Robin *Copsychus albospecularis*

White-rumped Shama *Copsychus malabaricus*

White-crowned Shama *Copsychus stricklandii* LR

White-browed Shama *Copsychus luzoniensis* LR

White-vented Shama *Copsychus niger*

Black Shama *Copsychus cebuensis* GT, LR

Rufous-tailed Shama *Trichixos pyrropyga* GT

White-throated Robin *Irania gutturalis*

White-bellied Robinchat *Cossyphicula roberti*

Mountain Robinchat *Cossypha isabellae*

Archer's Robinchat *Cossypha archeri*

Olive-flanked Robinchat *Cossypha anomala*

White-throated Robinchat *Cossypha humeralis*

Cape Robinchat *Cossypha caffra*

Blue-shouldered Robinchat *Cossypha cyanocampter*

Rüppell's Robinchat *Cossypha semirufa*

White-browed Robinchat *Cossypha heuglini*

Red-capped Robinchat *Cossypha natalensis*

Chorister Robinchat *Cossypha dichroa*

White-headed Robinchat *Cossypha heinrichi* GT

Snowy-headed Robinchat *Cossypha niveicapilla*

White-crowned Robinchat *Cossypha albicapilla*

Angola Cave-Chat *Xenocopsychus ansorgei* GT

Spot-throat *Modulatrix stictigula*

Dappled Mountain Robin *Phyllastrephu orostruthus* GT

Boulder Chat *Pinarornis plumosus*

Collared Palm Thrush *Cichladusa arquata*

Rufous-tailed Palm Thrush *Cichladusa ruficauda*

Spotted Palm Thrush *Cichladusa guttata*

Forest Scrub-Robin *Cercotrichas leucosticta*

Miombo Bearded Scrub-Robin *Cercotrichas barbata*

Eastern Bearded Scrub-Robin *Cercotrichas quadrivirgata*

Brown Scrub-Robin *Cercotrichas signata*

Brown-backed Scrub-Robin *Cercotrichas hartlaubi*

White-browed Scrub-Robin *Cercotrichas leucophrys*

Rufous-tailed Scrub-Robin *Cercotrichas galactotes*

African Scrub-Robin *Cercotrichas minor* LR

Kalahari Scrub-Robin *Cercotrichas paena*

Karoo Scrub-Robin *Cercotrichas coryphaeus*

Black Scrub-Robin *Cercotrichas podobe*

Herero Chat *Namibornis herero*

Ala Shan Redstart *Phoenicurus alaschanicus* GT, LR

Eversmann's Redstart *Phoenicurus erythronota*

Blue-capped Redstart *Phoenicurus coeruleocephalus*

Black Redstart *Phoenicurus ochruros*

Eurasian Redstart *Phoenicurus phoenicurus*

Hodgson's Redstart *Phoenicurus hodgsoni*

Blue-fronted Redstart *Phoenicurus frontalis*

White-throated Redstart *Phoenicurus schisticeps*

Daurian Redstart *Phoenicurus auroreus*

Moussier's Redstart *Phoenicurus moussieri*

Güldenstädt's Redstart *Phoenicurus erythrogaster*

White-capped Water-Redstart *Chaimarrornis leucocephalus*

Plumbeous Water-Redstart *Rhyacornis fuliginosus*

Luzon Water-Redstart *Rhyacornis bicolor* GT

White-bellied Redstart *Hodgsonius phaenicuroides*

White-tailed Robin *Myiomela leucura*

Sunda Robin *Myiomela diana*

Blue-fronted Robin *Cinclidium frontale*

dala Grandala *Grandala coelicolor*

_e_ Forktail *Enicurus scouleri*

_da_ Forktail *Enicurus velatus*

hestnut-naped Forktail *Enicurus ruficapillus* GT

Black-backed Forktail *Enicurus immaculatus*

Slaty-backed Forktail *Enicurus schistaceus*

White-crowned Forktail *Enicurus leschenaulti*

Spotted Forktail *Enicurus maculatus*

Purple Cochoa *Cochoa purpurea*

Green Cochoa *Cochoa viridis*

Javan Cochoa *Cochoa azurea* GT

Sumatran Cochoa *Cochoa beccarii* GT, LR

Whinchat *Saxicola rubetra*

Stoliczka's Bushchat *Saxicola macrorhyncha* GT

Hodgson's Bushchat *Saxicola insignis* GT

Fuerteventura Chat *Saxicola dacotiae* GT

Common Stonechat *Saxicola torquata*

African Stonechat *Saxicola axillaris* LR

Siberian Stonechat *Saxicola maura* LR

Réunion Stonechat *Saxicola tectes* LR

White-tailed Stonechat *Saxicola leucura*

Pied Stonechat *Saxicola caprata*

Jerdon's Bushchat *Saxicola jerdoni*

Grey Bushchat *Saxicola ferrea*

White-bellied Bushchat *Saxicola gutturalis* GT

Buff-streaked Chat *Oenanthe bifasciata*

White-crowned Black Wheatear *Oenanthe leucopyga*

Hooded Wheatear *Oenanthe monacha*

Black Wheatear *Oenanthe leucura*

Mountain Wheatear *Oenanthe monticola*

Somali Wheatear *Oenanthe phillipsi*

Northern Wheatear *Oenanthe oenanthe*

Mourning Wheatear *Oenanthe lugens*

South Arabian Wheatear *Oenanthe lugentoides* LR

Schalow's Wheatear *Oenanthe lugubris* LR

Finsch's Wheatear *Oenanthe finschii* LR

Variable Wheatear *Oenanthe picata*

Red-rumped Wheatear *Oenanthe moesta*

Pied Wheatear *Oenanthe pleschanka* LR

Cyprus Pied Wheatear *Oenanthe cypriaca*

Hume's Wheatear *Oenanthe alboniger*

Black-eared Wheatear *Oenanthe hispanica*

Red-tailed Wheatear *Oenanthe xanthoprymna*

Desert Wheatear *Oenanthe deserti*

Capped Wheatear *Oenanthe pileata*

Red-breasted Wheatear *Oenanthe bottae* LR

Heuglin's Wheatear *Oenanthe heuglini* LR

Isabelline Wheatear *Oenanthe isabellina*

Sicklewinged Chat *Cercomela sinuata*

Karoo Chat *Cercomela schlegelii*

Brown Rockchat *Cercomela fusca*

Tractrac Chat *Cercomela tractrac*

Red-tailed Chat *Cercomela familiaris*

Brown-tailed Chat *Cercomela scotocerca*

Sombre Rockchat *Cercomela dubia* PGT

Blackstart *Cercomela melanura*

Alpine Chat *Cercomela sordida*

Congo Moorchat *Myrmecocichla tholloni*

Northern Anteater Chat *Myrmecocichla aethiops*

Southern Anteater Chat *Myrmecocichla formicivora*

Sooty Chat *Myrmecocichla nigra*

Rüppell's Chat *Myrmecocichla melaena*

White-fronted Blackchat *Myrmecocichla albifrons*

White-headed Blackchat *Myrmecocichla arnott*

Mocking Cliffchat *Thamnolaea cinnamomeiventris*

White-crowned Cliffchat *Thamnolaea coronata* LR

White-winged Cliffchat *Thamnolaea semirufa*

Orthonychidae

Southern Logrunner *Orthonyx temminckii*

Spalding's Logrunner *Orthonyx spaldingii*

Cinclosomatidae

Papuan Whipbird *Androphobus viridis* PGT

Eastern Whipbird *Psophodes olivaceus*

Western Whipbird *Psophodes nigrogularis* GT

Mallee Whipbird *Psophodes leucogaster* GT, LR

Chirruping Wedgebill *Psophodes cristatus*

Chiming Wedgebill *Psophodes occidentalis* LR

Spotted Quail-Thrush *Cinclosoma punctatum*

Chestnut Quail-Thrush *Cinclosoma castanotus*

Cinnamon Quail-Thrush *Cinclosoma cinnamomeum*

Chestnut-breasted Quail-Thrush *Cinclosoma castaneothorax* LR

Ajax Quail-Thrush *Cinclosoma ajax*

Spotted Jewel-Babbler *Ptilorrhoa leucosticta*

Lowland Jewel-Babbler *Ptilorrhoa caerulescens*

Chestnut-backed Jewel-babbler *Ptilorrhoa castanonota*

Malaysian Rail-Babbler *Eupetes macrocerus* GT

Ifrita *Ifrita kowaldi*

omatastomidae

Isidor's Rufous Babbler *Garritornis isidorei* LR

Grey-crowned Babbler *Pomatostomus temporalis*

White-browed Babbler *Pomatostomus superciliosus*

Hall's Babbler *Pomatostomus halli* LR

Chestnut-crowned Babbler *Pomatostomus ruficeps*

maliidae

White-chested Jungle-Babbler *Trichastoma rostratum* GT

Sulawesi Jungle-Babbler *Trichastoma celebense*

Ferruginous Jungle-Babbler *Trichastoma bicolor*

Bagobo Babbler *Leonardina woodi* GT

Abbott's Babbler *Malacocincla abbotti*

Horsfield's Babbler *Malacocincla sepiarium*

Black-browed Babbler *Malacocincla perspicillata* GT

Short-tailed Babbler *Malacocincla malaccensis* GT

Ashy-headed Babbler *Malacocincla cinereiceps*

Buff-breasted Babbler *Pellorneum tickelli* LR

Temminck's Babbler *Pellorneum pyrrogenys*

Spot-throated Babbler *Pellorneum albiventre*

Marsh Babbler *Pellorneum palustre* GT

Puff-throated Babbler *Pellorneum ruficeps*

Brown-capped Jungle-Babbler *Pellorneum fuscocapillum*

Black-capped Jungle-Babbler *Pellorneum capistratum*

Moustached Tree-Babbler *Malacopteron magnirostre*

Sooty-capped Tree-Babbler *Malacopteron affine* GT

Scaly-crowned Tree-Babbler *Malacopteron cinereum*

Rufous-crowned Tree-Babbler *Malacopteron magnum* GT

Melodious Babbler *Malacopteron palawanense* GT

Grey-breasted Babbler *Malacopteron albogulare* GT

Blackcapped Illadopsis *Illadopsis cleaveri*

Scaly-breasted Illadopsis *Illadopsis albipectus*

Rufous-winged Illadopsis *Illadopsis rufescens* GT

Puvel's Illadopsis *Illadopsis puveli*

Pale-breasted Illadopsis *Illadopsis rufipennis*

Brown Illadopsis *Illadopsis fulvescens*

Mountain Illadopsis *Illadopsis pyrrhoptera*

Ruwenzori Hill Babbler *Illadopsis atriceps* LR

African Hill Babbler *Illadopsis abyssinica*

Grey-chested Illadopsis *Kakamega poliothorax*

Spotted Thrush-Babbler *Ptyrticus turdinus*

Large Scimitar-Babbler *Pomatorhinus hypoleucos*

Spot-breasted Scimitar-Babbler *Pomatorhinus erythrocnemis* LR

Rusty-cheeked Scimitar-Babbler *Pomatorhinus erythrogenys*

Indian Scimitar-Babbler *Pomatorhinus horsfieldii*

White-browed Scimitar-Babbler *Pomatorhinus schisticeps* LR

Chestnut-backed Scimitar-Babbler *Pomatorhinus montanus*

Streak-breasted Scimitar-Babbler *Pomatorhinus ruficollis*

Red-billed Scimitar-Babbler *Pomatorhinus ochraceiceps*

Coral-billed Scimitar-Babbler *Pomatorhinus ferruginosus*

Slender-billed Scimitar-Babbler *Xiphirhynchus superciliaris*

Short-tailed Scimitar-Babbler *Jabouilleia danjoui* GT

Long-billed Wren-Babbler *Rimator malacoptilus*

Bornean Wren-Babbler *Ptilocichla leucogrammica* GT

Striated Wren-Babbler *Ptilocichla mindanensis*

Falcated Wren-Babbler *Ptilocichla falcata* GT

Striped Wren-Babbler *Kenopia striata* GT

Rusty-breasted Wren-Babbler *Napothera rufipectus* LR

Black-throated Wren-Babbler *Napothera atrigularis* GT

Large Wren-Babbler *Napothera macrodactyla* GT

Marbled Wren-Babbler *Napothera marmorata*

Limestone Wren-Babbler *Napothera crispifrons*

Streaked Wren-Babbler *Napothera brevicaudata*

Mountain Wren-Babbler *Napothera crassa*

Rabor's Wren-Babbler *Napothera rabori* GT

Eyebrowed Wren-Babbler *Napothera epilepidota*

Scaly-breasted Wren-Babbler *Pnoepyga albiventer* LR

Nepal Wren-Babbler *Pnoepyga immaculata* LR

Pygmy Wren-Babbler *Pnoepyga pusilla*

Rufous-throated Wren-Babbler *Spelaeornis caudatus* GT

Rusty-throated Wren-Babbler *Spelaeornis badeigularis* GT, LR

Bar-winged Wren-Babbler *Spelaeornis troglodytoides*

Spotted Wren-Babbler *Spelaeornis formosus*

Long-tailed Wren-Babbler *Spelaeornis chocolatinus* LR

Tawny-breasted Wren-Babbler *Spelaeornis longicaudatus* GT

Wedge-billed Wren-Babbler *Sphenocichla humei* GT

Madagascar Jery *Neomixis tenella*

Southern Green Jery *Neomixis viridis*

Stripe-throated Jery *Neomixis striatigula*

Wedge-tailed Jery *Neomixis flavoviridis* GT

Rufous-fronted Babbler *Stachyris rufifrons*

Deignan's Babbler *Stachyris rodolphei*

Buff-chested Babbler *Stachyris ambigua* LR

Rufous-capped Babbler *Stachyris ruficeps*

Black-chinned Babbler *Stachyris pyrrhops*

Golden Tree-Babbler *Stachyris chrysaea*

Pygmy Tree-Babbler *Stachyris plateni* GT

Golden-crowned Babbler *Stachyris dennistouni* GT, LR

Black-crowned Babbler *Stachyris nigrocapitata* LR

Rusty-crowned Babbler *Stachyris capitalis*

Flame-templed Babbler *Stachyris speciosa* GT

Chestnut-faced Babbler *Stachyris whiteheadi*

Luzon Striped Babbler *Stachyris striata* GT

Negros Striped Babbler *Stachyris nigrorum* GT

Palawan Striped Babbler *Stachyris hypogrammica* GT

Panay Striped Babbler *Stachyris latistriata* GT, LR

White-breasted Babbler *Stachyris grammiceps* GT

Sooty Tree-Babbler *Stachyris herberti* GT

Grey-throated Babbler *Stachyris nigriceps*

Grey-headed Babbler *Stachyris poliocephala*

Spot-necked Babbler *Stachyris striolata*

Snowy-throated Babbler *Stachyris oglei* GT

White-necked Babbler *Stachyris leucotis* GT

Black-throated Babbler *Stachyris nigricollis* GT

White-bibbed Babbler *Stachyris thoracica*

Chestnut-rumped Babbler *Stachyris maculata* GT

Chestnut-winged Babbler *Stachyris erythropter*

Crescent-chested Babbler *Stachyris melanothorax*

Tawny-bellied Babbler *Dumetia hyperythra*

Dark-fronted Babbler *Rhopocichla atriceps*

Striped Tit-Babbler *Macronous gularis*

Grey-cheeked Tit-Babbler *Macronous flavicollis* LR

Grey-faced Tit-Babbler *Macronous kelleyi*

Brown Tit-Babbler *Macronous striaticeps*

Fluffy-backed Tit-Babbler *Macronous ptilosus* GT

Miniature Tit-Babbler *Micromacronus leytensis* PGT

Red-capped Babbler *Timalia pileata*

Oriental Yellow-eyed Babbler *Chrysomma sinense*

Jerdon's Babbler *Moupinia altirostre* GT

Rufous-tailed Babbler *Moupinia poecilotis*

Wrentit *Chamaea fasciata*

Spiny Babbler *Turdoides nipalensis*

Iraq Babbler *Turdoides altirostris*

Common Babbler *Turdoides caudatus*

Striated Babbler *Turdoides earlei* LR

White-throated Babbler *Turdoides gularis*

Slender-billed Babbler *Turdoides longirostris* GT

Large Grey Babbler *Turdoides malcolmi*

Arabian Babbler *Turdoides squamiceps*

Fulvous Babbler *Turdoides fulvus*

Scaly Chatterer *Turdoides aylmeri*

Rufous Chatterer *Turdoides rubiginosus*

Rufous Babbler *Turdoides subrufus*

Jungle-Babbler *Turdoides striatus*

Orange-billed Babbler *Turdoides rufescens* GT, LR

White-billed Babbler *Turdoides affinis*

Black-lored Babbler *Turdoides melanops*

Sharpe's Pied Babbler *Turdoides sharpei* LR

Dusky Babbler *Turdoides tenebrosus*

Blackcap Babbler *Turdoides reinwardtii*

Scaly Babbler *Turdoides squamulatus*

White-rumped Babbler *Turdoides leucopygius*

Angola Babbler *Turdoides hartlaubii* LR

Hinde's Pied Babbler *Turdoides hindei* GT, LR

Northern Pied Babbler *Turdoides hypoleucus*

Southern Pied Babbler *Turdoides bicolor*

African Brown Babbler *Turdoides plebejus*

White-headed Babbler *Turdoides leucocephalus* LR

Arrow-marked Babbler *Turdoides jardineii* LR

Bare-cheeked Babbler *Turdoides gymnogenys*

Chinese Babax *Babax lanceolatus*

Giant Babax *Babax waddelli* GT

Tibetan Babax *Babax koslowi* GT

Ashy-headed Laughingthrush *Garrulax cinereifrons* GT

Sunda Laughingthrush *Garrulax palliatus*

Rufous-fronted Laughingthrush *Garrulax rufifrons* GT

Masked Laughingthrush *Garrulax perspicillatus*

White-throated Laughingthrush *Garrulax albogularis*

White-crested Laughingthrush *Garrulax leucolophus*

Lesser Necklaced Laughingthrush *Garrulax monileger*

Greater Necklaced Laughingthrush *Garrulax pectoralis*

Black Laughingthrush *Garrulax lugubris*

Bare-headed Laughingthrush *Garrulax calvus* LR

Striated Laughingthrush *Garrulax striatus*

White-necked Laughingthrush *Garrulax strepitans*

Black-hooded Laughingthrush *Garrulax milleti* GT

Grey Laughingthrush *Garrulax maesi*

Rufous-necked Laughingthrush *Garrulax ruficollis*

Chestnut-backed Laughingthrush *Garrulax nuchalis* GT, LR

Black-throated Laughingthrush *Garrulax chinensis*

White-cheeked Laughingthrush *Garrulax vassali*

Yellow-throated Laughingthrush *Garrulax galbanus*

Wynaad Laughingthrush *Garrulax delesserti*

Rufous-vented Laughingthrush *Garrulax gularis* LR

Plain Laughingthrush *Garrulax davidi*

Snowy-cheeked Laughingthrush *Garrulax sukatschewi* GT

Moustached Laughingthrush *Garrulax cineraceus*

Rufous-chinned Laughingthrush *Garrulax rufogularis*

Chestnut-eared Laughingthrush *Garrulax kankakinhensis* LR

Barred Laughingthrush *Garrulax lunulatus*

White-speckled Laughingthrush *Garrulax bieti* GT, LR

Giant Laughingthrush *Garrulax maximus* LR

Spotted Laughingthrush *Garrulax ocellatus*

Grey-sided Laughingthrush *Garrulax caerulatus*

Rusty Laughingthrush *Garrulax poecilorhynchus*

Chestnut-capped Laughingthrush *Garrulax mitratus*

Spot-breasted Laughingthrush *Garrulax merulinus*

Hwamei *Garrulax canorus*

White-browed Laughingthrush *Garrulax sannio*

Nilgiri Laughingthrush *Garrulax cachinnans* GT

Grey-breasted Laughingthrush *Garrulax jerdoni* GT, LR

Streaked Laughingthrush *Garrulax lineatus*

Striped Laughingthrush *Garrulax virgatus*

Variegated Laughingthrush *Garrulax variegatus*

Brown-capped Laughingthrush *Garrulax austeni*

Blue-winged Laughingthrush *Garrulax squamatus*

Scaly Laughingthrush *Garrulax subunicolor*

Elliot's Laughingthrush *Garrulax elliotii*

Brown-cheeked Laughingthrush *Garrulax henrici*

Black-faced Laughingthrush *Garrulax affinis*

White-whiskered Laughingthrush *Garrulax morrisonianus* LR

Chestnut-crowned Laughingthrush *Garrulax erythrocephalus*

Golden-winged Laughingthrush *Garrulax ngoclinhensis* GT, LR

Collared Laughingthrush *Garrulax yersini* GT

Red-winged Laughingthrush *Garrulax formosus*

Red-tailed Laughingthrush *Garrulax milnei*

Red-faced Liocichla *Liocichla phoenicea*

Mount Omei Shan Liocichla *Liocichla omeiensis* GT, LR

Steere's Liocichla *Liocichla steerii*

Silver-eared Mesia *Leiothrix argentauris* LR

Red-billed Leiothrix *Leiothrix lutea* LR

Cutia *Cutia nipalensis*

Black-headed Shrike-Babbler *Pteruthius rufiventer*

White-browed Shrike-Babbler *Pteruthius flaviscapis*

Green Shrike-Babbler *Pteruthius xanthochlorus*

Black-eared Shrike-Babbler *Pteruthius melanotis*

Chestnut-fronted Shrike-Babbler *Pteruthius aenobarbus*

White-hooded Babbler *Gampsorhynchus rufulus*

Rusty-fronted Barwing *Actinodura egertoni*

Spectacled Barwing *Actinodura ramsayi*

Black-crowned Barwing *Actinodura sodangorum* GT

Hoary-throated Barwing *Actinodura nipalensis*

Streak-throated Barwing *Actinodura waldeni* LR

Streaked Barwing *Actinodura souliei*

Taiwan Barwing *Actinodura morrisoniana*

Blue-winged Minla *Minla cyanouroptera*

Chestnut-tailed Minla *Minla strigula*

Red-tailed Minla *Minla ignotincta*

Golden-breasted Fulvetta *Alcippe chrysotis*

Gold-fronted Fulvetta *Alcippe variegaticeps* GT

Yellow-throated Fulvetta *Alcippe cinerea*

Rufous-winged Fulvetta *Alcippe castaneceps*

White-browed Fulvetta *Alcippe vinipectus*

Chinese Fulvetta *Alcippe striaticollis*

Spectacled Fulvetta *Alcippe ruficapilla*

Streak-throated Fulvetta *Alcippe cinereiceps*

Brown-throated Fulvetta *Alcippe ludlowi* LR

Rufous-throated Fulvetta *Alcippe rufogularis*

Rusty-capped Fulvetta *Alcippe dubia* LR

Dusky Fulvetta *Alcippe brunnea*

Brown Fulvetta *Alcippe brunneicauda* GT, LR

Brown-cheeked Fulvetta *Alcippe poioicephala*

Javan Fulvetta *Alcippe pyrrhoptera* LR

Mountain Fulvetta *Alcippe peracensis* LR

Grey-cheeked Fulvetta *Alcippe morrisonia*

Nepal Fulvetta *Alcippe nipalensis*

Bush Blackcap *Lioptilus nigricapillus* GT

White-throated Mountain-Babbler *Kupeornis gilberti* GT

Red-collared Mountain-Babbler *Kupeornis rufocinctus* GT

Chapin's Mountain-Babbler *Kupeornis chapini* GT, LR

Abyssinian Catbird *Parophasma galinieri*

Capuchin Babbler *Phyllanthus atripennis*

Grey-crowned Crocias *Crocias langbianis* GT

Spotted Crocias *Crocias albonotatus* GT

Rufous-backed Sibia *Heterophasia annectens* LR

Rufous Sibia *Heterophasia capistrata*

Grey Sibia *Heterophasia gracilis*

Black-backed Sibia *Heterophasia melanoleuca*

Black-eared Sibia *Heterophasia desgodinsi* LR

White-eared Sibia *Heterophasia auricularis*

Beautiful Sibia *Heterophasia pulchella*

Long-tailed Sibia *Heterophasia picaoides*

Striated Yuhina *Yuhina castaniceps*

Chestnut-crested Yuhina *Yuhina everetti* LR

White-naped Yuhina *Yuhina bakeri*

Whiskered Yuhina *Yuhina flavicollis*

Burmese Yuhina *Yuhina humilis* LR

Stripe-throated Yuhina *Yuhina gularis*

White-collared Yuhina *Yuhina diademata*

Rufous-vented Yuhina *Yuhina occipitalis*

Taiwan Yuhina *Yuhina brunneiceps*

Black-chinned Yuhina *Yuhina nigrimenta*

White-bellied Yuhina *Yuhina zantholeuca* LR

Fire-tailed Myzornis *Myzornis pyrrhoura*

Döhrn's Thrush-Babbler *Horizorhinus dohrni*

White-throated Oxylabes *Oxylabes madagascariensis*

Yellow-browed Oxylabes *Crossleyia xanthophrys* GT

Crossley's Babbler *Mystacornis crossleyi*

Panuridae

Bearded Parrotbill *Panurus biarmicus*

Great Parrotbill *Conostoma oemodium*

Three-toed Parrotbill *Paradoxornis paradoxus*

Brown Parrotbill *Paradoxornis unicolor*

Grey-headed Parrotbill *Paradoxornis gularis*

Black-breasted Parrotbill *Paradoxornis flavirostris* GT

Spot-breasted Parrotbill *Paradoxornis guttaticollis* LR

Spectacled Parrotbill *Paradoxornis conspicillatus*

Vinous-throated Parrotbill *Paradoxornis webbianus*

Brown-winged Parrotbill *Paradoxornis brunneus* LR

Yunnan Parrotbill *Paradoxornis ricketti* LR

Ashy-throated Parrotbill *Paradoxornis alphonsianus* LR

Grey-hooded Parrotbill *Paradoxornis zappeyi* GT

Rusty-throated Parrotbill *Paradoxornis przewalskii* GT

Fulvous Parrotbill *Paradoxornis fulvifrons*

Black-throated Parrotbill *Paradoxornis nipalensis*

Golden Parrotbill *Paradoxornis verreauxi* LR

Black-browed Parrotbill *Paradoxornis atrosuperciliaris*

Short-tailed Parrotbill *Paradoxornis davidianus* GT

Greater Rufous-headed Parrotbill *Paradoxornis ruficeps*

Reed Parrotbill *Paradoxornis heudei* GT

Picathartidae

White-necked Picathartes *Picathartes gymnocephalus* GT

Grey-necked Picathartes *Picathartes oreas* GT

Polioptilidae

Collared Gnatwren *Microbates collaris*

Tawny-faced Gnatwren *Microbates cinereiventris*

Straight-billed Gnatwren *Ramphocaenus melanurus*

Blue-grey Gnatcatcher *Polioptila caerulea*

California Gnatcatcher *Polioptila californica* LR

Black-tailed Gnatcatcher *Polioptila melanura*

Cuban Gnatcatcher *Polioptila lembeyei*

White-lored Gnatcatcher *Polioptila albiloris*

Black-capped Gnatcatcher *Polioptila nigriceps* LR

Tropical Gnatcatcher *Polioptila plumbea*

Marañón Gnatcatcher *Polioptila maior* LR

Creamy-bellied Gnatcatcher *Polioptila lactea* GT

Guianan Gnatcatcher *Polioptila guianensis*

Slate-throated Gnatcatcher *Polioptila schistaceigula*

Masked Gnatcatcher *Polioptila dumicola*

Cisticolidae

Red-faced Cisticola *Cisticola erythrops*

Lepe Cistocola *Cisticola lepe* LR

Singing Cisticola *Cisticola cantans* LR

Whistling Cisticola *Cisticola lateralis*

Trilling Cisticola *Cisticola woosnami*

Chattering Cisticola *Cisticola anonymus*

Bubbling Cisticola *Cisticola bulliens*

Brown-backed Cisticola *Cisticola discolor* LR

Chubb's Cisticola *Cisticola chubbi*

Hunter's Cisticola *Cisticola hunteri*

Black-lored Cisticola *Cisticola nigriloris*

Rock-loving Cisticola *Cisticola emini* LR

Rock Cisticola *Cisticola aberrans*

Boran Cisticola *Cisticola bodessa*

Rattling Cisticola *Cisticola chinianus*

Ashy Cisticola *Cisticola cinereolus*

Red-pate Cisticola *Cisticola ruficeps*

Mongalla Cisticola *Cisticola mongalla* LR

Dorst's Cisticola *Cisticola dorsti* PGT, LR

Tinkling Cisticola *Cisticola rufilatus*

Grey-backed Cisticola *Cisticola subruficapillus*

Wailing Cisticola *Cisticola lais*

Lynes's Cisticola *Cisticola distinctus* LR

Tana River Cisticola *Cisticola restrictus* PGT

Churring Cisticola *Cisticola njombe*

Winding Cisticola *Cisticola galactotes*

Carruthers's Cisticola *Cisticola carruthersi*

Chirping Cisticola *Cisticola pipiens*

Levaillant's Cisticola *Cisticola tinniens*

Stout Cisticola *Cisticola robustus*

Angola Cisticola *Cisticola angolensis* LR

Aberdare Cisticola *Cisticola aberdare* GT

Croaking Cisticola *Cisticola natalensis*

Piping Cisticola *Cisticola fulvicapillus*

Tabora Cisticola *Cisticola angusticauda* LR

Slender-tailed Cisticola *Cisticola melanurus* PGT

Foxy Cisticola *Cisticola troglodytes*

Siffling Cisticola *Cisticola brachypterus*

Rufous Cisticola *Cisticola rufus*

Tiny Cisticola *Cisticola nanus*

Zitting Cisticola *Cisticola juncidis*

Socotra Cisticola *Cisticola haesitatus* GT

Madagascar Cisticola *Cisticola cherinus*

Desert Cisticola *Cisticola aridulus*

Spotted Cloud Cisticola *Cisticola textrix*

Black-necked Cisticola *Cisticola eximius*

Cloud-scraping Cisticola *Cisticola dambo*

Pectoral-patch Cisticola *Cisticola brunnescens*

Pale-crowned Cisticola *Cisticola cinnamomeus* LR

Wing-snapping Cisticola *Cisticola ayresii*

Golden-headed Cisticola *Cisticola exilis*

Socotra Warbler *Incana incana*

Streaked Scrub-Warbler *Scotocerca inquieta*

White-browed Chinese Warbler *Rhopophilus pekinensis*

Rufous-vented Prinia *Prinia burnesii* GT

Swamp Prinia *Prinia cinerascens* LR

Striated Prinia *Prinia criniger* LR

Javan Brown Prinia *Prinia polychroa*

Hill Prinia *Prinia atrogularis*

Grey-crowned Prinia *Prinia cinereocapilla* GT

Rufous-fronted Prinia *Prinia buchanani*

Rufescent Prinia *Prinia rufescens*

Grey-breasted Prinia *Prinia hodgsonii*

Graceful Prinia *Prinia gracilis*

Jungle Prinia *Prinia sylvatica*

Bar-winged Prinia *Prinia familiaris*

Yellow-bellied Prinia *Prinia flaviventris*

Ashy Prinia *Prinia socialis*

Tawny-flanked Prinia *Prinia subflava*

Pale Prinia *Prinia somalica*

Plain-colored Prinia *Prinia inornata* LR

Saffron-breasted Prinia *Prinia hypoxantha* LR

Black-chested Prinia *Prinia flavicans*

São Tomé Prinia *Prinia molleri*

White-chinned Prinia *Prinia leucopogon*

Sierra Leone Prinia *Prinia leontica* GT

Banded Prinia *Prinia bairdii*

Black-faced Prinia *Prinia melanops* LR

Roberts's Prinia *Prinia robertsi*

Rufous-eared Prinia *Prinia pectoralis*

Karoo Prinia *Prinia maculosa*

White-breasted Prinia *Phragmacia substriata*

Red-winged Warbler *Heliolais erythroptera*

Green Longtail *Urolais epichlora*

Red-winged Grey Warbler *Drymocichla incana*

Cricket Longtail *Spiloptila clamans*

Red-faced Warbler *Spiloptila rufifrons*

Bar-throated Apalis *Apalis thoracica* LR

Black-collared Apalis *Apalis pulchra*

Collared Apalis *Apalis ruwenzorii* LR

Black-capped Apalis *Apalis nigriceps*

Black-throated Apalis *Apalis jacksoni*

White-winged Apalis *Apalis chariessa* GT

Masked Apalis *Apalis binotata*

Mountain Masked Apalis *Apalis personata*

Rudd's Apalis *Apalis ruddi*

Yellow-breasted Apalis *Apalis flavida*

Brown-tailed Apalis *Apalis viridiceps* LR

Buff-throated Apalis *Apalis rufogularis*

Kungwe Apalis *Apalis argentea* GT, LR

Sharpe's Apalis *Apalis sharpii*

Gosling's Apalis *Apalis goslingi* LR

Bamenda Apalis *Apalis bamendae* GT, LR

Chestnut-throated Apalis *Apalis porphyrolaema*

Kabobo Apalis *Apalis kaboboensis* PGT, LR

Chapin's Apalis *Apalis chapini* LR

Black-headed Apalis *Apalis melanocephala*

Chirinda Apalis *Apalis chirindensis* LR

Grey Apalis *Apalis cinerea*

Brown-headed Apalis *Apalis alticola* LR

Karamoja Apalis *Apalis karamojae* GT

Fairy Warbler *Stenostira scita*

Buff-bellied Warbler *Phyllolais pulchella*

Green-backed Camaroptera *Camaroptera brachyura*

Grey-backed Camaroptera *Camaroptera brevicaudata* LR

Hartert's Camaroptera *Camaroptera harterti* LR

Yellow-browed Camaroptera *Camaroptera superciliaris*

Olive-green Camaroptera *Camaroptera chloronota*

Grey Wren-Warbler *Calamonastes simplex*

Pale Wren-Warbler *Calamonastes undosus* LR

Stierling's Wren-Warbler *Calamonastes stierlingi* LR

Thornbush Barred Wren-Warbler *Calamonastes fasciolatus*

Cinnamon-breasted Warbler *Euryptila subcinnamomea*

ylviidae

Chestnut-headed Tesia *Tesia castaneocoronata*

Javan Tesia *Tesia superciliaris*

Slaty-bellied Tesia *Tesia olivea*

Grey-bellied Tesia *Tesia cyaniventer*

Russet-capped Tesia *Tesia everetti* LR

Timor Stubtail *Urosphena subulata*

Bornean Stubtail *Urosphena whiteheadi*

Asian Stubtail *Urosphena squameiceps*

Pale-footed Bush-Warbler *Cettia pallidipes*

Manchurian Bush-Warbler *Cettia canturians* LR

Japanese Bush-Warbler *Cettia diphone*

Palau Bush-Warbler *Cettia annae*

Brown-flanked Bush-Warbler *Cettia fortipes* LR

Sunda Bush-Warbler *Cettia vulcania* LR

Aberrant Bush-Warbler *Cettia flavolivacea*

Philippine Bush-Warbler *Cettia seebohmi* LR

Chestnut-crowned Bush-Warbler *Cettia major*

Yellow-bellied Bush-Warbler *Cettia acanthizoides* LR

Grey-sided Bush-Warbler *Cettia brunnifrons*

Cetti's Bush-Warbler *Cettia cetti*

Tanimbar Bush-Warbler *Cettia carolinae* GT

Shade Warbler *Cettia parens*

Fiji Bush-Warbler *Cettia ruficapilla*

Little Rush Warbler *Bradypterus baboecala*

Grauer's Swamp-Warbler *Bradypterus graueri* GT

Dja River Warbler *Bradypterus grandis* GT

White-winged Scrub-Warbler *Bradypterus carpalis*

Bamboo Warbler *Bradypterus alfredi*

Knysna Scrub-Warbler *Bradypterus sylvaticus* GT

Cameroon Scrub-Warbler *Bradypterus lopezi*

Evergreen Forest Warbler *Bradypterus mariae* LR

African Scrub-Warbler *Bradypterus barratti*

Victorin's Scrub-Warbler *Bradypterus victorini*

Bangwa Forest Warbler *Bradypterus bangwaensis* GT, LR

Cinnamon Bracken Warbler *Bradypterus cinnamomeus*

Spotted Bush-Warbler *Bradypterus thoracicus*

David's Bush-Warbler *Bradypterus davidi* LR

Long-billed Bush-Warbler *Bradypterus major* GT

Chinese Bush-Warbler *Bradypterus tacsanowskius*

Brown Bush-Warbler *Bradypterus luteoventris*

Russet Bush-Warbler *Bradypterus mandelli* LR

Taiwan Bush-Warbler *Bradypterus alishanensis* LR

Sri Lanka Bush-Warbler *Bradypterus palliseri* GT

Long-tailed Bush-Warbler *Bradypterus caudatus*

Friendly Bush-Warbler *Bradypterus accentor*

Chestnut-backed Bush-Warbler *Bradypterus castaneus*

Black-headed Rufous Warbler *Bathmocercus cerviniventris* GT

Black-faced Rufous Warbler *Bathmocercus rufus* LR

Mrs Moreau's Warbler *Scepomycter winifredae* GT

Brown Emutail *Dromaeocercus brunneus*

Grey Emutail *Amphilais seebohmi*

Madagascar Brush-Warbler *Nesillas typica*

Subdesert Brush-Warbler *Nesillas lantzii* LR

Anjouan Brush-Warbler *Nesillas longicaudata* LR

Comoro Brush-Warbler *Nesillas brevicaudata* LR

Moheli Brush-Warbler *Nesillas mariae*

Aldabra Brush-Warbler *Nesillas aldabrana* E

Thamnornis Warbler *Thamnornis chloropetoides*

African Moustached Warbler *Melocichla mentalis*

Damara Rockjumper *Achaetops pycnopygius*

Cape Grassbird *Sphenoeacus afer*

Japanese Swamp-Warbler *Megalurus pryeri* GT

Tawny Grassbird *Megalurus timoriensis*

Striated Grassbird *Megalurus palustris*

Fly River Grassbird *Megalurus albolimbatus* GT

Little Grassbird *Megalurus gramineus*

New Zealand Fernbird *Megalurus punctatus*

Chatham Islands Fernbird *Megalurus rufescens* E

Rufous Songlark *Cincloramphus mathewsi*

Brown Songlark *Cincloramphus cruralis*

pinifexbird *Eremiornis carteri*

Buff-banded Grassbird *Buettikoferella bivittata*

New Caledonian Grassbird *Megalurulus mariei* PGT

Guadalcanal Thicketbird *Cichlornis whitneyi* GT

Bismarck Thicketbird *Cichlornis grosvenori* PGT

Bougainville Thicketbird *Cichlornis llaneae* PGT

Rusty Thicketbird *Ortygocichla rubiginosa*

Long-legged Thicketbird *Trichocichla rufa* PGT

Bristled Grassbird *Chaetornis striatus* GT

Rufous-rumped Grassbird *Graminicola bengalensis* GT

Broad-tailed Grassbird *Schoenicola platyura* GT

Fan-tailed Grassbird *Schoenicola brevirostris* LR

Lanceolated Warbler *Locustella lanceolata*

Common Grasshopper-Warbler *Locustella naevia*

Pallas's Grasshopper-Warbler *Locustella certhiola*

Middendorff's Grasshopper-Warbler *Locustella ochotensis* LR

Pleske's Grasshopper-Warbler *Locustella pleskei* GT

Eurasian River Warbler *Locustella fluviatilis*

Savi's Warbler *Locustella luscinioides*

Gray's Grasshopper-Warbler *Locustella fasciolata*

Stepanyan's Grasshopper-Warbler *Locustella amnicola* LR

Moustached Warbler *Acrocephalus melanopogon*

Aquatic Warbler *Acrocephalus paludicola* GT

Sedge Warbler *Acrocephalus schoenobaenus*

Streaked Reed-Warbler *Acrocephalus sorghophilus* GT

Black-browed Reed-Warbler *Acrocephalus bistrigiceps* LR

Paddyfield Warbler *Acrocephalus agricola*

Crimean Reed-Warbler *Acrocephalus septimus* LR

Blunt-winged Warbler *Acrocephalus concinens* LR

European Marsh Warbler *Acrocephalus palustris*

Eurasian Reed-Warbler *Acrocephalus scirpaceus*

South African Reed-Warbler *Acrocephalus baeticatus*

Mangrove Warbler *Acrocephalus avicenniae* LR

Blyth's Reed-Warbler *Acrocephalus dumetorum*

Great Reed-Warbler *Acrocephalus arundinaceus*

Large-billed Reed-Warbler *Acrocephalus orinus*

Clamorous Reed-Warbler *Acrocephalus stentoreus* LR

Australian Reed-Warbler *Acrocephalus australis* LR

Oriental Great Reed-Warbler *Acrocephalus orientalis* LR

Basra Reed-Warbler *Acrocephalus griseldis* GT, LR

Caroline Reed-Warbler *Acrocephalus syrinx*

Nightingale Reed-Warbler *Acrocephalus luscini* GT

Nauru Reed-Warbler *Acrocephalus rehsei* GT, LR

Laysan Millerbird *Acrocephalus familiaris* GT, LR

Nilhoa Millerbird *Acrocephalus kingi*

Polynesian Reed-Warbler *Acrocephalus aequinoctialis*

Long-billed Reed-Warbler *Acrocephalus caffer* GT

Marquesan Reed-Warbler *Acrocephalus mendanae* LR

Tuamotu Reed-Warbler *Acrocephalus atyphus*

Pitcairn Reed-Warbler *Acrocephalus vaughani* GT

Rimatara Reed-Warbler *Acrocephalus rimatarae* GT, LR

Cook Islands Reed-Warbler *Acrocephalus kerearako* GT

Henderson Island Reed-Warbler *Acrocephalus taiti* GT, LR

Greater Swamp-Warbler *Acrocephalus rufescens*

Cape Verde Islands Warbler *Acrocephalus brevipennis* GT

Lesser Swamp-Warbler *Acrocephalus gracilirostris*

Madagascar Swamp-Warbler *Acrocephalus newtoni*

Thick-billed Warbler *Acrocephalus aedon*

Booted Warbler *Acrocephalus caligata*

Rodriguez Brush-Warbler *Bebrornis rodericanus* GT

Seychelles Brush-Warbler *Bebrornis sechellensis* GT

Sykes's Warbler *Hippolais rama* LR

Üpcher's Warbler *Hippolais languida*

Eastern Olivaceous Warbler *Hippolais pallida*

Western Olivaceous Warbler *Hippolais opaca* LR

Olive-tree Warbler *Hippolais olivetorum*

Melodious Warbler *Hippolais polyglotta*

Icterine Warbler *Hippolais icterina*

African Yellow Warbler *Chloropeta natalensis*

Mountain Yellow Warbler *Chloropeta similis*

Papyrus Yellow Warbler *Chloropeta gracilirostris* GT

African Tailorbird *Orthotomus metopias*

Long-billed Tailorbird *Orthotomus moreaui* GT

Mountain Tailorbird *Orthotomus cuculatus*

Rufous-headed Tailorbird *Orthotomus heterolaemus* LR

Common Tailorbird *Orthotomus sutorius*

Dark-necked Tailorbird *Orthotomus atrogularis*

Philippine Tailorbird *Orthotomus castaneiceps* LR

Rufous-fronted Tailorbird *Orthotomus frontalis* LR

Grey-backed Tailorbird *Orthotomus derbianus*

Rufous-tailed Tailorbird *Orthotomus sericeus*

Ashy Tailorbird *Orthotomus ruficeps* LR

Olive-backed Tailorbird *Orthotomus sepium* LR

White-eared Tailorbird *Orthotomus cinereiceps*

Black-headed Tailorbird *Orthotomus nigriceps*

Yellow-breasted Tailorbird *Orthotomus samarensis* GT

White-tailed Warbler *Poliolais lopezi* GT

Grauer's Warbler *Graueria vittata*

Yellow-bellied Eremomela *Eremomela icteropygialis*

Salvadori's Eremomela *Eremomela salvadorii* LR

Yellow-vented Eremomela *Eremomela flavicrissalis*

Green-capped Eremomela *Eremomela scotops*

Smaller Green-backed Eremomela *Eremomela pusilla*

Green-backed Eremomela *Eremomela canescens* LR

Karoo Green Eremomela *Eremomela gregalis*

Rufous-crowned Eremomela *Eremomela badiceps*

Turner's Eremomela *Eremomela turneri* GT, LR

Black-necked Eremomela *Eremomela atricollis*

Burnt-necked Eremomela *Eremomela usticollis*

Rand's Warbler *Randia pseudozosterops*

Dark Newtonia *Newtonia amphichroa*

Common Newtonia *Newtonia brunneicauda*

Archbold's Newtonia *Newtonia archboldi*

Red-tailed Newtonia *Newtonia fanovanae* GT

Cryptic Warbler *Cryptosylvicola randrianasoloi*

Green Crombec *Sylvietta virens*

Lemon-bellied Crombec *Sylvietta denti*

White-browed Crombec *Sylvietta leucophrys*

Chapin's Crombec *Sylvietta chapini* LR

Northern Crombec *Sylvietta brachyura*

Somali Short-billed Crombec *Sylvietta philippae* PGT

Red-faced Crombec *Sylvietta whytii*

Red-capped Crombec *Sylvietta ruficapilla*

Long-billed Crombec *Sylvietta rufescens*

Somali Long-billed Crombec *Sylvietta isabellina*

Neumann's Warbler *Hemitesia neumanni*

Kemp's Longbill *Macrosphenus kempi* LR

Yellow Longbill *Macrosphenus flavicans*

Grey Longbill *Macrosphenus concolor*

Pulitzer's Longbill *Macrosphenus pulitzeri* GT

Kretschmer's Longbill *Macrosphenus kretschmeri*

São Tomé Shorttail *Amaurocichla bocagii* GT

Oriole Warbler *Hypergerus atriceps*

Grey-capped Warbler *Eminia lepida*

Yellow-bellied Hyliota *Hyliota flavigaster*

Southern Yellow-bellied Hyliota *Hyliota australis*

Usambara Hyliota *Hyliota usambarae* GT, LR

Violet-backed Hyliota *Hyliota violacea*

Green Hylia *Hylia prasina*

Yellow-throated Woodland-Warbler *Phylloscopus ruficapillus*

Laura's Woodland-Warbler *Phylloscopus laurae*

Red-faced Woodland-Warbler *Phylloscopus laetus*

Uganda Woodland-Warbler *Phylloscopus budongoensis*

Black-capped Woodland-Warbler *Phylloscopus herberti*

Brown Woodland-Warbler *Phylloscopus umbrovirens*

Willow-Warbler *Phylloscopus trochilus*

Common Chiffchaff *Phylloscopus collybita*

Iberian Chiffchaff *Phylloscopus ibericus* LR

Canary Islands Chiffchaff *Phylloscopus canariensis* LR

Caucasian Chiffchaff *Phylloscopus lorenzi* LR

Mountain Chiffchaff *Phylloscopus sindianus* LR

Plain Leaf-Warbler *Phylloscopus neglectus*

Wood Warbler *Phylloscopus sibilatrix*

Western Bonelli's Warbler *Phylloscopus bonelli*

Eastern Bonelli's Warbler *Phylloscopus orientalis* LR

Dusky Warbler *Phylloscopus fuscatus*

Smoky Warbler *Phylloscopus fuligiventer* LR

Tickell's Leaf-Warbler *Phylloscopus affinis*

Buff-throated Warbler *Phylloscopus subaffinis* LR

Sulphur-bellied Warbler *Phylloscopus griseolus*

Yellow-streaked Leaf-Warbler *Phylloscopus armandii*

Radde's Warbler *Phylloscopus schwarzi*

Buff-barred Warbler *Phylloscopus pulcher*

Ashy-throated Leaf-Warbler *Phylloscopus maculipennis*

Pallas's Leaf-Warbler *Phylloscopus proregulus*

Kansu Leaf-Warbler *Phylloscopus kansuensis*

Chinese Leaf-Warbler *Phylloscopus sichuanensis*

Lemon-rumped Warbler *Phylloscopus chloronotus* LR

Brooks's Leaf-Warbler *Phylloscopus subviridis*

Yellow-browed Leaf-Warbler *Phylloscopus inornatus*

Hume's Leaf-Warbler *Phylloscopus humei* LR

Arctic Warbler *Phylloscopus borealis*

Greenish Warbler *Phylloscopus trochiloides*

Pale-legged Leaf-Warbler *Phylloscopus tenellipes*

Sakhalin Leaf-Warbler *Phylloscopus borealoides* LR

Large-billed Leaf-Warbler *Phylloscopus magnirostris*

Tytler's Leaf-Warbler *Phylloscopus tytleri*

Western Crowned Leaf-Warbler *Phylloscopus occipitalis*

Eastern Crowned Leaf-Warbler *Phylloscopus coronatus* LR

Ijima's Leaf-Warbler *Phylloscopus ijimae* GT, LR

Emei Leaf-Warbler *Phylloscopus emeiensis* LR

Blyth's Leaf-Warbler *Phylloscopus reguloides*

White-tailed Leaf-Warbler *Phylloscopus davisoni*

Yellow-vented Warbler *Phylloscopus cantator*

Hainan Leaf-Warbler *Phylloscopus hainanus* PGT, LR

Sulphur-breasted Warbler *Phylloscopus ricketti* LR

Philippine Leaf-Warbler *Phylloscopus olivaceus* LR

Lemon-throated Leaf-Warbler *Phylloscopus cebuensis* LR

Mountain Leaf-Warbler *Phylloscopus trivirgatus*

Sulawesi Leaf-Warbler *Phylloscopus sarasinorum* LR

Timor Leaf-Warbler *Phylloscopus presbytes* LR

Island Leaf-Warbler *Phylloscopus poliocephalus* LR

San Cristobal Leaf-Warbler *Phylloscopus makirensis*

Kulambangra Leaf-Warbler *Phylloscopus amoenus* GT

Golden-spectacled Warbler *Seicercus burkii*

Eastern Golden Spectacled Warbler *Seicercus soror* LR

Emei Golden Spectacled Warbler *Seicercus omeiensis* LR

Grey-hooded Warbler *Seicercus xanthoschistos*

White-spectacled Warbler *Seicercus affinis*

Grey-cheeked Warbler *Seicercus poliogenys*

Chestnut-crowned Warbler *Seicercus castaniceps*

Yellow-breasted Warbler *Seicercus montis*

Sunda Warbler *Seicercus grammiceps*

Broad-billed Warbler *Tickellia hodgsoni*

Rufous-faced Warbler *Abroscopus albogularis*

Black-faced Warbler *Abroscopus schisticeps*

Yellow-bellied Warbler *Abroscopus superciliaris*

Banded Tit-Warbler *Parisoma boehmi*

Layard's Tit-Warbler *Parisoma layardi*

Southern Tit-Warbler *Parisoma subcaeruleum*

Brown Sylvia *Sylvia lugens*

Yemen Warbler *Sylvia buryi* GT

Blackcap *Sylvia atricapilla*

Garden Warbler *Sylvia borin*

Common Whitethroat *Sylvia communis*

Lesser Whitethroat *Sylvia curruca*

Desert Lesser Whitethroat *Sylvia minula* LR

Hume's Lesser Whitethroat *Sylvia althaea* LR

Desert Warbler *Sylvia nana*

Barred Warbler *Sylvia nisoria*

Western Orphean Warbler *Sylvia hortensis*

Eastern Orphean Warbler *Sylvia crassirostris* LR

Arabian Warbler *Sylvia leucomelaena*

Rüppell's Warbler *Sylvia rueppelli*

Sardinian Warbler *Sylvia melanocephala*

Cyprus Warbler *Sylvia melanothorax* LR

Ménétries' Warbler *Sylvia mystacea*

Subalpine Warbler *Sylvia cantillans*

Spectacled Warbler *Sylvia conspicillata*

Tristram's Warbler *Sylvia deserticola*

Dartford Warbler *Sylvia undata*

Marmora's Warbler *Sylvia sarda*

Balearic Warbler *Sylvia balearica* LR

Crested Tit-Warbler *Leptopoecile elegans*

White-browed Tit-Warbler *Leptopoecile sophiae*

Regulidae

Eurasian Firecrest *Regulus ignicapilla*

Flamecrest *Regulus goodfellowi*

European Goldcrest *Regulus regulus*

Tenerife Goldcrest *Regulus teneriffae* LR

Golden-crowned Kinglet *Regulus satrapa*

Ruby-crowned Kinglet *Regulus calendula*

Muscicapidae

Silverbird *Empidornis semipartitus*

Pale Flycatcher *Bradornis pallidus*

Chat Flycatcher *Bradornis infuscatus*

Marico Flycatcher *Bradornis mariquensis*

Small Grey Flycatcher *Bradornis pumilus* LR

African Grey Flycatcher *Bradornis microrhynchus*

Abyssinian Slaty Flycatcher *Melaenornis chocolatinus*

White-eyed Slaty Flycatcher *Melaenornis fischeri*

Angolan Slaty Flycatcher *Melaenornis brunneus*

Northern Black-Flycatcher *Melaenornis edolioides*

Southern Black-Flycatcher *Melaenornis pammelaina*

Yellow-eyed Black-Flycatcher *Melaenornis ardesiacus*

Nimba Flycatcher *Melaenornis annamarulae* GT

African Forest-Flycatcher *Fraseria ocreata*

White-browed Forest-Flycatcher *Fraseria cinerascens*

Fiscal Flycatcher *Sigelus silens*

Streaky-breasted Jungle-Flycatcher *Rhinomyia addita* GT

Russet-backed Jungle-Flycatcher *Rhinomyias oscillans*

Brown-chested Jungle-Flycatcher *Rhinomyias brunneata* GT, LR

Fulvous-chested Jungle-Flycatcher *Rhinomyias olivacea*

Grey-chested Jungle-Flycatcher *Rhinomyias umbratilis* GT

Rufous-tailed Jungle-Flycatcher *Rhinomyias ruficaudia*

Henna-tailed Jungle-Flycatcher *Rhinomyias colonus* GT

Eyebrowed Jungle-Flycatcher *Rhinomyias gularis*

White-browed Jungle-Flycatcher *Rhinomyias insignis* GT, LR

White-throated Jungle-Flycatcher *Rhinomyias albigularis* GT, LR

Slaty-backed Jungle-Flycatcher *Rhinomyias goodfellowi* GT, LR

Spotted Flycatcher *Muscicapa striata*

Gambaga Flycatcher *Muscicapa gambagae*

Grey-streaked Flycatcher *Muscicapa griseisticta*

Siberian Flycatcher *Muscicapa sibirica*

Asian Brown Flycatcher *Muscicapa dauurica*

Brown-streaked Flycatcher *Muscicapa williamsoni* LR

Ashy-breasted Flycatcher *Muscicapa randi* GT, LR

Sumba Brown Flycatcher *Muscicapa segregata* GT, LR

Brown-breasted Flycatcher *Muscicapa muttui*

Rusty-tailed Flycatcher *Muscicapa ruficauda*

Ferruginous Flycatcher *Muscicapa ferruginea*

African Sooty Flycatcher *Muscicapa infuscata*

Ussher's Flycatcher *Muscicapa ussheri*

Böhm's Flycatcher *Muscicapa boehmi*

Swamp Flycatcher *Muscicapa aquatica*

Olivaceous Flycatcher *Muscicapa olivascens*

Chapin's Flycatcher *Muscicapa lendu* GT

Itombwe Flycatcher *Muscicapa itombwensis* LR

African Dusky Flycatcher *Muscicapa adusta*

Little Grey Flycatcher *Muscicapa epulata*

Yellow-footed Flycatcher *Muscicapa sethsmithi*

Dusky Blue-Flycatcher *Muscicapa comitata*

Tessmann's Flycatcher *Muscicapa tessmanni* PGT

Cassin's Flycatcher *Muscicapa cassini*

Ashy Flycatcher *Muscicapa caerulescens*

Dull Blue-Flycatcher *Eumyias sordida* GT

Verditer Flycatcher *Eumyias thalassina*

Island Flycatcher *Eumyias panayensis*

Nilgiri Flycatcher *Eumyias albicaudata* GT

Indigo Flycatcher *Eumyias indigo*

Grey-throated Tit-Flycatcher *Myioparus griseigularis*

Grey Tit-Flycatcher *Myioparus plumbeus*

Grand Comoro Flycatcher *Humblotia flavirostris* GT

European Pied Flycatcher *Ficedula hypoleuca*

Collared Flycatcher *Ficedula albicollis*

Semi-collared Flycatcher *Ficedula semitorquata* LR

Yellow-rumped Flycatcher *Ficedula zanthopygia* LR

Narcissus Flycatcher *Ficedula narcissina*

Mugimaki Flycatcher *Ficedula mugimaki*

Slaty-backed Flycatcher *Ficedula hodgsonii*

Rufous-gorgeted Flycatcher *Ficedula strophiata*

Red-breasted Flycatcher *Ficedula parva*

Kashmir Flycatcher *Ficedula subrubra* GT, LR

White-gorgeted Flycatcher *Ficedula monileger*

Rufous-browed Malaysian Flycatcher *Ficedula solitaris*

Rufous-browed Flycatcher *Ficedula submoniliger* LR

Rufous-chested Flycatcher *Ficedula dumetoria* GT

Snowy-browed Flycatcher *Ficedula hyperythra*

Rufous-throated Flycatcher *Ficedula rufigula* GT

Little Slaty Flycatcher *Ficedula basilanica* GT

Cinnamon-chested Flycatcher *Ficedula buruensis*

Damar Flycatcher *Ficedula henrici* GT

Sumba Flycatcher *Ficedula harterti*

Palawan Flycatcher *Ficedula platenae* GT

Cryptic Flycatcher *Ficedula crypta* GT, LR

Lompobatang Flycatcher *Ficedula bonthaina* GT, LR

Furtive Flycatcher *Ficedula disposita* GT, LR

Little Pied Flycatcher *Ficedula westermanni*

Ultramarine Flycatcher *Ficedula superciliaris*

Slaty-blue Flycatcher *Ficedula tricolor*

Sapphire Flycatcher *Ficedula sapphira*

Black-and-orange Flycatcher *Ficedula nigrorufa* GT

Black-banded Flycatcher *Ficedula timorensis* GT

Blue-and-white Flycatcher *Cyanoptila cyanomelana*

Large Niltava *Niltava grandis*

Small Niltava *Niltava macgrigoriae*

Fujian Niltava *Niltava davidi*

Rufous-bellied Niltava *Niltava sundara*

Rufous-vented Niltava *Niltava sumatrana* LR

Vivid Niltava *Niltava vivida*

Timor Blue-Flycatcher *Cyornis hyacinthinus*

Blue-fronted Blue-Flycatcher *Cyornis hoevelli*

Matinan Blue-Flycatcher *Cyornis sanfordi* GT

White-tailed Flycatcher *Cyornis concretus*

Rück's Blue-Flycatcher *Cyornis ruckii* GT

Blue-breasted Flycatcher *Cyornis herioti*

Hainan Blue-Flycatcher *Cyornis hainanus*

White-bellied Blue-Flycatcher *Cyornis pallipes*

Pale-chinned Blue-Flycatcher *Cyornis poliogenys*

Pale Blue-Flycatcher *Cyornis unicolor*

Blue-throated Flycatcher *Cyornis rubeculoides*

Chinese Blue-Flycatcher *Cyornis glaucicomans* LR

Hill Blue-Flycatcher *Cyornis banyumas*

Palawan Blue-Flycatcher *Cyornis lemprieri* GT, LR

Bornean Blue-Flycatcher *Cyornis superbus*

Large-billed Blue-Flycatcher *Cyornis caerulatus* PGT

Malaysian Blue-Flycatcher *Cyornis turcosus* GT

Tickell's Blue-Flycatcher *Cyornis tickelliae*

Mangrove Blue-Flycatcher *Cyornis rufigastra*

Sulawesi Blue-Flycatcher *Cyornis omissus* LR

Pygmy Blue-Flycatcher *Muscicapella hodgsoni*

Grey-headed Canary Flycatcher *Culicicapa ceylonensis*

Citrine Canary Flycatcher *Culicicapa helianthea*

Platysteiridae

African Shrike-Flycatcher *Megabyas flammulatus*

Black-and-white Shrike-Flycatcher *Bias musicus*

Ward's Flycatcher *Pseudobias wardi*

Ruwenzori Batis *Batis diops*

Margaret's Batis *Batis margaritae*

Forest Batis *Batis mixta*

Reichenow's Batis *Batis reichenowi* LR

Malawi Batis *Batis dimorpha* LR

Cape Batis *Batis capensis*

Woodwards's Batis *Batis fratrum*

Chinspot Batis *Batis molitor*

Pale Batis *Batis soror*

Pririt Batis *Batis pririt*

Senegal Batis *Batis senegalensis*

Grey-headed Batis *Batis orientalis*

Black-headed Batis *Batis minor*

Pygmy Batis *Batis perkeo*

Angola Batis *Batis minulla*

Verreaux's Batis *Batis minima* GT

Ituri Batis *Batis ituriensis*

West African Batis *Batis occulta* LR

Fernando Po Batis *Batis poensis*

Scarlet-spectacled Wattle-eye *Platysteira cyanea*

White-fronted Wattle-eye *Platysteira albifrons* GT

Black-throated Wattle-eye *Platysteira peltata*

Bamenda Wattle-eye *Platysteira laticincta* GT, LR

White-spotted Wattle-eye *Dyaphorophyia tonsa*

Chestnut Wattle-eye *Dyaphorophyia castanea*

Red-cheeked Wattle-eye *Dyaphorophyia blissetti*

Black-necked Wattle-eye *Dyaphorophyia chalybea* LR

Jameson's Wattle-eye *Dyaphorophyia jamesoni* LR

Yellow-bellied Wattle-eye *Dyaphorophyia concreta*

Maluridae

Orange-crowned Fairywren *Clytomyias insignis*

Wallace's Fairywren *Sipodotus wallacii*

Broad-billed Fairywren *Malurus grayi*

White-shouldered Fairywren *Malurus alboscapulatus*

Red-backed Fairywren *Malurus melanocephalus*

White-winged Fairywren *Malurus leucopterus*

Superb Fairywren *Malurus cyaneus*

Splendid Fairywren *Malurus splendens*

Variegated Fairywren *Malurus lamberti*

Blue-breasted Fairywren *Malurus pulcherrimus*

Lovely Fairywren *Malurus amabilis* LR

Red-winged Fairywren *Malurus elegans*

Purple-crowned Fairywren *Malurus coronatus*

Emperor Fairywren *Malurus cyanocephalus*

Southern Emuwren *Stipiturus malachurus*

Rufous-crowned Emuwren *Stipiturus ruficeps*

Mallee Emuwren *Stipiturus mallee* GT, LR

Grey Grasswren *Amytornis barbatus*

Thick-billed Grasswren *Amytornis textilis* GT

Dusky Grasswren *Amytornis purnelli*

Kalkadoon Grasswren *Amytornis ballarae* LR

Black Grasswren *Amytornis housei*

White-throated Grasswren *Amytornis woodwardi* GT

Carpentarian Grasswren *Amytornis dorotheae* GT

Striated Grasswren *Amytornis striatus*

Short-tailed Grasswren *Amytornis merrotsyi* LR

Eyrean Grasswren *Amytornis goyderi*

Acanthizidae

Eastern Bristlebird *Dasyornis brachypterus* GT

Western Bristlebird *Dasyornis longirostris* GT, LR

Rufous Bristlebird *Dasyornis broadbenti* GT

Pilothird *Pycnoptilus floccosus*

Rock-Warbler *Origma solitaria*

Australian Fernwren *Oreoscopus gutturalis*

Rusty Mouse-Warbler *Crateroscelis murina*

Black-backed Mouse-Warbler *Crateroscelis nigrorufa*

Mountain Mouse-Warbler *Crateroscelis robusta*

Yellow-throated Sericornis *Sericornis citreogularis*

Spotted Sericornis *Sericornis maculatus* LR

Tasmanian Sericornis *Sericornis humilis* LR

White-browed Sericornis *Sericornis frontalis*

Tropical Scrubwren *Sericornis beccarii* LR

Perplexing Sericornis *Sericornis virgatus* LR

Large Sericornis *Sericornis nouhuysi*

Large-billed Sericornis *Sericornis magnirostris*

Atherton Sericornis *Sericornis keri*

Pale-billed Sericornis *Sericornis spilodera*

Buff-faced Sericornis *Sericornis perspicillatus*

Vogelkop Sericornis *Sericornis rufescens*

Grey-green Sericornis *Sericornis arfakianus* LR

Papuan Sericornis *Sericornis papuensis*

Scrubtit *Acanthornis magnus*

Redthroat *Pyrrholaemus brunneus*

Speckled Warbler *Pyrrholaemus sagittatus* GT

Striated Calamanthus *Calamanthus fuliginosus*

Rufous Calamanthus *Calamanthus campestris*

Western Fieldwren *Calamanthus montanellus* LR

Chestnut-rumped Hylacola *Hylacola pyrrhopygius*

Shy Hylacola *Hylacola cautus*

Papuan Thornbill *Acanthiza murina*

Western Thornbill *Acanthiza inornata*

Buff-rumped Thornbill *Acanthiza reguloides*

Slender-billed Thornbill *Acanthiza iredalei* GT

Mountain Thornbill *Acanthiza katherina*

Brown Thornbill *Acanthiza pusilla*

Broad-tailed Thornbill *Acanthiza apicalis* LR

Tasmanian Thornbill *Acanthiza ewingii*

Yellow-rumped Thornbill *Acanthiza chrysorrhoa*

Chestnut-rumped Thornbill *Acanthiza uropygialis*

Slaty-backed Thornbill *Acanthiza robustirostris*

Yellow Thornbill *Acanthiza nana*

Striated Thornbill *Acanthiza lineata*

Brown Weebill *Smicrornis brevirostris*

Grey Gerygone *Gerygone cinerea*

Green-backed Gerygone *Gerygone chloronotus*

Fairy Gerygone *Gerygone palpebrosa*

White-throated Gerygone *Gerygone olivacea*

Rufous-sided Gerygone *Gerygone dorsalis* LR

Yellow-bellied Gerygone *Gerygone chrysogaster*

Large-billed Gerygone *Gerygone magnirostris*

Biak Gerygone *Gerygone hypoxantha* GT

Golden-bellied Gerygone *Gerygone sulphurea* LR

Plain Gerygone *Gerygone inornata*

Treefern Gerygone *Gerygone ruficollis*

Western Gerygone *Gerygone fusca*

Lord Howe Island Gerygone *Gerygone insularis* E

Dusky Gerygone *Gerygone tenebrosa*

Mangrove Gerygone *Gerygone levigaster*

Fan-tailed Gerygone *Gerygone flavolateralis*

Brown Gerygone *Gerygone mouki*

Norfolk Island Gerygone *Gerygone modesta* GT LR

New Zealand Gray Gerygone *Gerygone igata*

Chatham Islands Gerygone *Gerygone albofrontata*

Southern Whiteface *Aphelocephala leucopsis*

Chestnut-breasted Whiteface *Aphelocephala pectoralis* GT

Banded Whiteface *Aphelocephala nigricincta*

Whitehead *Mohoua albicilla* LR

Yellowhead *Mohoua ochrocephala* GT

New Zealand Brown Creeper *Finschia novaeseelandiae*

Neosittidae

Black Sittella *Neositta miranda*

Varied Sittella *Neositta chrysoptera*

Papuan Sittella *Neositta papuensis* LR

Menuridae

Superb Lyrebird *Menura novaehollandiae*

Prince Albert's Lyrebird *Menura alberti* GT

Atrichornithidae

Noisy Scrubbird *Atrichornis clamosus* GT

Rufous Scrubbird *Atrichornis rufescens* GT

Monarchinae

Little Yellow Flycatcher *Erythrocercus holochlorus*

Chestnut-capped Flycatcher *Erythrocercus mccallii*

Livingstone's Flycatcher *Erythrocercus livingstonei*

African Blue-Flycatcher *Elminia longicauda*

White-tailed Blue-Flycatcher *Elminia albicauda*

Dusky Crested-Flycatcher *Trochocercus nigromitratus*

White-bellied Crested-Flycatcher *Trochocercus albiventris*

White-tailed Crested-Flycatcher *Trochocercus albonotatus*

Blue-headed Crested-Flycatcher *Trochocercus nitens*

African Crested-Flycatcher *Trochocercus cyanomelas*

Red-bellied Paradise-Flycatcher *Terpsiphone rufiventer* GT

Bedford's Paradise-Flycatcher *Terpsiphone bedfordi* GT, LR

Rufous-vented Paradise-Flycatcher *Terpsiphone rufocinerea*

Bates's Paradise-Flycatcher *Terpsiphone batesi* LR

African Paradise-Flycatcher *Terpsiphone viridis*

Asian Paradise-Flycatcher *Terpsiphone paradisi*

Black Paradise-Flycatcher *Terpsiphone atrocaudata* GT

Blue Paradise-Flycatcher *Terpsiphone cyanescens* GT

Rufous Paradise-Flycatcher *Terpsiphone cinnamomea*

São Tomé Paradise-Flycatcher *Terpsiphone atrochalybeia*

Madagascar Paradise-Flycatcher *Terpsiphone mutata*

Seychelles Paradise-Flycatcher *Terpsiphone corvina* GT

Mascarene Paradise-Flycatcher *Terpsiphone bourbonnensis*

Rufous-winged Philentoma *Philentoma pyrhopterum*

Maroon-breasted Philentoma *Philentoma velatum* GT

Short-crested Monarch *Hypothymis helenae* GT

Black-naped Monarch *Hypothymis azurea*

Pacific Small Monarch *Hypothymis puella* LR

Celestial Monarch *Hypothymis coelestis* GT

Cerulean Paradise-Flycatcher *Eutrichomyias rowleyi* GT

Elepaio *Chasiempis sandwichensis* GT

Rarotonga Monarch-Flycatcher *Pomarea dimidiata* GT

Tahiti Monarch-Flycatcher *Pomarea nigra* GT

Marquesas Flycatcher *Pomarea mendozae* GT

Allied Flycatcher *Pomarea iphis* GT

Large Monarch *Pomarea whitneyi* GT

Small Slaty Monarch *Mayrornis schistaceus* GT

Ogea Monarch *Mayrornis versicolor* GT

White-tipped Slaty Flycatcher *Mayrornis lessoni*

Buff-bellied Monarch *Neolalage banksiana*

Southern Shrikebill *Clytorhynchus pachycephaloides*

Fiji Shrikebill *Clytorhynchus vitiensis*

Black-throated Shrikebill *Clytorhynchus nigrogularis* GT

Rennell Shrikebill *Clytorhynchus hamlini*

Truk Monarch *Metabolus rugensis* GT

Black Monarch *Monarcha axillaris*

Rufous Monarch *Monarcha rubiensis*

Island Monarch *Monarcha cinerascens*

Black-faced Monarch *Monarcha melanopsis*

Black-winged Monarch *Monarcha frater*

Bougainville Monarch *Monarcha erythrostictus*

Chestnut-bellied Monarch-Flycatcher *Monarcha castaneiventris*

Richards's Monarch *Monarcha richardsii*

White-eared Monarch *Monarcha leucotis*

Loetoe Monarch *Monarcha castus* LR

White-naped Monarch *Monarcha pileatus* LR

Spot-winged Monarch *Monarcha guttulus*

Black-bibbed Monarch *Monarcha mundus*

Flores Mountain Monarch *Monarcha sacerdotum* GT

Black-chinned Monarch *Monarcha boanensis* GT

Spectacled Monarch *Monarcha trivirgatus*

White-tailed Monarch *Monarcha leucurus* GT

White-tipped Monarch *Monarcha everetti* GT, LR

Black-tipped Monarch *Monarcha loricatus* LR

Kofiau Monarch *Monarcha julianae* PGT

Black-and-white Monarch *Monarcha manadensis*

Biak Monarch *Monarcha brehmii* GT

Admiralty Islands Monarch *Monarcha infelix* GT

White-breasted Monarch *Monarcha menckei* GT

New Britain Pied Monarch *Monarcha verticalis*

Solomon Islands Pied Monarch *Monarcha barbatus* GT

Kulambangra Monarch *Monarcha browni* GT

San Cristobal Monarch *Monarcha viduus*

Black-and-yellow Monarch *Monarcha chrysomela*

Yap Island Monarch *Monarcha godeffroyi* GT

Tinian Island Monarch *Monarcha takatsukasae* GT

Australian Pied Monarch *Arses kaupi*

Rufous-collared Monarch *Arses insularis* LR

Australian Frilled Monarch *Arses telescophthalmus*

Frill-necked Monarch *Arses lorealis* LR

Guam Myiagra-Flycatcher *Myiagra freycineti* E, LR

Mangrove Flycatcher *Myiagra erythrops* LR

Micronesian Flycatcher *Myiagra oceanica*
Ponapé Flycatcher *Myiagra pluto* LR
Helmeted Flycatcher *Myiagra galeata*
Black Myiagra-Flycatcher *Myiagra atra* GT
Leaden Flycatcher *Myiagra rubecula*
Solomons Flycatcher *Myiagra ferrocyanea*
San Cristobal Myiagra-Flycatcher *Myiagra cervinicauda*
Melanesian Flycatcher *Myiagra caledonica*
Vanikoro Flycatcher *Myiagra vanikorensis*
Samoan Flycatcher *Myiagra albiventris* GT
Blue-crested Flycatcher *Myiagra azureocapilla*
Broad-billed Myiagra *Myiagra ruficollis*
Satin Myiagra-Flycatcher *Myiagra cyanoleuca*
Shining Myiagra-Flycatcher *Myiagra alecto*
Dull Flycatcher *Myiagra hebetior*
Restless Flycatcher *Myiagra inquieta*
Paperback Flycatcher *Myiagra nana* LR
Silktail *Lamprolia victoriae* GT
Yellow-breasted Boatbill *Machaerirhynchus flaviventer*
Black-breasted Boatbill *Machaerirhynchus nigripectus*
Lowland Peltops *Peltops blainvillii*
Mountain Peltops *Peltops montanus*

Rhipidurinae

Yellow-bellied Fantail *Rhipidura hypoxantha*
Blue Fantail *Rhipidura superciliaris*
Blue-headed Fantail *Rhipidura cyaniceps*
Rufous-tailed Fantail *Rhipidura phoenicura*
Black-and-cinnamon Fantail *Rhipidura nigrocinnamomea*
Spot-breasted Fantail *Rhipidura albogularis* LR
White-bellied Fantail *Rhipidura euryura*
White-browed Fantail *Rhipidura aureola*
Pied Fantail *Rhipidura javanica*
Willie Wagtail *Rhipidura leucophrys*
White-throated Fantail *Rhipidura albicollis*
Spotted Fantail *Rhipidura perlata*
Brown-capped Fantail *Rhipidura diluta* LR
Northern Fantail *Rhipidura rufiventris*
Cockerell's Fantail *Rhipidura cockerelli* GT, LR
Cinnamon-tailed Fantail *Rhipidura fuscorufa* GT, LR
Friendly Fantail *Rhipidura albolimbata*
Sooty Thicket-Fantail *Rhipidura threnothorax*

Chestnut-bellied Fantail *Rhipidura hyperythra*
Black Thicket-Fantail *Rhipidura maculipectus*
White-bellied Thicket-Fantail *Rhipidura leucothorax*
Black Fantail *Rhipidura atra*
New Zealand Fantail *Rhipidura fuliginosa*
Grey Fantail *Rhipidura albiscapa* LR
Mangrove Fantail *Rhipidura phasiana* LR
Brown Fantail *Rhipidura drownei*
Dusky Fantail *Rhipidura tenebrosa* GT
Rennell Fantail *Rhipidura rennelliana*
Streaked Fantail *Rhipidura spilodera*
Samoan Fantail *Rhipidura nebulosa*
Dimorphic Rufous Fantail *Rhipidura brachyrhyncha*
Kandavu Fantail *Rhipidura personata*
Streaky-breasted Fantail *Rhipidura dedemi*
Tawny-backed Fantail *Rhipidura superflua*
Rusty-bellied Fantail *Rhipidura teysmanni*
Long-tailed Fantail *Rhipidura opistherythra* GT
Palau Fantail *Rhipidura lepida*
Grey-breasted Rufous Fantail *Rhipidura rufidorsa*
New Britain Fantail *Rhipidura dahli*
St Matthias Fantail *Rhipidura matthiae* GT
Malaita Fantail *Rhipidura malaitae* GT
Ponapé Fantail *Rhipidura kubaryi* LR
Rufous Fantail *Rhipidura rufifrons*
Arafura Fantail *Rhipidura dryas* LR
Manus Fantail *Rhipidura semirubra* GT, LR

Petroicidae

Greater New Guinea Thrush *Amalocichla sclateriana*
Lesser New Guinea Thrush *Amalocichla incerta*
River Flycatcher *Monachella muelleriana*
Jacky Winter *Microeca fascinans*
Lemon-bellied Flycatcher *Microeca flavigaster*
Kimberley Flycatcher *Microeca tormenti* LR
Tanimbar Microeca Flycatcher *Microeca hemixantha* GT, LR
Yellow-legged Flyrobin *Microeca griseoceps*
Olive Microeca *Microeca flavovirescens*
Papuan Microeca *Microeca papuana*
Garnet Robin *Eugerygone rubra*
Forest Robin-Flycatcher *Petroica bivittata*
Rock Robin-Flycatcher *Petroica archboldi* PGT

Pacific Robin *Petroica multicolor*

Scarlet Robin *Petroica boodang* LR

Red-capped Robin *Petroica goodenovii*

Flame Robin-Flycatcher *Petroica phoenicea*

Pink Robin-Flycatcher *Petroica rodinogaster*

Rose Robin-Flycatcher *Petroica rosea*

New Zealand Tomtit *Petroica macrocephala*

New Zealand Robin *Petroica australis*

Chatham Islands Robin *Petroica traversi* GT

Hooded Robin *Petroica cucullata*

Dusky Robin *Melanodryas vittata*

White-faced Robin *Tregellasia leucops*

Pale-yellow Robin *Tregellasia capito*

Eastern Yellow Robin *Eopsaltria australis*

Western Yellow Robin *Eopsaltria griseogularis* LR

White-breasted Robin *Eopsaltria georgiana*

Yellow-bellied Robin *Eopsaltria flaviventris*

Mangrove Robin *Peneoenanthe pulverulenta*

Black-chinned Robin *Poecilodryas brachyura*

Black-sided Robin *Poecilodryas hypoleuca*

Olive-yellow Robin *Poecilodryas placens* GT

Black-throated Robin *Poecilodryas albonotata*

White-browed Robin *Poecilodryas superciliosa*

Buff-sided Robin *Poecilodryas cerviniventris*

White-winged Robin *Peneothello sigillatus* LR

Smoky Robin *Peneothello cryptoleucus*

Blue-grey Robin *Peneothello cyanus*

White-rumped Robin *Peneothello bimaculatus*

Ashy Robin *Heteromyias albispecularis*

Grey-headed Robin *Heteromyias cinereifrons* LR

Green-backed Robin *Pachycephalopsis hattamensis*

Eastern White-eyed Robin *Pachycephalopsis poliosoma*

Southern Scrub-Robin *Drymodes brunneopygia*

Northern Scrub-Robin *Drymodes superciliaris*

Pachycephalidae

Wattled Shrike-Tit *Eulacestoma nigropectus*

Eastern Shrike-Tit *Falcunculus frontatus*

Western Shrike-Tit *Falcunculus leucogaster* LR

Northern Shrike-Tit *Falcunculus whitei* LR

Crested Bellbird *Oreoica gutturalis*

Golden-faced Pachycare *Pachycare flavogrisea*

Mottled Whistler *Rhagologus leucostigma*

Olive-flanked Whistler *Hylocitrea bonensis*

Maroon-backed Whistler *Coracornis raveni*

Rufous-naped Whistler *Aleadryas rufinucha*

Olive Whistler *Pachycephala olivacea*

Red-lored Whistler *Pachycephala rufogularis* GT

Gilbert's Whistler *Pachycephala inornata*

Mangrove Whistler *Pachycephala grisola*

Palawan Whistler *Pachycephala plateni* LR

Green-backed Whistler *Pachycephala albiventris* LR

White-vented Whistler *Pachycephala homeyeri* LR

Island Whistler *Pachycephala phaionotus*

Rusty Whistler *Pachycephala hyperythra*

Brown-backed Whistler *Pachycephala modesta*

Yellow-bellied Whistler *Pachycephala philippinensis*

Sulphur-bellied Whistler *Pachycephala sulfuriventer*

Bornean Mountain Whistler *Pachycephala hypoxantha*

Vogelkop Whistler *Pachycephala meyeri*

Sclater's Whistler *Pachycephala soror*

Grey Whistler *Pachycephala simplex*

Grey-headed Whistler *Pachycephala griseiceps* LR

Fawn-breasted Whistler *Pachycephala orpheus*

Common Golden Whistler *Pachycephala pectoralis*

Tongan Whistler *Pachycephala jacquinoti* GT

Mangrove Golden Whistler *Pachycephala melanura*

Yellow-fronted Whistler *Pachycephala flavifrons*

New Caledonian Whistler *Pachycephala caledonica*

Hooded Whistler *Pachycephala implicata*

Bare-throated Whistler *Pachycephala nudigula*

Lorentz's Whistler *Pachycephala lorentzi*

Schlegel's Whistler *Pachycephala schlegelii*

Yellow-backed Whistler *Pachycephala aurea*

Rufous Whistler *Pachycephala rufiventris*

Black-headed Whistler *Pachycephala monacha* LR

White-bellied Whistler *Pachycephala leucogastra* LR

Wallacean Whistler *Pachycephala arctitorquis* LR

Drab Whistler *Pachycephala griseonota* LR

White-breasted Whistler *Pachycephala lanioides*

Sooty Shrike-Thrush *Colluricincla umbrina*

Pachycephalidae

Little Shrike-Thrush *Colluricincla megarhyncha*

Pachycephalidae

Sangihe Shrike-Thrush *Colluricincla sanghirensis* GT, LR

Pachycephalidae

Bower's Shrike-Thrush *Colluricincla boweri*

Grey Shrike-Thrush *Colluricincla harmonica*

Sandstone Shrike-Thrush *Colluricincla woodwardi*

Morningbird *Colluricincla tenebrosa*

Variable Pitohui *Pitohui kirhocephalus*

Hooded Pitohui *Pitohui dichrous*

White-bellied Pitohui *Pitohui incertus* GT

Rusty Pitohui *Pitohui ferrugineus*

Crested Pitohui *Pitohui cristatus*

Black Pitohui *Pitohui nigrescens*

Piopio *Turnagra capensis* E20

Aegithalidae

Eurasian Long-tailed-Tit *Aegithalos caudatus*

White-cheeked Long-tailed-Tit *Aegithalos leucogenys*

Black-throated Long-tailed-Tit *Aegithalos concinnus*

White-throated Long-tailed-Tit *Aegithalos niveogularis* LR

Rufous-fronted Long-tailed-Tit *Aegithalos iouschistos*

Black-browed Long-tailed-Tit *Aegithalos bonvaloti* LR

Sooty Long-tailed-Tit *Aegithalos fuliginosus*

Plain Bushtit *Psaltriparus minimus*

Pygmy Tit *Psaltria exilis*

Remizidae

Eurasian Penduline-Tit *Remiz pendulinus*

Remizidae

Black-headed Penduline-Tit *Remiz macronyx* LR

White-crowned Penduline-Tit *Remiz coronatus* LR

Chinese Penduline-Tit *Remiz consobrinus* LR

Sennar Penduline-Tit *Anthoscopus punctifrons*

Yellow Penduline-Tit *Anthoscopus parvulus*

Mouse-colored Penduline-Tit *Anthoscopus musculus*

Forest Penduline-Tit *Anthoscopus flavifrons*

African Penduline-Tit *Anthoscopus caroli*

Buff-bellied Penduline-Tit *Anthoscopus sylviella* LR

Cape Penduline-Tit *Anthoscopus minutus*

Verdin *Auriparus flaviceps*

Fire-capped Tit *Cephalopyrus flammiceps*

Tit-Hylia *Pholidornis rushiae*

Paridae

Black-bibbed Marsh Tit *Poecile hypermelaena* LR

Caspian Tit *Poecile hyrcana* LR

Songar Tit *Poecile songara* LR

Marsh Tit *Poecile palustris*

Sombre Tit *Poecile lugubris*

Willow Tit *Poecile montana* LR

Black-capped Chickadee *Poecile atricapillus*

Carolina Chickadee *Poecile carolinensis*

Mexican Chickadee *Poecile sclateri*

Mountain Chickadee *Poecile gambeli*

White-browed Tit *Poecile superciliosa*

Rusty-breasted Tit *Poecile davidi*

Siberian Chickadee *Poecile cincta*

Boreal Chickadee *Poecile hudsonica*

Chestnut-backed Chickadee *Poecile rufescens*

Rufous-vented Tit *Periparus rubidiventris*

Rufous-naped Black Tit *Periparus rufonuchalis* LR

Spot-winged Black Tit *Periparus melanolophus* LR

Coal Tit *Periparus ater*

Yellow-bellied Tit *Pardaliparus venustulus*

Elegant Tit *Pardaliparus elegans*

Palawan Tit *Pardaliparus amabilis* GT

Crested Tit *Lophophanes cristatus*

Grey-crested Tit *Lophophanes dichrous*

Northern Grey Tit *Melaniparus thruppi* LR

Southern Grey Tit *Melaniparus afer*

Ashy Tit *Melaniparus cinerascens* LR

Miombo Grey Tit *Melaniparus griseiventris*

Carp's Tit *Melaniparus carpi* LR

Southern Black Tit *Melaniparus niger*

Northern Black Tit *Melaniparus guineensis* LR

White-winged Black Tit *Melaniparus leucomelas*

White-bellied Tit *Melaniparus albiventris*

White-backed Black Tit *Melaniparus leuconotus*

Dusky Tit *Melaniparus funereus*

Stripe-breasted Tit *Melaniparus fasciiventer*

Red-throated Tit *Aegithospiza fringillinus*

Rufous-bellied Tit *Aegithospiza rufiventris*

Cinnamon-breasted Tit *Aegithospiza pallidiventris* LR

Great Tit *Parus major*

Turkestan Great Tit *Parus bokharensis* LR

Green-backed Tit *Parus monticolus*

White-naped Black Tit *Parus nuchalis* GT

Black-lored Yellow-Tit *Machlolophus xanthogenys*

Yellow-cheeked Tit *Machlolophus spilonotus* LR

Yellow Tit *Machlolophus holsti* GT

Blue Tit *Cyanistes caeruleus*

Azure Tit *Cyanistes cyanus*

Yellow-breasted Tit *Cyanistes flavipectus* LR

Varied Tit *Sittiparus varius*

White-fronted Tit *Sittiparus semilarvatus* GT

Bridled Titmouse *Baeolophus wollweberi*

Oak Titmouse *Baeolophus inornatus*

Juniper Titmouse *Baeolophus ridgwayi* LR

Tufted Titmouse *Baeolophus bicolor*

Black-crested Titmouse *Baeolophus atricristatus* LR

Sultan Tit *Melanochlora sultanea*

Yellow-browed Tit *Sylviparus modestus*

Sittidae

European Nuthatch *Sitta europaea*

Chestnut-vented Nuthatch *Sitta nagaensis* LR

Kashmir Nuthatch *Sitta cashmirensis* LR

Chestnut-bellied Nuthatch *Sitta castanea* LR

White-tailed Nuthatch *Sitta himalayensis*

White-browed Nuthatch *Sitta victoriae* GT

Pygmy Nuthatch *Sitta pygmaea*

Brown-headed Nuthatch *Sitta pusilla*

Corsican Nuthatch *Sitta whiteheadi*

Yunnan Nuthatch *Sitta yunnanensis* GT

Red-breasted Nuthatch *Sitta canadensis* LR

Chinese Nuthatch *Sitta villosa* LR

Krüper's Nuthatch *Sitta krueperi*

Algerian Nuthatch *Sitta ledanti* GT

White-cheeked Nuthatch *Sitta leucopsis*

White-breasted Nuthatch *Sitta carolinensis*

Western Rock Nuthatch *Sitta neumayer*

Eastern Rock Nuthatch *Sitta tephronota*

Velvet-fronted Nuthatch *Sitta frontalis*

Yellow-billed Nuthatch *Sitta solangiae* GT

Sulphur-billed Nuthatch *Sitta oenochlamys* LR

Blue Nuthatch *Sitta azurea*

Giant Nuthatch *Sitta magna* GT

Beautiful Nuthatch *Sitta formosa* GT

Tichidromidae

Wallcreeper *Tichodroma muraria*

Certhiidae

Eurasian Treecreeper *Certhia familiaris*

American Treecreeper *Certhia americana*

Short-toed Treecreeper *Certhia brachydactyla*

Bar-tailed Treecreeper *Certhia himalayana*

Rusty-flanked Treecreeper *Certhia nipalensis*

Brown-throated Treecreeper *Certhia discolor*

Spotted Creeper *Salpornis spilonotus*

Rhabdornithidae

Stripe-breasted Rhabdornis *Rhabdornis inornatus*

Long-billed Rhabdornis *Rhabdornis grandis* LR

Stripe-sided Rhabdornis *Rhabdornis mysticalis*

Climacteridae

Red-browed Treecreeper *Climacteris erythrops*

White-browed Treecreeper *Climacteris affinis*

Brown Treecreeper *Climacteris picumnus*

Rufous Treecreeper *Climacteris rufa*

Black-tailed Treecreeper *Climacteris melanura*

White-throated Treecreeper *Cormobates leucophaeus*

Papuan Treecreeper *Cormobates placens*

Melanocharitidae

Obscure Berrypecker *Melanocharis arfakiana* PGT

Black Berrypecker *Melanocharis nigra*

Mid-mountain Berrypecker *Melanocharis longicauda*

Fan-tailed Berrypecker *Melanocharis versteri*

Streaked Berrypecker *Melanocharis striativentris*

Spotted Berrypecker *Melanocharis crassirostris* LR

Yellow-bellied Longbill *Toxorhamphus novaeguineae*

Slaty-chinned Longbill *Toxorhamphus poliopterus*

Grey-bellied Longbill *Toxorhamphus iliolophus*

Pygmy Longbill *Oedistoma pygmaeum*

Dicaeidae

Olive-backed Flowerpecker *Prionochilus olivaceus*

Yellow-breasted Flowerpecker *Prionochilus maculatus*

Crimson-breasted Flowerpecker *Prionochilus percussus*

Palawan Flowerpecker *Prionochilus plateni*

Yellow-rumped Flowerpecker *Prionochilus xanthopygius*

Scarlet-breasted Flowerpecker *Prionochilus thoracicus* GT

Golden-rumped Flowerpecker *Dicaeum annae*

Thick-billed Flowerpecker *Dicaeum agile*

Striped Flowerpecker *Dicaeum aeruginosum* LR

Brown-backed Flowerpecker *Dicaeum everetti* GT

Whiskered Flowerpecker *Dicaeum proprium* GT

Yellow-vented Flowerpecker *Dicaeum chrysorrheum*

Yellow-bellied Flowerpecker *Dicaeum melanoxanthum*

Legge's Flowerpecker *Dicaeum vincens* GT

Yellow-sided Flowerpecker *Dicaeum aureolimbatum*

Olive-capped Flowerpecker *Dicaeum nigrilore*

Flame-crowned Flowerpecker *Dicaeum anthonyi* GT

Bicolored Flowerpecker *Dicaeum bicolor*

Cebu Flowerpecker *Dicaeum quadricolor* GT

Red-striped Flowerpecker *Dicaeum australe*

Visayan Flowerpecker *Dicaeum haematostictum* GT, LR

Scarlet-collared Flowerpecker *Dicaeum retrocinctum* GT

Orange-bellied Flowerpecker *Dicaeum trigonostigma*

Buzzing Flowerpecker *Dicaeum hypoleucum*

Pale-billed Flowerpecker *Dicaeum erythrorynchos*

Plain Flowerpecker *Dicaeum concolor*

Pygmy Flowerpecker *Dicaeum pygmaeum*

Crimson-crowned Flowerpecker *Dicaeum nehrkorni*

Flame-breasted Flowerpecker *Dicaeum erythrothorax*

Ashy Flowerpecker *Dicaeum vulneratum*

Olive-crowned Flowerpecker *Dicaeum pectorale*

Red-capped Flowerpecker *Dicaeum geelvinkianum* LR

Louisiade Flowerpecker *Dicaeum nitidum* LR

Red-banded Flowerpecker *Dicaeum eximium*

Solomon Islands Flowerpecker *Dicaeum aeneum*

San Cristobal Flowerpecker *Dicaeum tristrami*

Black-fronted Flowerpecker *Dicaeum igniferum*

Red-chested Flowerpecker *Dicaeum maugei*

Fire-breasted Flowerpecker *Dicaeum ignipectus*

Black-sided Flowerpecker *Dicaeum monticolum* LR

Grey-sided Flowerpecker *Dicaeum celebicum*

Blood-breasted Flowerpecker *Dicaeum sanguinolentum*

Mistletoebird *Dicaeum hirundinaceum*

Scarlet-backed Flowerpecker *Dicueum cruentatum*

Scarlet-headed Flowerpecker *Dicaeum trochileum*

Paramythiidae

Tit Berrypecker *Oreocharis arfaki*

Crested Berrypecker *Paramythia montium*

Pardalotidae

Forty-spotted Pardalote *Pardalotus quadragintus* GT

Spotted Pardalote *Pardalotus punctatus*

Red-browed Pardalote *Pardalotus rubricatus*

Yellow-tipped Pardalote *Pardalotus striatus* LR

Red-tipped Pardalote *Pardalotus ornatus* LR

Striated Pardalote *Pardalotus substriatus* LR

Black-headed Pardalote *Pardalotus melanocephalus* LR

Nectariniidae

Ruby-cheeked Sunbird *Chalcoparia singalensis*

Scarlet-tufted Sunbird *Deleornis fraseri*

Grey-headed Sunbird *Deleornis axillaris* LR

Plain-backed Sunbird *Anthreptes reichenowi* GT

Anchieta's Sunbird *Anthreptes anchietae*

Plain Sunbird *Anthreptes simplex*

Brown-throated Sunbird *Anthreptes malacensis*

Red-throated Sunbird *Anthreptes rhodolaema* GT

Mouse-brown Sunbird *Anthreptes gabonicus*

Western Violet-backed Sunbird *Anthreptes longuemarei*

Kenya Violet-backed Sunbird *Anthreptes orientalis*

Ulluguru Violet-backed Sunbird *Anthreptes neglectus*

Violet-tailed Sunbird *Anthreptes aurantium*

Little Green Sunbird *Anthreptes seimundi*

Green Sunbird *Anthreptes rectirostris*

Banded Sunbird *Anthreptes rubritorques* GT, LR

Collared Sunbird *Hedydipna collaris*

Western Pygmy Sunbird *Hedydipna platura*

Nile Valley Sunbird *Hedydipna metallica* LR

Amani Sunbird *Hedydipna pallidigaster* GT

Purple-naped Sunbird *Hypogramma hypogrammicum*

Reichenbach's Sunbird *Anabathmis reichenbachii*

Príncipe Sunbird *Anabathmis hartlaubii*

Newton's Yellow-breasted Sunbird *Anabathmis newtonii*

São Tomé Giant Sunbird *Dreptes thomensis* GT

Orange-breasted Sunbird *Anthobophes violacea*

Green-headed Sunbird *Cyanomitra verticalis*

Bannerman's Sunbird *Cyanomitra bannermani*

Blue-throated Brown Sunbird *Cyanomitra cyanoluema*

Cameroon Sunbird *Cyanomitra oritis*

Blue-headed Sunbird *Cyanomitra alinae*

Eastern Olive Sunbird *Cyanomitra olivacea*

Western Olive Sunbird *Cyanomitra obscura* LR

Mouse-colored Sunbird *Cyanomitra veroxii*

Buff-throated Sunbird *Chalcomitra adelberti*

Carmelite Sunbird *Chalcomitra fuliginosa*

Green-throated Sunbird *Chalcomitra rubescens*

Amethyst Sunbird *Chalcomitra amethystina*

Scarlet-chested Sunbird *Chalcomitra senegalensis*

Hunter's Sunbird *Chalcomitra hunteri* LR

Socotra Sunbird *Chalcomitra balfouri*

Purple-rumped Sunbird *Leptocoma zeylonica*

Crimson-backed Sunbird *Leptocoma minima*

Purple-throated Sunbird *Leptocoma sperata*

Black Sunbird *Leptocoma sericea*

Copper-throated Sunbird *Leptocoma calcostetha*

Tacazze Sunbird *Nectarinia tacazze*

Bocage's Sunbird *Nectarinia bocagii*

Purple-breasted Sunbird *Nectarinia purpureiventris*

Malachite Sunbird *Nectarinia famosa*

Red-tufted Malachite Sunbird *Nectarinia johnstoni*

Bronze Sunbird *Nectarinia kilimensis*

Golden-winged Sunbird *Drepanorhynchus reichenowi*

Bates's Sunbird *Paradeleornis batesi*

Fernando Po Sunbird *Cinnyris ursulae* GT

Olive-bellied Sunbird *Cinnyris chloropygius*

Tiny Sunbird *Cinnyris minullus*

Miombo Double-collared Sunbird *Cinnyris manoensis*

Southern Double-collared Sunbird *Cinnyris chalybeus*

Neergaard's Sunbird *Cinnyris neergaardi* GT

Stuhlmann's Sunbird *Cinnyris stuhlmanni* LR

Prigogine's Sunbird *Cinnyris prigoginei* LR

Montane Double-collared Sunbird *Cinnyris ludovicensis* LR

Northern Double-collared Sunbird *Cinnyris reichenowi* LR

Greater Double-collared Sunbird *Cinnyris afer*

Regal Sunbird *Cinnyris regius*

Rockefeller's Sunbird *Cinnyris rockefelleri* GT

Eastern Double-collared Sunbird *Cinnyris mediocris*

Moreau's Sunbird *Cinnyris moreaui* GT

Loveridge's Sunbird *Cinnyris loveridgei*

Beautiful Sunbird *Cinnyris pulchellus*

Mariqua Sunbird *Cinnyris mariquensis*

Shelley's Sunbird *Cinnyris shelleyi*

Congo Black-bellied Sunbird *Cinnyris congensis*

Red-chested Sunbird *Cinnyris erythrocerca*

Smaller Black-bellied Sunbird *Cinnyris nectarinioides*

Purple-banded Sunbird *Cinnyris bifasciatus*

Tsavo Sunbird *Cinnyris tsavoensis* LR

Kenya Violet-breasted Sunbird *Cinnyris chalcomelas*

Pemba Sunbird *Cinnyris pembae*

Orange-tufted Sunbird *Cinnyris bouvieri*

Palestine Sunbird *Cinnyris oseus*

Shining Sunbird *Cinnyris habessinicus*

Splendid Sunbird *Cinnyris coccinigaster*

Johanna's Sunbird *Cinnyris johannae*

Superb Sunbird *Cinnyris superbus*

Coppery Sunbird *Cinnyris cupreus*

Rufous-winged Sunbird *Cinnyris rufipennis* GT

Oustalet's Sunbird *Cinnyris oustaleti*

Southern White-bellied Sunbird *Cinnyris talatala*

Yellow-bellied Sunbird *Cinnyris venustus*

Dusky Sunbird *Cinnyris fuscus*

Purple Sunbird *Cinnyris asiaticus*

Olive-backed Sunbird *Cinnyris jugularis*

Apricot-breasted Sunbird *Cinnyris buettikoferi* LR

Flame-breasted Sunbird *Cinnyris solaris*

Souimanga Sunbird *Cinnyris sovimanga*

Abbott's Sunbird *Cinnyris abbotti* LR

Madagascar Green Sunbird *Cinnyris notatus*

Comoro Green Sunbird *Cinnyris moebii* LR

Seychelles Sunbird *Cinnyris dussumieri*

Humblot's Sunbird *Cinnyris humbloti*

Anjouan Sunbird *Cinnyris comorensis*

Mayotte Sunbird *Cinnyris coquerellii*

Loten's Sunbird *Cinnyris lotenius*

Grey-hooded Sunbird *Aethopyga primigenius* GT

Apo Sunbird *Aethopyga boltoni* GT

Lina's Sunbird *Aethopyga linaraborae* GT, LR

Flaming Sunbird *Aethopyga flagrans*

Metallic-winged Sunbird *Aethopyga pulcherrima*

Elegant Sunbird *Aethopyga duyvenbodei* GT

Lovely Sunbird *Aethopyga shelleyi*

Mrs Gould's Sunbird *Aethopyga gouldiae*

Green-tailed Sunbird *Aethopyga nipalensis*

White-flanked Sunbird *Aethopyga eximia*

Fork-tailed Sunbird *Aethopyga christinae*

Black-throated Sunbird *Aethopyga saturata*

Western Crimson Sunbird *Aethopyga vigorsii* LR

Crimson Sunbird *Aethopyga siparaja*

Javan Sunbird *Aethopyga mystacalis*

Temminck's Sunbird *Aethopyga temminckii* LR

Fire-tailed Sunbird *Aethopyga ignicauda*

Little Spiderhunter *Arachnothera longirostra*

Thick-billed Spiderhunter *Arachnothera crassirostris*

Long-billed Spiderhunter *Arachnothera robusta*

Spectacled Spiderhunter *Arachnothera flavigaster*

Yellow-eared Spiderhunter *Arachnothera chrysogenys*

Naked-faced Spiderhunter *Arachnothera clarae*

Grey-breasted Spiderhunter *Arachnothera modesta* LR

Streaky-breasted Spiderhunter *Arachnothera affinis*

Streaked Spiderhunter *Arachnothera magna*

Bornean Spiderhunter *Arachnothera everetti* LR

Whitehead's Spiderhunter *Arachnothera juliae*

Zosteropidae

Chestnut-flanked White-eye *Zosterops erythropleurus*

Japanese White-eye *Zosterops japonicus*

Lowland White-eye *Zosterops meyeni* LR

Enggano White-eye *Zosterops salvadorii*

Oriental White-eye *Zosterops palpebrosus*

Sri Lanka White-eye *Zosterops ceylonensis*

Bridled White-eye *Zosterops conspicillatus*

Rota Bridled White-eye *Zosterops rotensis* GT

Caroline White-eye *Zosterops semperi* LR

Plain White-eye *Zosterops hypolais* GT, LR

Black-capped White-eye *Zosterops atricapillus*

Everett's White-eye *Zosterops everetti*

Golden-green White-eye *Zosterops nigrorum*

Mountain White-eye *Zosterops montanus*

Yellow-spectacled White-eye *Zosterops wallacei*

Javan White-eye *Zosterops flavus* GT, LR

Lemon-bellied White-eye *Zosterops chloris* LR

Australian Pale White-eye *Zosterops citrinellus* LR

Pale-bellied White-eye *Zosterops consobrinorum* PGT

Pearl-bellied White-eye *Zosterops grayi* GT, LR

Golden-bellied White-eye *Zosterops uropygialis* GT

Black-ringed White-eye *Zosterops anomalus*

Creamy-throated White-eye *Zosterops atriceps*

Black-crowned White-eye *Zosterops atrifrons*

New Guinea Black-fronted White-eye *Zosterops minor* LR

White-throated White-eye *Zosterops meeki* PGT, LR

Black-headed White-eye *Zosterops hypoxanthus* LR

Biak White-eye *Zosterops mysorensis* GT

Yellow-bellied Mountain White-eye *Zosterops fuscicapillus*

Buru Island White-eye *Zosterops buruensis*

Ambon White-eye *Zosterops kuehni* GT

New Guinea White-eye *Zosterops novaeguineae*

Yellow-throated White-eye *Zosterops metcalfii*

Christmas Island White-eye *Zosterops natalis* GT

Australian Yellow White-eye *Zosterops luteus*

Louisiades White-eye *Zosterops griseotinctus*

Rennell Island White-eye *Zosterops rennellianus* LR

Banded White-eye *Zosterops vellalavella* GT, LR

Ganongga White-eye *Zosterops splendidus* GT, LR

Splendid White-eye *Zosterops luteirostris* GT, LR

Kulambangra White-eye *Zosterops kulambangrae* LR

Solomon Islands White-eye *Zosterops rendovae*

Kulambangra Mountain White-eye *Zosterops murphyi*

Grey-throated White-eye *Zosterops ugiensis* LR

Malaita White-eye *Zosterops stresemanni*

Santa Cruz White-eye *Zosterops sanctaecrucis*

Samoan White-eye *Zosterops samoensis* GT

Dusky White-eye *Zosterops finschii*

Grey White-eye *Zosterops cinereus* LR

Layard's White-eye *Zosterops explorator*

Yellow-fronted White-eye *Zosterops flavifrons*

Small Lifou White-eye *Zosterops minutus*

Green-backed White-eye *Zosterops xanthochrous*

Western Silvereye *Zosterops gouldi* LR

Silvereye *Zosterops lateralis*

Lord Howe Island White-eye *Zosterops tephropleurus* GT, LR

Robust White-eye *Zosterops strenuus* E

Slender-billed White-eye *Zosterops tenuirostris* GT

White-chested White-eye *Zosterops albogularis* GT

Large Lifou White-eye *Zosterops inornatus*

White-breasted White-eye *Zosterops abyssinicus*

Cape White-eye *Zosterops pallidus*

African Yellow White-eye *Zosterops senegalensis*

Pemba White-eye *Zosterops vaughani* LR

Grand Comoro White-eye *Zosterops kirki* LR

Réunion Grey White-eye *Zosterops borbonicus*

Mauritius Grey White-eye *Zosterops mauritianus* LR

Príncipe White-eye *Zosterops ficedulinus* GT

Annobón White-eye *Zosterops griseovirescens* GT

Madagascar White-eye *Zosterops maderaspatanus*

Mayotte White-eye *Zosterops mayottensis* LR

Broad-ringed White-eye *Zosterops poliogaster* LR

Seychelles White-eye *Zosterops modestus* GT

Comoro White-eye *Zosterops mouroniensis* GT

Réunion Olive White-eye *Zosterops olivaceus*

Mauritius Olive White-eye *Zosterops chloronothos* GT

Yap Olive White-eye *Zosterops oleagineus* GT

Bare-eyed White-eye *Woodfordia superciliosa*

Sanford's White-eye *Woodfordia lacertosa* GT

Great Truk White-eye *Rukia ruki* GT

Ponapé White-eye *Rukia longirostra* GT

Large Palau White-eye *Megazosterops palauensis* GT

Golden White-eye *Cleptornis marchei* GT

Bonin Islands White-eye *Apalopteron familiare* GT

Bicolored White-eye *Tephrozosterops stalkeri*

Rufous-throated White-eye *Madanga ruficollis* GT

Grey-hooded White-eye *Lophozosterops pinaiae*

Black-masked White-eye *Lophozosterops goodfellowi*

Streak-headed White-eye *Lophozosterops squamiceps*

Javan Grey-throated White-eye *Lophozosterops javanicus*

Yellow-browed White-eye *Lophozosterops superciliaris*

Crested White-eye *Lophozosterops dohertyi*

Pygmy White-eye *Oculocincta squamifrons*

Spot-breasted White-eye *Heleia muelleri* GT

Thick-billed White-eye *Heleia crassirostris*

Mountain Black-eye *Chlorocharis emiliae*

Cinnamon Ibon *Hypocryptadius cinnamomeus*

Fernando Po Speirops *Speirops brunneus* GT

Príncipe Speirops *Speirops leucophoeus* GT

Mount Cameroon Speirops *Speirops melanocephalus* GT, LR

Black-capped Speirops *Speirops lugubris*

Promeropidae

Gurney's Sugarbird *Promerops gurneyi*

Cape Sugarbird *Promerops cafer*

Meliphagidae

Olive Straightbill *Timeliopsis fulvigula*

Tawny Straightbill *Timeliopsis griseigula*

Long-billed Honeyeater *Melilestes megarhynchus*

Bougainville Honeyeater *Melilestes bougainvillei*

Green-backed Honeyeater *Glycichaera fallax*

Scaly-crowned Honeyeater *Lichmera lombokia*

Olive Honeyeater *Lichmera argentauris*

Indonesian Honeyeater *Lichmera limbata* LR

Brown Honeyeater *Lichmera indistincta*

Dark-brown Honeyeater *Lichmera incana*

Silver-eared Honeyeater *Lichmera alboauricularis*

White-tufted Honeyeater *Lichmera squamata*

Buru Honeyeater *Lichmera deningeri* PGT

Seram Honeyeater *Lichmera monticola*

Yellow-eared Honeyeater *Lichmera flavicans*

Black-chested Honeyeater *Lichmera notabilis* GT

White-streaked Honeyeater *Trichodere cockerelli*

Drab Myzomela *Myzomela blasii*

White-chinned Myzomela *Myzomela albigula* PGT

Ashy Myzomela *Myzomela cineracea* LR

Red-throated Myzomela *Myzomela eques*

Dusky Myzomela *Myzomela obscura*

Red Myzomela *Myzomela cruentata*

Papuan Black Myzomela *Myzomela nigrita*

Olive-yellow Myzomela *Myzomela pulchella*

Crimson-hooded Myzomela *Myzomela kuehni* GT

Sumba Myzomela *Myzomela dammermani* LR

Red-headed Myzomela *Myzomela erythrocephala*

Mountain Myzomela *Myzomela adolphinae*

Sulawesi Myzomela *Myzomela chloroptera* LR

Wakolo Myzomela *Myzomela wakoloensis* LR

Banda Myzomela *Myzomela boiei* LR

Scarlet Myzomela *Myzomela sanguinolenta*

New Caledonian Myzomela *Myzomela caledonica* LR

Cardinal Myzomela *Myzomela cardinalis*

Rotuma Myzomela *Myzomela chermesina* GT, LR

Micronesian Myzomela *Myzomela rubratra* LR

Scarlet-bibbed Myzomela *Myzomela sclateri*

Bismarck Black Myzomela *Myzomela pammelaena* LR

Scarlet-naped Myzomela *Myzomela lafargei*

Black-headed Myzomela *Myzomela melanocephala*

Yellow-vented Myzomela *Myzomela eichhorni*

Red-bellied Myzomela *Myzomela malaitae* GT

Sooty Myzomela *Myzomela tristrami*

Orange-breasted Myzomela *Myzomela jugularis*

Black-bellied Myzomela *Myzomela erythromelas*

Red-rumped Myzomela *Myzomela vulnerata*

Red-collared Myzomela *Myzomela rosenbergii*

White-fronted Chat *Ephthianura albifrons*

Crimson Chat *Ephthianura tricolor*

Orange Chat *Ephthianura aurifrons*

Yellow Chat *Ephthianura crocea*

Gibberbird *Ashbyia lovensis*

Banded Honeyeater *Certhionyx pectoralis*

Black Honeyeater *Certhionyx niger*

Pied Honeyeater *Certhionyx variegatus*

Large Spot-breasted Honeyeater *Meliphaga mimikae*

Forest White-eared Honeyeater *Meliphaga montana*

Hill-forest Honeyeater *Meliphaga orientalis*

Scrub White-eared Honeyeater *Meliphaga albonotata*

Puff-backed Honeyeater *Meliphaga aruensis*

Mimic Honeyeater *Meliphaga analoga*

Tagula Honeyeater *Meliphaga vicina* PGT

Graceful Honeyeater *Meliphaga gracilis*

Yellow-spotted Honeyeater *Meliphaga notata*

Yellow-gaped Honeyeater *Meliphaga flavirictus*

Lewin's Honeyeater *Meliphaga lewinii*

White-lined Honeyeater *Meliphaga albilineata*

Streak-breasted Honeyeater *Meliphaga reticulata*

Guadalcanal Honeyeater *Guadalcanaria inexpectata*

Yellow Honeyeater *Lichenostomus flavus*

Singing Honeyeater *Lichenostomus virescens*

Varied Honeyeater *Lichenostomus versicolor*

Mangrove Honeyeater *Lichenostomus fasciogularis*

Grey-fronted Honeyeater *Lichenostomus plumulus*

Yellow-faced Honeyeater *Lichenostomus chrysops*

Eungella Honeyeater *Lichenostomus hindwoodi*

Purple-gaped Honeyeater *Lichenostomus cratitius*

Grey-headed Honeyeater *Lichenostomus keartlandi*

Fuscous Honeyeater *Lichenostomus fuscus*

Yellow-tinted Honeyeater *Lichenostomus flavescens* LR

White-plumed Honeyeater *Lichenostomus penicillatus*

Yellow-plumed Honeyeater *Lichenostomus ornatus*

White-eared Honeyeater *Lichenostomus leucotis*

Yellow-throated Honeyeater *Lichenostomus flavicollis*

Yellow-tufted Honeyeater *Lichenostomus melanops*

White-gaped Honeyeater *Lichenostomus unicolor*

Bridled Honeyeater *Lichenostomus frenatus*

Black-throated Honeyeater *Lichenostomus subfrenatus*

Obscure Honeyeater *Lichenostomus obscurus*

Tawny-breasted Honeyeater *Xanthotis flaviventer*

Spotted Honeyeater *Xanthotis polygramma*

Macleay's Honeyeater *Xanthotis macleayana*

Kadavu Honeyeater *Xanthotis provocator*

Wattled Honeyeater *Foulehaio carunculata*

Orange-cheeked Honeyeater *Oreornis chrysogenys*

Brown-headed Honeyeater *Melithreptus brevirostris*

White-naped Honeyeater *Melithreptus lunatus*

White-throated Honeyeater *Melithreptus albogularis*

Black-headed Honeyeater *Melithreptus affinis*

Black-chinned Honeyeater *Melithreptus gularis*

Strong-billed Honeyeater *Melithreptus validirostris* LR

Golden-backed Honeyeater *Melithreptus laetior* LR

Blue-faced Honeyeater *Entomyzon cyanotis*

Stitchbird *Notiomystis cincta* GT

Plain Honeyeater *Pycnopygius ixoides*

Marbled Honeyeater *Pycnopygius cinereus*

Streak-headed Honeyeater *Pycnopygius stictocephalus*

White-streaked Friarbird *Melitograis gilolensis*

Meyer's Friarbird *Philemon meyeri*

Brass's Friarbird *Philemon brassi* GT

Little Friarbird *Philemon citreogularis*

Grey Friarbird *Philemon kisserensis* LR

Timor Friarbird *Philemon inornatus*

Dusky Friarbird *Philemon fuscicapillus* GT

Grey-necked Friarbird *Philemon subcorniculatus*

Black-faced Friarbird *Philemon moluccensis*

Helmeted Friarbird *Philemon buceroides*

Melville Island Friarbird *Philemon gordoni*

New Guinea Friarbird *Philemon novaeguineae* LR

New Britain Friarbird *Philemon cockerelli*

New Ireland Friarbird *Philemon eichhorni*

White-naped Friarbird *Philemon albitorques*

Silver-crowned Friarbird *Philemon argenticeps*

Noisy Friarbird *Philemon corniculatus*

New Caledonian Friarbird *Philemon diemenensis*

Leaden Honeyeater *Ptiloprora plumbea*

Olive-streaked Honeyeater *Ptiloprora meekiana*

Rufous-sided Honeyeater *Ptiloprora erythropleura*

Rufous-backed Honeyeater *Ptiloprora guisei*

Mayr's Honeyeater *Ptiloprora mayri* LR

Black-backed Honeyeater *Ptiloprora perstriata*

Sooty Melidectes *Melidectes fuscus*

Bismarck Melidectes *Melidectes whitemanensis*

Long-bearded Melidectes *Melidectes princeps* GT

Short-bearded Melidectes *Melidectes nouhuysi*

Cinnamon-browed Melidectes *Melidectes ochromelas*

Vogelkop Melidectes *Melidectes leucostephes*

Belford's Melidectes *Melidectes belfordi*

Yellow-browed Melidectes *Melidectes rufocrissalis*

Huon Wattled Melidectes *Melidectes foersteri*

Ornate Melidectes *Melidectes torquatus*

San Cristobal Melidectes *Melidectes sclateri*

Arfak Melipotes *Melipotes gymnops*

Huon Melipotes *Melipotes ater*

Common Melipotes *Melipotes fumigatus*

Dark-eared Myza *Myza celebensis*

White-eared Myza *Myza sarasinorum*

Green Honeyeater *Gymnomyza viridis* GT

Black-breasted Honeyeater *Gymnomyza samoensis* GT

Red-faced Honeyeater *Gymnomyza aubryana* GT

Kaua'i O'o *Moho braccatus* E

Oahu O'o *Moho apicalis* E

Bishop's O'o *Moho bishopi* E

Hawaii O'o *Moho nobilis* E

Kioea *Chaetoptila angustipluma* E

Tawny-crowned Honeyeater *Glyciphila melanops*

Crescent Honeyeater *Phylidonyris pyrrhoptera*

New Holland Honeyeater *Phylidonyris novaehollandiae*

White-cheeked Honeyeater *Phylidonyris nigra*

White-fronted Honeyeater *Phylidonyris albifrons*

Barred Honeyeater *Phylidonyris undulata*

New Hebrides Honeyeater *Phylidonyris notabilis*

Bar-breasted Honeyeater *Ramsayornis fasciatus*

Brown-backed Honeyeater *Ramsayornis modestus*

Striped Honeyeater *Plectorhyncha lanceolata*

Grey Honeyeater *Conopophila whitei*

Rufous-banded Honeyeater *Conopophila albogularis*

Rufous-throated Honeyeater *Conopophila rufogularis*

Painted Honeyeater *Grantiella picta* GT

Regent Honeyeater *Xanthomyza phrygia* GT

Eastern Spinebill *Acanthorhynchus tenuirostris*

Western Spinebill *Acanthorhynchus superciliosus*

Bell Miner *Manorina melanophrys*

Noisy Miner *Manorina melanocephala*

Yellow-throated Miner *Manorina flavigula*

Black-eared Miner *Manorina melanotis* GT, LR, GD

New Zealand Bellbird *Anthornis melanura*

Spiny-cheeked Honeyeater *Acanthagenys rufogularis*

Western Wattlebird *Anthochaera lunulata* LR

Brush Wattlebird *Anthochaera chrysoptera* LR

Red Wattlebird *Anthochaera carunculata*

Yellow Wattlebird *Anthochaera paradoxa*

Tui *Prosthemadera novaeseelandiae*

Dicruridae

Pygmy Drongo *Chaetorhynchus papuensis*

Square-tailed Drongo *Dicrurus ludwigii*

Shining Drongo *Dicrurus atripennis*

Common Drongo *Dicrurus adsimilis*

Velvet-mantled Drongo *Dicrurus modestus* GT, LR

Comoro Drongo *Dicrurus fuscipennis* GT

Aldabra Drongo *Dicrurus aldabranus* GT

Crested Drongo *Dicrurus forficatus*

Mayotte Drongo *Dicrurus waldenii* GT

Black Drongo *Dicrurus macrocercus* LR

Ashy Drongo *Dicrurus leucophaeus*

White-bellied Drongo *Dicrurus caerulescens*

Crow-billed Drongo *Dicrurus annectans*

Bronzed Drongo *Dicrurus aeneus*

Lesser Racquet-tailed Drongo *Dicrurus remifer*

Balicassio *Dicrurus balicassius*

Sulawesi Drongo *Dicrurus montanus* LR

Spangled Drongo *Dicrurus bracteatus* LR

Wallacean Drongo *Dicrurus densus* LR

Sumatran Drongo *Dicrurus sumatranus* GT, LR

New Ireland Drongo *Dicrurus megarhynchus*

Hair-crested Drongo *Dicrurus hottentottus*

Andaman Drongo *Dicrurus andamanensis* GT

Greater Racquet-tailed Drongo *Dicrurus paradiseus*

Callaeidae

Kokako *Callaeas cinerea* GT

Saddleback *Callaeas carunculatus* GT

Huia *Heteralocha acutirostris* E20

Grallinidae

Magpie-Lark *Grallina cyanoleuca*

Torrent-Lark *Grallina bruijni*

White-winged Chough *Corcorax melanorhamphos*

Apostlebird *Struthidea cinerea*

Artamidae

Ashy Woodswallow *Artamus fuscus*

White-breasted Woodswallow *Artamus leucorynchus*

Ivory-backed Woodswallow *Artamus monachus*

Papuan Woodswallow *Artamus maximus*

Bismarck Woodswallow *Artamus insignis*

Fiji Woodswallow *Artamus mentalis* LR

Masked Woodswallow *Artamus personatus*

White-browed Woodswallow *Artamus superciliosus*

Black-faced Woodswallow *Artamus cinereus*

Dusky Woodswallow *Artamus cyanopterus*

Little Woodswallow *Artamus minor*

Cracticidae

Black-backed Butcherbird *Cracticus mentalis*

Grey Butcherbird *Cracticus torquatus*

Silver-backed Butcherbird *Cracticus argenteus* LR

Pied Butcherbird *Cracticus nigrogularis*

Hooded Butcherbird *Cracticus cassicus*

Tagula Butcherbird *Cracticus louisiadensis* PGT

Black Butcherbird *Cracticus quoyi*

Australasian Magpie *Gymnorhina tibicen*

Bornean Bristlehead *Pityriasis gymnocephala* GT

Pied Currawong *Strepera graculina*

Black Currawong *Strepera fuliginosa*

Grey Currawong *Strepera versicolor*

Ptilonorhynchidae

White-eared Catbird *Ailuroedus buccoides*

Green Catbird *Ailuroedus crassirostris*

Spotted Catbird *Ailuroedus melanotis* LR

Tooth-billed Catbird *Scenopoeetes dentirostris*

Archbold's Bowerbird *Archboldia papuensis* GT

Sanford's Bowerbird *Archboldia sanfordi* LR

Vogelkop Gardener-Bowerbird *Amblyornis inornatus*

Macgregor's Gardener-Bowerbird *Amblyornis macgregoriae*

Streaked Bowerbird *Amblyornis subalaris*

Golden-fronted Bowerbird *Amblyornis flavifrons*

Newton's Golden Bowerbird *Prionodura newtoniana*

Flame Bowerbird *Sericulus aureus*

Fire-maned Bowerbird *Sericulus bakeri* GT

Regent Bowerbird *Sericulus chrysocephalus*

Satin Bowerbird *Ptilonorhynchus violaceus*

Western Bowerbird *Chlamydera guttata* LR

Spotted Bowerbird *Chlamydera maculata*

Great Grey Bowerbird *Chlamydera nuchalis*

Yellow-breasted Bowerbird *Chlamydera lauterbachi*

Fawn-breasted Bowerbird *Chlamydera cerviniventris*

Paradisaeidae

Loria's Bird-of-Paradise *Loria loriae*

Paradisaeidae

Crested Bird-of-Paradise *Cnemophilus macgregorii*

Yellow-breasted Bird-of-Paradise *Loboparadisea sericea* GT

Macgregor's Bird-of-Paradise *Macgregoria pulchra* GT

Paradise-Crow *Lycocorax pyrrhopterus*

Glossy-mantled Manucode *Manucodia atra*

Jobi Manucode *Manucodia jobiensis*

Crinkle-collared Manucode *Manucodia chalybata*

Curl-crested Manucode *Manucodia comrii*

Australian Trumpetbird *Phonygammus keraudrenii*

Paradise Riflebird *Ptiloris paradiseus*

Victoria's Riflebird *Ptiloris victoriae*

Eastern Riflebird *Ptiloris intercedens* LR

Magnificent Riflebird *Ptiloris magnificus*

Wallace's Standardwing *Semioptera wallacii*

Twelve-wired Bird-of-Paradise *Seleucidis melanoleuca*

Long-tailed Paradigalla *Paradigalla carunculata* GT

Short-tailed Paradigalla *Paradigalla brevicauda*

Black-billed Sicklebill *Drepanornis albertisii*

Pale-billed Sicklebill *Drepanornis bruijnii* GT

Black Sicklebill *Epimachus fastuosus* GT

Brown Sicklebill *Epimachus meyeri*

Arfak Astrapia *Astrapia nigra*

Splendid Astrapia *Astrapia splendidissima*

Ribbon-tailed Astrapia *Astrapia mayeri* GT

Princess Stephanie's Astrapia *Astrapia stephaniae*

Huon Astrapia *Astrapia rothschildi*

Superb Bird-of-Paradise *Lophorina superba*

Western Parotia *Parotia sefilata*

Queen Carola's Parotia *Parotia carolae*

Lawes's Parotia *Parotia lawesii*

Eastern Parotia *Parotia helenae* LR

Wahnes's Parotia *Parotia wahnesi* GT

King of Saxony's Bird-of-Paradise *Pteridophora alberti*

King Bird-of-Paradise *Cicinnurus regius*

Magnificent Bird-of-Paradise *Diphyllodes magnificus*

Wilson's Bird-of-Paradise *Diphyllodes respublica* GT

Greater Bird-of-Paradise *Paradisaea apoda*

Raggiana Bird-of-Paradise *Paradisaea raggiana* LR

Lesser Bird-of-Paradise *Paradisaea minor* LR

Goldie's Bird-of-Paradise *Paradisaea decora* GT, LR

Red Bird-of-Paradise *Paradisaea rubra* GT, LR

Emperor's Bird-of-Paradise *Paradisaea guilielmi* GT

Blue Bird-of-Paradise *Paradisaea rudolphi* GT

Lesser Melampitta *Melampitta lugubris*

Greater Melampitta *Melampitta gigantea*

Corvidae

Crested Jay *Platylophus galericulatus* GT

Black Jay *Platysmurus leucopterus* GT

Pinyon Jay *Gymnorhinus cyanocephalus*

Blue Jay *Cyanocitta cristata*

Steller's Jay *Cyanocitta stelleri*

Island Scrub-Jay *Aphelocoma insularis* GT, LR

Western Scrub-Jay *Aphelocoma californica* LR

Florida Scrub-Jay *Aphelocoma coerulescens* GT

Grey-breasted Jay *Aphelocoma ultramarina*

Unicolored Jay *Aphelocoma unicolor*

White-collared Jay *Cyanolyca viridicyana*

Black-collared Jay *Cyanolyca armillata* LR

Turquoise Jay *Cyanolyca turcosa* LR

Beautiful Jay *Cyanolyca pulchra* GT

Azure-hooded Jay *Cyanolyca cucullata*

Black-throated Jay *Cyanolyca pumilo*

Dwarf Jay *Cyanolyca nana* GT

White-throated Jay *Cyanolyca mirabilis* GT

Silvery-throated Jay *Cyanolyca argentigula*

Bushy-crested Jay *Cissilopha melanocyanea*

San Blas Jay *Cissilopha sanblasiana*

Yucatan Jay *Cissilopha yucatanicus*

Beechey's Jay *Cissilopha beecheii*

Azure Jay *Cyanocorax caeruleus* GT

Purplish Jay *Cyanocorax cyanomelas*

Violaceous Jay *Cyanocorax violaceus*

Curl-crested Jay *Cyanocorax cristatellus*

Azure-naped Jay *Cyanocorax heilprini*

Cayenne Jay *Cyanocorax cayanus*

Black-chested Jay *Cyanocorax affinis*

Plush-crested Jay *Cyanocorax chrysops*

White-naped Jay *Cyanocorax cyanopogon* LR

White-tailed Jay *Cyanocorax mystacalis*

Tufted Jay *Cyanocorax dickeyi* GT

Inca Jay *Cyanocorax yncas*

Mexican Jay *Cyanocorax luxuosus* LR

Brown Jay *Psilorhinus morio*

White-throated Magpie-Jay *Calocitta formosa*

Black-throated Magpie-Jay *Calocitta colliei* LR

Eurasian Jay *Garrulus glandarius*

Black-headed Jay *Garrulus lanceolatus*

Purple Jay *Garrulus lidthi* GT

Grey Jay *Perisoreus canadensis*

Siberian Jay *Perisoreus infaustus*

Sichuan Jay *Perisoreus internigrans* GT

Sri Lanka Blue-Magpie *Urocissa ornata* GT

Taiwan Blue-Magpie *Urocissa caerulea*

Yellow-billed Blue-Magpie *Urocissa flavirostris*

Red-billed Blue-Magpie *Urocissa erythrorhyncha*

White-winged Magpie *Urocissa whiteheadi*

Green-Magpie *Cissa chinensis*

Indochinese Green-Magpie *Cissa hypoleuca* LR

Short-tailed Green-Magpie *Cissa thalassina*

Azure-winged Magpie *Cyanopica cyana*

Rufous Treepie *Dendrocitta vagabunda*

Sumatran Treepie *Dendrocitta occipitalis*

Grey Treepie *Dendrocitta formosae*

Bornean Treepie *Dendrocitta cinerascens* LR

White-bellied Treepie *Dendrocitta leucogastra* PGT

Collared Treepie *Dendrocitta frontalis*

Andaman Treepie *Dendrocitta bayleyi* GT

Black Racquet-tailed Treepie *Crypsirina temia*

Hooded Racquet-tailed Treepie *Crypsirina cucullata* GT

Ratchet-tailed Treepie *Temnurus temnurus*

Common Magpie *Pica pica*

Black-billed Magpie *Pica hudsonia* LR

Yellow-billed Magpie *Pica nuttalli*

Stresemann's Bush-Crow *Zavattariornis stresemanni* GT

Mongolian Ground-Jay *Podoces hendersoni*

Xinjiang Ground-Jay *Podoces biddulphi* GT

Pander's Ground-Jay *Podoces panderi*

Pleske's Ground-Jay *Podoces pleskei*

Hume's Ground-Jay *Pseudopodoces humilis*

Clark's Nutcracker *Nucifraga columbiana*

Spotted Nutcracker *Nucifraga caryocatactes*

Larger Spotted Nutcracker *Nucifraga multipunctata* LR

Red-billed Chough *Pyrrhocorax pyrrhocorax*

Yellow-billed Chough *Pyrrhocorax graculus*

Piapiac *Ptilostomus afer*

Eurasian Jackdaw *Corvus monedula*

Daurian Jackdaw *Corvus dauuricus* LR

House Crow *Corvus splendens*

Slender-billed Crow *Corvus enca*

Violaceus Crow *Corvus violaceus* LR

Banggai Crow *Corvus unicolor* GT

Piping Crow *Corvus typicus*

Flores Crow *Corvus florensis* GT

New Caledonian Crow *Corvus moneduloides*

Marianas Crow *Corvus kubaryi* GT

Long-billed Crow *Corvus validus*

Bougainville Crow *Corvus meeki* LR

White-billed Crow *Corvus woodfordi*

Brown-headed Crow *Corvus fuscicapillus* GT

Grey Crow *Corvus tristis*

Hawaiian Crow *Corvus hawaiiensis* GT

Cape Crow *Corvus capensis*

Eurasian Rook *Corvus frugilegus*

American Crow *Corvus brachyrhynchos*

Northwestern Crow *Corvus caurinus* LR

Tamaulipas Crow *Corvus imparatus*

Sinaloa Crow *Corvus sinaloae* LR

Fish Crow *Corvus ossifragus*

Hispaniolan Palm Crow *Corvus palmarum* GT

Cuban Palm Crow *Corvus minutus* GT, LR

Jamaican Crow *Corvus jamaicensis*

Cuban Crow *Corvus nasicus*

White-necked Crow *Corvus leucognaphalus* GT

Carrion Crow *Corvus corone*

Hooded Crow *Corvus cornix* LR

Collared Crow *Corvus torquatus*

Large-billed Crow *Corvus macrorhynchos*

Jungle Crow *Corvus levaillantii* LR

Torresian Crow *Corvus orru*

Little Crow *Corvus bennetti*

Australian Raven *Corvus coronoides*

Relict Raven *Corvus boreus* LR

Forest Raven *Corvus tasmanicus*

Little Raven *Corvus mellori*

African Pied Crow *Corvus albus*

Chihuahuan Raven *Corvus cryptoleucus*

Brown-necked Raven *Corvus ruficollis*

Dwarf Raven *Corvus edithae* LR

Common Raven *Corvus corax*

Fan-tailed Raven *Corvus rhipidurus*

White-naped Raven *Corvus albicollis*

Thick-billed Raven *Corvus crassirostris*

Oriolidae

Brown Oriole *Oriolus szalayi*

Dusky Oriole *Oriolus phaeochromus*

Grey-collared Oriole *Oriolus forsteni*

Black-eared Oriole *Oriolus bouroensis*

Olive-brown Oriole *Oriolus melanotis*

Olive-backed Oriole *Oriolus sagittatus*

Australian Yellow Oriole *Oriolus flavocinctus*

Dark-throated Oriole *Oriolus xanthonotus* GT

Philippine Oriole *Oriolus steerii* LR

White-lored Oriole *Oriolus albiloris* LR

Isabela Oriole *Oriolus isabellae* GT

Eurasian Golden Oriole *Oriolus oriolus*

African Golden Oriole *Oriolus auratus*

Black-naped Oriole *Oriolus chinensis*

Slender-billed Oriole *Oriolus tenuirostris* LR

Green-headed Oriole *Oriolus chlorocephalus*

São Tomé Oriole *Oriolus crassirostris* GT

Western Black-headed Oriole *Oriolus brachyrhynchus*

Dark-headed Oriole *Oriolus monacha*

Montane Oriole *Oriolus percivali*

African Black-headed Oriole *Oriolus larvatus*

Black-winged Oriole *Oriolus nigripennis*

Black-hooded Oriole *Oriolus xanthornus*

Black Oriole *Oriolus hosii* GT
Black-and-crimson Oriole *Oriolus cruentus*
Maroon Oriole *Oriolus traillii*
Silver Oriole *Oriolus mellianus* GT
Green Figbird *Sphecotheres viridis*
Australasian Figbird *Sphecotheres vieilloti* LR
Wetar Figbird *Sphecotheres hypoleucus* GT, LR

Sturnidae

New Hebrides Starling *Aplonis zelandica* GT
Santo Mountain Starling *Aplonis santovestris* GT
Ponapé Starling *Aplonis pelzelni* GT
Samoan Starling *Aplonis atrifusca*
Kosrae Starling *Aplonis corvina* E
Mysterious Starling *Aplonis mavornata* E
Rarotonga Starling *Aplonis cinerascens* GT
Polynesian Starling *Aplonis tabuensis*
Striated Starling *Aplonis striata*
Tasman Island Starling *Aplonis fusca* E
Micronesian Starling *Aplonis opaca*
Singing Starling *Aplonis cantoroides*
Tanimbar Starling *Aplonis crassa* GT
Atoll Starling *Aplonis feadensis* GT
Rennell Island Starling *Aplonis insularis* LR
San Cristobal Starling *Aplonis dichroa* LR
Large Glossy-Starling *Aplonis grandis*
Island Starling *Aplonis mysolensis*
Long-tailed Starling *Aplonis magna* LR
Short-tailed Glossy-Starling *Aplonis minor*
Asian Glossy-Starling *Aplonis panayensis*
Metallic Starling *Aplonis metallica*
Grant's Starling *Aplonis mystacea* GT
White-eyed Glossy-Starling *Aplonis brunneicapilla* GT
Golden-breasted Myna *Mino anais*
Yellow-faced Myna *Mino dumontii*
Long-tailed Myna *Mino kreffti* LR
Sulawesi Crested Myna *Basilornis celebensis*
Helmeted Myna *Basilornis galeatus* GT
Long-crested Myna *Basilornis corythaix*
Mount Apo Myna *Basilornis miranda* GT
Coleto *Sarcops calvus*
White-necked Myna *Streptocitta albicollis*
Bare-eyed Myna *Streptocitta albertinae* GT
Fiery-browed Myna *Enodes erythrophris*
Finch-billed Myna *Scissirostrum dubium*

Madagascar Starling *Saroglossa aurata*
Spot-winged Starling *Saroglossa spiloptera*
Rodrigues Starling *Necrospar rodericanus* E
Réunion Starling *Fregilupus varius* E
Golden-crested Myna *Ampeliceps coronatus*
Common Hill-Myna *Gracula religiosa*
Southern Hill-Myna *Gracula indica* LR
Engganno Hill-Myna *Gracula enganensis* LR
Nias Hill-Myna *Gracula robusta* LR
Sri Lanka Myna *Gracula ptilogenys* GT
White-vented Myna *Acridotheres grandis* LR
Crested Myna *Acridotheres cristatellus*
Javan Myna *Acridotheres javanicus* LR
Pale-bellied Myna *Acridotheres cinereus* LR
Jungle Myna *Acridotheres fuscus*
Collared Myna *Acridotheres albocinctus*
Bank Myna *Acridotheres ginginianus*
Common Myna *Acridotheres tristis*
Vinous-breasted Myna *Acridotheres burmannicus*
Black-winged Myna *Acridotheres melanopterus* GT
Bali Myna *Leucopsar rothschildi* GT
Asian Pied Starling *Gracupica contra*
Black-collared Starling *Gracupica nigricollis*
Daurian Starling *Sturnia sturnina*
Chestnut-cheeked Starling *Sturnia philippensis*
White-shouldered Starling *Sturnia sinensis*
Chestnut-tailed Starling *Sturnia malabarica*
White-headed Starling *Sturnia erythropygia*
White-faced Starling *Sturnia senex* GT
Brahminy Starling *Temenuchus pagodarum*
Rosy Starling *Pastor roseus*
Red-billed Starling *Sturnus sericeus*
White-cheeked Starling *Sturnus cineraceus*
Common Starling *Sturnus vulgaris*
Spotless Starling *Sturnus unicolor*
Wattled Starling *Creatophora cinerea*
Red-shouldered Glossy-Starling *Lamprotornis nitens*
Blue-eared Glossy-Starling *Lamprotornis chalybaeus*
Lesser Blue-eared Glossy-Starling *Lamprotornis chloropterus*
Southern Blue-eared Glossy-Starling *Lamprotornis elisabeth* LR

Bronze-tailed Glossy-Starling *Lamprotornis chalcurus*

Splendid Glossy-Starling *Lamprotornis splendidus*

Príncipe Glossy-Starling *Lamprotornis ornatus*

Iris Glossy-Starling *Lamprotornis iris* PGT

Purple Glossy-Starling *Lamprotornis purpureus*

Rüppell's Long-tailed Glossy-Starling *Lamprotornis purpuropterus*

Northern Long-tailed Glossy-Starling *Lamprotornis caudatus*

Golden-breasted Starling *Lamprotornis regius*

Meves's Glossy-Starling *Lamprotornis mevesii*

Burchell's Glossy-Starling *Lamprotornis australis*

Sharp-tailed Glossy-Starling *Lamprotornis acuticaudus*

Black-bellied Glossy-Starling *Lamprotornis corruscus*

Superb Starling *Lamprotornis superbus*

Hildebrandt's Starling *Lamprotornis hildebrandti*

Shelley's Starling *Lamprotornis shelleyi*

Chestnut-bellied Starling *Lamprotornis pulcher*

Purple-headed Glossy-Starling *Hylopsar purpureiceps*

Copper-tailed Glossy-Starling *Hylopsar cupreocauda* GT

Violet Starling *Cinnyricinclus leucogaster*

African Pied Starling *Spreo bicolor*

Fischer's Starling *Spreo fischeri*

Ashy Starling *Spreo unicolor*

White-crowned Starling *Spreo albicapillus*

Slender-billed Chestnut-winged Starling *Onychognathus tenuirostris*

Common Chestnut-winged Starling *Onychognathus fulgidus*

Waller's Chestnut-winged Starling *Onychognathus walleri*

Somali Starling *Onychognathus blythii*

Socotra Starling *Onychognathus frater* GT

Tristram's Starling *Onychognathus tristramii*

Pale-winged Starling *Onychognathus nabouroup*

Bristle-crowned Starling *Onychognathus salvadorii*

White-billed Starling *Onychognathus albirostris*

Neumann's Starling *Onychognathus neumanni* LR

Red-winged Starling *Onychognathus morio*

Narrow-tailed Starling *Poeoptera lugubris*

Stuhlmann's Starling *Poeoptera stuhlmanni*

Kenrick's Starling *Poeoptera kenricki*

Abbott's Starling *Pholia femoralis* GT

Sharpe's Starling *Pholia sharpii*

White-collared Starling *Grafisia torquata*

Magpie Starling *Speculipastor bicolor*

White-winged Starling *Neocichla gutturalis*

Yellow-billed Oxpecker *Buphagus africanus*

Red-billed Oxpecker *Buphagus erythrorhynchus*

Emberizidae

Crested Bunting *Melophus lathami*

Slaty Bunting *Latoucheornis siemsseni*

Corn Bunting *Miliaria calandra*

Yellowhammer *Emberiza citrinella*

Pine Bunting *Emberiza leucocephalos*

Rock Bunting *Emberiza cia*

Godlewski's Bunting *Emberiza godlewskii* LR

Siberian Meadow Bunting *Emberiza cioides*

Jankowski's Bunting *Emberiza jankowskii* GT

White-capped Bunting *Emberiza stewarti*

Cinereous Bunting *Emberiza cineracea* GT

Grey-necked Bunting *Emberiza buchanani*

Ortolan Bunting *Emberiza hortulana*

Cretzschmar's Bunting *Emberiza caesia*

Cirl Bunting *Emberiza cirlus*

Striolated Bunting *Emberiza striolata*

Lark-like Bunting *Emberiza impetuani*

Cinnamon-breasted Bunting *Emberiza tahapisi*

Socotra Bunting *Emberiza socotrana* GT

Cape Bunting *Emberiza capensis*

Ochre-rumped Bunting *Emberiza yessoensis* GT

Tristram's Bunting *Emberiza tristrami*

Yellow-browed Bunting *Emberiza chrysophrys*

Yellow-throated Bunting *Emberiza elegans*

Koslov's Bunting *Emberiza koslowi* GT

Chestnut-eared Bunting *Emberiza fucata*

Little Bunting *Emberiza pusilla*

Rustic Bunting *Emberiza rustica*

Yellow-breasted Bunting *Emberiza aureola*

Golden-breasted Bunting *Emberiza flaviventris*

Somali Golden-breasted Bunting *Emberiza poliopleura* LR

Brown-rumped Bunting *Emberiza affinis*

Cabanis' Bunting *Emberiza cabanisi*

Black-headed Bunting *Emberiza melanocephala* LR

Red-headed Bunting *Emberiza bruniceps*

Chestnut Bunting *Emberiza rutila*

Japanese Yellow Bunting *Emberiza sulphurata* GT

Black-faced Bunting *Emberiza spodocephala*

Grey Bunting *Emberiza variabilis*

Pallas's Bunting *Emberiza pallasi*

Common Reed-Bunting *Emberiza schoeniclus*

McCown's Longspur *Calcarius mccownii*

Lapland Longspur *Calcarius lapponicus*

Smith's Longspur *Calcarius pictus*

Chestnut-collared Longspur *Calcarius ornatus*

Snow Bunting *Plectrophenax nivalis*

McKay's Bunting *Plectrophenax hyperboreus* GT, LR

Lark Bunting *Calamospiza melanocorys*

Red Fox-Sparrow *Passerella iliaca*

Sooty Fox-Sparrow *Passerella unalaschcensis* LR

Slate-colored Fox-Sparrow *Passerella schistacea* LR

Song Sparrow *Melospiza melodia*

Lincoln's Sparrow *Melospiza lincolnii*

Swamp Sparrow *Melospiza georgiana*

Rufous-collared Sparrow *Zonotrichia capensis*

Harris's Sparrow *Zonotrichia querula*

White-crowned Sparrow *Zonotrichia leucophrys*

White-throated Sparrow *Zonotrichia albicollis*

Golden-crowned Sparrow *Zonotrichia atricapilla*

Volcano Junco *Junco vulcani*

Dark-eyed Junco *Junco hyemalis*

Guadalupe Junco *Junco insularis* GT, LR

Grey-headed Junco *Junco caniceps* LR

Yellow-eyed Junco *Junco phaeonotus*

Baird's Junco *Junco bairdi* LR

Savannah Sparrow *Passerculus sandwichensis*

Large-billed Sparrow *Passerculus rostratus* LR

Nelson's Sharp-tailed Sparrow *Ammodramus nelsoni*

Seaside Sparrow *Ammodramus maritimus*

Saltmarsh Sharp-tailed Sparrow *Ammodramus caudacutus* GT

Baird's Sparrow *Ammodramus bairdii*

Le Conte's Sparrow *Ammodramus leconteii*

Henslow's Sparrow *Ammodramus henslowii*

Grasshopper Sparrow *Ammodramus savannarum*

Grassland Sparrow *Myospiza humeralis*

Yellow-browed Sparrow *Myospiza aurifrons*

Sierra Madre Sparrow *Xenospiza baileyi* GT

American Tree Sparrow *Spizella arborea*

Chipping Sparrow *Spizella passerina*

Field Sparrow *Spizella pusilla*

Worthen's Sparrow *Spizella wortheni* GT, LR

Black-chinned Sparrow *Spizella atrogularis*

Clay-colored Sparrow *Spizella pallida*

Brewer's Sparrow *Spizella breweri*

Timberline Sparrow *Spizella taverneri* LR

Vesper Sparrow *Pooecetes gramineus*

Lark Sparrow *Chondestes grammacus*

Black-throated Sparrow *Amphispiza bilineata*

Bell's Sage Sparrow *Amphispiza belli*

Sage Sparrow *Amphispiza nevadensis* LR

Five-striped Sparrow *Amphispiza quinquestriata*

Bridled Sparrow *Aimophila mystacalis*

Black-chested Sparrow *Aimophila humeralis*

Stripe-headed Sparrow *Aimophila ruficauda*

Cinnamon-tailed Sparrow *Aimophila sumichrasti* GT

Stripe-capped Sparrow *Aimophila strigiceps*

Rufous-winged Sparrow *Aimophila carpalis*

Tumbes Sparrow *Aimophila stolzmanni*

Bachman's Sparrow *Aimophila aestivalis* GT

Botteri's Sparrow *Aimophila botterii*

Cassin's Sparrow *Aimophila cassinii*

Rufous-crowned Sparrow *Aimophila ruficeps*

Oaxaca Sparrow *Aimophila notosticta* GT

Rusty Sparrow *Aimophila rufescens*

Zapata Sparrow *Torreornis inexpectata* GT

Striped Sparrow *Oriturus superciliosus*

Peruvian Sierra-Finch *Phrygilus punensis* LR

Black-hooded Sierra-Finch *Phrygilus atriceps* LR

Grey-hooded Sierra-Finch *Phrygilus gayi*

Patagonian Sierra-Finch *Phrygilus patagonicus*

Mourning Sierra-Finch *Phrygilus fruticeti*

Plumbeous Sierra-Finch *Phrygilus unicolor*

Red-backed Sierra-Finch *Phrygilus dorsalis*

White-throated Sierra-Finch *Phrygilus erythronotus*

Ash-breasted Sierra-Finch *Phrygilus plebejus*

Carbonated Sierra-Finch *Phrygilus carbonarius*

Band-tailed Sierra-Finch *Phrygilus alaudinus*

Canary-winged Finch *Melanodera melanodera*

Yellow-bridled Finch *Melanodera xanthogramma*

Slaty Finch *Haplospiza rustica*

Uniform Finch *Haplospiza unicolor*

Peg-billed Finch *Acanthidops bairdii*

Black-crested Finch *Lophospingus pusillus*

Grey-crested Finch *Lophospingus griseocristatus*

Long-tailed Reed-Finch *Donacospiza albifrons*

Gough Island Finch *Rowettia goughensis* GT

Nightingale Finch *Nesospiza acunhae* GT

Wilkins's Finch *Nesospiza wilkinsi* GT

White-winged Diuca-Finch *Diuca speculifera*

Common Diuca-Finch *Diuca diuca*

Short-tailed Finch *Idiopsar brachyurus*

Cinereous Finch *Piezorhina cinerea*

Slender-billed Finch *Xenospingus concolor* GT

Great Inca-Finch *Incaspiza pulchra*

Rufous-backed Inca-Finch *Incaspiza personata* LR

Grey-winged Inca-Finch *Incaspiza ortizi* GT

Buff-bridled Inca-Finch *Incaspiza laeta*

Little Inca-Finch *Incaspiza watkinsi* GT

Bay-chested Warbling-Finch *Poospiza thoracica*

Bolivian Warbling-Finch *Poospiza boliviana*

Plain-tailed Warbling-Finch *Poospiza alticola* GT

Rufous-sided Warbling-Finch *Poospiza hypochondria*

Rusty-browed Warbling-Finch *Poospiza erythrophrys*

Cinnamon Warbling-Finch *Poospiza ornata*

Black-and-rufous Warbling-Finch *Poospiza nigrorufa*

Black-and-chestnut Warbling-Finch *Poospiza whitii* LR

Red-rumped Warbling-Finch *Poospiza lateralis*

Rufous-breasted Warbling-Finch *Poospiza rubecula* GT

Chestnut-breasted Mountain-Finch *Poospiza caesar*

Collared Warbling-Finch *Poospiza hispaniolensis*

Ringed Warbling-Finch *Poospiza torquata*

Black-capped Warbling-Finch *Poospiza melanoleuca*

Cinereous Warbling-Finch *Poospiza cinerea* GT, LR

Cochabamba Mountain-Finch *Compospiza garleppi* GT

Tucumán Mountain-Finch *Compospiza baeri* GT, LR

Puna Yellow-Finch *Sicalis lutea*

Stripe-tailed Yellow-Finch *Sicalis citrina*

Bright-rumped Yellow-Finch *Sicalis uropygialis*

Citron-headed Yellow-Finch *Sicalis luteocephala*

Greater Yellow-Finch *Sicalis auriventris*

Greenish Yellow-Finch *Sicalis olivascens*

Patagonian Yellow-Finch *Sicalis lebruni*

Orange-fronted Yellow-Finch *Sicalis columbiana*

Saffron Yellow-Finch *Sicalis flaveola*

Grassland Yellow-Finch *Sicalis luteola*

Misto Yellow-Finch *Sicalis luteiventris* LR

Raimondi's Yellow-Finch *Sicalis raimondii* LR

Sulphur-throated Finch *Sicalis taczanowskii*

Wedge-tailed Grass-Finch *Emberizoides herbicola*

Lesser Grass-Finch *Emberizoides ypiranganus*

Duida Grass-Finch *Emberizoides duidae* GT

Great Pampa-Finch *Embernagra platensis*

Pale-throated Sierra-Finch *Embernagra longicauda* GT

Blue-black Grassquit *Volatinia jacarina*

Buffy-fronted Seedeater *Sporophila frontalis* GT

Temminck's Seedeater *Sporophila falcirostris* GT

Slate-colored Seedeater *Sporophila schistacea*

Grey Seedeater *Sporophila intermedia*

Plumbeous Seedeater *Sporophila plumbea*

Variable Seedeater *Sporophila corvina* LR

Wing-barred Seedeater *Sporophila americana*

Caquetá Seedeater *Sporophila murallae* LR

White-collared Seedeater *Sporophila torqueola*

Rusty-collared Seedeater *Sporophila collaris*

Lesson's Seedeater *Sporophila bouvronides* LR

Lined Seedeater *Sporophila lineola*

Black-and-white Seedeater *Sporophila luctuosa*

Yellow-bellied Seedeater *Sporophila nigricollis*

Dubois' Seedeater *Sporophila ardesiaca*

Hooded Seedeater *Sporophila melanops* GT

Double-collared Seedeater *Sporophila caerulescens*

White-throated Seedeater *Sporophila albogularis*

Grey-backed Seedeater *Sporophila leucoptera*

Black-backed Seedeater *Sporophila bicolor*

Parrot-billed Seedeater *Sporophila peruviana*

Drab Seedeater *Sporophila simplex*

Tumaco Seedeater *Sporophila insulata* GT

Black-and-tawny Seedeater *Sporophila nigrorufa* GT

Capped Seedeater *Sporophila bouvreuil*

Ruddy-breasted Seedeater *Sporophila minuta*

Tawny-bellied Seedeater *Sporophila hypoxantha* LR

Rufous-rumped Seedeater *Sporophila hypochroma* GT

Dark-throated Seedeater *Sporophila ruficollis* GT

Marsh Seedeater *Sporophila palustris* GT

Chestnut-bellied Seedeater *Sporophila castaneiventris*

Chestnut Seedeater *Sporophila cinnamomea* GT

Narosky's Seedeater *Sporophila zelichi* GT, LR, PH

Black-bellied Seedeater *Sporophila melanogaster* GT

Chestnut-throated Seedeater *Sporophila telasco*

Nicaraguan Seed-Finch *Oryzoborus nuttingi*

Large-billed Seed-Finch *Oryzoborus crassirostris*

Great-billed Seed-Finch *Oryzoborus maximiliani*

Black-billed Seed-Finch *Oryzoborus atrirostris*

Lesser Seed-Finch *Oryzoborus angolensis*

Thick-billed Seed-Finch *Oryzoborus funereus* LR

Blue Seedeater *Amaurospiza concolor*

Blackish-blue Seedeater *Amaurospiza moesta* GT

Cuban Bullfinch *Melopyrrha nigra*

White-naped Seedeater *Dolospingus fringilloides*

Band-tailed Seedeater *Catamenia analis*

Plain-colored Seedeater *Catamenia inornata*

Paramo Seedeater *Catamenia homochroa*

Colombian Seedeater *Catamenia oreophila* LR

Dull-colored Grassquit *Tiaris obscura*

Cuban Grassquit *Tiaris canora*

Yellow-faced Grassquit *Tiaris olivacea*

Black-faced Grassquit *Tiaris bicolor*

Sooty Grassquit *Tiaris fuliginosa*

Yellow-shouldered Grassquit *Loxipasser anoxanthus*

Puerto Rican Bullfinch *Loxigilla portoricensis*

Greater Antillean Bullfinch *Loxigilla violacea*

Lesser Antillean Bullfinch *Loxigilla noctis*

St Lucia Black Finch *Melanospiza richardsoni* GT

Large Ground-Finch *Geospiza magnirostris*

Medium Ground-Finch *Geospiza fortis*

Small Ground-Finch *Geospiza fuliginosa*

Sharp-beaked Ground-Finch *Geospiza difficilis*

Small Cactus Finch *Geospiza scandens*

Large Cactus Finch *Geospiza conirostris*

Vegetarian Finch *Camarhynchus crassirostris*

Large Insectivorous Tree-Finch *Camarhynchus psittacula*

Medium Tree-Finch *Camarhynchus pauper* GT

Small Insectivorous Tree-Finch *Camarhynchus parvulus*

Woodpecker Finch *Camarhynchus pallidus*

Mangrove Finch *Camarhynchus heliobates* GT

Warbler Finch *Certhidea olivacea*

Cocos Island Finch *Pinaroloxias inornata* GT

Collared Towhee *Pipilo ocai* LR

Eastern Towhee *Pipilo erythrophthalmus*

Spotted Towhee *Pipilo maculatus*

Socorro Towhee *Pipilo socorroensis* LR

Canyon Towhee *Pipilo fuscus*

California Towhee *Pipilo crissalis* LR

Abert's Towhee *Pipilo aberti*

White-throated Towhee *Pipilo albicollis*

Green-tailed Towhee *Chlorura chlorura*

Rusty-crowned Ground-Sparrow *Melozone kieneri* LR

Prevost's Ground-Sparrow *Melozone biarcuatum*

White-eared Ground-Sparrow *Melozone leucotis*

Pectoral Sparrow *Arremon taciturnus*

Half-collared Sparrow *Arremon semitorquatus* LR

São Francisco Sparrow *Arremon franciscanus* GT

Saffron-billed Sparrow *Arremon flavirostris*

Orange-billed Sparrow *Arremon aurantiirostris*

Golden-winged Sparrow *Arremon schlegeli*

Black-capped Sparrow *Arremon abeillei*

Olive Sparrow *Arremonops rufivirgatus*

Tocuyo Sparrow *Arremonops tocuyensis*

Green-backed Sparrow *Arremonops chloronotus*

Black-striped Sparrow *Arremonops conirostris*

White-naped Brushfinch *Atlapetes albinucha*

Yellow-throated Brushfinch *Atlapetes gutturalis* LR

Pale-naped Brushfinch *Atlapetes pallidinucha*

Bolivian Brushfinch *Atlapetes rufinucha*

Rufous-naped Brushfinch *Atlapetes latinuchus* LR

Vilcabamba Brushfinch *Atlapetes terborghi* GT, LR

White-rimmed Brushfinch *Atlapetes leucopis*

Santa Marta Brushfinch *Atlapetes melanocephalus*

Rufous-capped Brushfinch *Atlapetes pileatus*

Olive-headed Brushfinch *Atlapetes flaviceps* GT

Dusky-headed Brushfinch *Atlapetes fuscoolivaceus* GT

Tricolored Brushfinch *Atlapetes tricolor*

Moustached Brushfinch *Atlapetes albofrenatus*

Slaty Brushfinch *Atlapetes schistaceus*

Rusty-bellied Brushfinch *Atlapetes nationi*

Bay-crowned Brushfinch *Atlapetes seebohmi* LR

White-winged Brushfinch *Atlapetes leucopterus*

White-headed Brushfinch *Atlapetes albiceps* LR

Pale-headed Brushfinch *Atlapetes pallidiceps* GT

Rufous-eared Brushfinch *Atlapetes rufigenis* GT

Ochre-breasted Brushfinch *Atlapetes semirufus*

Tepui Brushfinch *Atlapetes personatus*

Fulvous-headed Brushfinch *Atlapetes fulviceps*

Yellow-striped Brushfinch *Buarremon citrinellus*

Plain-breasted Brushfinch *Buarremon apertus* LR

Chestnut-capped Brushfinch *Buarremon brunneinucha*

Green-striped Brushfinch *Buarremon virenticeps*

Stripe-headed Brushfinch *Buarremon torquatus*

Black-headed Brushfinch *Buarremon atricapillus* LR

Black-spectacled Brushfinch *Buarremon melanops* GT, LR

Large-footed Finch *Pezopetes capitalis*

Yellow-thighed Finch *Pselliophorus tibialis*

Yellow-green Finch *Pselliophorus luteoviridis* GT, LR

Olive Finch *Lysurus castaneiceps*

Sooty-faced Finch *Lysurus crassirostris*

Tanager Finch *Oreothraupis arremonops* GT

Black-backed Bush-Tanager *Urothraupis stolzmanni*

Coal-crested Finch *Charitospiza eucosma* GT

Many-colored Chaco-Finch *Saltatricula multicolor*

Black-masked Finch *Coryphaspiza melanotis* GT

Grey Pileated-Finch *Coryphospingus pileatus*

Red Pileated-Finch *Coryphospingus cucullatus*

Crimson-breasted Finch *Rhodospingus cruentus*

Plushcap *Catamblyrhynchus diadema*

Yellow Cardinal *Gubernatrix cristata* GT

Red-crested Cardinal *Paroaria coronata*

Red-cowled Cardinal *Paroaria dominicana*

Red-capped Cardinal *Paroaria gularis*

Crimson-fronted Cardinal *Paroaria baeri* LR

Yellow-billed Cardinal *Paroaria capitata*

Dickcissel *Spiza americana*

Mexican Yellow Grosbeak *Pheucticus chrysopeplus*

Black-thighed Grosbeak *Pheucticus tibialis* LR

Southern Yellow Grosbeak *Pheucticus chrysogaster* LR

Black-backed Grosbeak *Pheucticus aureoventris*

Rose-breasted Grosbeak *Pheucticus ludovicianus*

Black-headed Grosbeak *Pheucticus melanocephalus*

Northern Cardinal *Cardinalis cardinalis*

Vermilion Cardinal *Pyrrhuloxia phoeniceus*

Pyrrhuloxia *Pyrrhuloxia sinuatus*

Yellow-green Grosbeak *Caryothraustes canadensis*

Black-faced Grosbeak *Caryothraustes poliogaster* LR

Yellow-shouldered Grosbeak *Parkerthraustes humeralis*

Crimson-collared Grosbeak *Rhodothraupis celaeno*

Red-and-black Grosbeak *Periporphyrus erythromelas*

Slate-colored Grosbeak *Saltator grossus*

Black-throated Grosbeak *Saltator fuliginosus*

Black-headed Saltator *Saltator atriceps*

Buff-throated Saltator *Saltator maximus*

Black-winged Saltator *Saltator atripennis*

Green-winged Saltator *Saltator similis*

Greyish Saltator *Saltator coerulescens*

Orinocan Saltator *Saltator orenocensis*

Thick-billed Saltator *Saltator maxillosus* PGT

Black-cowled Saltator *Saltator nigriceps* LR

Golden-billed Saltator *Saltator aurantiirostris*

Masked Saltator *Saltator cinctus* GT

Black-throated Saltator *Saltator atricollis*

Rufous-bellied Saltator *Saltator rufiventris* GT

Lesser Antillean Saltator *Saltator albicollis*

Streaked Saltator *Saltator striatipectus* LR

Indigo Grosbeak *Cyanoloxia glaucocaerulea*

Blue-black Grosbeak *Cyanocompsa cyanoides*

Ultramarine Grosbeak *Cyanocompsa brissonii*

Blue Bunting *Cyanocompsa parellina*

Blue Grosbeak *Passerina caerulea*

Indigo Bunting *Passerina cyanea*

Lazuli Bunting *Passerina amoena*

Varied Bunting *Passerina versicolor*

Painted Bunting *Passerina ciris*

Rose-bellied Bunting *Passerina rositae* GT

Orange-breasted Bunting *Passerina leclancherii*

Blue Finch *Porphyrospiza caerulescens* GT

Brown Tanager *Orchesticus abeillei* GT

Cinnamon Tanager *Schistochlamys ruficapillus*

Black-faced Tanager *Schistochlamys melanopis*

White-banded Tanager *Neothraupis fasciata* GT

White-rumped Tanager *Cypsnagra hirundinacea*

Black-and-white Tanager *Conothraupis speculigera* GT

Cone-billed Tanager *Conothraupis mesoleuca* GT

Red-billed Pied Tanager *Lamprospiza melanoleuca*

Magpie Tanager *Cissopis leveriana*

Grass-green Tanager *Chlorornis riefferii*

Scarlet-throated Tanager *Compsothraupis loricata*

White-capped Tanager *Sericossypha albocristata*

Puerto Rican Tanager *Nesospingus speculiferus*

Common Bush-Tanager *Chlorospingus ophthalmicus*

Tacarcuna Bush-Tanager *Chlorospingus tacarcunae* LR

Pirre Bush-Tanager *Chlorospingus inornatus* LR

Dotted Bush-Tanager *Chlorospingus punctatus* LR

Dusky Bush-Tanager *Chlorospingus semifuscus*

Sooty-capped Bush-Tanager *Chlorospingus pileatus*

Yellow-whiskered Bush-Tanager *Chlorospingus parvirostris*

Yellow-throated Bush-Tanager *Chlorospingus flavigularis*

Yellow-green Bush-Tanager *Chlorospingus flavovirens* GT

Ashy-throated Bush-Tanager *Chlorospingus canigularis*

Grey-hooded Bush-Tanager *Cnemoscopus rubrirostris*

Black-capped Hemispingus *Hemispingus atropileus*

Orange-browed Hemispingus *Hemispingus calophrys*

Parodi's Hemispingus *Hemispingus parodii*

Superciliaried Hemispingus *Hemispingus superciliaris*

Grey-capped Hemispingus *Hemispingus reyi* GT

Oleaginous Hemispingus *Hemispingus frontalis*

Black-eared Hemispingus *Hemispingus melanotis*

Western Hemispingus *Hemispingus ochraceus* LR

Piura Hemispingus *Hemispingus piurae* LR

Slaty-backed Hemispingus *Hemispingus goeringi* GT

Rufous-browed Hemispingus *Hemispingus rufosuperciliaris* GT

Black-headed Hemispingus *Hemispingus verticalis*

Drab Hemispingus *Hemispingus xanthophthalmus*

Three-striped Hemispingus *Hemispingus trifasciatus*

Chestnut-headed Tanager *Pyrrhocoma ruficeps*

Fulvous-headed Tanager *Thlypopsis fulviceps*

Rufous-chested Tanager *Thlypopsis ornata*

Brown-flanked Tanager *Thlypopsis pectoralis*

Orange-headed Tanager *Thlypopsis sordida*

Buff-bellied Tanager *Thlypopsis inornata*

Rust-and-yellow Tanager *Thlypopsis ruficeps*

Guira Tanager *Hemithraupis guira*

Rufous-headed Tanager *Hemithraupis ruficapilla*

Yellow-backed Tanager *Hemithraupis flavicollis*

Black-and-yellow Tanager *Chrysothlypis chrysomelas*

Scarlet-and-white Tanager *Erythrothlypis salmoni*

Hooded Tanager *Nemosia pileata*

Cherry-throated Tanager *Nemosia rourei* GT

Black-crowned Palm-Tanager *Phaenicophilus palmarum*

Grey-crowned Palm-Tanager *Phaenicophilus poliocephalus* GT

Eastern Chat-Tanager *Calyptophilus frugivorus* GT

Western Chat-Tanager *Calyptophilus tertius* LR

Rosy Thrush-Tanager *Rhodinocichla rosea*

Dusky-faced Tanager *Mitrospingus cassinii*

Olive-backed Tanager *Mitrospingus oleagineus*

Carmiol's Tanager *Chlorothraupis carmioli*

Olive Tanager *Chlorothraupis frenata* LR

Lemon-spectacled Tanager *Chlorothraupis olivacea* LR

Ochre-breasted Tanager *Chlorothraupis stolzmanni*

Olive-green Tanager *Orthogonys chloricterus*

Grey-headed Tanager *Eucometis penicillata*

Fulvous Shrike-Tanager *Lanio fulvus*

White-winged Shrike-Tanager *Lanio versicolor*

White-throated Shrike-Tanager *Lanio leucothorax* LR

Black-throated Shrike-Tanager *Lanio aurantius* LR

Rufous-crested Tanager *Creurgops verticalis*

Slaty Tanager *Creurgops dentata*

Sulphur-rumped Tanager *Heterospingus rubrifrons* LR

Scarlet-browed Tanager *Heterospingus xanthopygius*

Flame-crested Tanager *Tachyphonus cristatus*

Natterer's Tanager *Tachyphonus nattereri* LR

Yellow-crested Tanager *Tachyphonus rufiventer*

Fulvous-crested Tanager *Tachyphonus surinamus*

White-shouldered Tanager *Tachyphonus luctuosus*

Tawny-crested Tanager *Tachyphonus delatrii*

Ruby-crowned Tanager *Tachyphonus coronatus*

White-lined Tanager *Tachyphonus rufus*

Red-shouldered Tanager *Tachyphonus phoenicius*

Black-goggled Tanager *Trichothraupis melanops*

Red-crowned Ant-Tanager *Habia rubica*

Black-cheeked Ant-Tanager *Habia atrimaxillaris* GT

Red-throated Ant-Tanager *Habia fuscicauda* LR

Sooty Ant-Tanager *Habia gutturalis* GT

Crested Ant-Tanager *Habia cristata*

Flame-colored Tanager *Piranga bidentata*

Hepatic Tanager *Piranga flava*

Highland Hepatic Tanager *Piranga lutea* LR

Northern Hepatic Tanager *Piranga hepatica* LR

Summer Tanager *Piranga rubra*

Rose-throated Tanager *Piranga roseogularis*

Scarlet Tanager *Piranga olivacea*

Western Tanager *Piranga ludoviciana*

White-winged Tanager *Piranga leucoptera*

Red-headed Tanager *Piranga erythrocephala*

Red-hooded Tanager *Piranga rubriceps*

Vermilion Tanager *Calochaetes coccineus*

Crimson-collared Tanager *Ramphocelus sanguinolentus*

Masked Crimson Tanager *Ramphocelus nigrogularis*

Crimson-backed Tanager *Ramphocelus dimidiatus*

Huallaga Tanager *Ramphocelus melanogaster* LR

Silver-beaked Tanager *Ramphocelus carbo*

Brazilian Tanager *Ramphocelus bresilius*

Passerini's Tanager *Ramphocelus passerinii*

Cherrie's Tanager *Ramphocelus costaricensis* LR

Flame-rumped Tanager *Ramphocelus flammigerus*

Lemon-rumped Tanager *Ramphocelus icteronotus* LR

Western Spindalis *Spindalis zena*

Jamaican Spindalis *Spindalis nigricephala* LR

Hispaniolan Spindalis *Spindalis dominicensis* LR

Puerto Rican Spindalis *Spindalis portoricensis* LR

Blue-grey Tanager *Thraupis episcopus*

Sayaca Tanager *Thraupis sayaca* LR

Glaucous Tanager *Thraupis glaucocolpa* LR

Azure-shouldered Tanager *Thraupis cyanoptera* GT

Golden-chevroned Tanager *Thraupis ornata*

Yellow-winged Tanager *Thraupis abbas*

Palm Tanager *Thraupis palmarum*

Blue-capped Tanager *Thraupis cyanocephala*

Blue-and-yellow Tanager *Thraupis bonariensis*

Blue-backed Tanager *Cyanicterus cyanicterus*

Blue-and-gold Tanager *Bangsia arcaei* GT

Black-and-gold Tanager *Bangsia melanochlamys* GT

Golden-chested Tanager *Bangsia rothschildi*

Moss-backed Tanager *Bangsia edwardsi*

Gold-ringed Tanager *Bangsia aureocincta* GT

Hooded Mountain-Tanager *Buthraupis montana*

Black-chested Mountain-Tanager *Buthraupis eximia*

Golden-backed Mountain-Tanager *Buthraupis aureodorsalis* GT

Masked Mountain-Tanager *Buthraupis wetmorei* GT

Orange-throated Tanager *Wetmorethraupis sterrhopteron* GT

Santa Marta Mountain-Tanager *Anisognathus melanogenys* LR

Lacrimose Mountain-Tanager *Anisognathus lacrymosus*

Scarlet-bellied Mountain-Tanager *Anisognathus igniventris*

Blue-winged Mountain-Tanager *Anisognathus somptuosus*

Black-chinned Mountain-Tanager *Anisognathus notabilis*

Diademed Tanager *Stephanophorus diadematus*

Purplish-mantled Tanager *Iridosornis porphyrocephala* GT, LR

Yellow-throated Tanager *Iridosornis analis*

Golden-collared Tanager *Iridosornis jelskii*

Golden-crowned Tanager *Iridosornis rufivertex*

Yellow-scarfed Tanager *Iridosornis reinhardti* LR

Buff-breasted Mountain-Tanager *Dubusia taeniata*

Chestnut-bellied Mountain-Tanager *Delothraupis castaneoventris*

Fawn-breasted Tanager *Pipraeidea melanonota*

Jamaican Euphonia *Euphonia jamaica*

Plumbeous Euphonia *Euphonia plumbea*

Scrub Euphonia *Euphonia affinis*

Yellow-crowned Euphonia *Euphonia luteicapilla*

Purple-throated Euphonia *Euphonia chlorotica*

Trinidad Euphonia *Euphonia trinitatis* LR

Velvet-fronted Euphonia *Euphonia concinna*

Orange-crowned Euphonia *Euphonia saturata*

Finsch's Euphonia *Euphonia finschi*

Violaceous Euphonia *Euphonia violacea*

Thick-billed Euphonia *Euphonia laniirostris*

Yellow-throated Euphonia *Euphonia hirundinacea*

White-lored Euphonia *Euphonia chrysopasta*

Green-chinned Euphonia *Euphonia chalybea* GT

Elegant Euphonia *Euphonia elegantissima* LR

Golden-rumped Euphonia *Euphonia cyanocephala* LR

Blue-hooded Euphonia *Euphonia musica*

Fulvous-vented Euphonia *Euphonia fulvicrissa*

Spot-crowned Euphonia *Euphonia imitans*

Olive-backed Euphonia *Euphonia gouldi*

Bronze-green Euphonia *Euphonia mesochrysa*

White-vented Euphonia *Euphonia minuta*

Tawny-capped Euphonia *Euphonia anneae*

Orange-bellied Euphonia *Euphonia xanthogaster*

Rufous-bellied Euphonia *Euphonia rufiventris*

Chestnut-bellied Euphonia *Euphonia pectoralis*

Golden-sided Euphonia *Euphonia cayennensis*

Yellow-collared Chlorophonia *Chlorophonia flavirostris*

Blue-naped Chlorophonia *Chlorophonia cyanea*

Chestnut-breasted Chlorophonia *Chlorophonia pyrrhophrys*

Blue-crowned Chlorophonia *Chlorophonia occipitalis*

Golden-browed Chlorophonia *Chlorophonia callophrys* LR

Glistening-green Tanager *Chlorochrysa phoenicotis*

Orange-eared Tanager *Chlorochrysa calliparaea*

Multicolored Tanager *Chlorochrysa nitidissima* GT

Plain-colored Tanager *Tangara inornata*

Azure-rumped Tanager *Tangara cabanisi* GT

Grey-and-gold Tanager *Tangara palmeri*

Turquoise Tanager *Tangara mexicana*
Paradise Tanager *Tangara chilensis*
Seven-colored Tanager *Tangara fastuosa* GT
Green-headed Tanager *Tangara seledon*
Red-necked Tanager *Tangara cyanocephala*
Brassy-breasted Tanager *Tangara desmaresti*
Gilt-edged Tanager *Tangara cyanoventris*
Blue-whiskered Tanager *Tangara johannae* GT
Green-and-gold Tanager *Tangara schrankii*
Emerald Tanager *Tangara florida*
Golden Tanager *Tangara arthus*
Silver-throated Tanager *Tangara icterocephala*
Saffron-crowned Tanager *Tangara xanthocephala*
Golden-eared Tanager *Tangara chrysotis*
Flame-faced Tanager *Tangara parzudakii*
Yellow-bellied Tanager *Tangara xanthogastra*
Spotted Tanager *Tangara punctata*
Speckled Tanager *Tangara guttata*
Dotted Tanager *Tangara varia*
Rufous-throated Tanager *Tangara rufigula*
Bay-headed Tanager *Tangara gyrola*
Rufous-winged Tanager *Tangara lavinia*
Burnished-buff Tanager *Tangara cayana*
Lesser Antillean Tanager *Tangara cucullata*
Black-backed Tanager *Tangara peruviana* GT
Chestnut-backed Tanager *Tangara preciosa*
Scrub Tanager *Tangara vitriolina*
Green-capped Tanager *Tangara meyerdeschauenseei* GT
Rufous-cheeked Tanager *Tangara rufigenis*
Golden-naped Tanager *Tangara ruficervix*
Metallic-green Tanager *Tangara labradorides*
Blue-browed Tanager *Tangara cyanotis*
Blue-necked Tanager *Tangara cyanicollis*
Golden-hooded Tanager *Tangara larvata*
Masked Tanager *Tangara nigrocincta*
Spangle-cheeked Tanager *Tangara dowii*
Green-naped Tanager *Tangara fucosa* GT, LR
Beryl-spangled Tanager *Tangara nigroviridis*
Blue-and-black Tanager *Tangara vassorii*
Black-capped Tanager *Tangara heinei*
Sira Tanager *Tangara phillipsi* GT, LR
Silver-backed Tanager *Tangara viridicollis*
Straw-backed Tanager *Tangara argyrofenges*
Black-headed Tanager *Tangara cyanoptera*

Opal-rumped Tanager *Tangara velia*
Opal-crowned Tanager *Tangara callophrys*
Yellow-collared Tanager *Iridophanes pulcherrima*
Turquoise Dacnis *Pseudodacnis hartlaubi* GT
White-bellied Dacnis *Dacnis albiventris*
Black-faced Dacnis *Dacnis lineata*
Yellow-tufted Dacnis *Dacnis egregia* LR
Yellow-bellied Dacnis *Dacnis flaviventer*
Black-legged Dacnis *Dacnis nigripes* GT
Scarlet-thighed Dacnis *Dacnis venusta*
Blue Dacnis *Dacnis cayana*
Viridian Dacnis *Dacnis viguieri* GT
Scarlet-breasted Dacnis *Dacnis berlepschi* GT
Green Honeycreeper *Chlorophanes spiza*
Short-billed Honeycreeper *Cyanerpes nitidus*
Shining Honeycreeper *Cyanerpes lucidus* LR
Purple Honeycreeper *Cyanerpes caeruleus*
Red-legged Honeycreeper *Cyanerpes cyaneus*
Tit-like Dacnis *Xenodacnis parina*
Giant Conebill *Oreomanes fraseri* GT
Cinnamon-bellied Flowerpiercer *Diglossa baritula*
Slaty Flowerpiercer *Diglossa plumbea* LR
Rusty Flowerpiercer *Diglossa sittoides* LR
White-sided Flowerpiercer *Diglossa albilatera*
Chestnut-bellied Flowerpiercer *Diglossa gloriosissima* GT, LR
Glossy Flowerpiercer *Diglossa lafresnayii*
Moustached Flowerpiercer *Diglossa mystacalis* LR
Merida Flowerpiercer *Diglossa gloriosa* LR
Black Flowerpiercer *Diglossa humeralis* LR
Black-throated Flowerpiercer *Diglossa brunneiventris* LR
Grey-bellied Flowerpiercer *Diglossa carbonaria*
Venezuelan Flowerpiercer *Diglossa venezuelensis* GT
Scaled Flowerpiercer *Diglossa duidae*
Greater Flowerpiercer *Diglossa major*
Indigo Flowerpiercer *Diglossopis indigotica*
Golden-eyed Flowerpiercer *Diglossopis glauca*
Bluish Flowerpiercer *Diglossopis caerulescens*
Masked Flowerpiercer *Diglossopis cyanea*
Orangequit *Euneornis campestris*
Swallow-Tanager *Tersina viridis*

Coerebidae

Bananaquit *Coereba flaveola*

Peucedramiidae

Olive Warbler *Peucedramus taeniatus*

Parulidae

Bachman's Warbler *Vermivora bachmanii* GT

Golden-winged Warbler *Vermivora chrysoptera*

Blue-winged Warbler *Vermivora pinus*

Tennessee Warbler *Vermivora peregrina*

Orange-crowned Warbler *Vermivora celata*

Nashville Warbler *Vermivora ruficapilla*

Virginia's Warbler *Vermivora virginiae*

Colima Warbler *Vermivora crissalis* GT

Lucy's Warbler *Vermivora luciae*

Flame-throated Warbler *Parula gutturalis*

Crescent-chested Warbler *Parula superciliosa*

Northern Parula *Parula americana*

Tropical Parula *Parula pitiayumi* LR

Black-and-white Warbler *Mniotilta varia*

Golden Warbler *Dendroica petechia*

American Yellow Warbler *Dendroica aestiva* LR

Cerulean Warbler *Dendroica cerulea*

Black-throated Blue Warbler *Dendroica caerulescens*

Plumbeous Warbler *Dendroica plumbea*

Arrowhead Warbler *Dendroica pharetra*

Elfin Woods Warbler *Dendroica angelae* GT

Pine Warbler *Dendroica pinus*

Chestnut-sided Warbler *Dendroica pensylvanica*

Grace's Warbler *Dendroica graciae*

Adelaide's Warbler *Dendroica adelaidae*

Barbuda Warbler *Dendroica subita* LR

St Lucia Warbler *Dendroica delicata* LR

Olive-capped Warbler *Dendroica pityophila*

Yellow-throated Warbler *Dendroica dominica*

Blackburnian Warbler *Dendroica fusca*

Black-throated Grey Warbler *Dendroica nigrescens*

Townsend's Warbler *Dendroica townsendi*

Hermit Warbler *Dendroica occidentalis*

Golden-cheeked Warbler *Dendroica chrysoparia* GT

Black-throated Green Warbler *Dendroica virens*

Prairie Warbler *Dendroica discolor*

Vitelline Warbler *Dendroica vitellina* GT, LR

Palm Warbler *Dendroica palmarum*

Kirtland's Warbler *Dendroica kirtlandii* GT

Cape May Warbler *Dendroica tigrina*

Magnolia Warbler *Dendroica magnolia*

Yellow-rumped Warbler *Dendroica coronata*

Blackpoll Warbler *Dendroica striata*

Bay-breasted Warbler *Dendroica castanea*

American Redstart *Setophaga ruticilla*

Whistling Warbler *Catharopeza bishopi* GT

Ovenbird *Seiurus aurocapillus*

Northern Waterthrush *Seiurus noveboracensis*

Louisiana Waterthrush *Seiurus motacilla*

Swainson's Warbler *Helmitheros swainsonii*

Worm-eating Warbler *Helmitheros vermivorus*

Prothonotary Warbler *Protonotaria citrea*

Common Yellowthroat *Geothlypis trichas*

Belding's Yellowthroat *Geothlypis beldingi* GT, LR

Altamira Yellowthroat *Geothlypis flavovelata* GT, LR

Bahama Yellowthroat *Geothlypis rostrata*

Olive-crowned Yellowthroat *Geothlypis semiflava*

Black-polled Yellowthroat *Geothlypis speciosa* GT

Hooded Yellowthroat *Geothlypis nelsoni*

Chiriquí Yellowthroat *Geothlypis chiriquensis* LR

Masked Yellowthroat *Geothlypis aequinoctialis*

Black-lored Yellowthroat *Geothlypis auricularis* LR

Southern Yellowthroat *Geothlypis velata* LR

Grey-crowned Yellowthroat *Geothlypis poliocephala*

Kentucky Warbler *Oporornis formosus*

Connecticut Warbler *Oporornis agilis*

Mourning Warbler *Oporornis philadelphia*

MacGillivray's Warbler *Oporornis tolmiei* LR

Green-tailed Ground-Warbler *Microligea palustris*

White-winged Warbler *Xenoligea montana* GT

Yellow-headed Warbler *Teretistris fernandinae*

Oriente Warbler *Teretistris fornsi*

Semper's Warbler *Leucopeza semperi* GT

Hooded Warbler *Wilsonia citrina*

Wilson's Warbler *Wilsonia pusilla*

Canada Warbler *Wilsonia canadensis*

American Red-faced Warbler *Cardellina rubrifrons*

Red Warbler *Ergaticus ruber*

Pink-headed Warbler *Ergaticus versicolor* GT, LR

Painted Whitestart *Myioborus pictus*

Slate-throated Whitestart *Myioborus miniatus*

Guaiquinima Whitestart *Myioborus cardonai* GT

White-faced Whitestart *Myioborus albifacies*

Tepui Whitestart *Myioborus castaneocapillus* LR

Brown-capped Whitestart *Myioborus brunniceps*

Paria Whitestart *Myioborus pariae* GT

Collared Whitestart *Myioborus torquatus*

Golden-fronted Whitestart *Myioborus ornatus* LR

Spectacled Whitestart *Myioborus melanocephalus* LR

White-fronted Whitestart *Myioborus albifrons* GT

Yellow-crowned Whitestart *Myioborus flavivertex*

Neotropic Fan-tailed Warbler *Euthlypis lachrymosa*

Grey-and-gold Warbler *Basileuterus fraseri*

Two-banded Warbler *Basileuterus bivittatus*

Golden-bellied Warbler *Basileuterus chrysogaster*

Chocó Warbler *Basileuterus chlorophrys* LR

Citrine Warbler *Basileuterus luteoviridis*

Pale-legged Warbler *Basileuterus signatus*

Black-crested Warbler *Basileuterus nigrocristatus*

Flavescent Warbler *Basileuterus flaveolus*

Grey-headed Warbler *Basileuterus griseiceps* GT

White-rimmed Warbler *Basileuterus leucoblepharus*

White-striped Warbler *Basileuterus leucophrys*

Neotropical River Warbler *Basileuterus rivularis*

Buff-rumped Warbler *Basileuterus fulvicauda* LR

Santa Marta Warbler *Basileuterus basilicus* GT

Grey-throated Warbler *Basileuterus cinereicollis* GT

White-lored Warbler *Basileuterus conspicillatus* GT, LR

Russet-crowned Warbler *Basileuterus coronatus*

Golden-crowned Warbler *Basileuterus culicivorus*

White-bellied Warbler *Basileuterus hypoleucus* LR

Three-striped Warbler *Basileuterus tristriatus*

Rufous-capped Warbler *Basileuterus rufifrons*

Golden-browed Warbler *Basileuterus belli*

Black-cheeked Warbler *Basileuterus melanogenys*

Pirre Warbler *Basileuterus ignotus* GT

Three-banded Warbler *Basileuterus trifasciatus*

Pardusco *Nephelornis oneilli*

Wrenthrush *Zeledonia coronata*

Red-breasted Chat *Granatellus venustus*

Grey-throated Chat *Granatellus sallaei*

Rose-breasted Chat *Granatellus pelzelni*

Yellow-breasted Chat *Icteria virens*

Chestnut-vented Conebill *Conirostrum speciosum*

White-eared Conebill *Conirostrum leucogenys*

Bicolored Conebill *Conirostrum bicolor*

Pearly-breasted Conebill *Conirostrum margaritae*

Cinereous Chat *Conirostrum cinereum*

Tamarugo Conebill *Conirostrum tamarugense* GT

White-browed Conebill *Conirostrum ferrugineiventre*

Rufous-browed Conebill *Conirostrum rufum*

Blue-backed Conebill *Conirostrum sitticolor*

Capped Conebill *Conirostrum albifrons*

Drepanididae

Lana'i Hookbill *Dysmorodrepanis munroi* E

Laysan Finch *Telespiza cantans* GT

Nihoa Finch *Telespiza ultima* GT

O'u *Psittirostra psittacea* GT

Palila *Loxioides bailleui* GT

Lesser Koa-Finch *Rhodacanthis flaviceps* E

Greater Koa-Finch *Rhodacanthis palmeri* E

Kona Finch *Chloridops kona* E

Maui Parrotbill *Pseudonestor xanthophrys* GT

Kaua'i Amakihi *Viridonia stejnegeri* GT, LR

Hawaii Amakihi *Viridonia virens*

O'ahu Amakihi *Viridonia flava* GT, LR

Anianiau *Viridonia parva* GT

Greater Amakihi *Viridonia sagittirostris* E

Greater Akialoa *Hemignathus ellisianus* LR

Lesser Akialoa *Hemignathus obscurus* E
Nukupu'u *Hemignathus lucidus* GT
Akiapolaa'u *Hemignathus munroi* GT
Akikiki *Oreomystis bairdi* GT
Hawaii Creeper *Oreomystis mana* GT
Maui Alauahio *Paroreomyza montana* GT, LR
Kakawahie *Paroreomyza flammea* E
O'ahu 'Alauahio *Paroreomyza maculata* GT
Akeke'e *Loxops caeruleirostris* GT
Akepa *Loxops coccineus* GT
Ula-ai-hawane *Ciridops anna* E
Iiwi *Vestiaria coccinea* GT
Hawaii Mamo *Drepanis pacifica* E
Black Mamo *Drepanis funerea* E
Akohekohe *Palmeria dolei* GT
Apapane *Himatione sanguinea*
Po'o-uli *Melamprosops phaeosoma* GT

Vireonidae

Rufous-browed Peppershrike *Cyclarhis gujanensis*
Black-billed Peppershrike *Cyclarhis nigrirostris*
Chestnut-sided Shrike-Vireo *Vireolanius melitophrys*
Green Shrike-Vireo *Vireolanius pulchellus*
Yellow-browed Shrike-Vireo *Vireolanius eximius* LR
Slaty-capped Shrike-Vireo *Vireolanius leucotis*
Slaty Vireo *Vireo brevipennis*
Hutton's Vireo *Vireo huttoni*
Black-capped Vireo *Vireo atricapillas* GT
White-eyed Vireo *Vireo griseus*
Mangrove Vireo *Vireo pallens* LR
St Andrew Vireo *Vireo caribaeus* GT, LR
Cuban Vireo *Vireo gundlachii* LR
Thick-billed Vireo *Vireo crassirostris* LR
Cozumel Vireo *Vireo bairdi*
Chocó Vireo *Vireo masteri* GT
Grey Vireo *Vireo vicinior*
Bell's Vireo *Vireo bellii*
Dwarf Vireo *Vireo nelsoni* LR
Jamaican White-eyed Vireo *Vireo modestus*
Flat-billed Vireo *Vireo nanus*
Puerto Rican Vireo *Vireo latimeri*
Blue Mountain Vireo *Vireo osburni* GT
Carmiol's Vireo *Vireo carmioli*
Blue-headed Vireo *Vireo solitarius*

Plumbeous Vireo *Vireo plumbeus* LR
Cassin's Vireo *Vireo cassinii* LR
Yellow-throated Vireo *Vireo flavifrons*
Red-eyed Vireo *Vireo olivaceus*
Noronha Vireo *Vireo gracilirostris* GT, LR
Yellow-green Vireo *Vireo flavoviridis* LR
Yucatan Vireo *Vireo magister*
Black-whiskered Vireo *Vireo altiloquus*
Golden Vireo *Vireo hypochryseus*
Philadelphia Vireo *Vireo philadelphicus*
Western Warbling Vireo *Vireo swainsonii* LR
Eastern Warbling Vireo *Vireo gilvus*
Brown-capped Vireo *Vireo leucophrys* LR
Grey-eyed Greenlet *Hylophilus amaurocephalus* LR
Rufous-crowned Greenlet *Hylophilus poicilotis*
Lemon-chested Greenlet *Hylophilus thoracicus*
Grey-chested Greenlet *Hylophilus semicinereus*
Ashy-headed Greenlet *Hylophilus pectoralis*
Tepui Greenlet *Hylophilus sclateri*
Buff-cheeked Greenlet *Hylophilus muscicapinus*
Brown-headed Greenlet *Hylophilus brunneiceps*
Rufous-naped Greenlet *Hylophilus semibrunneus*
Golden-fronted Greenlet *Hylophilus aurantiifrons*
Dusky-capped Greenlet *Hylophilus hypoxanthus*
Scrub Greenlet *Hylophilus flavipes* LR
Olivaceous Greenlet *Hylophilus olivaceus*
Tawny-crowned Greenlet *Hylophilus ochraceiceps*
Lesser Greenlet *Hylophilus decurtatus*

Fringillidae

European Chaffinch *Fringilla coelebs*
Blue Chaffinch *Fringilla teydea* GT
Brambling *Fringilla montifringilla*
Red-fronted Serin *Serinus pusillus*
European Serin *Serinus serinus*
Syrian Serin *Serinus syriacus* GT, LR
Canary *Serinus canaria*
Citril Finch *Serinus citrinella*
Corsican Finch *Serinus corsicana* LR
Tibetan Siskin *Serinus thibetanus*
Yellow-crowned Canary *Serinus canicollis*
Abyssinian Siskin *Serinus nigriceps*

Western Citril *Serinus frontalis* LR

African Citril *Serinus citrinelloides*

East African Citril *Serinus hypostictus* LR

Black-faced Canary *Serinus capistratus*

Papyrus Serin *Serinus koliensis* LR

Forest Canary *Serinus scotops*

White-rumped Seedeater *Serinus leucopygius*

Arabian Yellow-rumped Serin *Serinus rothschildi* LR

Abyssinian Yellow-rumped Seedeater *Serinus xanthopygius* LR

Kenyan Yellow-rumped Seedeater *Serinus reichenowi* LR

Yellow-throated Serin *Serinus flavigula* GT, LR

Salvadori's Serin *Serinus xantholaema* GT, LR

Lemon-breasted Seedeater *Serinus citrinipectus*

Yellow-fronted Serin *Serinus mozambicus*

Southern Yellow-rumped Seedeater *Serinus atrogularis*

Abyssinian Grosbeak Canary *Serinus donaldsoni*

Kenya Grosbeak Canary *Serinus buchanani* LR

Yellow Canary *Serinus flaviventris*

White-bellied Serin *Serinus dorsostriatus*

Brimstone Serin *Serinus sulphuratus*

White-throated Canary *Serinus albogularis*

Stripe-breasted Serin *Serinus reichardi*

West African Serin *Serinus canicapillus* LR

Streaky-headed Serin *Serinus gularis*

Black-eared Serin *Serinus mennelli*

Brown-rumped Serin *Serinus tristriatus*

Ankober Serin *Serinus ankoberensis* GT

Yemen Serin *Serinus menachensis*

Streaky Serin *Serinus striolatus*

Yellow-browed Seedeater *Serinus whytii* LR

Thick-billed Serin *Serinus burtoni*

Kipengere Seedeater *Serinus melanochrous* GT, LR

White-winged Seedeater *Serinus leucopterus*

Príncipe Seedeater *Serinus rufobrunneus*

Cape Siskin *Serinus totta*

Drakensberg Siskin *Serinus symonsi* LR

Black-headed Canary *Serinus alario*

Damara Canary *Serinus leucolaema* LR

Mountain Serin *Serinus estherae*

São Tomé Grosbeak *Neospiza concolor* GT

Oriole Finch *Linurgus olivaceus*

Golden-winged Grosbeak *Rhynchostruthus socotranus*

European Greenfinch *Carduelis chloris*

Oriental Greenfinch *Carduelis sinica*

Himalayan Greenfinch *Carduelis spinoides*

Vietnamese Greenfinch *Carduelis monguilloti* GT, LR

Black-headed Greenfinch *Carduelis ambigua* LR

Eurasian Siskin *Carduelis spinus*

Pine Siskin *Carduelis pinus*

Black-capped Siskin *Carduelis atriceps* LR

Andean Siskin *Carduelis spinescens*

Yellow-faced Siskin *Carduelis yarrellii* GT

Red Siskin *Carduelis cucullata* GT

Thick-billed Siskin *Carduelis crassirostris*

Hooded Siskin *Carduelis magellanica*

Antillean Siskin *Carduelis dominicensis*

Saffron Siskin *Carduelis siemiradzkii* GT, LR

Olivaceous Siskin *Carduelis olivacea*

Black-headed Siskin *Carduelis notata*

Yellow-bellied Siskin *Carduelis xanthogastra*

Black Siskin *Carduelis atrata*

Yellow-rumped Siskin *Carduelis uropygialis*

Black-chinned Siskin *Carduelis barbata*

American Goldfinch *Carduelis tristis*

Lesser Goldfinch *Carduelis psaltria*

Lawrence's Goldfinch *Carduelis lawrencei*

European Goldfinch *Carduelis carduelis*

Arctic Redpoll *Acanthis hornemanni* LR

Common Redpoll *Acanthis flammea*

Lesser Redpoll *Acanthis cabaret* LR

Twite *Acanthis flavirostris*

Eurasian Linnet *Acanthis cannabina*

Yemeni Linnet *Acanthis yemenensis*

Warsangli Linnet *Acanthis johannis* GT

Hodgson's Mountain-Finch *Leucosticte nemoricola*

Brandt's Mountain-Finch *Leucosticte brandti*

Sillem's Mountain-Finch *Leucosticte sillemi* PGT, LR

Arctic Rosy-Finch *Leucosticte arctoa*

Grey-crowned Rosy-Finch *Leucosticte tephrocotis* LR

Black Rosy-Finch *Leucosticte atrata* LR

Brown-capped Rosy-Finch *Leucosticte australis* LR

Red-browed Finch *Callacanthis burtoni*

Crimson-winged Finch *Rhodopechys sanguinea*

Desert-Finch *Rhodopechys obsoleta*

Trumpeter-Finch *Bucanetes githagineus*

Mongolian Finch *Bucanetes mongolicus* LR

Long-tailed Rosefinch *Uragus sibiricus*

Przewalski's Rosefinch *Urocynchramus pylzowi*

Blanford's Rosefinch *Carpodacus rubescens*

Dark Rosefinch *Carpodacus nipalensis*

Common Rosefinch *Carpodacus erythrinus*

Purple Finch *Carpodacus purpureus*

Cassin's Finch *Carpodacus cassinii*

House Finch *Carpodacus mexicanus*

Beautiful Rosefinch *Carpodacus pulcherrimus*

Stresemann's Rosefinch *Carpodacus eos* LR

Pink-browed Rosefinch *Carpodacus rodochrous*

Vinaceus Rosefinch *Carpodacus vinaceus*

Dark-rumped Rosefinch *Carpodacus edwardsii*

Sinai Rosefinch *Carpodacus synoicus*

Pallas's Rosefinch *Carpodacus roseus*

Three-banded Rosefinch *Carpodacus trifasciatus*

Spot-winged Rosefinch *Carpodacus rodopeplus*

White-browed Rosefinch *Carpodacus thura*

Red-mantled Rosefinch *Carpodacus rhodochlamys*

Eastern Great Rosefinch *Carpodacus rubicilloides*

Caucasian Great Rosefinch *Carpodacus rubicilla*

Red-breasted Rosefinch *Carpodacus puniceus*

Tibetan Rosefinch *Carpodacus roborowskii*

Bonin Islands Grosbeak *Chaunoproctus ferreorostris* E

Pine Grosbeak *Pinicola enucleator*

Red-headed Rosefinch *Propyrrhula subhimachala*

Scarlet Finch *Haematospiza sipahi*

Parrot Crossbill *Loxia pytyopsittacus*

Scottish Crossbill *Loxia scotica* PGT, LR

Common Crossbill *Loxia curvirostra*

Hispaniolan Crossbill *Loxia megaplaga* GT, LR

White-winged Crossbill *Loxia leucoptera*

Brown Bullfinch *Pyrrhula nipalensis*

Philippine Bullfinch *Pyrrhula leucogenis*

Orange Bullfinch *Pyrrhula aurantiaca*

Red-headed Bullfinch *Pyrrhula erythrocephala*

Beavan's Bullfinch *Pyrrhula erythaca*

Common Bullfinch *Pyrrhula pyrrhula*

Azores Bullfinch *Pyrrhula murina* GT, LR

Hawfinch *Coccothraustes coccothraustes*

Evening Grosbeak *Hesperiphona vespertina*

Hooded Grosbeak *Hesperiphona abeillei*

Chinese Grosbeak *Eophona migratoria*

Japanese Grosbeak *Eophona personata*

Black-and-yellow Grosbeak *Mycerobas icterioides*

Collared Grosbeak *Mycerobas affinis*

Spotted-winged Grosbeak *Mycerobas melanozanthos*

White-winged Grosbeak *Mycerobas carnipes*

Gold-naped Finch *Pyrrhoplectes epauletta*

Estrildidae

Woodhouse's Antpecker *Parmoptila woodhouse*

Red-fronted Antpecker *Parmoptila rubrifrons*

Jameson's Antpecker *Parmoptila jamesoni* LR

White-breasted Negrofinch *Nigrita fusconota*

Chestnut-breasted Negrofinch *Nigrita bicolor*

Pale-fronted Negrofinch *Nigrita luteifrons*

Grey-headed Negrofinch *Nigrita canicapilla*

Fernando Po Oliveback *Nesocharis shelleyi* LR

White-collared Oliveback *Nesocharis ansorgei*

Grey-headed Oliveback *Nesocharis capistrata*

Crimson-winged Pytilia *Pytilia phoenicoptera*

Lineated Pytilia *Pytilia lineata* LR

Red-faced Pytilia *Pytilia hypogrammica*

Orange-winged Pytilia *Pytilia afra*

Green-winged Pytilia *Pytilia melba*

Red-faced Crimsonwing *Cryptospiza reichenovii*

Ethiopian Crimsonwing *Cryptospiza salvadorii*

Dusky Crimsonwing *Cryptospiza jacksoni*

Shelley's Crimsonwing *Cryptospiza shelleyi* GT

Crimson Seedcracker *Pyrenestes sanguineus*

Black-bellied Seedcracker *Pyrenestes ostrinus*

Lesser Seedcracker *Pyrenestes minor*

Grant's Bluebill *Spermophaga poliogenys*

Western Bluebill *Spermophaga haematina*

Red-headed Bluebill *Spermophaga ruficapilla* LR

Brown Twinspot *Clytospiza monteiri*

Green-backed Twinspot *Mandingoa nitidula*

Rosy Twinspot *Hypargos margaritatus*

Red-throated Twinspot *Hypargos niveoguttatus*

Dybowski's Twinspot *Euschistospiza dybowskii*

Dusky Twinspot *Euschistospiza cinereovinacea*

Black-bellied Firefinch *Lagonosticta rara*

Bar-breasted Firefinch *Lagonosticta rufopicta*

Brown Firefinch *Lagonosticta nitidula* LR

Red-billed Firefinch *Lagonosticta senegala*

Kulikoro Firefinch *Lagonosticta virata* LR

Rock Firefinch *Lagonosticta sanguinodorsalis* LR

African Firefinch *Lagonosticta rubricata*

Pale-billed Firefinch *Lagonosticta landanae* LR

Jameson's Firefinch *Lagonosticta rhodopareia*

Chad Firefinch *Lagonosticta umbrinodorsalis* LR

Black-throated Firefinch *Lagonosticta larvata*

Black-faced Firefinch *Lagonosticta vinacea* LR

Blue-cheeked Cordonbleu *Uraeginthus angolensis*

Red-cheeked Cordonbleu *Uraeginthus bengalus*

Blue-capped Cordonbleu *Uraeginthus cyanocephalus*

Common Grenadier *Uraeginthus granatina*

Purple Grenadier *Uraeginthus ianthinogaster*

Lavender Waxbill *Estrilda caerulescens*

Black-tailed Lavender Waxbill *Estrilda perreini*

Cinderella Waxbill *Estrilda thomensis* GT

Swee Waxbill *Estrilda melanotis*

Yellow-bellied Waxbill *Estrilda quartinia* LR

Anambra Waxbill *Estrilda poliopareia* GT, LR

Fawn-breasted Waxbill *Estrilda paludicola*

Abyssinian Waxbill *Estrilda ochrogaster* LR

Orange-cheeked Waxbill *Estrilda melpoda*

Crimson-rumped Waxbill *Estrilda rhodopyga*

Arabian Waxbill *Estrilda rufibarba*

Black-rumped Waxbill *Estrilda troglodytes*

Common Waxbill *Estrilda astrild*

Black-lored Waxbill *Estrilda nigriloris* PGT, LR

Black-crowned Waxbill *Estrilda nonnula*

Black-headed Waxbill *Estrilda atricapilla*

Kandt's Waxbill *Estrilda kandti* LR

Black-faced Waxbill *Estrilda erythronotos*

Red-rumped Waxbill *Estrilda charmosyna*

Red Avadavat *Amandava amandava*

Green Avadavat *Amandava formosa* GT

Zebra Waxbill *Amandava subflava*

African Quailfinch *Ortygospiza atricollis*

Black-chinned Quailfinch *Ortygospiza gabonensis* LR

Common Locustfinch *Ortygospiza locustella*

Painted Finch *Emblema pictum*

Beautiful Firetail *Stagonopleura bella*

Red-eared Firetail *Stagonopleura oculata*

Diamond Firetail *Stagonopleura guttata* GT

Crimson-sided Mountain-Finch *Oreostruthus fuliginosus*

Red-browed Firetail *Neochmia temporalis* LR

Crimson Finch *Neochmia phaeton*

Star Finch *Neochmia ruficauda* GT

Plum-headed Finch *Aidemosyne modesta*

Zebra Finch *Taeniopygia guttata*

Chestnut-eared Finch *Taeniopygia castanotis* LR

Double-barred Finch *Taeniopygia bichenovii*

Masked Finch *Poephila personata*

Long-tailed Finch *Poephila acuticauda*

Black-throated Finch *Poephila cincta*

Tawny-breasted Parrotfinch *Erythrura hyperytra*

Pin-tailed Parrotfinch *Erythrura prasina*

Green-faced Parrotfinch *Erythrura viridifacies* GT

Three-colored Parrotfinch *Erythrura tricolor*

Red-eared Parrotfinch *Erythrura coloria* GT

Blue-faced Parrotfinch *Erythrura trichroa*

Papuan Parrotfinch *Erythrura papuana* LR

Red-throated Parrotfinch *Erythrura psittacea*

Fiji Parrotfinch *Erythrura pealii*

Red-headed Parrotfinch *Erythrura cyaneovirens*

Royal Parrotfinch *Erythrura regia* GT, LR

Pink-billed Parrotfinch *Erythrura kleinschmidti* GT

Gouldian Finch *Chloebia gouldiae* GT

Madagascar Munia *Lemuresthes nana*

African Silverbill *Euodice cantans* LR

Indian Silverbill *Euodice malabarica*

Grey-headed Silverbill *Euodice griseicapilla*

Bronze Mannikin *Lonchura cucullata*

Black-and-white Mannikin *Lonchura bicolor*

Brown-backed Munia *Lonchura nigriceps* LR

Magpie Munia *Lonchura fringilloides*

White-rumped Munia *Lonchura striata*

Javan White-bellied Munia *Lonchura leucogastroides*

Dusky Munia *Lonchura fuscans*

Black-faced Munia *Lonchura molucca*

Black-throated Munia *Lonchura kelaarti*

Scaly-breasted Munia *Lonchura punctulata*

White-bellied Munia *Lonchura leucogastra*

Streak-headed Mannikin *Lonchura tristissima*

White-spotted Mannikin *Lonchura leucosticta*

Chestnut-and-white Munia *Lonchura quinticolor*

Cream-bellied Munia *Lonchura pallidiventer* LR, PH

Black-headed Munia *Lonchura malacca*

Chestnut Munia *Lonchura atricapilla* LR

White-capped Munia *Lonchura ferruginosa* LR

White-headed Munia *Lonchura maja*

Pale-headed Munia *Lonchura pallida*

Great-billed Munia *Lonchura grandis*

Grey-banded Mannikin *Lonchura vana* GT

Grey-headed Mannikin *Lonchura caniceps*

Grey-crowned Munia *Lonchura nevermanni*

Black Mannikin *Lonchura stygia* GT

New Britain Mannikin *Lonchura spectabilis*

New Ireland Munia *Lonchura forbesi*

Hunstein's Munia *Lonchura hunsteini*

New Hanover Munia *Lonchura nigerrima* LR

Yellow-rumped Munia *Lonchura flaviprymna*

Chestnut-breasted Munia *Lonchura castaneothorax*

Grand Valley Munia *Lonchura teerinki*

Eastern Alpine Munia *Lonchura monticola* LR

Snow Mountain Munia *Lonchura montana*

Thick-billed Munia *Lonchura melaena*

Timor Dusky Sparrow *Lonchura fuscata* GT

Java Sparrow *Lonchura oryzivora* GT

Pictorella Finch *Heteromunia pectoralis* GT

Red-headed Finch *Amadina erythrocephala*

Cut-throat Finch *Amadina fasciata*

Viduidae

Village Indigobird *Vidua chalybeata*

Jambandu Indigobird *Vidua raricola*

Baka Indigobird *Vidua larvaticola*

Jos Plateau Indigobird *Vidua maryae* LR

Quailfinch Indigobird *Vidua nigeriae* LR, PH

Purple Indigobird *Vidua purpurascens*

Variable Indigobird *Vidua funerea*

Pale-winged Indigobird *Vidua wilsoni*

Cameroon Indigobird *Vidua camerunensis* LR, PH

Steel-blue Whydah *Vidua hypocherina*

Twinspot Indigobird *Vidua codringtoni* LR

Straw-tailed Whydah *Vidua fischeri*

Shaft-tailed Whydah *Vidua regia*

Pin-tailed Whydah *Vidua macroura*

Eastern Paradise-Whydah *Vidua paradisaea*

Togo Paradise-Whydah *Vidua togoensis* LR

Long-tailed Paradise-Whydah *Vidua interjecta* LR

Northern Paradise-Whydah *Vidua orientalis*

Broad-tailed Paradise-Whydah *Vidua obtusa* LR

Ploceidae

White-billed Buffalo-Weaver *Bubalornis albirostris*

Red-billed Buffalo-Weaver *Bubalornis niger* LR

White-headed Buffalo-Weaver *Dinemellia dinemelli*

White-browed Sparrow-Weaver *Plocepasser mahali*

Chestnut-crowned Sparrow-Weaver *Plocepasser superciliosus*

Donaldson-Smith's Sparrow-Weaver *Plocepasser donaldsoni*

Chestnut-mantled Sparrow-Weaver *Plocepasser rufoscapulatus*

Rufous-tailed Weaver *Histurgops ruficauda*

Grey-capped Social-Weaver *Pseudonigrita arnaudi*

Black-capped Social-Weaver *Pseudonigrita cabanisi*

Common Social-Weaver *Philetairus socius*

Scaly Weaver *Sporopipes squamifrons*

Speckle-fronted Weaver *Sporopipes frontalis*

Baglafecht Weaver *Ploceus baglafecht*

Bannerman's Weaver *Ploceus bannermani* GT

Black-chinned Weaver *Ploceus nigrimentum* GT

Bertrand's Weaver *Ploceus bertrandi*

Bates's Weaver *Ploceus batesi* GT

Slender-billed Weaver *Ploceus pelzelni*

Loango Weaver *Ploceus subpersonatus* GT

Little Weaver *Ploceus luteolus*

Lesser Masked-Weaver *Ploceus intermedius*

Spectacled Weaver *Ploceus ocularis*

Black-necked Weaver *Ploceus nigricollis*

Strange Weaver *Ploceus alienus*

Black-billed Weaver *Ploceus melanogaster*

Cape Weaver *Ploceus capensis*

Bocage's Weaver *Ploceus temporalis*

African Golden-Weaver *Ploceus subaureus*

Holub's Golden-Weaver *Ploceus xanthops*

Kilombero Weaver *Ploceus burnieri* GT, LR

Orange Weaver *Ploceus aurantius*

Príncipe Golden-Weaver *Ploceus princeps*

Golden Palm Weaver *Ploceus bojeri*

Taveta Golden-Weaver *Ploceus castaneiceps*

Southern Brown-throated Weaver *Ploceus xanthopterus*

Heuglin's Masked-Weaver *Ploceus heuglini*

Northern Brown-throated Weaver *Ploceus castanops*

Rüppell's Weaver *Ploceus galbula*

Victoria Masked-Weaver *Ploceus victoriae* PGT

Northern Masked-Weaver *Ploceus taeniopterus*

Southern Masked-Weaver *Ploceus velatus*

Ruwet's Masked-Weaver *Ploceus ruweti* PGT, LR

Katanga Masked-Weaver *Ploceus katangae* LR

Tanzanian Masked-Weaver *Ploceus reichardi* LR

Vitelline Masked-Weaver *Ploceus vitellinus* LR

Speke's Weaver *Ploceus spekei*

Fox's Weaver *Ploceus spekeoides*

Village Weaver *Ploceus cucullatus*

Layard's Weaver *Ploceus nigriceps* LR

Giant Weaver *Ploceus grandis*

Vieillot's Black Weaver *Ploceus nigerrimus*

Weyns's Weaver *Ploceus weynsi*

Clarke's Weaver *Ploceus golandi* GT

Salvadori's Weaver *Ploceus dichrocephalus*

Yellow-backed Weaver *Ploceus melanocephalus*

Jackson's Golden-backed Weaver *Ploceus jacksoni*

Cinnamon Weaver *Ploceus badius*

Chestnut Weaver *Ploceus rubiginosus*

Golden-naped Weaver *Ploceus aureonucha* GT

Yellow-mantled Weaver *Ploceus tricolor*

Maxwell's Black Weaver *Ploceus albinucha*

Nelicourvi Weaver *Ploceus nelicourvi*

Sakalava Weaver *Ploceus sakalava* LR

Asian Golden-Weaver *Ploceus hypoxanthus* GT

Finn's Weaver *Ploceus megarhynchus* GT

Black-breasted Weaver *Ploceus benghalensis*

Streaked Weaver *Ploceus manyar*

Baya Weaver *Ploceus philippinus*

Dark-backed Weaver *Ploceus bicolor*

Western Golden-backed Weaver *Ploceus preussi*

Yellow-capped Weaver *Ploceus dorsomaculatus*

Olive-headed Weaver *Ploceus olivaceiceps* GT

Usambara Weaver *Ploceus nicolli* GT

Brown-capped Weaver *Ploceus insignis*

Bar-winged Weaver *Ploceus angolensis*

São Tomé Weaver *Ploceus sanctithomae*

Compact Weaver *Pachyphantes superciliosus*

Yellow-legged Malimbe *Malimbus flavipes* GT

Red-crowned Malimbe *Malimbus coronatus*

Black-throated Malimbe *Malimbus cassini*

Rachel's Malimbe *Malimbus racheliae*

Gola Malimbe *Malimbus ballmanni* GT

Red-vented Malimbe *Malimbus scutatus*

Ibadan Malimbe *Malimbus ibadanensis* GT

Gray's Malimbe *Malimbus nitens*

Red-bellied Malimbe *Malimbus erythrogaster*

Red-headed Malimbe *Malimbus rubricollis*

Crested Malimbe *Malimbus malimbicus*

Red-headed Anaplectes *Anaplectes rubriceps*

Cardinal Quelea *Quelea cardinalis*

Red-headed Quelea *Quelea erythrops*

Red-billed Quelea *Quelea quelea*

Madagascar Red Fody *Foudia madagascariensis*

Mascarene Fody *Foudia eminentissima*

Red Forest Fody *Foudia omissa* LR

Aldabra Red Fody *Foudia aldabrana* LR

Mauritius Fody *Foudia rubra* GT

Seychelles Fody *Foudia sechellarum* GT

Rodrigues Fody *Foudia flavicans* GT

Bob-tailed Weaver *Brachycope anomala*

Yellow-crowned Bishop *Euplectes afer*

Fire-fronted Bishop *Euplectes diadematus*

Zanzibar Bishop *Euplectes nigroventris*

Black Bishop *Euplectes gierowii*

Black-winged Red Bishop *Euplectes hordeaceus*

Northern Red Bishop *Euplectes franciscanus* LR

Southern Red Bishop *Euplectes orix*

Golden-backed Bishop *Euplectes aureus*

Yellow Bishop *Euplectes capensis*

Fan-tailed Widowbird *Euplectes axillaris*

Yellow-mantled Widowbird *Euplectes macrourus*

Hartlaub's Marsh Widowbird *Euplectes hartlaubi*

Buff-shouldered Widowbird *Euplectes psammocromius*

Long-tailed Widowbird *Euplectes progne*

White-winged Widowbird *Euplectes albonotatus*

Red-collared Widowbird *Euplectes ardens*

Jackson's Widowbird *Euplectes jacksoni* GT

Parasitic Weaver *Anomalospiza imberbis*

Grosbeak Weaver *Amblyospiza albifrons*

Passeridae

Saxaul Sparrow *Passer ammodendri*

House Sparrow *Passer domesticus*

Spanish Sparrow *Passer hispaniolensis* LR

Sind Sparrow *Passer pyrrhonotus*

Somali Sparrow *Passer castanopterus*

Cinnamon Sparrow *Passer rutilans*

Plain-backed Sparrow *Passer flaveolus*

Dead Sea Sparrow *Passer moabiticus*

Iago Sparrow *Passer iagoensis* LR

Southern Rufous Sparrow *Passer motitensis*

Cape Sparrow *Passer melanurus*

Socotra Sparrow *Passer insularis* LR

Kenya Rufous Sparrow *Passer rufocinctus* LR

Grey-headed Sparrow *Passer griseus*

Swainson's Sparrow *Passer swainsonii* LR

Parrot-billed Sparrow *Passer gongonensis* LR

Swahili Sparrow *Passer suahelicus* LR

Southern Grey-headed Sparrow *Passer diffusus* LR

Desert Sparrow *Passer simplex*

Eurasian Tree Sparrow *Passer montanus*

Sudan Golden Sparrow *Auripasser luteus*

Arabian Golden Sparrow *Auripasser euchlorus* LR

Chestnut Sparrow *Sorella eminibey*

Pale Rock-Sparrow *Carpospiza brachydactyla*

Yellow-spotted Petronia *Petronia pyrgita* LR

Yellow-throated Petronia *Petronia xanthocollis* LR

Rock Petronia *Petronia petronia*

South African Petronia *Petronia supercilliaris*

Bush Petronia *Petronia dentata*

White-winged Snowfinch *Montifringilla nivalis*

Tibetan Snowfinch *Montifringilla adamsi* LR

Theresa's Snowfinch *Montifringilla theresae*

White-rumped Snowfinch *Pyrgilauda taczanowskii*

Père David's Snowfinch *Pyrgilauda davidiana*

Rufous-necked Snowfinch *Pyrgilauda ruficollis*

Plain-backed Snowfinch *Pyrgilauda blanfordi*

Icteridae

Casqued Oropendola *Clypicterus oseryi*

Crested Oropendola *Psarocolius decumanus*

Green Oropendola *Psarocolius viridis*

Dusky-green Oropendola *Psarocolius atrovirens*

Russet-backed Oropendola *Psarocolius angustifrons*

Chestnut-headed Oropendola *Zarhynchus wagleri*

Band-tailed Oropendola *Ocyalus latirostris*

Montezuma Oropendola *Gymnostinops montezuma* LR

Baudó Oropendola *Gymnostinops cassini* GT, LR

Para Oropendola *Gymnostinops bifasciatus*

Olive Oropendola *Gymnostinops yuracares* LR

Black Oropendola *Gymnostinops guatimozinus* LR

Yellow-rumped Cacique *Cacicus cela*

Red-rumped Cacique *Cacicus haemorrhous*

Scarlet-rumped Cacique *Cacicus microrhynchus* LR

Subtropical Cacique *Cacicus uropygialis*

Golden-winged Cacique *Cacicus chrysopterus*

Selva Cacique *Cacicus koepckeae* GT

Southern Mountain Cacique *Cacicus chrysonotus*

Northern Mountain Cacique *Cacicus leucoramphus* LR

Ecuadorian Cacique *Cacicus sclateri*

Solitary Cacique *Cacicus solitarius*

Yellow-winged Cacique *Cacicus melanicterus*

Yellow-billed Cacique *Amblycercus holosericeus*

Yellow-backed Oriole *Icterus chrysater*

Yellow Oriole *Icterus nigrogularis*

Jamaican Oriole *Icterus leucopteryx*

Orange Oriole *Icterus auratus*

Yellow-tailed Oriole *Icterus mesomelas*

White-edged Oriole *Icterus graceannae*

Spot-breasted Oriole *Icterus pectoralis*

Altamira Oriole *Icterus gularis*

Streak-backed Oriole *Icterus pustulatus*

Troupial *Icterus icterus*

Orange-backed Troupial *Icterus croconotus* LR

Campo Troupial *Icterus jamacaii* LR

Baltimore Oriole *Icterus galbula*

Bullock's Oriole *Icterus bullockii* LR

Abeillé's Oriole *Icterus abeillei* LR

Orchard Oriole *Icterus spurius*

Moriche Oriole *Icterus chrysocephalus* LR

Hooded Oriole *Icterus cucullatus*

Epaulette Oriole *Icterus cayanensis*

Orange-crowned Oriole *Icterus auricapillus*

Greater Antillean Oriole *Icterus dominicensis*

Central American Black-cowled Oriole *Icterus prosthemelas* LR

Black-vented Oriole *Icterus wagleri*

Montserrat Oriole *Icterus oberi* GT

Bar-winged Oriole *Icterus maculialatus*

Scott's Oriole *Icterus parisorum*

St Lucia Oriole *Icterus laudabilis* GT

Audubon's Oriole *Icterus graduacauda*

Martinique Oriole *Icterus bonana* GT

Jamaican Blackbird *Nesopsar nigerrimus* GT

Oriole Blackbird *Gymnomystax mexicanus*

Yellow-headed Blackbird *Xanthocephalus xanthocephalus*

Saffron-cowled Blackbird *Xanthopsar flavus* GT

Yellow-eyed Blackbird *Agelaius xanthophthalmus*

Yellow-winged Blackbird *Agelaius thilius*

Red-winged Blackbird *Agelaius phoeniceus*

Red-shouldered Blackbird *Agelaius assimilis* LR

Tricolored Blackbird *Agelaius tricolor*

Yellow-hooded Blackbird *Agelaius icterocephalus*

Tawny-shouldered Blackbird *Agelaius humeralis*

Yellow-shouldered Blackbird *Agelaius xanthomus* GT

Unicolored Blackbird *Agelaius cyanopus*

Chestnut-capped Blackbird *Agelaius ruficapillus*

White-browed Blackbird *Leistes superciliaris* LR

Red-breasted Blackbird *Leistes militaris*

Peruvian Meadowlark *Sturnella bellicosa* LR

Pampas Meadowlark *Sturnella militaris* GT, LR

Long-tailed Meadowlark *Sturnella loyca*

Eastern Meadowlark *Sturnella magna*

Lilian's Meadowlark *Sturnella lilianae* LR

Western Meadowlark *Sturnella neglecta*

Yellow-rumped Marshbird *Pseudoleistes guirahuro*

Brown-and-yellow Marshbird *Pseudoleistes virescens*

Scarlet-headed Blackbird *Amblyramphus holosericeus*

Red-bellied Grackle *Hypopyrrhus pyrohypogaster* GT

Austral Blackbird *Curaeus curaeus*

Forbes Blackbird *Curaeus forbesi* GT

Chopi Blackbird *Gnorimopsar chopi*

Bolivian Blackbird *Oreopsar bolivianus*

Velvet-fronted Grackle *Lampropsar tanagrinus*

Colombian Mountain Grackle *Macroagelaius subalaris* GT

Tepui Mountain Grackle *Macroagelaius imthurni* LR

Cuban Blackbird *Dives atroviolacea*

Melodious Blackbird *Dives dives*

Scrub Blackbird *Dives warszewiczi*

Great-tailed Grackle *Quiscalus mexicanus*

Boat-tailed Grackle *Quiscalus major*

Slender-billed Grackle *Quiscalus palustris* E

Nicaraguan Grackle *Quiscalus nicaraguensis*

Common Grackle *Quiscalus quiscula*

Greater Antillean Grackle *Quiscalus niger*

Lesser Antillean Grackle *Quiscalus lugubris*

Rusty Blackbird *Euphagus carolinus*

Brewer's Blackbird *Euphagus cyanocephalus*

Bay-winged Cowbird *Molothrus badius*

Screaming Cowbird *Molothrus rufoaxlllaris*

Shiny Cowbird *Molothrus bonariensis*

Bronzed Cowbird *Molothrus aeneus*

Brown-headed Cowbird *Molothrus ater*

Giant Cowbird *Molothrus oryzivorus*

Bobolink *Dolichonyx oryzivorus*

Index of Common Names for the World Bird List

Index to the Almanac